# The Penguin Good

HUON HOOKE discovered wine while working as a raw and slightly astringent cadet reporter on *The Murrumbidgee Irrigator* in the New South Wales Riverina. He followed the flow south to the Albury *Border Morning Mail* where he matured somewhat (with the help of local Rutherglen muscat) and then across to the Barossa where he further ripened, studying wine marketing in the warm climate of Roseworthy College. He spent a while mellowing in the cellars of Best's and Yellowglen where he worked vintages, finally reaching marketability when he arrived in Sydney in 1982 to work in wine retailing. A fiercely independent freelancer, he has supported himself solely from writing, lecturing, judging and educating for sixteen years. Currently he writes weekly columns in the *Sydney Morning Herald* and *Good Weekend*, also appearing regularly in *The Wine Magazine* and *Decanter*, and contributes sporadically to many other publications. He judges about ten shows a year and is chairman of several, and runs wine courses in Sydney where he lives. He chairs the judging of Australia's Wine List of the Year Awards (see inside) and occasionally finds time to relax and enjoy a glass of the fluid in question while watching the cricket, reading, listening to music or poisoning friends with his cooking. He published a biography, *Max Schubert Winemaker*, in 1994, *Words on Wine* in 1997, and *The Penguin Wine Cellar Book* in 1999.

RALPH KYTE-POWELL was introduced to wine as a boy by a father who sipped table wines long before such things became fashionable. He joined his dad at wine tastings and on vineyard trips, and cellared his first bottle of wine in his bedroom cupboard as a teenager in the late sixties. On leaving school he studied law at Melbourne University until the first-year exams exposed just how much time he'd spent studying, and how much he'd spent drinking wine. He was tossed out of university, of course, and the world of wine beckoned. Since then he's worked for some of Australia's leading wine merchants at both the wholesale and retail level. He's worked in wineries at vintage in Australia and France, managed a wine store, worked as a sommelier and a restaurant manager, lectured on wine, been part-owner and licensee of a successful small hotel, and judged at regional wine shows. He started writing about wine in 1993 in response to a request from Geoff Slattery, a friend who was starting up the *Melbourne Weekly* magazine. Since then he's written extensively on the subject in various magazines and newspapers, and had a regular radio spot. Currently he writes weekly columns in the *Age* and *Sunday Life!*, contributes to other magazines, and is a judge of Australia's Wine List of the Year Awards. He enjoys cooking too, attempting ridiculously complex dishes with mixed success. And, of course, he still enjoys a good bottle of wine.

2001–2002

the penguin good australian

# WINE guIDE

HUON HOOKE & RALPH KYTE-POWELL

Penguin Books

Penguin Books Australia Ltd
487 Maroondah Highway, PO Box 257
Ringwood, Victoria 3134, Australia
Penguin Books Ltd
Harmondsworth, Middlesex, England
Penguin Putnam Inc.
375 Hudson Street, New York, New York 10014, USA
Penguin Books Canada Limited
10 Alcorn Avenue, Toronto, Ontario, Canada M4V 3B2
Penguin Books (NZ) Ltd
Cnr Rosedale and Airborne Roads, Albany, Auckland, New Zealand
Penguin Books (South Africa) (Pty) Ltd
24 Sturdee Avenue, Rosebank, Johannesburg 2196, South Africa
Penguin Books India (P) Ltd
11, Community Centre, Panchsheel Park, New Delhi 110 017, India

First published by Penguin Books Australia Ltd 2001

10 9 8 7 6 5 4 3 2 1

Cover design by Sandy Cull, Penguin Design Studio
Front cover photograph by Julie Anne Renouf
Cover image: Stelton corkscrew, courtesy of Jarass Pty Ltd
Author photograph of Huon Hooke and
Ralph Kyte-Powell at Walter's Wine Bar,
Southgate, Melbourne, by Rick de Carteret
Typeset in Stone Sans by Post Pre-press Group, Brisbane, Queensland
Printed and bound in Australia by McPherson's Printing Group, Maryborough, Victoria

National Library of Australia
Cataloguing in Publication data:

Hooke, Huon.
    The Penguin good Australian wine guide 2001–2002.

    ISBN 0 14 300011 X.

    1. Wine and wine making – New Zealand. 2. Wine and wine
    making – Australia. I. Kyte-Powell, Ralph. II. Title.

641.220994

www.penguin.com.au

# Contents

ACKNOWLEDGEMENTS

The authors wish to thank all those people in the wine industry who helped make this book possible. Instead of listing them and risking omissions, thanks to all – including the dedicated folk at Penguin Books who worked on this book.

# Introduction

2000–2001 was the year wine lost its innocence.

It was the year wine became more of a commodity than ever, with speculators cashing in and hordes of people rushing to get involved in an industry they increasingly see as one in which money can be made. And it was the year winemaking became just another business to invest in, to trade on the stock exchange; a new player in the corporate chess game. Oh for the days when big business left the wine industry pretty well alone, because the old joke about making a small fortune in wine by starting with a large one was true!

Over the past couple of decades, wine in Australia had shrugged off its stigma as the snob's drink and become the people's drink. Once the exclusive tipple of the wealthy and privileged elite, wine by the end of the 1980s was being enjoyed by people from all walks of life and most socio-economic levels. It had broken down the barriers. It was afford-able and accessible. But by the end of the twentieth century, we were in danger of losing those gains as wine again looked like becoming a social-climber's ladder, an elitist's prop – like a Prada handbag, a snow-capped fountain pen or a Rolex watch. The conspicuous consumption of rare and expensive wine is now being used increasingly as a symbol of status – albeit a crass one.

Yep, you guessed it: we're angry! But there's nothing anyone can do about it. So-called 'collectable wines' are here to stay. They're no longer just a phenomenon, they're part of the day-to-day reality of wine biz. It's simply a reflection of success. The 'western' world is an increasingly affluent place, wine is affordable to more people, and winemaking is now quite profitable. Even where wineries aren't profitable (and there are still plenty of these) the scent of money inevitably attracts investors, and some of them are interested only in making more money. This is a new thing for the wine industry to reckon with: in the past it was passion alone that drove many of our fine-wine producers. Money was a secondary consideration to the desire to make great wine. The days of the benevolent shareholder, who didn't expect an immediate return on investment but who was content to enjoy the perks, seem to have vanished.

Equally inevitably, profitability has led to wine businesses becoming publicly funded and Stock Exchange-listed. Now, the key people at the top of at least 20 Australian wine companies probably spend the first hour of each day scanning the share prices and angsting over their company's financial performance. They worry about whether the analysts are recommending people buy, hold or sell their shares – and the effect this has on the share price and hence the value of every move they make. They worry about being taken over. The wine comes second. And this, we believe, is a terrible thing for the quality wine industry. We wonder why wine producers are so desperate to 'grow' their enterprises, for this is what drives them into 'going public' and becoming vulnerable to takeover and the whole damn nightmare.

This was the year Wild Duck Creek Duck Muck, a thick, soupy 15 to 17 per cent alcohol red wine originally made for fun, brought over US$1000 at auctions, and the year when the maker of Three Rivers Shiraz saw fit to raise his price from $65 to $600 a bottle from one vintage to the next. Sure, one half of our brain says: 'Go for it! If there's someone loony enough to pay that sort of money for a fluid that'll become urine within hours of swigging it down, why not go for the jugular? It's what the market will bear, isn't it?'

And the other half of us says: 'This is so breathtakingly stupid, it's sickening.'

The authors sat down one evening and demolished a steak and a bottle of Barwang cabernet, a $25 wine, and loved it to death. As long as there's value like that in the wine world, we will continue to enjoy the wine business.

To most wine drinkers, perhaps, these concerns are in some other realm, some vinous equivalent of Las Vegas or Hollywood. A place we're all fascinated with, but not somewhere we'd really want to live. Most regular wine drinkers we meet are still interested in knowing what's good value under $15. The other stuff is in Cloud Cuckoo Land. And that's why we produce this book. We, like you, love wine, and we love finding a really good wine at a fair price, and we can't afford these millionaire's wines any more than you can. Good, affordable wine at a fair price: that's what this book is all about.

The 2001 vintage was another record, thanks to the thousands of hectares of new vineyards that were established in the late '90s. The total crush was 1,426,000 tonnes, an increase of 280,000 tonnes (or 25 per cent) on the previous record, set in 2000. For the first time, more red grapes were harvested than white, which indicates the world's rapidly increasing thirst for red wine. This trend was starkly evident in the intake of Beringer Blass, the new name for Foster's wine interest Mildara Blass after it merged with California's Beringer. This group crushed no less than 73 per cent red grapes. That probably reflects the fact that although white wine still outsells red in Australia, largely because of casks, the group makes no cask wine. And it exports a lot of red to the red-thirsty Asian nations where there's a strong belief in red wine's health-giving effects. Hey, we agree with you guys!

The year's biggest story in winery amalgamations was the merger of Southcorp and Rosemount, accompanied by wisecracks about Rosecorp and rude suggestions about Southmount. It was a Rosemount-led executive team that emerged, with Rosemount's Keith Lambert as chief executive, Chris Hancock as marketing manager of global brands and Philip Shaw as chief winemaker. On paper, Penfolds' John Duval is on equal footing with Shaw, but Shaw has far wider responsibilities and was certainly the man in the driving seat during the restructure. He was pivotal in rationalising winemaker numbers. First up, most of the white winemaking team from Nuriootpa got their marching orders, including the man behind Yattarna and Tollana, Neville Falkenberg. Ian McKenzie left Great Western after bringing his retirement plans forward. The Oatley family pocketed a heap of cash, and then spent some of it buying more Southcorp shares. Bob Oatley was to join son Sandy and son-in-law Lambert on the board late in 2001.

One stated reason for the takeover was the desire to keep the great brands Lindemans, Penfolds and Rosemount in Australian hands. But we can't see any reason why – next time the Southcorp share price heads south – one of the *seriously* big global drinks companies wouldn't make a play for Southcorp. Another belief in the Rosemount camp was that overseas mergers for either company (à la Beringer Blass or BRL Hardy getting into bed with Kendall Jackson or Constellation) were unnecessary; Australia has all the resources both companies need to become the global players they want to be. We certainly agree with that.

2001 was also the year when the most ambitious and original wine-retailing adventure for donkey's years, Wine Planet, wobbled out of orbit and finally crashed. This pioneering on-line wine retailer, haemorrhaging cash, became the subject of a takeover offer in April from Foster's. Foster's already owned 25 per cent of Wine Planet through its Cellarmasters arm, and must have rued the day it got involved. The wine trade, perceiving a conflict of interest in Foster's selling wine in competition with the traditional retail trade, embarked on a partial boycott of Mildara Blass products, which must have hurt Mildara. The leading objector was Australia's biggest wine retailer, Coles Myer/Liquorland. Wine Planet's share price had been on a slippery slope and tottered to 22 cents amid its final throes, after having a $1.07 peak for the year. The final scenario was that Foster's paid $42 million to close it down. Officially, Foster's will 'restructure Wine Planet into an international wine e-tailing business in support of our European and Asian wine clubs', according to Foster's chief Ted Kunkel. It was an ignominious end for what was truly an exciting, adventurous business, whose web site came closer than anyone to exploiting the web's potential to broadcast an immediate news service.

Meanwhile, the other high-profile Australia-based wine web site, Winepros, seemed destined to limp along without any significant revenue-earning activities. Its first year's trading brought a net loss of $3.8 million on revenue of just $426,000. Most of that was interest on the cash reserves ($10.6 million) left over from its float, while sales produced a miserable $44,000. Wine-lovers are making hay though: the portal provides a terrific quantity of information – much of it free – which includes Jancis Robinson's entire *Oxford Companion to Wine* and Clive Coates' excellent magazine, *The Vine*.

Other hatches, matches and dispatches (aka births, deaths and marriages): Mountadam sold to Veuve Clicquot, following negotiations conducted between Adam Wynn and David Hohnen, founder of Cape Mentelle and Cloudy Bay – which are both wholly owned by Veuve Clicquot and, through it, Louis Vuitton Moët Hennessy. These owners seem both benign and non-interferist, providing the money needed for development and basically leaving the key people to run their own companies as they see fit. Mountadam immediately announced it was expanding its vineyard by 100 hectares.

Banksia Wines, which was formed by the Tatachilla/St Hallett merger, took over the Hillstowe business (sans vineyards) and looked set for more acquisitions.

The 'Mouth of the Hunter', Murray Tyrrell AM, died at the age of 79. Tyrrell was one of the outstanding wine people of our time, and played a key role in pioneering chardonnay and pinot noir. He was a great believer in, and promoter of, the Hunter Valley. Tyrrell focused on vineyard rather than winery as the main source of quality, long before it became fashionable in Australia.

Claudio Alcorso, creator of Moorilla Estate and the modern-day pioneer of Tasmania's wine industry, also died. And we lost a friend, the respected Melbourne wine writer Tony Hitchin, 64, former editor of *Epicurean* magazine and wine columnist for the *Sunday Herald Sun*.

Wolf Blass won the Maurice O'Shea Award, and six months later collected an Order of Australia, accepting both with his customary lack of false modesty. Vanya Cullen was the Qantas/*Gourmet Traveller Wine* magazine Winemaker of the Year 2000. Langton's Fine Wine Auctions sold a 44-vintage set of Penfolds Grange for a hammer price of $159,000 – a new record.

Wine Australia 2000 was hailed as the best ever, with 33,000 visitors passing through the doors – an increase of nearly 20 per cent on the previous event in 1998. Organisers said it met all its objectives: to increase attendance, attract more overseas trade and media, attract younger consumers, and help wineries find agents in other states and countries. The next challenge would be for Sydney to host an even better and more relevant exhibition in 2002.

Mount View Estate and Lake's Folly were both sold to private owners, the first by the Tulloch family, the second by founder Max Lake's family. There was a spate of sell-offs in the Hunter, taking advantage of high prices and strong demand for wine properties. Terrace Vale sold to a private investor for nearly $2.5 million; and Lesnik's Wilderness Estate went too. Upper Hunter-based Barrington Estate, which already has the Yarraman Road and other minor brands and is based in the former Rosemount Wybong winery, got aggressive, taking over first Hayshed Hill in Margaret River, then McLaren Vale's Haselgrove, and then Mount Avoca in the Pyrenees.

Palandri, the most talked-about, big new winegrowing venture in

Western Australia, bought Rosabrook Estate and signalled its intent to buy Amberley Estate, both of Margaret River. Palandri already owns Baldivis Estate and it launched a $15 range, Aurora, and a repackaged range of Baldivis wines. Palandri had already established a winery in Margaret River, and 210 hectares of new vineyards in the Frankland region with another 140 planned for 2001.

Also in the West, Xanadu went public and soon afterwards declared its intention to take over part of Normans, another public company which had wobbled into financial trouble. In the Barossa, Simeon Wines, Australia's third-biggest winemaker which so far has existed as a contract bulk winemaker, took over the Barossa firm Yaldara, and then announced a joint venture with Brian McGuigan Wines. Simeon will make McGuigan's South Australian wines while McGuigans, with their marketing nous, will manage the Yaldara cellar door sales and no doubt market a new crop of wines.

Dromana Estate also went public and at the same time took over Mornington Vineyards Estate. The group also includes the Yarra Valley Hills brand. The former Yarra Valley Hills winery was taken over by a syndicate led by Master of Wine Martin Williams and renamed Warranwood. Dan Crane (ex-Barrington Estate) joined Williams, and the duo will make Williams' own Métier wines, as well as several boutique-sized southern Victorian brands, plus Will Taylor Wines (of South Australia). The Upper Hunter's Reynolds Wine Co was sold to the ambitious public company Cabonne Limited, near Orange. Cabonne has almost 1,000 hectares of vineyards in three cool-climate locations in the New South Wales central ranges, and is using Reynolds as its premium brand, while Jon Reynolds is effectively chief winemaker. Other brands are Little Boomey (export) and Cabonne.

Got all that? Phew!

After years of family disagreements, which saw him exit the winery for a time, John Cassegrain, his wife Eva and partners bought back the

Cassegrain winery, near Port Macquarie. While he no longer has the grapes from all the vineyards the family developed in the Hastings Valley, John Cassegrain is excited about the chance to access fruit from Tenterfield, Inverell and east of Tamworth, as well as Canberra, Orange, the Hunter and Coonawarra.

Highly respected and long-serving BRL Hardy winemaker, Tim James, moved to Wirra Wirra to replace Tony Jordan as managing director. James worked for Hardys for 24 years and for the last five years was group technical manager. He's highly valued as a taster and is a senior judge at Adelaide, Sydney, the national show in Canberra, the Hunter Valley, Cowra and Barossa Valley shows. Founder and chairman Greg Trott said Wirra was in the midst of rapid expansion, with its winemaking capacity recently doubled to 2,500 tonnes and a building program under way. Wirra is also involved in a new 100-hectare vineyard on the Finniss River, in the south of the Fleurieu Peninsula.

On the marketing front, the irrepressible Zar Brooks left D'Arenberg for Chain of Ponds, and Hugh Cuthbertson left Beringer Blass to focus on the new brand Cheviot Bridge. The latter is based on several vineyards at Yea including those of the Cuthbertson family, and has big growth plans.

Wine exports continued to boom, setting new records for value and volume. In the year ended March, the volume of wine exported grew 21 per cent over the previous year, to reach 326 million litres, and the value grew 26 per cent, to reach A$1.57 billion. New milestones were passed in two of the top 10 export destinations. Sales to the US topped A$400 million for the first time and sales to Japan topped A$40 million. The top five destinations were the UK with 157 million litres (48 per cent of all exports), the US with 64 million litres (20 per cent), New Zealand with 21 million litres (6.4 per cent), Canada with 15 million litres (4.6 per cent) and Germany with 10 million litres (3.1 per cent). Japan ranked seventh with 5.5 million litres (1.7 per cent).

In mid-2001, Australia became the number one wine exporter to the UK, elbowing France aside. And earlier in the year, Australia became the third-biggest wine exporter to the US after France and Italy. According to Austrade: 'Australian wine exports to the US have skyrocketed by 40 per cent in the last 12 months.'

The new National Wine Centre in Adelaide was almost complete at the time of going to press. Peak wine industry bodies such as the Australian Wine & Brandy Corporation and the Winemakers Federation of Australia had moved in. Despite the extraordinary heat during Adelaide's 2000–01 summer, the building was on schedule to be finished by the official opening date in July. The centre will act as an exhibition, education, tasting and sales facility for wineries in all 61 Australian regions. The address is: corner of Botanic and Hackney Roads, Adelaide. All wineries are to be invited to put their wines on for tasting on a rotational basis. Information: (08) 8222 9200. Web site: www.wineaustralia.com.au

Evans & Tate pulled off a seemingly impossible feat: it won the trophy for the best red wine at both International Wine Challenges run by Britain's *WINE* magazine – with the same wine. The judgings were held in London in 2000 and several months later in Hong Kong in early 2001. The wine is E&T's 1999 Margaret River Shiraz, a very oaky but undoubtedly powerful red. It was on sale for about $26. In London in late 2000, it won the awards for best shiraz and best red wine, then in Hong Kong, the equivalent trophy, for best red wine. The chances of this happening would be akin to finding a needle in a haystack.

In a year which saw wine companies all round the world getting a sudden attack of insecurity, which launched them on an orgy of acquisitions and mergers, BRL Hardy formed an alliance with the second-biggest US winemaker, Constellation. Then followed the failure of BRL's much-publicised bid to land another major US wine company, Kendall Jackson.

Globalisation is a cyclone that threatens the individuality of many excellent wine companies, and we only hope it doesn't compromise their wines. The newly formed colossus Beringer Blass bought 51 per cent of Matua Valley, one of New Zealand's top six winemakers, for A$9.3 million. The agreement is that Beringer Blass can buy the remaining 49 per cent over the next three years, subject to the authorities approving. Founders Bill and Ross Spence are staying on for the time being.

Australia has a new wine producer every 72 hours, according to the best barometer of these things, *The Australian and New Zealand Wine Industry Directory*. The 2001 edition shows that allowing for closures and amalgamations, there was a net gain of 121 producers to 1,318 in Australia during 2000. This was a 10 per cent increase during 1999. Over the past decade, the Australian wine industry has seen a net average gain of about 70 wine producers every year. Most of them are very small: many are grapegrowers who've decided to bottle some of their crop to sell under their own label. Amazingly, 1,035 of the total 1,318 process less than 250 tonnes of grapes a year. And 667 crush less than 50 tonnes – truly microscopic!

A new, groovier than groovy wine and lifestyle magazine for young people was launched. *Wine-X* is aimed at 18 to 39 year-olds and it's a spin-off from an American mag. The first issue was published in December 2000. The covers depict images such as a bucket's-eye view of a girl spitting red wine. It features younger writers such as Ben Canaider, Zar Brooks and Kate McIntyre, and others just breaking into the field. There's fashion, food, 'hangover cures', beer, CD reviews, books, oddball grape varieties, cigars, surfing, tour reports, and everything has heaps of attitude. The tasting pages are called (what else but) X-rated. The tasting notes are quite amusing but we're not sure we'd be buying wine on their recommendation. Allusions to music, sport, cars, famous people and sex are everywhere. The froth and fun are there in spades, and if it brings more under-40s into wine, it can't be bad.

Chardonnay continued to dominate the white wine market, increasing its share of sales at what seems an unstoppable rate. But chardonnay is the most disappointing wine style that we taste. The vast majority are plain, ordinary wines – not bad, not faulty, but boring. We would much rather drink riesling. Riesling is consistently delicious, and refreshing; it's great with a variety of foods, it can be cellared with positive results, and it's usually cheaper than even the bog-standard chardonnays.

On the riesling front, at least 15 Clare Valley producers opted to bottle all or part of their 2001 vintage riesling under Stelvin screw-caps. These protect the delicate flavours of riesling from the scourge of wine: cork taint. The Clare winemakers estimate cork taint affects at least 5 per cent of wines bottled under natural cork. Three cheers, we reckon. New Zealand looks like taking up the baton, too, with makers of Marlborough sauvignon blanc moving to follow suit. However, we wait with bated breath to see what sort of bottle they put the screw-cap on: the Stelvin finish looks great on a tall riesling bottle, but we're not sure about the claret and burgundy shapes used for most sauvignon blanc.

Riesling lovers cheered on 31 December 2000: the phase-out day for using the word 'riesling' as a generic name on wine packaging. This should be the final nail in the coffin of Australia's long history of passing off non-riesling wines as riesling varietals. A varietal wine must contain at least 85 per cent of the named grape variety: in this case, true riesling. By the phase-out date, the misuse of the R word was pretty well confined to cask wines, which must now be labelled 'soft dry white', 'fresh fruity white', etc.

A strange process of consolidation continues in liquor retailing, almost in parallel with the amalgamations of wine companies. The main protagonist is Woolworths, whose aggressive buying of independent liquor stores and small chains such as Toohey Brothers (New South Wales), Booze Brothers (South Australia) and Liberty Liquor (Western Australia-based) is making everybody twitchy. Woolies is apparently trying to equal or even exceed the dominant liquor retail power of Coles Myer (Liquorland and Vintage Cellars). This is stimulating other major players – notably Theo's – to also get acquisitive, and there seems no end to the takeovers. Coles in turn swallowed Australian Liquor Group (ALG), which was the expanded, renamed and floated Philip Murphy group that began in Melbourne and suffered delusions of grandeur.

It's likely there'll be scarcely any high-quality wine retail business remaining independent when the smoke and dust settles. Whether this is a good or bad thing for the wine-buyer is not easy to divine. The chains have become much better at fine-wine retailing in recent years, led by Coles' stunningly successful Vintage Cellars sub-chain of premium stores. Taking Vintage Cellars' lead, Woolies announced it was re-badging a number of its flagship stores as a new premium brand, First Estate. It will retain its Macs Cellars brand for mid-market stores. For discount, high-volume stores it's starting a new brand, BWS, which stands for beer, wine and spirits. Whatever happens, winemakers are likely to find the tough job of getting their product on shop shelves even harder, especially if managers of chain stores are restricted in their power to select stock for their own shops.

This scenario, plus the increased competition resulting from the fact that a new wine producer is being born every 72 hours, means small wineries will become more and more focused on winery tourism. They'll think up more enticements such as swish tasting rooms, educational facilities, winery and vineyard tours, concerts and cricket matches, as well as offering food.

And, with the increasing demand on the really big-name, small-producer wines, expect to see more of them being sold exclusively via mail order and/or the internet, but rarely in shops.

It's the way of the world.

# Red Wine: the Bigger the Better?

A few years ago we were reading one of those glossy British wine magazines. Such publications often describe tastings by panels of commentators and wine trade people, some with impressively hyphenated names, and a smattering of them followed by the prized letters MW (Master of Wine). Only a cynical few would doubt their credentials to pass judgement on wine.

In this issue top Australian shiraz was the wine under the microscope. We read on with interest and an increasing level of uneasiness. The winners of the coveted top ratings all represented a style in which the characteristic traits of Aussie wine were so exaggerated that they became caricatures. They were big black bruisers – over-the-top doses of super-ripe fruit, new oak, walls of tannin, and headachy alcohol levels. The most statuesque of these wines are meals in themselves, rather than harmonious accompaniments to good food and company. And the wines that were downpointed and criticised in that tasting, for not having 'true Australian shiraz character' believe it or not, were mostly suave food-friendly wines of finesse, elegance and balance.

We suppose it must suit many people to be able to pigeon-hole wines, as these caricatures have become the international norm for high-quality Australian wine. Top shiraz, by these standards, is thick and purple, sweet with berry flavour, sometimes very woody, and big in grippy tannins. In the same league, cabernet sauvignon is similarly constructed and almost interchangeable with shiraz. Any other styles are also-rans.

Now some would say that this is the natural style of wine that's made in a warm country like Australia, where abundant sunshine gives plenty of everything. They're right to an extent, and we would agree that there is certainly a place for these wines in the scheme of things. They are uniquely Australian and provide many a memorable experience. (In fact there are some very Australian gastronomic events involving large helpings of high-quality, charry barbecued meat where these big reds are compulsory.) Given bottle-age some will mature into flavoursome classics and provide exciting drinking experiences in the future. It's when these big reds become the *only* Australian wines that are synonymous with quality on the world stage that it's a worry.

We put the magazine away. Something seemed out of whack with the tasting; surely not all foreign wine people were looking for these Australian caricatures. Why don't they praise our elegant wines as well? But if you seek out other overseas assessments of Aussie wines, the story remains the same. And in the influential world of American wine commentators, it's worst of all. The highest scoring wines in most US assessments are almost without exception the biggest and brawniest. When it comes to Aussie wine bigger is better, bodyslammers are preferred over ballerinas, vulgarity is prized over refinement. Even the language of American wine commentary reinforces the message with such descriptors as 'super-extracted', 'beyond massive', 'gargantuan', 'monster', and being 'like a dry vintage port' seen as communicating the greatest virtues. Alcohol levels of 15–16 per cent and more (around the strength of many sherries, and only slightly less than some ports and liqueur muscats) are deemed desirable and an ability to remain open for days without oxidising is seen as a big positive.

Such is the all-pervading nature of this bigger-is-better message that some Australian winemakers are getting on the bandwagon. Since positive American reviews of a wine can result in US consumers rushing to the stores for it and buying all they can irrespective of price, a growing number of Aussies are seeing big wines as a pot of gold. The best examples of the genre are being exported in quantity, and there are wines made in this caricature style for the USA that are never sold in Australia. Others are being sold here initially, then re-sold to the Americans by entrepreneurial liquor stores, restaurants and the like. As a result prices of these wines have started to climb, in some cases astronomically.

Another factor in the popularising of the caricature style is a burgeoning auction market, which does much to promote the prestige and desirability of this type of wine. International interest in the big Aussie red pushes the auction circus along and the local scene follows. It seems that nearly every producer in South Australia's Barossa Valley, and increasingly in other regions, has a super-premium red. These wines are sold with spiels that make much of ancient vines, forests of new oak and traditional methods, yet many are like peas in a pod – impenetrable in colour, hugely ripe in fruit character, very oaky, highly alcoholic and expensive. Although Penfolds Grange pioneered the territory, the smaller players are now embracing the style enthusiastically, with an eye to getting rich quick, usually involving a big input of US dollars.

On the home front the story's the same, with fashion following these big, alcoholic, often super-oaky caricatures, and the intrinsic value of many elegant reds has decreased as a result. Retail wine merchants who privately denigrate the heftiest examples of the big reds and the American fashion for them, quote American reviews in newsletters and advertisements, as though these international imprimaturs are badges of acceptability. Who said our cultural cringe was dead?

Maybe the competitive Australian Wine Show system has been partly to blame as well. These shows give out medals and trophies that translate into marketing success in a way that few others do – medals mean dollars on the bottom line for most wineries. And how do you get the medals in the first place? You have to make sure your wine gets noticed by the judges in a masked line-up ahead of its competitors, and the sure-fire way in some shows is to make wine in the caricature style. Tasted alongside the caricatures, anything of delicacy and refinement seems wishy-washy and neutral.

Just how long this fashion will last is anybody's guess, but our view is that sooner or later both foreign and domestic markets will start to look beyond the caricatures. We're already seeing this happen with chardonnay; some previously massively styled wines and some super-oaky ones are now trending towards something a bit more gentle and friendly. With reds change is slow in coming, but there are signs. Visiting British wine gurus are becoming more and more aware of refined Australian wines from cooler regions and are starting to spread the message. Locals are growing inquisitive about such styles and some momentum is building. If consumers of high-priced red wines, particularly the international ones, do start looking at the broader palette of Australian wines, some winemakers who've cashed in on fashion may suffer from credibility problems in the future. If they do, it's nice to know that all the while there has been another band of dedicated Australian winemakers working away, making a second tier of great wines that rely on factors other than muscle and alcohol, massive extract and new oak. For serious consumers this means that our most subtle, best-balanced, easiest-drinking red wines might remain relatively good value, at least until the Yanks discover them!

*The Penguin Good Australian Wine Guide* has a place for all wines in its pages. We mark them for quality and value as we see them, but it's important in using this book not to rely solely on the ratings. Drink the biggies by all means, but don't ignore the others. Look at our tasting notes to see which are the caricatures, which are the big reds, which are the elegant types, and what lies in between.

To help out, here's our list of ten of our big reds and ten of our best elegant styles from the *Guide*.

## THE BIGGIES

Fox Creek Reserve Shiraz

Hamilton Fullers Barn Shiraz

Hillstowe Mary's Hundred Shiraz

Jim Barry The Armagh Shiraz

Langmeil The Freedom Shiraz

Rosemount Balmoral Syrah

Seppelt Dorrien Cabernet Sauvignon

Torbreck Runrig Shiraz Viognier

Warrenmang Estate Shiraz

Wynns John Riddoch Cabernet Sauvignon

## THE ELEGANTS

Bannockburn by Farr Pinot Noir

Clonakilla Shiraz Viognier

Cullen Cabernet Merlot

Diamond Valley Close Planted Pinot Noir

Grosset Gaia

Lenswood Vineyards Palatine

Paringa Estate Shiraz

Petaluma Coonawarra

Seppelt Great Western Shiraz

Zema Estate Cabernet Sauvignon

# Exotic Beauties

Feel like a change? Are you bored with a constant diet of chardonnay, cabernet sauvignon and shiraz? So, it seems, are an increasing number of Australian wine consumers and winemakers. As a result a growing number of small plots of vines with unfamiliar names and obscure ancestry are springing up in the most unexpected places.

Some of these new-wave grape varieties are well known to fans of European wine, while others confound even the most well-versed. To help you navigate through the more arcane grape names that you might encounter on Australian wine bottles in the future, here is our brief guide to some that you are likely to see on the shelves. So equipped, you'll find the delights (and shortcomings) of these more unusual grapes and their wines won't be such a mystery.

## THE REDS

### Sangiovese

One of the great red wine grapes of the world, sangiovese is responsible, wholly or in part, for most of the best wines of Tuscany and Emilia-Romagna in Central Italy. Chianti, Vino Nobile di Montepulciano and Brunello di Montalcino are among its finest expressions. Its wines are characterised by typically Italian 'savoury' aromas and flavours with cherry, tobacco, earth and nutty characters to the fore. It also has attractive succulence from good acidity, and tannins tend to be firm. In Australia its story goes back to the '60s when Montrose at Mudgee pioneered a number of Italian grapes. Subsequent plantings at McLaren Vale and Clare in South Australia, the King Valley in Victoria and elsewhere around the country have been very successful, making wines that capture varietal personality very well. Suitable for planting in a range of climatic conditions, sangiovese looks to have a good future here. Examples worth trying come from Montrose, Coriole, Pizzini, Garry Crittenden's series 'i', Pikes and Primo Estate.

## Nebbiolo

This is the great grape of Piedmont in Italy's north west, where it makes almost immortal wines that have a peculiarly 'foreign' personality that takes some getting used to. The colour is usually paler than most reds and the nose is complex and unusual. Aromas of rose petals, earth, licorice, mocha and hot tar mark the varietal character, and the palate is robust, typically with huge slabs of super-grippy tannins. This tannic assault can be intimidating to the uninitiated but with bottle-age it can make sense. In Italy long ageing can help these wines develop surprising subtlety; in Australia we simply don't know yet. Australian nebbiolos to try come from Victoria's King Valley, and include Garry Crittenden's series 'i' and Brown Brothers.

## Barbera

Barbera originated in northern Italy, probably in Piedmont where it is the most widely planted red grape. The wine it makes is medium-bodied and relatively low in tannins, but with high acidity. Varietal keys are cherry, hazelnut, earth and herbs, put together in a savoury Italian way, rather than the fruity Australian. This makes it a good wine to drink young with appropriate cuisine, although it will take a few years' age too. Occasionally it is given some new oak which makes it into a more substantial, complex drop. In Australia Montrose at Mudgee were pioneers and there are also plantings in Victoria's King Valley. Wines to look for are Garry Crittenden's series 'i', Montrose and Brown Brothers.

## Dolcetto

Most people who try a good dolcetto will be impressed. It's a likeable red that suits the sort of lifestyle and much of the cuisine of contemporary

Australians. Originally from Piedmont in Italy, it makes low-acid, fruity wine of good flavour intensity. Reminiscent of cherries, aniseed and almond syrup, it epitomises the savoury/fruity style of Italian red wine. It's made quickly to keep extraction of tannins to a minimum, and is designed to be consumed young while its fruit lasts. It's said that it gives the Piedmontese something to drink while they're waiting for their barbera, and then their nebbiolo, to mature. In Australia dolcetto has a much longer history than the other trendy Italian grapes, going back to the 1800s in parts of Victoria and South Australia, although today the remnant plots of those earlier plantings are small. New plantings should guarantee a future for Australian dolcetto. Wines to try are Best's Great Western and Garry Crittenden's series 'i'.

## Lagrein

A native of the Trentino–Alto–Aldige region of north east Italy, lagrein is an obscure grape that produces wines of good colour and tannic backbone in its home vineyards. Traditionally it's been firm to the point of bitterness, but a new generation of Italian winemakers are taming its aggression to make softer wine. It provides these characteristics in a cooler climate, which is why the only planting in Australia is in Victoria's Macedon Ranges. There it makes wine of deep purple colour with a peppery, cherry-fruited personality, lean structure and a dry finish. It could be a bit riper in flavour, but it shows promise. Perhaps other cool-climate makers might give it a go, but so far the only Australian example to try is Cobaw Ridge.

## Marzemino

Another of the native vines of Italy's Trentino, marzemino makes a simple medium-bodied red of no great distinction. At its best it's fresh and fruity but not really memorable. Its future in this country probably rests with the cultural interests of some Italian–Australians; it doesn't have the oomph to attract a wider following. The only Australian example we've seen so far is from the Michelini winery at Myrtleford in Victoria's high country.

## Petit Verdot

Petit verdot is one of the classic red grapes of Bordeaux in France. There it plays a minor role in blends with cabernet sauvignon, merlot and cabernet franc, giving depth of colour, tannic backbone and acidity to the blend. It ripens very late, so it can provide problems for the French, whose vineyards are often cooler than ours, but there's no doubting its quality. In Australia it's been around since the wine boom of the 1960s, but until recently only as a component in Bordeaux-inspired blends. This has changed somewhat with a number of South Australian Riverland growers, headed by Kingston Estate's Bill Moularadellis, growing petit verdot for use in straight varietal table wine. Results in the warm Murray Valley have been good, perhaps due to conditions suiting its late-ripening tendencies. Some of the wines we've seen so far have relied too much on oak, but it has a solid, cabernet-like feel that is appealing. Petit verdot looks a variety to watch in the future, both as a blender and straight. Try Kingston Estate or Pirramimma to get the idea.

## Tempranillo

Spain's best red grape, tempranillo, claims the famous Rioja region in the north of the country as its home, but it translates well to other parts of the Iberian Peninsula. It's a very versatile red grape, being just as suitable for light, fruity young reds for early drinking as it is for more substantial wines with varying combinations of cask- and bottle-age. It can be blended successfully with other grapes, principally grenache and others in traditional wines, and more excitingly with cabernet sauvignon in some modern ones. It's medium-bodied with balanced tannins, and has a raspberryish quality as well as more earthy and spicy notes. In Australia tempranillo is a newcomer that should translate well to our climate and evolving drinking habits. It's very food-friendly in much the same way as sangiovese. The only problem is finding it. A number of vineyards are trialling tempranillo, or committing themselves to future production, but the only example we've seen so far was a fairly pedestrian wine made by Brown Brothers in north east Victoria. With tempranillo it's a case of 'watch this space'; the variety promises well.

## Gamay

Beaujolais is a light red from southern Burgundy in France. Its incomparably juicy, gulpable, soft character comes in part from the gamay grape it's made from, and in part from its method of production, which involves fermentation of whole rather than crushed grapes. This means less extract of harsh tannins, keeping the wine fruity and easy to drink. It was once all the rage in Australia, but its star has dimmed a great deal. A few small patches of gamay have been grown in Australia from time to time, but only recently has anything of excitement come of it. Yet gamay made in the style of Beaujolais should be ideal for a warm country like Australia, where a cool glass of light red like this would suit alfresco summer dining perfectly. Two producers taking it seriously are the small Eldridge Estate on the Mornington Peninsula where two delicious versions of gamay are made, and Sorrenberg at Beechworth. Whether these inspire others is a moot point, but they should. Try their efforts and see if you agree with us.

## THE WHITES

### Verduzzo

From Friuli in Italy's north east, verduzzo is made into either a dry white or a semi-sweet version. It has peachy fruit and high acidity, and it develops honeyed richness with age. The sweeter version is often made from semi-dried grapes in the Italian *passito* manner. In Australia there is only one pocket of verduzzo that we know of: Bianchet in Victoria's Yarra Valley has made a speciality of it for some years. The dry wines have sometimes been sold with quite a few years' bottle-age, sometimes too much in our opinion, with maderised aromas and flavours dominating the smooth fruit character. A sweet version is a recent addition. The Bianchet vineyard has changed hands recently, so we'll see what happens to verduzzo in the future, but in our view it's unlikely to become the next big thing in Australian wine.

## Arneis

Arneis is a white grape from Piedmont that had all but disappeared until recently. Possibly its capricious habits in the vineyard had something to do with its lack of popularity. The only Australian example we've seen so far comes under the Garry Crittenden 'i' range, which figures since Mr Crittenden's passion for Italian wine has translated into some pioneering work with those varieties over here. Arneis has the typically northern Italian characteristics of stone-fruit and almond aromas and soft flavours. It may just be a little too obscure to enjoy wide popularity in Australia.

## Viognier

Viognier is everybody's darling these days, with winemakers all over the world inspired by the popularity of the French white Rhone Condrieu to have a go at it. Viognier makes very distinctive wine with an extraordinary aromatic richness. It has powerful aromas of apricots and other stone fruit, along with a heady floral perfume that suggests floral pot-pourri, or your grandma's chest of drawers. The wine is alcoholic and broad to taste, due to relatively low acidity. All this suggests early consumption, as it tends to go to fat with age. Australian examples are getting better and more interesting all the time, which isn't really surprising since in France it usually thrives alongside shiraz, and there's plenty of shiraz in Oz. There are many examples to try but a good starting point are Yalumba's various efforts from South Australia's Eden Valley under the Heggies, Yalumba and Virgilius labels.

## Roussanne

Along with marsanne and viognier, roussanne is an important white grape from France's Rhone Valley. It makes elegant wines with an aroma reminiscent of heathland undergrowth, herbs and citrus. Along with viognier, roussanne shares a certain trendiness, probably following the current American fixation with everything to do with the Rhone Valley. It's often blended with marsanne to add cut and complexity. Look out for Don Lewis's efforts with such blends at Mitchelton, and also the rare, expensive and delicious Giaconda Aeolia made from straight roussanne. St Huberts regularly makes a straight varietal too. A promising variety; expect to hear more of it.

## Cortese

A white grape from north west Italy, cortese is responsible for the white wine known as Gavi. At its best it has a depth, richness and acid structure that makes it a substantial companion to the rich seafood of the Ligurian coast nearby. Australia's only cortese so far is an agreeably soft dry white with pear-like fruit made from young vines grown at Lost Valley, near Strath Creek in central Victorian high country. More may follow.

# The Rating System

The rating system used in this guide is designed to give you an immediate assessment of a wine's attributes, as they will affect your purchasing decision. The symbols provide at-a-glance information, and the written descriptions go into greater depth. Other wine guides are full of numbers, but this one places importance on the written word.

The authors assess quality and value; provide an estimate of cellaring potential and optimum drinking age; and give notes on source, grape variety, organic cultivation where applicable, decanting, and alcohol content. We list previous outstanding vintages where we think they're relevant.

We assess quality using a cut-down show-judging system, marking out of a possible 10. Wine show judges score out of 20 points – three for nose, seven for colour, 10 for palate – but any wine scoring less than 10 is obviously faulty, so our five-glass range (with half-glass increments) indicates only the top 10 points. When equated to the show system, three glasses is roughly equivalent to a bronze medal, and five glasses, our highest award, equals a high gold medal or trophy-standard wine.

Value is arrived at primarily by balancing absolute quality against price. But we do take some account of those intangible attributes that make a wine more desirable, such as rarity, great reputation, glamour, outstanding cellarability, and so on. We take such things into account because they are part of the value equation for most consumers.

If a wine scores more for quality than for value, it does not mean the wine is overpriced. As explained below, any wine scoring three stars for value is fairly priced. Hence, a wine scoring five glasses and five stars is extraordinary value for money. Very few wines manage this feat. And, of course, good and bad value for money can be found at $50 just as it can at $5.

If there are more stars than glasses, you are looking at unusually good value. We urge readers not to become star-struck: a three-glass three-star wine is still a good drink.

Where we had any doubt about the soundness of a wine, a second bottle was always sampled.

## Quality

| | |
|---|---|
| 🍷🍷🍷🍷🍷 | The acme of style, a fabulous, faultless wine that Australia should be proud of. |
| 🍷🍷🍷🍷🍷 | A marvellous wine that is so close to the top it almost doesn't matter. |
| 🍷🍷🍷🍷 | An exciting wine that has plenty of style and dash. You should be proud to serve this. |
| 🍷🍷🍷🍷 | Solid quality with a modicum of style; good drinking. |
| 🍷🍷🍷 | Decent, drinkable wine good for everyday quaffing. You can happily serve this to family and friends. |
| 🍷🍷🍷 | Sound, respectable wines, but the earth won't move. |
| 🍷🍷 | Just okay but, in quality terms, starting to look a little wobbly. |

*(Lower scores are not usually included.)*

## Value

| | |
|---|---|
| ★★★★★ | You should feel guilty for paying so little: this is great value for money. |
| ★★★★⭐ | Don't tell too many people because the wine will start selling and the maker will put the price up. |
| ★★★★ | If you complain about paying this much for a wine, you've got a death adder in your pocket. |
| ★★★⭐ | Still excellent wine, but the maker is also making money. |
| ★★★ | Fair is fair, this is a win–win exchange for buyer and maker. |

| ★★⁺ | They are starting to see you coming, but it's not a total rip-off. |
| ★★ | This wine will appeal to label drinkers and those who want to impress their bank manager. |
| ★⁺ | You know what they say about fools and their money . . . |
| ★ | Makes the used-car industry look saintly. |

## Grapes

Grape varieties are listed in order of dominance; percentages are cited when available.

## Region

Where the source of the grapes is known, the region is stated. If there is more than one region, they are listed in order of dominance. Many large commercial blends have so many source regions that they are not stated.

## Cellar

Any wine can of course be drunk immediately, but for maximum pleasure we recommend an optimum drinking time, assuming correct cellaring conditions. We have been deliberately conservative, believing it's better to drink a wine when it's a little too young than to risk waiting until it's too old.

An upright bottle ▮ indicates that the wine is ready for drinking now. It may also be possible to cellar it for the period shown. Where the bottle is lying on its side ➠ the wine is not ready for drinking now and should be cellared for the period shown.

▮ Drink now: there will be no improvement achieved by cellaring.

▮ 3 Drink now or during the next three years.

➠ 3–7 Cellar for three years at least before drinking; can be cellared for up to seven years.

➠ 10+ Cellar for 10 years or more; it will be at its best in 10 years.

## Alcohol by Volume

Australian labelling laws require that alcohol content be shown on all wine labels. It's expressed as a percentage of alcohol by volume, e.g. 12.0% A/V means that 12 per cent of the wine is pure alcohol.

## Recommended Retail Price

Prices were arrived at either by calculating from the trade wholesale using a standard full bottle shop mark-up, or by using a maker-nominated recommended retail price. In essence, however, there is no such thing as RRP because retailers use different margins. The prices in this book are indicative of those in Sydney and Melbourne, but they will still vary from shop to shop and city to city. They should only be used as a guide. Cellar-door prices have been quoted when the wines are not available in the retail trade.

## ⓢ Special

The wine is likely to be 'on special', so it will be possible to pay less than the recommended retail price. Shop around.

## ⊕ Organic

The wine has passed the tests required to label it as 'organically grown and made'.

## 🍾 Decant

The wine will be improved by decanting.

# Best Wines

Handing out awards in a guide such as this is always a tricky business. It's the most difficult task of all. Why? Because there are so many deserving wines. But the factors that bring us back to earth with a thud every year are **price** and **availability**. So many of the best wines are either very expensive, or made in tiny quantities that never begin to supply the demand for them. Often both.

So we take the attitude that our awards must be as user-friendly as possible. We could fill these pages with nothing but scarce, hideously pricey wines – but, apart from their makers, who would thank us for that?

So most of the award winners are wines that were available at the time of going to press and looked as though they would still be around when the book was due to hit the shops. This is not always easy to manage – to use a gross understatement. Take pinot noir for instance. Virtually all the better pinots made in this country are produced in small quantities and are in big demand, so the 'Sold out!' sign goes up distressingly quickly.

Unfortunately, this voracious demand-pull is being witnessed not only with the fashionable pinots, but with more and more of Australia's great red wines of other varieties, and also some whites.

It should be no surprise by now that the best value in cheaper wines is increasingly confined to the biggest companies. And this year's value awards go to the likes of BRL Hardy, Southcorp and Orlando Wyndham because they're the wineries with 'economies of scale' who can produce wine cheaply enough to sell it at modest prices. The days when smaller-sized wineries tried to cover a wide range of price points have long gone. They simply cannot afford to any longer. Not only that, but the quality of the mass-produced, big-company wines is so good that 'declassified' off-cuts from boutique wineries seldom make the grade. Some of these so-called failures are flogged off as cleanskins, so beware!

The good news for us punters is that there's likely to be a lot more inexpensive wine floating around soon because of the grape glut. Record quantities of wine are on the bulk market right now, and this is likely to become an Australian Wine Lake if the 2002 vintage is at all bountiful. A lot of wine companies and vineyards will go broke but drinkers will have a field day.

Our Penguin Wine of the Year is what we consider to be an under-sung style from an under-sung region: Great Western. It's a shiraz – Australia's signature grape – but from a region and maker that both deserve to be icons. We like the Great Western shiraz style: it's elegant, refined, intensely flavoured, well-structured, ages long-term and builds fabulous complexity of character as it matures.

The Best Cabernet and Best Red Blend are both from the 1999 vintage, whose repute will probably suffer because it follows a highly touted vintage, 1998. In fact, we are finding many excellent reds from '99 now, most notably from Coonawarra, where the weather problems that affected some other regions didn't cause too much grief.

So, the message is, '98 is an excellent year for red wine but don't overlook the '99s – there are some gems and, as a vintage, it is far from being a 'lesser' year like '95, and better than an 'ordinary' year like '97.

Cheers!

## PENGUIN WINE OF THE YEAR and BEST RED WINE
**Seppelt Great Western Vineyards Shiraz 1997**
Shiraz puts the Great into Great Western, and we reckon this wine deserves a place among the hierarchy of Australia's best reds. What a superb wine to mark the 150th year of Seppelt and the year of wine-maker Ian McKenzie's retirement! (See page 191.)

## BEST WHITE WINE and BEST CHARDONNAY
**Yering Station Reserve 1999**
Tom Carson continues to craft a startlingly good array of diverse wines at the Yarra Valley's showpiece winery. This chardonnay manages that difficult act of combining subtlety with power and complexity. (See page 362.)

## BEST SPARKLING
**Chandon Blanc de Blancs 1997**
Not for the first time, we've been thoroughly seduced by the Chandon Blanc de Blancs, which is more often than not the best fizz in the Chandon portfolio. Pristine flavour and delicacy. (See page 368.)

## BEST FORTIFIED
**Lindemans Celebration Spirit Tawny Port**
Not quite all the mementoes of the Sydney Olympic Games were flim-flam. This is a serious tawny of depth and character in a uniquely Aussie style, of which we can all be proud. (See page 393.)

## PICKS OF THE BUNCH

## BEST CABERNET SAUVIGNON
**Brand's 1999**
Brand's wines are impressing us more and more, while owner McWilliams continues to hold the prices down. We think this deserves

the strongest approval. And the '99s are in no way a come-down from the '98s. (See page 69.)

## BEST PINOT NOIR
**Bannockburn By Farr 1999**

Gary Farr makes a distinctive and fascinating style of pinot at Bannockburn Vineyards, so it was a thrill to see an equally lovely wine emerge from Farr's own vineyard next door, under this exciting new label. (See page 61.)

## BEST SHIRAZ
**Penfolds Magill Estate 1998**

We think this is the best Magill Estate shiraz to date, a statuesque red from the cradle of Grange, made in the traditional way in the old Magill winery by rising star Peter Gago. (See page 167.)

## BEST RED BLEND/OTHER VARIETY
**Tim Adams The Fergus 1999**

This is one of the most serious grenache-based reds around, a solid wine from a dependable maker. Tim Adams turns out some of Clare's most honest, natural and well-priced wines. (See page 207.)

## BEST RIESLING
**Heggies 2000**

After a chequered career, Heggies Riesling is back on track. It's now a slightly riper style than some of the earlier low-alcohol efforts. The 2000 is bursting with Eden Valley charm and fruit. (See page 274.)

## BEST SAUVIGNON BLANC
**Lenswood Vineyards 2000**

The Adelaide Hills are arguably Australia's best region for this grape and Tim Knappstein is one of our most dedicated winemakers. The result? A delicious wine with ripe, non-pungent flavours. (See page 286.)

## BEST SEMILLON
### Brokenwood ILR Aged Reserve 1996
Iain Riggs is dedicated to pushing the boundaries of the few grape varieties that excel in the Hunter Valley. His semillon ageing program is starting to bear seriously tasty fruit. The '96 is right up there, with the Hunter's best. (See page 240.)

## BEST SWEET WINE
### Pipers Brook Cuvée Clark Reserve 2000
A brilliant sticky from Tassie, a state that yields remarkably little botrytis wine considering the quality that's possible. The only thing wrong with this stunner is the small quantity made. (See page 315.)

## BEST WHITE BLEND/OTHER VARIETY
### Delatite Dead Man's Hill Gewurztraminer 2000
This rich, complex, pungent wine is more Alsatian than most of the few other, mostly tokenistic, gewurztraminers in Australia. The 2000 vintage gave Delatite an especially lovely wine. More, please! (See page 257.)

## BARGAINS

## BEST BARGAIN RED
### Banrock Station Cave Cliff Merlot 2000
It's a rare thing when both our spoilt authors admit they have (separately) drunk the best part of a bottle of a sub-$12 wine, and enjoyed every drop! Even rarer when the grape is merlot. Enough said. (See page 62.)

## BEST BARGAIN WHITE
### Tollana Chardonnay 1999
This has some of the hallmarks of much dearer Southcorp chardonnays such as Penfolds Adelaide Hills and Yattarna. It's incredibly good value and we hope the new Southcorp regime doesn't lop the Tollana brand, as some insiders predict. (See page 347.)

## BEST BARGAIN BUBBLY
**Wyndham Estate Vintage Chardonnay Brut 1999**
Eureka! A modestly priced fizz that actually tastes good, and isn't loaded with sweetness. Soft, simple, fruity – and very affordable. (See page 382.)

## BEST BARGAIN FORTIFIED
**Brown Brothers Reserve Muscat**
This had us scratching our heads: did someone mix up the tasting glasses or is this inexpensive muscat really as good as it seems? Happily, the wine **is** that good. (See page 386.)

## BEST NEW PRODUCER
**Bannockburn By Farr**
Gary Farr is hardly a novice winemaker: he's been a brilliant one-man band at Bannockburn Vineyards near Geelong since its genesis in the mid-'70s. He's the winemaker and manager but, contrary to common assumption, not the owner. In 2000, Farr shocked and surprised the wine world with a new range of wines he'd been quietly working on since 1994 – the year he and his wife Robyn planted vines on their own land adjoining Bannockburn Vineyards. The 1999 chardonnay, pinot noir, shiraz and viognier, from the first crop of these baby vines, were released under a simple label branded 'Bannockburn By Farr'. Each of them is exceptional and our spies tell us the 2000s, to be released late in 2001 (and probably just labelled 'By Farr'), are at least as good. These are astonishing wines and further proof – if any were really needed – that Gary Farr is a rare talent.

# Top-quality Wines

This year for the first time we include a table of the Top Wines of the *Guide*. This makes it easier for you to see at a glance which wines we liked the most, accompanied by their prices and value-for-money ratings.

And what a shopping list it is! There are five sparklings, 18 fortifieds, 66 reds and 47 whites – 136 wines in total – which all receive five-glass ratings for quality. The breakdown accurately reflects the state of Aussie wine: this country is very strong in reds, and our fortifieds, while a relatively small part of the market (and of this *Guide*), are of quite exceptional quality. Go get 'em!

| Wine | Price | Value |
| --- | --- | --- |
| RED WINES | | |
| Wynns Shiraz 1999 | $16.50 | ★★★★★ |
| Tim Adams The Fergus 1999 | $20.65 | ★★★★★ |
| Seppelt Chalambar Shiraz 1999 | $21.00 | ★★★★★ |
| Brand's Cabernet Sauvignon 1999 | $23.00 | ★★★★★ |
| Starvedog Lane Shiraz 1998 | $25.00 | ★★★★★ |
| Cheviot Bridge Cabernet Merlot 1999 | $27.00 | ★★★★★ |
| Wynns Cabernet Sauvignon 1998 | $27.00 | ★★★★★ |
| Torbreck The Steading 1999 | $32.50 | ★★★★★ |
| Ainsworth Reserve Shiraz 2000 | $34.00 | ★★★★★ |
| Jamiesons Run McShane's Block Shiraz 1998 | $35.00 | ★★★★★ |
| Penfolds Bin 389 Cabernet Shiraz 1998 | $35.00 | ★★★★★ |
| Penfolds Magill Estate 1998 | $60.00 | ★★★★★ |

| | | |
|---|---|---|
| Rosevears Estate Pinot Noir 1999 | $27.00 | ★★★★⁺ |
| Lindemans Steven Vineyard Hunter Shiraz | $30.75 | ★★★★⁺ |
| Jamiesons Run Alexander's Block | | |
|     Cabernet Sauvignon 1998 | $35.00 | ★★★★⁺ |
| Paringa Estate Shiraz 2000 | $35.00 | ★★★★⁺ |
| Plantagenet Shiraz 1998 | $35.00 | ★★★★⁺ |
| Tower Estate Cabernet Sauvignon 1999 | $35.00 | ★★★★⁺ |
| Hewitson l'Oizeau Shiraz 1998 | $36.80 | ★★★★⁺ |
| Bannockburn By Farr Pinot Noir 1999 | $41.00 | ★★★★⁺ |
| Murdock Cabernet Sauvignon 1998 | $42.00 | ★★★★⁺ |
| Parker Estate Terra Rossa First Growth 1998 | $69.50 | ★★★★⁺ |
| Cullen Cabernet Merlot 1999 | $70.00 | ★★★★⁺ |
| | | |
| Providence Miguet Pinot Noir 1999 | $27.25 | ★★★★ |
| Hugo Reserve Shiraz 1998 | $28.00 | ★★★★ |
| Rothvale Luke's Shiraz 2000 | $28.00 | ★★★★ |
| Lenton Brae Margaret River 1998 | $30.00 | ★★★★ |
| Warrenmang Cabernet Sauvignon 1999 | $30.00 | ★★★★ |
| Best's Great Western Shiraz Bin 0 1999 | $33.00 | ★★★★ |
| Lake Breeze Winemaker's Selection | | |
|     Cabernet Sauvignon 1998 | $33.50 | ★★★★ |
| Burge Family Winemakers Olive Hill Shiraz | | |
|     Grenache Mourvèdre 1999 | $35.00 | ★★★★ |
| Seppelt Great Western Shiraz 1997 | $37.00 | ★★★★ |
| Parker Estate Terra Rossa Merlot 1998 | $39.50 | ★★★★ |
| Hillstowe Mary's Hundred Shiraz 1998 | $45.00 | ★★★★ |
| Meerea Park Alexander Munro Shiraz 1999 | $45.00 | ★★★★ |
| Paringa Estate Pinot Noir 2000 | $45.00 | ★★★★ |
| Armstrong Shiraz 1999 | $48.00 | ★★★★ |
| Clonakilla Shiraz Voignier 2000 | $48.00 | ★★★★ |
| Taylors St Andrews Cabernet Sauvignon 1997 | $48.50 | ★★★★ |
| Giaconda Cabernet Sauvignon 1999 | $55.00 | ★★★★ |

| | | |
|---|---|---|
| Petaluma Merlot 1998 | $55.00 | ★★★★ |
| Rosemount Mountain Blue Shiraz Cabernet 1998 | $55.00 | ★★★★ |
| Grosset Gaia 1999 | $56.00 | ★★★★ |
| Majella The Malleea 1999 | $57.00 | ★★★★ |
| Seppelt Dorrien Cabernet Sauvignon 1996 | $57.00 | ★★★★ |
| Mount Langi Ghiran Langi Shiraz 1999 | $60.00 | ★★★★ |
| Rosemount Balmoral Syrah 1998 | $70.00 | ★★★★ |
| | | |
| St Huberts Reserve Cabernet Sauvignon 1998 | $42.00 | ★★★⸍ |
| Nicholas McLaren Vale Shiraz 1998 | $53.00 | ★★★⸍ |
| Diamond Valley Vineyards Close Planted | | |
| Pinot Noir 1999 | $59.50 | ★★★⸍ |
| Petaluma Coonawarra Unfiltered 1999 | $59.60 | ★★★⸍ |
| Giaconda Warner Vineyard Shiraz 1999 | $60.00 | ★★★⸍ |
| Penley Estate Cabernet Sauvignon 1998 | $60.00 | ★★★⸍ |
| Warrenmang Black Puma Shiraz 1998 | $60.00 | ★★★⸍ |
| Langmeil The Freedom Shiraz 1998 | $61.00 | ★★★⸍ |
| Hardys Thomas Hardy Cabernet Sauvignon 1994 | $72.00 | ★★★⸍ |
| Penfolds RWT Barossa Shiraz 1998 | $95.00 | ★★★⸍ |
| Wynns John Riddoch Cabernet Sauvignon 1998 | $95.00 | ★★★⸍ |
| | | |
| Apsley Gorge Pinot Noir 2000 | $46.00 | ★★★ |
| Lenswood Vineyards The Palatine 1998 | $52.00 | ★★★ |
| Happs Three Hills Shiraz 1999 | $70.00 | ★★★ |
| Brokenwood Graveyard Vineyard 1999 | $90.00 | ★★★ |
| Tarrawarra MDB Pinot Noir 1998 | $95.00 | ★★★ |
| Jim Barry The Armagh 1998 | $145 | ★★★ |
| | | |
| Dalwhinnie Eagle Shiraz 1998 | $160 | ★★⸍ |
| | | |
| Penfolds Grange 1996 | $300–350 | ★ |

## WHITE WINES

| | | |
|---|---|---|
| Huntington Estate Semillon 2000 | $12.50 | ★★★★★ |
| Mitchelton Blackwood Park Riesling 2000 | $15.00 | ★★★★★ |
| Richmond Grove Watervale Riesling 2000 | $15.80 | ★★★★★ |
| Heggies Riesling 2000 | $16.50 | ★★★★★ |
| Hewitson Eden Valley Riesling 2000 | $18.55 | ★★★★★ |
| Diamond Valley Yarra Valley Chardonnay 1999 | $20.60 | ★★★★★ |
| Delatite Dead Man's Hill Gewurztraminer 2000 | $22.00 | ★★★★★ |
| Belgenny Vineyard Partners Reserve | | |
|     Chardonnay 2000 | $23.00 | ★★★★★ |
| Petaluma Riesling 2000 | $23.50 | ★★★★★ |
| Dalrymple Sauvignon Blanc 2000 | $24.00 | ★★★★★ |
| Hunter's Chardonnay 1997 | $24.00 | ★★★★★ |
| Tamar Ridge Josef Chromy Selection | | |
|     Riesling 1999 | $24.20 | ★★★★★ |
| Derwent Estate Chardonnay 2000 | $25.00 | ★★★★★ |
| Mount Horrocks Riesling 2000 | $25.00 | ★★★★★ |
| Pewsey Vale The Contours Riesling 1996 | $25.00 | ★★★★★ |
| Cullen Semillon Sauvignon Blanc 2000 | $28.00 | ★★★★★ |
| Fromm La Strada Dry Riesling 2000 | $29.00 | ★★★★★ |
| Tollana Bay F2 Reserve Riesling 1994 | $29.00 | ★★★★★ |
| Brokenwood ILR Aged Reserve Semillon 1996 | $35.00 | ★★★★★ |
| Lindemans Classic Hunter Semillon | | |
|     Bin 7871 1991 | $44.00 | ★★★★★ |
| Yering Station Reserve Chardonnay 1999 | $50.00 | ★★★★★ |
| | | |
| Freycinet Riesling 2000 | $19.35 | ★★★★¹ |
| Isabel Estate Sauvignon Blanc 2000 | $23.00 | ★★★★¹ |
| Providence Miguet Chardonnay 2000 | $25.50 | ★★★★¹ |
| Moss Wood Semillon 2000 | $26.00 | ★★★★¹ |
| Penfolds Clare Valley Reserve Aged Riesling 1997 | $29.00 | ★★★★¹ |
| Grosset Watervale Riesling 2000 | $30.00 | ★★★★¹ |

| | | |
|---|---|---|
| Shaw and Smith Reserve Chardonnay 1999 | $31.00 | ★★★★┤ |
| Cape Mentelle Chardonnay 1999 | $32.50 | ★★★★┤ |
| Grosset Polish Hill 2000 | $35.00 | ★★★★┤ |
| | | |
| Giesen Marlborough Sauvignon Blanc 2000 | $17.50 | ★★★★ |
| Rothbury Estate Brokenback Semillon 1998 | $21.00 | ★★★★ |
| Balgownie Estate Chardonnay 2000 | $30.00 | ★★★★ |
| Cloudy Bay Chardonnay 1999 | $32.40 | ★★★★ |
| Pipers Brook Cuvée Clark Reserve 2000 | $34.00 | ★★★★ |
| Hotham Bridgeland Chardonnay 2000 | $35.00 | ★★★★ |
| McWilliams Mount Pleasant Lovedale Semillon 1996 | $40.00 | ★★★★ |
| Bannockburn Chardonnay 1999 | $47.00 | ★★★★ |
| Tyrrells Vat 1 Semillon 1995 | $50.00 | ★★★★ |
| Leeuwin Estate Art Series Chardonnay 1998 | $75.50 | ★★★★ |
| Giaconda Chardonnay 1999 | $85.00 | ★★★★ |
| | | |
| Highfield Marlborough Sauvignon Blanc 2000 | $27.00 | ★★★┤ |
| Stonier Reserve Chardonnay 1999 | $39.00 | ★★★┤ |
| | | |
| Yalumba Hand-Picked Riesling 2000 | $29.00 | ★★★ |
| Pierro Chardonnay 1999 | $57.00 | ★★★ |
| Giaconda Aeolia 2000 | $85.00 | ★★★ |

## SPARKLING WINES

| | | |
|---|---|---|
| Seppelt Original Sparkling Shiraz 1996 | $19.00 | ★★★★★ |
| Chandon Blanc de Blancs 1997 | $34.00 | ★★★★┤ |
| Tamar Ridge RV Sparkling 1995 | $25.00 | ★★★★ |
| Chandon Vintage Brut 1997 | $33.50 | ★★★★ |
| Seppelt Show Sparkling Shiraz 1990 | $65.00 | ★★★★ |

## FORTIFIED WINES

| | | |
|---|---|---|
| Seppelt Show Amontillado DP 116 | $20.00 (375 ml) | ★★★★★ |
| Seppelt Show Fino DP 117 | $20.00 (375 ml) | ★★★★★ |
| Seppelt Show Oloroso DP 38 | $20.00 (375 ml) | ★★★★★ |
| Lindemans Celebration Spirit Tawny Port | $26.00 | ★★★★★ |
| Seppelt Para Liqueur 21 Year Old Vintage Tawny 1980 | $42.00 | ★★★★★ |
| Galway Pipe 20 Year Old Tawny Port | $45.00 | ★★★★★ |
| Morris Old Premium Liqueur Muscat | $46.00 (500 ml) | ★★★★★ |
| Morris Old Premium Liqueur Tokay | $46.00 (500 ml) | ★★★★★ |
| | | |
| Morris Old Premium Amontillado Sherry | $46.00 (500 ml) | ★★★★⁺ |
| Chambers Special Tokay | $50.00 (375 ml) | ★★★★⁺ |
| | | |
| Lauriston Show Port | $29.00 (500 ml) | ★★★★ |
| Chambers Special Muscat | $30.00 (375 ml) | ★★★★ |
| All Saints Grand Rutherglen Muscat | $32.00 (375 ml) | ★★★★ |
| All Saints Grand Rutherglen Tokay | $32.00 (375 ml) | ★★★★ |
| Hardys Show Port | $43.00 | ★★★★ |
| All Saints Rare Rutherglen Muscat | $65.00 (375 ml) | ★★★★ |
| All Saints Rare Rutherglen Tokay | $65.00 (375 ml) | ★★★★ |
| Seppelt Show Tawny DP 90 | $90.00 (500 ml) | ★★★★ |

# Best-value Wines

Every year when we release this *Guide*, the most-asked question is: 'What's the best value?' So, to make it easier for you to find the best-value wines, we've decided to list them, using $15 as the cut-off price. They are listed in descending order of value-for-money, using our ratings (one to five stars), and the prices are included, so you can easily spot the best buys. To save space, we've left out the quality ratings (out of five glasses) but you can easily check these by turning to the review pages.

There's a particularly large number of white wines in the list, which closely mirrors the state of the market. Due to massive planting of white varieties in the mid to late 1990s, there is a lot of good-value white wine around. Red, on the other hand, has been in short supply, which puts pressure on the cheaper brands. This is likely to change soon, as huge new plantings of red grapes are starting to come on-stream from the 2001 vintage.

The prices quoted here are full retail prices, but don't forget that most of these wines can often be found discounted. You will quite likely find them substantially cheaper if you shop around, especially if you purchase by the dozen. Retailers commonly charge around 10 per cent less for a case purchase, as an incentive to buy more. Take advantage!

| Wine | Price | Value |
|------|-------|-------|
| **RED WINES** | | |
| Normans Encounter Bay Shiraz 1999 | $12.00 | ★★★★★ |
| Leasingham Bastion Shiraz Cabernet 1999 | $14.00 | ★★★★★ |

| | | |
|---|---|---|
| Orlando Jacob's Creek Reserve | | |
| Cabernet Sauvignon 1998 | $14.95 | ★★★★★ |
| De Bortoli Windy Peak Pinot Noir 2000 | $15.00 | ★★★★★ |
| | | |
| Lindemans Bin 50 Shiraz 1999 | $9.30 | ★★★★┥ |
| Deakin Estate Cabernet Sauvignon 2000 | $10.00 | ★★★★┥ |
| D'Arenberg The Stump Jump Grenache | | |
| Shiraz 1999 | $11.00 | ★★★★┥ |
| Banrock Station Cave Cliff Merlot 2000 | $13.00 | ★★★★┥ |
| Grant Burge Barossa Vines Shiraz 1999 | $14.95 | ★★★★┥ |
| Salena Estate Shiraz 1999 | $15.00 | ★★★★┥ |
| | | |
| Ashwood Grove Shiraz 1999 | $9.50 | ★★★★ |
| Deakin Estate Merlot 2000 | $10.00 | ★★★★ |
| Blues Point Shiraz Cabernet 1999 | $11.00 | ★★★★ |
| Normans Encounter Bay Cabernet Sauvignon 1999 | $12.00 | ★★★★ |
| Banrock Station Cabernet Merlot 2000 | $12.50 | ★★★★ |
| Rouge Homme Shiraz Cabernet 1999 | $14.40 | ★★★★ |
| Orlando Jacob's Creek Reserve Shiraz 1998 | $14.95 | ★★★★ |
| Miranda High Country Merlot 1999 | $15.00 | ★★★★ |
| Palandri Aurora Cabernet Shiraz 2000 | $15.00 | ★★★★ |
| Palandri Aurora Shiraz 2000 | $15.00 | ★★★★ |
| Salena Estate Cabernet Sauvignon 1999 | $15.00 | ★★★★ |

WHITE WINES

| | | |
|---|---|---|
| De Bortoli Sacred Hill Traminer Riesling 2000 | $7.00 | ★★★★★ |
| McWilliams Hanwood Chardonnay 2000 | $11.00 | ★★★★★ |
| Tollana Eden Valley Riesling 2000 | $11.60 | ★★★★★ |
| Trentham Estate Sauvignon Blanc 2000 | $12.00 | ★★★★★ |
| Wynns Riesling 2000 | $12.00 | ★★★★★ |
| Huntington Estate Semillon 2000 | $12.50 | ★★★★★ |
| De Bortoli Windy Peak Rhine Riesling 2000 | $14.00 | ★★★★★ |

| | | |
|---|---|---|
| Jim Barry Watervale Riesling 2000 | $14.50 | ★★★★★ |
| Seppelt Corella Ridge Chardonnay 1998 | $14.50 | ★★★★★ |
| Tollana Chardonnay 1999 | $14.50 | ★★★★★ |
| McWilliams Eden Valley Riesling 1997 | $15.00 | ★★★★★ |
| McWilliams Mount Pleasant Hunter Valley | | |
|     Chardonnay 1998 | $15.00 | ★★★★★ |
| Mitchelton Blackwood Park Riesling 2000 | $15.00 | ★★★★★ |
| Pewsey Vale Riesling 2000 | $15.00 | ★★★★★ |
| | | |
| Tyrrells Long Flat White 2001 | $9.70 | ★★★★┥ |
| Penfolds Rawsons Retreat Semillon | | |
|     Chardonnay 2000 | $10.20 | ★★★★┥ |
| R.L. Buller & Son Victoria Chardonnay 1999 | $11.00 | ★★★★┥ |
| Charles Sturt University Chardonnay 2000 | $12.00 | ★★★★┥ |
| St Hallett Poacher's Blend 2000 | $12.50 | ★★★★┥ |
| Wolf Blass Yellow Label Riesling 2000 | $12.95 | ★★★★┥ |
| The Mill Cowra Chardonnay 2000 | $13.45 | ★★★★┥ |
| Rothbury Estate Verdelho 2000 | $13.75 | ★★★★┥ |
| Dowie Doole Chenin Blanc 2000 | $14.00 | ★★★★┥ |
| Hungerford Hill Cowra Chardonnay 1999 | $14.85 | ★★★★┥ |
| McWilliams Mount Pleasant Hunter Valley | | |
|     Chardonnay 1999 | $15.00 | ★★★★┥ |
| Palandri Aurora Chardonnay 2000 | $15.00 | ★★★★┥ |
| Palandri Aurora Semillon Sauvignon Blanc 2000 | $15.00 | ★★★★┥ |
| Seppelt Mornington Peninsula Pinot Gris | $15.00 | ★★★★┥ |
| | | |
| Lindemans Bin 65 Chardonnay 2000 | $9.30 | ★★★★ |
| Jindalee Chardonnay 2000 | $10.00 | ★★★★ |
| Deakin Estate Chardonnay 2000 | $10.50 | ★★★★ |
| Deakin Estate Sauvignon Blanc 2000 | $10.50 | ★★★★ |
| Trentham Estate Murphy's Lore Semillon | | |
|     Chardonnay 2000 | $10.65 | ★★★★ |

| | | |
|---|---|---|
| Seaview Chardonnay 1999 | $11.00 | ★★★★ |
| Westend Richland Sauvignon Blanc 2000 | $11.00 | ★★★★ |
| Deen De Bortoli Vat 7 Chardonnay 2000 | $11.75 | ★★★★ |
| Peter Lehmann Semillon Chardonnay 2000 | $11.80 | ★★★★ |
| Lindemans Limestone Coast Chardonnay 2000 | $12.00 | ★★★★ |
| Normans Encounter Bay Chardonnay 2000 | $12.00 | ★★★★ |
| Ashwood Grove Chardonnay 2000 | $12.50 | ★★★★ |
| Orlando Trilogy Semillon Sauvignon Blanc Muscadelle 2000 | $13.00 | ★★★★ |
| Talijancich Voices 1998 | $13.70 | ★★★★ |
| Bushrangers Bounty Chardonnay 2000 | $14.00 | ★★★★ |
| Lake Breeze Chardonnay 2000 | $14.00 | ★★★★ |
| The Gorge Verdelho 2001 | $14.00 | ★★★★ |
| Trentham Estate Chardonnay 2000 | $14.00 | ★★★★ |
| Water Wheel Bendigo Chardonnay 2000 | $14.00 | ★★★★ |
| Wynns Chardonnay 2000 | $14.00 | ★★★★ |
| Schinus Sauvignon Blanc 2000 | $15.00 | ★★★★ |
| Tarline Chardonnay 2000 | $15.00 | ★★★★ |

## SPARKLING WINES

| | | |
|---|---|---|
| Hardy's Omni Red | $10.00 | ★★★★★ |
| Banrock Station Sparkling Shiraz | $12.80 | ★★★★★⁺ |
| Deakin Estate Brut | $10.50 | ★★★★ |
| Fleur de Lys Chardonnay Pinot Noir Pinot Meunier | $12.60 | ★★★★ |
| Miranda High Country Sparkling Chardonnay 1999 | $13.00 | ★★★★ |
| Wyndham Estate Vintage Chardonnay Brut 1999 | $13.50 | ★★★★ |

FORTIFIED WINES

| | | |
|---|---|---|
| Seppelt Trafford Tawny DP 30 | $12.00 | ★★★★┥ |
| Lindemans Macquarie Tawny Port | $12.50 | ★★★★┥ |
| | | |
| Brown Brothers Reserve Port | $13.50 | ★★★★ |
| Angoves Fino Dry Flor | $14.90 | ★★★★ |

# Australia's Wine List of the Year Awards

Quality of wine service in Australia has assumed a position of importance unheard of a couple of decades ago. Things have changed from the days when licensed restaurants provided a lacklustre range of so-so wines, marked-up to extortionate prices, and sometimes served by staff whose wine knowledge was sadly lacking. Back then if you wanted to enjoy a really good bottle of wine with your meal, and didn't have a tycoon's bank balance, you often took it along to a BYO restaurant, or simply stayed at home.

Times have changed, and the emphasis on professionalism that has marked the Australian gastronomic scene in recent years has brought about a revolution in restaurant wine service. Many more restaurants are licensed these days and a good wine list is seen as important in a very competitive marketplace. Now wine lists are much more likely to be chosen with real thought to offer a well-balanced selection of wines, appropriate to the style of the establishment, and at a range of fair prices. Good wines by the glass have generally replaced the anonymous and usually disappointing 'house wine' of yesteryear with wines of character, value and interest.

To help direct you to restaurants that do a great job with their wines, each year this *Guide* brings you the results of Australia's Restaurant Wine List of the Year Awards. Sponsored by wholesale wine and spirit merchants Tucker Seabrook & Co., it's an Australia-wide competition, with the Awards judged by a 12-member panel which includes both authors of the *Guide*, with Huon Hooke as chairman.

We can thoroughly recommend the following Award-winning establishments to you. You can be sure of a decent bottle at a fair price at any of them.

## NATIONAL WINNER

Circa, The Prince, Vic.   ♉♉♉

## HALL OF FAME NATIONAL WINNERS

*(previous National Winners maintaining three-glass ratings)*

The Melbourne Wine Room, Vic. (2000 winner)   ♉♉♉

Syracuse Restaurant and Wine Bar, Vic. (1999 winner)   ♉♉♉

Forty One, NSW (1998 winner)   ♉♉♉

France-Soir, Vic. (1997 winner)   ♉♉♉

Walter's Wine Bar, Vic. (1996 winner)   ♉♉♉

Dear Friends Garden Restaurant, WA (1995 winner)   ♉♉♉

## HALL OF FAME CATEGORY & STATE WINNERS

*(three-time State or Category winners who have maintained their rating)*

The Grape Food and Wine Bar, Qld   ♉♉♉

Universal Wine Bar, SA   ♉♉♉

Chloe's Restaurant, SA   ♉♉♉

Stephenies Restaurant, WA   ♉♉♉

Caffe Della Piazza, ACT   ♉♉♉

Hanuman Thai, NT   ♉♉

## 2001 STATE & TERRITORY WINNERS

ACT   China Tea Club   ♉♉

NSW   Wine Banc   ♉♉♉

NT   Blush Wine Bar   ♉

Qld   Downs Club   ♉♉♉

SA   Blakes Restaurant   ♉♉♉

Tas.   Franklin Manor   ♉♉♉

Vic.   Circa, The Prince   ♉♉♉

WA   Altos   ♉♉♉

## 2001 CATEGORY WINNERS

Best Restauarant   Circa, The Prince, Vic.   ♥♥♥

Best Small Wine List   Balmain Eating House, NSW   ♥♥

Best Club Restaurant   Downs Club, Qld   ♥♥♥

Best Pub Restaurant   Ozone Hotel, Vic.   ♥♥♥

Best Café/Brasserie/Trattoria   Grape Wine and Food Bar, Qld   ♥♥♥

Best Country/Regional Restaurant   Franklin Manor, Tas.   ♥♥♥

Tony Hitchin Award for Best New Restaurant   Celsius, NSW   ♥♥♥

## VERY HIGHLY RECOMMENDED   ♥♥♥

**ACT**

Café Della Piazza

**NSW**

Aria; Banc Restaurant; Bather's Pavilion; Buon Ricordo; Celsius Restaurant; Darling Mills; Forty One Restaurant; International Restaurant Bar; La Grillade Restaurant; Marque Restaurant; MG Garage; Restaurant VII; Seven Mile Café; Tetsuya's; Watermark Restaurant; Wine Banc

**Queensland**

Downs Club; Grape Wine and Food Bar

**South Australia**

Blakes Restaurant; Chloe's Restaurant; Universal Wine Bar

**Tasmania**

Calstock Country Guest House; Franklin Manor

**Victoria**

Bar Corvina; B-Coz Restaurant; Charcoal Grill on the Hill; Circa, The Prince; Donovans; The European; France-Soir; Jacques Reymond Restaurant; Lake House; Langton's Restaurant and Wine Bar; Le Restaurant; Marchetti's Latin Restaurant; Mask of China Restaurant; The Melbourne Supper Club; Melbourne Wine Room; Number 8 Restaurant & Winebar; One Fitzroy Street; Ozone Hotel; Syracuse Restaurant & Bar; Walters Wine Bar

**Western Australia**

Altos; Dear Friends Restaurant; Friends Restaurant; Stephenies Restaurant

HIGHLY RECOMMENDED  ♥♥

**ACT**

Atlantic Restaurant; Chairman and Yip Restaurant; China Tea Club; Juniperberry Restaurant

**NSW**

Armstrongs Brasserie; Arte E Cucina; Balmain Eating House; Bistro Moncur; Club Grill; Courtney's Brasserie; The Credo; Darleys Restaurant; Grappa Ristorante E Bar; Hermitage at Hunter Resort; Jonah's; Kables Restaurant The Regent Sydney; KoK (Shirk) Restaurant; Lilians Restaurant; Longrain; Mixing Pot Restaurant; Old George & Dragon Restaurant; Otto Ristorante Italiano; Pavilion on the Park; Prime; Quay Restaurant; Salt; Summit Restaurant

**Northern Territory**

Hanuman Restaurant

**Queensland**

Circa Restaurant; Isis Brasserie; Jameson's Restaurant; Marco Polo East West Cuisine; Ristorante Fellini; Rumba Wine Bar; Sails Beach Restaurant; Season Restaurant; Vanitas; Volare Restaurant

**South Australia**

Chesser Cellars; Cibo Ristorante; Durhams Restaurant; The George Wine Bar; The Manse Restaurant; Melting Pot Restaurant

**Tasmania**

Stillwater River Café Restaurant & Wine Bar

**Victoria**

The Baths; Beaumaris Pavilion; Blakes Restaurant; Café Latte; Caterina's Cucina e Bar; Cecconis Restaurant; Chine on Paramount; Choi's Restaurant; Cicciolina; Circ; Edwards Waterfront; Eleonore's; Enzo; The European Grill;

Grossi Florentino; Hotel Australia; Isthmus of Kra; Joseph's Restaurant; Kudos Restaurant Wine Bar; Linden Tree Restaurant; Marchetti's Tuscan Grill; Matteo's; Oscar W's Wharfside Redgum Grill & Deck Bar; Owensville; Pearl; Red Emperor Chinese Restaurant; Restaurant Saucier; Ristorante Strega; Royal Mail Hotel; Scusa Mi Ristorante; Sempre Caffe E Paninoteca; Stokehouse – Upstairs; Stonelea Country Estate; Vault Bar & Restaurant; Vue de Monde

### Western Australia

Balthazar; Frasers Restaurant; Subiaco Wine Room; Witch's Cauldron Restaurant

## RECOMMENDED ♀

### ACT

Dijon Restaurant; Fig Café; Hermitage Restaurant & Wine Bar; Mezzalira Ristorante; Rubicon; Silo Bakery

### NSW

Aqua Dining; Archies on the Park; Bay Views Restaurant & Function Centre; Beppi's Restaurant; Biba Restaurant Bar; Boomerang; Boronia House; Canterbury Hurlstone Park RSL; Criterion Restaurant; The Dining Room; Ecco Mosman Restaurant; Feast Restaurant; Fins Seafood Restaurant; Harbourside Restaurant; Heritage Court Restaurant; Jaspers Restaurant; Jitterbug Mood; Kingsleys Steakhouse; L'Unico; Mezzaluna Restaurant; Milsons Restaurant; Neptune Palace; Nobles Restaurant; Pavilion Café; Pruniers Restaurant; Quay East Restaurant; Restaurant Balzac; The Saltwater Grill; Scratchleys on the Wharf Restaurant; Shiki Japanese Restaurant; Tongarra Restaurant; Tory's Seafood Restaurant; Union Hotel Dining Room; Volnay Restaurant; Zacks on Bent Street

### Northern Territory

Blush Wine Bar; Cornucopia Museum Café; Delicious Blue; Ten Litchfield Espresso Bar Café

### Queensland

Aqua; Baguette Restaurant; Bedarra Island Resort; Bretts Wharf Restaurant & Function Centre; Cha Char Char Wine Bar & Grill; Champagne Brasserie; The

Clubhouse; E'cco Bistro; Friday's; Gerties Bar & Restaurant; Il Mondo Restaurant; The Melrose; Morgans Seafood Restaurant; Mt Coot-tha Summit Restaurant; Red Ochre Grill; Ricky Ricardo's; Venice Café Bar

### South Australia

93 The American Eatery; Anchorage at Victor Harbor; The Oxford Hotel; Sage & Muntries Café; Tatehams Restaurant

### Tasmania

Alexander's Restaurant

### Victoria

Barwon Heads Golf Club; Benbrook at Lalor House; Birches; Caffe E Cucina; Cavalli Restaurant & Bar; China Max; Cincotta's Café & Bar; Clancy's Restaurant; Dish Restaurant; East Empress Restaurant; Emeu Inn Restaurant; Ezard at Adelphi; Fawkner Park Hotel; George Public Bar; Grand; Haggers Restaurant; Hairy Canary; Il Bacaro; Jason's Terrace; Jus Restaurant & Wine Bar; Koh Samui Thai Restaurant; Le Nouveau 28; Marine Café; Mark's Restaurant; Mecca Restaurant; Mercer's Restaurant; Mietta's Queenscliff Hotel; Near East Restaurant; Nikitas Greek Tavern; Plume Chinese Cuisine; Poffs Restaurant; The Point; Portofino by the Sea; Potters Cottage Restaurant; r.bar; Red Orange Restaurant & Bar; Reifs Restaurant & Bar; Richmond Hill Café & Larder; Ristorante Masani; Ruby Ruby; Sails on the Bay Restaurant; Shakahari Vegetarian Restaurant; Sharkfin House; Stokehouse – Downstairs; Tiger Bar; Turf Accountants Bar & Grill Veludo; Verona Restaurant (Gateway on Monash); Victoria Hotel; Vista Bar and Bistro; Vue Grand Hotel; Whirrakee Restaurant & Wine Bar; Woodman Estate

### Western Australia

Code Bar and Café; Gershwins Restaurant; Globe Wine Bar & Restaurant; Jacksons Restaurant; Tsunami Sushi Bar

# The Best Sommeliers

While our wine lists have improved out of sight in recent years, the person who serves you your wine in a restaurant has taken a turn for the better too. The wine waiter of old is now the 'sommelier', and although there's a whiff of pretension about the use of this French term, its widespread adoption has paralleled a great improvement in standards. The best Australian sommeliers now have broad-ranging wine knowledge, experienced palates, a good understanding of food, skill in handling all types of wines, and a sympathetic appreciation of the role that different wines can have in complementing a fine dining experience.

Each year there are two competitions aimed at finding the best of these great Australian sommeliers. The Champagne Devaux Young Sommelier of the Year aims at finding the best young (under 30) man or woman, via some very testing examinations and practical exercises. This competition is held under the chairmanship of Huon Hooke, co-author of this *Guide*, and assessment is done by an experienced panel. The winner for 2001 is Nicole Tuckwell from Melbourne's Jacques Reymond's Restaurant. The prize is a trip to France as a guest of Champagne Devaux.

The second national competition for sommeliers is the Sommelier of the Year, sponsored by Rosemount Estate and the Australian Sommeliers Association with assistance from Riedel glassware. Once again a comprehensive examination and practical assessment takes place, with a first prize of a trip for two to the United Kingdom and Europe plus a selection of Riedel glassware. The winner for the year 2000 was Nick Stock of Armstrong's Restaurant in Brisbane. The winner of the 2001 Sommelier of the Year will have just been announced as this edition of *The Penguin Good Australian Wine Guide* goes on sale. Stay tuned . . .

# Red Wines

## Abercorn Shiraz

Tim and Connie Stevens are making some of the most memorable shiraz in Mudgee these days. They recently built a smart new cellar-door sales outlet beside the vineyard. Their property is next door to Huntington Estate – not a bad address.

*Previous outstanding vintage: '98*

CURRENT RELEASE 1999   This seems more elegant than the two preceding vintages, but no less impressive. The bouquet is dominated by vanillin charred oak at this tender age, while the flavour is sweet and cherry/plummy, with a smooth texture and a measure of elegance. The finish is tight but supple, and it promises to cellar well. Great with lamb chops smeared with truffle paste.

| | |
|---|---|
| Quality | 🍷🍷🍷🍷🍷 |
| Value | ★★★★ |
| Grapes | shiraz |
| Region | Mudgee, NSW |
| Cellar | 🍾 10+ |
| Alc./Vol. | 14.0% |
| RRP | $25.00 🍾 |

## Ainsworth Reserve Shiraz

New wines from new wineries that really stop us in our tracks are few and far between, but every year there are a couple of standouts. This is one of them.

CURRENT RELEASE 2000   A robust young shiraz packed with personality. The nose has clean plum, berry and choc-mint aromas of good concentration, wrapped up in a good measure of smoky oak. The palate is medium in body with a mouth-coating texture and intense minty berry flavours. Despite its concentration it doesn't weigh you down and finishes friendly with smooth, ripe tannins. A good companion for venison.

| | |
|---|---|
| Quality | 🍷🍷🍷🍷🍷 |
| Value | ★★★★★ |
| Grapes | shiraz |
| Region | Yarra Valley, Vic. |
| Cellar | 🍾 5 |
| Alc./Vol. | 13.0% |
| RRP | $34.00 |

## All Saints Cabernet Sauvignon

| | |
|---|---|
| Quality | ▼▼▼⬚ |
| Value | ★★★ |
| Grapes | cabernet sauvignon |
| Region | Rutherglen, Vic. |
| Cellar | ▮ 5 |
| Alc./Vol. | 14.0% |
| RRP | $18.70 |

The winemaking team at All Saints must have shares in a Kentucky oak plantation, such is their devotion to American oak character in their red wines. A pity, since they must have some valuable old-vine fruit to work with. CURRENT RELEASE 1999 The nose has charry, vanillin, sweet American oak aromas above all, with some dark berry touches hidden in there somewhere. The palate is medium-bodied and sweet fruit still plays a cameo role, but it's bludgeoned into submission by all that oak. Dry oaky tannins add notable astringency on the finish. Serve it with charry grilled meats.

## All Saints Carlyle Shiraz

| | |
|---|---|
| Quality | ▼▼▼▼ |
| Value | ★★⬚ |
| Grapes | shiraz |
| Region | Rutherglen, Vic. |
| Cellar | ⬤ 1–8+ |
| Alc./Vol. | 14.0% |
| RRP | $37.40 |

With this, the team at All Saints has gone the whole hog in an attempt to make an unashamedly ballsy Aussie red. Wine from 80-year-old vines, oaked to the hilt, unfined, unfiltered, and very alcoholic, made on the 'bigger is better' principle.
CURRENT RELEASE 1998 Loads of sweet vanillin and toasty oak lead the way here. A nucleus of blackberry syrup-like fruit doesn't quite match all that tall timber. The palate follows the same pattern: concentrated dark berry flavour layered with huge amounts of sweet oak in a full-bodied package, finishing with very grippy tannins. Our rating for this wine comes with the proviso that you have to be an oak-fiend to like it. Drink it with smoky barbecued rump steak.

## All Saints Shiraz

| | |
|---|---|
| Quality | ▼▼▼⬚ |
| Value | ★★★ |
| Grapes | shiraz |
| Region | Rutherglen, Vic. |
| Cellar | ⬤ 1–6 |
| Alc./Vol. | 14.5% |
| RRP | $17.70 |

These days All Saints red wines have been restyled to hold their own among the modern reds of other regions. Oak has played a part in this renewal, perhaps too big a part. CURRENT RELEASE 1998 Deep colour suggests weight and concentration here, an impression reinforced by an inky nose, with sweet American oak contributing a notable vanillin/mocha input. The palate is firm and oaky with a core of sweet blackberry fruit. A high level of extract and that woodiness make it taste a bit harsh. All up a rather unyielding sort of wine that needs age. It should suit chargrilled steaks.

## Amberley Cabernet Merlot

Amberley is at the northern end of the Margaret River vineyard region, an area without a real consistency of regional style compared to the middle and southern parts. In fact the red wine made at Amberley has a lot in common with the mid-section; it's rich with plenty of stuffing yet still elegant.

CURRENT RELEASE 1999　The nose shows intense berry fruit with attractive barrel-derived complexities. In the mouth it's quite a structured wine with ripe tannins and good acidity providing the skeleton to support intense but not overblown fruit flavour. It will build flesh on those bones with medium-term cellaring. Serve it with porterhouse and maitre d'hotel butter.

| | |
|---|---|
| Quality | 🍷🍷🍷🍷 |
| Value | ★★★⸙ |
| Grapes | cabernet sauvignon; merlot; cabernet franc |
| Region | Margaret River, WA |
| Cellar | 🍾 8 |
| Alc./Vol. | 13.5% |
| RRP | $28.00 |

## Andraos Brothers Olde Winilba Cabernet Sauvignon

It's great to see the old Sunbury vineyards in action again. Winilba was the first in the early 1860s and was soon after joined by Craiglee and Goonawarra. All three are now producing wine again after a long hiatus.

CURRENT RELEASE 1998　Like its shiraz sibling, this is an honest, traditional red with a friendly nose of earth, berries and integrated subtle oak. The palate is smooth and soft with attractive fruit sweetness in the middle. Tannins are ripe and mellow. Overall it's a wine that seems somehow older than its years, but that's not a criticism: it drinks very well. Will go well with osso buco.

| | |
|---|---|
| Quality | 🍷🍷🍷🍷 |
| Value | ★★★ |
| Grapes | cabernet sauvignon |
| Region | Sunbury, Vic. |
| Cellar | 🍾 2 |
| Alc./Vol. | 13.5% |
| RRP | $45.00 |

## Andraos Brothers Olde Winilba Grandfather's Reserve Shiraz

Like the historic Craiglee and Goonawarra vineyards, Winilba is an original Sunbury property of the 1800s, now resurrected by the Andraos family.

CURRENT RELEASE 1998　Rather old-fashioned in style, this pricey Sunbury shiraz has blackberry and raspberry aromas with smoky, earthy touches and dry vanillin-oak influence. The palate is quite substantial with adequate ripeness and good length. It tastes very traditional, without the overt fruitiness that marks modern young Australian shiraz. Ripe tannins are in good balance. A worthwhile companion to braised lamb.

| | |
|---|---|
| Quality | 🍷🍷🍷🍷 |
| Value | ★★⸙ |
| Grapes | shiraz |
| Region | Sunbury, Vic. |
| Cellar | 🍾 5 |
| Alc./Vol. | 13.5% |
| RRP | $70.00 |

## Andrew Harris Cabernet Sauvignon

| | |
|---|---|
| Quality | ▓▓▓▒ |
| Value | ✱✱✱ |
| Grapes | cabernet sauvignon |
| Region | Mudgee, NSW |
| Cellar | ▬ 1–6 |
| Alc./Vol. | 13.5% |
| RRP | $15.80 |

First planted only a decade ago, this vineyard near Mudgee has grown like Topsy into a substantial regional player. As well as providing grapes for the Andrew Harris label, much of the crop is sold to other makers.

CURRENT RELEASE 1999   This is very deeply coloured in true Mudgee fashion, and it won't get any awards for delicacy. The nose has blackberry, mint and gum-tree aromas of some power, with a little vanillin oak mixed in. The palate is medium-bodied and robust in flavour with pretty powerful tannins. Try it with braised lamb and root vegetables.

## Andrew Harris Shiraz

| | |
|---|---|
| Quality | ▓▓▓▒ |
| Value | ✱✱✱ |
| Grapes | shiraz |
| Region | Mudgee, NSW |
| Cellar | ▬ 1–5 |
| Alc./Vol. | 13.0% |
| RRP | $15.80 |

Mudgee is a good source of the honest, hearty reds that Australians love, and shiraz is a star. Andrew Harris is a well-priced example.

CURRENT RELEASE 1999    Plum, spice and minty aromas of good concentration combined with a touch of sweet oak mark the nose of this friendly young red. The palate is quite solid with good depth of smooth berry flavour followed by firm, slightly astringent tannins. Good with meaty sausages and horseradish-flavoured mash.

## Angoves Sarnia Farm Cabernet Sauvignon

| | |
|---|---|
| Quality | ▓▓▓▓ |
| Value | ✱✱✱✦ |
| Grapes | cabernet sauvignon |
| Region | Padthaway, SA |
| Cellar | ▮ 3 |
| Alc./Vol. | 13.0% |
| RRP | $17.75 |

Most Angoves' table wines fit in the everyday quaffer category, but with Sarnia Farm the company lifted its sights a little.

CURRENT RELEASE 1998    Quite intense on the nose, this shows a leafy, minty edge to blackcurranty fruit that's fresh and appetising. In the mouth it's medium-bodied with reasonable concentration of cabernet fruit, leaf and oak. The palate is clean-tasting and quite fine in texture with balanced tannins. Try it with loin of lamb with mint crust.

## Annie's Lane Cabernet Merlot

Beringer Blass have messed around with so many labels in recent years that it's a bit hard to keep track of what's what. Annie's Lane would once have been labelled Quelltaler or Eaglehawk or Black Opal. Why can't wine marketers leave well enough alone? CURRENT RELEASE 1999 These wines are great quality at a good price but without strong brand recognition – that's good news for the consumer. This cab blend has a dense-packed nose of blackberries, ironstone and smooth oak. On the palate blackberry-ish fruit intensity, sweet oak and well-modulated tannins make for fine drinking. Roast an eye fillet to go with this one.

| | |
|---|---|
| Quality | 🍷🍷🍷🍷 |
| Value | ★★★★★ |
| Grapes | cabernet sauvignon; merlot |
| Region | Clare & Barossa Valleys, SA |
| Cellar | 🍷 5 |
| Alc./Vol. | 13.5% |
| RRP | $17.50 |

## Annie's Lane Shiraz

Annie's Lane runs through the old Quelltaler Estate that produces these wines. It's named after Annie Wayman, a local identity in the 1800s. Maker: Caroline Dunn. *Previous outstanding vintages: '96, '98* CURRENT RELEASE 1999 A raw youngster with an unevolved inky nose of dark berry fruit, blackcurrants and mocha. Dusty oak plays a part too and the palate is tightly constructed with intense berry and mineral flavours, and ripe tannins. It's a bit less substantial in mid-palate fruit at this stage than the very good '98, and not as soft. Oak is more noticeable, perhaps due to vintage conditions, but it remains a good example of the genre. Serve it with a rare porterhouse.

| | |
|---|---|
| Quality | 🍷🍷🍷 |
| Value | ★★★↓ |
| Grapes | shiraz |
| Region | Clare Valley, SA |
| Cellar | 1–7 |
| Alc./Vol. | 13.5% |
| RRP | $17.00 |

## Apsley Gorge Pinot Noir

Brian Franklin fell in love with pinot noir and chardonnay, and planted a vineyard on Tasmania's sunny east coast near Bicheno. The early wines were made by Andrew Hood, the '99 onwards by Franklin. CURRENT RELEASE 2000 This won the pinot trophy at the 2001 Boutique Winery Awards and is thoroughly delightful. The bouquet is complex, with ripe cherry and vanilla plus some feral notes adding interest. Texture is a feature: it's silky smooth and fleshy, with supple tannins. It has richness and body, and would go well with barbecued quail.

| | |
|---|---|
| Quality | 🍷🍷🍷🍷 |
| Value | ★★★ |
| Grapes | pinot noir |
| Region | East Coast, Tas. |
| Cellar | 🍷 4+ |
| Alc./Vol. | 14.0% |
| RRP | $46.00 |

## Arlewood Cabernet Merlot

| | |
|---|---|
| Quality | ♥ ♥ ♥ ♥ |
| Value | ★ ★ ★ ┥ |
| Grapes | cabernet sauvignon; merlot |
| Region | Margaret River, WA |
| Cellar | ▮ 5 |
| Alc./Vol. | 13.4% |
| RRP | $22.00 |

Arlewood's new owners have ambitious plans for the future and who can blame them, it seems the whole world wants Margaret River wine! CURRENT RELEASE 1999   A deeply coloured young wine with an attractive perfumed nose of dark berry fruit, light minty scents and restrained pencil-shavings oak character. In the mouth it has good intensity and medium body with good length and a pleasantly dry finish. Try it with risotto topped with crisp pancetta.

## Arlewood Cabernet Reserve

| | |
|---|---|
| Quality | ♥ ♥ ♥ ♥ |
| Value | ★ ★ ★ |
| Grapes | cabernet sauvignon; merlot; cabernet franc |
| Region | Margaret River, WA |
| Cellar | ▮ 5 |
| Alc./Vol. | 13.5% |
| RRP | $29.00 |

A recent change of ownership at Arlewood has meant a different approach with winemaking, and from the 2000 vintage wine will be contract-made at Voyager Estate instead of Chateau Xanadu. CURRENT RELEASE 1998   There's loads of piquant mintiness to this young cab. The nose has it, along with some tangy blackcurrant aromas. Well-integrated spicy oak sits in good balance. In the mouth there's a pepperminty edge to dark fruit flavour. It's a medium-bodied wine of smooth mouth-feel. Firm tannins underpin it all well. A particular style that will suit some, but it's well made and tasty. Try it with roast lamb and . . . you guessed it, mint sauce.

## Armstrong Shiraz

| | |
|---|---|
| Quality | ♥ ♥ ♥ ♥ ♥ |
| Value | ★ ★ ★ ★ |
| Grapes | shiraz |
| Region | Great Western, Vic. |
| Cellar | ⬤━ 1–10+ |
| Alc./Vol. | 13.0% |
| RRP | $48.00 |

Tony Royal was a winemaker before taking on the job of heading up French barrel-maker Seguin Moreau's Australian operation. He keeps his winemaking hand in by producing this excellent shiraz from his own vineyard at Great Western. *Previous outstanding vintages: '97, '98* CURRENT RELEASE 1999   The Great Western region should be much better known as a source of fine red wines. This is a classic example: complex, strongly regional with an intense nose of spices, pepper, leather and mint. Stylish French oak is folded in without a ripple. It tastes powerful yet smoothly ripe. A tight structure of fine-grained tannins backs things up nicely, and it should cellar very well. Serve it with cassoulet.

# Arrowfield Cabernet Merlot

There have been lots of changes of direction at Arrowfield over the years, and they've left the brand with a rather confused identity.

CURRENT RELEASE 1999    Reasonable value here in a cab blend with a savoury nose of berries, dried herbs and a little smoky oak. The palate has fruit-sweet blackberry flavour that's direct and easy to understand. Oak makes a balanced seasoning and it finishes with restrained powdery tannins. Try it with veal escalopes overbaked with cheese.

| | |
|---|---|
| Quality | ♟ ♟ ♟ |
| Value | ★ ★ ★ |
| Grapes | cabernet sauvignon; merlot |
| Region | Hunter Valley, NSW |
| Cellar | ▮ 3 |
| Alc./Vol. | 13.0% |
| RRP | $12.95 |

# Aruna McLaren Vale Shiraz

This is a newie from some Hunter-based entrepreneurs known as Winetrust Estates. 'Aruna' means 'the charioteer of the sun', an obscure reference to its Hunter Valley location.

CURRENT RELEASE 1999    A deep purplish–red wine with a lot of charry, smoky oak on the nose, imparting hints of clove, vanilla and coffee. Berry fruit sits comfortably in the middle of the oak, and the medium-weight palate finishes long, soft and toasty. There's quite a big measure of fruit and alcoholic sweetness in this wine that won't be to everyone's taste. With short- to medium-term ageing it should come together more. Serve it with calf's liver and onions.

| | |
|---|---|
| Quality | ♟ ♟ ♟ ♟ |
| Value | ★ ★ ✦ |
| Grapes | shiraz |
| Region | McLaren Vale, SA |
| Cellar | ▮ 3 |
| Alc./Vol. | 14.6% |
| RRP | $30.00 |

# Ashwood Grove Shiraz

The Murray Valley vineyards were once a source of wine that had the discerning drinker casting around for a cold beer. But these days they have become great sources of tasty table wines that won't break the bank. Good on 'em.

CURRENT RELEASE 1999    A straightforward, no-fuss red wine of a sort that international wine drinkers can't get enough of. The nose is a spicy fruitcake of sweet berry aromas that leads to a medium-bodied mouthful, ripe and chewy textured, trimmed in quite firm tannins. Spicy berry flavour dominates, making it an easy-to-like proposition in its youth, yet one that should improve with short-term cellaring. Try it with grilled lamb chops.

| | |
|---|---|
| Quality | ♟ ♟ ♟ ♟ |
| Value | ★ ★ ★ ★ |
| Grapes | shiraz |
| Region | Murray Valley, Vic. |
| Cellar | ▮ 3 |
| Alc./Vol. | 13.5% |
| RRP | $9.50 ⑤ |

## Baileys Shiraz

| | |
|---|---|
| Quality | ♛ ♛ ♛ ♛ |
| Value | ★ ★ ★ ⟩ |
| Grapes | shiraz |
| Region | Glenrowan, Vic. |
| Cellar | ➥ 2–10 |
| Alc./Vol. | 13.5% |
| RRP | $18.50 |

This is Baileys junior shiraz, fitting in under the 1904 Block and 1920s Block wines. Of course, there's nothing junior about any Baileys reds – they all have a good measure of testosterone.

CURRENT RELEASE 1998    As usual, this is a typically hefty member of the Baileys clan. The colour is deep and the nose has big, powerful sweet fruit smells. Lately a touch of sweet oak of the US type has been creeping into the wine, to the chagrin of traditionalists. But the real story remains the big fruit, big flavour and the full-Nelson grip of big tannins, and that hasn't gone away. Try it with a rib roast of beef.

## Baldivis Estate Cabernet Merlot

| | |
|---|---|
| Quality | ♛ ♛ |
| Value | ★ |
| Grapes | cabernet sauvignon; merlot |
| Region | Margaret River, WA |
| Cellar | ▮ 1 |
| Alc./Vol. | 14.0% |
| RRP | $28.00 |

Baldivis Estate has been a rather eccentric operation in the past, but we can now expect some entrepreneurial dynamism from new owners, Palandri. The new white wines are promising, the reds less so.

CURRENT RELEASE 2000    This young cabernet blend has a strong sulfide character on the nose and palate that obscures some good fruit underneath. The authors sometimes disagree and throw childish tantrums over such things, but in this case they are in accord. It's a pity, but we think it's a bit over the top, and really shouldn't have been released onto the market.

## Balgownie Estate Shiraz

| | |
|---|---|
| Quality | ♛ ♛ ♛ ♛ |
| Value | ★ ★ ★ ⟩ |
| Grapes | shiraz |
| Region | Bendigo, Vic. |
| Cellar | ➥ 3–12+ |
| Alc./Vol. | 13.5% |
| RRP | $29.00 ▮ |

Balgownie has increased its plantings at Maiden Gully and employed a new winemaker, Tobias Ansted, formerly of Windowrie Estate. He's only the third winemaker in 33 years.

CURRENT RELEASE 1999    The traditional big, dense Balgownie red-wine style is still in evidence. It's not a wine of great elegance but if flavour is your target, this has spadefuls. There are dry spice and toasty oak aromas, and the mouth-feel is thick, chewy and tannic, bordering on heavy-handed. Cellar, then serve with steak and kidney pie.

## Bannockburn By Farr Pinot Noir

Late in 2000, Gary Farr shocked and surprised wine lovers with a new range of wines he'd been quietly working on since 1994, when he and his wife Robyn planted vines on their own land adjoining Bannockburn. The 1999 chardonnay, pinot noir, shiraz and viognier are the first crop from these vines.

**CURRENT RELEASE 1999    This is classic Farr pinot: very complex even in youth, with spicy, foresty, leather and meaty aromas, reflecting whole-bunch ferments, stalk inclusion and fine oak. It 'comes up' well in the glass, revealing its great depth and multi-layered flavours and textures. Great stuff! Have it with barbecued marinated quails.**

| | |
|---|---|
| Quality | 🍷🍷🍷🍷🍷 |
| Value | ★★★★⬩ |
| Grapes | pinot noir |
| Region | Geelong, Vic. |
| Cellar | 🍷 5+ |
| Alc./Vol. | 14.0% |
| RRP | $41.00 |

 Penguin Best Pinot Noir

## Bannockburn Pinot Noir

Bannockburn's Gary Farr has been re-nominated for *The Wine Magazine*'s Winemaker of the Year Award. Will he carry it off this time? Stay tuned.

CURRENT RELEASE 1999    The '99 has the Bannockburn hallmarks: tobacco, forest-floor, undergrowth characters from whole-bunch fermentation, but it doesn't have the customary depth of sweet fruit and profound palate strength. It's a lighter-weight wine, quite forward in development. The usual silky texture is there, and it's a very pleasant drop. Drink it soon, perhaps with turkey.

| | |
|---|---|
| Quality | 🍷🍷🍷🍷 |
| Value | ★★★ |
| Grapes | pinot noir |
| Region | Geelong, Vic. |
| Cellar | 🍷 3 |
| Alc./Vol. | 14.0% |
| RRP | $50.00 |

## Bannockburn Saignée

Saignée is a process whereby the winemaker drains part of the juice from a fermenter of crushed grapes, in order to increase the skin-to-juice ratio and concentrate the resulting wine. Maker: Gary Farr.

CURRENT RELEASE 1999    Although it comes about as a sort of by-product of winemaking, this delicious wine leaves most other Aussie rosés in the shade. Drinkability is the key. A light orange–pink shade, it has complex nutty, strawberry, cherry and toast aromas. The taste is fruity, fleshy and more-ish, with its silky, slurpy, smooth texture a highlight. It should be served cool with antipasto.

| | |
|---|---|
| Quality | 🍷🍷🍷🍷 |
| Value | ★★★★ |
| Grapes | pinot noir; shiraz; etc. |
| Region | Geelong, Vic. |
| Cellar | 🍷 1 |
| Alc./Vol. | 13.5% |
| RRP | $20.50 |

## Bannockburn Shiraz

| | |
|---|---|
| Quality | ❦❦❦❦❦ |
| Value | ★★★❧ |
| Grapes | shiraz |
| Region | Geelong, Vic. |
| Cellar | ▮ 10+ |
| Alc./Vol. | 14.5% |
| RRP | $50.00 ▮ |

That old Farr magic again! The boy has a knack with shiraz. And pinot. And chardonnay. And viognier . . . CURRENT RELEASE 1999 This is a highly aromatic shiraz, exuding complex pepper, spice and slightly vegetal cool-grown aromas that are really seductive. There is no greenness in the tannins: they're smooth and fine, the palate flavours being multi-layered and excitingly Northern Rhone-like. It's a classy, fruit-driven shiraz with great length and balance. Lovely now with spicy meatballs, and will repay cellaring.

## Banrock Station Cabernet Merlot

| | |
|---|---|
| Quality | ❦❦❦ |
| Value | ★★★★ |
| Grapes | cabernet sauvignon; merlot |
| Region | Murray Valley, SA |
| Cellar | ▮ 3 |
| Alc./Vol. | 12.5% |
| RRP | $12.50 ⑤ |

BRL Hardy's clever promotion, whereby every bottle sold sends a donation to Landcare Australia and Wetland Care Australia, has raised many thousands of dollars for those causes in recent years. CURRENT RELEASE 2000 The colour is medium–light red–purple and it has a simple but clean aroma of vanilla and raspberry. There's a hint of gaminess and it's light and fairly short on the palate, some rustic tannins bringing up the rear. It's well priced and would suit herbed rissoles.

## Banrock Station Cave Cliff Merlot

| | |
|---|---|
| Quality | ❦❦❦❦ |
| Value | ★★★★❧ |
| Grapes | merlot |
| Region | Murray Valley, SA |
| Cellar | ▮ 2 |
| Alc./Vol. | 13.0% |
| RRP | $13.00 ⑤ |

Penguin Best Bargain Red

This is a worthy follow-up to the '99 vintage, and we've made the comment before, that Cave Cliff puts many fancy-priced merlots from fashionable regions to shame. **CURRENT RELEASE 2000 First: the grapes were ripe. Second: the wine is soft and easy to drink. Third: it tastes good! You'd be shocked at how many merlots double and treble the price don't satisfy one of these criteria. This giant-killer smells appealingly of raspberry, blueberry and mulberry, without obvious oak to clutter it. The taste is light but soft and nicely balanced. Nothing out of place. It has some fruit sweetness and just a slight grip to clean the finish. Serve with meatballs and pocket the change.**

## Barak's Bridge Cabernet Sauvignon Franc Merlot

Barak's Bridge was actually a log which had fallen over the Yarra River, allowing the natives to cross the torrent on a natural 'bridge'. Maker: Tom Carson. CURRENT RELEASE 1999 This is Yering Station's second-string cab blend, and a very agreeable drop it is. It smells of mulberry, with a crushed-leaf overtone, and the palate has attractive cabernet flavour and surprisingly good extract. It's smooth, fleshy and very drinkable as a youngster. It goes well with veal parmigiana.

| | |
|---|---|
| Quality | 🍷 🍷 🍷 |
| Value | ★ ★ ★ |
| Grapes | cabernet sauvignon; cabernet franc; merlot |
| Region | Yarra Valley, Vic. |
| Cellar | 🍾 3 |
| Alc./Vol. | 13.0% |
| RRP | $16.50 Ⓢ |

## Barambah Ridge Reserve Shiraz

The grapes were grown in Queensland's Burnett Valley, where the shiraz vines are trained on a Scott Henry trellis. Scott Henry was an American rocket scientist. Viticulture is not exactly rocket science, to coin a phrase.
CURRENT RELEASE 2000 We take it all back, Scott! This is a real eye-opener. It's a lovely big, rich, ripe shiraz filled with fruitcake, chocolate, plum-cake and vanillin oak scents. It's smooth and flavoursome, almost jammy on the palate, and has generous but not obtrusive oak handling. It drinks well now with roast lamb, and could be cellared.

| | |
|---|---|
| Quality | 🍷 🍷 🍷 🍷 |
| Value | ★ ★ ★ ★ |
| Grapes | shiraz |
| Region | Burnett Valley, Qld |
| Cellar | 🍾 8+ |
| Alc./Vol. | 13.3% |
| RRP | $19.50 |

## Basedow Johannes Shiraz

Another Grange pretender . . . but it doesn't get close to the target. It's a tribute to Johannes Basedow, who founded the wine company in 1896, exactly 100 years before this was vintaged.
CURRENT RELEASE 1996 The colour has developed a brick-red edge, while the bouquet reveals herbal, sappy and green-mint aromas – rather pungent and almost like naphthalene. The oak has mellowed into the wine nicely. There's a lot of drying tannin to finish, and the mellow flavour dips a little in the mid-palate. Serve it with fungal food flavours, such as beef stroganoff.

| | |
|---|---|
| Quality | 🍷 🍷 🍷 🍷 |
| Value | ★ ★ |
| Grapes | shiraz |
| Region | Barossa Valley, SA |
| Cellar | 🍾 5 |
| Alc./Vol. | 13.4% |
| RRP | $80.00 🍾 |

## Batista Pinot Noir

| | |
|---|---|
| Quality | ▼▼▼▼▼ |
| Value | ★★★★ |
| Grapes | pinot noir |
| Region | Pemberton– Manjimup, WA |
| Cellar | ▮ 5 |
| Alc./Vol. | 13.5% |
| RRP | $28.00 |

Batista is the classically elegant label of Bob Peruch, who planted vines in the Middlesex region of Pemberton in the early 1990s – mostly pinot noir. If this is what the young vines produce, we can't wait till they mature! CURRENT RELEASE 1998    This is a bold attempt at a serious pinot. The colour is deep and the bouquet complex, echoing spices, toasty oak, leathery/meaty undertones and a half-hidden layer of ripe plum. It's full-bodied, with chewy tannins and considerable power. The use of oak hasn't been spared. Tasted in early 2001, it could still benefit from a year. Food: kangaroo tail stew.

## Belgenny Vineyard Cabernet Sauvignon

| | |
|---|---|
| Quality | ▼▼▼▼ |
| Value | ★★★ |
| Grapes | cabernet sauvignon |
| Region | Hunter Valley, NSW |
| Cellar | ▮ 6 |
| Alc./Vol. | 14.5% |
| RRP | $23.00 |

The Belgenny wines are made by contractor Greg Silkman, whose business was based at the Monarch winery, at McGuigan Wine Village, but is moving to another winery in Palmers Lane, Pokolbin. CURRENT RELEASE 1999    A decent if slightly old-fashioned wine, it smells of earthy, walnutty, oak and secondary characters, together with some age development. There are some floral, almost spirit-like high notes and the palate is big, soft, chewy and rustic with abundant sweet fruit flavour. It goes well with osso bucco.

## Best's Great Western Cabernet Sauvignon

| | |
|---|---|
| Quality | ▼▼▼▼▼ |
| Value | ★★★↓ |
| Grapes | cabernet sauvignon 90%; merlot 10% |
| Region | Great Western, Vic. |
| Cellar | ➤ 2–10+ |
| Alc./Vol. | 14.0% |
| RRP | $33.00 ▮ |

Best's has 40 hectares of vines at Great Western, some of which date back to the 1860s. But cabernet sauvignon came to Concongella relatively recently. Makers: Viv Thomson and Hamish Seabrook. CURRENT RELEASE 1998    The pungent aromas remind of cassis, peppermint, blackcurrant and crushed vine leaves. It is still quite raw and underdeveloped. The palate is slightly aggressive and it begs to be left in a dark place for a few years. This is one of the better cabs we've seen from Best's. When mature, it will suit aged Heidi gruyère.

## Best's Great Western Shiraz Bin 0

This style of shiraz needs time to reveal its true worth. It's infanticide to drink wines like this straight away. They're sensitively made, without a lot of oak or other 'hurry up' factors to bring them forward to early drinkability. But with age they leave the flatteringly soft, oaky reds way behind.

*Previous outstanding vintages: '88, '90, '91, '92, '94, '97, '98*

CURRENT RELEASE 1999    The colour is deep, dark and vivid; the nose has fresh perfumes of cherries, berries and subtle spices, with a gentle overlay of oak. The taste is lively and jumping with freshness. It's medium- to full-bodied and carries some firm astringency which will soften with age. Like a tightly clenched fist at the moment, it will open out and reward patience. Then serve it with roast lamb.

| | |
|---|---|
| Quality | 🍷🍷🍷🍷🍷 |
| Value | ★★★★ |
| Grapes | shiraz |
| Region | Great Western, Vic. |
| Cellar | ➥ 4–17+ |
| Alc./Vol. | 14.0% |
| RRP | $33.00 |

## Best's Pinot Meunier

Best's was started in 1866 by Henry Best, younger brother of Joseph Best, who started what is now Seppelt across the highway in Great Western a year earlier. Growers and makers: the Thomson family.

CURRENT RELEASE 2000    The Thomsons have struck a whimsical new label for this varietal, which has been their signature wine for many years. The nose is slightly cherry, strawberry and just a trifle herbal. The palate is tart, firm and lean, and just misses out in the texture department. It should probably be approached more as a Beaujolais style than as a serious red, and could be served chilled. Try it with antipasto.

| | |
|---|---|
| Quality | 🍷🍷🍷 |
| Value | ★★★ |
| Grapes | pinot meunier |
| Region | Great Western, Vic. |
| Cellar | 3+ |
| Alc./Vol. | 12.5% |
| RRP | $21.00 |

## Bethany Cabernet Merlot

| | |
|---|---|
| Quality | ♥ ♥ ♥ ♥ |
| Value | ★ ★ ★ |
| Grapes | cabernet sauvignon; merlot |
| Region | Barossa Valley, SA |
| Cellar | 🍶 5 |
| Alc./Vol. | 13.0% |
| RRP | $23.40 |

Bethany was one of the original settlements in the Barossa, and still retains some fine old historic stone buildings. The Schrapels have a history in the town that stretches back as long as anybody's – to 1844 when the first Schrapel arrived in Adelaide.

CURRENT RELEASE 1999    The colour is somewhat developed: slightly dilute and brick-reddish. It has greenish stalky aromas together with gumleaf and earth. There are meaty, gamy flavours to taste, which are soft and open-knit, winding toward an earthy finish. Barossa cabernet was not at its best in '99, but it drinks quite well young, with herbed meatballs.

## Bethany Grenache

| | |
|---|---|
| Quality | ♥ ♥ ♥ ♥ |
| Value | ★ ★ ★ ✦ |
| Grapes | grenache |
| Region | Barossa Valley, SA |
| Cellar | 🍶 3 |
| Alc./Vol. | 14.0% |
| RRP | $16.50 |

The drought year resulted in 'disappointingly low' crops at Bethany, but the upside was extra-good depth of flavour thanks to the concentration effect.

CURRENT RELEASE 2000    The colour is lightish red–purple and it smells of cherry-essence and confectionery. It's lightly wooded and fruity, with some spiciness, and there's no denying the grapes were ripe. The palate is full, sweet, round and smooth, with evidence of high alcohol strength and lots of charm. It would drink well with chipolatas.

## Bethany Shiraz Cabernet

| | |
|---|---|
| Quality | ♥ ♥ ♥ |
| Value | ★ ★ ★ |
| Grapes | shiraz; cabernet sauvignon |
| Region | Barossa Valley, SA |
| Cellar | ➖ 1–5+ |
| Alc./Vol. | 13.0% |
| RRP | $16.50 |

Wow, they're pushing 'em out young! At one year, this is very fresh juice. The back label gives you the entire family history to keep you occupied while you're drinking it. Makers: Geoff and Rob Schrapel.

CURRENT RELEASE 2000    It has a nice purple–red colour but smells kind of raw. Greenish vegetal and peppercorn aromas lack some of the usual Barossa sunny charm. It smacks of slightly underripe grapes – or maybe young vines? It's a decent red with plenty of flavour, and will probably be smoother and more interesting in a year or two.

## Bleasdale Generations Shiraz

This is the first vintage of a wine commemorating five generations of Potts family involvement at Bleasdale since founder Frank Potts. Their faces are ranged on a strip-label that encircles the neck of the bottle. The grapes came from the Borrett family vineyard. Maker: Michael Potts.

CURRENT RELEASE 1997   The colour is dark red–purple and the wine shows concentration and richness. In typical Langhorne style it's fleshy and luxurious, with smooth, chewy tannin and high density. The mellow flavours are of vanilla, fruitcake and chocolate, and there is evidence of generous oak treatment and elevated alcohol. It goes well with meaty lasagne.

| | |
|---|---|
| Quality | ♀ ♀ ♀ ♀ |
| Value | ★ ★ ★ |
| Grapes | shiraz |
| Region | Langhorne Creek, SA |
| Cellar | ▮ 5+ |
| Alc./Vol. | 14.5% |
| RRP | $38.00 ▮ |

## The Blend Cabernet Sauvignon

This is the second in a series started by the Boutique Wineries Association, and includes wines blended by Ralph Fowler from Majella, Hamilton, Stephen John, Saddlers Creek, Reynolds and Fowler himself.

CURRENT RELEASE 1998   Oak dominates the nose at present, but this is likely to be swallowed up given a little cellaring time. It is quite rich and intense in the mouth, and the fruit flavours seem ripe and harmonious. The tannins are fine and well balanced. Age it, then serve with cheese, such as Heidi gruyère.

| | |
|---|---|
| Quality | ♀ ♀ ♀ ♀ ♀ |
| Value | ★ ★ ★ |
| Grapes | cabernet sauvignon |
| Region | Langhorne Creek, |
| | Clare Valley, |
| | Coonawarra |
| | & McLaren Vale, SA |
| | & Orange, NSW |
| Cellar | ➥ 2–10+ |
| Alc./Vol. | 13.2% |
| RRP | $50.00 ▮ |

## Blue Pyrenees Victoria Cabernet Sauvignon

In 2000, this winery came out with a cheaper 'Victoria' range of reds and whites, blended from estate fruit as well as bought-in material. The label is similar to the estate wines, but the word 'estate' is absent from the title. Confusing? We think so.

CURRENT RELEASE 1999   It's a good wine. The hue is deep purple–red and the aromas are of chocolate, vanilla and walnut, reflecting well-meshed fruit and oak characters. Mellow for its age, smooth and savoury, it has medium weight, some density and ready drinkability. You could serve it with brasato.

| | |
|---|---|
| Quality | ♀ ♀ ♀ ♀ |
| Value | ★ ★ ★ ★ |
| Grapes | cabernet sauvignon |
| Region | Pyrenees, Vic. |
| Cellar | ▮ 5+ |
| Alc./Vol. | 14.0% |
| RRP | $17.00 Ⓢ |

## Blues Point Shiraz Cabernet

| | |
|---|---|
| Quality | ♥ ♥ ♥ |
| Value | ★ ★ ★ ★ |
| Grapes | shiraz; |
| | cabernet sauvignon |
| Region | not stated |
| Cellar | 🍷 2 |
| Alc./Vol. | 13.0% |
| RRP | $11.00 Ⓢ |

One of the authors put some blue bottles out for the glass recycling chaps. They politely left them in a neat pile on the nature strip. Do they all end up as landfill? And is that doing the environment a favour?

CURRENT RELEASE 1999    The colour is a shade light, and it doesn't have a lot of cabernet varietal character, but it's a perfectly pleasant drink. It has a lollyish cherry/plum aroma and is admirably soft and smooth on the tongue. There's no great depth or persistence, but it's fruity and good easy drinking. It goes well with cocktail frankfurts.

## Bowen Estate Cabernet Sauvignon Merlot Cabernet Franc

| | |
|---|---|
| Quality | ♥ ♥ |
| Value | ★ ★ |
| Grapes | cabernet sauvignon; |
| | merlot; |
| | cabernet franc |
| Region | Coonawarra, SA |
| Cellar | 🍷 4 |
| Alc./Vol. | 14.0% |
| RRP | $24.80 |

Alas and alack! The Bowen Estate reds are very up-and-down these days, too often tasting thin and unripe. Especially the odd years, for some reason. It's a mystery, coming from what used to be such a reliable source.

CURRENT RELEASE 1999    Have the yields got out of control? This wine is disappointingly light in colour and vegetal, with a weak, short palate. It is not totally without charms: there are mulberry, blackcurrant, crushed-leaf aromas. But it's a far cry from what it ought to be. We suggest pairing it with vitello tonnato.

## Boyntons Alluvium Reserve

| | |
|---|---|
| Quality | ♥ ♥ ♥ ♥ ♥ |
| Value | ★ ★ ★ ⁴ |
| Grapes | cabernet sauvignon; |
| | merlot; petit verdot |
| Region | Ovens Valley, Vic. |
| Cellar | ➥ 2–10+ |
| Alc./Vol. | 14.0% |
| RRP | $38.00 🍷 |
| | (cellar door) |

The name relates to the alluvial soils washed through such North East Victorian alpine river valleys as the King, Buffalo and Ovens, on which vineyards are cultivated. This is a new flagship wine for Boyntons.

CURRENT RELEASE 1998    A seriously structured red which needs time in the cellar. The bouquet has toasty, pencil-shavings wood and lightly herbal, red-berry scents. The palate is quite complex with abundant mouth-coating tannins firming up the lingering finish. It would go well with a rare porterhouse steak.

## Brand's Cabernet Sauvignon

Brand's wines have been showing a great deal of class in recent years, and this one continues the happy trend. It's got more gold medals on its chest than Idi Amin. Winemakers are Jim Brand and Jim Brayne.
**CURRENT RELEASE 1999    This is high-fidelity Coonawarra! Blackcurrant jam, cassis, Ribena – all of the above. It tastes like a protectively made wine: clean, fresh and fruity, with oodles of grapey charm and panache. It speaks throatily to us of both Coonawarra and cabernet. While it will surely be long-lived, it's amazingly enjoyable right now, especially with grilled pork sausages and 'dead horse'.**

| | |
|---|---|
| Quality | ❦ ❦ ❦ ❦ ❦ |
| Value | ★ ★ ★ ★ ★ |
| Grapes | cabernet sauvignon |
| Region | Coonawarra, SA |
| Cellar | 🍷 12+ |
| Alc./Vol. | 14.0% |
| RRP | $23.00 Ⓢ |

Penguin Best
Cabernet
Sauvignon

## Brand's Shiraz

Brand's or Laira? It's hard to know what's the real brand. Laira is the name of the property, the Brands are the founders and managers (but no longer the owners). The original owner, Captain Stentiford, named the place Laira after the square-rigger he once mastered. CURRENT RELEASE 1999    This is a clean, modern and fairly straight style of shiraz, smelling of raspberry, cherry and a hint of mint. Oak plays a minor role. It's light- to medium-bodied and has both balance and elegance. A lighter, traditional Coonawarra style. It goes well with minted lamb chops.

| | |
|---|---|
| Quality | ❦ ❦ ❦ ❦ |
| Value | ★ ★ ★ ⌐ |
| Grapes | shiraz |
| Region | Coonawarra, SA |
| Cellar | 🍷 6 |
| Alc./Vol. | 13.5% |
| RRP | $23.00 Ⓢ |

## Brand's Special Release Merlot

Brand's is now part of the McWilliam's portfolio, and the red wines have become a lot more oaky since the takeover. Is this a good thing? Yes and no. The '98 has come into balance nicely. Maker: Jim Brand.
*Previous outstanding vintage: '98*
CURRENT RELEASE 1999    The nose is all coconut and charred barrels at this stage. The wood sits apart from the wine, but it's still a baby and you have to have faith. The palate has plum and aniseed flavours. The wine has a great deal of focus and length, but we wish they'd been slightly subtler with the wood. Have patience. Then serve with beef olives.

| | |
|---|---|
| Quality | ❦ ❦ ❦ ❦ ❦ |
| Value | ★ ★ ★ ★ |
| Grapes | merlot |
| Region | Coonawarra, SA |
| Cellar | ➥ 1–8 |
| Alc./Vol. | 14.5% |
| RRP | $29.00 🍷 |

## Brokenwood Cabernet Sauvignon Merlot

| | |
|---|---|
| Quality | ▼▼▼▼ |
| Value | ★ ★ ┤ |
| Grapes | cabernet sauvignon; merlot |
| Region | McLaren Vale, SA & King Valley, Vic. |
| Cellar | ▮ 8 |
| Alc./Vol. | 13.5% |
| RRP | $28.30 |

Brokenwood is one of the success stories of the recent Aussie wine industry. It has 20 hectares of vineyards at Pokolbin, but also owns vineyards at Cowra and Beechworth, plus Seville Estate in the Yarra, and buys a lot more grapes in.

CURRENT RELEASE 1999   This takes a bit of time to open up and show its true merits. When it does, the bouquet shows sweet berry and cherry aromas coupled with vanilla bean, and the structure is smooth and medium-bodied, with savoury flavours and finishing with balanced but drying tannins. It would go a treat with a gourmet hamburger.

## Brokenwood Graveyard Vineyard

| | |
|---|---|
| Quality | ▼▼▼▼▼ |
| Value | ★ ★ ★ |
| Grapes | shiraz |
| Region | Hunter Valley, NSW |
| Cellar | ➡ 2–18+ |
| Alc./Vol. | 13.5% |
| RRP | $90.00 ▮ |

Funny name for a wine . . . but the land beneath the vines was once gazetted as the Pokolbin cemetery. A good thing it was never used for one: the vines might have been too vigorous. This wine has gradually built up a deservedly great reputation. Maker: Iain Riggs. *Previous outstanding vintages: '83, '85, '86, '88, '89, '90, '91, '93, '94, '95, '96, '98*

CURRENT RELEASE 1999   Can the Brokenwood crew pack more flavour and stuffing into a bottle than this? It's a whopper. Sniff the smoky barrel-ferment, meaty, gamy and oaky scents and for an instant you might think you're in the Barossa. The wine has firm, tight, gripping structure and the combination of fruit density, extract and solid tannin will preserve it for many years. As Hunter reds go, it's in a league of its own. Serve with charred rump steak.

## Brookland Valley Verse One Cabernet Merlot

| | |
|---|---|
| Quality | ▼▼▼▼ |
| Value | ★ ★ ★ ★ |
| Grapes | cabernet sauvignon; merlot |
| Region | Margaret River, WA |
| Cellar | ▮ 7 |
| Alc./Vol. | 13.5% |
| RRP | $21.00 Ⓢ |

Brookland Valley was begun by Malcolm and Dee Jones in 1984, then BRL Hardy acquired a half-share in 1997. Maker: Larry Cherubino.

CURRENT RELEASE 1999   Designed to drink early, this is Brookland's bistro-style red. It's dominated by gamy/meaty and berry fruit aromas rather than dominant oak, and is smoothly balanced to slip down easily. It's quite up-front for a Margaret River red: fresh and clean with good intensity. It goes well with barbecued kebabs.

## Brown Brothers Victoria Shiraz

Brown Brothers has long enjoyed a reputation as a
varietal wine specialist, and has a wider range of grape
varieties planted than most wine companies. They
were using varietal names like shiraz while most of
their competitors were stuck on claret and burgundy.
CURRENT RELEASE 1999   This is decent, although
one always hopes for more than one gets with Browns
shiraz. The bouquet is dominated by toasty, charred
oak, which donates vanilla and honeycomb scents.
The palate is slightly hollow and gives the impression it
relies a little on oak. It's a pleasant drink and would go
well with smoky barbecued sausages and tomato
sauce.

| | |
|---|---|
| Quality | ♉ ♉ ♉ |
| Value | ★ ★ ⟩ |
| Grapes | shiraz |
| Region | North East Vic. |
| Cellar | ▮ 4 |
| Alc./Vol. | 14.5% |
| RRP | $20.00 Ⓢ |

## Burge Family Winemakers Olive Hill Shiraz Grenache Mourvèdre

Rick Burge's reds have joined the legion of rich,
warm-area, small-output wines that have become
the darlings of wealthy Americans, who are paying
silly prices for them. Unfortunately.
CURRENT RELEASE 1999   This is an inky, concentrated
Barossa red with spicy, peppery mourvèdre fruit
characters leading the way. The palate is impressively
rich and solid, with lots of smooth tannin providing a
structure that's pleasing now, and will also help it age.
It would work a treat with steak and kidney pie.

| | |
|---|---|
| Quality | ♉ ♉ ♉ ♉ ♉ |
| Value | ★ ★ ★ ★ |
| Grapes | shiraz; grenache; mourvèdre |
| Region | Barossa Valley, SA |
| Cellar | ▮ 9+ |
| Alc./Vol. | 14.5% |
| RRP | $35.00 ▮ |

## Callanans Road Pinot Noir

A new second label for Tuck's Ridge on the
Mornington Peninsula. While the thought of a new
second-tier Mornington pinot noir filled the authors
with trepidation, this is actually pretty good.
CURRENT RELEASE 2000   Let's face it, most under
$20 pinot noirs really are bloody awful, so this came
as a surprise to us. It actually has *real* varietal character
with a nose of sweet red berries, undergrowth,
stems and a whisper of oak. It tastes direct and
uncomplicated with pleasant soft fruit, some savoury
notes and a dry finish. A good choice for roast pork.

| | |
|---|---|
| Quality | ♉ ♉ ♉ ♉ |
| Value | ★ ★ ★ |
| Grapes | pinot noir |
| Region | Mornington Peninsula, Vic. |
| Cellar | ▮ 2 |
| Alc./Vol. | 13.6% |
| RRP | $19.00 |

## Campbells Bobbie Burns Shiraz

| | |
|---|---|
| Quality | ♥♥♥♥ |
| Value | ★★★★ |
| Grapes | shiraz |
| Region | Rutherglen, Vic. |
| Cellar | ▮ 5+ |
| Alc./Vol. | 14.5% |
| RRP | $21.00 |

Bobbie Burns is consistently one of Rutherglen's most well-mannered red wines. Any uncouth regional traits like portiness, oxidation and flabbiness were bred out of it years ago. It's not quite a complete toff yet though.
CURRENT RELEASE 1999    This has an inviting nose of licorice, blackberries and earth with a touch of dusty oak for seasoning. It tastes ripe and plummy with hearty flavours, good depth, warmth and robust structure. Tradition is definitely served here, but it also has the clean-cut personality that today's red drinker looks for. Very much one of the new breed of Rutherglen red. Try it with good sausages, red cabbage and buttery mashed spuds.

## Campbells Shiraz Durif Cabernet

| | |
|---|---|
| Quality | ♥♥♥♥ |
| Value | ★★★⬩ |
| Grapes | shiraz; durif; cabernet sauvignon |
| Region | Rutherglen, Vic. |
| Cellar | ▮ 5 |
| Alc./Vol. | 13.5% |
| RRP | $15.70 |

Campbells do shiraz well and they're experts with durif, so why not a three-way blend with cabernet? It works quite well in an ocker Rutherglen sort of way.
CURRENT RELEASE 1999    The nose is rather old-fashioned in character with dark berry, mineral and barnyard aromas, and a leathery regional touch. In the mouth it's ripe-flavoured with a pleasant chewiness that enhances its straightforward feel. Dry tannins hold things together well. All in all an unfussed style for drinkers with traditional tastes. No worries with steak, eggs and chips.

## Campbells The Barkly Durif

| | |
|---|---|
| Quality | ♥♥♥♥ |
| Value | ★★⬩ |
| Grapes | durif |
| Region | Rutherglen, Vic. |
| Cellar | ▮ 5+ |
| Alc./Vol. | 14.5% |
| RRP | $40.00 |

Campbells' Barkly has been an attempt to lift the image of that old Rutherglen stager, durif. Trendy labelling, a big heavy bottle and a hefty price tag have combined to add some cachet, and some dollars to Campbells' bottom line, but the wine inside remains traditional North East Victoria.
CURRENT RELEASE 1997    A brick-red hue suggests a bit of bottle development in this big red. There's some maturity about the nose too, which is a complex pot-pourri of liqueur prune, mocha, exotic spiciness, vanilla and sweet porty aromas. That portiness follows through the palate which is very ripe-tasting, warm with alcohol and firmly tannic in true Rutherglen fashion. Fans will enjoy this with hearty casseroles and the like.

## Cape Mentelle Cabernet Sauvignon

Each year Cape Mentelle supremo, David Hohnen, hosts a gala cabernet tasting at the winery at Margaret River. As well as his own wine he opens cabernets of pedigree from all over the world.

*Previous outstanding vintages: '82, '83, '86, '88, '90, '91, '93, '94, '95, '96*

CURRENT RELEASE 1998    This wine has a minty, leafy edge – typical of southern Margaret River vineyards – to pure, intense blackcurrant fruit aromas and cedary high-quality French oak. In the mouth it has an essency, mouth-coating quality, still with that slightly green thread, and silky texture with fine balancing tannins. The equilibrium of this wine is very good with real length and true concentration, yet it remains fresh and appetising. Try it with little pink-roasted racks of lamb.

| | |
|---|---|
| Quality | 🍷🍷🍷🍷🍷 |
| Value | ★★★ |
| Grapes | cabernet sauvignon |
| Region | Margaret River, WA |
| Cellar | ➡ 1–8 |
| Alc./Vol. | 14.0% |
| RRP | $51.00 |

## Cape Mentelle Shiraz

Shiraz makes some special wines at Margaret River, although cabernet sauvignon is the district's primary red grape. Cape Mentelle's shiraz can be one of the best. Maker: John Durham.

*Previous outstanding vintages: '91, '93, '95, '97, '98*

CURRENT RELEASE 1999    There has been a learning curve on how to handle shiraz at Cape Mentelle, but the formula looks to be right in the '99. It's complex with gamy and earthy notes to blackberry fruit, peppery spice and balanced oak, and medium in body and intense with slightly French-accented flavour. A firm, angular spine of ripe tannins should support some bottle-age. Works well with pan-fried liver and onions.

| | |
|---|---|
| Quality | 🍷🍷🍷🍷🍷 |
| Value | ★★★✦ |
| Grapes | shiraz |
| Region | Margaret River, WA |
| Cellar | ➡ 1–8 |
| Alc./Vol. | 14.5% |
| RRP | $29.00 |

## Cape Mentelle Trinders Vineyard Cabernet Merlot

| | |
|---|---|
| Quality | 🍷🍷🍷🍷🍷 |
| Value | ★★★★ |
| Grapes | cabernet sauvignon; merlot; cabernet franc; petit verdot |
| Region | Margaret River, WA |
| Cellar | ➥ 1–8 |
| Alc./Vol. | 14.4% |
| RRP | $26.50 |

Trinders may be Cape Mentelle's junior cabernet, but it's still a serious wine. It seems to be getting more oak and better fruit selection than ever these days, making it a fine cellaring proposition.

CURRENT RELEASE 1999   A worthy understudy to Cape Mentelle's Cabernet Sauvignon at around half the price. The nose has black fruit aromas of good intensity with touches of mint and savoury capsicum. Spicy oak plays a supporting role throughout. The palate is quite complex in flavour and texture already, with sweet fruit and oak flavours interwoven with briary touches and fine-grained tannins. When mature it will suit braised lamb shanks admirably.

## Cape Mentelle Zinfandel

| | |
|---|---|
| Quality | 🍷🍷🍷🍷🍷 |
| Value | ★★★ |
| Grapes | zinfandel |
| Region | Margaret River, WA |
| Cellar | ➥ 2–10+ |
| Alc./Vol. | 15.0% |
| RRP | $32.50 |

Zinfandel is actually the primitivo of southern Italy, but it's become much more famous as California's zinfandel. Cape Mentelle pioneered Australian plantings and continues to make the best.

*Previous outstanding vintages: '81, '82, '85, '88, '91, '92, '95, '97, '98*

CURRENT RELEASE 1999   A great example of this exuberant red-wine style. Subtle it ain't. The colour is deep and the nose has a strongly aromatic, spicy, 'wild' personality, like a liquid Siena cake, rich in concentrated berries, plum and warm spices. These qualities carry on through the full-bodied, deeply flavoured palate, which is warm, chewy-textured and firm in grippy tannins. A big red to serve with oxtail.

## Cascabel Grenache et al

A cascabel is a small bell used in Spain as an adornment in processions and the like. It all figures when you know that winemaker Susana Fernandez is Spanish-born. CURRENT RELEASE 1999 Made in a savoury European style, this bright young red relies on aromas and flavours other than simple primary fruit for its appeal. The nose has pepper, earth and exotic spice aromas that suggest French Cotes du Rhone, and the lightish medium-bodied palate follows up harmoniously with dry, interesting savoury flavour and a chewy, dry finish. A bottle can disappear quickly with charcuterie and crusty bread.

| | |
|---|---|
| Quality | ♟ ♟ ♟ ♟ |
| Value | ✱ ✱ ✱ |
| Grapes | grenache; shiraz; mourvèdre |
| Region | McLaren Vale, SA |
| Cellar | ▮ 3 |
| Alc./Vol. | 13.5% |
| RRP | $20.50 |

## Castle Rock Pinot Noir

We've long thought that Castle Rock was a name to watch for wines of class and subtlety. Whites have been a high point so far, but pinot noir shows promise too. CURRENT RELEASE 1999 In some quarters Western Australia's Great Southern is touted as a great pinot noir region but the authors aren't convinced just yet. This '99 is one of the better efforts, a lighter style with pleasant strawberryish fruit aromas and a bit of savoury complexity in some briary, undergrowthy touches. The palate is fresh, light and dry with medium-intensity red fruit flavour and a soft finish. Try it with cold cuts.

| | |
|---|---|
| Quality | ♟ ♟ ♟ ♟ |
| Value | ✱ ✱ ✱ ✱ |
| Grapes | pinot noir |
| Region | Great Southern, WA |
| Cellar | ▮ 2 |
| Alc./Vol. | 11.5% |
| RRP | $22.50 |

## Chapel Hill Cabernet Sauvignon

At Chapel Hill they use super-ripe grapes, plenty of oak, and lots of T.L.C. to provide some statuesque reds that reward cellaring well. Maker: Pam Dunsford. CURRENT RELEASE 1999 A very deep concentrated colour is in keeping with this wine's substantial constitution. The nose has big ripe blackcurrant fruit along with touches of violets, mocha and cedar. The palate is solid and immature, but the seeds of greatness are there in deep black-fruit flavour, attractive chewy texture, great balance and a firm backbone of tannins. Should develop into a typically flavoursome Aussie cabernet to serve with a roast leg of lamb.

| | |
|---|---|
| Quality | ♟ ♟ ♟ ♟ ♟ |
| Value | ✱ ✱ ✱ ✱ |
| Grapes | cabernet sauvignon |
| Region | McLaren Vale & Coonawarra, SA |
| Cellar | ➡ 2–10 |
| Alc./Vol. | 13.5% |
| RRP | $24.50 |

## Chapel Hill The Vicar

| | |
|---|---|
| Quality | ♟ ♟ ♟ ♟ ♟ |
| Value | ★ ★ ★ ⟩ |
| Grapes | shiraz; |
| | cabernet sauvignon |
| Region | McLaren Vale & |
| | Coonawarra, SA |
| Cellar | 🍾 8+ |
| Alc./Vol. | 13.7% |
| RRP | $35.00 |

The chapel where the vicar once gave sermons to the faithful is now the Chapel Hill winery cellar door. CURRENT RELEASE 1998   As with most of Pam Dunsford's Chapel Hill reds this is a wine of some power. The colour is very dense and purplish, and the nose is still rather tight and closed with very concentrated blackberry, mint and spice notes dressed in a cedary sweet mix of French and American oak. The palate is full-bodied with ripely concentrated blackberry fruit, spicy notes, some spicy wood flavours and firm dry tannins. Try it with grilled eye fillet medallions.

## Chapoutier Mount Benson Shiraz

| | |
|---|---|
| Quality | ♟ ♟ ♟ ♟ ♟ |
| Value | ★ ★ ★ ⟩ |
| Grapes | shiraz |
| Region | Mount Benson, SA |
| Cellar | 🍾 4 |
| Alc./Vol. | 13.0% |
| RRP | $25.00 |

The Australian outpost of Rhone red wine producer Michel Chapoutier has a clever bilingual label – on one side this wine is 'Shiraz Red Wine', on the other 'Syrah Vin Rouge'. Not surprisingly it's an Aussie red with a French accent. CURRENT RELEASE 1999   There's a definite 'foreign' feel to this wine. It has deep colour and a nose and palate with loganberry and plum fruit mixed in with some earthy and slightly feral touches. It's fine-textured and lasts long in the mouth with a sinewy line of tannins throughout to give structure. Serve it with Lyonnaise sausages with potatoes and onions.

## Charles Melton Grenache

| | |
|---|---|
| Quality | ♟ ♟ ♟ ♟ |
| Value | ★ ★ ★ |
| Grapes | grenache |
| Region | Barossa Valley, SA |
| Cellar | 🍾 5 |
| Alc./Vol. | 15.0% |
| RRP | $24.00 |

Charles Melton was one of the first to realise what a treasure South Australia's ancient gnarled grenache vines were. At a time when growers couldn't pull their grenache out quickly enough, Melton endowed it with a new respectability. Nowadays such grapes attract a premium. How times change. CURRENT RELEASE 1998   This has the prerequisite chocolatey-rich, stewed-berries sort of character that immediately identifies very ripe Barossa grenache. Earthy notes, meatiness and vanillin oak are interwoven with that very ripe fruit to give the wine complexity. It's full-bodied, warm in alcohol and firm in tannins and would stand up well to a hearty casserole.

## Charles Melton Rose of Virginia

This is one of Australia's best rosés. It's fruity and fresh yet it has more substance than most competitors. By the way, Virginia is Charlie Melton's charming wife.
CURRENT RELEASE 2000     This has a deeper pink colour than most rosés. In fact it's almost magenta for the colour-conscious among you. The nose is grapey and sweet with red berry grenache aromas and a hint of rose petals. The raspberryish flavour flirts with sweetness although the overall impression is dry. It finishes clean and soft. It's a bit more substantial than most pink fripperies, and is suited to more robust cuisine. Try it with paella.

| | |
|---|---|
| Quality | ♟♟♟♟♟ |
| Value | ★★★★❯ |
| Grapes | grenache |
| Region | Barossa Valley, SA |
| Cellar | ▌ 2 |
| Alc./Vol. | 12.5% |
| RRP | $17.00 |

## Chateau Leamon Reserve Cabernet Sauvignon

Chateau Leamon's Reserves are strongly regional styles that will bring a smile to the dial of most Bendigo red fans. Maker: Ian Leamon.
CURRENT RELEASE 1999     There's a pungency about this wine that's very much a Bendigo trait. The nose has minty overtones to black plum aromas, meatiness and smoky oak. In the mouth it's quite big and hefty in body and texture, with aromatic, slightly medicinal fruit, warm spirity touches and firm tannins. At the moment it's hard to drink more than a small glass, but some cellar time will mellow things somewhat. Try it with barbecue pork ribs.

| | |
|---|---|
| Quality | ♟♟♟♟ |
| Value | ★★★ |
| Grapes | cabernet sauvignon |
| Region | Bendigo, Vic. |
| Cellar | ⬤ 2–8 |
| Alc./Vol. | 15.0% |
| RRP | $39.00 |

## Chateau Leamon Reserve Shiraz

Ian Leamon's Reserve wines are some of the Bendigo region's biggest and oakiest reds. They probably need long age to sort out their strong flavours, although in some vintages we wonder whether the oak will outlast the fruit character.
CURRENT RELEASE 1999     An over-the-top effort with powerful oak-derived vanilla and mocha characteristics, a jammy, spicy core of blackberryish shiraz fruit, and the lift and warmth of a goodly belt of alcohol. It's a mite raw, oaky and tannic in its youth but a long stretch in the bottle may well temper those extrovert personality traits. Try it with a roast rib of beef.

| | |
|---|---|
| Quality | ♟♟♟♟ |
| Value | ★★★ |
| Grapes | shiraz |
| Region | Bendigo, Vic. |
| Cellar | ⬤ 2–8+ |
| Alc./Vol. | 15.0% |
| RRP | $39.00 |

## Chestnut Grove Merlot

| | |
|---|---|
| Quality | ❦❦❦❦❦ |
| Value | ★★★ |
| Grapes | merlot |
| Region | Great Southern, WA |
| Cellar | ▮ 5 |
| Alc./Vol. | 14.0% |
| RRP | $36.00 |

A large, mature chestnut tree at the vineyard's highest point gives its name to this wine. Merlot is a speciality here. The maker is Kim Horton who came from Houghtons (no, this isn't a spelling error!).

CURRENT RELEASE 1999   Wine consumers, winemakers and the authors of this book are getting more of a handle on Aussie merlot these days due to wines like this. The nose has mellow varietal clues like plummy fruit, spicy fruitcake and mint-leaf aromas, seasoned with balanced vanillin oak. The lush palate has good depth and persistence. Cedary oak slots in well with the smooth fruit, and tangy acidity coupled to dry tannins gives underlying structure. A good wine for braised duck.

## Cheviot Bridge Cabernet Merlot

| | |
|---|---|
| Quality | ❦❦❦❦❦ |
| Value | ★★★★★ |
| Grapes | cabernet sauvignon; cabernet franc; merlot |
| Region | Murrindindi, Vic. |
| Cellar | ▮ 5 |
| Alc./Vol. | 13.0% |
| RRP | $27.00 |

Cheviot Bridge supremo Hugh Cuthbertson speaks of making wines 'that you can sit down and drink a bottle of'. By this he means wines that aren't aggressive or thunderingly big, like the ones that American wine gurus go ape over. This cabernet speaks volumes for his approach.

CURRENT RELEASE 1999   A sweet-fruited nose introduces this delicious youngster. Although it's a cool-climate wine it has none of the greenness that blights so many. There are succulent blackcurrant, green olive and subtle cigar-box aromas. The palate is savoury and more-ish with soft, ripe tannins and a long, gentle, fragrant finish. It's 'light' in the best sense of the term, and yes, you *can* knock off a bottle quite easily. Try it with pot-roasted rabbit.

# Cheviot Bridge Shiraz

Cheviot Bridge is an ambitious new enterprise based on vineyards near Murrindindi in the highlands above Victoria's Yarra Valley. The initial wines look very promising.
CURRENT RELEASE 1999    This quietly complex shiraz is an interesting first effort, made in a style that has more to it than simple grape and oak-derived characters. Plummy fruit leads the way along with meaty, savoury notes and some light earthiness. The palate is smooth and 'winey' with subtle flavours and moderate tannins. Try it with Moroccan lamb stew and fruity couscous.

| | |
|---|---|
| Quality | ▼▼▼▼ |
| Value | ★★★ |
| Grapes | shiraz |
| Region | Yea, Vic. |
| Cellar | ▮ 3 |
| Alc./Vol. | 13.0% |
| RRP | $27.00 |

CURRENT RELEASE 2000    This steps up a notch from the '99 with more substance, richness and depth, yet it remains true to the easy-drinking philosophy of the proprietors. The nose has plum, cherry and sweet spice aromas with very subdued oak input and an attractive savouriness. In the mouth it's smooth and gentle with silky texture and a reserved, long flavour that's fragrant and fruity. A touch of charry oak sits quietly in the background.

| | |
|---|---|
| Quality | ▼▼▼▼▼ |
| Value | ★★★★↘ |
| Grapes | shiraz |
| Region | Yea, Vic. |
| Cellar | ▮ 5 |
| Alc./Vol. | 13.0% |
| RRP | $27.00 |

# Clairault Cabernet Merlot

The Cape Clairault vineyard is a little to the north of the Willyabrup cluster of vineyards at Margaret River. Quality in this central part of the region is good.
CURRENT RELEASE 1999    A competently made young Margaret River red which is a bit more supple and less well-defined than the best of its neighbours. The colour is medium to deep red and the nose has subdued plum and berry fruit with some oaky spice. The palate is smooth and fine in texture, and very soft in fruit, with mellow fine-grained tannins underneath. A softer regional red that will go well with coq au vin rouge de Margaret River.

| | |
|---|---|
| Quality | ▼▼▼▼ |
| Value | ★★★ |
| Grapes | cabernet sauvignon; merlot |
| Region | Margaret River, WA |
| Cellar | ▮ 4 |
| Alc./Vol. | 13.5% |
| RRP | $25.00 |

## Classic McLaren La Testa The Blend

| | |
|---|---|
| Quality | ♟ ♟ ♟ ♟ ♟ |
| Value | ★ ★ ★ |
| Grapes | grenache; shiraz; cabernet sauvignon |
| Region | McLaren Vale, SA |
| Cellar | ♦ 8+ |
| Alc./Vol. | 14.5% |
| RRP | $60.00 ♦ |

Tony DeLisio has been growing grapes in McLaren Vale for many years and only recently decided to take the next step and make some wine. Roman Bratasiuk helped set him on his way. The result was fame and fortune (and huge prices) in the US.

CURRENT RELEASE 1999    This is arguably the pick of DeLisio's bevy of powerful reds. La Testa is his reserve label and The Blend is a robust style with plenty of oak and tannin giving a chunky structure. There are decadent dark-chocolate, plum, blackberry and vanilla aromas and there's enough flavour to get truly lost in! The palate has excellent focus and balance. Sydney's Ultimo Wine Centre is one of the few stockists.

## Clonakilla Cabernet Merlot

| | |
|---|---|
| Quality | ♟ ♟ ♟ ♟ ♟ |
| Value | ★ ★ ★ ★ ♦ |
| Grapes | cabernet sauvignon; merlot |
| Region | Canberra region, NSW |
| Cellar | ♦ 5 |
| Alc./Vol. | 13.5% |
| RRP | $28.00 |

Clonakilla was established at Murrumbateman in 1971. Although actually in New South Wales, this winery comes under the Canberra district umbrella.

CURRENT RELEASE 2000    The cab blend at Clonakilla tends to be overlooked, but it shouldn't be. The latest edition has sweet black-fruit aromas with a hint of earth and some herbal touches. Oak is very subtle, allowing the grapes to make a statement unencumbered by too much wood. The palate has direct berry-fruit flavours that are smooth in texture, long and moderate in tannins. Try it with chargrilled vegetables.

## Clonakilla Hilltops Shiraz

| | |
|---|---|
| Quality | ♟ ♟ ♟ ♟ ♟ |
| Value | ★ ★ ★ ★ ♦ |
| Grapes | shiraz |
| Region | Hilltops, NSW |
| Cellar | ♦ 4 |
| Alc./Vol. | 13.0% |
| RRP | $18.00 (mailing list) |

Tim Kirk makes excellent shiraz from his family's small Canberra district vineyard, but there's never enough to go around. So he's made a batch of very good shiraz he obtained from the Hilltops region of New South Wales.

CURRENT RELEASE 2000    This wine is fruit-driven with a rich nose of raspberry and cherry fruit, mated to some of those meaty, savoury notes that mark the house style. A touch of bacony oak and some feral aromas keep you coming back for a refill. In the mouth it has medium body and good length of flavour. There's not quite the velvet of the estate-grown Shiraz Viognier, but it's pretty good. Veal with a wild mushroom sauce works a treat here.

## Clonakilla Shiraz Viognier

We reckon this is the Canberra district's best wine. Unusually for an Australian red wine it has a little of the white-grape viognier blended in to add fragrance and finesse, a common practice in France's Rhone Valley. *Previous outstanding vintages: '94, '95, '97, '98, '99* CURRENT RELEASE 2000    The 2000 encapsulates Tim Kirk's Rhone-inspired style perfectly. It's very complex, even in youth, with undergrowthy, meaty, savoury notes to peppery, black cherry-like shiraz fruit. The palate has the usual silky feel, finishing in soft fine tannins and a whisper of cedary oak. Be adventurous and serve pigeon (squab for those with delicate sensibilities) with a gamy sauce.

| | |
|---|---|
| Quality | ♟ ♟ ♟ ♟ ♟ |
| Value | ★ ★ ★ ★ |
| Grapes | shiraz; viognier |
| Region | Canberra region, NSW |
| Cellar | ⬤ 1–6 |
| Alc./Vol. | 13.0% |
| RRP | $48.00 |

## Cockatoo Ridge Reserve Shiraz

Big doses of high-toast American oak play a big part in this reserve wine. Apparently, many Australian winemakers, perhaps correctly, think that the taste of oak is what consumers both here and overseas want. CURRENT RELEASE 1998    This is a smartly put-together wine with the typically mod-Australian nose of sweet blackberry fruit, spices and a big measure of sweet oak. In the mouth it has medium body and good persistence with the chocolate, vanilla and singed-wood flavours derived from oak barrels registering quite strongly. Barbecue a piece of rump steak to go with this.

| | |
|---|---|
| Quality | ♟ ♟ ♟ ♟ |
| Value | ★ ★ ★ |
| Grapes | shiraz |
| Region | Limestone Coast, SA |
| Cellar | ▮ 5 |
| Alc./Vol. | 14.0% |
| RRP | $20.00 |

## Cockfighter's Ghost Premium Reserve Cabernet Sauvignon

Although Cockfighter's Ghost wines are based in the Hunter Valley, they also bottle parcels of wine from much further afield. This cabernet comes from Coonawarra in South Australia.
CURRENT RELEASE 1999    There are pungent peppermint and subdued blackcurrant fruit aromas, coupled to cedary oak. It all adds up to a rather angular nose that needs time to soften and open up. The palate is medium-weight and tightly structured with good length but it's not a very giving wine in youth. Give it time to get it all happening. A good drop for roast lamb.

| | |
|---|---|
| Quality | ♟ ♟ ♟ ♟ |
| Value | ★ ★ ★ |
| Grapes | cabernet sauvignon |
| Region | Coonawarra, SA |
| Cellar | ⬤ 2–7 |
| Alc./Vol. | 14.0% |
| RRP | $28.95 |

## Coldstream Hills Briarston

| | |
|---|---|
| Quality | 🍷🍷🍷🍷 |
| Value | ★★★ |
| Grapes | cabernet sauvignon; merlot |
| Region | Yarra Valley, Vic. |
| Cellar | 🍾 2 |
| Alc./Vol. | 13.0% |
| RRP | $26.00 |

Briarston is one of the vineyards associated with Coldstream Hills. It gives its name to this, the Coldstream Hills standard Bordeaux blend.

CURRENT RELEASE 1998    An easy-to-like wine with no aggressive tendencies. The nose is rather loose-knit with mulchy, plummy and blackberry aromas of moderate richness, seasoned with a touch of lightly applied charry oak. In the mouth it has good texture, depth and richness with soft fine-grained tannins, making it perfect now with Toulouse sausages and white beans.

## Coldstream Hills Merlot

| | |
|---|---|
| Quality | 🍷🍷🍷🍷 |
| Value | ★★★ |
| Grapes | merlot |
| Region | Yarra Valley, Vic. |
| Cellar | 🍾 2 |
| Alc./Vol. | 13.5% |
| RRP | $28.00 |

Formerly owned by wine guru James Halliday, this beautifully situated property has been a Southcorp outpost since 1996. Merlot performs well at Coldstream Hills, particularly in warm years like '98, and usually comes in top-shelf Reserve mode as well as this less elevated version.

CURRENT RELEASE 1998    Good merlot fruit aromas on the nose are earthy, mulberry and blackberry-scented with an interesting, light, undergrowthy thread throughout. It's all very merlot and the palate has smooth easy texture and berry fruit flavour. Once again there's that slight earthiness and the tannins are fine-grained and fairly soft. Serve with cheese tarts.

## Connor Park Shiraz

| | |
|---|---|
| Quality | 🍷🍷🍷🍷 |
| Value | ★★★★⁴ |
| Grapes | shiraz |
| Region | Bendigo, Vic. |
| Cellar | ➡ 2–6 |
| Alc./Vol. | 14.0% |
| RRP | $18.00 |

Each year Bendigo winemakers release a special mixed dozen to showcase the region's shiraz. This is one of the dozen. It's available through winery cellar doors in the district.

CURRENT RELEASE 1999    Perhaps the old vines, dating back to the '60s, explain the inky concentration of this young shiraz which has black plum, blackberry and ironstone aromas, plus the requisite amounts of regional mintiness. The medium-bodied palate is dense and tightly constructed with a reduced, almost 'boiled down' fruit character, ahead of some ripe tannins. An unusual regional red that needs some bottle-age to sort itself out. Try it with roast veal.

## Coolangatta Estate Eileen Chambourcin

Alexander Berry, the first to grow wine grapes in the Shoalhaven area, didn't have chambourcin, but it's a vine that's well suited to the region. It makes an unusual style of wine: the closest thing is probably Friulian refosco. Maker: Andrew Spinaze.

CURRENT RELEASE 2000 The colour is a quite alarming vivid neon purple. The typical chambourcin aroma reminds of charcoal and cherries. It's lean and light- to medium-bodied, with prominent acid and a subtle tannin grip. Unlike many chambourcins, this has some middle palate. It would go with meatballs in a tomato sauce.

| | |
|---|---|
| **Quality** | 🍷🍷🍷🍷 |
| **Value** | ★★★½ |
| **Grapes** | chambourcin |
| **Region** | Shoalhaven, NSW |
| **Cellar** | 🍾 5 |
| **Alc./Vol.** | 13.7% |
| **RRP** | $19.00 (cellar door) |

## Coriole Sangiovese

Coriole planted sangiovese in the 1980s, which makes them one of the Australian pioneers of this now popular Italian grape variety.

CURRENT RELEASE 1999 An authentic varietal wine, Coriole's '99 Sangiovese has that cherry, undergrowth and mocha mystery that makes this variety so different and appealing. The palate is typically dry and structured with a lean core of understated earthy cherry fruit. It finishes with quite a firm grip which will melt away with the appropriate food: try baby lamb or kid wet-roasted with a little balsamic.

| | |
|---|---|
| **Quality** | 🍷🍷🍷½ |
| **Value** | ★★★ |
| **Grapes** | sangiovese |
| **Region** | McLaren Vale, SA |
| **Cellar** | 🍾 4 |
| **Alc./Vol.** | 14.0% |
| **RRP** | $17.95 |

## Craiglee Cabernet Sauvignon

Shiraz is the Sunbury district's main claim to fame today, just as it was over a century ago, but cabernet can also work well in the hands of Craiglee's Patrick Carmody.

CURRENT RELEASE 1999 With more cool-climate character than usual, this still shows good ripeness via some mulberry and light blackberry aromas along with a touch of mint. Oak is handled with restraint, and it tastes pleasantly of berries with savoury, briary touches. Tannins are well integrated and non-threatening. A tasty, middleweight red which is a shade simpler in personality than Craiglee's best. Serve it with scaloppine.

| | |
|---|---|
| **Quality** | 🍷🍷🍷🍷 |
| **Value** | ★★★ |
| **Grapes** | cabernet sauvignon |
| **Region** | Sunbury, Vic. |
| **Cellar** | 🍾 5 |
| **Alc./Vol.** | 13.5% |
| **RRP** | $30.00 |

## Craiglee Shiraz

| | |
|---|---|
| Quality | 🍷🍷🍷🍷 |
| Value | ★★★★ |
| Grapes | shiraz |
| Region | Sunbury, Vic. |
| Cellar | ➾ 2–6+ |
| Alc./Vol. | 13.0% |
| RRP | $35.00 |

With the vintage variations of this mild Sunbury climate, some years provide wines of full flavour and concentration; others make wines of finesse and delicacy. They're always interesting and rarely less than very good. *Previous outstanding vintages: '86, '88, '90, '91, '92, '93, '94, '96, '97, '98*

CURRENT RELEASE 1999    A slightly lighter-styled Craiglee than '97 or '98, this still has the savoury balance between peppery spice, cherry-berry fruit and subtle undergrowthy touches that marks the house style. A hint of spicy, camphory oak peeks through, and the flavour is nicely spicy/fruity and well balanced. It needs time to build the extras that bottle-age brings. Serve it with lamb pastries.

## Cranswick Estate Vignette Cabernet Merlot

| | |
|---|---|
| Quality | 🍷🍷🍷 |
| Value | ★★★ |
| Grapes | cabernet sauvignon; merlot |
| Region | Riverina, NSW |
| Cellar | 🍷 2 |
| Alc./Vol. | 13.0% |
| RRP | $12.60 |

Cranswick Estate has expanded from its Griffith base into other broad-acre vineyard territory like the Murray Valley, via a merger with Alambie wines. Most of their wines are budget-oriented.

CURRENT RELEASE 1999    The nose is lightly aromatic with hints of blackcurrant, dried leaves and a slightly gamy note. In the mouth it has savoury flavours that once again suggest herbs along with hints of currants and aniseed. It finishes clean with light dry tannins. Try it with spaghetti and ragu.

## Cullen Cabernet Merlot

| | |
|---|---|
| Quality | 🍷🍷🍷🍷🍷 |
| Value | ★★★★⧹ |
| Grapes | cabernet sauvignon; merlot; cabernet franc |
| Region | Margaret River, WA |
| Cellar | ➾ 3–12+ |
| Alc./Vol. | 13.5% |
| RRP | $70.00 |

One of Australia's great red wines, made by a wonderful daughter and mother combination, using absolutely perfectionist techniques in both vineyard and winery.

CURRENT RELEASE 1999    The '98 was a hard act to follow, but this isn't far behind. It's supremely elegant, and perhaps a bit shy in its youth, but the building blocks of excellence are all there. An intense yet beguilingly fresh nose ties together aromas of violets, blackcurrants, crushed vine leaves and cedary-sweet oak. The palate follows with great balance and intensity, and long flavour, finishing with lovely fine-grained tannins. Give it a couple of years (at least) and serve with spring lamb.

## Currency Creek Ostrich Hill Shiraz

This isolated vineyard is found near Goolwa, close to the mouth of Lake Alexandrina where the Murray flows into the sea. The nearest wine region of reasonable size is at Langhorne Creek.

CURRENT RELEASE 1999   There's some intense, ripe shiraz fruit in the spice, blackberry and plum aromas of this wine. There's also the 'coconut rough' and vanilla caramel influences of a fair bit of American oak, but the balance isn't out of whack. It tastes juicy, intense and full-flavoured with good depth, against a background of fine, dry tannins. A worthy representative of an out-of-the-way pocket of viticulture. Serve it with a rare thick T-bone steak.

| | |
|---|---|
| Quality | ♟♟♟♟♟ |
| Value | ★★★★ |
| Grapes | shiraz |
| Region | Currency Creek, SA |
| Cellar | ➡ 1–8 |
| Alc./Vol. | 14.0% |
| RRP | $20.00 |

## D'Arenberg D'Arry's Original

An institution, D'Arry's Original was once known as D'Arenberg Burgundy and enjoyed a loyal following among people who didn't mind the sulfide aromas it sometimes had. These days it's fresher and more modern, but only just.

*Previous outstanding vintages: '86, '87, '88, '91, '94, '96, '97, '98*

CURRENT RELEASE 1999   There's good depth in this vintage of D'Arry's. It has a complex nose with less earth than usual but more spicy, peppery notes seasoning the plummy fruit. The palate is warm and savoury with a whisker less flavour ripeness than we're used to. That said, it's still a time capsule of how things used to be, only better. Try it with good Irish stew.

| | |
|---|---|
| Quality | ♟♟♟♟ |
| Value | ★★★★ |
| Grapes | shiraz; grenache |
| Region | McLaren Vale, SA |
| Cellar | ♟ 10 |
| Alc./Vol. | 14.5% |
| RRP | $20.90 Ⓢ |

## D'Arenberg The Stump Jump Grenache Shiraz

| | |
|---|---|
| Quality | ▯ ▯ ▯ ▯ |
| Value | ★ ★ ★ ★ ✦ |
| Grapes | grenache; shiraz |
| Region | McLaren Vale, SA |
| Cellar | ▮ 3 |
| Alc./Vol. | 14.5% |
| RRP | $11.00 $ |

The legendary D'Arenberg back labels are an absolute mine of historical information. This one tells us that many of the original McLaren Vale vineyards were cleared using South Australian-invented stump-jump ploughs. Now we know.

CURRENT RELEASE 1999   No finesse here, this is a bit rough and ready, with a stewed red berries sort of nose with some spice and earth to it. The palate is medium-bodied with deep, ripe, earthy berry flavours of old-fashioned, rustic interest. Tannins are moderate and the flavour is surprisingly persistent. Not a bad entrant in the 'more bang for your buck' stakes. Try it with lup cheong (steamed Chinese sausage) and steamed rice.

## Dalwhinnie Eagle Shiraz

| | |
|---|---|
| Quality | ▯ ▯ ▯ ▯ ▯ |
| Value | ★ ★ ✦ |
| Grapes | shiraz |
| Region | Pyrenees, Vic. |
| Cellar | ▮ 15+ |
| Alc./Vol. | 14.0% |
| RRP | $160 ▮ |

Dalwhinnie's David Jones plans to make more 'luxury, single block' wines in future. Eagle is a small-production wine (210 dozen) from the heart of the original vineyard, made by Jones using Burgundian methods. *Previous outstanding vintages: '86, '92, '97*

CURRENT RELEASE 1998   What a wine! Totally hand-made, this is at least as good as the heroic '97. Whole-bunch fermented, foot trodden, basket pressed, and it's stunning! The bouquet is many-layered, with foresty whole-bunch characters mingling with spice and berry flavours. In the mouth it's sumptuously fleshy, smooth and rich, somewhat akin to a top-notch Hermitage. Just a pity about the price. Enjoy it with duck confit.

## Dalwhinnie Moonambel Cabernet

| | |
|---|---|
| Quality | ▯ ▯ ▯ ▯ ▯ |
| Value | ★ ★ ★ ✦ |
| Grapes | cabernet sauvignon |
| Region | Pyrenees, Vic. |
| Cellar | ➥ 5–18+ |
| Alc./Vol. | 13.0% |
| RRP | $46.00 |

This is one of the most formidable reds in the country. Some say it's like the Monty Python line: for laying down and avoiding! We think differently.

CURRENT RELEASE 1999   It's tempting to say 'Throw away the key' here. It needs plenty of time. A pity it's released so young. It has a dark colour, and the dried-banana and bay-leaf aromas are quite unevolved. The palate is very deep and has a vice-like grip. It goes well with rare roast beef after extended breathing; that is, 24 hours!

# Dalwhinnie Shiraz

The Joneses of Dalwhinnie have gradually bought more land over the last decade, doubling the area under vines to 26 hectares. Recent plantings include sangiovese and viognier. Don Lewis made this wine at Mitchelton.
CURRENT RELEASE 1999    Another fine Dalwhinnie shiraz, although not as mind-blowing as the '98 or '97. There are slightly unintegrated dried-banana, dried-spice, bay-leaf and oaky scents and it's leaner and less powerful in the mouth than the '98. The flavour is still traditional Dalwhinnie and the finish is extended by gripping tannins. Cellar, then drink with braised beef.

| | |
|---|---|
| Quality | ♟♟♟♟♟ |
| Value | ★★★★ |
| Grapes | shiraz |
| Region | Pyrenees, Vic. |
| Cellar | ← 1–10+ |
| Alc./Vol. | 14.0% |
| RRP | $51.00 |

# De Bortoli Gulf Station Pinot Noir

The Gulf Station in the Yarra Valley is worth a visit for a glimpse of country life in the time when the squatter reigned. De Bortoli's Yarra vineyard is planted on ground that was once part of Gulf Station, hence the name.
CURRENT RELEASE 2000    A bright-coloured young pinot that opens up with a surge of juicy plummy fruit aroma which is just touched by a whisper of oak. In the mouth it's light and juicy with fruity flavour and medium body. A pleasant, simply constructed pinot noir to drink young and fresh. Serve it with a ham dish.

| | |
|---|---|
| Quality | ♟♟♟♟ |
| Value | ★★★★⁺ |
| Grapes | pinot noir |
| Region | Yarra Valley, Vic. |
| Cellar | 2 |
| Alc./Vol. | 13.0% |
| RRP | $16.50 (S) |

# De Bortoli Windy Peak Pinot Noir

Between their Riverina and Yarra Valley estates, De Bortoli now have several ranges of wines at different price points and in different styles. There should be something for everyone. Windy Peak is one of the most reliable brands of reasonably priced wines from the Yarra Valley.
CURRENT RELEASE 2000    This pinot gives varietal flavour that some wines at twice the price lack. It has earthy strawberry aromas with some dried undergrowth and light oak. It tastes smooth with good intensity of varietal flavour and a clean, soft finish. Serve it with a terrine.

| | |
|---|---|
| Quality | ♟♟♟♟ |
| Value | ★★★★★ |
| Grapes | pinot noir |
| Region | various, Vic. |
| Cellar | 2 |
| Alc./Vol. | 13.0% |
| RRP | $15.00 (S) |

## De Bortoli Yarra Valley Pinot Noir

| | |
|---|---|
| Quality | ▇▇▇▇ |
| Value | ★★★ |
| Grapes | pinot noir |
| Region | Yarra Valley, Vic. |
| Cellar | ▌ 5 |
| Alc./Vol. | 13.0% |
| RRP | $35.00 |

For people with no experience of making pinot noir table wines before they bought their Yarra Valley property in 1987, the De Bortoli clan has learnt quickly, making fine pinots across a variety of price points. Good on 'em, we say.

CURRENT RELEASE 1999    In '99 this pinot looks to have a bit less concentration than the last couple, but it retains a varietally correct stance. The nose has earthy, undergrowthy aromas interwoven with plummy, spicy fruit. There's a bit more oak too, and this conceals the fruit intensity somewhat. The palate is rich and long but once again not as sumptuous as some vintages. It's still a very good wine and maybe all it needs is time. Try it with rabbit casserole.

## Deakin Estate Cabernet Sauvignon

| | |
|---|---|
| Quality | ▇▇▇▇ |
| Value | ★★★★┥ |
| Grapes | cabernet sauvignon |
| Region | Murray Valley, Vic. |
| Cellar | ▌ 3 |
| Alc./Vol. | 13.5% |
| RRP | $10.00 ⑤ |

Deakin Estate's advertising depicts a clergyman in various scenes involving bottles of wine – a play on words, doncha know – and we wonder what the church thinks.

CURRENT RELEASE 2000    Ten bucks can still secure a decent drink of red, even in this age of rising prices and premium red-grape shortage. This has an excellent cherry red–purple colour and a reserved aroma of toasty wood, berries and vanilla: youthful, pleasant but not complex. It has very reasonable weight and depth of flavour, and finishes with light but slightly rough tannin. It would go well with meatballs.

## Deakin Estate Merlot

| | |
|---|---|
| Quality | ▇▇▇ |
| Value | ★★★★ |
| Grapes | merlot |
| Region | Murray Valley, Vic. |
| Cellar | ▌ 2 |
| Alc./Vol. | 14.0% |
| RRP | $10.00 ⑤ |

Merlot is the buzz grape of the moment, but without due reason, in our book. Too many merlots are green, skinny and over-priced. At least this one isn't pretending to be Chateau Petrus.

CURRENT RELEASE 2000    This is merlot gone feral! The colour is medium–deep red–purple and it smells very gamy, as well as cherry-like. The palate is soft, fruit-sweet and gentle, which is better than some merlots twice its price. Serve it with lamb's fry and bacon.

# Deakin Estate Shiraz

Red wine quality in the hot, irrigated Riverland districts has received a boost in recent years from such innovations as regulated deficit irrigation and partial root-zone drying. The former enables growers to avoid over-watering the vines, and the latter helps raise grape quality by mildly stressing the vine.
CURRENT RELEASE 2000    This is pretty much on the money for a $9 to $10 wine. It has a good full purple–red colour and smells of plummy, earthy, meaty regional shiraz fruit. It's a simple wine, fairly light and perhaps a trifle weak, but it's a clean, well-made and attractive drink that's fair value at the price. It's young and slightly raw, and there's negligible tannin to get in the way of your enjoyment. Try it with meatballs.

| | |
|---|---|
| Quality | ♟ ♟ ♟ |
| Value | ★ ★ ★ ⟩ |
| Grapes | shiraz |
| Region | Murray Valley, Vic. |
| Cellar | ▮ 3 |
| Alc./Vol. | 13.5% |
| RRP | $10.00 ⑤ |

# Deen De Bortoli Vat 8 Shiraz

Deen's father Vittorio De Bortoli arrived in Griffith from Italy in 1923, and made his first wine in 1928. You could say he started something. Today, the company is one of the 10 biggest in Australia.
CURRENT RELEASE 2000    A nice quaffing red at a decent price is all they're aiming for here. The colour is lightish red–purple and it has a light aroma of minty, herbal fruit – uncluttered by wood. It's light-bodied with clean mulberry flavour and a dash of drying tannin to close. It goes well with spaghetti bolognaise.

| | |
|---|---|
| Quality | ♟ ♟ ♟ |
| Value | ★ ★ ★ ⟩ |
| Grapes | shiraz |
| Region | Riverina, NSW |
| Cellar | ▮ 3 |
| Alc./Vol. | 12.5% |
| RRP | $11.75 ⑤ |

# Devil's Lair Fifth Leg

This is the value bet at Devil's – it's a similar style with quality not far different from the pricey Margaret River cabernet. This one's likely to mature more quickly because of the grape mix. Maker: Janice McDonald.
CURRENT RELEASE 1999    This is intended as an earlier drinking style but it will certainly benefit from cellaring. The bouquet offers charcuterie and smoked-meats scents and it's a little underdeveloped for a bistro wine. It's quite firm and tight and begs for a little cellar time to complex further. There's a hint of hollowness in the middle but it's a pretty smart red. Serve with washed-rind cheeses.

| | |
|---|---|
| Quality | ♟ ♟ ♟ ♟ |
| Value | ★ ★ ★ ★ |
| Grapes | cabernet sauvignon; shiraz; merlot; cabernet franc; petit verdot |
| Region | Margaret River, WA |
| Cellar | ▬ 1–8+ |
| Alc./Vol. | 14.0% |
| RRP | $24.00 ▮ |

## Devil's Lair Margaret River

**Quality** 🍷🍷🍷🍷½
**Value** ★★★½
**Grapes** cabernet sauvignon
**Region** Margaret River, WA
**Cellar** 2–12+
**Alc./Vol.** 13.5%
**RRP** $44.00

We can see why winemaker Stuart Pym moved from Voyager Estate to Devil's when he had the chance; both make excellent whites but the quality of Devil's red grapes is much higher.

CURRENT RELEASE 1998 This is all cabernet, and a seriously structured cabernet it is too. There are subtle charcuterie and smoked-meat aromas, coupled with fine toasty oak. In the mouth it is very lively and a tad astringent – just needing time. Buried deep within are some delicious cabernet berry flavours. Tight structure and firm tannins complete the picture. Cellar, then try it with hard cheeses.

## Diamond Valley Vineyards Close Planted Pinot Noir

**Quality** 🍷🍷🍷🍷🍷
**Value** ★★★½
**Grapes** pinot noir
**Region** Yarra Valley, Vic.
**Cellar** 4
**Alc./Vol.** 12.5%
**RRP** $59.50

The grapes come from a single patch of vines, which were planted close together, Burgundy style. In 1999, only 103 dozen bottles were produced, so it's very scarce. Makers: David and Jamie Lance.

CURRENT RELEASE 1999 Simply delicious! This sent us into transports of delight. It's a succulent, seductive, sweetly flavoured wine which is lovely alone but even better with food, such as salmon risotto. Medium–light red–purple colour; fresh raspberry, cherry nose with straw and sappy notes. It's fleshy and sweet, ripe tasting but modest in alcohol strength. Very fine pinot.

## Diamond Valley Yarra Valley Pinot Noir

**Quality** 🍷🍷🍷🍷½
**Value** ★★★★½
**Grapes** pinot noir
**Region** Yarra Valley, Vic.
**Cellar** 4
**Alc./Vol.** 13.0%
**RRP** $24.50

The blue-label Diamond Valley pinot is now known as the Yarra Valley pinot, and is made from grapes purchased from other local growers. It gets the same treatment as the estate wines but is lighter, less expensive and destined for earlier drinking. It often wins high awards all the same.

CURRENT RELEASE 2000 The fruit shows seductively sweet, fully ripe flavours in the cherry/plum spectrum with a discreet embellishment of vanillin oak. It is not especially complex but is beautifully textured and supple, with succulent sweet fruit and good length. It drinks well with duck risotto.

## Dowie Doole Cabernet Sauvignon

Dowie Doole is the unlikely named resulting from the joining of resources of two grapegrowers, Drew Dowie and Norm Doole. The wines are made at Boar's Rock by the highly experienced Brian Light.

CURRENT RELEASE 1999 This has nice fruit concentration and a degree of elegance. Berry fruit and oak flavours are finely melded, together with sandy tannins. The palate has good length. It's a bit young now, but should drink well between, say, 2003 and 2008. Like many Aussie reds, it's been thrust onto the market too soon. Try it with a rare and bloody steak.

**Quality** 🍷🍷🍷🍷½
**Value** ★★★★
**Grapes** cabernet sauvignon
**Region** McLaren Vale, SA
**Cellar** 2–7+
**Alc./Vol.** 13.5%
**RRP** $21.50

## Dowie Doole Merlot

McLaren Vale seems to be dominating the merlot market by sheer weight of numbers. It is a good red wine region but we're not convinced it can produce the best Australian merlots. Coonawarra leads the charge at present.

CURRENT RELEASE 1999 This is a somewhat callow young red, showing herbaceous and slightly raw berry-like fruit aromas and some coffee/vanillin oak that has yet to fully integrate. There are meaty/gamy and tobacco aromas, too. It is very soft on the tongue and falls away at the finish. Still, it's an enjoyable drink, with a salami sandwich.

**Quality** 🍷🍷🍷½
**Value** ★★★
**Grapes** merlot
**Region** McLaren Vale, SA
**Cellar** 1–5
**Alc./Vol.** 14.0%
**RRP** $21.00

## Dromana Estate Pinot Noir

| | |
|---|---|
| Quality | ♥ ♥ ♥ ♥ |
| Value | ★ ★ ★ |
| Grapes | pinot noir |
| Region | Mornington Peninsula, Vic. |
| Cellar | ▮ 2 |
| Alc./Vol. | 13.0% |
| RRP | $30.00 |

Garry and Margaret Crittenden have suddenly 'grown up' Dromana Estate, by floating it on the stock exchange and merging it with Mornington Estate and Yarra Valley Hills. They now have 24 different wines under five brands. Ulp!

CURRENT RELEASE 1999    The colour is medium–light red–purple and there's an appealing fragrance of spicy, strawberry, slightly herbal pinot fruit. It's light-bodied and fairly straightforward to taste, without a great deal of excitement. There's a hint of greenness in the fruit, but it's a pretty, ready-drinking style. Try beef carpaccio.

| | |
|---|---|
| Quality | ♥ ♥ ♥ ♥ ♥ |
| Value | ★ ★ ★ ★ |
| Grapes | pinot noir |
| Region | Mornington Peninsula, Vic. |
| Cellar | ▮ 5 |
| Alc./Vol. | 13.0% |
| RRP | $30.00 |

CURRENT RELEASE 2000    Winemakers Judy Gifford and Garry Crittenden are getting there! This is the most delicious pinot we've seen from Dromana. There's no hint of greenness: it's lovely and ripe, seductively flavoured, smooth and complex, with a power of sweet cherry fruit. There are grace notes of gaminess, spices and balanced oak, and it sustains your interest to the last drop. It goes well with shepherd's pie.

## E&C Cabernet Sauvignon

| | |
|---|---|
| Quality | ♥ ♥ ♥ ♥ |
| Value | ★ ★ ★ ★ ¹ |
| Grapes | cabernet sauvignon |
| Region | McLaren Vale, SA |
| Cellar | ▮ 5+ |
| Alc./Vol. | 14.0% |
| RRP | $16.50 |

The heritage in history and goodwill of names like Seaview means little to some marketing types. Thus the name disappears from the best Seaview wines, replaced by E&C. Despite that, this standard cabernet is a very good wine in keeping with Seaview tradition.

CURRENT RELEASE 1999    Good depth of colour introduces a flavoursome wine with intense plum, sweet spice and earthy touches. It has a ripe, concentrated palate that combines that plummy fruit with toasty oak and chewy tannins in attractive balance. Good value and a great partner for rare roast beef.

## Elderton Command Shiraz

Command started life as one of those macho, woody-tasting Barossa wines that seemed dedicated to keeping the oak industry buoyant. These days butch new oak is still a big factor, but the fruit stands up to it a bit more. CURRENT RELEASE 1996    This fits into the syrupy, oaky style beloved of some of our overseas colleagues. It has a powerful bouquet that lacks refinement, but it does come good with aromas of liqueur cherry chocolates, stewed blackberries, coffee and potent, raw, new-sawn oak. The solid texture, super-concentrated flavour and tightly knit tannins make this a wine to drink with a brontosaurus steak.

| | |
|---|---|
| Quality | ▮▮▮▮ |
| Value | ★★ |
| Grapes | shiraz |
| Region | Barossa Valley, SA |
| Cellar | ➡ 2–10 |
| Alc./Vol. | 14.5% |
| RRP | $75.00 ▮ |

## Eldridge Gamay

There was a time when bright young things guzzled French Beaujolais like there was no tomorrow. Trendiness is fickle, and when the fashion passed Beaujolais-type wines became decidedly uncool. Pity really, since light reds like this gamay, served cool, are ideal for slaking Aussie summer thirsts. CURRENT RELEASE 2000    Although most of the 2000 will have disappeared from the stores by now, this wine is worth checking out each vintage. This local beaujolais look-alike of delicious drinkability is bright and purplish. The nose is vibrant with appetising red-berry and plum aromas, and a sappy edge. In the mouth it is light yet tasty with a juicy surge of fruit and a friendly soft finish. Excellent served chilled with some antipasto.

| | |
|---|---|
| Quality | ▮▮▮▮▮ |
| Value | ★★★★ |
| Grapes | gamay |
| Region | Mornington Peninsula, Vic. |
| Cellar | ▮ 1 |
| Alc./Vol. | 13.3% |
| RRP | $20.00 |

## Element Shiraz Cabernet

Everyone seems to be courting the affections (and affectations) of that groovy group known in marketing hype as Generation X. Sandalford's entrant in the game is Element with an arty new-age label that fits the scene well.
CURRENT RELEASE 2000    Straightforward and fresh, this young red has a nose of berries, mint and earthy touches. The palate has good balance and an easy tannin finish, making it a good everyday drink that's not too demanding. Stirfry some beef and Chinese rice noodles for this one.

| | |
|---|---|
| Quality | ▮▮▮ |
| Value | ★★★ |
| Grapes | shiraz; cabernet sauvignon |
| Region | various, WA |
| Cellar | ▮ 2 |
| Alc./Vol. | 13.0% |
| RRP | $12.00 ⓢ |

## Elgee Park Family Reserve Pinot Noir

| | |
|---|---|
| Quality | ♉ ♉ ♉ ♉ |
| Value | ✶ ✶ ✶ ⰾ |
| Grapes | pinot noir |
| Region | Mornington Peninsula, Vic. |
| Cellar | ⌀ 4 |
| Alc./Vol. | 13.0% |
| RRP | $30.00 |

The Myer family of retail fame turned their entrepreneurial talents to wine when they pioneered the Mornington Peninsula wine industry in the early '70s. Their Elgee Park property inspired lots of others. CURRENT RELEASE 1999   A pinot with a bit more rustic, feral personality than some of its pristine Peninsula neighbours. Succulent cherry and red-berry aromas have some earthy and slightly animal touches to them and there's a briary, foresty feel. The palate's a bit 'wild' as well with rich gamy flavours of good depth and easy texture. It finishes fine and long. This would sit well with duck dishes.

## Elmswood Estate Cabernet Sauvignon

| | |
|---|---|
| Quality | ♉ ♉ ♉ ⰾ |
| Value | ✶ ✶ ✶ |
| Grapes | cabernet sauvignon |
| Region | Yarra Valley, Vic. |
| Cellar | ⌀ 3 |
| Alc./Vol. | 12.7% |
| RRP | $25.00 |

Another new name from Victoria where it's hard to keep up with the growth in vineyards. Unlike many, Elmswood's Yarra vines are quite mature. CURRENT RELEASE 1999   This is a very soft cabernet with sweet plum, earth and barnyardy aromas robed in balanced oak. There's almost a pinot-ish feel to it. In the mouth that impression carries on via savoury, smoky flavours and soft tannins. An ideal cab for people who find the big, firm style a bit much to take. This would drink well with Lyonnaise sausage.

## Evans and Tate Barrique 61 Cabernet Merlot

| | |
|---|---|
| Quality | ♉ ♉ ♉ ⰾ |
| Value | ✶ ✶ ✶ |
| Grapes | cabernet sauvignon; merlot |
| Region | Margaret River, WA |
| Cellar | ⌀ 3 |
| Alc./Vol. | 14.0% |
| RRP | $19.85 |

This is one of Evans and Tate's mid-range wines, slotting in a bit below the Margaret River flagships. These days it's all Margaret River grapes too. CURRENT RELEASE 1999   Cabernet sauvignon qualities dominate in this wine which has an intense nose of crushed blackcurrants, leaves and all. The palate is dry and angular with more of that lively, leafy cab character. It finishes fresh in acidity and moderate in tannins. A good partner for some grilled lamb cutlets.

## Evans and Tate Margaret River Cabernet Sauvignon

Margaret River is one of the greatest new wine regions to be established since the planting boom of the '60s. And vineyard growth continues apace, particularly at Evans and Tate.

CURRENT RELEASE 1998  An emphatic wine with a nose of mint, herbs, blackcurrant and a hint of prune. The leafy, foresty notes are noticeable but don't dominate, and there's a cedary austerity that comes from a healthy helping of French oak. The palate follows suit with strong cabernet varietal notes, savoury flavours, the taste of oak, and fresh acidity which gives it a mouth-watering tang. Medium-bodied with relatively soft tannins, this is a red that grows on you the more you sip it. Try it with roast lamb.

| | |
|---|---|
| Quality | ▼▼▼▼▽ |
| Value | ★★★↦ |
| Grapes | cabernet sauvignon |
| Region | Margaret River, WA |
| Cellar | ➥ 1–6 |
| Alc./Vol. | 13.5% |
| RRP | $39.75 |

## Evans and Tate Margaret River Shiraz

Much ballyhoo surrounded the 1999 vintage of this wine being named Best Red Wine out of 4875 entrants in Britain's International Wine Challenge (not all of them shirazes, of course). As with many international awards and opinions, we wonder why it was chosen above many others. Yes, it is a very good drop, but the best in the world?

CURRENT RELEASE 1999  The colour is very deep and the nose has a lot of concentration. Toasty oak plays a role and spicy cherry and plum fruit dovetail in nicely on the nose. In the mouth it's very rich and fleshy with dark cherry fruit, a notable seasoning of charry oak, good length and balanced dry tannins. This goes well with osso buco braised in red wine.

| | |
|---|---|
| Quality | ▼▼▼▼▽ |
| Value | ★★★↦ |
| Grapes | shiraz |
| Region | Margaret River, WA |
| Cellar | ➥ 1–5+ |
| Alc./Vol. | 14.0% |
| RRP | $27.50 |

## Evans and Tate Redbrook Shiraz

| | |
|---|---|
| Quality | ♟ ♟ ♟ ♟ ♟ |
| Value | ★ ★ ★ |
| Grapes | shiraz |
| Region | Margaret River, WA |
| Cellar | ⬥ 1–10 |
| Alc./Vol. | 14.0% |
| RRP | $50.00 |

Redbrook is a flagship label for Evans and Tate.
Sometimes this red is a blend of grape varieties
but the latest version is a straight shiraz.
CURRENT RELEASE 1998    Oak plays a big part in the
Redbrooks, but if the fruit's up to it, why not? This shiraz
has a subdued, seamless nose that combines ripe, very
concentrated dark fruit with high-quality oak in good
measure. In the mouth it shows more of the same, and
the tight, concentrated flavour and texture floods all the
way down the palate without letting up. This still needs
time but it should end up a very tasty piece of work.
Cellar it, then serve it with spit-roasted lamb.

## Fire Gully Cabernet Sauvignon Merlot

| | |
|---|---|
| Quality | ♟ ♟ ♟ |
| Value | ★ ★ ◗ |
| Grapes | cabernet sauvignon; |
| | merlot |
| Region | Margaret River, WA |
| Cellar | ⬥ 1–6 |
| Alc./Vol. | 13.5% |
| RRP | $29.50 |

The Fire Gully wines are produced by Mike Peterkin, of
Pierro, from grapes grown elsewhere in Margaret River
by Ellis and Marg Butcher.
CURRENT RELEASE 1999    The nose reveals slightly stalky
cabernet fruit, together with berry aromas and a trace of
tomato. The palate is medium-bodied with balanced fruit
and oak flavours, but the tannins are a touch green. We
wonder if it will ever lose that hard edge. It benefits from
food, so try it with herbed beef rissoles.

## Fire Gully Pinot Noir

| | |
|---|---|
| Quality | ♟ ♟ ♟ ♟ |
| Value | ★ ★ ★ |
| Grapes | pinot noir |
| Region | Margaret River & |
| | Albany, WA |
| Cellar | ◖ 3 |
| Alc./Vol. | 13.5% |
| RRP | $20.15 |

Winemaker Mike Peterkin bases these wines on the
Willyabrup vineyard of Marg and Ellis Butcher, but
the '99 pinot includes some grapes from Albany down
south, which should be cooler than Margaret River.
CURRENT RELEASE 1999    There is a touch of
development here and the fruit has a distinctly gamy
edge. It's medium–light red–purple and smells earthy,
vegetal and gamy. It's fairly light on the palate with
savoury flavours and a dry aftertaste. Serve it with
grilled quail.

## The Fleurieu Shiraz

Fleurieu is the official name of the zone that includes the McLaren Vale region. This wine is pieced together every year by donations from wineries in the region, and sold at the McLaren Vale Visitors' Centre to raise funds for the centre. It's a worthy cause. Contact: (08) 8323 8999. Blender: Mike Farmilo.

*Previous outstanding vintages: '94, '95*

CURRENT RELEASE 1998    There was no wine in '97 or '96, but this is a ripper. Nice deep red–purple colour; subdued but deep bouquet; concentrated, full-bodied, savoury palate with generous fruit sweetness balanced by drying tannins. It has heaps of secondary, developed flavours and is well on the way to being a complex drink. It lingers long. Try it with aged cheddar.

| | |
|---|---|
| Quality | 🍷🍷🍷🍷🍷 |
| Value | ★★★★ |
| Grapes | shiraz |
| Region | McLaren Vale, SA |
| Cellar | ➖ 2–12+ |
| Alc./Vol. | 14.0% |
| RRP | $35.00 |

## Fonty's Pool Pinot Noir

There's no grape like pinot for degree of difficulty. To plant a new vineyard in an untried site, and try to make fine pinot straight away is a tough call. It seems to take longer than any other grape to perfect. Maker: Eloise Jarvis.

CURRENT RELEASE 1999    There's a lot of vanillin oak at first which dominates the bouquet. It's slightly edgy, with some volatility – and alcohol which shows through. There is a little elusive fruit sweetness on the mid-palate but it's an edgy wine that struggles to find its balance. Serve it with veal sweetbreads.

| | |
|---|---|
| Quality | 🍷🍷🍷🍷 |
| Value | ★★★ |
| Grapes | pinot noir |
| Region | Manjimup, WA |
| Cellar | 🍷 4 |
| Alc./Vol. | 14.0% |
| RRP | $25.00 |

## Fossil Creek Cabernet Merlot

The Cowra region makes decent ready-drinking red wines but we've yet to see anything really impressive. At least they are well priced and represent good value.

CURRENT RELEASE 1999    The colour is a bit on the light side, but the wine has pleasing, soft, fruit-driven flavour that's nicely balanced for early drinking. It's slightly minty to sniff, and tastes of sweet berries, finishing with soft, mild tannin. It would go well with pasta and ham-based sauce, such as fusilli vesuvio.

| | |
|---|---|
| Quality | 🍷🍷🍷🍷 |
| Value | ★★★⊣ |
| Grapes | cabernet sauvignon; merlot |
| Region | Cowra, NSW |
| Cellar | 🍷 4 |
| Alc./Vol. | 13.5% |
| RRP | $18.00 |

## Fox Creek Reserve Shiraz

| | |
|---|---|
| Quality | 🍷🍷🍷🍷 |
| Value | ★★★ |
| Grapes | shiraz |
| Region | McLaren Vale, SA |
| Cellar | ➥ 4–12+ |
| Alc./Vol. | 14.5% |
| RRP | $60.00 |

This has become one of the icon wines of McLaren Vale. By 'icon', we don't mean we like it. Icons are things people put on pedestals and worship. In wine, an icon is something that's very famous, costs a lot of money and attracts a lot of attention. But whether you'd want to actually *drink* it is another question altogether.

*Previous outstanding vintages: '94, '96, '98*

CURRENT RELEASE 1999    An initially impressive wine: dense purple colour, massively proportioned and powerful in aroma and flavour. In 10 years it could well make a good drink, but right now it's far too oaky, tannic, thick and heavy. Texture is syrupy and oak and tannin create an astringency that at two years of age is unpleasant. Cellar, then serve with hard cheeses.

## Frankland Estate Isolation Ridge Cabernet Sauvignon

| | |
|---|---|
| Quality | 🍷🍷🍷 |
| Value | ★★✦ |
| Grapes | cabernet sauvignon |
| Region | Great Southern, WA |
| Cellar | 🍾 5+ |
| Alc./Vol. | 12.5% |
| RRP | $23.50 |

Frankland Estate is very much a family affair, with Barrie Smith and Judi Cullam's grown children involved and working alongside their parents.

CURRENT RELEASE 1998    This is a slightly feral style which might bother the technocrats but may please those who dislike fruit-bomb reds. You'll find pronounced meaty, gamy, sweaty/vegetal and pencil-shavings characters rising from the glass, and the wine is showing some early development. It has earthy tannins and a decidedly rustic bent. Try it with barbecued snags.

## Frankland Estate Isolation Ridge Shiraz

| | |
|---|---|
| Quality | 🍷🍷🍷🍷 |
| Value | ★★★✦ |
| Grapes | shiraz |
| Region | Great Southern, WA |
| Cellar | 🍾 9 |
| Alc./Vol. | 13.5% |
| RRP | $28.00 |

The '99s are back on track after some rather odd '98s and '97s. The Cullams and Smiths of Frankland Estate are more interested in making wines with character than wines that doff their lids to conventional notions of quality. They're on the edge.

CURRENT RELEASE 1999    This is a little beauty. It speaks clearly of the coolish meso-climate of the vineyard, with its markedly peppery, spicy aromas. It's lean, clean and elegantly medium-bodied; the flavours seem properly ripe and it is a satisfying drink. There are vanilla elements on the palate and the firm chewy tannins are in harmony. Try it with guinea fowl cooked with grapes.

## Fromm La Strada Pinot Noir

New Zealand's Marlborough region isn't just sauvignon blanc. Fromm's winery produces many different wines in different grades. Some are brilliant, some are oaky, some just okay, but they are never boring.
CURRENT RELEASE 1999   Kiwi pinot noir enjoys a deservedly lustrous reputation. This is Fromm's standard La Strada label, a wine with less oak than the Reserve version. It has a ripe but fine nose reminiscent of raspberry eau de vie, along with earthy and undergrowthy interest. In the mouth it's silky textured and long in juicy flavour with ripe tannins to back it up. Try it with roast pigeons.

| | |
|---|---|
| Quality | ♥ ♥ ♥ ♥ |
| Value | ★ ★ ⟩ |
| Grapes | pinot noir |
| Region | Marlborough, NZ |
| Cellar | 🍾 3 |
| Alc./Vol. | 14.0% |
| RRP | $42.00 |

## The Gap Shiraz Cabernet Sauvignon

Established in 1974 as Boroka, this 9-hectare vineyard near Halls Gap in the scenic Grampians is now part of the Mount Langi Ghiran organisation. The wines are only sold ex-vineyard. Makers: Trevor Mast and Andrew McLoughney.
CURRENT RELEASE 1998   This is fresh and young for its age. It smells of raspberry jam and blackcurrant cordial, with grassy and minty overtones – perhaps from the cabernet component. In the mouth, it's lively, intense and lingering. A very fruit-dominant style that would go great guns with a barbecue in the bush.

| | |
|---|---|
| Quality | ♥ ♥ ♥ ♥ |
| Value | ★ ★ ★ ⟩ |
| Grapes | shiraz; cabernet sauvignon |
| Region | Grampians, Vic. |
| Cellar | 🍾 6+ |
| Alc./Vol. | 13.5% |
| RRP | $26.00 (cellar door) |

## Gapsted Ballerina Canopy Cabernet Sauvignon

We always approach less well-known wines from cooler regions with a mixture of positive anticipation and a wee bit of trepidation. The Victorian High Country is one such place but standards are improving all the time.
CURRENT RELEASE 1998   This has a crowd-pleasing sort of nose, reminiscent of sweet berries, mint, caramel and vanilla. American oak plays a notable part in its make-up bestowing a lot of toasty, vanillin touches to the palate as well. Minty fruit flavour fills the mid-palate ahead of big, grippy tannins. Perhaps a little too oak-driven, but still good, flavourful drinking at the price. A good wine for assorted barbecued meats.

| | |
|---|---|
| Quality | ♥ ♥ ♥ ♥ |
| Value | ★ ★ ★ ⟩ |
| Grapes | cabernet sauvignon |
| Region | King & Alpine Valleys, Vic. |
| Cellar | 🍾 4 |
| Alc./Vol. | 14.0% |
| RRP | $20.00 |

## Gapsted Ballerina Canopy Durif

| | |
|---|---|
| Quality | ♀♀♀♀ |
| Value | ✱✱✱ |
| Grapes | durif |
| Region | King Valley, Vic. |
| Cellar | ▮ 5 |
| Alc./Vol. | 14.5% |
| RRP | $30.00 |

Durif is usually found in rather warmer vineyards than Victoria's King Valley, but the Gapsted crowd are an adventurous lot. They have some tempranillo planted, and even vines with such household names as petit manseng and saperavi!

CURRENT RELEASE 1998    The Gapsted people like a bit of woodiness in their wines, as evidenced by this durif. Sweet coconutty American oak dominates the nose and also adds mocha touches to a core of syrupy berry fruit. In the mouth the oakfest continues with vanilla, cedar and toasty influences dominating but not obliterating berry flavour. It finishes with a drying, firm backbone of strong (you guessed it) oak. Drink it with meat grilled over a wood fire.

## Gapsted Ballerina Canopy Merlot

| | |
|---|---|
| Quality | ♀♀♀♀ |
| Value | ✱✱✱┩ |
| Grapes | merlot |
| Region | King & Alpine Valleys, Vic. |
| Cellar | ▮ 3 |
| Alc./Vol. | 14.0% |
| RRP | $20.00 |

Ballerina Canopy is a type of trellising for vines which helps them achieve optimum ripeness despite cooler climatic conditions. It works well at Gapsted. Maker: Michael Cope-Williams.

CURRENT RELEASE 1998    Lots of character here with distinct merlot fruit aromas of plum pudding and leafy notes, wrapped up in Gapsted's trademark sweet vanillin oak. The palate is chocolatey-rich, minty and long-flavoured with firm ripe tannins at the end. Serve it with stirfried Thai beef with fresh basil.

## Garry Crittenden i Barbera

| | |
|---|---|
| Quality | ♀♀♀♀ |
| Value | ✱✱✱┩ |
| Grapes | barbera |
| Region | King Valley, Vic. |
| Cellar | ▮ 2 |
| Alc./Vol. | 13.0% |
| RRP | $22.00 |

Garry Crittenden loves Italian wine. The 'i' range is his homage to wines that dare to be different in a world of homogenised cabernet, merlot and the like.

CURRENT RELEASE 1999    A purplish-hued youngster with earth, briar and mulch aromas that add a gamy tone to attractive cherry scents. The palate is juicy yet savoury with kernelly cherry fruit at the core and some vibrant acidity to enhance its more-ish character. A little bitterness on the finish melts away with appropriate food, maybe saltimbocca alla romana.

## Garry Crittenden i Sangiovese

As a pioneer of the Italian push, you'd expect Garry
Crittenden to make wines at the forefront of these
exciting developments. His sangiovese succeeds
admirably, giving us a true taste of Tuscany down under.
CURRENT RELEASE 2000    The nose is varietally just
right with light cherryish fruit mixed in with appealing
savoury notes reminiscent of oregano, aniseed and the
like. The palate follows that savoury theme well but it
has a degree of richness that's unusual. It's bigger and
more solid than the '99, with real density and length
ahead of a dry finish. Grilled herbed lamb cutlets here.

| | |
|---|---|
| Quality | ▼▼▼▼▼ |
| Value | ★★★★ |
| Grapes | sangiovese |
| Region | King Valley, Vic. |
| Cellar | ▌ 4 |
| Alc./Vol. | 14.0% |
| RRP | $22.00 |

## Gartelmann Diedrich Shiraz

The Diedrich in question was present owner Jorg
Gartelmann's grandfather. The appellation is reserved
for the best shiraz from this 30-year-old vineyard.
CURRENT RELEASE 1999    The colour is medium–
deep and the nose is Hunter Valley-savoury rather than
strongly fruity. There's a hint of leather and some
cherry fruit of good intensity on the nose. In the
mouth it follows the same pattern with a dry, savoury
palate. It isn't heavily built and has a pleasantly briary
texture, finishing in moderate tannins. Serve with
sautéed chicken livers on polenta.

| | |
|---|---|
| Quality | ▼▼▼▼ |
| Value | ★★★ |
| Grapes | shiraz |
| Region | Hunter Valley, NSW |
| Cellar | ▌ 4 |
| Alc./Vol. | 13.0% |
| RRP | $25.00 |

## Gemtree Shiraz

Paul and Jill Buttery have been McLaren Vale vignerons
for 20 years, but have only started selling their own
wine in the last couple of years.
CURRENT RELEASE 1999    This is the second Gemtree
vintage and it follows a tried and true Southern Vales
formula. The nose has a surge of ripe blackberries, juicy
and sweet, with an overlay of spice and a dressing of
vanillin oak. The palate is all honest Aussie red wine of
the type the world loves: rich, ripe and full of flavour
with smooth texture and fine tannins. All it needs is a
few years to lose some slightly raw edges. A good match
for sautéed calf's liver, if you like that sort of thing.

| | |
|---|---|
| Quality | ▼▼▼▼▼ |
| Value | ★★★★ |
| Grapes | shiraz |
| Region | McLaren Vale, SA |
| Cellar | ▌ 8 |
| Alc./Vol. | 14.0% |
| RRP | $23.35 (mail order) |

## Geoff Hardy Kuitpo Shiraz

| | |
|---|---|
| Quality | ♟ ♟ ♟ ♟ ♟ |
| Value | ★ ★ ★ |
| Grapes | shiraz |
| Region | Adelaide Hills, SA |
| Cellar | ▮ 3 |
| Alc./Vol. | 14.0% |
| RRP | $33.00 Ⓥ |

Although the Kuitpo vineyard is only seven kilometres inland from McLaren Vale, its climate, location and wine styles put it into the Adelaide Hills region.
CURRENT RELEASE 1998    This has good deep colour and an attractive bouquet of ripe berry and black cherry fruit, some savoury notes and subtle oak. In the mouth it has lovely supple texture and rich berry fruit character. It's medium-bodied, intensely flavoured and long with very soft fine tannins. Would be a treat with a veal pie.

## Geoff Merrill Cabernet Merlot

| | |
|---|---|
| Quality | ♟ ♟ ♟ ♟ |
| Value | ★ ★ ⁴ |
| Grapes | cabernet sauvignon; merlot |
| Region | not stated |
| Cellar | ▮ 3 |
| Alc./Vol. | 13.5% |
| RRP | $20.50 |

These days Geoff Merrill wines don't rely solely on fruit from their native McLaren Vale region, sourcing from the Goulburn Valley and elsewhere.
CURRENT RELEASE 1998    This has a savoury nose of mulberry and some softer plummy notes underneath. The nose is of middling intensity, and so is the palate which features light berry fruit and medium tannins. A wine of rather ordinary personality that doesn't encourage superlatives. Try it with a minute steak.

## Geoff Merrill Shiraz

| | |
|---|---|
| Quality | ♟ ♟ ♟ ♟ |
| Value | ★ ★ ⁴ |
| Grapes | shiraz |
| Region | McLaren Vale, SA & Goulburn Valley, Vic. |
| Cellar | ▮ 5 |
| Alc./Vol. | 13.5% |
| RRP | $20.50 |

The Geoff Merrill wines were once rather eviscerated critters in the days of 'elegant' early-picked McLaren Vale reds. These days they have more generous constitutions. Interestingly the label describes McLaren Vale and the Goulburn Valley as 'cool-climate regions'.
CURRENT RELEASE 1998    This is an honest red with a rather countrified personality. It has spicy blackberry fruit, some lightly earthy and minerally touches that add savoury appeal, subtle oak input and moderate tannins. All in all a friendly red to drink with Middle-Eastern lamb pastries.

## Giaconda Cabernet Sauvignon

Cabernet doesn't attract as much attention as other wines in the Giaconda scheme of things, but at its best it's a top drop. As with all the Giaconda wines, scarcity is a problem; sometimes good restaurant wine lists are about the only source.

CURRENT RELEASE 1999    This was tasted alongside a young (1997) second-growth Bordeaux, and came out on top. Yes, Bordeaux needs time, but who has it these days? This young Giaconda has a voluptuous, complex nose of sweetly ripe, plummy cabernet fruit, touched by briar and subtle cedary/spicy oak. The palate is ripe and long, with concentrated lush blackcurrant fruit and classy oak, silky finesse of flavour and texture, and dry cedary tannins. Try it with roast lamb.

| | |
|---|---|
| Quality | ♥♥♥♥♥ |
| Value | ★★★★ |
| Grapes | cabernet sauvignon |
| Region | Beechworth, Vic. |
| Cellar | ➥ 2–6 |
| Alc./Vol. | 13.0% |
| RRP | $55.00 |

## Giaconda Warner Vineyard Shiraz

Although maker Rick Kinzbrunner has played with Beechworth shiraz before, this is the first 'serious' one for Giaconda. It's a spectacular debut, all the more so given the youth of the Warner shiraz vineyard. Like all the Giacondas, this is hard to find.

CURRENT RELEASE 1999    A real Rhone look-alike. The nose is exciting with pepper, spices, earth, smoky touches, and deep, foresty cherry fruit dissolved into a complex whole. The palate is smooth and elaborately flavoured, with slightly gamy fruit of great suppleness and super-length dovetailing into fine-grained, ripe tannins. Lovely with kangaroo.

| | |
|---|---|
| Quality | ♥♥♥♥♥ |
| Value | ★★★⁴ |
| Grapes | shiraz |
| Region | Beechworth, Vic. |
| Cellar | ➥ 1–5 |
| Alc./Vol. | 13.0% |
| RRP | $60.00 |

## The Gorge Shiraz

David Hook has been a contract winemaker in the Hunter for many years, and makes small quantities of his own wines on the side. He has 8 hectares of vines at Belford, and also has the premium brand Pothana.

CURRENT RELEASE 2000    Minty and toasty oak aromas are the feature of this smooth, open-knit wine. It has good flavour intensity and despite its youth is already drinking well. Soft tannins complete the picture. It would suit braised beef.

| | |
|---|---|
| Quality | ♥♥♥♥ |
| Value | ★★★★ |
| Grapes | shiraz |
| Region | Hunter Valley, NSW |
| Cellar | ▮ 5 |
| Alc./Vol. | 13.5% |
| RRP | $16.00 |

## Goundrey Cabernet Merlot

| | |
|---|---|
| Quality | ▼ ▼ ▼ ꜜ |
| Value | ★ ★ ★ |
| Grapes | cabernet sauvignon; merlot |
| Region | Great Southern, WA |
| Cellar | ▮ 4 |
| Alc./Vol. | 13.5% |
| RRP | $16.20 |

The Goundrey enterprise has gone ahead in leaps and bounds with new vineyard plantings and enlarged winery facilities. This is the 'cooking' label; there's also a very good Reserve range.

CURRENT RELEASE 1999    This has a softer, fruitier nose than some previous vintages. It's perfumed with blackberry and dark chocolate, with oak in a secondary role. The palate has adequate ripe berry and prune flavours which are shortened somewhat by a sinewy dry finish. Try it with homemade hamburgers.

## Gramp's Barossa Grenache

| | |
|---|---|
| Quality | ▼ ▼ ▼ ꜜ |
| Value | ★ ★ ★ |
| Grapes | grenache |
| Region | Barossa Valley, SA |
| Cellar | ▮ 3 |
| Alc./Vol. | 14.0% |
| RRP | $14.95 Ⓢ |

Barossa grenache never lets you down in sheer volume of flavour, but don't look for subtlety in it. Gramp's is better priced than some.

CURRENT RELEASE 1998    Not as sweet and 'hot' as usual, this has the traditional earthy raspberry/blackberry and meaty touches that make up typical varietal/regional character. The fresh-tasting middleweight palate has fair depth and light tannins. An everyday red to go with shepherd's pie.

## Grant Burge Barossa Vines Shiraz

| | |
|---|---|
| Quality | ▼ ▼ ▼ ꜜ |
| Value | ★ ★ ★ ★ ꜜ |
| Grapes | shiraz |
| Region | Barossa Valley, SA |
| Cellar | ▮ 2 |
| Alc./Vol. | 13.0% |
| RRP | $14.95 Ⓢ |

Barossa Vines wines are Grant Burge's cheapies. They offer real character on a budget and can stand up well to a lot of more costly drops.

CURRENT RELEASE 1999    The nose has berry aromas that are pleasantly sweet and not too light, along with some touches of earth and mint. In the mouth it has good depth with more than adequate weight and concentration for the price, finishing in some savoury, dry tannins. Good with roasted vegetable lasagne.

## Grant Burge Filsell Shiraz

Named after the Filsells who originally planted this Lyndoch vineyard, this shiraz is one of Grant Burge's typical oaky, generously flavoured reds.

CURRENT RELEASE 1999    Mr Burge reckons that his '99s aren't quite as opulent as the '98s, but this isn't far behind in our opinion. It has the consistent hallmarks: mocha, licorice, vanillin oak, tar and blackberries on the nose, and a rich, ripe palate that's fruit sweet and slightly raw-oaky. Tannins aren't overbearing, but ideally they do need the softening effect of time. Suits Lebanese shawarma kebab nicely.

| | |
|---|---|
| Quality | ♀♀♀♀ |
| Value | ★★★⁾ |
| Grapes | shiraz |
| Region | Barossa Valley, SA |
| Cellar | ⊸ 1–7 |
| Alc./Vol. | 14.5% |
| RRP | $27.30 |

## Grant Burge Hillcot Merlot

These days the mercurial Mr Burge makes a plethora of different wines, each reflecting a different vineyard, variety and quality, but the house red wine style – ripe fruit, plenty of sweet oak and easy drinkability – dominates other factors.

CURRENT RELEASE 1999    This has plentiful ripe raspberry-like aromas which have an attractive syrupy quality. Oak makes its presence felt by way of smoky vanillin barrel influence, but it's less noticeable than in other reds in the range. It tastes smooth and satisfying, ripe fruit, leafy touches and fine tannins combining in nice harmony. Serve this red with roast veal.

| | |
|---|---|
| Quality | ♀♀♀♀ |
| Value | ★★★⁾ |
| Grapes | merlot; |
| | cabernet sauvignon |
| Region | Barossa Valley, SA |
| Cellar | ▮ 4 |
| Alc./Vol. | 13.5% |
| RRP | $18.20 |

## Grant Burge Meshach

This has truly climbed into the ranks of the South Australian super-shiraz. It's always had the requisite power, the overt oakiness and the big structure, but now it's right in there price-wise with the damage nearing a hundred smackers!

*Previous outstanding vintages: '90, '91*

CURRENT RELEASE 1996    Another Meshach of blockbuster proportions, this wine has an almost 'boiled down' concentration with intense liqueur plum, chocolate and berry aromas. There's also a big dose of charry vanillin oak. The palate is dense and syrupy in texture, full-bodied and long tasting with big, ripe tannins underneath. Serve with hare.

| | |
|---|---|
| Quality | ♀♀♀♀⁙ |
| Value | ★★⁾ |
| Grapes | shiraz |
| Region | Barossa Valley, SA |
| Cellar | ⊸ 1–10+ |
| Alc./Vol. | 14.0% |
| RRP | $96.00 |

## Grant Burge Miamba Shiraz

| | |
|---|---|
| Quality | ♟♟♟♟ |
| Value | ★★★ |
| Grapes | shiraz |
| Region | Barossa Valley, SA |
| Cellar | 🍷 3 |
| Alc./Vol. | 14.5% |
| RRP | $20.00 |

A newie from Grant Burge, made from a nineteenth-century property once used by Orlando for 'Miamba Claret'. Amazingly in 1980 the vines were removed for pasture and only replanted by Grant Burge in 1987. CURRENT RELEASE 1999    A less concentrated Grant Burge red, with a nose of raspberry fruit and singed coconut oak. The palate is straightforward with a warm berry flavour and soft tannins. It lacks a little concentration in the mouth, but there's reasonable persistence. Serve it with grilled lamb cutlets.

## Grant Burge Shadrach

| | |
|---|---|
| Quality | ♟♟♟♟♟ |
| Value | ★★★ |
| Grapes | cabernet sauvignon |
| Region | Coonawarra & Barossa Valley, SA |
| Cellar | 🍷 10 |
| Alc./Vol. | 13.5% |
| RRP | $44.70 |

Shadrach, Meshach, Holy Trinity – biblical allusions feature a lot in the names of Grant Burge's wines, but then they've always been a religious lot in the Barossa. CURRENT RELEASE 1996    This has quite a lot in common with Grant Burge's Meshach Shiraz. Lots of oak for starters, and very ripe fruit character, but Shadrach has a bit more refinement in its youth. The nose has strong blackcurrant and blackberry aromas with a whisper of varietal earth and leaf. The oak is spicy and powerful but doesn't overwhelm the fruit. The tasty palate is full and long with great depth and ripe tannins. Chargrill some rump steak to go with this.

## Green Point McLaren Vale Shiraz

| | |
|---|---|
| Quality | ♟♟♟♟ |
| Value | ★★★★ |
| Grapes | shiraz |
| Region | McLaren Vale, SA |
| Cellar | 🍷 5 |
| Alc./Vol. | 14.0% |
| RRP | $27.00 |

Made by Chandon in the Yarra Valley, this is a departure from the usual Green Point table wines which are sourced from the same pinot noir and chardonnay grapes as the Chandon sparklers. CURRENT RELEASE 1999    This is so at odds with the normal Chandon style – perhaps management wants a slice of the action when it comes to the fruit-sweet, charry oak wines for which there seems to be increasing demand. Whatever the reason, this is a good example of that sort of shiraz with sweet blackberry, earth, and appreciable quantities of smoky, toasty oak. The flavours track the nose exactly, it's mouth-filling with good depth and length, and a signature of grippy tannins finishes things off. Try it with a beef claypot dish.

# Grosset Gaia

The Gaia vineyard stands apart from the rest of the Clare Valley, isolated in cooler high country, next to the ruins of an old coach stop on the way north. CURRENT RELEASE 1999  Gaia is a special wine, even when young. It smells harmonious right from the start with a fragrant nose of florals, leafy black fruit, cigar-boxy scents and subtle oak. The overall effect is of savoury complexity. It's perhaps a little more forward than last vintage, but still a wine for the future. The palate is fine, intense and rather Bordeaux-like with long flavour and a tight, sinewy tannin structure. Try it with roast lamb.

| | |
|---|---|
| Quality | ♥ ♥ ♥ ♥ ♥ |
| Value | ★ ★ ★ ★ |
| Grapes | cabernet sauvignon; cabernet franc; merlot |
| Region | Clare Valley, SA |
| Cellar | ➤ 2–10 |
| Alc./Vol. | 13.5% |
| RRP | $56.00 |

# Grove Estate The Partners Cabernet Sauvignon

Brian Mullany and his partners started growing grapes for Southcorp, supplying the Hungerford Hill brand from their 30-hectare vineyard, planted in 1990. They have some wine made locally for their own brand. CURRENT RELEASE 1999  The colour is bright and fresh and the grapes were properly ripe, going by the bright berryish cabernet fruit aromas. Wood is underplayed, and the wine has very attractive elegance and quite concentrated flavour, with a trace of tartness showing on the finish. Promising wine. Try it with saltbush mutton.

| | |
|---|---|
| Quality | ♥ ♥ ♥ ♥ |
| Value | ★ ★ ★ ⁴ |
| Grapes | cabernet sauvignon |
| Region | Hilltops, NSW |
| Cellar | ➤ 1–8+ |
| Alc./Vol. | 13.8% |
| RRP | $23.80 |

# Hamilton Burton's Vineyard Grenache Shiraz

Single-vineyard, old bush vines. Not a bad start. But why 15.5 per cent alcohol? The wine burns the palate with alcohol. Maker: Pip Treadwell. CURRENT RELEASE 1998  The colour is nice and deep but the bouquet is a combination of dusty oak and spirity, heady alcohol. It's a big, raunchy, gutsy wine with a grippy finish thanks to oak tannins and alcohol. It seems to need time, but just how cellaring will affect it is unclear. You could try serving it with smelly cheese, such as reblochon.

| | |
|---|---|
| Quality | ♥ ♥ ♥ ⁴ |
| Value | ★ ★ ⁴ |
| Grapes | grenache; shiraz |
| Region | McLaren Vale, SA |
| Cellar | ➤ 1–6+ |
| Alc./Vol. | 15.5% |
| RRP | $30.00 |

## Hamilton Centurion Shiraz

| | |
|---|---|
| Quality | 🍷🍷🍷🍷 |
| Value | ★★⸱ |
| Grapes | shiraz |
| Region | McLaren Vale, SA |
| Cellar | 🍷 8 |
| Alc./Vol. | 13.5% |
| RRP | $49.00 |

The grapes were harvested from ancient McLaren Vale vines planted in 1892. Dry-grown, hand-pruned, hand-tended, says the blurb. It won a gold medal at the 2000 Concours Mondiale in Brussels.

CURRENT RELEASE 1998    This split the panel in no uncertain terms. RKP liked its richness and weight while HH found a feral character he didn't like. There are strong pencil-shavings or graphite aromas together with liberal oak, and it has a very drying, savoury palate which carries plenty of extract and generous helpings of tannin. Try before you buy!

## Hamilton Estate Lot 148 Merlot

| | |
|---|---|
| Quality | 🍷🍷🍷⸱ |
| Value | ★★★ |
| Grapes | merlot |
| Region | McLaren Vale, SA |
| Cellar | 🍷 5 |
| Alc./Vol. | 14.0% |
| RRP | $21.80 |

This company, one of many manifestations of the venerable Hamilton clan in South Australia, used to be called Richard Hamilton, after its owner. It has 55 hectares of vineyards in McLaren Vale and fields a full range of table wines.

CURRENT RELEASE 1999    This is a firm, somewhat claret-styled merlot with straightforward but pleasant flavour and some fresh oak, which is rather obvious on the nose at this stage. There's plenty of clean, fresh berry flavour as well. It needs a year or two. Then serve with shish kebabs.

## Hamilton's Ewell Vineyards Fullers Barn Shiraz

| | |
|---|---|
| Quality | 🍷🍷🍷⸱ |
| Value | ★★★ |
| Grapes | shiraz |
| Region | Barossa Valley, SA |
| Cellar | ➡ 2–10 |
| Alc./Vol. | 15.5% |
| RRP | $26.00 🍷 |

This is 'the other Hamilton' – it's not Richard Hamilton's company, nor Hugh Hamilton's, but Mark Hamilton's. Ewell is a very old family trade name, and this company was established in 1991. They're getting into the swing of creating brand names.

CURRENT RELEASE 1998    This is a pretty over-the-top drop. The colour is dark and blackish; the nose reveals blackberry jam and sweaty, gamy aromas, and the palate confirms the porty impression. There is a certain over-ripe fruit character throughout, and it lacks vibrancy. Sweet jammy fruit is countered by harsh, drying tannins. It needs rich food, such as osso bucco.

## Hamilton's Ewell Vineyards Stonegarden Grenache

The small print says 'Mature Vines'. How old is 'mature'? It's often hard to say because really old vineyards contain replacements for vines that die for various reasons. Stonegarden was originally planted near Springton by Oscar Benno Seppelt in the 1850s. It's passed through the hands of various members of the Hamilton family; now lawyer Mark Hamilton and his wife, Deborah, own it.
CURRENT RELEASE 1999   This lighter style of grenache smells of berry-jam and confectionery, and little sign of wood. It's full, soft and broad on the palate with diffused rather than focused flavour. A pleasant, interesting red. Try it with grilled pork chops.

| | |
|---|---|
| Quality | 🍷🍷🍷🍷 |
| Value | ★★★ |
| Grapes | grenache |
| Region | Eden Valley, SA |
| Cellar | 🍾 4 |
| Alc./Vol. | 13.5% |
| RRP | $20.00 |

## Hanging Rock Central Highlands Pinot Noir

Winemaker John Ellis has taken the bold step of declaring that he would bottle all his wines with plastic cork-substitute stoppers. So far he seems to have kept his word. The fruit here comes from Faraday, Strathbogie Ranges and Tallarook, all in Victoria.
CURRENT RELEASE 1999   This is a decent pinot but lacks the textural charm that distinguishes the best pinots. The colour and aroma are both fresh and vibrant, and the bouquet reveals vanillin oak sitting slightly apart from the fruit. There's a hint of leather and some distracting tartness. It's quite big and has a firm, chewy oak-tannic palate. It has plenty of flavour. Try with shish kebabs.

| | |
|---|---|
| Quality | 🍷🍷🍷🍷 |
| Value | ★★★⁺ |
| Grapes | pinot noir |
| Region | various, Vic. |
| Cellar | 🍾 4 |
| Alc./Vol. | 13.0% |
| RRP | $20.00 |

## Hanging Rock Victoria Cabernet Merlot

Hanging Rock is the largest winery in the 'greater Macedon region', and takes grapes from all over Victoria as well as its own 12-hectare plantings. Much of its output is contract winemaking for small growers.
CURRENT RELEASE 1999   This is an appealing, fruit-dominant, well-proportioned red that drinks well young. The colour is only of medium depth, and it smells berry, gamy, and vanilla/coconut. It's light- to medium-bodied, with little tannin, some juiciness and elegant balance. Drink with a cheesy risotto.

| | |
|---|---|
| Quality | 🍷🍷🍷🍷 |
| Value | ★★★⁺ |
| Grapes | cabernet sauvignon; merlot |
| Region | King Valley, Swan Hill & Echuca, Vic. |
| Cellar | 🍾 5 |
| Alc./Vol. | 13.0% |
| RRP | $20.00 |

## Happs Three Hills Charles Andreas

| | |
|---|---|
| Quality | ♥♥♥♥♦ |
| Value | ★★★ |
| Grapes | cabernet sauvignon 50%; merlot 25%; cabernet franc 25% |
| Region | Margaret River, WA |
| Cellar | ⬤ 2–10+ |
| Alc./Vol. | 14.3% |
| RRP | $70.00 🍾 |

The Happ family has vineyards in the two extremities of Margaret River: Dunsborough in the north and Karridale in the south. This is part of a new super-duper range and was sourced purely from Karridale, where winemaker Erl Happ is now sourcing his best grapes.
CURRENT RELEASE 1999    This is a dense, slightly closed wine which is saying 'go away and leave me alone' for the moment. It has sweet berry flavours hidden deep within, and the substantial tannins hint at extended skin maceration and are quite formidable on the finish. It needs cellaring; then serve it with barbecued kangaroo fillets.

## Happs Three Hills Shiraz

| | |
|---|---|
| Quality | ♥♥♥♥♥ |
| Value | ★★★ |
| Grapes | shiraz |
| Region | Margaret River, WA |
| Cellar | ⬤ 2–10+ |
| Alc./Vol. | 14.0% |
| RRP | $70.00 🍾 |

Erl Happ is fascinated by the range of choice among the grapevine varieties, and has about 30 in his own vineyards. Shades of a boutique-sized Brown Brothers! This wine was grown at Karridale, where Happ is especially excited about nebbiolo.
CURRENT RELEASE 1999    The colour is dark purple–red and the wine presents as young for its age. It displays great concentration in every regard: ripe, almost jammy plum and vanilla aromas and vibrant, profound palate flavours. It's ultra-ripe, sweet and thoroughly seductive in the mouth. It has a great future, but would drink well now with roast venison.

## Hardys RR Cabernet Sauvignon

| | |
|---|---|
| Quality | ♥♥♦ |
| Value | ★★★ |
| Grapes | cabernet sauvignon |
| Region | not stated |
| Cellar | 🍾 1 |
| Alc./Vol. | 12.5% |
| RRP | $8.00 ⓢ |

If memory serves, the RR brand first appeared on a 'Rhine riesling' which Hardys were loath to give its proper name because of the negativity about riesling in the UK market. Now, RR is a full range of wines called Regional Reserve, although what region isn't exactly clear.
CURRENT RELEASE 2000    The colour is rather weak and it even looks cheap! The aromas are really light and simple, with more green herbal notes than dinky-di cabernet fruit. It's the same in the mouth: soft, light and sweetish, and slightly reductive into the bargain. It won't challenge the senses. Save it for lunch with the bank manager.

## Hardys Thomas Hardy Cabernet Sauvignon

The BRL Hardy group's flagship cabernet was named after the company's founder and his face adorns the label. Chief red winemaker Stephen Pannell held some stock of this great vintage back for further ageing and re-release. Smart move!

CURRENT RELEASE 1994 This is a wonderful red indeed! Great concentration, fabulous flavour, and extra bottle-age has worked its miracles. Toasty, roast-meat, smoky and blackberry flavours abound. It has no shortage of tannin but it's all smooth and supple: brilliantly drinkable. Serve with beef wellington.

**Quality** 🍷🍷🍷🍷🍷
**Value** ★★★½
**Grapes** cabernet sauvignon
**Region** Coonawarra, SA
**Cellar** 10
**Alc./Vol.** 14.0%
**RRP** $72.00

## Hardys Tintara Cellars Cabernet Sauvignon

The BRL Hardy people have two ranges of wines bearing the Tintara name, the more exxy one with the name Tintara etched into the glass, and this cheaper line, Tintara Cellars. Confusing for us mug punters!

CURRENT RELEASE 1999 This will appeal to lovers of complex, feral-tasting reds, and that includes us. The first impression is of gamy fruit, and the fleshy, meaty, almost animal characters continue throughout the wine, ending up with some earthy tannins. It has remarkably good concentration, depth and extract for the price. It doesn't lack persistence, either. A character wine! Try it with barbecued roo.

**Quality** 🍷🍷🍷🍷
**Value** ★★★★★
**Grapes** cabernet sauvignon
**Region** McLaren Vale, Coonawarra & Adelaide Hills, SA
**Cellar** 6+
**Alc./Vol.** 13.5%
**RRP** $16.00 (\$)

## Hardys Tintara Grenache

These old-fashioned-looking Tintara wines evoke past glories with a pair of traditionally made reds from shiraz and grenache. The best of Hardys' McLaren Vale vines are allowed to express themselves perfectly.

CURRENT RELEASE 1999 This has a purplish colour and a strong nose with more grenache varietal aromas than last year's edition. There's raspberry, blackberry and spicy fruitcake on the fruit-sweet nose along with a dab of dusty oak. In the mouth it has lovely texture and long plummy flavour, seasoned just right with charry oak. Tannins are grainy and ripe, adding firmness to the finish. Serve it with soy-braised and glazed beef ribs.

**Quality** 🍷🍷🍷🍷½
**Value** ★★★★
**Grapes** grenache
**Region** McLaren Vale, SA
**Cellar** 6
**Alc./Vol.** 14.5%
**RRP** $40.00

## Haselgrove Picture Series Shiraz

| | |
|---|---|
| Quality | 🍷🍷🍷 |
| Value | ★★★⭐ |
| Grapes | shiraz |
| Region | McLaren Vale, SA |
| Cellar | ➥ 1–5 |
| Alc./Vol. | 13.0% |
| RRP | $19.50 |

The picture on the label of this McLaren Vale shiraz is a painting of the Salopian Inn, a historic building that also houses one of the region's best places to eat, drink and be merry.

CURRENT RELEASE 1999    Unashamedly Southern Vales, this red has a bright colour and a nose that combines spicy blackberry aromas with strong regional earthy hints. Oak is folded in with care, and it tastes earthy and rich with old-fashioned sunshiny shiraz flavour. Tannins are quite astringent, detracting from the wine's softness at the moment, but it's still a pup and time will soften it and build personality.

## Hayshed Hill Pitchfork Red

| | |
|---|---|
| Quality | 🍷🍷🍷⭐ |
| Value | ★★★ |
| Grapes | not stated |
| Region | Margaret River, WA |
| Cellar | 🍾 4 |
| Alc./Vol. | 13.5% |
| RRP | $17.90 |

The Barrington Estate people, who own the Yarraman Road brand in the Hunter Valley, recently bought this Margaret River winery, established in 1987. The Pitchfork range of wines are designed as no-nonsense ready-drinkers. Maker: Peter Stanlake.

CURRENT RELEASE 2000    This is medium-bodied and soft, with lightly nutty oak and sweet berry aromas. It tastes ripe and smooth, the tannins are light, and it's very easy to drink now. It would partner veal saltimbocca.

## Heathcote Winery Curagee Shiraz

| | |
|---|---|
| Quality | 🍷🍷🍷🍷 |
| Value | ★★★ |
| Grapes | shiraz; viognier |
| Region | Heathcote, Vic. |
| Cellar | ➥ 2–10+ |
| Alc./Vol. | 14.0% |
| RRP | $45.00 🍾 |

Curagee is a Daung Wurrung tribal name for the Cambrian greenstone that forms the basis of the soils in the vineyard. This shiraz contains some viognier, following the Cote Rotie model. Maker: Mark Kelly.

CURRENT RELEASE 1998    This is pretty smart stuff, but it would be even better with less aroma of mint – which seems a regional attribute in these parts. There are raspberry, stalk and gumleaf nuances, and the wine is fairly firm and astringent in the mouth, with a suspicion of greenness. It's a robust and somewhat aggressive red which needs time. Then try it with parmesan cheese.

## Heathfield Ridge Merlot

The grapes come from a vineyard at Bool Lagoon, a famous wildlife reserve which lies west of Coonawarra and Wrattonbully. Maker: Pat Tocaciu.
CURRENT RELEASE 1999    This is not a bad opening shot for a new maker. It is a little acid on the palate but it smells invitingly of coffee, mocha and berry, with stalky/leafy high notes. The colour is nice and full. It's a respectable, if lean, style of red wine. Have it with Wiener schnitzel.

| | |
|---|---|
| Quality | ♟ ♟ ♟ ♟ |
| Value | ★ ★ ★ |
| Grapes | merlot |
| Region | Wrattonbully, SA |
| Cellar | 🍷 5 |
| Alc./Vol. | 13.8% |
| RRP | $20.00 |

## Henschke Keyneton Estate

This blended red is named in tribute to a Mr Keynes, after whom the local metropolis of Keyneton was named. Fifth-generation winemaker is Stephen Henschke.
CURRENT RELEASE 1998    This lovely, seamless red is smooth and delicious and instead of emphasising any particular varietal character, it's just a complex, nicely rounded red wine. It smells of raspberry and mint with slightly gamy, vegetal inflexions – typical of the area. The tannins are very soft and supple. It's a comfort drink. Serve with comfort food, like corned beef and white sauce.

| | |
|---|---|
| Quality | ♟ ♟ ♟ ♟ ♟ |
| Value | ★ ★ ★ ↘ |
| Grapes | shiraz 65%; cabernet sauvignon 30%; malbec 5% |
| Region | Eden Valley, SA |
| Cellar | 🍷 8+ |
| Alc./Vol. | 14.0% |
| RRP | $36.50 |

## Hewitson Barossa Shiraz

Dean Hewitson won the Best New Producer award in last year's edition of this *Guide*. We love the wines, the presentation, and the attitude of the man. Long may he reign.
CURRENT RELEASE 1999    This is quite a peppery number, tasting more like a cool-climate shiraz, which may reflect the difficult Barossa vintage in '99. The colour is encouraging: dark purple–red, and it smells stemmy with deeper licorice/anise notes. The palate is rich, with layers of flavour, ranging from pepper to spices to plum to licorice. It seems ripe enough and certainly needs time. Cellar, then serve with pepper steak.

| | |
|---|---|
| Quality | ♟ ♟ ♟ ♟ |
| Value | ★ ★ ★ ↘ |
| Grapes | shiraz |
| Region | Barossa Valley, SA |
| Cellar | ➻ 2–10 |
| Alc./Vol. | 14.0% |
| RRP | $36.80 🍷 |

## Hewitson l'Oizeau Shiraz

| | |
|---|---|
| Quality | ▮▮▮▮▮ |
| Value | ★★★★⭒ |
| Grapes | shiraz |
| Region | McLaren Vale, SA |
| Cellar | ▮ 12 |
| Alc./Vol. | 14.0% |
| RRP | $36.80 ▮ |

*Josephine l'Oizeau* was the name of a ship wrecked off McLaren Vale in 1856. She was carrying wine and spirits. The crew survived, but the bounty is still down there. Maker: Dean Hewitson.

CURRENT RELEASE 1998    Another champ from Mr Hewitson, who seems able to do no wrong. The colour is dark and the nose offers intriguing meaty, spicy and charred-oak complexities. The taste is very deep, concentrated and lingering, with lashings of fruit, oak and tannin all playing their part. The clincher, however, is a wonderfully rich, fleshy texture. It's a sumptuous drink. Try it with osso bucco.

## Hewitson Miss Harry

| | |
|---|---|
| Quality | ▮▮▮▮ |
| Value | ★★★⭒ |
| Grapes | mainly grenache, with shiraz and mourvèdre |
| Region | Barossa Valley, SA |
| Cellar | ▮ 5 |
| Alc./Vol. | 13.5% |
| RRP | $23.55 |

The subscript on the label is 'Dry Grown and Ancient', which describes the vines, we take it – not Miss Harry, who is Dean Hewitson's young daughter Harriet.
CURRENT RELEASE 2000    Just a babe, this one. Its colour is a glowing purple–red and it smells of grenache: sweet, simple, lollyish and undeveloped. Oak, if present at all, is in the background. It's light-bodied, smooth and sweetly fruity, bursting with cherry, aniseed, chocolate and vanilla flavours. A well-made wine that's easy to enjoy young, with duck-neck sausages.

## Highfield Marlborough Pinot Noir

| | |
|---|---|
| Quality | ▮▮▮▮⭒ |
| Value | ★★★ |
| Grapes | pinot noir |
| Region | Marlborough, NZ |
| Cellar | ▮ 3 |
| Alc./Vol. | 13.5% |
| RRP | $56.00 |

The Marlborough region has lofty aspirations to become an important producer of pinot. It's a bit cool for the other red varieties, after all.
CURRENT RELEASE 1999    This wine is quite complex and its chief asset is a seductive, almost Burgundy-like texture, which is rare enough in New World pinot. The colour is medium–light and there's a hint of volatility, some banana-like oak and a dusty/stemmy, almost capsicum-like overtone. It comes into its own on the tongue, with a smooth mouth-feel and captivating flavour. It would suit roast guinea fowl.

## Hillstowe Mary's Hundred Shiraz

Hillstowe announced in May 2001 that it was merging with the Banksia group (St Hallett and Tatachilla), although the founding Laurie family will keep the vineyards and buildings. This wine is their flagship, named in honour of one of the colony's first women winemakers, Mary Laurie.

CURRENT RELEASE 1998   This big bouncy beauty boasts all the rich, ripe, dense characteristics that typify the best McLaren Vale shiraz. The colour is dark and the bouquet already complex, with fruitcake and preserved-plum aromas. A concentrated wine in every regard, it has almost fathomless depth and a big future. Great with osso bucco.

| | |
|---|---|
| Quality | ♀ ♀ ♀ ♀ ♀ |
| Value | ★ ★ ★ ★ |
| Grapes | shiraz |
| Region | McLaren Vale, SA |
| Cellar | 🍾 10+ |
| Alc./Vol. | 14.0% |
| RRP | $45.00 🍾 |

## Hochkirch Pinot Noir

Say that German name quickly and you sound like a cat with a furball in its throat. The Hochkirch vineyard is in the far south-west of Victoria, where Burgundy-like growing season temperatures make pinot noir a logical choice. Maker: John Nagorcka.

CURRENT RELEASE 1999   This has a deep colour with a slight murkiness, perhaps due to lack of filtration. The nose has classical varietal smells, still quite closed but already showing some pinot noir mystery. There are aromas of undergrowth, plums, stems, liqueur cherries and subtle oaky spice, ahead of a palate of varietal purity, richness and depth. There's a wild gamy rawness about it that's appealing to some, and the finish is a mite too astringent, bordering on bitter. Appropriate food is a must to appreciate this interesting wine fully – we tried it with Cantonese roast duck. Future vintages will be worth watching.

| | |
|---|---|
| Quality | ♀ ♀ ♀ ♀ |
| Value | ★ ★ ★ ★ ★ |
| Grapes | pinot noir |
| Region | Tarrington, Vic. |
| Cellar | 🍾 3 |
| Alc./Vol. | 13.0% |
| RRP | $20.00 |

## Hollick Cabernet Merlot

| | |
|---|---|
| Quality | ♥ ♥ ♥ ♥ |
| Value | ★ ★ ★ ⅃ |
| Grapes | cabernet sauvignon; merlot |
| Region | Coonawarra, SA |
| Cellar | ▮ 6 |
| Alc./Vol. | 13.0% |
| RRP | $24.00 ⑤ |

The Hollicks have 65 hectares of vineyards in Coonawarra and 30 hectares in Wrattonbully. Ian is president of the Winemakers' Forum, which represents the small wineries on the industry bodies.
CURRENT RELEASE 1999   This is a lighter-style Coonawarra – more traditional, if you like. It's unlike some of the reds-on-steroids we're seeing these days. The aromas are attractive mulberry, cassis and herbs, and the taste is clean, light- to medium-bodied and finely balanced. It has plum and cherry flavours and no excess of oak. It goes with Lebanese shawarma.

## Hollick Neilson's Block Merlot

| | |
|---|---|
| Quality | ♥ ♥ ♥ ♥ ♥ |
| Value | ★ ★ ★ ⅃ |
| Grapes | merlot |
| Region | Coonawarra, SA |
| Cellar | ▮ 8 |
| Alc./Vol. | 13.0% |
| RRP | $49.00 |

Ian Hollick is one of the stayers in the Coonawarra field. His uncle Bob was a viticulturist for Mildara as was Ian, before he struck out on his own with his wife, Wendy. His wines are mostly in the elegant traditional Coonawarra style.
CURRENT RELEASE 1999   The bouquet is subtle and restrained without the now-usual Coonawarra dominant oakiness. Straw, hay, earthy and slightly metallic scents greet the nose, and the palate has fresh raspberry flavours and vibrant acidity. It is lean and restrained with some aniseed and bright, berry-jam notes. Tannins are very discreet. Very drinkable, especially with vitello tonnato.

## Holm Oak Pinot Noir

| | |
|---|---|
| Quality | ♥ ♥ ♥ ♥ ♥ |
| Value | ★ ★ ★ ★ |
| Grapes | pinot noir |
| Region | West Tamar, Tas. |
| Cellar | ▮ 4+ |
| Alc./Vol. | 13.5% |
| RRP | $28.50 |

Nick and Cynthia Butler manage this 6-hectare vineyard at Rowella in the West Tamar, established in 1983. Nick is both winemaker and viticulturist. This wine won a gold medal at the 2001 Tasmanian Regional Wine Show.
CURRENT RELEASE 1999   Here is a chunky style of pinot. It has a slightly minty, herby nose with *sousbois* overtones, and there's evidence of slightly raisined fruit. The concentrated, rich palate has some grip from tannin. A solid wine with a future in the cellar. Try it with veal saltimbocca.

## Honeytree Estate Cabernet Sauvignon

This is an estate-grown Hunter wine that takes its name from a large honeytree (whatever that is) which once grew there. The 10-hectare vineyard was established in 1970 and has a new lease of life in recent years.

CURRENT RELEASE 1999 The colour is dark and promisingly deep; the bouquet has an overriding element of sawn planks, and charry oak flavours also permeate the palate. It's tannic and rustic, and should benefit from a little cellaring. Team it with barbecued steak.

| | |
|---|---|
| **Quality** | 🍷🍷🍷½ |
| **Value** | ★★★ |
| **Grapes** | cabernet sauvignon |
| **Region** | Hunter Valley, NSW |
| **Cellar** | 2–7 |
| **Alc./Vol.** | 13.6% |
| **RRP** | $20.00 |

## Hope Estate Cabernet Merlot

This is quite a substantial operation: it has 100 hectares of vineyards, 55 of them in the Broke Fordwich sub-region of the Hunter. Proprietor: Michael Hope. Maker: Peter Howland.

CURRENT RELEASE 1999 There's a whiff of volatile acidity here, but it needn't be a concern. The colour is pleasingly full and the bouquet carries fresh oak and berries, with a slight edginess. It has good weight and concentration in the mouth, and the finish is firm – completing a claret-like structure. Pair it with doner kebabs.

| | |
|---|---|
| **Quality** | 🍷🍷🍷½ |
| **Value** | ★★★ |
| **Grapes** | cabernet sauvignon 60%; merlot 40% |
| **Region** | Hunter Valley, NSW |
| **Cellar** | 5 |
| **Alc./Vol.** | 13.0% |
| **RRP** | $18.00 (S) |

## Houghton Cabernet Shiraz Merlot

Houghton is easily the biggest winery in Western Australia and is wholly owned by BRL Hardy. Chief winemaker is Larry Cherubino. This wine is part of its bread-and-butter, red-striped 'line range'.

CURRENT RELEASE 2000 This very gamy red wine will test some people's tolerance. It has a nice full colour but the mulberry/cabernet-led aromas are submerged under a very meaty pong. If you don't mind that, it's a good drink and fair value for money. It would work with a hamburger with the lot.

| | |
|---|---|
| **Quality** | 🍷🍷½ |
| **Value** | ★★★ |
| **Grapes** | cabernet sauvignon; shiraz; merlot |
| **Region** | various, WA |
| **Cellar** | 3 |
| **Alc./Vol.** | 13.5% |
| **RRP** | $12.00 (S) |

## Howard Park Leston Shiraz

| | |
|---|---|
| Quality | ▮▮▮▮ |
| Value | ★★★ |
| Grapes | shiraz |
| Region | Margaret River, WA |
| Cellar | ▬ 2–8+ |
| Alc./Vol. | 14.5% |
| RRP | $32.00 |

This is a new brand for Howard Park, which recently built a second winery at Margaret River and expanded its winemaking activities. This one's aged only in French oak. Maker: Michael Kerrigan.

CURRENT RELEASE 1999　There's plenty of raw muscle in this youngster. It needs time to mellow out a bit. The colour is full purple–red and it smells fresh, fruit-driven and edgy. There's good weight of undeveloped fruit in the mouth supported by pretty firm tannins. A gutsy wine that should reward keeping. Then try it with aged cheddar.

## Howard Park Scotsdale Cabernet Sauvignon

| | |
|---|---|
| Quality | ▮▮▮▮▮ |
| Value | ★★★⯪ |
| Grapes | cabernet sauvignon |
| Region | Great Southern, WA |
| Cellar | ▬ 3–10+ |
| Alc./Vol. | 12.5% |
| RRP | $32.00 ▮ |

Scotsdale is a village in the Great Southern. This wine, from two vineyards at Mount Barker and Frankland, and the Leston shiraz from Margaret River are the beginnings of a new regional/varietal portfolio from Howard Park.

CURRENT RELEASE 1999　The bouquet is dominated by dark-chocolate and vanilla aromas from toasty oak while the fruit is expressed more clearly on the palate. It has nice juicy berry cabernet flavours and a long, firmly tannic finish. The flavours and structure are very good and all it needs is time. Then drink with roast venison.

## Hugo Reserve Shiraz

| | |
|---|---|
| Quality | ▮▮▮▮▮ |
| Value | ★★★★ |
| Grapes | shiraz |
| Region | McLaren Vale, SA |
| Cellar | ▬ 2–12+ |
| Alc./Vol. | 14.5% |
| RRP | $28.00 (cellar door) |

This is a selection of fruit from the oldest vines in the 20-hectare vineyard. They were planted in 1960. The wine was given more time in oak, and newer oak, than the regular shiraz, which we reviewed in the last edition. Maker: John Hugo.

CURRENT RELEASE 1998　If big, ripe reds are your bag, this will please! It's a gorgeous, voluptuous, fleshy, ultra-ripe shiraz that shows plenty of oak and tannin at this stage. It needs time to integrate fully with the massive fruit and is just a bit four-square at present. It will be sensational in time. Then drink with aged cheddar.

## Hunter's Pinot Noir

Marlborough is New Zealand's great white hope as far as producing a decent red is concerned. The winemakers there want to do with pinot in red what they've done with sauvignon blanc in white. That's optimism! Maker: Gary Duke.

CURRENT RELEASE 1999    A very smart pinot from one of the less noisy pinot makers. The bouquet is a captivating fusion of strawberry, cherry, and hints of left-field animal complexities. In the mouth, it has the sort of sweet, supple texture that comes from a warmer ferment, and there are bitter-cherry and other less definable, but delicious, flavours. Very promising. Try it with duck risotto.

| | |
|---|---|
| Quality | 🍷🍷🍷🍷 |
| Value | ★★★¹ |
| Grapes | pinot noir |
| Region | Marlborough, NZ |
| Cellar | 🍾 4+ |
| Alc./Vol. | 13.5% |
| RRP | $27.00 |

## Ingoldby Cabernet Sauvignon

When Mildara Blass started absorbing small vineyards there was great trepidation. Would their names and indentities survive? Well, some have, some haven't, but thankfully some among them actually might have got better. Ingoldby is a case in point.

CURRENT RELEASE 1999    McLaren Vale red of real character at a good price. As usual, regional and winemaking factors take precedence over cabernet varietal clues, giving a nose of ripe berries, earth and well-modulated dusty oak. The medium-weight palate has balanced, mellow berry and plum flavour which is rich and smooth. It finishes with enough dry tannins for structure. Good with roast beef.

| | |
|---|---|
| Quality | 🍷🍷🍷🍷 |
| Value | ★★★★ |
| Grapes | cabernet sauvignon |
| Region | McLaren Vale, SA |
| Cellar | 🍾 4 |
| Alc./Vol. | 13.5% |
| RRP | $17.00 Ⓢ |

## Ingoldby Road Block Grenache Shiraz

| | |
|---|---|
| Quality | ♟ ♟ ♟ ♟ |
| Value | ★ ★ ★ |
| Grapes | grenache; shiraz |
| Region | McLaren Vale, SA |
| Cellar | 🍾 3 |
| Alc./Vol. | 14.5% |
| RRP | $19.00 |

Grenache and shiraz blends were the source of much of the 'claret' that inspired Aussie wine drinkers three decades ago. After years on the outer, now it's a cool thing to drink again.

CURRENT RELEASE 1998    This has a full-on nose that is big on immediate appeal but light on subtlety; there's a blackberry liqueur-like sweetness with notes of aniseed, warm spices and sweet oak. In the mouth the theme continues with rather jammy raspberry and blackberry flavours balanced with vanillin oak. It makes a smooth, full-bodied mouthful, soft in ripe tannins, with an aftertaste that echoes that sweet-fruited palate long after it's gone down the hatch. The stuff of happy backyard barbecues.

## Ingoldby Shiraz

| | |
|---|---|
| Quality | ♟ ♟ ♟ ♟ |
| Value | ★ ★ ★ ★ ¹ |
| Grapes | shiraz |
| Region | McLaren Vale, SA |
| Cellar | 🍾 5 |
| Alc./Vol. | 13.5% |
| RRP | $17.00 Ⓢ |

Thirty-odd years ago, the late Jim Ingoldby generously gave a dozen shiraz to a precocious little twerp visiting the winery with his parents. They should have been cellared and savoured with due ceremony, but the undeserving recipient (RK-P) guzzled most of them at boozy student parties in the '70s. Pearls before swine.

CURRENT RELEASE 1999    The Ingoldby range of wines give a lot of bang for your buck. This is a very inviting regional shiraz that isn't as traditional as those barnyardy old-style wines that have returned to favour in recent years. The nose is clean and modern with cherry, blackberry and dark-chocolate aromas mixing it with balanced vanillin oak. It tastes satisfyingly mellow and ripe with smooth drink-me-now texture and ripe tannins. Serve it with veal ragu lasagne.

## James Busby Barossa Cabernet Sauvignon

The James Busby range is a merchant's label owned by Coles Liquorland. The wines are made under contract by Grant Burge. They're also available from Vintage Cellars shops.

CURRENT RELEASE 1998    The wine is showing some early development and has a dry, dusty oak character that suggests it spent a long time in wood. It lacks primary fruit but is a good drink, despite being somewhat closed and savoury on the palate. There are some chewy tannins on the finish and it has solid persistence. It's probably in a development stage, and is a sensible partner for a lamb shawarma.

| | |
|---|---|
| Quality | ♟ ♟ ♟ ♟ |
| Value | ★ ★ ★ ✦ |
| Grapes | cabernet sauvignon |
| Region | Barossa Valley, SA |
| Cellar | ▯ 4 |
| Alc./Vol. | 13.0% |
| RRP | $15.40 Ⓢ |

## Jamiesons Run Alexander's Block Cabernet Sauvignon

Mildara, or should we say Beringer Blass, has distanced itself from the Jamiesons Run brand: there is no longer any mention of Mildara on the label. From the t'rific '98 harvest, the Coonawarra crew produced a bevy of special bottlings. This is one.

CURRENT RELEASE 1998    Concentrated fruit shows! The colour is dense and it smells and tastes rich. Typical Mildara minty, slightly eucalyptus aromas, and liberal oak come through in the bouquet, and there's evidence of high-quality barrels, well handled. It's a gutsy, powerful, delicious red which needs time. Cellar, then serve with barbecued butterflied leg of lamb.

| | |
|---|---|
| Quality | ♟ ♟ ♟ ♟ ♟ |
| Value | ★ ★ ★ ★ ✦ |
| Grapes | cabernet sauvignon |
| Region | Coonawarra, SA |
| Cellar | ➥ 2–12+ |
| Alc./Vol. | 13.0% |
| RRP | $35.00 |

## Jamiesons Run Coonawarra

This is one of Beringer Blass's (née Mildara's) great success stories. It's consistently good value for money and you always know what you're buying: the style is pretty constant.

CURRENT RELEASE 1998    Jammo's is a satisfying wine at an affordable price, and most vintages are good cellaring propositions into the bargain. The '98 is showing some development now, with bay-leaf, earth and dried-banana aromas. It's likewise savoury and drying in the mouth, building interesting flavour complexities, finishing with chewy, puckery tannins. It would go well with osso bucco.

| | |
|---|---|
| Quality | ♟ ♟ ♟ ♟ |
| Value | ★ ★ ★ ★ |
| Grapes | cabernet sauvignon; shiraz; merlot |
| Region | Coonawarra, SA |
| Cellar | ▯ 8 |
| Alc./Vol. | 13.0% |
| RRP | $18.65 Ⓢ |

## Jamiesons Run McShane's Block Shiraz

| | |
|---|---|
| Quality | ♟ ♟ ♟ ♟ ♟ |
| Value | ★ ★ ★ ★ ★ |
| Grapes | shiraz |
| Region | Coonawarra, SA |
| Cellar | 🍶 15+ |
| Alc./Vol. | 13.5% |
| RRP | $35.00 |

Yet another 'brand extension' for Mildara's stunningly successful Jamiesons Run. This was matured in 30 per cent French oak, the rest American. Maker: David 'Honky Petanquie' O'Leary.

CURRENT RELEASE 1998    Another ripper from the deft hand of O'Leary. It has a stunning array of aromas, from blackberry and cassis to cedar and smoky oak scents, and much more. The flavours are deep and layered with sweet berry fruit and smooth tannins finely melded. It has superb fleshiness, density and balance. No doubt the great year helped with its concentration and persistence. Try it with lamb fillets and pesto.

## Jeanneret Denis Shiraz

| | |
|---|---|
| Quality | ♟ ♟ ♟ ♟ ♟ |
| Value | ★ ★ ★ ⁹ |
| Grapes | shiraz |
| Region | Clare Valley, SA |
| Cellar | 🍶 12+ |
| Alc./Vol. | 14.0% |
| RRP | $55.00 🍷 |

This is Ben Jeanneret's tribute to his father Denis, who founded the family wine enterprise. Only 150 dozen were produced, from 138-year-old, dry-grown vines, and aged for 24 months in French oak.

CURRENT RELEASE 1998    It's soaked up that oak like a sponge. The wine has a fine oak/fruit balance, and is very intense without being too big or heavy. Indeed, it's an elegant shiraz, scented with cherries, plums and mint. It's medium- to full-bodied and very stylish. The finish lingers on and on. A superb wine which deserves pink-roasted leg of lamb.

## Jeanneret Grenache Shiraz

| | |
|---|---|
| Quality | ♟ ♟ ♟ ♟ |
| Value | ★ ★ ★ ★ |
| Grapes | grenache 70%; shiraz 30% |
| Region | Clare Valley, SA |
| Cellar | 🍶 8 |
| Alc./Vol. | 14.0% |
| RRP | $16.00 (cellar door) |

Few grenaches aren't improved by a little shiraz. Appropriately for a mainly grenache wine, this was stored in older barrels. Maker: Ben Jeanneret.

CURRENT RELEASE 1999    The colour is youthful and the bouquet invites you in, with aromas of licorice, cherry and subtle spices. The flavours turn chocolatey and vanillin in the mouth where it has a pleasing fleshy texture, more cherry fruit and good balance. It would drink well with grilled chorizo.

## Jim Barry Cabernet Sauvignon

Jim Barry himself established this family winery in 1959. It now has 200 hectares of vineyards at Clare, Watervale and Penola (Coonawarra). His three sons Peter, Mark and John all work in the business today. CURRENT RELEASE 1999  This is a solid red richly endowed with customary deep Clare minty/berry and earthy flavours. The colour is deep and there are dusty oak characters in the bouquet, which are repeated in the mouth resulting in a dry, savoury finish with some tannin grip. It is a good food wine. Try it with Lebanese shish kebabs.

| | |
|---|---|
| Quality | ▮▮▮▮ |
| Value | ★★★⁴ |
| Grapes | cabernet sauvignon |
| Region | Clare Valley, SA |
| Cellar | ▮ 8 |
| Alc./Vol. | 14.0% |
| RRP | $25.00 Ⓢ |

## Jim Barry McCrae Wood Shiraz

McCrae Wood was the name of the chap who owned the vineyard before Jim Barry. The wines are second-in-line to The Armagh in the Barry portfolio, although they lack the class of that wine. Maker: Mark Barry. CURRENT RELEASE 1998  Trademark minty, stalky, peppercorn aromas burst from the glass, and in the mouth these are joined by raspberry, redcurrant and blueberry flavours. It's tight and lean, and finishes firm, with some greener flavours that add bitterness. It needs time, then try it with Irish stew.

| | |
|---|---|
| Quality | ▮▮▮▮ |
| Value | ★★★ |
| Grapes | shiraz |
| Region | Clare Valley, SA |
| Cellar | ➤ 3–12+ |
| Alc./Vol. | 13.5% |
| RRP | $40.00 ▮ |

## Jim Barry The Armagh

The name of the Armagh sub-region is a reminder that it was an Irishman, James Gleeson, who first settled in the Clare Valley. Made from old, unwatered, low-yielding vines, The Armagh was one of the first Grange pretenders, and we'd have to admit it succeeds. *Previous outstanding vintages: '90, '91, '92, '93, '95, '96* CURRENT RELEASE 1998  Could this be the best Armagh ever? It is a gob-smacker. Armagh has always had great fruit concentration but the complexity and structure nowadays are better than ever. The colour is suitably dark; the bouquet suggests coffee, vanilla, toasty oak and smoked oyster. There's a lot of oak character, cleverly infused, and the palate is big, deep and dense, with all the thunderous power and relentless momentum of a freight train. Great with aged cheddar.

| | |
|---|---|
| Quality | ▮▮▮▮▮ |
| Value | ★★★ |
| Grapes | shiraz |
| Region | Clare Valley, SA |
| Cellar | ➤ 2–15+ |
| Alc./Vol. | 14.5% |
| RRP | $145.00 ▮ |

## Jindalee Cabernet Sauvignon

| | |
|---|---|
| Quality | ▼▼▼ |
| Value | ★★★↓ |
| Grapes | cabernet sauvignon |
| Region | Murray Valley, Vic. |
| Cellar | ▮ 3 |
| Alc./Vol. | 13.5% |
| RRP | $10.00 ⓢ |

The owners of Jindalee Wines have around 400 hectares of vineyards either producing or under development in the Murray–Darling region. That's a lot of vino!
CURRENT RELEASE 2000    For a mere tenner, this is a pretty reasonable red wine. It has direct, fruity, cherry aromas with some herbal notes and a toasty oak-chip overtone. This offers some vanilla but is mercifully not overdone. In the mouth, it's clean, light, simple and perfectly adequate. Smooth, low-tannin, well-made quaffing red. Serve it with pork sausages and 'dead horse'.

## Jindalee Merlot

| | |
|---|---|
| Quality | ▼▼▮ |
| Value | ★★★↓ |
| Grapes | merlot |
| Region | Murray–Darling, Vic. |
| Cellar | ▮ 3 |
| Alc./Vol. | 14.0% |
| RRP | $10.00 ⓢ |

Curiously, Jindalee is a Geelong-based wine company, and there's a Geelong address on the label. But its inexpensive, good-value wines come from the Murray Valley in northern Victoria.
CURRENT RELEASE 2000    Just an infant, this wine smells raw and somewhat unformed. The nose offers cherry-pip and plum essence aromas, with overtones of herbs and grapeskins. In the mouth, it has a simple, basic light-bodied flavour and some rather coarse tannins. It's good value and will be best from late 2001 to early 2002. Try it with rissoles.

## Jindalee Shiraz

| | |
|---|---|
| Quality | ▼▼▮ |
| Value | ★★★↓ |
| Grapes | shiraz |
| Region | Murray–Darling, Vic. |
| Cellar | ▮ 2 |
| Alc./Vol. | 13.5% |
| RRP | $10.00 ⓢ |

The folks at Jindalee have bought the former Idyll vineyard – which works well, as they're based in nearby Geelong. They've repackaged the wines as Fettler's Rest. Meanwhile the Jindalee range comes from Sunraysia.
CURRENT RELEASE 2000    The colour is pale but of good purple–red hue, and it smells of mint, cherry and green herbs. It's very light and simple, and lacks strength on the palate. The balance is acceptable and it's very drinkable at the price. It goes with bangers and mash.

## Juniper Estate Shiraz

Juniper Estate is the reborn Wrights, in the heart of Willyabrup. The estate wines are made from the 25-year-old vines on the property; Juniper Crossing wines are a mix of estate and bought-in fruit. Maker: Mark Messenger.

CURRENT RELEASE 1999    An infant loaded with potential! At present the bouquet is rather raw and immature, but shows beautifully sweet ripe fruit and a slightly meaty, gamy overtone, while the palate is big and richly fruity, with assertive tannin and again, undeveloped flavour. It shows great promise. Cellar, then drink with a chunky beef pie.

| | |
|---|---|
| Quality | 🍷🍷🍷🍷 |
| Value | ★★★★ |
| Grapes | shiraz |
| Region | Margaret River, WA |
| Cellar | 2–12+ |
| Alc./Vol. | 14.0% |
| RRP | $19.00 (cellar door) |

## Kaesler Old Vine Shiraz

Those old plots of Barossa vines that were being ripped out and otherwise desecrated only a couple of decades ago, are now gaining quite a lot of notoriety. The 1893 vintage Kaesler vineyard is one such property.

CURRENT RELEASE 1998    This wine is very much par for the course when it comes to the currently popular style of Barossa shiraz. The nose has earthy-sweet blackberry aromas with some leafy plum, spice and the vanillin aromas of American oak. In the mouth it has that lovely smooth fruit intensity of old-vine shiraz, a coconutty oak-derived touch, and the flavour lasts long and easy ahead of mild, dry tannins. Serve it with goulash.

| | |
|---|---|
| Quality | 🍷🍷🍷🍷 |
| Value | ★★★ |
| Grapes | shiraz |
| Region | Barossa Valley, SA |
| Cellar | 5 |
| Alc./Vol. | 14.0% |
| RRP | $60.00 |

## Kangarilla Road Shiraz

Shiraz and McLaren Vale go hand in hand and Kangarilla Road's smartly presented version epitomises the regional style well.

CURRENT RELEASE 1999    The nose is pleasantly complex, with a core of blackberry and liqueurish raspberry fruit mixed in with clean earthy aromas and spicy oak in good harmony. The medium-bodied palate has an attractive feel, with ripe berry flavour of moderate intensity leading through to a medium-grip, dry tannin finish. A very tasty wine, ideal for barbecued spare ribs.

| | |
|---|---|
| Quality | 🍷🍷🍷🍷 |
| Value | ★★★★ |
| Grapes | shiraz |
| Region | McLaren Vale, SA |
| Cellar | 4 |
| Alc./Vol. | 13.8% |
| RRP | $19.00 |

## Kangarilla Road Zinfandel

| | |
|---|---|
| Quality | ♥ ♥ ♥ ♥ |
| Value | ★ ★ ⬧ |
| Grapes | zinfandel |
| Region | McLaren Vale, SA |
| Cellar | ▮ 2 |
| Alc./Vol. | 14.6% |
| RRP | $32.00 |

'California's own wine grape' zinfandel has now been positively identified as the primitivo grape of Southern Italy. In the USA it makes wines that range from dense, dark biggies to washed-out sweet pink ones of amazing yuckiness.

CURRENT RELEASE 1999    This is a wine of contradictions. On the nose its fruit character is light with a loganberry sort of aroma and a gentle dusting of oak. Similarly it has quite a fresh, easy palate with soft tannins. Yet with an alcohol level that doesn't give a lot of change out of 15 per cent, you would expect a bigger, warmer and headier drop. Despite all that, it's a pleasant enough drink. Enjoy it with grilled Provençale vegetables.

## Katnook Estate Shiraz

| | |
|---|---|
| Quality | ♥ ♥ ♥ ♥ ♥ |
| Value | ★ ★ ★ |
| Grapes | shiraz |
| Region | Coonawarra, SA |
| Cellar | ⬤— 1–8 |
| Alc./Vol. | 14.0% |
| RRP | $42.50 |

Katnook Estate's one-off super-premium shiraz, Prodigy, impressed us greatly in last year's *Guide*. Now it seems that shiraz has become a regular feature of the Katnook portfolio. Winemaker Wayne Stehbens handles it with great skill.

CURRENT RELEASE 1998    This has a promising, deep purplish colour. The nose is ripe and nicely intense with clean blackberry and earthy varietal aromas touched harmoniously by smoky, vanillin oak. It tastes smooth and concentrated with medium weight and good texture. Ripe, fruit-sweet berry flavours lead through balanced tannins on a dry finish. A tasty companion to spiced lamb kebabs.

## Kelly's Promise Cabernet Merlot

| | |
|---|---|
| Quality | ♥ ♥ ♥ |
| Value | ★ ★ ★ |
| Grapes | cabernet sauvignon; merlot |
| Region | South East Australia |
| Cellar | ▮ 2 |
| Alc./Vol. | 13.5% |
| RRP | $12.00 |

The new Andrew Garrett wines range across a broad spread of prices and quality levels. Finding your way through them can be a bit confusing. Kelly's Promise is a cheaper label.

CURRENT RELEASE 1999    A red that introduces itself with some spicy plummy fruit and a lick of smoky oak. It's only of middling intensity, but pleasant enough. In the mouth it's lightish–medium in body and rather plain to taste, finishing soft and easy. Try it with simple pasta dishes.

## Kelly's Promise Shiraz

It's hard to keep track of all of Andrew Garrett's new labels and enterprises. This one springs from his ambitious McLaren Vale project.
CURRENT RELEASE 2000   A simple commercial red wine that relies a lot on fruit sweetness for its appeal. Blackberry fruit errs on the jammy side and a lick of sweet oak reinforces things. The palate is medium in body and a bit one-dimensional in flavour, and the finish is very soft. Try it with spaghetti bolognese.

| | |
|---|---|
| Quality | ▮ ▮ ▮ |
| Value | ★ ★ ★ |
| Grapes | shiraz |
| Region | South East Australia |
| Cellar | ▮ 1 |
| Alc./Vol. | 13.5% |
| RRP | $12.00 |

## Kingston Estate Petit Verdot

Petit verdot is a curiosity in Australia and it's none too common in its place of origin, Bordeaux. Some of our Murray Valley growers are playing around with it and Kingston's Bill Moularadellis reckons it suits the region perfectly.
CURRENT RELEASE 1999   This has an appetising nose of currants, dark fruits, licorice and a notable dose of cedary sweet oak. There's good intensity in the mouth with chewy texture and oaky dark fruit flavour, leading through to firm, ripe tannins. It's a straightforward wine with a lot of hearty appeal. Try it with Greek-inspired roast lamb.

| | |
|---|---|
| Quality | ▮ ▮ ▮ ▯ |
| Value | ★ ★ ★ |
| Grapes | petit verdot |
| Region | Murray Valley, SA |
| Cellar | ▬ 1–4 |
| Alc./Vol. | 14.5% |
| RRP | $14.95 |

## Knappstein Shiraz

Andrew Hardy makes an excellent range of wines from Clare Valley grapes in a middle of the road style, not super-modern, nor ultra-traditional.
CURRENT RELEASE 1999   An example of just how good shiraz can be if it's given French oak rather than the ubiquitous American. The nose has cherry liqueur fruit aromas of surprising intensity. There's also a suggestion of sweet spices and a deftly handled, light seasoning of cedary oak. It's medium-bodied, with a fleshy middle palate full of ripe cherry and berry flavours, and gently spicy French oak. Firm tannins are slightly astringent in youth but will soften with bottle-age. Serve with lamb kebabs.

| | |
|---|---|
| Quality | ▮ ▮ ▮ ▮ ▯ |
| Value | ★ ★ ★ ★ |
| Grapes | shiraz |
| Region | Clare Valley, SA |
| Cellar | ▮ 8 |
| Alc./Vol. | 14.2% |
| RRP | $22.00 |

## Knight Granite Hills Shiraz

| | |
|---|---|
| Quality | ♟ ♟ ♟ ⸹ |
| Value | ★ ★ ★ |
| Grapes | shiraz |
| Region | Macedon Ranges, Vic. |
| Cellar | ▮ 4 |
| Alc./Vol. | 14.5% |
| RRP | $27.30 |

Grown in the beautiful boulder-strewn part of Victoria's Macedon region, the Knight wines gave many people their first taste of peppery cool-grown shiraz back in the early '80s.

CURRENT RELEASE 1998   Sunny years like '98 tend to temper the overtly peppery spice in wines like this. It's still there, but it's secondary to aromas of mulberry, blackcurrant, herbs and a slightly vegetal touch. The palate is medium-bodied with easy berry flavours, tangy acidity and moderate tannins. Ideally it could do with more stuffing, but it's pleasant enough served alongside pasta with pesto.

## Kopparossa Shiraz

| | |
|---|---|
| Quality | ♟ ♟ ♟ ♟ |
| Value | ★ ★ ★ ★ |
| Grapes | shiraz |
| Region | Coonawarra, SA |
| Cellar | ▮ 5 |
| Alc./Vol. | 13.5% |
| RRP | $20.00 |

The new Kopparossa label will be borne by wines from three of South Australia's cool-climate wine regions, Coonawarra, the Adelaide Hills and Naracoorte/ Padthaway. The actual Kopparossa vineyard of Mike Press and Gavin Hogg is near Naracoorte.

CURRENT RELEASE 1998   There's quite a bit of charry barrel ferment character in this young shiraz, but ripe sweet fruit is there at the core, making for a very tasty red. It's medium-bodied, satisfying and long-tasting with the soft tannins that Coonawarra is famous for. Try it with chargrilled steaks.

## Lake Breeze Bernoota Shiraz Cabernet

| | |
|---|---|
| Quality | ♟ ♟ ♟ ♟ ⸹ |
| Value | ★ ★ ★ ★ ★ |
| Grapes | shiraz 50%; cabernet sauvignon 50% |
| Region | Langhorne Creek, SA |
| Cellar | ▮ 10+ |
| Alc./Vol. | 14.5% |
| RRP | $20.50 |

This topped the red blends class in the 2001 Boutique Winery Awards, a fine achievement for a mid-priced red. It's actually the Follett family's bread-and-butter label. Bernoota is the name of the family homestead, meaning 'camp among the trees'.

CURRENT RELEASE 1999   Coconut aromas from American oak are evident in the bouquet, which is still young and yet to fully meld. The wine is rich and fleshy, with ample soft berry flavours of fully ripe grapes, and plenty of extract. The texture is beautifully smooth and there's no shortage of ripe tannin, giving an appealing chunkiness. It would be a treat with shish kebabs.

## Lake Breeze Cabernet Sauvignon

The lake in question is Lake Alexandrina, where the Murray River empties into the sea, via the lake and The Coorong. Langhorne Creek is just a short hop from the lake.

CURRENT RELEASE 1999    This is a stylish red which belies the reports of the district having a dire vintage in '99. It is a tad more elegant than usual, however. The oak–fruit balance is pleasing and the palate is smooth and harmonious, with a nice touch of richness. It would drink well with roast leg of lamb.

| | |
|---|---|
| Quality | ♟♟♟♟ |
| Value | ★★★★ |
| Grapes | cabernet sauvignon |
| Region | Langhorne Creek, SA |
| Cellar | ▮ 10 |
| Alc./Vol. | 14.0% |
| RRP | $23.00 |

## Lake Breeze Winemaker's Selection Cabernet Sauvignon

Because '98 was such a great vintage, winemaker Greg Follett made a barrel selection, of just 360 cases, and released a winemaker's selection. There's a shiraz and a cabernet. Both are ripsnorters.

CURRENT RELEASE 1998    Langhorne Creek is one of our best (and most under-sung) cabernet regions. This showcases the power and length, the depth and concentration, the region can deliver. The bouquet reveals beef-stock, clove and nutmeg spice aromas. In the mouth you find chewy tannins, sumptuous depth of fruit and loads of extract, resulting in a fine, fleshy texture. Cellar, then serve with hearty beef casserole.

| | |
|---|---|
| Quality | ♟♟♟♟♟ |
| Value | ★★★★ |
| Grapes | cabernet sauvignon |
| Region | Langhorne Creek, SA |
| Cellar | ⇌ 2–20+ |
| Alc./Vol. | 15.0% |
| RRP | $33.50 ▮ |

## Lamonts Shiraz

Winemaker Mark Warren reckons he has trouble getting the grapes off in time, which explains the alcohol reading. They ripen fast in yonder Swan Valley! This wine should be just coming on sale as this edition is published. Grab some!

CURRENT RELEASE 1999    Here is a thumper of a shiraz! Big, bold and brassy, it's jam-packed with anise/licorice, berry jam and fruitcake aromas. Full-bodied, rich and chunky, it seems to somehow keep all its components in balance. Drink with barbecued roo.

| | |
|---|---|
| Quality | ♟♟♟♟♟ |
| Value | ★★★★ |
| Grapes | shiraz |
| Region | Swan Valley, WA |
| Cellar | ▮ 8+ |
| Alc./Vol. | 14.9% |
| RRP | $24.00 (cellar door) |

## Langmeil Barossa Shiraz

| | |
|---|---|
| Quality | ♥ ♥ ♥ ♥ |
| Value | ★ ★ ★ |
| Grapes | shiraz |
| Region | Barossa Valley, SA |
| Cellar | ▮ 6 |
| Alc./Vol. | 14.0% |
| RRP | $23.20 |

For a Barossa shiraz, this is a tad on the green side. It's not uncommon for a '99. No doubt it's a symptom of the wet vintage. Langmeil's top shiraz is The Freedom. CURRENT RELEASE 1999 The colour is nice and deep while the aromas are dominated by green peppercorn and stalky/sappy notes. It is certainly aromatic. The palate reveals plummy fruit-dominant flavours and fleshy characteristics, finishing with green, slightly bitter tannins that we wonder if the wine can overcome. Try it with peppered steak.

## Langmeil Cabernet Sauvignon

| | |
|---|---|
| Quality | ♥ ♥ ♥ ♥ |
| Value | ★ ★ ★ ✦ |
| Grapes | cabernet sauvignon |
| Region | Barossa Valley, SA |
| Cellar | ▮ 6 |
| Alc./Vol. | 14.0% |
| RRP | $20.30 |

Langmeil is a partnership between the Bitter and Lindner families. They've breathed new life into an old property: Langmeil is one of the original Barossa settlements (along with Bethany), and the first vines on the property were planted in the 1840s. CURRENT RELEASE 1999 This is a lighter, more elegant style than usually seen in the Barossa. The aromas are minty, herbaceous and Ribena-like, but there is no greenness in the palate flavour or tannins. It's light-to medium-bodied, with attractive sweet fruit and good persistence. Easy to enjoy, with pasta and a tomato-based sauce.

## Langmeil Selwin's Lot 36

| | |
|---|---|
| Quality | ♥ ♥ ♥ ♥ |
| Value | ★ ★ ★ ✦ |
| Grapes | cabernet sauvignon; grenache; shiraz |
| Region | Barossa Valley, SA |
| Cellar | ▮ 5+ |
| Alc./Vol. | 14.0% |
| RRP | $17.50 |

Q: Who was Selwin? A: The last member of the Auricht family to farm the original vineyard, planted by his forebears, at the village of Langmeil. Lot 36 is the site of the present-day winery. CURRENT RELEASE 1998 These guys just don't know how to make bad red wine. This is one of their cheaper wines, but it's right on form. Aromas of cherry, spice, earth and vanilla are captivating. Then follows a firm, slightly drying palate with a core of sweet plum/berry fruit which lingers nicely. It's a fine drink now and should keep for years. Serve with braised lamb shanks.

## Langmeil The Freedom Shiraz

The Auricht family – seeking freedom from religious persecution in Poland – planted the first shiraz vines at Langmeil in the mid-1840s. This is made from the few acres that remain: dry-grown, hand-pruned, hand-picked and yielding 1.5 to 2 tonnes an acre. CURRENT RELEASE 1998    You'll get religion after drinking this. It's a great wine! The colour is dark and dense; the bouquet showcases concentrated fruit of a blackberry, blackcurrant nature, with oak tucked well into the background. It's rich, dense and chewy in the mouth, with great flavour and texture. It's full-bodied and very long. It'll live for ages and go well with mature parmesan cheese.

| | |
|---|---|
| Quality | ♥ ♥ ♥ ♥ ♥ |
| Value | ★ ★ ★ ↓ |
| Grapes | shiraz |
| Region | Barossa Valley, SA |
| Cellar | ▮ 20 |
| Alc./Vol. | 14.5% |
| RRP | $61.00 ▮ |

## Lark Hill Pinot Noir

The Canberra region should be ideally suited to pinot red wine, but the right results have been a long time coming. Lark Hill produces the goods most consistently. Maker: Sue Carpenter.
*Previous outstanding vintages: '96, '97, '98, '99*
CURRENT RELEASE 2000    The cool-climate origins of this wine show clearly in its herbal, somewhat vegetal characters and its slightly elevated acidity. There are hints of stalk inclusion in the ferment, along with cherry and undergrowth characters. It's quite complex and will appeal to those who favour a stemmy style of pinot. Try it with Chinese duck with taro.

| | |
|---|---|
| Quality | ♥ ♥ ♥ ♥ |
| Value | ★ ★ ★ |
| Grapes | pinot noir |
| Region | Canberra region, NSW |
| Cellar | ▮ 4 |
| Alc./Vol. | 13.5% |
| RRP | $30.00 |

## Lark Hill Shiraz

This is Lark Hill's first shiraz. David and Sue Carpenter took grapes from vineyards in lower, warmer sites than their own at Bungendore. The fruit was from a second flowering after a severe frost in '98.
CURRENT RELEASE 1999    An impressive first effort. It's an intensely spicy, peppery cool-climate style, but it tastes as though the grapes were properly ripe. It has minty overtones and the palate is full of plush fruit that's soft and lacks the harsh green tannins that spoil unripe wines. The structure is fine and it has admirable balance and length. Drinks nicely with beef and vegie hotpot.

| | |
|---|---|
| Quality | ♥ ♥ ♥ ♥ |
| Value | ★ ★ ★ ↓ |
| Grapes | shiraz |
| Region | Canberra region, NSW |
| Cellar | ▮ 6+ |
| Alc./Vol. | 13.5% |
| RRP | $26.00 |

## Leasingham Bastion Shiraz Cabernet

| | |
|---|---|
| Quality | ♥♥♥♥ |
| Value | ★★★★★ |
| Grapes | shiraz; cabernet sauvignon |
| Region | Clare Valley, SA |
| Cellar | 🍷 5+ |
| Alc./Vol. | 13.5% |
| RRP | $14.00 Ⓢ |

Bastion indeed! Bastion of what? The last bastion of good value in moderately priced red wine, perhaps? Hmmm. That's probably not so far-fetched. Try the wine and you'll see what we mean. Maker: Kerri Thompson.

CURRENT RELEASE 1999    Not only is this remarkable value for a wine made from Clare grapes, it offers better depth of flavour and body than pretty well anything else at $10–$14. The nose offers plenty of nicely integrated toasty oak suggesting vanilla and cedar, and in the mouth it's dense, rich and chunky. The chewy tannins may not be elegant, but its key asset is generous flavour and a modicum of Clare regional style. It will even reward cellaring. Try it with osso bucco.

## Leasingham Bin 61 Shiraz

| | |
|---|---|
| Quality | ♥♥♥♥ |
| Value | ★★★♪ |
| Grapes | shiraz |
| Region | Clare Valley, SA |
| Cellar | ➖ 1–8+ |
| Alc./Vol. | 14.0% |
| RRP | $22.00 Ⓢ 🍾 |

Along with Bin 56, Bin 61 is one of the long-standing labels of Leasingham. This vintage won two trophies at Brisbane in 2000, by which time the wine would have been bottled. That makes the result more credible. Maker: Kerri Thompson.

CURRENT RELEASE 1998    Like most BRL reds, the colour is incredibly dark and vivid. The nose is a departure for this wine: markedly vegetal with pungent pepper/spice and compost/herbal notes. It is quite oaky and tannic on the tongue and needs time. It's a bit astringent now. Cellar, then serve with rare, peppered steak.

## Leconfield Cabernet

| | |
|---|---|
| Quality | ♥♥ |
| Value | ★★ |
| Grapes | cabernet sauvignon; merlot; cabernet franc; petit verdot |
| Region | Coonawarra, SA |
| Cellar | 🍷 3 |
| Alc./Vol. | 13.5% |
| RRP | $30.00 |

The wheels have really fallen off Leconfield in recent years. It's quite a while since we were impressed by a cabernet. Perhaps the yields are too high: certainly, the wines taste thin, short and unripe.

CURRENT RELEASE 1999    Even the colour isn't good: it looks older than it is. The aromas suggest crushed leaves, mint, green herbs and Ribena cordial. The taste is sweetly Ribena/vegetal and short, with a hollow middle and harsh green tannins bringing up the rear. We can't recommend this.

## Leeuwin Estate Prelude Vineyard Cabernet Merlot

Leeuwin is famous for its chardonnay, while its cabernet-style reds have been less consistently convincing, although they're built in an ambitiously big, power-packed style.
CURRENT RELEASE 1998   This is a wine that demands to be decanted and given plenty of air. We changed our minds about it as it breathed. It started out with sweaty, herbal and tobacco aromas, which changed to reveal more red-berry smells and fuller palate flavour. It's fruit-driven, focused and elegant, with a tight spine of tannin. This is different – and tasty! Try it with vitello tonnato.

| | |
|---|---|
| Quality | ♱ ♱ ♱ ♱ |
| Value | ★ ★ ★ ┥ |
| Grapes | cabernet sauvignon; merlot |
| Region | Margaret River, WA |
| Cellar | 🍶 6 |
| Alc./Vol. | 14.5% |
| RRP | $29.00 🍶 |

## Lenswood Vineyards Pinot Noir

Tim Knappstein has been on his Arthurian quest, in hot pursuit of the pinot noir holy grail, for about a decade. He gets a little closer to pinning it down every year.
CURRENT RELEASE 1999   The colour is medium–light purple–red and it smells of oak, sweet cherries and a curious hint of dandelion. It's light- to medium-bodied and the flavours are savoury, secondary – rather than primary – and quite drying on the finish. Oak is the dominant flavour and aroma at this stage. It should be best from 2002, with roast duck.

| | |
|---|---|
| Quality | ♱ ♱ ♱ ♱ |
| Value | ★ ★ ┥ |
| Grapes | pinot noir |
| Region | Adelaide Hills, SA |
| Cellar | ➾ 1–5 |
| Alc./Vol. | 13.5% |
| RRP | $49.00 |

## Lenswood Vineyards The Palatine

The inspiration for this wine came from a vineyard called The Palatine, appropriately sited in a lower, and therefore warmer, part of the Adelaide Hills, more suited to growing these grapes than Lenswood.
CURRENT RELEASE 1998   Tim Knappstein has crafted a classy cool-climate cabernet-based red, which happily tastes nice and ripe. It's very concentrated, tightly structured and firm. The fruit is sweet and fully ripe: a welcome improvement on some green early attempts. It's expensive, but very good, and warrants cautious cellaring for two to eight years. Serve with venison casserole.

| | |
|---|---|
| Quality | ♱ ♱ ♱ ♱ ♱ |
| Value | ★ ★ ★ |
| Grapes | cabernet sauvignon 52%; merlot 31%; malbec 17% |
| Region | Adelaide Hills, SA |
| Cellar | ➾ 2–8+ |
| Alc./Vol. | 13.5% |
| RRP | $52.00 🍶 |

## Lenton Brae Margaret River

| | |
|---|---|
| Quality | 🍷🍷🍷🍷🍷 |
| Value | ★★★★ |
| Grapes | cabernet sauvignon 75%; merlot 18%; petit verdot 7% |
| Region | Margaret River, WA |
| Cellar | ⬤ 2–14+ |
| Alc./Vol. | 14.0% |
| RRP | $30.00 🍾 |

It's always reassuring to see a nice, long, springy, high-quality cork come out of an expensive bottle of red. Especially if it's a red with pretensions to long-term cellaring, like this one. The wine won't last if the cork conks out. Maker: Ed Tomlinson.

CURRENT RELEASE 1998    This is a powerful but rather closed cabernet blend, which responds well to aeration. It's unready now but has tremendous potential. The aromas are of sweet berries and barbecued meat, with an intriguingly feral side. The palate is tannic and there's plenty of evidence of liberal oaking. The texture is very appealing: it has high extract, fleshiness, and a very long finish. Cellar, then serve with a hard cheese.

| | |
|---|---|
| Quality | 🍷🍷🍷🍷🍷 |
| Value | ★★★★ |
| Grapes | cabernet sauvignon; merlot; petit verdot |
| Region | Margaret River, WA |
| Cellar | ⬤ 3–15+ |
| Alc./Vol. | 14.0% |
| RRP | $30.00 🍾 |

CURRENT RELEASE 1999    Another solid, powerful red which will need cellaring to show its best. It's full-bodied and robustly structured, with gripping tannins and plenty of oak, which needs time to integrate further. The palate is quite savoury and the finish drying: an impressive youngster that's best served with rare steak – or cellared.

## Leo Buring Clare Valley Shiraz

| | |
|---|---|
| Quality | 🍷🍷🍷🍷 |
| Value | ★★★ |
| Grapes | shiraz |
| Region | Clare Valley, SA |
| Cellar | ⬤ 1–7+ |
| Alc./Vol. | 14.0% |
| RRP | $25.00 ⑤ 🍾 |

This has already thrown a substantial crust, a phenolic deposit that sticks to the bottle wall. It's not a bad sign, and means they haven't filtered it too hard. On the other hand, a stronger fining might have softened that oaky finish . . .

CURRENT RELEASE 1998    It has a very dark, almost black colour, and the bouquet reveals generous use of charred oak barrels. The taste is dense and chewy, robust and serious, which is all very fine until you come to the slightly bitter, oak-tannin finish. It's good, but just a bit timbery for us. Serve it with charred snags at a barbecue.

## Leo Buring DR 488 Cabernet Sauvignon

Leo Buring released a couple of old reds out of the blue. Perhaps they'd been forgotten; lost in a dark corner of the winery. It's not likely to happen in future: it looks as though Buring (and other brands) will be severely rationalised in the new Rosemount/Southcorp combine. CURRENT RELEASE 1985 A very mature, soft, mellow old red, this. Its colour is medium–light brick red to tawny, and it smells of smoked oyster, charcuterie and aged mulberry fruit. Light-bodied and slightly faded, it's a very pleasant old blast from the past, now on a gentle downhill slide. Enjoy solo, or with mild cheeses.

| | |
|---|---|
| Quality | ♀ ♀ ♀ ⸙ |
| Value | ★ ★ ⸙ |
| Grapes | cabernet sauvignon |
| Region | Coonawarra & Barossa Valley, SA |
| Cellar | 🍷 1 |
| Alc./Vol. | 12.5% |
| RRP | $60.00 |

## Lillydale Cabernet Merlot

Lillydale Vineyards was begun by Alex and Judith White in 1975. It's now owned by McWilliams and has 13 hectares of vines in the Seville sub-region. CURRENT RELEASE 1999 This doesn't shout 'Yarra Valley!' to us, but it's a very good wine. It is surprisingly chocolaty and it's likely that cleverly handled oak is concealing the regional flavours at this tender age. There is a glimpse of mulberry fruit in the mouth. It is very soft and approachable all the same. It would partner a beef and mushroom casserole.

| | |
|---|---|
| Quality | ♀ ♀ ♀ ♀ |
| Value | ★ ★ ★ ★ |
| Grapes | cabernet sauvignon; merlot |
| Region | Yarra Valley, Vic. |
| Cellar | 🍷 8+ |
| Alc./Vol. | 13.0% |
| RRP | $21.00 Ⓢ |

## Lindemans Bin 45 Cabernet Sauvignon

Instead of a cork, Lindemans' bin wines have a plastic plug called a Supremecorq. They are okay for the short term, but we wouldn't recommend keeping such wines for longer than a few months. CURRENT RELEASE 2000 This is very presentable at the price. It looks good, with a medium purple–red hue, and it smells of chocolate, vanilla and plum – not especially cabbish, but that's no matter. It's light-bodied, simple and stalky in the mouth. The finish is short but what's there is acceptable. Try it with stirfried pork and laugh all the way to the bank.

| | |
|---|---|
| Quality | ♀ ♀ ⸙ |
| Value | ★ ★ ★ ⸙ |
| Grapes | cabernet sauvignon |
| Region | South East Australia |
| Cellar | 🍷 2 |
| Alc./Vol. | 13.0% |
| RRP | $9.30 Ⓢ |

## Lindemans Bin 50 Shiraz

**Quality** 🍷🍷🍷½
**Value** ★★★★½
**Grapes** shiraz
**Region** South East Australia
**Cellar** 2
**Alc./Vol.** 13.5%
**RRP** $9.30 ($)

'Ah've bin everywhere, man, ah've bin everywhere'. Lindemans' bin wines sure do go everywhere these days. Southcorp can thank their Lucky Starrs.

CURRENT RELEASE 1999 Great value here! The nose is spicy and slightly vegetal; the taste is medium-bodied and very appealing for the price. It's not green, thin and nasty like a lot of sub-$10 reds. The finish carries a satisfying tannin grip that's in balance with the fruit, and the flavours linger well. You're tough to please if you don't enjoy this. It goes with quiche lorraine.

## Lindemans Limestone Ridge

**Quality** 🍷🍷🍷🍷
**Value** ★★★
**Grapes** shiraz; cabernet sauvignon
**Region** Coonawarra, SA
**Cellar** 3–15+
**Alc./Vol.** 13.0%
**RRP** $52.00 ($)

This is one of Lindemans' two single-vineyard Coonawarra wines (the other is St George). The vineyard is planted 7:1 shiraz to cabernet sauvignon, and the make-up of the wine varies according to the season.

*Previous outstanding vintages: '86, '88, '90, '91, '94, '96, '97*

CURRENT RELEASE 1998 As usual, the wine is very oaky in its youth and must be cellared. The aromas are of pronounced coconut American oak and fresh red berries – quite undeveloped. On entry, the wine is rather tart and oaky, seeming to lack flesh and charm, but experience indicates it will fill out and show better integration in time. It's just a pity a lot of it is drunk too soon. Cellar, then serve with a meaty casserole.

## Lindemans St George Cabernet Sauvignon

**Quality** 🍷🍷🍷🍷½
**Value** ★★★½
**Grapes** cabernet sauvignon
**Region** Coonawarra, SA
**Cellar** 4–17+
**Alc./Vol.** 13.0%
**RRP** $50.00 ($)

The grapes are all grown on the 12-hectare St George vineyard and the wine made its appearance with the 1973 vintage. The style has improved markedly since the mid-'80s. Makers: Greg Clayfield and Philip John.

*Previous outstanding vintages: '86, '88, '90, '91, '97*

CURRENT RELEASE 1998 Very much in the modern St George style – lean, elegant, tautly structured and showing some acidity – but the oak seems more subtle than usual upon release. Deep purple–red hue; nicely ripened mulberry, cassis, blackberry aromas entwined with fine oak characters. It's a very clean wine, still a bit 'elbows and knees' at present, but should be long-lived. Cellar, then try it with pink roast lamb.

## Lindemans Steven Vineyard Hunter Shiraz

Some of Lindemans' best red grapes each year come from the Steven Vineyard at Pokolbin. Hence the wines are bottled separately and sold at a premium over the regular Hunter shiraz. It was planted in 1968, first vintage 1975. Maker: Pat Auld.

CURRENT RELEASE 1997 Bin 9425. Lindemans had a better vintage in '97 than most. This shows some development in colour and flavour, with green-pepper, earthy, vegetal and plummy aromas already building leather and licorice characters with age. It is very firmly tannic in the mouth and demands patient cellaring. It's very intense and long, and promises a great and distinctive wine in the future. Drink with steak and kidney pie.

| | |
|---|---|
| Quality | 🍷🍷🍷🍷🍷 |
| Value | ★★★★½ |
| Grapes | shiraz |
| Region | Hunter Valley, NSW |
| Cellar | 2–10+ |
| Alc./Vol. | 13.0% |
| RRP | $30.75 |

## Lindenderry Pinot Noir

The Lindenderry vineyard at Red Hill on the Mornington Peninsula also boasts some of the best dining and accommodation in the region. The wines are made by Lindsay McCall at Paringa Estate.

CURRENT RELEASE 1999 This has a typical medium-red pinot colour. The nose has deep red fruit aromas along with some sappy, foresty bits, all wrapped up in smoky, savoury French oak. The palate has quite rich undergrowthy fruit character with a good measure of that savoury oak blended in. Fresh acidity keeps it lively and the finish is firm, long and aromatic. Try it with tea-smoked duck.

| | |
|---|---|
| Quality | 🍷🍷🍷🍷½ |
| Value | ★★★ |
| Grapes | pinot noir |
| Region | Mornington Peninsula, Vic. |
| Cellar | 1–5 |
| Alc./Vol. | 13.5% |
| RRP | $35.00 |

## Madfish WA Premium Red

The Madfish wines have balance and character, without delivering a body blow like some young reds. Maker: Michael Kerrigan.

CURRENT RELEASE 1999 This medium-coloured young red has a nose of sweet clean red and black berries, which is warm and inviting. Some mellow oak adds a dimension without taking over. In the mouth it has smooth flavour, medium body and it finishes dry with a little firmness. A wine to drink young, perhaps with Italian sausages.

| | |
|---|---|
| Quality | 🍷🍷🍷🍷 |
| Value | ★★★½ |
| Grapes | cabernet sauvignon; cabernet franc; merlot; shiraz |
| Region | South West WA |
| Cellar | 2 |
| Alc./Vol. | 14.0% |
| RRP | $17.00 |

## Maglieri Cabernet Sauvignon

| | |
|---|---|
| Quality | 🍷🍷🍷🍷 |
| Value | ★★★★ |
| Grapes | cabernet sauvignon |
| Region | McLaren Vale, SA |
| Cellar | ⬤ 1–8 |
| Alc./Vol. | 13.5% |
| RRP | $20.00 |

For many years the Maglieri winery lived a double life. On the one hand it was the home of Australian lambrusco, a sweet sparkling confection of dubious vinous value but great commercial appeal; and on the other hand as a producer of concentrated, high-quality McLaren Vale red wines. Now Beringer Blass call the tune.

CURRENT RELEASE 1999    A deep-coloured young McLaren Vale cabernet with a well-concentrated nose of jammy blackberry fruit, minerals and smoky/savoury, subtle oak. In the mouth it has smooth berry flavour that's suitably intense, oak flavour is restrained and provides a pleasant smoky seasoning ahead of some dry, mouth-puckering tannins. Handles T-bone steaks well. Oh, and it's great value too.

## Maglieri Merlot

| | |
|---|---|
| Quality | 🍷🍷🍷🍷 |
| Value | ★★★ |
| Grapes | merlot |
| Region | McLaren Vale, SA |
| Cellar | ⬤ 3 |
| Alc./Vol. | 12.5% |
| RRP | $20.00 |

Merlot is everybody's darlin', but everyone sees it differently. Varietal character is lost in a lot, and frankly there are too many high-priced wines from young vines around. There are also a lot of cheap and cheerfuls, and not enough in the middle, which is where the Maglieri version sits. Maker: John Loxton.

CURRENT RELEASE 1999    A friendly merlot from McLaren Vale, this has clean, juicy berry fruit aroma with attractive earthiness. In the mouth it's soft and approachable with nice leafy berry flavours, subtle oak and dry tannins on a long finish. No great complexity, just pleasant unfussed drinking. Good with little veal scaloppine.

## Maglieri Shiraz

One of the McLaren Vale bastions of the Mildara Blass empire, the Maglieri enterprise continues to make excellent shiraz that has never enjoyed the recognition it deserves. Maker is still John Loxton.

CURRENT RELEASE 1999   Generous wines like this are a McLaren Vale stock-in-trade, but few do it as well or as consistently as Maglieri. The nose is deliciously ripe and smooth with liqueur cherry and spice aromas that are pure, and uncomplicated by heavy-handed oak input. The palate follows suit perfectly with fleshy texture and succulent flavour, coupled to pleasantly chewy tannins on the long finish. Works well with braised steak and onions.

| | |
|---|---|
| Quality | ♥♥♥♥♥ |
| Value | ★★★★ |
| Grapes | shiraz |
| Region | McLaren Vale, SA |
| Cellar | 5 |
| Alc./Vol. | 13.5% |
| RRP | $21.00 |

## Main Ridge Half Acre Pinot Noir

Nat and Rosalie White preside with great good humour over a very cool vineyard spot on the Mornington Peninsula. On a cold winter's day there's a distinctly European feel to things here, reinforced by the small scale of the operation.

CURRENT RELEASE 1999    Nat White's pinots often do battle with a greenish thread through them. So it is with the '99 Half Acre; it has gentle, lightly sappy cherry fruit on the nose with subtle oak and that stemmy herbal note. The palate is silky with light, savoury plummy fruit flavours and some undergrowth/ herb complexity, ahead of a dry long finish. Will suit grilled quails with grapes.

| | |
|---|---|
| Quality | ♥♥♥ |
| Value | ★★ |
| Grapes | pinot noir |
| Region | Mornington Peninsula, Vic. |
| Cellar | 3 |
| Alc./Vol. | 14.0% |
| RRP | $45.00 (cellar door) |

## Majella Cabernet

| | |
|---|---|
| **Quality** | 🍷🍷🍷🍷½ |
| **Value** | ★★★★ |
| **Grapes** | cabernet sauvignon |
| **Region** | Coonawarra, SA |
| **Cellar** | 3–12+ |
| **Alc./Vol.** | 13.5% |
| **RRP** | $31.00 |

Majella is a gem of a Coonawarra estate, run with perfectionist zeal by 'Prof' Lynn. It was once the source of fruit that went into some of the big-name Coonawarra wines.

CURRENT RELEASE 1999 Like all Majella reds, this has a lot of oak, which dominates a bit at the moment. Underneath there's a tight core of sweet, floral cabernet with densely packed blackcurrant and dark berry fruit waiting to emerge. The palate is similarly closed up and oaky at the moment, but that deep, dark fruit is there in the middle, tasting fine, intense and juicy. Mouth-watering acidity emphasises the juicy yet austere cabernet flavour. Give it time to develop, then serve it with roast lamb.

## Majella Shiraz

| | |
|---|---|
| **Quality** | 🍷🍷🍷🍷½ |
| **Value** | ★★★★ |
| **Grapes** | shiraz |
| **Region** | Coonawarra, SA |
| **Cellar** | 3–10 |
| **Alc./Vol.** | 13.5% |
| **RRP** | $29.00 |

The Majella wines are made from what are reputedly some of the best grapes in Coonawarra. Our experience of them confirms it.

*Previous outstanding vintages: '97, '98*

CURRENT RELEASE 1999 All the Majella '99s are pretty special, in keeping with this estate's recent track record. The dense purple–black colour heralds a wine of substance. On the nose and palate it's closed up and tight, with less voluptuous fruit than the '98 at this stage. There's lots of oak giving dusty graphite aromas, and lush blackberry, cherry jam and spice characters are there, but still part-hidden in youth. The palate follows the nose faithfully – tight and closed, yet long and intense – and it reveals more with decanting. Cellar this wine for future enjoyment, perhaps with a lamb dish.

# Majella The Malleea

The traditional cabernet–shiraz blend, using fruit of the highest quality, coupled to lots of the best oak, has forged this entrant in the Coonawarra flagship stakes. *Previous outstanding vintages: '97, '98*
CURRENT RELEASE 1999   This Malleea is still very tight and closed, and dominated by spicy oak. Blackcurrant, olive and cedar aromas meet the nose, giving it a penetrating pristine fruit character more akin to straight cabernet than this blend. In the mouth it's concentrated and ripe with the depth and silkiness that is a Majella hallmark, along with an austerity that marks the '99s. Oak makes a big impact and it finishes long with ripe, well-integrated tannins. Try it with beef with olives.

| | |
|---|---|
| Quality | 🍷🍷🍷🍷🍷 |
| Value | ★★★★ |
| Grapes | cabernet sauvignon; shiraz |
| Region | Coonawarra, SA |
| Cellar | �‐ 3–15 |
| Alc./Vol. | 13.5% |
| RRP | $57.00 |

# Maxwell Reserve Shiraz

Maxwells don't just make wine, they make mead as well, ideal for any flaxen-plaited Nordic warriors who may be passing. For us wine drinkers there's good shiraz too.
CURRENT RELEASE 1998   A traditional type of red of depth and complexity, which has a rich and spicy nose of blueberry-like fruit aromas, along with some briar, mint and chocolate notes. It's very mouth-filling and sweet-fruited with a savoury minty touch, long flavour and firm, dry tannins. Oak is well blended without any sharp edges. Try it with roast beef and Yorkshire pud.

| | |
|---|---|
| Quality | 🍷🍷🍷🍷 |
| Value | ★★★ |
| Grapes | shiraz |
| Region | McLaren Vale, SA |
| Cellar | 🍾 4 |
| Alc./Vol. | 14.0% |
| RRP | $36.00 |

# McGuigan Bin 2000 Shiraz

Brian McGuigan was behind the success of Wyndham Estate wines for many years. His McGuigan wines follow a similar commercially inspired formula.
CURRENT RELEASE 2000   The nose has light, sweet aromas of red and black fruits with a hint of aniseed. In the mouth it's light and soft in texture, with a surprising level of sweetness that carries through to the finish which is soft, unstructured, and a little cloying. Obviously designed for early consumption, this oddball drop should appeal to people who don't really like red wine. Serve it with Big Macs, Whoppers and the like.

| | |
|---|---|
| Quality | 🍷🍷🍶 |
| Value | ★★⊣ |
| Grapes | shiraz |
| Region | various, South East Australia |
| Cellar | 🍾 1 |
| Alc./Vol. | 13.5% |
| RRP | $14.00 Ⓢ |

## McGuigan Bin 4000 Cabernet Sauvignon

| | |
|---|---|
| **Quality** | 🍷🍷🍷½ |
| **Value** | ★★★½ |
| **Grapes** | cabernet sauvignon |
| **Region** | not stated |
| **Cellar** | 1 |
| **Alc./Vol.** | 13.0% |
| **RRP** | $14.00 ($) |

Bin numbers in the thousands seem a bit ridiculous to us. It gets us wondering what Bin 3999 or Bin 4001 is like.

CURRENT RELEASE 2000 This is one of the best of the current crop of McGuigan bin number wines, although it's still no trophy winner. The nose has pleasant and appetising light berry and earth touches with a dab of oak, and the palate has fruity flavour and good texture, although it's fairly light and short. Easy drinking with a pizza.

## McWilliams Mount Pleasant Maurice O'Shea Shiraz

| | |
|---|---|
| **Quality** | 🍷🍷🍷½ |
| **Value** | ★★½ |
| **Grapes** | shiraz |
| **Region** | Hunter Valley, NSW |
| **Cellar** | 1 |
| **Alc./Vol.** | 12.5% |
| **RRP** | $36.00 |

This Mount Pleasant wine, once known as OP & OH in the code of legendary winemaker Maurice O'Shea, has had a makeover in his honour and now heads the Mount Pleasant line-up.

CURRENT RELEASE 1997 The colour is quite deep and the nose has the usual Hunter earthiness with plum and berry-fruit aromas woven in. It smells more developed than the colour or vintage date would suggest. The palate follows suit, tasting almost as if it has dried out a lot with age. We would like to have seen a bit more freshness and depth of flavour, and the finish is rather attenuated. Try it with goat's cheese ravioli.

## McWilliams Mount Pleasant Merlot

| | |
|---|---|
| **Quality** | 🍷🍷🍷🍷 |
| **Value** | ★★★★ |
| **Grapes** | merlot |
| **Region** | Hunter Valley, NSW |
| **Cellar** | 5 |
| **Alc./Vol.** | 14.0% |
| **RRP** | $18.00 |

Merlot isn't Hunter Valley traditional, but these days there are a lot of things there that aren't. As with other red varieties, regional factors can dominate varietal.

CURRENT RELEASE 1999 This is very much a Hunter regional red; if you want to see what pristine merlot character is, go elsewhere for it. The nose has a very Hunter combination of slightly leathery notes, earthiness and shy berry fruit, with oak in light coffee-like barrel-ferment touches. In the mouth it has robust berry flavour, again with savoury Huntery notes. It's medium-bodied and has good persistence of flavour with balanced tannins. A straightforward, tasty wine to enjoy with good homemade pasties.

## McWilliams Mount Pleasant Rosehill Shiraz

Once labelled RH Hermitage, in the odd terminology previously used to describe the individual vineyard wines of Mount Pleasant, this wine comes from 56-year-old shiraz grown at Rosehill vineyard. Maker: Phil Ryan.

CURRENT RELEASE 1998    Hunter shiraz is an odd critter; fans love it, others can't understand all the fuss. This is an interesting example with subdued aromas of cherries, earth and dried leaves, combined in almost Italianate savouriness. The palate is savoury rather than very fruit-sweet, and has a pleasant medium-bodied feel to it, ahead of a quite astringent, slightly stemmy finish. Needs food, like saltimbocca alla romana, to show its best.

| | |
|---|---|
| Quality | ♟ ♟ ♟ ♟ |
| Value | ★ ★ ★ ✦ |
| Grapes | shiraz |
| Region | Hunter Valley, NSW |
| Cellar | 🍾 6 |
| Alc./Vol. | 14.0% |
| RRP | $29.00 |

## McWilliams Riverina Tyrian

Tyrian is an Australian grape variety, bred by the CSIRO from the Spanish sumoll and cabernet sauvignon. Like those other Aussie-bred types, tarrango and taminga, it's going to find it hard to compete with the well-known European-origin grapes.

CURRENT RELEASE 2000    This has a deep, dense colour and the nose is one of those surging youthful affairs that are big on fruit, low on complexity. There's a floral touch to soft berry fruit and more savoury, spicy notes. The palate has medium body and subtle oak flavour, ending with middling tannin grip. Needs some age but should still be at its best reasonably young. Try it with pizza.

| | |
|---|---|
| Quality | ♟ ♟ ♟ ♟ |
| Value | ★ ★ ★ ✦ |
| Grapes | tyrian |
| Region | Riverina, NSW |
| Cellar | 🍾 3 |
| Alc./Vol. | 12.5% |
| RRP | $17.00 |

## Meadowbank Henry James Pinot Noir

| | |
|---|---|
| Quality | ▼▼▼▼▽ |
| Value | ★★★★⟩ |
| Grapes | pinot noir |
| Region | Derwent Valley, Tas. |
| Cellar | 🍾 5+ |
| Alc./Vol. | 14.0% |
| RRP | $35.00 |

The Ellis family's wine pursuits have undergone rapid growth in recent years. They now have 22 hectares under vine at Cambridge and by the Derwent River at Glenora. This reserve pinot is made by Andrew Hood. *Previous outstanding vintage: '98*

CURRENT RELEASE 2000    An excellent year for Tassie pinot, and here is a lovely wine, laden with properly ripe sweet cherry and plum flavours, in a relatively 'straight' style. The palate is plump and sweetly ripe, with vanilla from the oak still discernible, although this will vanish into the wine with a little bottle-age. It's a pinot with a future. Try it with roast guinea fowl.

## Meerea Park Alexander Munro Shiraz

| | |
|---|---|
| Quality | ▼▼▼▼▼ |
| Value | ★★★★ |
| Grapes | shiraz |
| Region | Hunter Valley, NSW |
| Cellar | � 3–12+ |
| Alc./Vol. | 13.5% |
| RRP | $45.00 |

Rhys Eather is one of our favourite Hunter Valley winemakers; he seems capable of getting something extra out of fruit from this sometimes over-rated region, and succeeds in making wines of rare concentration and style. CURRENT RELEASE 1999    A big regional red that kicks sand in the faces of some of the Hunter pretenders. It has a deep colour with earthy subtle plum fruit of real intensity. There's a hint of 'crushed ants' character and light touches of cloves and spices from lots of good oak. Grippy tannins support that ripe fruit and oak. This is a distinguished red of tight structure with a big future. Cellar some away, then enjoy it with braised lamb shanks.

## Meerea Park Cabernet Sauvignon Merlot

| | |
|---|---|
| Quality | ▼▼▼▼▽ |
| Value | ★★★⟩ |
| Grapes | cabernet sauvignon; merlot |
| Region | McLaren Vale, SA; Hunter Valley, NSW; King Valley, Vic. |
| Cellar | ➡ 2–8+ |
| Alc./Vol. | 13.5% |
| RRP | $22.00 |

Although they are Hunter Valley-based, the Meerea Park people seek out grapes from other regions to give this red character and consistency. Maker: Rhys Eather. CURRENT RELEASE 1999    At first there was a hint of earthiness that in other times might have been called 'sweaty saddle' in the Hunter or 'cowshed' in McLaren Vale. But with breathing the wine reveals a big young red with some butch charry oak and concentrated blackberry and blackcurrant fruit. It's almost a shiraz-like cabernet blend of intense long flavour, with loads of wood and robust construction. Strong grippy tannins ensure good ageing. Serve with kangaroo.

## Metala Original Plantings Shiraz

The grapes that go into this wine come from shiraz planted in 1891 and 1894 at Langhorne Creek. Those old vines give wine of great depth and intensity.
CURRENT RELEASE 1998 Low-yielding old-vine shiraz adds an extra dimension of intensity and we see it here. There's a tight core of dried berries, black fruits, dark chocolate, smoke and mint on both nose and palate. It has absorbed a good deal of oak and there's a hint of the bourbon barrel about it. The flavour is sweet, warm and concentrated with good depth, length and finely balanced ripe tannins. A wine of power and personality to serve with roast beef.

**Quality** 🍷🍷🍷🍷½
**Value** ★★★½
**Grapes** shiraz
**Region** Langhorne Creek, SA
**Cellar** 2–10+
**Alc./Vol.** 14.5%
**RRP** $35.00

## Metala Shiraz Cabernet

Metala's white label is another of those old designs that have barely changed in forty years. It once bore the venerable Stonyfell name, now long gone. Maker: Nigel Dolan.
CURRENT RELEASE 1999 There's a touch of class about this wine. The nose has sweet dark berry, cassis liqueur and mint-leaf aromas of good intensity, with oak only used as a restrained backdrop. The palate has medium body with attractive length of rather gentle flavour with no harsh traits. The finish has adequate ripe tannins for longevity but it drinks well now too. Try it with claypot beef and green beans.

**Quality** 🍷🍷🍷🍷
**Value** ★★★★★
**Grapes** shiraz; cabernet sauvignon
**Region** Langhorne Creek, SA
**Cellar** 5
**Alc./Vol.** 14.0%
**RRP** $17.50 (S)

## Milburn Park Shiraz

Milburn Park is another Murray Valley range of wines with quality pretensions. Their credo is that their wines are 'Everyone's Victoria' rather than the 'highbrow' products of the cooler regions.
CURRENT RELEASE 1999 This is a pleasant enough little red wine, but it won't make the earth move, that's for certain. The nose seems a bit underdone with light raspberry aromas and a dab of oak. It's the same story in the mouth – reasonable body but a lack of fruit concentration makes it pretty forgettable. Easy to sip while you're casting an eye around for a better bottle. Serve it with simple pasta dishes.

**Quality** 🍷🍷🍷
**Value** ★★★
**Grapes** shiraz
**Region** Murray Valley, Vic.
**Cellar** 2
**Alc./Vol.** 12.5%
**RRP** $14.00

## Mildara Coonawarra Cabernet Sauvignon

| | |
|---|---|
| Quality | ♥ ♥ ♥ ♥ |
| Value | ★ ★ ★ ⅃ |
| Grapes | cabernet sauvignon |
| Region | Coonawarra, SA |
| Cellar | ▮ 6 |
| Alc./Vol. | 13.5% |
| RRP | $22.50 |

A venerable label that sometimes gets overlooked in favour of more fashionable names. Quality has been a little erratic too which hasn't helped, but it looks back on song in this much-lauded vintage.

CURRENT RELEASE 1998    A tasty number that takes us back to a time when Coonawarra cabs not only had blackcurranty fruit, but also a distinct touch of peppermint on the nose and palate. This wine is quite a refined package, but it lacks a little stuffing in our opinion, especially considering the concentration most '98 Coonawarra reds have. That said, it does have good balance and should develop medium-term into an elegant alternative to the big blockbusters. Sweet little spring lamb cutlets will be ideal here.

## Miranda High Country Merlot

| | |
|---|---|
| Quality | ♥ ♥ ♥ ⅃ |
| Value | ★ ★ ★ ★ |
| Grapes | merlot |
| Region | King & Ovens Valleys, Vic. |
| Cellar | ▮ 3 |
| Alc./Vol. | 13.5% |
| RRP | $15.00 ▮ |

Merlot performs well in Victoria's King Valley, and Miranda's has good varietal definition on a budget.

CURRENT RELEASE 1999    This is a fairly straightforward merlot that's been well put together to offer character on a budget. The nose has some pleasant raspberry, blackberry and leafy aromas dressed up with a dash of caramelly oak. In the mouth it's a no-fuss wine with direct berry flavours, soft texture and well-balanced tannins. Try it with pork chops.

## Miranda Mirrool Creek Durif

| | |
|---|---|
| Quality | ♥ ♥ ♥ ⅃ |
| Value | ★ ★ ★ ⅃ |
| Grapes | durif |
| Region | Riverina, NSW |
| Cellar | ▮ 2 |
| Alc./Vol. | 13.5% |
| RRP | $11.00 |

Durif was once the exclusive province of the Rutherglen district, but new plantings in Australia's hotter Riverland regions show real promise.

CURRENT RELEASE 2000    A super-youthful purple colour here indicates a wine of some intensity and the nose confirms it. It smells fruity and uncomplicated with berry and cherry aromas, and a touch of licorice which seems to be a durif varietal clue. The palate is suitably intense, yet doesn't stray into heaviness, remaining pleasantly fruity ahead of some firmness at the end for structure. A good first effort with durif from Griffith's Miranda family. Try it with pizza.

## Mitchelton Crescent Shiraz Mourvèdre Grenache

Mitchelton winemaker Don Lewis admits to a fascination with the Rhone varieties, and has played around with them a lot in recent years. His expertise with them has led to some interesting new wines.
CURRENT RELEASE 1999    A tasty red which combines attractive ripe fruit character with serious structure. The nose has rich fruitcake aromas with attractive spice and clean earthy aromas. The palate has a chewy, minerally quality that's robust and savoury. It has good body but it's not at all heavy, and dry tannins are well balanced. A fine match for a lamb casserole.

| | |
|---|---|
| Quality | ♟ ♟ ♟ ♟ |
| Value | ★ ★ ★ |
| Grapes | shiraz; mourvèdre; grenache |
| Region | various, Central Vic. |
| Cellar | ▮ 5 |
| Alc./Vol. | 13.5% |
| RRP | $24.95 |

## Mitchelton Print Shiraz

For each vintage of Print Shiraz, Mitchelton commissions an artist's print to adorn the label. The charming work *In Vino Veritas* on the 1997 vintage is by well-known Melbourne artist Mirka Mora.
CURRENT RELEASE 1997    As usual, the Print Shiraz is a strongly constructed red. It has the deep colour and viscous appearance that indicates plenty of extract and personality. The nose has lots of sweet oak with slightly jammy berry fruit in the middle, along with spice and smoky aromas. In the mouth it's very concentrated, with dense, solid flavour and texture, and big firm tannins. Built for the long haul, with age this characterful red will suit roast beef well.

| | |
|---|---|
| Quality | ♟ ♟ ♟ ♟ ♟ |
| Value | ★ ★ ★ ♦ |
| Grapes | shiraz |
| Region | Goulburn Valley & Heathcote, Vic. |
| Cellar | ➡ 1–10+ |
| Alc./Vol. | 14.0% |
| RRP | $50.00 |

## Mitchelton Shiraz

Shiraz is a staple in most Central Victorian vineyards, giving wines that vary from fresh peppery, savoury types to big, hairy-chested blockbusters. At Mitchelton the wines have plenty of personality and concentration. Maker: Don Lewis.
CURRENT RELEASE 1999    A modern type of regional shiraz with a nose and palate of dark berries and sweet spices. It's a smooth wine with satisfying syrupy fruit flavour at the core, medium to full body, and attractively gritty tannins. The best 'standard' Mitchelton shiraz for a while. Try it with lamb fillets and pesto.

| | |
|---|---|
| Quality | ♟ ♟ ♟ ♟ |
| Value | ★ ★ ★ |
| Grapes | shiraz |
| Region | Goulburn Valley, Vic. |
| Cellar | ▮ 5 |
| Alc./Vol. | 14.0% |
| RRP | $21.95 |

## Moondah Brook Cabernet Sauvignon

| | |
|---|---|
| Quality | ♥♥♥♥ |
| Value | ★★★★⧸ |
| Grapes | cabernet sauvignon |
| Region | various, WA |
| Cellar | ▮ 6 |
| Alc./Vol. | 13.5% |
| RRP | $19.00 Ⓢ |

Moondah Brook reds originally came from the torrid climes of the Swan Valley. The quest for quality has meant a shift away from those original sources of grapes, to more southerly vineyards. This pair of reds offer fantastic value year in, year out for people who want lots of honest flavour in their wine.

CURRENT RELEASE 1999    The '99 has a deep colour and a fragrant nose of juicy blackberry and leafy blackcurrant fruit, well balanced with savoury charry, vanillin wood. In the mouth it has ripe flavour and good texture with fine tannins. Another friendly cab from this reliable label. Pot-roasted veal would go well here.

## Moondah Brook Shiraz

| | |
|---|---|
| Quality | ♥♥♥♥ |
| Value | ★★★★⧸ |
| Grapes | cabernet sauvignon |
| Region | various, WA |
| Cellar | ➞ 1–6 |
| Alc./Vol. | 13.5% |
| RRP | $19.00 Ⓢ |

Thirty-odd years ago shiraz like this was unknown in Western Australia. Wines were often porty, maderised, and jammy, whereas today's breed offers modern, world-class wines like this great-value drop. Maker: Larry Cherubino.

CURRENT RELEASE 1999    The colour is a promising dense purple–crimson. On the nose there's a good measure of charry oak and chocolate/coffee aromas surrounding ripe, spicy blackberry and plum fruit. In the mouth it has plenty of ripeness and a little less body than some past editions. Blackberry, vanilla and toasty oak are the main flavours and there is a firm grip of tannins to back things up. Just the wine for chargrilled porterhouse.

## Moondarra Pinot Noir

| | |
|---|---|
| Quality | ♥♥♥♥ |
| Value | ★★ |
| Grapes | pinot noir |
| Region | Gippsland Rivers, Vic. |
| Cellar | ▮ 4 |
| Alc./Vol. | 12.5% |
| RRP | $100 |

Neil Prentice has a penchant for different grape varieties and out-of-the-way vineyards. North of Moe in Victoria, Moondarra is certainly out of the way.

CURRENT RELEASE 1999    A red wine of substance with an equally substantial price tag. It has a rich nose with plum, mint, chocolate and undergrowth scents and a dash of cedary oak. The palate has good depth and weight, ripe berry flavours and a lick of sweet oak. It's a satisfying dry red all right, but is it perhaps a mite too robust and lacking in finesse for a pinot? People with very deep pockets who think pinot is for wimps will be well served by it. Try it with coq au vin.

## Moorilla Estate Reserve Cabernet Sauvignon

Moorilla's Reserves are wines that the makers consider have special merit. This 'Winter Collection' label is dedicated to former winemaker Jason Winter, a victim of the Port Arthur massacre in 1996.
CURRENT RELEASE 1997    A wine that sparked some disagreement between our feisty authors. HH liked it more than RK-P. It has good colour and smells of mulch, tobacco and shy blackcurranty fruit that may suggest problems with ripeness. The palate is light, angular and tannic. Try it with roast veal.

| | |
|---|---|
| Quality | ▮▮▮▯ |
| Value | ✷✷ |
| Grapes | cabernet sauvignon; merlot |
| Region | Derwent Valley, Tas. |
| Cellar | ▮ 2 |
| Alc./Vol. | 12.5% |
| RRP | $45.00 |

## Moorilla Estate Reserve Pinot Noir

A series of dream vintages have helped Tassie winemakers fashion better pinot noirs than ever before. Purchase carefully though, since standards still vary considerably. Moorilla's Reserve is one of the most reliable labels.
*Previous outstanding vintage: '97*
CURRENT RELEASE 1999    Good pinot can combine delicacy with intensity like no other red grape. Here is a case in point. Fine, complex cherry, plum, spice and almond aromas combine with some of the mysterious undergrowthy scents that seduce pinot-philes. In the mouth it has plummy fruit, silky texture and a soft, fragrant finish that lasts long. Support the lovely Apple Isle and drink this with chargrilled Tasmanian salmon.

| | |
|---|---|
| Quality | ▮▮▮▮▯ |
| Value | ✷✷✷✦ |
| Grapes | pinot noir |
| Region | Derwent Valley, Tas. |
| Cellar | ▮ 4 |
| Alc./Vol. | 13.0% |
| RRP | $45.00 |

## Morris Blue Imperial

Blue imperial is another name for the French grape cinsault, the stuff of many a vin ordinaire over there. Here it makes wine of much more rugged personality.
CURRENT RELEASE 1998    There are some interestingly different varietal cues here but regional factors are still strong. The nose has blackcurrant jam, mint, tar and vanilla aromas, and the palate is rather foursquare, without subtlety or finesse, but refinement isn't what Rutherglen red is all about anyway, is it? It tastes of dark berries with minerally, gravelly hints in flavour and texture. Firm, dry tannins bring up the rear. A wine for a hearty lamb casserole.

| | |
|---|---|
| Quality | ▮▮▮▯ |
| Value | ✷✷✷ |
| Grapes | cinsault |
| Region | Rutherglen, Vic. |
| Cellar | ▮ 5 |
| Alc./Vol. | 14.4% |
| RRP | $20.00 |

## Morris Durif

| | |
|---|---|
| Quality | ♥♥♥♥ |
| Value | ★★★⦾ |
| Grapes | durif |
| Region | Rutherglen, Vic. |
| Cellar | 🍷 4 |
| Alc./Vol. | 14.1% |
| RRP | $23.00 |

Rutherglen durif is one of Australia's true regional styles and Morris has been doing it well for many years. A recent retrospective tasting of older Morris durifs showed a slight change in style over the years to a more modern, slightly more oak-influenced wine, but one in which varietal character remained paramount.

*Previous outstanding vintages: '90, '94, '97*

CURRENT RELEASE 1997    Never a blushing violet, this deep-coloured red has loads of traditional Rutherglen character. It's powerful and rather old-fashioned with a porty veneer to jammy dark-berry and vanilla-essence aromas. The palate is full-bodied with smooth plum and berry flavours, alcoholic warmth and dry tannins. Serve it with steak and kidney pie.

## Moss Wood Glenmore Cabernet Sauvignon

| | |
|---|---|
| Quality | ♥♥♥♥ |
| Value | ★★★ |
| Grapes | cabernet sauvignon |
| Region | Margaret River, WA |
| Cellar | ➥ 1–8+ |
| Alc./Vol. | 14.0% |
| RRP | $32.00 |

In 1997 Moss Wood bottled their first Glenmore, made from fruit from their viticulturist Ian Bell's vineyard nearby. Originally made to supplement the estate label's wine, it appears as a regular fixture.

CURRENT RELEASE 1999    This has deep colour and the aromatic concentration on the nose that's a mark of central Margaret River. The nose has blackcurrant fruit with bitter chocolate, green foliage and subtle cigar-box smells. In the mouth it has intensity without great weight, and some of the lushness of texture that's a Moss Wood hallmark. There's also a stemmy almost bitter touch that keeps it from a higher rating. Try it with venison.

## Mount Avoca Shiraz

| | |
|---|---|
| Quality | ♥♥♥♥ |
| Value | ★★★ |
| Grapes | shiraz |
| Region | Pyrenees, Vic. |
| Cellar | 🍷 4 |
| Alc./Vol. | 13.5% |
| RRP | $18.70 |

This is one of the longest established of the Pyrenees wineries. Mount Avoca's founders, John and Arda Barry, sold the vineyard to the Barrington Estate group in mid-2001.

CURRENT RELEASE 1999    The nose is of low–medium intensity with blackberry and plum aromas, some hints of dried herbs and dusty oak. The palate has tasty berry flavour with mouth-watering acidity for freshness, and light tannins. Easy drinking with bocconcini, prosciutto and basil pizza.

## Mount Chalambar Cherry Tree Shiraz

The Ararat–Stawell–Great Western wines have a distinctly different feel from those of the nearby Pyrenees. We say *vive la différence*! Mount Chalambar is an exclusivity of Melbourne merchant Dan Murphy these days.
CURRENT RELEASE 1998    From Trevor Mast of Mount Langi Ghiran, this red has dusty and minerally touches to sweet juicy raspberry and earth aromas. The palate is in similar juicy, earthy style with a soft easy feel and low oak influence. The friendly personality of this red is enhanced by well-modulated fine-grained tannins. Serve it with lamb kebabs off the barbecue.

| | |
|---|---|
| Quality | ♥♥♥♥ |
| Value | ★★★ |
| Grapes | shiraz |
| Region | Great Western, Vic. |
| Cellar | 3 |
| Alc./Vol. | 13.5% |
| RRP | $14.00 |

## Mount Difficulty Pinot Noir

Despite what Kiwis think, most Australians don't care at all about cross-Tasman rivalry. This is just as well, as the new crop of New Zealand pinot noirs could give the Aussies some difficulty.
CURRENT RELEASE 1999    The best New Zealand pinots are lovely satisfying wines that capture the fruity/savoury magic of the variety better than many Oz examples. This has attractive raspberry, cherry and spice aromas with savoury woodsmoke touches and a hint of lead pencil-like high-quality oak. The velvety palate is rich and ripe, with some alcoholic warmth and sweetness, a balanced input from smoky oak and a very long finish. Just right with Cantonese roast duck.

| | |
|---|---|
| Quality | ♥♥♥♥♥ |
| Value | ★★★ |
| Grapes | pinot noir |
| Region | Central Otago, NZ |
| Cellar | 4 |
| Alc./Vol. | 14.5% |
| RRP | $46.00 |

## Mount Horrocks Cabernet Merlot

Mount Horrocks' red wines are among the Clare Valley hierarchy, made in a more elegant style than most.
CURRENT RELEASE 1999    This thankfully offers an alternative to the 'bigger is better' type of red. There's a friendly nose of soft black and red berries. Deftly handled, well-integrated French oak seasons things nicely. The palate has delicious smooth fruit-sweetness, medium body and good length. Slightly firm tannins unperpin things well and suggest some ageing potential. Less robust than the '98 edition, this is a good wine for a wild mushroom ragout.

| | |
|---|---|
| Quality | ♥♥♥♥♥ |
| Value | ★★★★ |
| Grapes | cabernet sauvignon; merlot |
| Region | Clare Valley, SA |
| Cellar | 6 |
| Alc./Vol. | 13.5% |
| RRP | $30.00 |

## Mount Langi Ghiran Billi Billi Creek

| | |
|---|---|
| Quality | ❦❦❦❦ |
| Value | ★★★ |
| Grapes | shiraz; grenache; cabernet sauvignon |
| Region | McLaren Vale & Barossa Valley, SA; Grampians, Vic. |
| Cellar | ▮ 2 |
| Alc./Vol. | 13.5% |
| RRP | $17.00 |

The Billi Billi Creek weaves its way through the town of Buangor and the vineyard country of Mount Langi Ghiran. Despite the name this wine is a multi-regional blend. CURRENT RELEASE 1999    Designed to broaden the reach of Mount Langi Ghiran wines, Billi Billi is an uncomplicated young drop which fits under the estate wines in the Langi hierarchy. The nose is savoury and spicy with some white-pepper notes adding zip to fresh raspberry-like fruit aromas. The palate has a straightforward spice and berry flavour of reasonable substance. The finish is dry, bordering on bitter – a quality that won't appeal to everyone. Try it with fontina cheese-sauced pasta.

## Mount Langi Ghiran Cliff Edge Shiraz

| | |
|---|---|
| Quality | ❦❦❦❦❦ |
| Value | ★★★★ |
| Grapes | shiraz |
| Region | Grampians, Vic. |
| Cellar | ➥ 2–7 |
| Alc./Vol. | 14.5% |
| RRP | $28.00 |

The Cliff Edge vineyard is a wind-blown block set against the 540 metre cliff face of Mount Langi. Since it was netted six years ago, its crops have increased to the point where the wine can be bottled separately. CURRENT RELEASE 1999    There's a peppery/spicy introduction on the nose that evokes the Rhone, and the fruit aromas of cherry liqueur and almond reinforce it. The middleweight palate is fragrant with dark fruits, but there's a slight lack of concentration meaning less richness and generosity than the estate's main shiraz. It's still pretty good though. The finish is firm in tannins and the aftertaste is long. Serve it with a lamb and chickpea casserole.

## Mount Langi Ghiran Joanna Cabernet Sauvignon

| | |
|---|---|
| Quality | ❦❦❦❦❦ |
| Value | ★★★✦ |
| Grapes | cabernet sauvignon |
| Region | Limestone Coast, SA |
| Cellar | ▮ 5 |
| Alc./Vol. | 13.0% |
| RRP | $28.00 |

Joanna is a new vineyard area in the expanding Limestone Coast region surrounding the long-established Coonawarra. CURRENT RELEASE 1998    This has a super-deep purple colour and classy cassis aromas with a minty edge. There's a good measure of richness, and in true Mount Langi style oak is a sideshow here; the fruit is the main act. It has a medium-bodied palate with tangy, juicy flavour and balanced tannins. It doesn't quite follow through with the same intensity as other Langi wines, but attractive nonetheless. Try it with rare roast beef.

## Mount Langi Ghiran Langi Cabernet Sauvignon Merlot

Shiraz has always been the unchallenged star at Mount Langi Ghiran, but this cabernet blend has been creeping up in profile and price recently. CURRENT RELEASE 1998   A delightful wine with a superfine cabernet bouquet of dark berries, dark chocolate and smoky, spicy oak. It tastes smooth and elegantly flavoured, with intense tangy fruit-sweetness in the middle and great palate structure. This is a rather gentle, persistent wine with impeccable clarity of flavour and excellent balance. Be warned! A bottle of this, once opened, will empty with indecent speed. Serve it with herbed minute steak.

| | |
|---|---|
| Quality | 🍷🍷🍷🍷 |
| Value | ★★★★ |
| Grapes | cabernet sauvignon; merlot |
| Region | Grampians, Vic. |
| Cellar | 🍾 8 |
| Alc./Vol. | 14.0% |
| RRP | $42.00 |

## Mount Langi Ghiran Langi Shiraz

This is one of Australia's outstanding shiraz vineyards. Its wine is made to allow the grapes full expression, unencumbered by over-use of oak.
*Previous outstanding vintages: '86, '89, '90, '93, '94, '95, '96, '97, '98*
CURRENT RELEASE 1999   Central Victorian shiraz doesn't come much more complex or better than this. It really tests our catalogue of descriptors. The nose has dark plum, black cherry, sweet spice, pepper, and savoury meaty notes. There are also touches of undergrowth and vanilla caramel. The tangy palate has lovely creamy texture with intense fruit, impeccable balance, good length and ripe tannins. Serve it with game pie.

| | |
|---|---|
| Quality | 🍷🍷🍷🍷🍷 |
| Value | ★★★★ |
| Grapes | shiraz |
| Region | Grampians, Vic. |
| Cellar | ➡ 1–8+ |
| Alc./Vol. | 14.5% |
| RRP | $60.00 🍾 |

## Mount Mary Pinot Noir

| | |
|---|---|
| Quality | ♥♥♥♥ |
| Value | ★★★ |
| Grapes | pinot noir |
| Region | Yarra Valley, Vic. |
| Cellar | ➡ 1–5 |
| Alc./Vol. | 13.0% |
| RRP | $80.00 (ex-winery) |

Mount Mary is often included in lists of Australia's best pinot noirs. Unhappily for consumers it is also rare and expensive. In the best vintages it can be a superb essay in finesse.

*Previous outstanding vintages: '90, '91, '94, '96*

CURRENT RELEASE 1998   As usual, this is a pale, elegant wine with a delicate nose suggesting cherries, raspberries, light earthiness and restrained oak. In the mouth it continues light and fine with tangy acidity, but it does seem to be in a bit of a hole early on. Past experience tells us that fine pinot noirs like Mount Mary can go into a trough before emerging with time. Give it time, then sip alongside pot-roasted rabbit.

## Mount Mary Quintet

| | |
|---|---|
| Quality | ♥♥♥♥♥ |
| Value | ★★★ |
| Grapes | cabernet sauvignon; cabernet franc; merlot; malbec; petit verdot |
| Region | Yarra Valley, Vic. |
| Cellar | ➡ 1–6+ |
| Alc./Vol. | 12.5% |
| RRP | $80.00 (ex-winery) |

Mount Mary proprietor, Dr John Middleton, deliberately stays away from the overdone blockbuster style of some Australian cabernet blends. He has produced some of Australia's best reds.

*Previous outstanding vintages: '84, '88, '90, '91, '94, '95, '97*

CURRENT RELEASE 1998   In true Mount Mary style this is all about understated elegance. It seems a little closed up at the moment, but Mount Marys are built to last so this needs keeping to be at its best. At present it offers a subtle, aromatic nose reminiscent of blackcurrant pastilles, flowers and leaves. Oak provides a cedary backdrop. The palate is fragrant with delicate flavours, great length and fine tannins. Perfect with pink baby racks of lamb.

## Mountadam Cabernet Sauvignon

| | |
|---|---|
| Quality | ♥♥♥♡ |
| Value | ★★ |
| Grapes | cabernet sauvignon |
| Region | Eden Valley, SA |
| Cellar | ▮ 4 |
| Alc./Vol. | 14.5% |
| RRP | $36.00 |

Adam Wynn has run his own race with this Eden Valley vineyard, making some eclectic wine styles and some very good, more mainstream ones. Now in alliance with Cape Mentelle of Margaret River, it will be interesting to see what happens in the future.

CURRENT RELEASE 1997   The colour is a rather advanced brick-red here, and it smells of green herbs, plum and briar dressed in some smart cedary oak. The palate is slightly mulchy/herbal with light fruit flavour, mintiness and a bit of tannic grip. A disappointing vintage after a '96 that impressed us greatly. Try it with baby lamb cutlets.

## Munari Cabernet Sauvignon

This young Heathcote vineyard is still finding its way, and wine quality can be a bit erratic, but good examples like this make the future bright.
CURRENT RELEASE 2000    Central Victorian cabernet in the first flight of youth is rarely as easy to sip as this. It's less macho than some previous Munari reds we've tasted – not a bad thing. The nose has sweet blackcurrant, spice and notably regional minty aromas, and some gamy and mulchy notes add a savoury 'wildness' to it. The palate is satisfying if a little rustic, with a hint of eucalypt, ripe berry and mint flavours, ahead of a dry tannin finish. Serve it with a homemade meat pie.

| | |
|---|---|
| Quality | ▾▾▾▾ |
| Value | ★★★ |
| Grapes | cabernet sauvignon |
| Region | Heathcote, Vic. |
| Cellar | ➟ 2–6 |
| Alc./Vol. | 14.4% |
| RRP | $35.00 |

## Murdock Cabernet Sauvignon

New names are popping up all the time in the Australian wine scene, but few get it absolutely right from the word go. Murdock has, and we look forward to future releases with great anticipation. Maker: Peter Bissell.
CURRENT RELEASE 1998    Wow, this is a real find! Low-yielding, mature vines and a superb vintage have combined to make this an exciting debut. Everything is in the right place: dark berry, plum, violet and chocolatey aromas of super concentration, edged with lightly smoky mocha oak; a ripe and intense palate, with penetrating black-fruit cabernet flavour, a seamless texture, finely integrated oak and savoury fine-grained tannins. Try it with braised lamb and white beans.

| | |
|---|---|
| Quality | ▾▾▾▾▾ |
| Value | ★★★★⸌ |
| Grapes | cabernet sauvignon |
| Region | Coonawarra, SA |
| Cellar | ▮ 8 |
| Alc./Vol. | 13.5% |
| RRP | $42.00 |

## Neagles Rock Cabernet Sauvignon

The owners, Jane Willson and Steve Wiblin, worked as marketers for various major wine companies before striking out on their own. They bought an established vineyard at Clare.
CURRENT RELEASE 1999    An elegantly weighted red, this is not a typical blood-and-thunder Clare style but exercises some restraint. It is very approachable now, and has a bouquet of smoked meats, good-quality toasty oak and a medium-weight palate. There's a touch of mint and it has the balance to drink well young. Try it with minted roast lamb.

| | |
|---|---|
| Quality | ▾▾▾▾ |
| Value | ★★★★ |
| Grapes | cabernet sauvignon |
| Region | Clare Valley, SA |
| Cellar | ▮ 7 |
| Alc./Vol. | 13.5% |
| RRP | $22.50 |

## Neagles Rock Grenache

| | |
|---|---|
| Quality | ♥ ♥ ♥ ♥ |
| Value | ★ ★ ★ ↓ |
| Grapes | grenache; shiraz |
| Region | Clare Valley, SA |
| Cellar | ▌ 4 |
| Alc./Vol. | 14.5% |
| RRP | $17.50 |

We've yet to see a grenache that didn't (or wouldn't) benefit from a little shiraz boost. According to the label, this has the 'subtlest addition' of same. It gives a bit more structure and depth.

CURRENT RELEASE 1999    The colour is nice and youthful and the aromas are fresh and cherry-like, without obvious wood influence. It tastes light and lively in the mouth with a smooth, low-tannin palate and is dangerously easy to drink young. It could even take a slight chill without detriment. Drink with roast pork loin.

## Neagles Rock Shiraz

| | |
|---|---|
| Quality | ♥ ♥ ♥ ♥ |
| Value | ★ ★ ★ ★ |
| Grapes | shiraz |
| Region | Clare Valley, SA |
| Cellar | ➡ 1–10+ |
| Alc./Vol. | 14.5% |
| RRP | $22.50 |

Doin' the Neagle Rock. Hey, hey, hey! Daddy Cool fans should stock up on this one. Makers: Jane Willson and Steve Wiblin.

CURRENT RELEASE 1999    A very decent red; more than a party wine. It has a deep purple–red hue and smells of dark chocolate, honey and charred oak, which will integrate better with the wine, given time. The palate has good depth and a degree of richness, and concludes with firm but supple tannins. The finish is quite drying. In a year or two, it will go well with parmesan cheese.

## Nepenthe The Fugue

| | |
|---|---|
| Quality | ♥ ♥ ♥ ♥ |
| Value | ★ ★ ★ ↓ |
| Grapes | cabernet sauvignon; merlot; cabernet franc |
| Region | Adelaide Hills, SA |
| Cellar | ➡ 1–7+ |
| Alc./Vol. | 14.0% |
| RRP | $30.00 |

A fugue is a musical form favoured by J.S. Bach and other contrapuntalists. It's also the name of a curly sculpture in the Nepenthe vineyard, which gave its name to this wine. Maker: Peter Leske.

CURRENT RELEASE 1999    This is much more chocolatey than you might expect of a cool-climate cabernet. The bouquet reveals considerable oak involvement, with vanilla/chocolate/mocha characters, evidence of sweet ripe fruit, and the profile is smooth and friendly. It has good weight and flavour, supple tannins and would go well with braised lamb shanks.

## Neudorf Nelson Pinot Noir

This Kiwi winery is famous for its Moutere Chardonnay – Moutere being the sub-district of the Nelson region – but this is a pretty serious pinot. The vineyard soil is a particular kind of dirt, known as Moutere clay. Maker: Tim Finn.

CURRENT RELEASE 1999   The bouquet displays sappy, undergrowth and slightly animal complexities while the mouth-flavours are deliciously ripe and fruit-sweet. It has impressive concentration and subtlety, plus a fleshy richness and marvellous texture – which is so important in pinot. Try it with marinated, spit-roasted quail.

| | |
|---|---|
| Quality | 🍷🍷🍷🍷🍷 |
| Value | ★★★⁺ |
| Grapes | pinot noir |
| Region | Nelson, NZ |
| Cellar | 🍷 4 |
| Alc./Vol. | 13.5% |
| RRP | $35.60 |

## Nicholas McLaren Vale Shiraz

This comes out under the aegis of Springwood Park, one of Andrew Garrett's (relatively) new labels. Nicholas is one of his young sons. The other is Tom (see under T for).

CURRENT RELEASE 1998   Concentration is the keyword for this big beauty. The colour is a young-looking purple–red and it smells invitingly of fruitcake, plum and toast, with wood and grape well integrated. In the mouth it's very big, solid, chewy and forceful, and the finish lingers on and on. It should have a great future if cellared. Then try it with devilled kidneys.

| | |
|---|---|
| Quality | 🍷🍷🍷🍷🍷 |
| Value | ★★★⁺ |
| Grapes | shiraz |
| Region | McLaren Vale, SA |
| Cellar | ➥ 1–15 |
| Alc./Vol. | 14.0% |
| RRP | $53.00 🍷 |

## Ninth Island Pinot Noir

Ninth Island is the lowest-priced label of Pipers Brook and can often stand for good but straightforward wines with a decidedly cool-climate accent.

CURRENT RELEASE 2000   True to form, this is a fruit-driven wine with little or no evidence of wood-ageing, and a frisky hint of greenness to its fruit. The colour is medium purple–red and it smells of sweet cherry/plum confectionery, with grass/hay notes. The palate flavour is an intriguing combination of sweet fruit and tartness, without much complexity. It would go well chilled at lunch with a frittata.

| | |
|---|---|
| Quality | 🍷🍷🍷 |
| Value | ★★⁺ |
| Grapes | pinot noir |
| Region | northern Tas. |
| Cellar | 🍷 2 |
| Alc./Vol. | 13.3% |
| RRP | $23.70 |

## Normans Encounter Bay Cabernet Sauvignon

| | |
|---|---|
| Quality | 🍷🍷🍷 |
| Value | ★★★★ |
| Grapes | cabernet sauvignon |
| Region | not stated |
| Cellar | 🍾 4 |
| Alc./Vol. | 13.5% |
| RRP | $12.00 Ⓢ |

Encounter Bay is just off the tip of the Fleurieu Peninsula. It's where a French expedition led by Baudin met an English one led by Flinders, totally by chance, back in 1802. Both were mapping the coast and despite their countries being at war, not a shot was fired.
CURRENT RELEASE 1999　The nose has dominant charry wood aromas – probably from oak chips – and the flavours are basic, light- to medium-bodied and fruity, with a pleasant raspberry character. The finish has a light grip and it drinks well now, with Lebanese felafel.

## Normans Encounter Bay Shiraz

| | |
|---|---|
| Quality | 🍷🍷🍷🍷 |
| Value | ★★★★★ |
| Grapes | shiraz |
| Region | not stated |
| Cellar | 🍾 7 |
| Alc./Vol. | 14.0% |
| RRP | $12.00 Ⓢ |

This won a gold medal at the Atlanta Wine Summit 2000, whatever that is. We would certainly award it a gold medal if value-for-money were the criterion!
CURRENT RELEASE 1999　This is a real find. It's outstanding value, and tastes like some wines double the price. There are sweet vanilla, cherry, toasty barrel aromas and, in the mouth, tight fine tannins and some potential to cellar. The taste is elegant and lively. It would suit pink lamb cutlets.

## Normans Old Vine Shiraz

| | |
|---|---|
| Quality | 🍷🍷🍷🍷 |
| Value | ★★★★↓ |
| Grapes | shiraz |
| Region | Barossa Valley & McLaren Vale, SA |
| Cellar | 🍾 8+ |
| Alc./Vol. | 14.0% |
| RRP | $22.60 🍾 |

When the wine industry's buoyant, it's no wonder everyone's floating. (Sorry about that.) In early 2001, the public wine company Normans merged with Xanadu of Margaret River while Xanadu also floated. Maker: Peter Fraser.
CURRENT RELEASE 1998　Here's one for those who like the soft, rich, smooth-as-plush style of South Australian shiraz. The bouquet offers lovely, rich fruitcake and dark chocolate aromas while the palate is big and chewy, with supple tannins and plenty of persistence. It would do justice to roast saddle of hare with demiglaze.

## Old Station Grenache Shiraz

The old railway line through the Clare Valley has now been resurrected as the Riesling Trail walking track. Old Station vineyard runs alongside where Watervale station once stood.
CURRENT RELEASE 1999    A very traditional drop with a rich, warm nose, which is very dry-grown grenache. Sweet berries, spice, meaty and earthy aromas give it an old-fashioned appeal. The palate has succulent red and black berry flavors and dry but not aggressive tannins. An honest red that would suit a steak and kidney pie well.

| | |
|---|---|
| Quality | ♟ ♟ ♟ ♟ |
| Value | ★ ★ ★ ⧩ |
| Grapes | grenache; shiraz |
| Region | Clare Valley, SA |
| Cellar | ▮ 6 |
| Alc./Vol. | 14.0% |
| RRP | $17.50 |

## Orlando Jacob's Creek Grenache Shiraz

Jacob's Creek flows all over the world these days and it's perhaps the best-known ambassador for Australian wine there is. It remains a reasonable drop at a fair price; just don't expect the earth to move when you sip it.
CURRENT RELEASE 2000    A light red of good character, simple and non-challenging, an ideal quaffer on a tight budget. Nose and palate have a juicy-sweet raspberry and blackberry character with some spicy and earthy notes. It has reasonable intensity of flavour, and the tannins are soft and friendly, making it easy to glug down. It suits an informal picnic of pâté and crusty bread.

| | |
|---|---|
| Quality | ♟ ♟ ♟ |
| Value | ★ ★ ★ |
| Grapes | grenache; shiraz |
| Region | various, SA |
| Cellar | ▮ 1 |
| Alc./Vol. | 13.0% |
| RRP | $10.00 Ⓢ |

## Orlando Jacob's Creek Reserve Cabernet Sauvignon

We reported on Jacob's Creek's inexorable march for world domination in the last edition. Now they have a Reserve label that has caused a stir in the hotly contested under $15 price category with its high quality.
CURRENT RELEASE 1998    A wine of real depth and impact at a very good price. This purplish young cabernet has an attractive nose with a surprisingly classy feel. There are ripe dark berries, floral notes and balanced vanillin oak, all in harmony. It's medium in body with good intensity and mouth-feel, ahead of an attractively grippy finish. Buy it by the case as it should develop well in bottle. A good all-rounder to serve with most meat dishes and hearty pastas.

| | |
|---|---|
| Quality | ♟ ♟ ♟ ♟ |
| Value | ★ ★ ★ ★ ★ |
| Grapes | cabernet sauvignon |
| Region | various, SA |
| Cellar | ▮ 5 |
| Alc./Vol. | 13.0% |
| RRP | $14.95 Ⓢ |

## Orlando Jacob's Creek Reserve Shiraz

| | |
|---|---|
| Quality | ▼▼▼▼ |
| Value | ★★★★ |
| Grapes | shiraz |
| Region | various, SA |
| Cellar | ▮ 3 |
| Alc./Vol. | 13.5% |
| RRP | $14.95 ⑤ |

Shiraz is Australia's world success story and Orlando have the formula for success here: bottle a good example, give it a very reasonable price, add the Jacob's Creek name, emphasise the Reserve part, and you should have a world-beater.

CURRENT RELEASE 1998   A great partner for the other Jacob's Creek Reserves, this shiraz has a ripe blackberry aroma and flavour that's fruit-sweet and appealing. Oak is restrained, in welcome contrast to some of the opposition, and the flavour is soft, fruit-sweet and easy with friendly tannins. An easy-drinking red to take to one of our dwindling number of BYOs.

## Orlando St Hugo Cabernet Sauvignon

| | |
|---|---|
| Quality | ▼▼▼▼ |
| Value | ★★★ |
| Grapes | cabernet sauvignon |
| Region | Coonawarra, SA |
| Cellar | ▮ 5 |
| Alc./Vol. | 14.0% |
| RRP | $32.00 |

Coonawarra is a source of flagship reds for many wineries outside the region. St Hugo's consistent quality shows us why this is so.

*Previous outstanding vintages: '88, '90, '91, '92, '94, '96*

CURRENT RELEASE 1997   The nose has minty Coonawarra notes and cassis-like fruit aromas. Sweet oak contributes a vanillin aspect without obscuring the cabernet fruit. In the mouth the black fruit/mint/vanilla bit carries on with good intensity and length, finishing with fine, dry tannins. It isn't as concentrated or as lush as the 1996 vintage but it still has a touch of class. Try it with wet-roasted lamb with onions.

## Padthaway Estate Cabernet Sauvignon

| | |
|---|---|
| Quality | ▼▼▼ |
| Value | ★★★ |
| Grapes | cabernet sauvignon |
| Region | Padthaway, SA |
| Cellar | ➥ 1–5+ |
| Alc./Vol. | 12.5% |
| RRP | $19.00 |

This winery is the only one in Australia to have an authentic Champagne grape press, with a wooden slatted basket – like they used to use in Champagne. They make good fizz too.

CURRENT RELEASE 1999   There's quite a fulsome measure of oak overlying some greener fruit characters here. The nose is all chocolate, vanilla and Padthaway regional mint, while the palate flavours are leafy and oaky with somewhat rustic tannins. It's disjointed now but could improve. Try it with pie floater.

## Palandri Aurora Cabernet Shiraz

Palandri tried to take over Amberley Estate but last reports were that the deal did not go ahead. Whatever happens, Palandri will need a major brand if it's to move large quantities of wine quickly. A public company has to feed its shareholders.

CURRENT RELEASE 2000   The colour is full purple–red and the aromas are hi-fi cabernet: pristine blackcurrant. It is all about fruit, not oak. The palate flavours are similarly bright and lively, if a tad short, and the acid is noticeable; a minor quibble. It goes well with egg and bacon pie.

| | |
|---|---|
| Quality | ♥ ♥ ♥ ♦ |
| Value | ★ ★ ★ ★ |
| Grapes | cabernet sauvignon; shiraz |
| Region | various, WA |
| Cellar | ▮ 4 |
| Alc./Vol. | 13.5% |
| RRP | $15.00 ⑤ |

## Palandri Aurora Shiraz

Aurora – great name! Can't believe no one else has picked that one up. The antipodes' own aurora is, of course, the Aurora Australis. Not many Aussies have ever seen it, though.

CURRENT RELEASE 2000   This is just a young freshie, but it has all the nice fruit flavours you'd want in an inexpensive, early-drinking shiraz: sweet berry, herbal, green-mint aromas without obvious wood. There's plenty of flavour for the price, and even a hint of good tannin structure. It's a suitable partner for beef tartare.

| | |
|---|---|
| Quality | ♥ ♥ ♥ ♦ |
| Value | ★ ★ ★ ★ |
| Grapes | shiraz |
| Region | various, WA |
| Cellar | ▮ 5 |
| Alc./Vol. | 13.5% |
| RRP | $15.00 ⑤ |

## Panorama Vineyard Pinot Noir

The vineyard was established by Steve Ferencz in 1974. Michael and Sharon Vishacki bought it a few years ago and built a (sorely needed) new winery. The vineyard had made good pinot before, but the Vishackis' 1998 vintage won the trophy for best pinot at the Tasmanian Regional Wine Show in 2000. This vintage could even surpass it.

CURRENT RELEASE 2000   Nothing like Burgundy, but it's a lovely pinot noir! The colour is deep and youthful; the aromas are of vanilla, chocolate, ripe cherry and spice. It's full, smooth and rounded in the mouth: a big generous mouthful of flavour, but soft and voluptuous and drinking superbly already. It would go well with lasagne.

| | |
|---|---|
| Quality | ♥ ♥ ♥ ♥ ♦ |
| Value | ★ ★ ★ ★ ♦ |
| Grapes | pinot noir |
| Region | southern Tas. |
| Cellar | ▮ 4+ |
| Alc./Vol. | 14.0% |
| RRP | $25.00 |

## Paracombe Cabernet Sauvignon

| | |
|---|---|
| Quality | ▼ ▼ ▼ |
| Value | ★ ★ ★ |
| Grapes | cabernet sauvignon |
| Region | Adelaide Hills, SA |
| Cellar | ▮ 5 |
| Alc./Vol. | 14.0% |
| RRP | $25.00 (cellar door) |

This 12-hectare vineyard is run by the Drogemuller family in the Adelaide Hills district of Paracombe. Paul Drogemuller manages the vineyard and the wines are made under contract at Petaluma.

CURRENT RELEASE 1998  The cool-climate origin of the grapes is readily apparent in the sappy, stalky aromas of this cabernet. The panoply of underbrush aromas includes a tinge of green tomato. The tannins are somewhat harsh on the finish and the length of aftertaste is modest. Those who enjoy the greener spectrum of cabernet flavours may like this. Serve with beef casserole.

## Paracombe Shiraz

| | |
|---|---|
| Quality | ▼ ▼ ▼ ▼ |
| Value | ★ ★ ★ |
| Grapes | shiraz |
| Region | Adelaide Hills, SA |
| Cellar | ▮ 5 |
| Alc./Vol. | 14.5% |
| RRP | $25.00 (cellar door) |

The original Penfolds St Henri Claret was based on shiraz grown at Paracombe. There are lots of Para names around Adelaide: the Para River in the Barossa; South Para reservoir in the hills, and so on.

CURRENT RELEASE 1998  There are some compost-like vegetal characters coming from the high-altitude fruit, and an unusual linseed-oil character from the oak. It's medium-bodied and smoothly structured, with pleasant fruit sweetness and reasonable length. An easy-drinking style to pair with gourmet sausages.

## Paringa Estate Pinot Noir

| | |
|---|---|
| Quality | ▼ ▼ ▼ ▼ ▼ |
| Value | ★ ★ ★ ★ |
| Grapes | pinot noir |
| Region | Mornington Peninsula, Vic. |
| Cellar | � 1–7+ |
| Alc./Vol. | 14.5% |
| RRP | $45.00 (cellar door) |

Lindsay and Margaret McCall have a classic site: a steep north-facing slope that acts as a sun and heat trap. It's what the viticultural gurus slaver over: a hot site in a cool climate. Lindsay reckons 2000 was his best pinot vintage yet.

*Previous outstanding vintages: '97, '98*

CURRENT RELEASE 2000  This is a big pinot! Very ripe fruit endows it with sweet, ripe-cherry aromas and in the maker's typical style, there's a veneer of vanillin oak still showing at this early stage. It's very deeply flavoured and long in the mouth, with high alcohol in harmony and quite a splash of tannin firming the finish. It should be long-lived. Drink with Peking duck.

## Paringa Estate Shiraz

The degree of difficulty in getting shiraz ripe on the Mornington Peninsula is pretty high. Lindsay McCall manages it most years, with a double pike and back flip as well. Gold medal at the 2001 Boutique Wine Awards. CURRENT RELEASE 2000   Very Rhone-ish – and more-ish – stuff! It's spicy and white-peppery in true cool-climate mode, but properly ripe, with cherry and dark-berry aromas as well. There's a meaty aspect to the flavour and the palate structure is chunky, rich and deep, with a deliciously velvety texture. A masterful wine, to serve with beef stroganoff.

| | |
|---|---|
| Quality | ﹖﹖﹖﹖﹖ |
| Value | ★★★★﹜ |
| Grapes | shiraz |
| Region | Mornington Peninsula, Vic. |
| Cellar | ▮ 6 |
| Alc./Vol. | 13.5% |
| RRP | $35.00 (cellar door) |

## Parker Estate Terra Rossa Merlot

John Parker has been around wine a long time. One of the original partners of Hungerford Hill, which began in the Hunter; he saw the potential of Coonawarra straightaway and planted a sizeable vineyard there. Only 500 cases were made. CURRENT RELEASE 1998   Sautéed meats, charcuterie, all sorts of lovely complex red-wine smells emerge from this bottle. Toasty oak, smoked meats, nutmeg and spices. The wine has been subjected to considerable oak treatment but it's layered and supple. A delicious merlot and one of the few whose price shouldn't attract criticism. Serve with pink lamb backstraps.

| | |
|---|---|
| Quality | ﹖﹖﹖﹖﹖ |
| Value | ★★★★ |
| Grapes | merlot |
| Region | Coonawarra, SA |
| Cellar | ⬤ 1–7+ |
| Alc./Vol. | 13.5% |
| RRP | $39.50 ▮ (cellar door) |

## Parker Estate Terra Rossa First Growth

The Parker First Growth wines sit happily among Coonawarra's greatest. CURRENT RELEASE 1998   Hugh Johnson once called Coonawarra Australia's Medoc. Comparisons are odious, but we think that if most Medoc wine was as good as this, the French would be ecstatic. It's a concentrated young cabernet blend with a lovely deep complex nose of cassis, mocha, cedar, floral scents and clean earth. Despite all that concentration, it has balance and poise. The palate is long and lush with seamless, profound flavour, beautifully integrated with fine-grained ripe tannins and classy oak. A wine to age, then open it with roast fillet of beef.

| | |
|---|---|
| Quality | ﹖﹖﹖﹖﹖ |
| Value | ★★★★﹜ |
| Grapes | cabernet sauvignon; merlot; cabernet franc |
| Region | Coonawarra, SA |
| Cellar | ⬤ 2–15 |
| Alc./Vol. | 14.0% |
| RRP | $69.50 ▮ |

## Paul Conti Medici Ridge Pinot Noir

| | |
|---|---|
| Quality | ▼▼▼▼ |
| Value | ★★★⸜ |
| Grapes | pinot noir |
| Region | mainly Pemberton–Manjimup, WA |
| Cellar | ▮ 4 |
| Alc./Vol. | 14.0% |
| RRP | $24.00 (cellar door) |

Paul Conti and his son Jason make some excellent, and wildly underrated, wines in the Wanneroo district, north of Perth. Most of the fruit for this was sourced, wisely, from down south: Middlesex in the Warren Valley.
CURRENT RELEASE 1999    This is an attractive wine, proving once again that Pemberton–Manjimup has lots of pinot potential. The nose carries some earthy tinges plus sweet plum, licorice fruit, and the quite high level of alcohol shows. There's big fruit flavour with some jammy characters, plus a definite tannin grip. Try it with saddle of hare.

## Pauletts Polish Hill River Shiraz

| | |
|---|---|
| Quality | ▼▼▼▼ |
| Value | ★★★★ |
| Grapes | shiraz |
| Region | Clare Valley, SA |
| Cellar | ▮ 10+ |
| Alc./Vol. | 13.5% |
| RRP | $19.80 |

Neil Paulett worked at Penfolds and Rosemount before deciding on Clare as a place to put down roots. He bought land in the Polish area in 1982. While getting started on his own place, he worked at Stanley Leasingham.
CURRENT RELEASE 1998    Not too many bad reds were made in '98. This is a typically smooth, fleshy example, smelling of plum and herb and toasty oak – but fruit leads the charge. It has good density and texture and is medium- to full-bodied. The tannins are smooth. It drinks well already, with beef stroganoff.

## Penfolds Bin 28 Kalimna

| | |
|---|---|
| Quality | ▼▼▼▼⸜ |
| Value | ★★★★★ |
| Grapes | shiraz |
| Region | mainly McLaren Vale, Padthaway, Barossa & Clare Valleys, SA |
| Cellar | ▮ 12+ |
| Alc./Vol. | 14.0% |
| RRP | $23.00 Ⓢ ▮ |

In one of those typical Australian acts of poetic licence, this is no longer a single-vineyard wine, nor even single-region wine. At what point this change occurred we are not told, but we suspect it's been a long-term trend.
*Previous outstanding vintages: '82, '83, '86, '87, '90, '91, '92, '93, '94, '96*
CURRENT RELEASE 1998    An outstanding Bin 28! Sumptuously rich and complex, it features the earthier aromas typical of warmer-climate reds; hints of cedar, dark-chocolate and toasty oak surging from the glass. The profile is rich and chunky, voluptuously smooth and full of the sweet flavour of ripe grapes. Great with civet of hare.

## Penfolds Bin 128 Coonawarra

With a history stretching back to 1962, this is one of Penfolds' few single-region wines. It emerged from Max Schubert's many red winemaking experiments. *Previous outstanding vintages: '78, '80, '82, '86, '88, '90, '91, '93, '94, '96*
CURRENT RELEASE 1998  This is one of the better Bin 128s in recent times. It's crammed with dark-chocolate, dark-berry aromas and is relatively rich and fleshy on the palate. There's little of the usual peppery Coonawarra signature and you can taste the warmer year. It's quite savoury and the tannins are fine and smooth. Serve it with slow-braised meats.

| | |
|---|---|
| Quality | ♥♥♥♥ |
| Value | ★★★★ |
| Grapes | shiraz |
| Region | Coonawarra, SA |
| Cellar | 🍾 10+ |
| Alc./Vol. | 13.5% |
| RRP | $23.00 Ⓢ 🍾 |

## Penfolds Bin 138 Old Vine Shiraz Grenache Mourvèdre

Penfolds has added a bin number to its Rhone blend this year for the first time. The wine is always made from three varieties, but the mix varies according to season. It was aged in older oak, the youngest barrels being six years old.
*Previous outstanding vintages: '94, '96*
CURRENT RELEASE 1998  The Penfolds signature taste is there despite the absence of new oak character. And again, this model wine avoids the portiness so common in other makers' Rhone blends. It's a complex, rustic, savoury red with significant peppery mourvèdre character plus some hints of confectionery from grenache. A well-balanced, fleshy, friendly wine, with a hint of ironstone. It's seductively smooth and more-ish on the palate. Try steak and kidney pie.

| | |
|---|---|
| Quality | ♥♥♥♥♥ |
| Value | ★★★★♪ |
| Grapes | shiraz 55%; grenache 25%; mourvèdre 20% |
| Region | Barossa Valley, SA |
| Cellar | 🍾 7 |
| Alc./Vol. | 14.0% |
| RRP | $23.00 Ⓢ |

## Penfolds Bin 389 Cabernet Shiraz

| | |
|---|---|
| Quality | 🍷🍷🍷🍷🍷 |
| Value | ★★★★★ |
| Grapes | cabernet sauvignon 57%; shiraz 41%; mystery 2% |
| Region | Padthaway, Bordertown, McLaren Vale, Barossa & Clare Valleys, SA |
| Cellar | ➥ 2–20+ |
| Alc./Vol. | 14.0% |
| RRP | $35.00 Ⓢ 🍾 |

The traditional Aussie cab shiraz has to some extent been replaced by cabernet merlots of late, but it's good to see some companies carrying on the tradition. The first vintage was 1960 and it earnt the nickname 'poor man's Grange', although these days no poor man could afford it. Interestingly, only 22 per cent of the oak was new.
*Previous outstanding vintages: '66, '70, '71, '80, '83, '86, '87, '90, '91, '92, '94, '96, '97*
CURRENT RELEASE 1998    A great 389! The nose is somewhat 'quiet' at present: undeveloped, with coconut/toasty American oak and rich fruit aromas. It's full-bodied, chewy and tannic, and needs time. There's tremendous concentration and fleshy density, in typical savoury Penfolds house style, and the whole thing has an endless finish. Cellar it, then serve with hard cheeses.

## Penfolds Grange

| | |
|---|---|
| Quality | 🍷🍷🍷🍷🍷 |
| Value | ★ |
| Grapes | shiraz; cabernet sauvignon |
| Region | various, SA |
| Cellar | ➥ 5–20+ |
| Alc./Vol. | 14.0% |
| RRP | $300–$350 🍾 |

Ah, Grange, we remember it fondly. It used to be a wine people drank. You'd empty the piggy bank to buy a bottle for a special birthday or to celebrate a promotion. Now the only people who can afford it are the mega-wealthy, who increasingly reside in the US of A.
*Previous outstanding vintages: '53, '55, '62, '63, '66, '71, '72, '76, '80, '83, '86, '88, '90, '91, '94*
CURRENT RELEASE 1996    This is touted as the greatest vintage since the '90, and sure it's a tremendous wine but, like the '90, we're not sure the fuss is justified – let alone the price. It has the trademark Grange dense blackish red–purple colour, the toasty oak, mocha, vanilla, ground-coffee smells, tremendously complex with a hint of mint and buried cherries. It has the assertive tannin grip, the powerful, muscular body and long licorice/blackberry finish. It's a long way from drinking at its peak. And we're sure it will mature into a great wine. So if you own some, drink it, perhaps with aged cheddar, but don't sell it.

## Penfolds Magill Estate

This is the most hand-made of all Penfolds wines, produced by Peter Gago in the old Magill bluestone cellars, using the same techniques and open fermenters as the historic Max Schubert wines of the '40s and '50s. The grapes are all from the 5 hectares of remaining Magill Estate vines. The fruit travels just a few hundred metres from vine to crusher. It's Penfolds' only single-vineyard wine.

*Previous outstanding vintages: '83, '86, '89, '90, '91, '93, '95, '96*

**CURRENT RELEASE 1998    Could this be the best Magill Estate ever? Very possibly. The colour is dense dark red; the aromas are quite undeveloped and in the blackberry, dark-cherry spectrum, overlaid with cedary, scented French oak. On nose and palate it shows a tightness, fineness and elegance that bodes well for the future. It's packed with flavour that lingers long after you swallow. Wonderful wine! Cellar, then serve with rump steak.**

| | |
|---|---|
| Quality | 🍷🍷🍷🍷🍷 |
| Value | ★★★★★ |
| Grapes | shiraz |
| Region | Adelaide, SA |
| Cellar | 🍾 2–15 |
| Alc./Vol. | 13.5% |
| RRP | $60.00 ⑤ |

Penguin Best Shiraz

## Penfolds Rawsons Retreat

What's in a name? Very little – Rawson was the second name of Christopher Penfold, who established the Penfold wine name. Where did he retreat to? Nobody's letting on.

CURRENT RELEASE 2000    As you'd expect at the price, this is a simple, grapey wine which is dominated by rather raw fruit and some herbal/anise flavours, probably from not-so-ripe grapes. The colour is promising, and it's light, soft, simple and fair quaffing at the price. You get what you pay for. A decent pizza wine.

| | |
|---|---|
| Quality | 🍷🍷🍷 |
| Value | ★★★⁺ |
| Grapes | shiraz; cabernet sauvignon; ruby cabernet |
| Region | not stated |
| Cellar | 🍾 2 |
| Alc./Vol. | 13.0% |
| RRP | $9.00 ⑤ |

## Penfolds RWT Barossa Shiraz

| | |
|---|---|
| Quality | 🍷🍷🍷🍷🍷 |
| Value | ★★★⟩ |
| Grapes | shiraz |
| Region | Barossa Valley, SA |
| Cellar | ➥ 2–20+ |
| Alc./Vol. | 14.0% |
| RRP | $95.00 🍾 |

A great wine company keeps inventing outstanding new wines, and Penfolds has done this with RWT and, to a lesser degree, Yattarna. The main differences from Grange are fruit style and sourcing (all Barossa), French oak and earlier release. Makers: John Duval and team.
CURRENT RELEASE 1998    The '97 debut was very good, but the '98 is in an altogether higher realm. This is a great wine: a real superstar. Powerful yet elegant, finely structured but firm and tight; possessed of tremendous intensity and persistence. The flavours remind of anise and blackberry, with cedary French oak yet to completely integrate. It will improve over many years in the cellar. Then serve with rare roast beef. A wine to walk over hot coals for.

## Penley Estate Cabernet Sauvignon

| | |
|---|---|
| Quality | 🍷🍷🍷🍷🍷 |
| Value | ★★★⟩ |
| Grapes | cabernet sauvignon |
| Region | Coonawarra, SA |
| Cellar | ➥ 3–17+ |
| Alc./Vol. | 14.0% |
| RRP | $60.00 🍾 |

After a slightly wobbly '97, the Penley cab is back on track with a sensational wine from the great '98 harvest. It reminds us of Penfolds' Bin 707 style. Funny, owner Kym Tolley used to make those wines!
CURRENT RELEASE 1998    The colour is dark blackish red–purple and this is a brooding infant of a wine with a tremendous future. Lavish toasty oak is a feature of the bouquet, and if you look hard you'll find blackberry cabernet fruit, yet to fully emerge. It's a dense, rich, concentrated and at the moment slightly chewy wine. Cellar, then have it with aged tilsit cheese.

## Penley Estate Hyland Shiraz

| | |
|---|---|
| Quality | 🍷🍷🍷🍷🍷 |
| Value | ★★★★ |
| Grapes | shiraz |
| Region | Coonawarra, SA |
| Cellar | 🍷 12+ |
| Alc./Vol. | 14.0% |
| RRP | $18.00 |

The Hyland name comes from the brothers Frank and Leslie Penfold Hyland and their father Thomas Hyland, who married Georgina Penfold. The good lady was Kym Tolley's great grandmother.
CURRENT RELEASE 1999    Pristine Coonawarra here: the terroir comes rocketing through the wine. You certainly won't sleep while sipping this delicious drop. Its raspberry, cherry aromas are clean and concentrated, while the taste is fine and lively, with elegant cassis fruit, measured tannins and a lingering aftertaste. It goes well with lamb backstraps and pesto.

## Penley Estate Phoenix Cabernet Sauvignon

Nothing to do with rising from the ashes. The Phoenix name is an old Tolley family brand-name from 1888, which Kym Tolley resurrected for his second-string cabernet.

CURRENT RELEASE 1999   While it's always a little leafier than the flagship cab, the Phoenix regularly gives us pleasure in a more fruit-led, elegant, ready-drinking style. There are cassis/Ribena and crushed-leaf aromas, but no mid-palate thinness. It has elegance, and a full middle with attractive red-berry flavours. Try it with pink lamb chops.

| | |
|---|---|
| Quality | ♥ ♥ ♥ ♥ |
| Value | ★ ★ ★ ★ |
| Grapes | cabernet sauvignon |
| Region | Coonawarra, SA |
| Cellar | ▮ 6 |
| Alc./Vol. | 13.5% |
| RRP | $20.50 |

## Penley Estate Shiraz Cabernet

Has Kym Tolley been navel-gazing too long? Thus speaks the deep and meaningful, soul-searching back-label: 'Experience was earnt, tradition was given, but my wine reflects what I feel.' Amen.

CURRENT RELEASE 1998   The colour is dark and youthful at three years old. The bouquet is deep and reveals a lot of toasty oak plus other, semi-hidden complexities. In the mouth it's full-bodied and loaded with sweet blackberry, blackcurrant flavours and vanilla from barrels. It's smooth and oaky – but not overdone – and the finish is clean and tidy. It would suit rump steak marinated in red wine.

| | |
|---|---|
| Quality | ♥ ♥ ♥ ♥ |
| Value | ★ ★ ★ � |
| Grapes | shiraz; cabernet sauvignon |
| Region | Coonawarra, McLaren Vale & Barossa Valley, SA |
| Cellar | ➡ 1–10+ |
| Alc./Vol. | 14.0% |
| RRP | $28.00 |

## Petaluma Coonawarra Unfiltered

| | |
|---|---|
| Quality | 🍷🍷🍷🍷🍷 |
| Value | ★★★⯪ |
| Grapes | cabernet sauvignon 60%; merlot 40% |
| Region | Coonawarra, SA |
| Cellar | ➥ 3–18+ |
| Alc./Vol. | 13.5% |
| RRP | $59.60 🍾 |

Sounds like a pack of cigarettes, doesn't it? But that's what it says on the label, God's honour. Coonawarra's '99 growing season had a heat summation of 1575 degree days Celsius, which means it was hotter than the norm – which is 1414. Maker: Brian Croser and team. *Previous outstanding vintages: '79, '86, '88, '90, '91, '92, '94, '95, '96, '97, '98*

CURRENT RELEASE 1999    Subdued aromatics seem to be a trait of the '99 Coonawarras. This has a quite elusive bouquet, with just a whiff of cassis. But the right sorts of cabernet flavours are all present and correct on the palate. Blackberry and blackcurrant flavours of great elegance and intensity show through; the oak is in the background and the persistence is very impressive. The tannins form a fine, tight backbone. Cellar, then serve with hard cheeses.

## Petaluma Merlot

| | |
|---|---|
| Quality | 🍷🍷🍷🍷🍷 |
| Value | ★★★★ |
| Grapes | merlot |
| Region | Coonawarra, SA |
| Cellar | 🍷 10+ |
| Alc./Vol. | 14.0% |
| RRP | $55.00 |

Brian Croser is a devotee of merlot in Coonawarra. He thinks it's better suited to the area than shiraz, which has been the mainstay of Coonawarra since the nineteenth century. Perhaps time will prove him correct, but merlot has an awful lot of ground to make up on shiraz's track record.

CURRENT RELEASE 1998    This is simply one of the best merlots Petaluma has made. The colour is very deep purple–red; the bouquet is fresh and vibrant, and perfumed with violets and dark berries. The oak character is subtle but slightly off-key. In the mouth, it's still a trifle firm but has terrific flavour and concentration. It packs a punch and lingers well with a satisfying finish. Try boeuf à la mode.

## Peter Lehmann Clancy's Legendary Red

This was originally called Clancy's Gold Preference. Qué? No one understood that one, either. It's hardly old enough to be a legend. It's actually known simply as Clancy's.

CURRENT RELEASE 1999    This has lightened off a trifle over the years. It's a light–medium bodied, fruit-driven red which smells of raspberry, herbs and mint. It's quite lean but has length and structure, with more tannin than you might expect, going on nose and colour. It's an easy-drinking red to schlock with Barossa mettwurst.

| | |
|---|---|
| Quality | ▼▼▼⬚ |
| Value | ★★★⬧ |
| Grapes | shiraz; cabernet sauvignon; merlot; cabernet franc |
| Region | various, SA |
| Cellar | 🍶 4 |
| Alc./Vol. | 13.0% |
| RRP | $16.30 Ⓢ |

## Peter Lehmann Shiraz

When the Lehmann team changed their labels to reproductions of original artworks, and opted for a non-traditional bottle, their sales grew wings. So much for feel-good, down-home Barossa legend stuff! CURRENT RELEASE 1999    As Roy and HG might say, this is a lightweight with a welterweight punch. It offers depth and character above its station. Dusty, toasty nut, plum and chocolate aromas – there's more than just simple fruit here. It has plenty of grunt, very good depth of vanilla/plum flavour and an attractive, smooth grip to close. It would suit lamb navarin.

| | |
|---|---|
| Quality | ▼▼▼▼ |
| Value | ★★★★⬧ |
| Grapes | shiraz |
| Region | Barossa Valley, SA |
| Cellar | 🍶 10+ |
| Alc./Vol. | 14.0% |
| RRP | $21.50 Ⓢ |

## Peter Lehmann The Seven Surveys

We won't give you the full name: it would take up too much room. It's a triple-varietal Rhone blend and is named after the seven surveys William Jacob (he of Jacobs Creek) completed in 1840, which defined the Barossa Valley.

CURRENT RELEASE 1998    Love the style: it's an effective antidote to the fruit-bombs so prevalent in this country. The flavours are savoury, showing complex secondary development, and remind us of earth, meat-stock, dried spices and old leather. It's showing some matured character – with a dry and slightly dusty finish, warmed by the heat of alcohol. It's a good style to pair with food. Try braised lamb shanks.

| | |
|---|---|
| Quality | ▼▼▼⬚ |
| Value | ★★★ |
| Grapes | mourvèdre; shiraz; grenache |
| Region | Barossa Valley, SA |
| Cellar | 🍶 4+ |
| Alc./Vol. | 14.0% |
| RRP | $21.50 |

## Phillip Island Wines Cabernet Sauvignon

**Quality** 🍷🍷🍷🍷
**Value** ★★★
**Grapes** cabernet sauvignon
**Region** Gippsland, Vic.
**Cellar** 8
**Alc./Vol.** 13.0%
**RRP** $27.00

The Lance family of Diamond Valley planted a vineyard in an untested locality: the beach holiday destination Phillip Island in Westernport Bay, best known for penguins and motorbike racing. The 2-hectare site turned out to be disastrous from a wind point of view, but was saved by wind netting.

CURRENT RELEASE 1999 The grapes were all grown on the island, and the wine has a ripe but cool-climate aroma of blackberry, cherry, cassis and vanilla. It is clean and well balanced, and the palate is smooth, medium-bodied and well proportioned. Fine tannins provide a firm finish. It would drink well with roast leg of lamb.

## Picarus Limestone Coast Cabernet Sauvignon

**Quality** 🍷🍷🍷½
**Value** ★★★
**Grapes** cabernet sauvignon
**Region** Coonawarra, Mount Benson & Padthaway, SA
**Cellar** 6+
**Alc./Vol.** 12.7%
**RRP** $27.00

Picarus is a negociant label, started by Sydneysiders Mark Arnold and John Baruzzi. Arnold is a wine marketer and former retailer; Baruzzi was until lately a Hunter Valley winemaker.

CURRENT RELEASE 1998 Elegance is the order of the day here. It's a discreet wine, typical of the Limestone Coast region. Aromas are of mulberry, cherries and herbs with some vegetal aspects. There are some coconutty/oak nuances peeping through the fruit. It's lean and lacks a little mid-palate punch, but is a pleasing drink with braised lamb shanks.

## Picarus Limestone Coast Shiraz

**Quality** 🍷🍷🍷🍷½
**Value** ★★★★
**Grapes** shiraz
**Region** Naracoorte, Coonawarra, Mount Benson & Padthaway, SA
**Cellar** 10
**Alc./Vol.** 13.2%
**RRP** $27.00

Picarus . . . wasn't that the brother of the chap who flew too close to the sun and melted his wax wings? This is a new label but they've gone to a lot of trouble to make it look distinguished and worthy of your $27. The brand is part of Winetrust Estates, which has on its board a cluster of people from the heydays of Camperdown Cellars.

CURRENT RELEASE 1999 A quite complex style with lots of barrel-ferment and fruit concentration – without being overdone. It smells of toasty oak and savoury secondary characters. The palate offers plenty of flavour with a sweet core of ripe blackberry/cranberry-flavoured grapes. It's rich and fleshy with smooth tannins and fine balance. Very more-ish! Try it with aged cheddar.

## Picarus Reserve-1 Cabernet Sauvignon

There's a theory in the wine business that if you produce little enough of a wine, you can charge whatever you like for it. This runs out at 100 dozen. The label reassures us that the grapes came from an old, low-yielding single vineyard.
CURRENT RELEASE 1997    The colour is light–medium in depth, and it smells oaky. Toasty barrels, vanilla, dusty cedar . . . but not a lot of ripe fruit. Acid is noticeable in the mouth with greenish flavours, grippy tannins and charry oak flavours. If someone gives you a bottle, re-gift.

| | |
|---|---|
| Quality | ♟ ♟ ♟ |
| Value | ★ ⟩ |
| Grapes | cabernet sauvignon |
| Region | Coonawarra, SA |
| Cellar | ⬥ 1–5+ |
| Alc./Vol. | 12.0% |
| RRP | $80.00 |

## Picarus Reserve-A Shiraz

This is a much better wine than the cabernet, which may reflect the relative merits of the vintages. Half the wine was barrel-fermented and the wood was half each American and French. A major selling-point of the Reserve reds seems to be the news that only 100 dozen were bottled.
CURRENT RELEASE 1998    This is delicious stuff: warm and friendly and bursting with joyously ripe flavour. The fruit and oak are well married and we liked the supple, silky texture. There's plenty of toasty oak and the style reflects the warm vintage and region. The finish is firm and it will repay cellaring. Try it with a daube of beef.

| | |
|---|---|
| Quality | ♟ ♟ ♟ ♟ ⟩ |
| Value | ★ ★ ⟩ |
| Grapes | shiraz |
| Region | Padthaway, SA |
| Cellar | ⬥ 1–12+ |
| Alc./Vol. | 14.0% |
| RRP | $80.00 ▮ |

## Pikes Premio Sangiovese

Tuscany comes to the Clare Valley. Neil Pike is drinking lots of espresso these days and shouting things like ecco!, oggi! and pronto! into his mobile phone.
*Previous outstanding vintage: '97*
CURRENT RELEASE 1998    This does a decent job of capturing the savouriness and austere grip of some Chiantis. It has a leathery, earthy developed bouquet and is filled with secondary, savoury flavours, capped off by a firm tannic finish. It has plenty of stuffing and needs food. Try it with brasato.

| | |
|---|---|
| Quality | ♟ ♟ ♟ ♟ |
| Value | ★ ★ ★ ★ |
| Grapes | sangiovese 94%; cabernet sauvignon 4%; merlot 2% |
| Region | Clare Valley, SA |
| Cellar | ▮ 6 |
| Alc./Vol. | 14.0% |
| RRP | $27.50 ▮ |

## Pikes Shiraz Grenache Mourvèdre

| | |
|---|---|
| Quality | ▼▼▼◗ |
| Value | ★★★ |
| Grapes | shiraz; grenache; mourvèdre |
| Region | Clare Valley, SA |
| Cellar | ▮ 5 |
| Alc./Vol. | 14.0% |
| RRP | $24.00 |

This is what's commonly referred to these days as a 'Rhone blend'. There are plenty of GSMs and this is an SGM. But what would happen if you had an MSG? Not a great marketing angle. (Psst: see under Peter Lehmann.) CURRENT RELEASE 1999   This is a decent drink with an unusual spectrum of flavours. We detect meaty, gamy, tobacco flavours and a hint of tomato bush, and the oak influence is nicely restrained. It's medium-bodied, smooth, and well-balanced for current drinking. Good with shepherd's pie.

## Pirramimma McLaren Vale Shiraz

| | |
|---|---|
| Quality | ▼▼▼▼◗ |
| Value | ★★★★ |
| Grapes | shiraz |
| Region | McLaren Vale, SA |
| Cellar | ➠ 1–12+ |
| Alc./Vol. | 14.0% |
| RRP | $26.50 ▮ |

Pirramimma is one of the low-profile – and therefore widely underrated – wineries of the Vale. This spent two years in new American oak barrels. Maker: Geoff Johnston. CURRENT RELEASE 1998   The colour is dark and serious-looking; the bouquet is similarly dense and rich with dark-chocolate, toasty oak, plum and vanilla aromas. The taste is robust and chunky, with masses of chewy oak tannins and a finish like a vise. It needs time, then serve it with boeuf à la mode.

## Pirramimma Stock's Hill Shiraz

| | |
|---|---|
| Quality | ▼▼▼▼ |
| Value | ★★★★★ |
| Grapes | shiraz |
| Region | McLaren Vale, SA |
| Cellar | ➠ 1–9+ |
| Alc./Vol. | 14.0% |
| RRP | $15.90 ⑤ |

Stock's Hill is the name of the vineyard where the grapes are grown. This is a reliable label for good value, and puts a lot of fancy-priced shirazes to shame. Maker: Geoff Johnston, whose family has been making wine for over a century. CURRENT RELEASE 1999   The colour is deep and promising. The nose offers toasty-barrel, plum, chocolate and vanilla scents. It's full-bodied and quite tannic, which bodes well for its future in the cellar. This is serious wine! It has real density and concentration, and drinks well with a standing rib roast of beef.

## Plantagenet Cabernet Sauvignon

The Great Southern is the poor relation compared to Margaret River: it's more remote and far-flung, with fewer wineries and a more troublesome climate. Plantagenet has been an exemplary winery for over two decades. Maker: Gavin Berry.

*Previous outstanding vintages: '81, '83, '85, '86, '90, '91, '94*

CURRENT RELEASE 1998    This is released a year older than most cabernets, and the slow-evolving (but long-keeping) style merits the extra time. The aromas evoke dusty oak, cassis and blackcurrants, with a little crushed leafiness. In the mouth, it is an elegant, fine style which may have a slight dip in the mid-palate but the finish is long and the tannins are fine and supple. It's worth cellaring. Then serve with aged cheddar.

| | |
|---|---|
| Quality | ♟♟♟♟♙ |
| Value | ★★★★ |
| Grapes | cabernet sauvignon |
| Region | Great Southern, WA |
| Cellar | ➤ 2–12+ |
| Alc./Vol. | 13.5% |
| RRP | $28.00 |

## Plantagenet Shiraz

Founder Tony Smith sold Plantagenet some years ago to a Perth liquor wholesaler, Lionel Sampson & Co. Winemaker is still the reliable Gavin Berry.

CURRENT RELEASE 1998    A simply delicious shiraz, this southern belle from Western Australia oozes class. It smells of mixed exotic spices, cherry and plum with oak sensibly tucked in the background. There's a signature twist of herbs as well. In the mouth it's tight, firm, intense and very long. This is classy cool-grown Oz shiraz. Drink it with aged Heidi gruyère cheese.

| | |
|---|---|
| Quality | ♟♟♟♟♟ |
| Value | ★★★★⟩ |
| Grapes | shiraz |
| Region | Great Southern, WA |
| Cellar | ▮ 12+ |
| Alc./Vol. | 13.5% |
| RRP | $35.00 |

## Plunkett Merlot

| | |
|---|---|
| Quality | ♟♟♟♟ |
| Value | ★★★ |
| Grapes | merlot |
| Region | Strathbogie Ranges, Vic. |
| Cellar | ♦ 5 |
| Alc./Vol. | 13.0% |
| RRP | $19.35 |

The Plunkett family has big vineyard holdings but their winemaking is boutique-sized. They have cellar door sales on the Hume Freeway near Avenel. Maker: Sam Plunkett.

CURRENT RELEASE 1998    A taut and twitchy style of cool-climate merlot. It has raspberry, mint and crushed-leaf aromas and these translate onto a lean and slightly acid palate. It has very light tannin and extract and is light-to medium-bodied. It would suit pan-fried veal cutlets.

| | |
|---|---|
| Quality | ♟♟♟♟ |
| Value | ★★★ |
| Grapes | merlot |
| Region | Strathbogie Ranges, Vic. |
| Cellar | ♦ 4 |
| Alc./Vol. | 13.0% |
| RRP | $19.35 (cellar door) |

CURRENT RELEASE 1999    This is light-bodied and leafy/minty flavoured, but quite palatable – especially with food. The colour is medium red and it smells of mint, raspberry and leaf, while the taste is light and somewhat lean, with slightly prominent acid and a sharp-edged cool-climate greenness. Try it with lamb and mint sauce.

## Portree Macedon Pinot Noir

| | |
|---|---|
| Quality | ♟♟♟♟ |
| Value | ★★★ |
| Grapes | pinot noir |
| Region | Macedon Ranges, Vic. |
| Cellar | ♦ 3 |
| Alc./Vol. | 12.5% |
| RRP | $24.00 (cellar door) |

Portree is a tiny winery at Lancefield in the Macedon Ranges region. The vineyard is 5 hectares and was established in 1983. The label proudly proclaims this wine as unfiltered. Maker: Ken Murchison.

CURRENT RELEASE 1999    It's a lighter and fairly straightforward style, and smells of cherry and vanilla, vaguely reminiscent of cough medicine. The palate is light and lean, dry on the finish and just a little bit meagre. It's not without its charms and is a pleasing drink right now, with tuna carpaccio.

## Prentice Pinot Noir

Neil Prentice has a negociant-style business, buying grapes from various regions in Victoria and having them made in other people's wineries. His Whitlands pinot has been consistently impressive. But you need zoom vision to read the ant-sized print on his labels! CURRENT RELEASE 1999   This opens up with delicious strawberry/cherry aromas, with cherry-brandy overtones plus hints of sap and stalks. It turns minty with extended airing. The palate is smooth, elegant, complex and stylish. Its texture is a highlight. There's more than a streak of Burgundy here. Try it with smoked chicken.

| | |
|---|---|
| Quality | ♟♟♟♟♟ |
| Value | ★★★★ |
| Grapes | pinot noir |
| Region | King Valley, Vic. |
| Cellar | ▮ 4 |
| Alc./Vol. | 12.5% |
| RRP | $28.00 |

## Preston Peak Cabernets Merlot

This vineyard and winery are at Preston in the Granite Belt, with vineyards at Wyberba (9 hectares) and Preston (1.5 hectares).
CURRENT RELEASE 1999   This red seems to reflect a cool growing season, with marked capsicum and pea-pod aromas over dusty, raspberry fruit. It's lean and angular to taste, with a firm tannin finish. It may benefit from cellaring, but the tannins are on the green side. Try it with baked, stuffed capsicums.

| | |
|---|---|
| Quality | ♟♟♟ |
| Value | ★★↗ |
| Grapes | cabernet franc 35%; cabernet sauvignon 29%; merlot 31%; shiraz 5% |
| Region | Granite Belt, Qld |
| Cellar | ▮ 6 |
| Alc./Vol. | 13.0% |
| RRP | $26.00 |

## Providence Miguet Pinot Noir

Owner Stuart Bryce cut off 40 per cent of the bunches to make a more concentrated pinot. The wine won trophies for best pinot noir and best wine of show at the 2001 Tasmanian Regional Wine Show.
CURRENT RELEASE 1999   The sacrifice worked: it's a delicious wine, with concentrated wild cherry aromas of great complexity. There are subtle undergrowth, smoky and meaty nuances. The mouth flavours of sweetly ripe dark fruits are opulent and silky smooth. Try it with confit of duck.

| | |
|---|---|
| Quality | ♟♟♟♟♟ |
| Value | ★★★★ |
| Grapes | pinot noir |
| Region | Pipers River, Tas. |
| Cellar | ▮ 4 |
| Alc./Vol. | 13.5% |
| RRP | $27.25 (cellar door) |

## R.L. Buller & Son Beverford Shiraz

| | |
|---|---|
| Quality | ❦❦❦❦ |
| Value | ★★★❧ |
| Grapes | shiraz |
| Region | Murray Valley, Vic. |
| Cellar | ❦ 5 |
| Alc./Vol. | 14.0% |
| RRP | $17.00 ⑤ |

Beverford is Bullers' vineyard on the Murray, near Swan Hill. Good name for a wine. 'Care for a bevvy or two from Beverford?' could catch on. Maker: Richard Buller Jnr.

CURRENT RELEASE 1999 Strictly for lovers of big, hot-climate reds. It has a slightly oxidised, porty bouquet and the raisins-and-licorice theme continues on the palate. Plummy fruit also chimes in. There's not a lot of finesse but it does have plenty of flavour. It doesn't stint on value. Try it with steak and kidney pie.

## R.L. Buller & Son Magee Cabernet Shiraz

| | |
|---|---|
| Quality | ❦❦❦ |
| Value | ★★★ |
| Grapes | cabernet sauvignon; shiraz |
| Region | Murray Valley, Vic. |
| Cellar | ❦ 4 |
| Alc./Vol. | 13.5% |
| RRP | $14.00 ⑤ |

Love that ye olde wine companye title. It makes us hanker for the olde days when port was the preferred tipple and Rutherglen was top of the pops. Maker: Richard Buller Jnr.

CURRENT RELEASE 1999 The colour is slightly forward for a two-year-old and the bouquet is dominated by a toasted oak-chip aroma. There is a kind of burnt-fruit, barbecued aroma as well. It is smooth, light- to medium-bodied and fruit-sweet on the palate. It's ready to drink without further ado. Try it with barbecued sausages.

## Red Edge Cabernet Sauvignon

| | |
|---|---|
| Quality | ❦❦❦❦❦ |
| Value | ★★★★❧ |
| Grapes | cabernet sauvignon |
| Region | Heathcote, Vic. |
| Cellar | ➡ 2–10 |
| Alc./Vol. | 13.9% |
| RRP | $30.00 |

Heathcote red grapes are at a premium these days and wines from this area near Bendigo are climbing in price. Recently RK-P had a *South Australian* wine producer, on condition of anonymity, confide that he thought Heathcote shiraz was the best in Australia!

CURRENT RELEASE 1999 This is a complex young cabernet with real potential. It has very deep purplish colour and an aromatic nose of blackcurrants, violets, earth, minerals and herby regional notes. The palate has intense cassis flavour with a leafy edge. It's still quite austere in youth with a tight backbone of big firm tannins, but given time it should be a beauty. Serve it with a rich lamb casserole.

## Redbank Percydale Cabernet Merlot

Redbank has burst its banks and run all over the state! This is one of a series of snappily labelled new wines from Redbank, sourced in the main from other regions.

CURRENT RELEASE 1999 This has a pretty good colour but the nose is dumb and unevolved. The palate flavours show vanilla, caramel and dark chocolate from charred-oak and fruit/wood interactions. It's quite smooth and there are tomato, leaf and berry flavours as well. Straightforward but pleasant wine, to go with casseroled kid.

| | |
|---|---|
| **Quality** | 🍷🍷🍷½ |
| **Value** | ★★★ |
| **Grapes** | cabernet sauvignon |
| **Region** | King Valley, Vic. |
| **Cellar** | 5 |
| **Alc./Vol.** | 14.0% |
| **RRP** | $21.00 (S) |

## Redgate Cabernet Merlot

The Ullinger family have owned and operated this winery and its 20-hectare vineyard since they established it in 1977. Winemaker is Andrew Forsell. Like nearby Redgate Beach, it's named after a shipwreck.

CURRENT RELEASE 1999 This is a distinctive regional style. It smells leafy but ripe, with deep minty and dark-berry fruit flavours, a hint of chocolate and a tightly wound, concentrated palate. It has a dense tannin structure suggesting post-fermentation skin maceration, and it needs time to mellow and soften. Then serve it with aged cheeses.

| | |
|---|---|
| **Quality** | 🍷🍷🍷🍷½ |
| **Value** | ★★★★ |
| **Grapes** | cabernet sauvignon; merlot |
| **Region** | Margaret River, WA |
| **Cellar** | 3–12+ |
| **Alc./Vol.** | 13.8% |
| **RRP** | $29.50 (cellar door) |

## Redman Cabernet Sauvignon

These wines are made in traditional Coonawarra style, and tend to get left behind in the rush for the big, high-alcohol, oaky styles that are popular today. They age well and should not be overlooked.

CURRENT RELEASE 1999 This is a finely scented cabernet, where fruit does all the talking – as opposed to oak. It is light-bodied and seems fairly modest in alcohol, which would be par for the Redman course. It has elegance in its favour. It brings to mind Owen Redman's phrase 'dinner claret' – and would be well suited to minted, pink-roasted lamb.

| | |
|---|---|
| **Quality** | 🍷🍷🍷🍷 |
| **Value** | ★★★½ |
| **Grapes** | cabernet sauvignon |
| **Region** | Coonawarra, SA |
| **Cellar** | 12+ |
| **Alc./Vol.** | 13.0% |
| **RRP** | $26.50 |

## Redman Cabernet Sauvignon Merlot

| | |
|---|---|
| Quality | 🍷🍷🍷🍷 |
| Value | ★★★ |
| Grapes | cabernet sauvignon; merlot |
| Region | Coonawarra, SA |
| Cellar | 🍶 6+ |
| Alc./Vol. | 13.0% |
| RRP | $28.00 Ⓢ |

Bill Redman, grandfather of the present incumbents Bruce and Malcolm, arrived in Coonawarra exactly 100 years ago, as a 14-year-old looking for work. He was put to work at the old Riddoch winery for one pound a week.

*Previous outstanding vintage: '96*

CURRENT RELEASE 1997   The colour is slightly developed and the nose reveals this to be a lighter-weight red, with gently leafy and raspberry fruit characters, and subtle oak. It is lean and somewhat angular in the mouth, lacking the fleshy richness some makers are achieving in Coonawarra these days. It is true to the family's traditional style and is a very easy wine to drink. It goes well with herbed roast veal.

## Redman Shiraz

| | |
|---|---|
| Quality | 🍷🍷🍷 |
| Value | ★★★★ |
| Grapes | shiraz |
| Region | Coonawarra, SA |
| Cellar | 🍶 10+ |
| Alc./Vol. | 13.0% |
| RRP | $18.00 Ⓢ |

The Redmans have been making a lighter-bodied style of shiraz ever since Bill Redman's day in the first half of the twentieth century. It's not an attention-seeking style but very drinkable and ages surprisingly well.

CURRENT RELEASE 1999   There's nothing about this wine that jumps up and grabs you, but it is a very more-ish drink. Straightforward cherry fruit nose with a high-note of violets. Elegant weight in the mouth – fruit-driven – with perhaps a little more tannin than usual. A hint of anise to close. Goes well with pasta and bolognese sauce.

## Richmond Grove Cabernet Shiraz Merlot

| | |
|---|---|
| Quality | 🍷🍷🍷 |
| Value | ★★★★ |
| Grapes | cabernet sauvignon; shiraz; merlot |
| Region | not stated |
| Cellar | 🍶 5 |
| Alc./Vol. | 13.0% |
| RRP | $7.00 (375 ml) Ⓢ |

This blend was recently released in half-bottles, as part of Orlando's push to capture the small-format market. (It also released 187.5 ml quarter-bottles of various Poet's Corner and Wyndham Estate wines – all good value for money.)

CURRENT RELEASE 1999   The sticker says it won a gold medal at the Hobart Show, and while we can't see a gold medal in it, we'd admit it's a pleasant, lighter-bodied, easy-drinking style. It has soft minty, leafy, uncomplicated cabernet flavours and light supple tannins that don't get in the way. It's a juicy, fruit-led red which slips down the throat with ease. It goes with veal saltimbocca.

## Riddoch Cabernet Merlot

The name of John Riddoch is everywhere in the Coonawarra region. And fair enough too: the man founded the wine industry there and his descendants are still in the district. Maker: Wayne Stehbens.
CURRENT RELEASE 1999    This wine is soft and showing forward development, and is apparently designed to drink young. There are gamy and meaty aromas, with some vegetal overtones. It's quite light-bodied, and finishes fairly short, with some tobacco and humus characters. It could go with veal schnitzel.

| | |
|---|---|
| Quality | ♥ ♥ ♥ |
| Value | ★ ★ ★ |
| Grapes | cabernet sauvignon; merlot |
| Region | Coonawarra, SA |
| Cellar | ▮ 4 |
| Alc./Vol. | 13.5% |
| RRP | $20.00 ⑤ |

## Riddoch Cabernet Shiraz

The label tells us the wine's namesake, John Riddoch, lived from 1804 to 1901, or 97 years. Another advertisement for the health-giving properties of wine in moderation? Maker: Wayne Stehbens.
CURRENT RELEASE 1999    This brand, the second label of Katnook, is among the most reliable on the market, and here's another example. It has a deep, dark red–purple colour and smells invitingly of blackberry and cassis, cabernet leading the charge. Toasty oak provides a grace note. The palate has richness, fruit sweetness and depth, and the wine is chock-full of interest. Smooth tannin completes the picture. A stylish red to serve with pink lamb chops.

| | |
|---|---|
| Quality | ♥ ♥ ♥ ♥ ♥ |
| Value | ★ ★ ★ ★ |
| Grapes | cabernet sauvignon; shiraz |
| Region | Coonawarra, SA |
| Cellar | ▮ 10+ |
| Alc./Vol. | 14.0% |
| RRP | $20.00 ⑤ |

## Riddoch Shiraz

Wayne Stehbens has been making shiraz for the Riddoch brand for a long time, but only recently under the Katnook label. His first Katnook effort, the '97, won the Jimmy Watson Trophy and, as silly as we think that trophy is, the wine is superb.
CURRENT RELEASE 1999    The colour is only medium–deep and the bouquet has some vegetal, leafy components as well as discreet berries. There's plenty of chewy tannin on a medium-bodied frame. Berry and vanilla flavours appear on the palate. It's a decent early-drinking wine that could improve in the short term. It suits grilled T-bone steak.

| | |
|---|---|
| Quality | ♥ ♥ ♥ ♥ |
| Value | ★ ★ ★ |
| Grapes | shiraz |
| Region | Coonawarra, SA |
| Cellar | ▮ 5 |
| Alc./Vol. | 14.0% |
| RRP | $20.00 ⑤ |

## Rosemount Balmoral Syrah

| | |
|---|---|
| Quality | 🍷🍷🍷🍷🍷 |
| Value | ★★★★ |
| Grapes | shiraz |
| Region | McLaren Vale, SA |
| Cellar | ➛ 2–15+ |
| Alc./Vol. | 14.5% |
| RRP | $70.00 🍾 |

Que syrah, syrah? It's a whim of marketing that this shiraz has always been labelled syrah. The Kiwis would take issue: some of them believe their syrah is a different grape from our shiraz, and that we should not call our shiraz syrah. *Previous outstanding vintages: '90, '91, '92, '94, '96, '97* CURRENT RELEASE 1998    Typical Balmoral: it deserves its status as an icon of McLaren Vale shiraz. If you love the fruitcakey, plum-pudding, chocolatey style of warm-grown Oz shiraz, this is your bag. Balmoral does the style better than most. Very deep purple–red hue; very rich bouquet, laced with stacks of toasted oak, and dense in every regard. Texture is a feature: it's silky smooth and lavish as plush. A superb wine, to drink with standing beef rib roast.

## Rosemount Hill of Gold Cabernet Sauvignon

| | |
|---|---|
| Quality | 🍷🍷🍷🍷 |
| Value | ★★★⁺ |
| Grapes | cabernet sauvignon |
| Region | Mudgee, NSW |
| Cellar | ➛ 2–10 |
| Alc./Vol. | 13.5% |
| RRP | $20.00 ⑤ |

When Rosemount merged with Southcorp in 2001, many saw it as a reverse takeover because the top jobs were mostly filled by Rosemount bods. Including chief winemaker, Philip Shaw. CURRENT RELEASE 1999    This is a deep and chunky red, with liberal tannins typical of the Mudgee district, but it avoids the rusticity of many of its contemporaries. The bouquet is shy, with discreet berry and lightly leafy scents. It tastes flavoursome, with plenty of fruit-sweet berry nuances and smooth but chunky tannins. Clean and well-made, it should cellar well. Try it with steak and kidney pie.

## Rosemount Hill of Gold Shiraz

| | |
|---|---|
| Quality | 🍷🍷🍷🍷 |
| Value | ★★★⁺ |
| Grapes | shiraz |
| Region | Mudgee, NSW |
| Cellar | ➛ 1–6+ |
| Alc./Vol. | 13.5% |
| RRP | $20.00 ⑤ |

Henschke, seeking to protect its Hill of Grace trademark, challenged Rosemount's right to use the name Hill of Gold, but lost the court action. The wines are very different in style. Maker: Philip Shaw. CURRENT RELEASE 1999    This is a baby wine with a vivid young colour and slightly subdued nose which has yet to develop into a bouquet. There are perfumed oak scents and the wine has good presence in the mouth. It's smooth and rich and finishes with definite tannins. It would team well with lamb navarin.

## Rosemount Mountain Blue Shiraz Cabernet

Rosemount rarely puts a foot wrong. After many years of buying grapes from Mudgee, it bought some existing vineyards and land, and started developing Mudgee brands, including Hill of Gold. Mountain Blue is the first – and best – of them. Maker: Philip Shaw.
*Previous outstanding vintages: '95, '96, '97*
CURRENT RELEASE 1998    Lashings of oak are all part of the style, and given a year or two's ageing this wine will be nicely in balance. It has a very deep red–purple hue; the aromas are of high-quality, well-seasoned oak and somewhat subdued plum/spice fruit. It is very tight and firmly tannic in the mouth and, while concentrated and very long, it's not showing a lot of fruit at this stage. The finish is dry and savoury. It would go with pork ribs and plum sauce.

| | |
|---|---|
| Quality | 🍷🍷🍷🍷🍷 |
| Value | ★★★★ |
| Grapes | shiraz; cabernet sauvignon |
| Region | Mudgee, NSW |
| Cellar | ⬥ 2–17+ |
| Alc./Vol. | 14.5% |
| RRP | $55.00 |

## Rosemount Shiraz

Rosemount's diamond label wines, especially the reds, offer tremendously good value, and winemaker Philip Shaw manages to do this very consistently year to year.
CURRENT RELEASE 2000    It's just a baby but one of Shaw's great talents is to make his cheaper reds deliciously drinkable at a young age. The bean-counters must be eternally grateful. The bouquet offers simple, sweet cherry and plum fruit, with a slightly burnt aspect. It's clean and fruit-driven with a smooth and well-balanced palate. Better in a few months. Goes with lamb chops.

| | |
|---|---|
| Quality | 🍷🍷🍷🍷 |
| Value | ★★★★★ |
| Grapes | shiraz |
| Region | McLaren Vale, SA; Hunter Valley, NSW; & others |
| Cellar | 🍷 5 |
| Alc./Vol. | 13.5% |
| RRP | $16.00 Ⓢ |

## Rosevears Estate Pinot Noir

In Tasmania's sunny Tamar Valley, Dr Mike Beamish and his backers have built a spiffing new winery with an excellent restaurant, which takes advantage of the area's beautiful views. They make fine wine as well.
CURRENT RELEASE 1999    This is a surprise packet. It's a nicely fruit-accented style with a sweet cherry fragrance and some almost-jammy, super-ripe notes. The structure is deep and tightly framed, with some tannin to close. It's seductive now and will surely improve in the short term. Serve with roast guinea fowl.

| | |
|---|---|
| Quality | 🍷🍷🍷🍷🍷 |
| Value | ★★★★⁴ |
| Grapes | pinot noir |
| Region | West Tamar, Tas. |
| Cellar | 🍷 5 |
| Alc./Vol. | 13.0% |
| RRP | $27.00 |

## Rothbury Estate Brokenback Shiraz

| | |
|---|---|
| Quality | ♟♟♟♟ |
| Value | ★★★ |
| Grapes | shiraz |
| Region | Hunter Valley, NSW |
| Cellar | ▮ 6 |
| Alc./Vol. | 12.0% |
| RRP | $28.70 |

Like our own dear Kylie Minogue, this tries hard to be more than it is. It won a gold medal as an unfinished wine (Hunter Show, '99) and comes from a good source; Brokenback is a fine vineyard of old, low-yielding vines. CURRENT RELEASE 1999  This will disappoint some people because of its rather weak colour and light body, but it is a fine, smooth, well-proportioned Hunter 'burgundy' style. With the right food, it would be as good as a pinot. Raspberry aromas mingle with pepper and herbs, and the oak is gently played. The tannins are fine and tight. It should develop lovely Hunter character with a little age. It suits grilled quail wrapped in prosciutto.

## Rothvale Luke's Shiraz

| | |
|---|---|
| Quality | ♟♟♟♟♟ |
| Value | ★★★★ |
| Grapes | shiraz |
| Region | Hunter Valley, NSW |
| Cellar | ➥ 2–10+ |
| Alc./Vol. | 14.0% |
| RRP | $28.00 ▮ |
| | (cellar door) |

Max Patton and family have 20 hectares of vines on Deasy's Road, Pokolbin. Max's son Luke is chief executive and assistant to his dad as winemaker and viticulturist. This was top shiraz at the 2001 Boutique Wine Awards. CURRENT RELEASE 2000  It's a strongly built red, very much at the big end of Hunter style. It's very youthful, vibrant and a bit unready now. Intense aromas of cherry and raspberry are highly attractive and the wine is full-bodied and quite tannic with a slightly aggressive finish. It needs time in the cellar and should turn into a splendid bottle in time.

## Rouge Homme Shiraz Cabernet

| | |
|---|---|
| Quality | ♟♟♟♟ |
| Value | ★★★★ |
| Grapes | shiraz; |
| | cabernet sauvignon |
| Region | Coonawarra, SA |
| Cellar | ➥ 1–9+ |
| Alc./Vol. | 13.5% |
| RRP | $14.40 Ⓢ |

The back label reminds us the Rouge Homme tradition began way back in 1952. And a proud tradition it is too. It would be a pity if it got sidelined in the Southcorp–Rosemount cabinet reshuffle. Maker: Paul Gordon. CURRENT RELEASE 1999  The colour is a promisingly dark purple–red, and it smells subdued, but with latent berry and oak flavours. The palate is quite big and climaxes with a tannic grip. There are some gamy flavours and the wine is more rustic than you might expect from Coonawarra. It should reward cellaring, and goes well with grilled, marinated lamb backstraps.

# Ryecroft Cabernet Shiraz

Although it has a history going back to the 1800s, Ryecroft these days is a sous-marque of Rosemount. Aside from Ryecroft, Rosemount was (until the recent merger) a surprisingly successful single-brand company. CURRENT RELEASE 2000   Who else but Philip Shaw and team could make this baby so appealing so young? The nose is all grapey raspberry and mint, a tad raw, but the palate is sweet and berryish, with minimal tannin and no obvious oak. There's a nice light grip to close. A handy little quaffing red to drink young. It goes with honey-glazed pork.

| | |
|---|---|
| Quality | 🍷🍷🍷 |
| Value | ★★★ |
| Grapes | cabernet sauvignon; shiraz |
| Region | not stated |
| Cellar | 🍷 3 |
| Alc./Vol. | 13.5% |
| RRP | $13.25 Ⓢ |

# Rymill MC2 Merlot Cabernet Franc Cabernet Sauvignon

Whew! They coined the name MC2 to avoid having to use the full name all the time. But somehow it doesn't solve the problem, does it? Maker: John Innes. CURRENT RELEASE 1999   The aromas are very subdued and the question is whether they'll build with cellar time. In the mouth, it has plenty of muscle, but also gripping tannins, which give a mouth-puckering toughness. Any fruit flavour is well and truly buried. We suggest cellaring, then try it with braised venison.

| | |
|---|---|
| Quality | 🍷🍷🍷 |
| Value | ★★★ |
| Grapes | merlot; cabernet franc; cabernet sauvignon |
| Region | Coonawarra, SA |
| Cellar | 🍷 2–8+ |
| Alc./Vol. | 14.0% |
| RRP | $18.00 🍷 |

# Saddler's Creek Equus McLaren Shiraz

Saddler's Creek make two Equus shirazes, one from their Hunter Valley base, one from McLaren Vale. CURRENT RELEASE 1998   This McLaren Vale version is made in a no-holds-barred style with plenty of sweet American oak. The nose has notes of dark berries, plum pud and licorice, with a strong overlay of toasty, coconut and vanillin oak. The concentrated palate follows suit exactly as expected with lots of deep ripe fruit and lots of that Yankee wood. Tannins are relatively moderate and there's a sweet, long, oaky aftertaste. Slap a T-bone on the barbie for this one.

| | |
|---|---|
| Quality | 🍷🍷🍷🍷 |
| Value | ★★★ |
| Grapes | shiraz |
| Region | McLaren Vale, SA |
| Cellar | 🍷 8 |
| Alc./Vol. | 14.0% |
| RRP | $40.00 |

## Salena Estate Cabernet Sauvignon

| | |
|---|---|
| Quality | ♥♥♥♀ |
| Value | ★★★★ |
| Grapes | cabernet sauvignon |
| Region | Murray Valley, SA |
| Cellar | ▮ 2 |
| Alc./Vol. | 13.5% |
| RRP | $15.00 |

Cabernet sauvignon has come ahead in leaps and bounds in Australia's irrigated vineyard areas. Yield control, improved viticulture and better winery techniques mean that wines like this can cut it easily in competition with those from warmer dryland vineyards. CURRENT RELEASE 1999　This has an attractively fresh nose, even though there's a fair whack of charry/sweet vanillin oak to it. Ripe black-fruit and berry aromas are there too, and the palate follows suit. Toasty, smoky, sweet oak flavours are interwoven with ripe berries in a medium-bodied package, and tannins are well modulated. Will suit lamb kebabs.

## Salena Estate Shiraz

| | |
|---|---|
| Quality | ♥♥♥♥ |
| Value | ★★★★♀ |
| Grapes | shiraz |
| Region | Murray Valley, SA |
| Cellar | ▮ 2 |
| Alc./Vol. | 13.8% |
| RRP | $15.00 |

Salena Estate is a new name to watch from South Australia's Murray Valley. The quality revolution that's taken place there in recent years has been exciting to watch.
CURRENT RELEASE 1999　Value for money is the thing here. This crowd-pleasing red offers no-fuss character and enjoyment at the same price as some pretty ordinary plonk. The nose is filled with intense dark berry aromas, spice, and liberal smoky oak. In the mouth it has succulent chewy ripe fruit of medium weight and some attractive spice, backed up by pleasantly dry, balanced tannins. A good red for chargrilled meats Turkish style.

## Salisbury Estate Cabernet Merlot

| | |
|---|---|
| Quality | ♥♥♥ |
| Value | ★★★ |
| Grapes | cabernet sauvignon; merlot |
| Region | Murray Valley, Vic. |
| Cellar | ▮ 1 |
| Alc./Vol. | 12.5% |
| RRP | $9.60 |

Salisbury's Murray Valley wines are very much in the cheap and cheerful mould. They are wines to drink young without too much analysis.
CURRENT RELEASE 2000　Not bad budget-wise, this inexpensive cabernet blend has a lightweight nose of sweet raspberries and herbs. The palate is a little light-on with a simple fruity flavour that falls away a bit in the middle. The finish is agreeably soft. Try it with burgers.

## Saltram Mamre Brook Cabernet Sauvignon

Like many of the prestigious labels of yesterday, Mamre Brook now occupies the middle ground of Australian wine. And unlike the variable quality of the expensive Mamre Brooks of thirty years ago, these days the wines are consistently good.

CURRENT RELEASE 1999  This has a robust nose which leans on a good measure of toasty, vanillin American oak, but dark plum and berry fruit character, and dark chocolatey notes keep it alive. The palate has concentrated fruit-sweet berry flavours, finely integrated with the oak. The dense texture and strength of flavour make it a chewy mouthful, and firm dry tannins support it nicely. It should cellar well. A solid red for a roast scotch fillet of beef.

| | |
|---|---|
| Quality | ♥♥♥♥♥ |
| Value | ★★★★→ |
| Grapes | cabernet sauvignon |
| Region | Barossa Valley, SA |
| Cellar | ➡ 2–8+ |
| Alc./Vol. | 14.5% |
| RRP | $21.00 |

## Sandalford Cabernet Sauvignon

A steady improvement in Sandalford's wines is continuing under the winemaking direction of Paul Boulden.

CURRENT RELEASE 1998  An attractive wine with a fragrant nose of aromatic berries and some minty/leafy touches, with oak playing a very subdued role. In the mouth it has blackcurrant/berry flavour of good intensity and more smooth depth than the nose would suggest. Tannins are ripe and fine-grained. A civilised red that improves with time in the glass. Serve it with veal chops.

| | |
|---|---|
| Quality | ♥♥♥♥ |
| Value | ★★★→ |
| Grapes | cabernet sauvignon |
| Region | Margaret River & Mount Barker, WA |
| Cellar | ▮ 6 |
| Alc./Vol. | 13.5% |
| RRP | $22.00 |

## Sandalford Shiraz

Sandalford's red wines don't quite get the accolades they deserve yet, but we think the shiraz is pretty good and getting better.

CURRENT RELEASE 1998  This is a rich, complex Western Australian shiraz that combines youthful dark cherry, earth and herby aromas with a hint of leathery maturity. Oak is well modulated. It's ripe-tasting and medium-bodied with good balance and a nicely chewy texture. A good drink-now proposition with Chinese braised beef and rice stick noodles, but worth a few years' cellar time as well.

| | |
|---|---|
| Quality | ♥♥♥♥♥ |
| Value | ★★★★→ |
| Grapes | shiraz |
| Region | Margaret River, Mount Barker, Frankland River & Swan Valley, WA |
| Cellar | ▮ 5 |
| Alc./Vol. | 13.5% |
| RRP | $22.00 |

## Sandhurst Ridge Cabernet Sauvignon

| | |
|---|---|
| Quality | ♥ ♥ ♥ ♥ ♥ |
| Value | ★ ★ ★ |
| Grapes | cabernet sauvignon |
| Region | Bendigo, Vic. |
| Cellar | ➥ 2–8 |
| Alc./Vol. | 13.0% |
| RRP | $34.00 |

Sandhurst Ridge is at Marong, the cradle of modern Bendigo region viticulture where Stuart Anderson planted his ground-breaking Balgownie vineyard in 1969. By the way, Sandhurst was Bendigo's original name.
CURRENT RELEASE 1999    In keeping with the Greblo brothers' house style, helped by another drought year in Victoria, this is a concentrated young wine with an intense nose of boiled-down blackcurrants, ink, and lead-pencils oak. The palate has the same sort of intensity with very tight curranty fruit flavour, a good dose of oak and a long finish. Dry tannins give some austerity to the flavour, which needs some years to evolve. In old Bendigo braised mutton would be the choice here.

## Sandhurst Ridge Shiraz

| | |
|---|---|
| Quality | ♥ ♥ ♥ ♥ |
| Value | ★ ★ ★ |
| Grapes | shiraz |
| Region | Bendigo, Vic. |
| Cellar | ➥ 2–8 |
| Alc./Vol. | 13.5% |
| RRP | $27.00 |

Central Victoria is spoken of in some circles as potentially Australia's greatest shiraz region. Sandhurst Ridge, near Bendigo, is one of the newer vineyards.
CURRENT RELEASE 1999    This young shiraz has quite strong regional character which manifests itself as a leafy character – minty and perhaps a hint of eucalypt. This gives the nose attractive freshness surrounding blackberry fruit aromas and a touch of sweet oak. The palate is full-flavoured and medium- to full-bodied with intense dark berry flavour and cedary oak. Dry tannins provide an attractive savoury signature. Try it with Turkish lamb pizza.

## Scarpantoni Block 3 Shiraz

| | |
|---|---|
| Quality | ♥ ♥ ♥ ♥ ♥ |
| Value | ★ ★ ★ ★ ♦ |
| Grapes | shiraz |
| Region | McLaren Vale, SA |
| Cellar | ➥ 1–5+ |
| Alc./Vol. | 14.5% |
| RRP | $23.00 |

Scarpantoni's reds offer plenty of big McLaren Vale flavour, which sometimes errs on the side of over-extraction. These emphatic qualities make them a very desirable commodity. Maker: Michael Scarpantoni.
CURRENT RELEASE 1999    Here is a big nose with ripe blackberry and sweet plum aromas of good concentration, an attractive mocha barrel-ferment touch, and a liberal seasoning of vanillin American oak. The palate is full-bodied and warmly satisfying with a strong core of ripe sweet fruit flavour, more tasty oak, good length and easy, relatively soft tannins. Lamb shaslicks would be excellent with this.

## Scarpantoni Cabernet Sauvignon

Cabernet in McLaren Vale often makes wines of less distinct varietal character than elsewhere. Yet their generous style means that it doesn't really matter, unless you're a real stickler for such things. Scarpantoni's French-oaked example is an exception.

CURRENT RELEASE 1999 There's a classy feel to this young cabernet with refined blackcurrant/berry fruit character, licorice and a hint of dark chocolate on the nose, all dressed up with a Bordeaux-like whiff of cedary oak. Good intensity of fruit in the mouth gives generous flavour which remains quite elegant for the Southern Vales. Fine-grained tannins carry a soft finish.

| | |
|---|---|
| Quality | 🍷🍷🍷🍷½ |
| Value | ★★★★★ |
| Grapes | cabernet sauvignon |
| Region | McLaren Vale, SA |
| Cellar | 5 |
| Alc./Vol. | 13.5% |
| RRP | $23.00 |

## Schinus Merlot

The Schinus range of wines gives Dromana Estate a budget-priced range, just the thing to improve cash-flow in expensive vineyard territory like the Mornington Peninsula. The wines are mainly sourced outside the region and can be pretty good.

CURRENT RELEASE 2000 This merlot is a great summer-weight red. The nose is fresh with succulent plum and cherry aromas, touched by a hint of sweet spice. It tastes gentle, soft and fruity, light-to-middling in body, and finishes soft and clean. Easy to sip with quails off the barbecue or chargrilled.

| | |
|---|---|
| Quality | 🍷🍷🍷½ |
| Value | ★★★½ |
| Grapes | merlot |
| Region | Goulburn Valley, Vic. & McLaren Vale, SA |
| Cellar | 2 |
| Alc./Vol. | 13.0% |
| RRP | $15.00 |

## Seaview Shiraz

Yet another label change gives the Seaview reds yet another look. The wines are now firmly locked into the bargain basement.

CURRENT RELEASE 2000 The colour is of medium depth and the nose has light earthy raspberry fruit aromas. It tastes straightforward with simple berry flavours touched by some charry oak. The finish is soft and easy. An unchallenging red to drink with lamb chops.

| | |
|---|---|
| Quality | 🍷🍷🍷 |
| Value | ★★★ |
| Grapes | shiraz |
| Region | not stated |
| Cellar | 2 |
| Alc./Vol. | 12.5% |
| RRP | $10.75 (S) |

## Seppelt Chalambar Shiraz

| | |
|---|---|
| Quality | ♟ ♟ ♟ ♟ ♟ |
| Value | ★ ★ ★ ★ ★ |
| Grapes | shiraz |
| Region | various, Vic. |
| Cellar | ▮ 7 |
| Alc./Vol. | 14.0% |
| RRP | $21.00 |

If we had a time machine, it would be great to go back and see how the legendary Chalambars of the 1950s and '60s stacked up against the current crop. Both the old and the new have enjoyed rave reviews over the years.
CURRENT RELEASE 1999    Chalambar continues to give excellent wine at a good price. This has a modern nose that's aromatic with peppery spice and seductively ripe black cherry fruit and chocolatey notes. Oak takes a back seat. In the mouth it continues juicy, ripe and spicy with real length and concentration, yet it's soft and approachable right now. It finishes long and fine with mild tannins. An adventurous combination with sautéed kidneys and Madeira sauce.

## Seppelt Dorrien Cabernet Sauvignon

| | |
|---|---|
| Quality | ♟ ♟ ♟ ♟ ♟ |
| Value | ★ ★ ★ ★ |
| Grapes | cabernet sauvignon |
| Region | Barossa Valley, SA |
| Cellar | ▮ 10 |
| Alc./Vol. | 13.0% |
| RRP | $57.00 |

It's pity that more wasn't made of the Seppelt 150th Anniversary in 2001. The name is one of Australia's greatest, and it's via the Seppelt connection that the Southcorp empire has gained some of Australia's best vineyard plots. Dorrien is one of them, providing benchmark cabernet to rival the best.
*Previous outstanding vintages: '82, '84, '87, '89, '90, '91, '92, '94*
CURRENT RELEASE 1996    Despite over five years of age this cabernet is still young. The colour is deep and dense, and the nose still has strong primary fruit characters in the blackcurrant liqueur and blackberry range. That fruit is fragrantly sweet with well-integrated spicy oak married into it seamlessly. The palate is juicy and long in lush sweet fruit, with fine-grained tannins dovetailed perfectly into it. Excellent with roast leg of lamb.

## Seppelt Drumborg Cabernet Sauvignon

Drumborg is Seppelt's outpost in the cool windswept terrain north of Portland in south-western Victoria. Things can get pretty marginal down there, therefore reds like this are only made every so often.

CURRENT RELEASE 1996   The word elegant is often misused when it comes to red wines. More often than not for 'elegant' read 'unripe', but this red fits the elegant descriptor well. It has distinct leafy, herby notes on the nose, but also tight blackcurrant and redcurrant fruit aromas that are blended into balanced spicy, cedary oak. There is good depth of flavour of the zippy blackcurrant type. It's medium-bodied and tangy, with nice length and moderate tannins. Simply made for racks of spring lamb.

| | |
|---|---|
| Quality | ★★★★½ |
| Value | ★★★ |
| Grapes | cabernet sauvignon |
| Region | Drumborg, Vic. |
| Cellar | 6+ |
| Alc./Vol. | 13.0% |
| RRP | $45.00 |

## Seppelt Great Western Vineyards Shiraz

Once a simple white label with a coat of arms and the words 'Seppelt Great Western' had the same cachet as the similarly plain-labelled Penfolds Bin Reds. A succession of differing managements, marketing strategies, and experts have conspired to reduce its status. Pity, since the wines are time-honoured Australian classics.

**CURRENT RELEASE 1997   An impenetrably deep youthful appearance looks the goods here, and the bouquet is lovely. With air it evolves with slightly Rhone-ish savouriness, subtle cherry and berry fruit, earth, undergrowth, a touch of walnut, and charry oak. The palate is the best part with a velvety texture and a deep rich flavour that lasts and lasts. This is one of those subtle reds that you keep going back to. Try it with roast beef and baked vegetables.**

| | |
|---|---|
| Quality | ★★★★★ |
| Value | ★★★★ |
| Grapes | shiraz |
| Region | Great Western, Vic. |
| Cellar | 8 |
| Alc./Vol. | 13.5% |
| RRP | $37.00 |

Penguin Wine
of the Year
&
Best Red Wine

## Seppelt Moyston Cabernet Shiraz

| | |
|---|---|
| Quality | ▼▼▼ |
| Value | ★★★ |
| Grapes | cabernet sauvignon; shiraz |
| Region | various, South East Australia |
| Cellar | ▮ 1 |
| Alc./Vol. | 13.0% |
| RRP | $9.00 ⑤ |

Moyston was once a stablemate for Chalambar in the old Seppelt scheme of things, Moyston was a 'claret' and Chalambar a 'burgundy', but both relied on Great Western shiraz for their high quality. These days Moyston is a bargain-basement brand of anonymous origins.
CURRENT RELEASE 1998 A simple dry red that's fair enough for the price. There's a bit of plummy fruit-sweetness to it on the nose, and it tastes of middleweight black fruit, backed by soft tannins. A quaffer to enjoy with fast food.

## Seppelt Terrain Series Shiraz

| | |
|---|---|
| Quality | ▼▼▼▼ |
| Value | ★★★▸ |
| Grapes | shiraz |
| Region | various, South East Australia |
| Cellar | ▮ 2 |
| Alc./Vol. | 13.5% |
| RRP | $11.50 |

Seppelt-branded wines cover all price points but there's a slightly confused feel about what fits where and why. Overall quality is good, due in no small part to the many years' work of recently retired chief winemaker Ian McKenzie.
CURRENT RELEASE 1998 This and its cabernet sibling have appealed to us quite a bit in recent years. The shiraz has deep colour and good concentration of blackberry and warm spice character. The palate is medium-weight with spicy berry jam shiraz flavour and mild tannins. Serve it with a mixed grill.

## Settlers Rise Montville Shiraz Cabernet Sauvignon

| | |
|---|---|
| Quality | ▼▼▼ |
| Value | ★★▸ |
| Grapes | shiraz; cabernet sauvignon |
| Region | Granite Belt, Burnett & Inglewood, Qld |
| Cellar | ▮ 2 |
| Alc./Vol. | 13.0% |
| RRP | $18.00 |

When most Aussies think of Queensland they don't think of vineyards. Coconut palms, pineapple plantations, mango trees, bananas – yes. Rows of vines – no. But in southern Queensland there's a fledgeling wine industry that's only just developing momentum. Maker: Peter Scudamore-Smith.
CURRENT RELEASE non-vintage Beneath a gaudy label is a simple sort of red wine with good colour and a pleasant nose of black fruits with light floral touches, earth and oak. It's rather plain without great weight and presence, but it tastes clean and pleasantly fresh. It's also good to note that it doesn't have any overt hot-climate characters. Try it with pork schnitzels.

## Sevenhill Shiraz

Some Christian groups have been heading the anti-alcohol lobby for centuries, but thankfully the Catholics don't share all that temperance stuff. Otherwise this lovely establishment wouldn't exist! CURRENT RELEASE 1999 This has a deep, dense colour. The nose is very concentrated in true Clare Valley fashion, and the palate follows through with power and intensity. It has blackberry, mint and a sort of dissolved mineral character that is a part of some traditionally made Clare reds. Oak is very much in the background and it has a big grip of tannin to hold it all together. A potent regional red that should be given long age, then it will go well with roast beef and Yorkshire pud.

| | |
|---|---|
| Quality | 🍷🍷🍷🍷 |
| Value | ★★★★⁴ |
| Grapes | shiraz |
| Region | Clare Valley, SA |
| Cellar | ➖ 2–12 |
| Alc./Vol. | 13.8% |
| RRP | $23.00 |

## Seville Estate Pinot Noir

Seville Estate has become more of a mainstream name since its takeover by Brokenwood with a new cellar door for visitors and some second labels to increase volume. CURRENT RELEASE 1999 The label boasts that this is unfiltered, the new catchword with the wine gurus of the USA, and sheep-like we follow. Of course, some of the greatest wines in the world are filtered and some aren't, so who cares? This has correct lightish pinot colour and the nose has strong undergrowthy and earthy scents as well as light plum and cherry fruit. It has a slight green thread but not too much for comfort. In the mouth it's better with some richness and depth ahead of a clean dry finish. Try it with duck.

| | |
|---|---|
| Quality | 🍷🍷🍷🍷 |
| Value | ★★★⁴ |
| Grapes | pinot noir |
| Region | Yarra Valley, Vic. |
| Cellar | 🍷 3 |
| Alc./Vol. | 14.0% |
| RRP | $26.00 |

## Shadowfax Pinot Noir

| | |
|---|---|
| Quality | ♼♼♼♼ |
| Value | ★★★★ |
| Grapes | pinot noir |
| Region | Geelong & Yarra Valley, Vic. |
| Cellar | ▯ 1 |
| Alc./Vol. | 13.0% |
| RRP | $26.00 |

Shadowfax is at Werribee, very close to the sprawl of Melbourne's suburbs, but the wines can be blended from other southern vineyards. Quality so far under winemaker Matt Harrop's direction has been promising. CURRENT RELEASE 2000    A bright young pinot with some juicy red-fruit and sappy aromas that are very fragrant and appealing. In the mouth it's uncomplicated, light and flavoursome with soft red-berry flavours of good length and moderate intensity. Unlike many cool-climate pinots there are no stemmy, green influences. The aftertaste is long, soft and sweet. There should be more pleasant, easy-to-glug pinot noirs like this one. Drink it in the first flush of youth with a terrine and crusty bread.

## Shottesbrooke Cabernet Sauvignon Merlot Malbec

| | |
|---|---|
| Quality | ♼♼♼♼ |
| Value | ★★★ |
| Grapes | cabernet sauvignon; merlot; malbec |
| Region | McLaren Vale, SA |
| Cellar | ▯ 5 |
| Alc./Vol. | 14.0% |
| RRP | $22.50 |

Honest regional red wines are Shottesbrooke's main claim to fame, sometimes with a touch of elegance that some of the neighbours lack.
CURRENT RELEASE 1999    A more mainstream McLaren Vale red than some Shottesbrookes, this has an earthy dark berry aroma that relies on fruit, with oak as a lightly applied condiment. The palate follows in line with the nose with earthy fruit, good depth and dry tannins. An easy-drinking cab which will suit sautéed kidneys well.

## Shottesbrooke Eliza Shiraz

| | |
|---|---|
| Quality | ♼♼♼♼♽ |
| Value | ★★★ |
| Grapes | shiraz |
| Region | McLaren Vale, SA |
| Cellar | ▯ 5 |
| Alc./Vol. | 13.5% |
| RRP | $36.50 |

A limited release of old-vine shiraz, named after a former owner of the oldest part of what is now Shottesbrooke. This is a limited release special. Maker: Nick Holmes.
CURRENT RELEASE 1998    This has deep colour and a really pure McLaren Vale shiraz nose that suggests old-vine concentration and softness in its smooth plummy aromas. In the mouth it's fruit-sweet, ripe and long-tasting with a hint of charry oak to season it. Tannins are very soft, making it an approachable, well-made wine right now. Serve it with fillet steak.

## Shottesbrooke Shiraz

Nick Holmes' Shottesbrooke wines sometimes have a bit more elegance than other McLaren Vale makers, perhaps due to having access to fruit from the higher-altitude, cooler Myponga vineyard.

CURRENT RELEASE 1999 The nose indicates a well-made, attractive McLaren Vale shiraz with blackberry and spice varietal aromas and a subdued hint of oak. The palate is medium-bodied with good fruit character and mouth-feel, but it finishes rather hard with astringent tannins. It's definitely too soon to drink now, but we suspect with a couple of years it will develop into the flavoursome, honest style the region is famous for. Serve it with grilled cavapcici (spiced skinless sausages).

| | |
|---|---|
| Quality | 🍷🍷🍷🍷 |
| Value | ★★★ |
| Grapes | shiraz |
| Region | McLaren Vale, SA |
| Cellar | 🍾 2–6 |
| Alc./Vol. | 14% |
| RRP | $22.00 |

## Skillogalee The Cabernets

Good riesling and foursquare reds are Clare Valley stock-in-trade and that's where Skillogalee excels. Maker: David Palmer.

CURRENT RELEASE 1998 The '98 Clare reds have great depth of colour, matched by outstandings levels of ripeness and personality in the wines. This is a good example with loads of sweet, ripe blackcurrant and blackberry fruit, touched harmoniously by integrated vanillin oak. There's also a hint of leafiness, but it's far less pronounced than the minty style that the Skillogalee winery sometimes produces. Fine-grained, ripe tannins fold into the wine seamlessly and there's a long aftertaste. A good match for lamb with a redcurrant sauce.

| | |
|---|---|
| Quality | 🍷🍷🍷🍷🍷 |
| Value | ★★★★ |
| Grapes | cabernet sauvignon; cabernet franc; malbec |
| Region | Clare Valley, SA |
| Cellar | 🍾 6+ |
| Alc./Vol. | 13.0% |
| RRP | $26.50 |

## Smithbrook Merlot

| | |
|---|---|
| Quality | ❦❦❦❦ |
| Value | ★★★ |
| Grapes | merlot |
| Region | Pemberton, WA |
| Cellar | ➥ 2–6 |
| Alc./Vol. | 13.8% |
| RRP | $23.00 |

Petaluma's Brian Croser, head honcho of Smithbrook these days, has faith in the Pemberton region as a source of excellent merlot. Maker: Michael Symons.
CURRENT RELEASE 1999   Merlot madness hasn't quite hit as it has in the USA, but there are already a lot of them around and you can expect more. This Western Australian example has good colour and good varietals of medium intensity on the nose. The fruit aroma is quite juicy, suggesting ripe cherries, along with some spiciness and cedary-dry oak. In the mouth that succulent fruit character chimes in early, then it dissolves into a dry finish with marked tannic grip. A firmly constructed young merlot that could (and should) become more giving with time in bottle. Try it with minute steaks.

## Spring Vale Pinot Noir

| | |
|---|---|
| Quality | ❦❦❦❦ |
| Value | ★★★ |
| Grapes | pinot noir |
| Region | East Coast, Tas. |
| Cellar | ▮ 2 |
| Alc./Vol. | 13.5% |
| RRP | $35.00 |

Spring Vale is a small Tasmanian operation with wines made by contract winemaker Andrew Hood, who is responsible for many of the smaller Tassie growers' products.
CURRENT RELEASE 1999   This is a light fine Tasmanian pinot with no green or stemmy traits to put you off. It has a pleasant, delicate nose of red fruits, candy and a hint of cedar. In the mouth it has light plummy flavour with a hint of caramel. It's soft and friendly with good length and balance. Try it with Tasmanian salmon.

## St Hallett Gamekeeper's Reserve

| | |
|---|---|
| Quality | ❦❦❦❦ |
| Value | ★★★♦ |
| Grapes | not stated |
| Region | Barossa Valley, SA |
| Cellar | ▮ 2 |
| Alc./Vol. | 13.5% |
| RRP | $12.50 |

Lady Chatterley should have stuck to the Gamekeeper's Reserve and left the gamekeeper alone. Less trouble all round.
CURRENT RELEASE 2000   A rather rustic little number that would appeal to a gamekeeper, this has a savoury nose of spices, earth, meaty notes and sweet small berries. The palate has dark fruit and spice flavours of good intensity and it tastes dry and soft on the finish. Best in the first flush of youth, try this with pasta.

## St Hallett The Reward Cabernet Sauvignon

The Reward is St Hallett's super cabernet, only released in exceptional vintages. The '96 is only the second such wine, and we can't remember ever tasting the initial '93 edition, as nearly all of it was consumed by the St Hallett crew themselves!

CURRENT RELEASE 1996 A classic varietal/regional wine, this is very Barossa. The bouquet has sweet, fragrant blackcurrant fruit at the core, typically dressed up in lots of sweet oak. There's also a suggestion of austerity about it. The palate is tightly constructed, again with intense sweet cabernet fruit surrounded by vanillin oak. The mouth-feel is good and tannins are fine and soft. Roast a leg of lamb to go with this.

| | |
|---|---|
| **Quality** | 🍷🍷🍷🍷½ |
| **Value** | ★★★ |
| **Grapes** | cabernet sauvignon |
| **Region** | Barossa Valley, SA |
| **Cellar** | 🍾 5 |
| **Alc./Vol.** | 13.5% |
| **RRP** | $43.00 |

## St Huberts Cabernet Merlot

St Huberts was Hubert de Castella's showpiece estate in the Yarra Valley's halcyon days of the 1800s. Unlike nearby wineries Yering Station and Yeringberg, the original buildings didn't survive, so there isn't quite the same sense of history here.

CURRENT RELEASE 1999 This has a loose-knit forward aroma that suggests soft fruits like raspberries and blackcurrant with a hint of cedary oak. It's an agreeable nose that lacks the concentration this estate is capable of. The palate is smooth and easy to like with soft easy tannins. A wine to drink reasonably young with sautéed veal.

| | |
|---|---|
| **Quality** | 🍷🍷🍷½ |
| **Value** | ★★★ |
| **Grapes** | cabernet sauvignon; merlot |
| **Region** | Yarra Valley, Vic. |
| **Cellar** | 🍾 2 |
| **Alc./Vol.** | 13.0% |
| **RRP** | $22.50 |

## St Huberts Reserve Cabernet Sauvignon

The '98 St Huberts standard cabernet was very impressive and this new Reserve wine takes things a step further. Maker: Fiona Purnell.

CURRENT RELEASE 1998 A very deep dense colour looks the goods here. The bouquet is fragrant and pure with sweet cassis, spice and harmoniously integrated cedary oak in lovely balance. The palate is concentrated, but elegant and not at all heavy. The flavour is smooth, silky and long, almost gentle for a substantial reserve cabernet. Very fine ripe tannins finish a stylish wine in excellent balance. Serve it with roast loin of lamb.

| | |
|---|---|
| **Quality** | 🍷🍷🍷🍷🍷 |
| **Value** | ★★★½ |
| **Grapes** | cabernet sauvignon |
| **Region** | Yarra Valley, Vic. |
| **Cellar** | 🍾 6 |
| **Alc./Vol.** | 13.5% |
| **RRP** | $42.00 |

## St Matthias Pinot Noir

| | |
|---|---|
| Quality | 🍷 🍷 🍷 |
| Value | ★ ★ ⁺ |
| Grapes | pinot noir |
| Region | Tamar Valley, Tas. |
| Cellar | 🍷 2 |
| Alc./Vol. | 13.2% |
| RRP | $22.00 |

Grown on the Tamar River in northern Tasmania, and now owned by Hobart's Moorilla Estate, St Matthias is benefiting from its new proprietors' expertise.
CURRENT RELEASE 2000    A pinot noir that treads the line between ripeness and slightly green 'Tassie' characters. There are red fruit and sappy touches on the nose, but it also strays into minty, vegetal territory. The palate has plum fruit of medium intensity with acidity giving it a snappy tang, but green-ish and stemmy edges to the flavour don't flatter it. Try it with a warm quail salad.

## Stanley Brothers Thoroughbred Cabernet

| | |
|---|---|
| Quality | 🍷 🍷 🍷 🍷 |
| Value | ★ ★ ★ |
| Grapes | cabernet sauvignon |
| Region | Barossa Valley, SA |
| Cellar | 🍷 5 |
| Alc./Vol. | 14.0% |
| RRP | $24.50 |

Experienced winemaker Lindsay Stanley bought this Barossa vineyard in 1994. Since then it's been a rather low-key operation, but wine quality hasn't been bad.
CURRENT RELEASE 1998    This is a simple Barossa dry red without much lustre or complexity. What you get is light berry fruit aromas dressed in some coconutty oak. The flavour is straightforward and of medium intensity, and it has good balance in the mouth. A competent wine that lacks excitement. Try it with sausages.

## Stanton and Killeen Cabernet Sauvignon Cabernet Franc Merlot

| | |
|---|---|
| Quality | 🍷 🍷 🍷 🍷 |
| Value | ★ ★ ★ ⁺ |
| Grapes | cabernet sauvignon; cabernet franc; merlot |
| Region | Rutherglen, Vic. |
| Cellar | 🍷 7 |
| Alc./Vol. | 14.0% |
| RRP | $23.50 |

This is a very modern blend of grapes for the Rutherglen district. Traditionally most reds were made from super-ripe shiraz.
CURRENT RELEASE 1998    An attractive nose with blackcurrant and blackberry fruit to the fore with some savoury earth and mulberry aromas underneath. A balanced robe of vanillin oak dresses things up nicely. In the mouth it's more traditionally constructed with sweet fruit in the middle of good depth and persistence. Fine tannins impart pleasant grip to the finish. A satisfying, well-made red to serve with roast beef.

## Stanton and Killeen Jack's Block Shiraz

The Jack in question was the late Jack Stanton, partner in S&K and a Rutherglen identity for many decades. Maker: Chris Killeen.

CURRENT RELEASE 1998 The Stanton and Killeen reds are more modern in style than the Rutherglen traditionals, but they still have tons of character. This shiraz improved with breathing, evolving earthy dark-fruit aromas of ripe, rustic intensity. There's also a hint of spicy new oak in there. The palate is rich with ripe blackberry flavour, dressed with a dab of oak, and it has a satisfying, smooth texture and good underlying structure. Try it with a chargrilled porterhouse.

| | |
|---|---|
| **Quality** | 🍷🍷🍷🍷 |
| **Value** | *** |
| **Grapes** | shiraz |
| **Region** | Rutherglen, Vic. |
| **Cellar** | (bottle) 10 |
| **Alc./Vol.** | 14.5% |
| **RRP** | $29.00 |

## Starvedog Lane Cabernet Sauvignon

The Starvedog Lane wines come from Hahndorf, that little corner of South Australia where oompah-pah bands, lederhosen, wurst and sauerkraut don't seem too out of place. Prosit!

CURRENT RELEASE 1998 Satisfyingly deep in colour, this has stylish concentration on the nose with juicy blackcurrant, dark-chocolate, spice and leafy aromas. The palate is ripe and fleshy with long blackcurrant, mint and oak flavours and firm, ripe tannins. An excellent cool-grown cabernet in fine Adelaide Hills style. Try it with butterflied and barbecued leg of lamb.

| | |
|---|---|
| **Quality** | 🍷🍷🍷🍷½ |
| **Value** | ****½ |
| **Grapes** | cabernet sauvignon |
| **Region** | Adelaide Hills, SA |
| **Cellar** | (bottle) 5+ |
| **Alc./Vol.** | 13.5% |
| **RRP** | $25.00 |

## Starvedog Lane Shiraz

This is a new label to watch. It's the result of a collaboration between BRL Hardy, who make the wines, and John and Helen Edwards, who own some of the vineyards responsible. Maker: Steve Pannell.

CURRENT RELEASE 1998 A very dense, deeply coloured shiraz that showcases cool-grown Adelaide Hills grapes in absolutely their best light. The nose is potent with dark berry and currant aromas, earthy touches, minty spices and subtle oak. In the mouth it has dense fruit character of great intensity, but no heaviness, stylish oak in the background and a fine structure of sinewy tannins to back it up. This is a complete wine of real potential. Try it with pot-roasted kid or baby lamb.

| | |
|---|---|
| **Quality** | 🍷🍷🍷🍷🍷 |
| **Value** | ***** |
| **Grapes** | shiraz |
| **Region** | Adelaide Hills, SA |
| **Cellar** | (bottle lying down) 2–8 |
| **Alc./Vol.** | 13.5% |
| **RRP** | $25.00 |

## Stefano Lubiana Primavera Pinot Noir

| | |
|---|---|
| Quality | ¶ ¶ ¶ ⫯ |
| Value | ★ ★ ⫯ |
| Grapes | pinot noir |
| Region | Derwent Valley, Tas. |
| Cellar | ▮ 1 |
| Alc./Vol. | 13.7% |
| RRP | $25.00 |

Stefano Lubiana is one of Tasmania's leaders when it comes to the capricious pinot noir grape. Primavera is his lighter, simpler version.

CURRENT RELEASE 2000    There's not a lot of stuffing here, but there's none of the awful green harshness we often see in 'second label' pinot noirs from cool-climate vineyards either. Instead there's a pleasant nose of light red berries and earth with hints of herbs. The palate is simple, fresh and fruity with a soft, easy finish, belying its relatively high alcohol. A wine to drink young and fresh with Tasmanian ocean trout.

## Stein's Robert Stein Reserve Shiraz

| | |
|---|---|
| Quality | ¶ ¶ ¶ ¶ |
| Value | ★ ★ ★ ⫯ |
| Grapes | shiraz |
| Region | Mudgee, NSW |
| Cellar | ⬷ 1–12+ |
| Alc./Vol. | 14.0% |
| RRP | $25.00 ▮ |
| | (cellar door) |

Bob Stein is descended from one of the German 'vine-dressers' brought to New South Wales by William Macarthur in the early 1800s to work on his Camden vineyard. Maker: Bob Stein.

CURRENT RELEASE 1998    Here's an attractive shiraz, showing peppermint and sweet berry aromas, and a typically tight, firm-tannin Mudgee palate. It is a wine of satisfying depth and nice fleshy texture, although the tannins are a little chewy on the finish. It will benefit from cellaring. Then it will go well with venison cutlets.

## Stonier Pinot Noir

| | |
|---|---|
| Quality | ¶ ¶ ¶ ¶ |
| Value | ★ ★ ★ |
| Grapes | pinot noir |
| Region | Mornington Peninsula, Vic. |
| Cellar | ▮ 2 |
| Alc./Vol. | 13.0% |
| RRP | $23.00 |

Pinot noir is one of Stonier's fortes; they make a Reserve wine that's more serious and substantial, and this less concentrated standard edition. Maker: Tod Dexter.

CURRENT RELEASE 2000    This is a bright young pinot with a light fruity nose of strawberry and a herbal, briary touch. The palate fulfils the requirements of a light red perfectly with tasty red berry-fruit flavour, soft mouth-feel and a gentle finish. That herbal thread tracks down the palate but doesn't quite stray into 'green' territory, thank goodness. A pleasant drink to enjoy with a selection of pâtés and terrines.

## Storm Ridge Merlot

At the Badger's Brook vineyard in the Yarra Valley, they keep the Storm Ridge label for wines made from non-estate fruit. This merlot predominantly comes from Victoria's High Country where the grape variety shows a lot of promise.

CURRENT RELEASE 1999 The colour is medium–dense, and the nose has authentic merlot aromas of plum and earth with a little whisper of sulfide giving it a European feel. The palate is smooth with soft tannins and a dry end. Try it with lamb's fry and bacon.

| | |
|---|---|
| **Quality** | 🍷🍷🍷½ |
| **Value** | ★★★ |
| **Grapes** | merlot; cabernet sauvignon |
| **Region** | Alpine & Yarra Valleys, Vic. |
| **Cellar** | 🍾 2 |
| **Alc./Vol.** | 13.7% |
| **RRP** | $21.00 |

## Storm Ridge Pinot Noir

In Victoria there's some talk of whether the Yarra Valley or the Mornington Peninsula is the best place for pinot noir. Amazingly Geelong and South Gippsland are often left out of the equation. Storm Ridge confuses the issue with a Yarra/Mornington blend.

CURRENT RELEASE 2000 This is a fresh pinot with varietal cherry and strawberry fruit on the nose, and a touch of smoky oak. It's sweet and fragrant, and the palate has intense red fruit flavours. It finishes long with good tannic structure for a young pinot and should evolve nicely over a couple of years. Try it with duckling with sour cherries.

| | |
|---|---|
| **Quality** | 🍷🍷🍷🍷 |
| **Value** | ★★★ |
| **Grapes** | pinot noir |
| **Region** | Yarra Valley & Mornington Peninsula, Vic. |
| **Cellar** | 1–4 |
| **Alc./Vol.** | 13.0% |
| **RRP** | $18.00 |

## T'Gallant Celia's White Pinot

This wine's about as white as Californian white zinfandel. That's to say, it's pink! Call it artistic licence . . . The grapes are red, but it's made much as you would make a chardonnay dry white wine, that is whole-bunch pressed, barrel-fermented, malolactic, etc.

CURRENT RELEASE 2000 The back label boasts about 'exquisite texture', and much as we hate to agree with label-speak, we do concur! The pale pink colour is turning onion-skin now, and the bouquet is smoky pinot with a trace of nutty oak. It really is rich and fleshy, complex, velvet-smooth and full of extract – a most satisfying rosé. Very, very drinkable with antipasto, but watch out for that alcohol!

| | |
|---|---|
| **Quality** | 🍷🍷🍷🍷½ |
| **Value** | ★★★½ |
| **Grapes** | pinot noir |
| **Region** | Mornington Peninsula, Vic. |
| **Cellar** | 🍾 2 |
| **Alc./Vol.** | 14.0% |
| **RRP** | $23.00 |

## T'Gallant Pinot Noir

| | |
|---|---|
| Quality | ♟ ♟ ♟ ♟ |
| Value | ✱ ✱ ✱ |
| Grapes | pinot noir |
| Region | Mornington Peninsula, Vic. |
| Cellar | ▮ 4 |
| Alc./Vol. | 14.0% |
| RRP | $29.00 |

T'Gallant's Kevin McCarthy is passionate about pinot noir and believes the site is the key to quality on the Mornington Peninsula. It's a fluky climate and a sheltered, north-facing, frost-free slope, on soil of moderate fertility, is the way to go. This wine is a blend of vineyards.
CURRENT RELEASE 2000   It's a pretty wine, and that's not a put-down. It's may lack a little in body, but the flavours are entertaining. There are sappy, stemmy aromas from whole-bunch fermentations, which will turn nicely undergrowthy in a year, some cherry and some other interesting pinoid complexities. The palate is smooth and sweet. Try it with minted lamb fillet.

## Tahbilk Cabernet Sauvignon

| | |
|---|---|
| Quality | ♟ ♟ ♟ ♟ |
| Value | ✱ ✱ ✱ |
| Grapes | cabernet sauvignon |
| Region | Goulburn Valley, Vic. |
| Cellar | ▮ 8 |
| Alc./Vol. | 13.0% |
| RRP | $20.00 |

Oddly the standard Tahbilk reds often seem to be more enjoyable wines than the expensive special prestige bins. They're still very traditional, but have a modicum of youthful fruit that makes them a more friendly drink.
CURRENT RELEASE 1998   This has traditional Tahbilk character but it also has youth on its side. The nose has berry fruit, earth and spice aromas, uncomplicated by the overt oak or barrel-ferment aromas that take over many a modern young red. The palate is soft with savoury earth and berry characters and surprisingly smooth but still dry tannins. Serve it with a beef casserole.

## Tahbilk Reserve Shiraz

| | |
|---|---|
| Quality | ♟ ♟ ♟ |
| Value | ✱ ✱ |
| Grapes | shiraz |
| Region | Goulburn Valley, Vic. |
| Cellar | ▮ 1 |
| Alc./Vol. | 12.5% |
| RRP | $64.50 |

The old-fashioned label on this special edition Tahbilk shiraz evokes a bygone age. So does the wine inside. It's like a time capsule showing where Australian wine used to be.
CURRENT RELEASE 1994   This has an aged brick-reddish colour and the nose is very old-fashioned and oxidative. The nose has leathery dry smells with old spice and desiccated-fruit aromas. The palate is medium-bodied with rather attenuated dried-out fruit and an aged astringency that's positively unwelcoming. This really is questionable value. Braised steak and onions may help.

# Talijancich Shiraz

This is Shaggy meets Julie Andrews: full of good intentions but a bit too funky to be respectable. Winemaker is James Talijancich.
CURRENT RELEASE 1999    The bouquet comes over all fumey and sump-oily with oddball secondary characters instead of primary fruit. In the mouth it's dry and savoury, with slightly chewy tannins. There's no shortage of flavour and those less-nitpicking souls will enjoy it. Take it to a smoky barbecue.

| | |
|---|---|
| Quality | ▼ ▼ ▼ |
| Value | ★ ★ ꝯ |
| Grapes | shiraz |
| Region | Swan Valley, WA |
| Cellar | ▮ 5 |
| Alc./Vol. | 14.0% |
| RRP | $29.00 ▮ |

# Taltarni Merlot

There is life at Taltarni after Dominique Portet and Greg Gallagher. Current winemaker is Shane Clohesy. But they're still leaving their reds in oak a long time: this spent two years in French barriques.
CURRENT RELEASE 1997    It's showing its age, with a medium–full brick-red colour and a dusty, earthy, somewhat dried-out bouquet. There's more than sufficient tannin and the impression on palate is dry, leathery and faintly bitter. It has good persistence but we'd love to see a bit more fruit. Try it with cassoulet.

| | |
|---|---|
| Quality | ▼ ▼ ▼ ꝯ |
| Value | ★ ★ ꝯ |
| Grapes | merlot |
| Region | Pyrenees, Vic. |
| Cellar | ▮ 5 |
| Alc./Vol. | 14.0% |
| RRP | $32.00 ▮ |

# Taltarni Rosé

Snappy packaging here! Colourful print on a clear-glass bottle makes it look all summery and fun. It's a time-honoured tradition at this winery to use malbec for rosé.
CURRENT RELEASE 2000    The colour is a fresh and vibrant medium–full pink–purple, and the aroma recalls freshly crushed vine-leaves and berries. It smells as though the grapes were picked early. It tastes very lean, tangy and dry, with some green-fruit nuances. The texture could be more palate-friendly. Try it with frittata.

| | |
|---|---|
| Quality | ▼ ▼ ▼ ꝯ |
| Value | ★ ★ ★ ꝯ |
| Grapes | malbec; shiraz |
| Region | Pyrenees, Vic. |
| Cellar | ▮ 2 |
| Alc./Vol. | 12.5% |
| RRP | $15.75 |

## Tarlina Coonawarra Cabernet Sauvignon

| | |
|---|---|
| Quality | 🍷🍷🍷🍷 |
| Value | ★★★↓ |
| Grapes | cabernet sauvignon |
| Region | Coonawarra, SA |
| Cellar | 🍷 6 |
| Alc./Vol. | 13.0% |
| RRP | $15.00 Ⓢ |

Where in tarnation is Tarlina? Well may you ask. It's a name that was dreamt up by the marketing boffins at Norman's for their newest brand. It apparently comes from an Aboriginal word meaning 'one', and represents the notion of one region, one grape variety.
CURRENT RELEASE 1998   A fresh, bouncy young wine, filled with the Ribena/cassis-like fruit typical of a lighter Coonawarra cab. There are leafy and blueberry cool-grown elements. It's fruit-driven and fairly straightforward, and goes with lamb shawarma.

## Tarrawarra MDB Pinot Noir

| | |
|---|---|
| Quality | 🍷🍷🍷🍷🍷 |
| Value | ★★★ |
| Grapes | pinot noir |
| Region | Yarra Valley, Vic. |
| Cellar | 🍷 5+ |
| Alc./Vol. | 14.0% |
| RRP | $95.00 (cellar door) |

We include this just for the record, as it's a rare, one-off barrel selection of great interest from one of Australia's finest pinot noir producers. The initials stand for Marc and Daniel Besen, the owners, and why the heck not! Not everyone can manage pinot of this quality! It's a cracker. Maker: Clare Halloran. Only 567 bottles made.
CURRENT RELEASE 1998   The bouquet is filled with barrel and *sousbois* characters and it has quite a spooky overtone of Burgundy. It's big on secondary (as opposed to grapey) flavours, is deep and long and improves with air. It'll be even better next year. Serve with roast guinea fowl.

## Tarrawarra Pinot Noir

| | |
|---|---|
| Quality | 🍷🍷🍷🍷 |
| Value | ★★★ |
| Grapes | pinot noir |
| Region | Yarra Valley, Vic. |
| Cellar | ➥ 1–4+ |
| Alc./Vol. | 14.0% |
| RRP | $46.50 |

Tarrawarra's is consistently one of the most convincing pinot noirs in Australia. The '99 saw just 25 per cent new oak, which is a blessing. It was a difficult vintage, with hot spells interspersed with rain. Maker: Clare Halloran.
*Previous outstanding vintages: '94, '96, '97, '98*
CURRENT RELEASE 1999   From a less than ideal vintage, this is a comedown from the stellar '98, but still a good wine. The colour is medium red–purple and it smells closed, with hints of plum and an overriding vegetable, celery-like aroma. There's a suggestion of raisined fruit. It has some of the desirable plum/cherry flavours but without great fluency. The tannins are smooth and supple, and it's not woody. It should repay short-term cellaring, then drink with meaty lasagne.

## Tatachilla McLaren Vale Cabernet Sauvignon

Chief winemaker Michael Fragos was a finalist in *Gourmet Traveller Wine Magazine*'s Winemaker of the Year award for 2000.

CURRENT RELEASE 1999    Another excellent red from this ultra-reliable maker. It's a little closed on the nose at present, showing traces of dominant toasty oak, but it should 'come up' with a little time in the cellar. It's a solidly built red which harbours sweet berry-jam and anise flavours. It's smooth, savoury and dry on the palate with fairly grippy tannins that need time. A cellar special. It will do justice to roast beef.

| | |
|---|---|
| Quality | ♥ ♥ ♥ ♥ ♥ |
| Value | ★ ★ ★ ★ ⁾ |
| Grapes | cabernet sauvignon |
| Region | McLaren Vale, SA |
| Cellar | ➥ 2–12+ |
| Alc./Vol. | 14.0% |
| RRP | $23.00 |

## Tatachilla McLaren Vale Shiraz

In 2000, Tatachilla united with St Hallett in Banksia Wines, a company designed to help both of them expand their sales in export destinations. Maker: Michael Fragos.

CURRENT RELEASE 1999    The deep, dark colour is impressive; so are the sweet plummy, oaky aromas and the chunky density of the palate. It has serious depth of flavour but just misses out on the finer points of nuance and elegance. Generous, chewy and ripe, it will satisfy most palates. Try it with stewed venison.

| | |
|---|---|
| Quality | ♥ ♥ ♥ ♥ ♥ |
| Value | ★ ★ ★ ★ ⁾ |
| Grapes | shiraz |
| Region | McLaren Vale, SA |
| Cellar | 8 |
| Alc./Vol. | 14.0% |
| RRP | $23.00 |

## Taylors Cabernet Sauvignon

In the UK, Taylors wines are labelled Wakefield Estate because of the obvious conflict of name with the great Portuguese port company. The new regime at Taylors of Neil Jericho and Adam Eggins has had a welcome effect on the reds.

CURRENT RELEASE 1999    This was released a shade immature for our tastes, but has the makings of a top bottle if cellared. The colour is a vivid purple–red, and it smells of youthful sweet, ripe blackberry fruit and smartly handled oak. The taste is fleshy and smoothly tannic. There are some 'cooked' aromas and hints of overripe fruit. It's keen value. Try it with rare roast beef.

| | |
|---|---|
| Quality | ♥ ♥ ♥ ♥ |
| Value | ★ ★ ★ ★ ⁾ |
| Grapes | cabernet sauvignon |
| Region | Clare Valley, SA |
| Cellar | ➥ 2–12 |
| Alc./Vol. | 13.5% |
| RRP | $17.00 Ⓢ |

## Taylors St Andrews Cabernet Sauvignon

| | |
|---|---|
| Quality | ♥ ♥ ♥ ♥ ♥ |
| Value | ★ ★ ★ ★ |
| Grapes | cabernet sauvignon |
| Region | Clare Valley, SA |
| Cellar | 🍷 10 |
| Alc./Vol. | 13.0% |
| RRP | $48.50 🍷 |

St Andrews is a historic old property with a derelict stone winery, which Taylors bought and replanted several years ago. The St Andrews brand has become their flagship label.

CURRENT RELEASE 1997    Very impressive, although it appears to be developing quite quickly. The colour is medium brick-red, and the bouquet shows mellow aged characters, reflected in the mouth. It has a liberal splash of coconutty, vanillin oak and some smoky barrel-ferment complexities. Lovely aged berry flavours abound on the palate, together with concentration and fleshiness. A satisfying red to go with aged cheeses.

## Thomas Shiraz

| | |
|---|---|
| Quality | ♥ ♥ ♥ ♥ |
| Value | ★ ★ ★ ✦ |
| Grapes | shiraz |
| Region | Hunter Valley, NSW & McLaren Vale, SA |
| Cellar | ⬤ 2–8+ |
| Alc./Vol. | 13.6% |
| RRP | $32.00 (cellar door) |

Andrew Thomas, former red winemaker at Tyrrells and son of McLaren Vale winemaker Wayne Thomas, is doing his own thing in the Hunter. Having been brought up in the Vale, and worked mostly in the Hunter, he's combined the two in this wine.

CURRENT RELEASE 1999    Lovely colour: it's a very deep, vivid purple–red. The wine shows good concentration all around. The bouquet holds clean, fresh, undeveloped plum and vanilla aromas. The palate is ripe and round, with chocolate/plum flavours well meshed, and plenty of grainy tannin that should help it age. It goes well with beef casserole.

## Tim Adams Aberfeldy Shiraz

| | |
|---|---|
| Quality | ♥ ♥ ♥ ♥ ♥ |
| Value | ★ ★ ★ ✦ |
| Grapes | shiraz |
| Region | Clare Valley, SA |
| Cellar | ⬤ 2–12+ |
| Alc./Vol. | 14.0% |
| RRP | $49.00 🍷 |

Aberfeldy was planted in 1904: it's the sort of dry-grown, low-yield, old-vine fruit that finds its way into many of South Australia's most statuesque reds. Winemaker Tim Adams put this shiraz into new American oak for 22 months, and it doesn't show.

CURRENT RELEASE 1999    This is a big but elegant red in which the fruit does the talking. The colour is a youthful purple–red and it smells grassy, herbal, minty and cherried. The flavours are likewise pristine: deep and sweet and finished off by a drying tannin grip that leaves a savoury impression. It's long and delicious, promising to last for many years. Drink with steak and kidney pie.

## Tim Adams Shiraz

Tim Adams gives full credit to his grapegrowers. The back label lists four separate vineyards by name. Hopefully, no one will use this information to poach his growers!

CURRENT RELEASE 1999 The grapes do all the talking here. It's a trad Clare style. The colour is deep purple–red; the aromas are undeveloped and raw: sweet, ripe and slightly straightforward Clare shiraz in an ultra-ripe, almost porty berry-jam spectrum. There's a hint of peppermint. It's big, full, soft and round in the mouth, and demands time to build complexity. Then have it with steak.

| | |
|---|---|
| **Quality** | 🍷🍷🍷🍷 |
| **Value** | ★★★★ |
| **Grapes** | shiraz |
| **Region** | Clare Valley, SA |
| **Cellar** | 2–10 |
| **Alc./Vol.** | 14.0% |
| **RRP** | $19.00 |

## Tim Adams The Fergus

This wine takes its name from the grapegrower, Ferg Mahon. It's mainly grenache, with a small benison of other varieties, and is given a short (nine-month) term in wood. Grenache tends to oxidise easily if left in barrel too long. The price is a gift.

**CURRENT RELEASE 1999 Truly scrumptious stuff! The colour is medium red with purple flashes. It smells pepperminty, clean and fragrant with licorice and sweet oak scents. It tastes very smooth and spicy, with dominant cherry/anise flavours, fine balance and length, finishing with a note of bitter cherry. Great with chicken liver and mushroom pâté.**

| | |
|---|---|
| **Quality** | 🍷🍷🍷🍷🍷 |
| **Value** | ★★★★★ |
| **Grapes** | grenache; cabernet sauvignon; cabernet franc; shiraz |
| **Region** | Clare Valley, SA |
| **Cellar** | 7 |
| **Alc./Vol.** | 14.0% |
| **RRP** | $20.65 |

Penguin Best Red Blend/ Other Variety

## Tin Cows Pinot Noir

The Tin Cows wines from Tarrawarra are a range of smartly packaged, well-made wines that used to go under the successful Tunnel Hill label. We wonder at the wisdom of replacing a widely accepted brand with an arty new one, but time will tell.

CURRENT RELEASE 2000 There's a hint of the Tarrawarra style in this young pinot but it's made to be a less concentrated, early-drinking type. The nose has correct, sappy, cherry and spiced plum varietal aromas that lead to a tasty palate of medium fruit intensity. The finish is dry and slightly hard. Try it with duck confit.

| | |
|---|---|
| **Quality** | 🍷🍷🍷½ |
| **Value** | ★★★ |
| **Grapes** | pinot noir |
| **Region** | Yarra Valley, Vic. |
| **Cellar** | 2 |
| **Alc./Vol.** | 13.5% |
| **RRP** | $25.00 |

## Tin Cows Shiraz

**Quality** 🍷🍷🍷½
**Value** ★★★
**Grapes** shiraz
**Region** Yarra Valley, Vic.
**Cellar** 3
**Alc./Vol.** 12.7%
**RRP** $25.00

The Tin Cows graze peacefully under a stand of trees at Tarrawarra. Once you realise that the Besen family who own the vineyard are great patrons of the arts you understand what they're doing there.

CURRENT RELEASE 1999 This is a rather wild, rustic cool-climate shiraz, quite at odds with the usual Australian style. The nose is smoky and earthy with a hint of game and a touch of caramel. Sweet berry and plum aromas and flavours track down the smooth palate which has a friendly soft finish. Try it with braised duck and winter vegetables.

## Tom King Valley Merlot

**Quality** 🍷🍷🍷🍷½
**Value** ★★★
**Grapes** merlot
**Region** King Valley, Vic.
**Cellar** 7
**Alc./Vol.** 14.5%
**RRP** $53.00 (S)

Tom Garrett is the son of winemaker Andrew Garrett. The young feller was only 12 when his name was immortalised as a brand-name. With good cellaring, it should see him to his twenty-first birthday party.

CURRENT RELEASE 1998 Three years of age before release have paid dividends: this is a smooth, fleshy, delicious drink, as merlot ought to be and so rarely is. The nose has complex burnt-toast, gamy, oaky and slight Vegemite-like aromas. It shows best on palate, where it has liberal sweet cherry and raspberry fruit buried inside a serious tannin structure. It has pleasing texture, good intensity and length. Try it with duck.

## Torbreck Runrig

**Quality** 🍷🍷🍷🍷½
**Value** ★★½
**Grapes** shiraz 97%; viognier 3%
**Region** Barossa Valley, SA
**Cellar** 3–15+
**Alc./Vol.** 14.5%
**RRP** $100.00

This is Torbreck's flagship, a shiraz modelled on Cote Rotie, where they traditionally blend a little viognier white wine into the red. This is thought to raise the acidity, intensify the colour (amazingly) and add complexity. Maker: Dave Powell.

CURRENT RELEASE 1998 From a great vintage, this is a massively concentrated, densely coloured wine. It's richly endowed with ripe plummy fruit and although more oaky than other Torbreck reds, it's not at all excessive. The downside is that it's too thick, heavy and tannic to enjoy for many years. The texture is dense and chewy, but the fruit-sweetness is seductive. Cellar, then serve with beef wellington.

## Torbreck The Descendant

Dave Powell created this wine from newer vineyards but using the same varietal mix and winemaking approach as his icon wine, Runrig. Hence, it's a descendant of Runrig.

CURRENT RELEASE 1999   It's built very much in the heroic style of Torbreck's other wines: thick and syrupy, with very dark colour and plenty of density. The difference with Powell's wines is that the oak is subtle compared to many other 'name' Barossa reds. There's an element of greenness in this one, with plum and plum-skin aromas, some garden herbs and somewhat straightforward flavour (at this early stage). It needs time; then serve with beef casserole.

| | |
|---|---|
| Quality | ￥ ￥ ￥ ￥ ￥ |
| Value | ★ ★ ★ ￧ |
| Grapes | shiraz 93%; viognier 7% |
| Region | Barossa Valley, SA |
| Cellar | ➡ 2–10+ |
| Alc./Vol. | 14.0% |
| RRP | $55.00 |

## Torbreck The Factor

Another new wine from Torbreck, made in minuscule quantity that will be hard to find and increasingly expensive. At least Dave Powell tells us he's calling a halt on new wines, and will be using any extra fruit to increase the 'make' of each.

CURRENT RELEASE 1998   All shiraz, aged in older barrels, this is a delicious, plump, satiny Barossa of the sort Powell seems to produce with ease. There are toasty barrel-aged aromas merging seamlessly with spicy, plummy, chocolatey fruit. Smooth, full-bodied, opulent in the mouth, it's beaut now but will surely cellar well. Try with stewed venison.

| | |
|---|---|
| Quality | ￥ ￥ ￥ ￥ ￥ |
| Value | ★ ★ ★ ★ |
| Grapes | shiraz |
| Region | Barossa Valley, SA |
| Cellar | ➡ 1–12+ |
| Alc./Vol. | 13.5% |
| RRP | $55.00 |

## Torbreck The Steading

| | |
|---|---|
| Quality | ♜♜♜♜♜ |
| Value | ★★★★★ |
| Grapes | grenache 60%; mataro 20%; shiraz 20% |
| Region | Barossa Valley, SA |
| Cellar | 🍾 12+ |
| Alc./Vol. | 14.5% |
| RRP | $32.50 🍾 |

Torbreck was established by ex-Rockford employee David Powell in 1994. He share-farms a number of small, old Barossa vineyards as well as his own small plantings. The wines have become darlings of the US collecting mafia. The winery is at Marananga.
*Previous outstanding vintages: '96, '97, '98*
CURRENT RELEASE 1999    This is our favourite of all the current Torbreck wines. It's power-packed and profound, but retains a degree of elegance. It has a deepish purple–red colour and smells ripely spicy, with subtle oak-matured, complex secondary characteristics that build into a haunting perfume if it's given time to breathe. It tastes supple and savoury with smooth yet drying tannins to close. Beautiful balance: a complex wine. Serve it with seared kangaroo fillets.

## Touchwood Pinot Noir

| | |
|---|---|
| Quality | ♜♜♜♜ |
| Value | ★★★⯪ |
| Grapes | pinot noir |
| Region | Coal Valley, Tas. |
| Cellar | 🍾 3 |
| Alc./Vol. | 13.5% |
| RRP | $25.00 (cellar door) |

This is a tiny, 5-hectare vineyard at Tea Tree in the Coal Valley, owned by the Sexton family. The wine was made by Alain Rousseau at Moorilla Estate.
CURRENT RELEASE 1999    An interesting pinot in a slightly feral, meaty style. The nose shows charred oak and perhaps a hint of sulfide, but nothing objectionable. It comes into its own on palate. Full-bodied and rich, it has very deep, persistent flavour and a lovely silky texture. It would go well with veal cutlets and roast tomato aioli.

## Tower Estate Cabernet Sauvignon

| | |
|---|---|
| Quality | ♜♜♜♜♜ |
| Value | ★★★★⯪ |
| Grapes | cabernet sauvignon |
| Region | Coonawarra, SA |
| Cellar | ➥ 3–15+ |
| Alc./Vol. | 14.0% |
| RRP | $35.00 🍾 (cellar door) |

Tower Estate is the new deluxe focal point of the Hunter. Attached to it is Tower Lodge, a luxury accommodation complex the likes of which the region has never seen before. Len Evans is behind it, so everything is in impeccable taste.
CURRENT RELEASE 1999    Serious vino! From grapes supplied by Yalumba, this is one of the more impressive '99 Coonawarras we've seen. Toasty oak dominates the bouquet at present but it's just an infant. The palate is deep, powerful and rich in ripe berry flavours. It's firmly tannic to close and just oozes style. It needs time and when mature will be great with aged hard cheeses.

## Trentham Estate Pinot Noir

Trentham Estate is named after Trentham Cliffs, a high place looking over the Murray River and home to the winery, restaurant and cellar-door sales of the Murphy family enterprise.

CURRENT RELEASE 2000   You'd have to say the Murray Valley ain't the preferred place to grow pinot for table wine. But the Murphys do a creditable job. The wine has simple plum-skin aromas with some green elements, and the flavour is plain, fruity and falls away on the finish, with prominent acidity. It's a decent wine at the price, and goes with veal parmigiana.

| | |
|---|---|
| Quality | ♥ ♥ ♥ |
| Value | ★ ★ ★ ⅃ |
| Grapes | pinot noir |
| Region | Murray Valley, NSW |
| Cellar | ▯ 2 |
| Alc./Vol. | 13.0% |
| RRP | $14.00 ⓢ |

## Turkey Flat Rosé

Turkey Flat is owned and run by the Schulz family at Tanunda. Its 36 hectares of vineyards contain some of the oldest vines in the Barossa, and that's saying something. Winemaker is Peter Schulz.

CURRENT RELEASE 2000   Made from an eclectic pot-pourri of grape varieties, this rosé has a hot purple–pink colour and a confection-like aroma recalling chocolate-coated raspberries. It's soft, light and very fruity, finishing with considerable sweetness, so we recommend a thorough chill. It could team well with devils on horseback.

| | |
|---|---|
| Quality | ♥ ♥ ♥ ⅃ |
| Value | ★ ★ ★ ⅃ |
| Grapes | grenache; shiraz; cabernet sauvignon |
| Region | Barossa Valley, SA |
| Cellar | ▯ 2 |
| Alc./Vol. | 14.0% |
| RRP | $18.60 |

CURRENT RELEASE 2001   This is something of a departure: previous vintages were made from grenache. A very appealing drink, even if it is kind of big for a rosé. The colour is medium–light hot pink–purple, and it has a charming aroma of soft, earthy, cherry-ish fruit. It's quite sweet at first, and fills out in the middle with ample grenache-like confectionery flavour, and tails off quickly, as you'd expect a rosé to do. It's very quaffable, served chilled with antipasti.

| | |
|---|---|
| Quality | ♥ ♥ ♥ ⅃ |
| Value | ★ ★ ★ ⅃ |
| Grapes | shiraz; grenache; cabernet sauvignon; dolcetto |
| Region | Barossa Valley, SA |
| Cellar | ▯ 2 |
| Alc./Vol. | 10.7% |
| RRP | $18.00 |

## Turkey Flat Shiraz

| | |
|---|---|
| Quality | ♥♥♥♥ |
| Value | ★★★ |
| Grapes | shiraz |
| Region | Barossa Valley, SA |
| Cellar | ➥ 2–8+ |
| Alc./Vol. | 14.0% |
| RRP | $44.00 🍾 |

The label proudly proclaims that this shiraz was based on the fruit of vines that were planted before the American Civil War, and the Russian Revolution, in 1847. Ponder on that!

CURRENT RELEASE 1999    This is a babe, and needs time to allow the vanilla and chocolate flavours from the barrels to mellow into the wine. There are plum aromas behind the toasty oak and it will certainly come good. It's soft, rich and rounded in the mouth, typical of the district, and just falls away slightly on the finish. The tannins are soft and generous. Drink with civet of hare.

## Tyrrells Brokenback Shiraz

| | |
|---|---|
| Quality | ♥♥♥♥ |
| Value | ★★★ |
| Grapes | shiraz |
| Region | Hunter Valley, NSW |
| Cellar | 🍾 7+ |
| Alc./Vol. | 13.5% |
| RRP | $22.00 Ⓢ |

This belongs in Tyrrells' individual vineyard range, with the (for Tyrrells) snappy modern packaging. It has less of the typical Hunter character than you might expect, but that's probably the '98 vintage talking.

CURRENT RELEASE 1998    It smells of plum, vanilla and chocolate with a suspicion of coconutty American oak. There are some meaty undertones and we suspect the traditional leathery/earthy regional character will show up with a little age. It has a lean, angular palate with a moderate grip. Plum-cherry fruit leads the way and it will reward short-term cellaring. It goes with minute steak.

## Tyrrells Rufus Stone Merlot

| | |
|---|---|
| Quality | ♥♥♥♥ |
| Value | ★★★⟩ |
| Grapes | merlot |
| Region | McLaren Vale, SA |
| Cellar | ➥ 1–10 |
| Alc./Vol. | 14.5% |
| RRP | $22.00 🍾 |

Tyrrells is a Hunter-based company but – at least for red wines – it's been roving far and wide for grapes to make more modern, full-flavoured wines that the market wants. Shades of Rosemount. Maker: Andrew Spinaze.

CURRENT RELEASE 1999    This is a very fresh style, verging on raw, and if the truth be known it's on sale a bit too soon. The colour is vivid purple and it smells of simple, quite undeveloped herbal/plum fruit. It appears to have been made very protectively – that is, with strict exclusion of air – making it taste a bit unfinished. The fruit quality is exceptional, though. Cellar, then serve with rack of venison.

## Tyrrells Stevens Reserve Shiraz

The grapes come from Neil and George Stevens' vineyard at Pokolbin. The oldest vines were planted in 1865. Maker: Andrew Spinaze.

CURRENT RELEASE 1997    Not a great year for Hunter reds, but the best growers turned in useful fruit. This has a typical ageing, medium–red colour. The bouquet carries some leathery, earthy regional character along with straw and raspberry/cherry characters. There are hints of jam and pencil-shavings. It's light- to medium-bodied in the mouth and the structure is soft and smooth in typical 'Hunter burgundy' style. The tannins are mellow already. Try it with ripe brie.

| | |
|---|---|
| Quality | ♖ ♖ ♖ ♖ |
| Value | ★ ★ ★ ⸱ |
| Grapes | shiraz |
| Region | Hunter Valley, NSW |
| Cellar | ▮ 6 |
| Alc./Vol. | 13.0% |
| RRP | $28.00 |

## Voyager Estate Cabernet Merlot

Voyager is the impressive winery and vineyard of Perth mining businessman Michael Wright. It has a 60-hectare vineyard which began life as Freycinet in 1978. The rose gardens and landscaped grounds are a sight to behold.

CURRENT RELEASE 1997    The colour shows some premature age and the wine smells very gamy, vegetal and minty. The impression of slightly underripe fruit is confirmed when you taste: it's just a wee bit hollow, with tart herbal and tomato flavours predominating. Try it with minted roast lamb.

| | |
|---|---|
| Quality | ♖ ♖ ♖ |
| Value | ★ ★ ⸱ |
| Grapes | cabernet sauvignon; merlot |
| Region | Margaret River, WA |
| Cellar | ▮ 4 |
| Alc./Vol. | 13.5% |
| RRP | $38.70 |

## Warrenmang Black Puma Shiraz

The Black Puma is a legendary creature that stalks the hills and valleys of Victoria's Pyrenees region. Proof of its existence is shaky, but go up there on a still night and you can *feel* something. Or maybe it's just the after-effects of big reds like this one.

CURRENT RELEASE 1998    These flavoursome reds became regional benchmarks in the '90s due to their great consistency. This is right in the mould: a concentrated nose of syrupy blackberries and chocolatey oak with less mint and eucalypt than some neighbours. The flavour is powerful, full-bodied and long with solid texture and firm tannins. Cellar, then serve with braised oxtail.

| | |
|---|---|
| Quality | ♖ ♖ ♖ ♖ ♖ |
| Value | ★ ★ ★ ⸱ |
| Grapes | shiraz |
| Region | Pyrenees, Vic. |
| Cellar | ⸱ 2–10+ |
| Alc./Vol. | 14.0% |
| RRP | $60.00 |

## Warrenmang Cabernet Sauvignon

| | |
|---|---|
| Quality | ♟ ♟ ♟ ♟ ♟ |
| Value | ★ ★ ★ ★ |
| Grapes | cabernet sauvignon |
| Region | Pyrenees, Vic. |
| Cellar | ➥ 3–10+ |
| Alc./Vol. | 13.5% |
| RRP | $30.00 |

The Bazzanis brought a great deal of restaurant and hospitality industry experience with them when they bought Warrenmang. It's a great base for touring the vineyards of the surrounding Pyrenees district.
CURRENT RELEASE 1999 Concentrated in true Pyrenees fashion, this young cabernet has a nose of potent plum and black-fruit aromas that are sweet and ripe, with leafy hints, some dark chocolatey richness and restrained oak treatment. The solid palate is full-bodied and crammed with ripe fruit flavour. Super-grippy tannins back things up but the fruit ripeness provides innate balance. A whopper with a big future that would suit a rib roast of beef superbly.

## Warrenmang Estate Shiraz

| | |
|---|---|
| Quality | ♟ ♟ ♟ ♟ ♟ |
| Value | ★ ★ ★ ✦ |
| Grapes | shiraz |
| Region | Pyrenees, Vic. |
| Cellar | ➥ 3–12 |
| Alc./Vol. | 15% |
| RRP | $35.00 |

Warrenmang's shiraz is now one of the Pyrenees' benchmark reds in the no-holds-barred style. It's a big wine that needs long age for its strong character to moderate.
CURRENT RELEASE 1999 More Pyrenees power from the Bazzanis at Warrenmang, this shiraz on steroids has a dark, impenetrable colour and a powerful nose brimming with spices, dark plum, tar, chocolate mints (really) and vanilla. The palate continues the butch theme with warm, super-concentrated berry flavours and a sturdy wall of grippy tannins. Braised oxtail with reduced pan juices would match.

## Water Wheel Cabernet Sauvignon

| | |
|---|---|
| Quality | ♟ ♟ ♟ |
| Value | ★ ★ ★ |
| Grapes | cabernet sauvignon |
| Region | Bendigo, Vic. |
| Cellar | ➥ 10+ |
| Alc./Vol. | 14.5% |
| RRP | $17.00 |

Water Wheel's cabernet usually isn't as generously constructed as the estate's justifiably sought-after shiraz. The pricing remains within very reasonable standards compared to other Bendigo reds.
CURRENT RELEASE 1999 A densely coloured, strongly extractive wine that opens with very concentrated dark-berry, licorice and softly sweet oak aromas. The palate has blackberry-like fruit of real depth and intensity, but halfway down super-aggressive tannins hit you with all the subtlety of a bulldozer. This great wall of tannin knocks the wine off balance and it doesn't recover. Time may help but we doubt it. To sip with steak.

# Water Wheel Shiraz

Bendigo shiraz has something of a cult following, making some very powerful wines that may well reward long cellaring. Water Wheel is a different kettle of fish, a wine that often has raw precocious appeal, yet one that will also keep well. Value is exemplary too. Maker: Peter Cumming.

CURRENT RELEASE 1999  The colour is deep and purplish, the nose is ripe – loads of juicy berry aroma and a dab of peppery spice, with only a trace of regional mintiness. The palate is lush and powerful with earthy, unevolved shiraz flavour of great purity, and it finishes firmly with big dry tannins. A great proposition for lovers of big Central Victorian reds. Try it with braised steak and kidney.

| | |
|---|---|
| Quality | 🍷🍷🍷🍷🍷 |
| Value | ★★★★★ |
| Grapes | shiraz |
| Region | Bendigo, Vic. |
| Cellar | ➥ 2–10 |
| Alc./Vol. | 14.5% |
| RRP | $18.00 |

# Wedgetail Pinot Noir

Occasionally an eagle surveys its domain from a post in this vineyard, hence the estate's name. Maker: Guy Lamothe.

CURRENT RELEASE 1999  There's freshness here and pleasant light aromas of strawberry, along with hints of leaf and subtle oak. The simply constructed palate has some silkiness and length with a subtle seasoning of oak. It's lightish- to medium-bodied and has good length, but lacks the velvety complexity of great pinot. The finish is clean with soft tannins. Try it with mushroom risotto.

| | |
|---|---|
| Quality | 🍷🍷🍷🍷 |
| Value | ★★★ |
| Grapes | pinot noir |
| Region | Yarra Valley, Vic. |
| Cellar | 🍾 2 |
| Alc./Vol. | 13.0% |
| RRP | $31.00 |

## Wedgetail Reserve Pinot Noir

| | |
|---|---|
| Quality | ▼▼▼▼ |
| Value | ★★ |
| Grapes | pinot noir |
| Region | Yarra Valley, Vic. |
| Cellar | ▮ 3 |
| Alc./Vol. | 13.0% |
| RRP | $58.00 |

We don't know how many Canadian winemakers there are in Australia, but we suspect that they probably don't have the numbers for an ice hockey team. Quebec-born Guy Lamothe is an ex-photographer with a passion for pinot that's taken him all the way to this small Yarra Valley estate.

CURRENT RELEASE 1999   The last Wedgetail ('98) we tasted had a 'dry-reddish' character and lacked the finesse of the best pinot noirs. This latest edition again has that feel, with a middling-intensity, almost Central Victorian nose of mint, berries, foliage and spicy/smoky French oak, but little pinot 'mystery'. The medium-intensity palate follows suit with pleasant herbal and cherry flavours robed in well-integrated oak, but without really positive varietal richness. Serve it with crumbed veal chops.

## Westend 3 Bridges Cabernet Sauvignon

| | |
|---|---|
| Quality | ▼▼▼▮ |
| Value | ★★★ |
| Grapes | cabernet sauvignon |
| Region | Riverina, NSW |
| Cellar | ▮ 3 |
| Alc./Vol. | 13.5% |
| RRP | $21.00 |

The Westend wines are at the forefront of the quality drive by many Riverina growers. They are making a concerted effort to lose the stigmatised description 'irrigated' in favour of a strong regional identity. Makers: Bill Calabria and James Ceccato.

CURRENT RELEASE 1998   Vanillin American oak plays a big part in these wines, although there's some pleasant soft berry fruit in there as well. The '98 is very much in the oak-dominant mode, but many Australians like the taste in their wines, so who are we to quibble? Well . . . we've no doubt this wine would be better if the juicy ripe fruit took centre stage. It's still a sound red that will accompany any charry barbecued meats well.

## Wetherall Shiraz

Like many people who started off growing grapes for others, the Wetheralls of Coonawarra decided to have a go for themselves in 1991, via Roseworthy graduate Michael Wetherall.
CURRENT RELEASE 1999    Shiraz and Coonawarra go together like football and meat pies, and this is a good example. It has very deep colour reflecting the concentration of the 1999 vintage. The nose has deep plum, blackberry and slightly raisiny fruit, along with a touch of sweet oak. In the mouth it's smoothly constructed with good intensity of berry flavour, some oaky hints and long, smooth tannins to finish. A tasty Coonawarra of good balance and gentle drinkability to go with a big platter of chargrilled and roasted vegetables.

| | |
|---|---|
| Quality | 🍷🍷🍷🍷🍷 |
| Value | ★★★★ |
| Grapes | shiraz |
| Region | Coonawarra, SA |
| Cellar | 🍾 4 |
| Alc./Vol. | 13.5% |
| RRP | $25.00 |

## Wicked Wines Greed

Is a table wine packed in a lurid iridescent red bottle all that wicked? Maybe, but don't dismiss the wine within out of hand because of the packaging.
CURRENT RELEASE 1999    Glitz aside, this BRL Hardy product should appeal to its target group (whoever they are) simply because it's reasonably priced and easy to drink. Plentiful ripe fruit dominates with attractive blackberry and cherry aromas. In the mouth the fruity theme continues in a lightish- to medium-bodied vein, and the finish is soft and easy. This non-threatening young red slips down readily with cheese and spinach ravioli.

| | |
|---|---|
| Quality | 🍷🍷🍷🍷 |
| Value | ★★★★ |
| Grapes | shiraz |
| Region | various |
| Cellar | 🍾 1 |
| Alc./Vol. | 13.5% |
| RRP | $12.00 $ |

## Willespie Cabernet Sauvignon

| | |
|---|---|
| Quality | 🍷🍷🍷🍷 |
| Value | ★★★ |
| Grapes | cabernet sauvignon |
| Region | Margaret River, WA |
| Cellar | 🍷 5 |
| Alc./Vol. | 13.8% |
| RRP | $35.00 |

At Willespie they hold onto vintages longer than most wineries who can't wait to get them into the marketplace. As a result the age of their current releases is often a year or so older than the competition. A pity more don't follow suit although it must be an expensive business.

CURRENT RELEASE 1997 This falls into the more herby, foresty type of Margaret River cabernet, but it doesn't have any unripe or green characters. The nose is savoury with mint, dark chocolate, blackcurrant and cedary oak aromas, and it tastes full and long with medium body and firm dry tannins. It's a well-balanced savoury style that would be great with lamb casserole and parsley dumplings.

## Willespie Shiraz

| | |
|---|---|
| Quality | 🍷🍷🍷🍷 |
| Value | ★★★ |
| Grapes | shiraz |
| Region | Margaret River, WA |
| Cellar | 🍷 5 |
| Alc./Vol. | 14.5% |
| RRP | $25.50 |

Willespie was founded in 1976 by Kevin and Marian Squance. It's in the Willyabrup sub-region of Margaret River.

CURRENT RELEASE 1998 A Margaret River shiraz of some concentration, with rich berry and herb aromas, and appropriate aromatic oak input serving to support the fruit character, rather than taking it over. The palate is smooth and attractively textured, and doesn't show its rather high alcohol. There are grainy tannins woven through rich fruit, finishing pleasantly dry and lightly grippy. Good with roast lamb.

## Willow Bridge Shiraz

| | |
|---|---|
| Quality | 🍷🍷🍷🍷 |
| Value | ★★★★ |
| Grapes | shiraz |
| Region | Geographe, WA |
| Cellar | 🍷 3 |
| Alc./Vol. | 14.5% |
| RRP | $22.00 |

The Western Australian vineyards south of Perth aren't generally regarded as prime shiraz country but they should be. Average quality is good and improving, and the best of them are excellent.

CURRENT RELEASE 1999 A nicely balanced, fruit-driven young shiraz with a nose of sweet spiced cherries and some foresty notes. There seems to have been some whole berry influence giving pronounced fruitiness and softness in the mouth. Oak plays little part in flavour development and tannins are moderate. Try it with Lebanese lamb pies.

## Willow Creek Shiraz

On paper, the Mornington Peninsula isn't exactly prime shiraz country, but a few producers are making a good fist of it. The wines will never be the testosterone-charged shiraz beloved of the Yanks and the investment crowd. CURRENT RELEASE 1999    The keys to cool-climate shiraz are all here, but there's no sign of the greenness that can beset it. It's very spicy with a peppery zip on the nose as well as mellow, cherry-like fruit. The palate is medium-weight and savoury to taste with spicy cherry flavour, good length and texture. Try it with peppery marinated chicken cooked on the barbecue.

| | |
|---|---|
| Quality | ♟ ♟ ♟ ♟ |
| Value | ★ ★ ★ ┤ |
| Grapes | shiraz |
| Region | Mornington Peninsula, Vic. |
| Cellar | ▮ 3 |
| Alc./Vol. | 12.5% |
| RRP | $23.00 |

## Wirra Wirra Church Block

Church Block was a favourite with the suits a while back, but they've moved on to more esoteric tipples these days. The wine remains an honest Southern Vale-ish red, despite the addition of grapes from the Limestone Coast further south. Maker: Ben Riggs. CURRENT RELEASE 1999    This latest has a rather hearty old-fashioned McLaren Vale aroma, reminiscent of vineyard soil, plummy fruit and sweet spices. The palate has good depth and oak is restrained throughout. The Wirra Wirra mob describe it as 'a wine you can drink a bottle of' and it does taste smooth and easy to guzzle down. A good match with slow-braised beef or lamb.

| | |
|---|---|
| Quality | ♟ ♟ ♟ ♟ |
| Value | ★ ★ ★ |
| Grapes | cabernet sauvignon; shiraz; merlot |
| Region | McLaren Vale & Limestone Coast, SA |
| Cellar | ▮ 3 |
| Alc./Vol. | 14.0% |
| RRP | $20.00 |

## Wolf Blass Black Label Cabernet Sauvignon Shiraz

Black Label is the red wine that heads the Wolf Blass range. It's a caricature-like essay in overdone American oak.
CURRENT RELEASE 1997    This may well be the most predictable red wine in Australia. You can always rely on it to take oakiness as far as it can. This has a bouquet and flavour of coconut, dust, vanilla and mocha aromas – all oak-derived. Oh, and there's sweet blackberry fruit in the midst of it all. The palate has a thick texture and a very dry finish of oaky tannins. Try it with a pepper steak.

| | |
|---|---|
| Quality | ♟ ♟ ♟ ♟ |
| Value | ★ ★ |
| Grapes | cabernet sauvignon; shiraz |
| Region | Langhorne Creek & Barossa Valley, SA |
| Cellar | ▮ 8 |
| Alc./Vol. | 14.0% |
| RRP | $110 |

## Wolf Blass Brown Label Shiraz

| | |
|---|---|
| Quality | ♟ ♟ ♟ ♟ |
| Value | ★ ★ ★ |
| Grapes | shiraz |
| Region | various, SA |
| Cellar | ➥ 3–8 |
| Alc./Vol. | 14.5% |
| RRP | $28.50 |

The Wolf Blass formula of loads of American oak married to very ripe grapes has continued without much change for many years now. The style seems dated to smarty-pantses like us, but it works well commercially, so if it ain't broke why fix it?

CURRENT RELEASE 1998   Very recognisable as a Wolf Blass red, this shiraz has an overt personality that puts subtlety on hold. Instead it has a lot of concentrated, syrupy, blackberry fruit, but even more sweet vanilla/coconut oak. In the mouth it continues this 'more of everything' theme, mainly with caramel/coconut oak, but there's unctuously ripe fruit flavour as well, lots of body and firm tannins. It's all a bit much for easy drinking and we would suggest age is nigh on essential to mellow things a little. Try it with rare roast beef.

## Wolf Blass Grey Label Cabernet Sauvignon

| | |
|---|---|
| Quality | ♟ ♟ ♟ ♟ |
| Value | ★ ★ ★ |
| Grapes | cabernet sauvignon |
| Region | various, SA |
| Cellar | ➥ 2–8 |
| Alc./Vol. | 14.0% |
| RRP | $33.00 |

The question of oak, too much or too little, that haunts so many modern Australian reds is a non-issue with Wolf Blass wines. 'No wood, no good' Mr Blass once said, and his successors believe that even more is even better.

CURRENT RELEASE 1997   This is so oak-dominated that it's hard to catch any fruit character at all amongst all the cooperage. Lashings of coconut, caramel and vanillin fill the bouquet, and the thick-tasting, full-bodied palate is simply over-the-top oaky. A wee bit of blackberry fruit peeks out from under the timber, and there's a firm structure of drying, oaky tannins. Try it with pot-roasted topside.

## Wolf Blass South Australia Shiraz

| | |
|---|---|
| Quality | ♟ ♟ ♟ ♟ |
| Value | ★ ★ ★ |
| Grapes | shiraz |
| Region | various, SA |
| Cellar | ▮ 3 |
| Alc./Vol. | 13.5% |
| RRP | $16.50 ▮ |

This is a junior label from the Wolf Blass stable that is designed as an early-drinking red, without the forests of Yankee oak.

CURRENT RELEASE 1999   A refreshing change for a Blass red, this has some attractive light raspberry/blackberry and earth aromas married nicely to a balanced touch of sweet oak. The palate continues with the easy raspberry fruit and sweet oak in a smooth, easy-to-like way. A simple but attractive wine to accompany a mixed grill.

## Wolf Blass Yellow Label Cabernet Sauvignon

The reds of Wolf Blass did more to popularise the flavour of new oak in red wines than most. Yellow Label was one of the trailblazers.
CURRENT RELEASE 1998   This seems slightly less woody than some of its predecessors, but it's still there in good measure contributing caramel and mocha notes on the nose. There's syrupy berry fruit as well, but wood-matured character takes front of stage. In the mouth it has good body and smooth tannins but the flavour remains a bit one-dimensional. Serve with veal chops pizzaiola.

| | |
|---|---|
| Quality | ♥♥♥♥ |
| Value | ★★★ |
| Grapes | cabernet sauvignon |
| Region | various, SA |
| Cellar | ▮ 4 |
| Alc./Vol. | 14.0% |
| RRP | $17.50 |

## Wyndham Estate Bin 999 Merlot

Merlot is looking a little like the flavour of the month in some quarters. Unfortunately many wines are expensive, and just as often rather disappointing. This one is inexpensive, but it does have a splash of varietal integrity.
CURRENT RELEASE 2000   This has a bright, encouraging, youthful colour and the nose has the sort of juicy, plummy and sappy aromas that make merlot so desirable in many overseas markets. In the mouth it needs a complexity transplant, but it's cheap! It tastes ripe fruit-sweet and soft, with friendly tannins. Try it with baked vegetable lasagne.

| | |
|---|---|
| Quality | ♥♥♥♥ |
| Value | ★★★→ |
| Grapes | merlot |
| Region | various |
| Cellar | ▮ 2 |
| Alc./Vol. | 12.5% |
| RRP | $14.00 |

## Wyndham Estate Show Reserve Mudgee Cabernet Sauvignon

The Wyndham name has long been associated with an unashamedly commercial range of red wines that sometimes toy with sweetness to appeal to the market. The Show Reserve wines are different.
CURRENT RELEASE 1996   This has deep colour and an appetising bouquet combining cabernet fruit aromas of the blackberry liqueur type, well-handled vanillin oak, and a hint of mocha. In the mouth it's a big smoothie, with ripe blackcurrant fruit flavour, balanced oak and fine tannins. A satisfying Mudgee red of good character.

| | |
|---|---|
| Quality | ♥♥♥♥♥ |
| Value | ★★★ |
| Grapes | cabernet sauvignon |
| Region | Mudgee, NSW |
| Cellar | ▮ 3 |
| Alc./Vol. | 14.0% |
| RRP | $45.00 |

## Wynns Cabernet Sauvignon

| | |
|---|---|
| Quality | 🍷🍷🍷🍷🍷 |
| Value | ★★★★★ |
| Grapes | cabernet sauvignon |
| Region | Coonawarra, SA |
| Cellar | ➡ 1–15 |
| Alc./Vol. | 13.5% |
| RRP | $27.00 ⑤ |

Few Australian red wines have a pedigree like this Wynns cabernet with the black label. The outstanding '98 vintage deserves a place in any cellar.
*Previous outstanding vintages: '71, '76, '82, '85, '86, '88, '90, '91, '93, '94, '96*
CURRENT RELEASE 1998    A year after our first tasting of this excellent vintage, it's even more of an Australian classic at a fair price. This deep purple wine has delicious juicy blackcurrant, aromas of violets and spicy oak in fine harmony on the nose. In the mouth it boasts lovely fruit-sweet flavour of real freshness and elegance. Cabernet sauvignon's natural austerity provides excellent balance of flavour, and smooth, fine tannins carry a long finish. This will build complexity with age, but it drinks well young too. Try it with pink-roasted racks of lamb.

## Wynns Cabernet Shiraz Merlot

| | |
|---|---|
| Quality | 🍷🍷🍷🍷 |
| Value | ★★★★★ |
| Grapes | cabernet sauvignon; shiraz; merlot |
| Region | Coonawarra, SA |
| Cellar | 🍷 6 |
| Alc./Vol. | 13.5% |
| RRP | $17.50 ⑤ |

The '98 Coonawarra reds are wines to buy in quantity and few offer better value than some of the Wynns. The Cabernet Shiraz Merlot is sold as the drink-now wine in the range, but that doesn't mean it's a lightweight.
CURRENT RELEASE 1998    There's something extra in this vintage. The nose has fragrant blackberry and blackcurrant smells and the palate is deep and velvety. Ripe fruit fills the mouth and oak is pleasantly subtle. A signature of soft tannins makes it an easy early-drinking red, but it will improve over the medium term as well. Great with herbed roast veal.

## Wynns John Riddoch Cabernet Sauvignon

Winemaker Sue Hodder has taken over the reins at Wynns Coonawarra Estate and is already making her mark with slightly more supple wines than earlier vintages.
*Previous outstanding vintages: '82, '86, '91, '94, '96*
CURRENT RELEASE 1998   In this vintage Coonawarra reds gained an extra dimension of lush fruit, the result of a near-perfect year. John Riddoch is very deep in colour and it shares the syrupy black-fruit characters of the other '98 Wynns red wines. Powerful new oak is folded into that profound fruit in a balanced way that doesn't overwhelm. In the mouth it's full-bodied and long-tasting with a balanced, firm underpinning of ripe tannins. A wine with a big future that will suit roast lamb perfectly.

| | |
|---|---|
| Quality | ▼▼▼▼▼ |
| Value | ★★★) |
| Grapes | cabernet sauvignon |
| Region | Coonawarra, SA |
| Cellar | ⬤ 2–15+ |
| Alc./Vol. | 13.5% |
| RRP | $95.00 |

## Wynns Michael Shiraz

In the past we've sometimes had a problem with the oak levels in Wynns Michael. Now there seems to be a slight reduction, or perhaps we're just getting used to it.
*Previous outstanding vintage: '90*
CURRENT RELEASE 1998   Real concentration here with a densely packed core of liqueurish blackberry fruit on nose and palate. The nose also has strong barrel influences which impart mocha and toasted coconut aromas in liberal measure. It tastes oaky, ripe and powerful with a mouth-coating smooth texture, persistent flavour and fine-grained ripe tannins. A big wine to serve with roast rib of beef.

| | |
|---|---|
| Quality | ▼▼▼▼▼ |
| Value | ★★★ |
| Grapes | shiraz |
| Region | Coonawarra, SA |
| Cellar | ⬤ 1–10+ |
| Alc./Vol. | 13.5% |
| RRP | $95.00 |

## Wynns Shiraz

**Quality** 🍷🍷🍷🍷🍷
**Value** ★★★★★
**Grapes** shiraz
**Region** Coonawarra, SA
**Cellar** 5
**Alc./Vol.** 13.5%
**RRP** $16.50 (S)

Few Australian wines have achieved anything like the consistency of quality of this famous line. Once an absolute bargain, the price has crept up, and for a while it looked as though quality was being compromised a little, but this vintage is exemplary.

*Previous outstanding vintages: '82, '86, '90, '91, '97, '98*

CURRENT RELEASE 1999 Everything you might want in Coonawarra shiraz is right here and it'll give you change out of $20. The nose has you interested straight away – dark cherry fruit, spices, a hint of pepper and restrained oak, intense and appetising. In the mouth it's medium in body with good concentration of spicy, cherry-like shiraz flavour, finishing in dusty, ripe tannins. Super value. Great with barbecued porterhouse.

## Xanadu Merlot

**Quality** 🍷🍷🍷🍷
**Value** ★★★
**Grapes** merlot
**Region** Margaret River, WA
**Cellar** 3–10+
**Alc./Vol.** 15.0%
**RRP** $45.00

Margaret River is a sort of Xanadu to an eclectic mix of wine people, surfies, hippies and escapees from the big smoke. Some of them only produce straight merlot when the Moon is in the seventh house and Jupiter aligns with Mars. A safer course is to do it when the fruit looks good enough to stand alone. Xanadu take the latter course.

CURRENT RELEASE 1999 This opens up with good varietal character which sums up the fascinating plum pudding-like aromas of ripe merlot, and a powerful load of spicy oak plays a part. The palate is big and robust with strong oaky berry flavour and a Great Wall of tannins at the end. The level of extract, oak, alcohol and tannic toughness suggests that this wine needs many long years to harmonise. At the moment it's a hard-tasting drop indeed. Forget about it for years, then serve it with merlot-braised oxtail.

## Yalumba Barossa Shiraz

Yalumba is Australia's oldest family-owned winery. The winery at Angaston in the foothills that lead up to Eden Valley is a picturesque destination for travellers. CURRENT RELEASE 1999   This is a traditional type of shiraz, with ripe fruit submerged in aromas of old leather chesterfields, boot polish and earth. That may sound awful, but in fact it's an appealing, savoury nose that keeps you going back for more. In the mouth there's soft, spicy fruit flavour with some earthy old oak notes. A balanced old-fashioned red that's a real crowd-pleaser.

| | |
|---|---|
| Quality | ♥♥♥♥ |
| Value | ★★★⁴ |
| Grapes | shiraz |
| Region | Barossa Valley, SA |
| Cellar | 🍾 6 |
| Alc./Vol. | 14.0% |
| RRP | $17.00 |

## Yalumba Galway Vintage Shiraz

Galway Vintage was once a sought-after high-quality label. Nowadays it's more of a cheap-and-cheerful drop. CURRENT RELEASE 1999   An attractive young red wine on a budget, this Galway has some sweet, spicy raspberry and blackberry aromas with touches of earth and sweet oak. Those fresh berry flavours mark the palate which is light- to medium-bodied, tasty and soft. Serve it with crispy prosciutto pizza.

| | |
|---|---|
| Quality | ♥♥♥ |
| Value | ★★★⁴ |
| Grapes | shiraz |
| Region | various, SA |
| Cellar | 🍾 3 |
| Alc./Vol. | 13.5% |
| RRP | $12.00 ⑤ |

## Yalumba Mawson's Cabernet Shiraz Merlot

Douglas Mawson took Yalumba wines to Antarctica with him and no doubt they had a bit to do with maintaining morale in that most trying of environments. This wine commemorates Yalumba's sponsorship of the expedition. CURRENT RELEASE 1998   Attractive blackberry and spice aromas from the shiraz component of this wine lead the way on the nose, but there's also a plummy note and a whiff of smoky vanillin oak. The palate is medium-bodied with middling fruit intensity and the soft tannins typical of Coonawarra reds. A good middle-of-the-road Coonawarra to try with beef olives.

| | |
|---|---|
| Quality | ♥♥♥♥ |
| Value | ★★★ |
| Grapes | cabernet sauvignon; shiraz; merlot |
| Region | Coonawarra, SA |
| Cellar | 🍾 4 |
| Alc./Vol. | 14.0% |
| RRP | $22.50 |

## Yalumba Merlot

| | |
|---|---|
| Quality | ▼▼▼⦚ |
| Value | ★★★⦚ |
| Grapes | merlot |
| Region | not stated |
| Cellar | ▮ 2 |
| Alc./Vol. | 14.0% |
| RRP | $12.00 |

Yalumba is one of the many wineries in Australia who have embraced merlot in anticipation of a trend. Statistics now tell us that the fashion has arrived. CURRENT RELEASE 1999    Merlot means many things to many people as we try to sort out just where it sits in Australia. This is a worthwhile effort with plum, raspberry and leafiness on the nose, along with a touch of spicy oak. It tastes smooth and easy with a dry finish. Good drinking with Chinese barbecued pork.

## Yalumba Shiraz Viognier

| | |
|---|---|
| Quality | ▼▼▼▼ |
| Value | ★★★ |
| Grapes | shiraz; viognier |
| Region | Barossa & Eden Valleys, SA |
| Cellar | ▮ 3 |
| Alc./Vol. | 14.5% |
| RRP | $35.00 |

In France's northern Rhone Valley, viognier is often blended with shiraz in small proportions to leaven the red grape's strong character, while adding fragrance and complexity. Yalumba is now trying out the combination. CURRENT RELEASE 1998    Viognier lends some aroma, but essentially the wine is all Barossa shiraz with ripe and succulent blackberry character, a touch of mint and standard issue oak. The palate is unexciting, with straightforward big flavour, smooth construction and dry tannins to finish. A satisfying red of good character, but given its pretensions it could offer more. As our school reports used to say, 'Could do better!'

## Yalumba The Menzies Cabernet Sauvignon

| | |
|---|---|
| Quality | ▼▼▼▼ |
| Value | ★★★⦚ |
| Grapes | cabernet sauvignon |
| Region | Coonawarra, SA |
| Cellar | ▮ 6+ |
| Alc./Vol. | 14.5% |
| RRP | $26.95 |

Do our prime ministers know a good wine from a bad one? Not that long ago John Howard was serving bargain-basement plonk to dignitaries at Kirribilli House and had to get a consultant in to lift his game. Howard's hero Bob Menzies was different, and his liking for a particular Yalumba red led to this label.
*Previous outstanding vintages: '90, '91, '94, '96*
CURRENT RELEASE 1997    A traditional Coonawarra red with a nose of penetrating blackcurrant aromas, a leafy touch, some spice and cedary oak. The palate is intense in dark berry and currant fruit with chocolatey barrel-ferment richness adding another dimension. Balanced dry tannins support things well, and despite rather high alcohol it remains balanced and likeable. Maintain tradition by serving a roast leg of lamb with it.

## Yalumba Tricentenary Vines Grenache

Three-hundred-year-old vines? What Yalumba mean is that these 1889-planted grenache vines' lives have *spanned* three centuries, the nineteenth, twentieth and twenty-first. But only just.
CURRENT RELEASE 1999    The nose is more subdued and interesting than some old-vine grenaches. Deep, earthy, red fruit aromas fill the nose. There's a minerally touch, some herbs and a little trace of volatility, as well as subdued old oak touches. In the mouth it has savoury dark-plum flavours of real warmth and overt fruit-sweetness, and old-fashioned tannins are firm yet ripe. Serve it with daube of beef.

| | |
|---|---|
| Quality | � ♛♛♛ |
| Value | ★★★↓ |
| Grapes | grenache |
| Region | Barossa Valley, SA |
| Cellar | ▮ 4 |
| Alc./Vol. | 14.5% |
| RRP | $35.00 |

## Yering Station Pinot Noir

Yering Station makes two different pinot noirs, each with a distinct style of its own. This is the standard label, a simpler wine than the spectacular Reserve.
CURRENT RELEASE 2000    A pleasant, light pinot that still has enough complexity and interest to elevate it a bit above the many poor pinot noirs on the Australian market. The earthy nose and palate have sappy touches to beetrooty, gamy varietal qualities. There's a well-handled dab of oak there too, but some hardness detracts from the palate. Best with food like Chinese barbecue pork.

| | |
|---|---|
| Quality | ♛♛♛ |
| Value | ★★↓ |
| Grapes | pinot noir |
| Region | Yarra Valley, Vic. |
| Cellar | ▮ 3 |
| Alc./Vol. | 13.0% |
| RRP | $24.00 |

## Yering Station Shiraz

Shiraz is making a resurgence in the Yarra Valley, which is a good thing. It's at its best in the warmer years.
CURRENT RELEASE 1999    This has a decidedly French feel, sharing some of the rustic elements you can find in Cote du Rhones. The nose has raspberry and herb aromas along with earthy, gamy touches and maybe little hints of aldehyde and hydrogen sulfide. The wild Frenchy feel continues on the palate, which has an attractively supple texture and a slightly stemmy finish. Served with Lyonnaise sausages or andouillettes, it all makes sense.

| | |
|---|---|
| Quality | ♛♛♛ |
| Value | ★★★ |
| Grapes | shiraz |
| Region | Yarra Valley, Vic. |
| Cellar | ▮ 2 |
| Alc./Vol. | 13.0% |
| RRP | $24.00 |

## Zema Estate Cabernet Sauvignon

| | |
|---|---|
| Quality | ♟♟♟♟♟ |
| Value | ★★★★↓ |
| Grapes | cabernet sauvignon |
| Region | Coonawarra, SA |
| Cellar | ▮ 8 |
| Alc./Vol. | 14.0% |
| RRP | $26.00 |

The Zema family has been making fine reds in Coonawarra since the early 1980s. Dimitrio Zema is the patriarch; his sons Matt and Nick make and market the wines. They still hand-prune their vines. The '98 was our best red wine in last year's *Guide*. *Previous outstanding vintages: '92, '94, '96, '97, '98* CURRENT RELEASE 1999   A typically elegant effort from Zema and a worthy follow-up to the fine '98. The aromas recall mint, cassis and Ribena, and it's a fruit-driven wine all round. Clean, sweet-berry, mint and blackcurrant flavours continue in the mouth. It is well balanced and refined, with discreet powdery tannins. Good with aged parmesan cheese.

## Zema Estate Cluny

| | |
|---|---|
| Quality | ♟♟♟♟ |
| Value | ★★★ |
| Grapes | cabernet sauvignon 55%; merlot 25%; cabernet franc 15%; malbec 5% |
| Region | Coonawarra, SA |
| Cellar | ➤ 2–8+ |
| Alc./Vol. | 13.5% |
| RRP | $26.00 |

This is a single-vineyard wine. The Cluny block was developed from bare ground by the Zema family, at the southern end of the famed Coonawarra terra rossa strip. *Previous outstanding vintage: '98* CURRENT RELEASE 1999   This is a typical lighter-bodied Coonawarra red, with carefully understated oak and no excess of alcohol or anything else. The colour is medium-depth purple–red and it smells sweetly of blackcurrant and raspberry. There are some herbal elements throughout, and it has a lean profile. A good food wine: try pink lamb backstraps.

## Zema Estate Shiraz

| | |
|---|---|
| Quality | ♟♟♟♟ |
| Value | ★★★↓ |
| Grapes | shiraz |
| Region | Coonawarra, SA |
| Cellar | ➤ 2–7+ |
| Alc./Vol. | 13.0% |
| RRP | $26.00 |

Dimitrio Zema migrated to South Australia from Calabria, Italy, where his father had made wine (doesn't everyone there?). He made enough money as a house painter to buy his first plot of land in Coonawarra in 1982. It's a great success story. CURRENT RELEASE 1999   True to form, Zema has made another elegant, sinewy style which perhaps shows a little more oak-derived flavour than usual. The colour is full purple–red and there's plenty of vanilla, chocolate and coffee-like aromas. It's soft and chewy with drying tannins, but perhaps lacks the customary fruit intensity. Try it with gourmet sausages.

# White Wines

## Ainsworth Chardonnay

Seville, in the fertile southern part of the Yarra Valley, is a little away from the main concentration of Lilydale vineyards. Denis and Kerri Craig's Ainsworth Estate is one of the promising newcomers in the area.
CURRENT RELEASE 2000    This is a subtle, civilised chardonnay that doesn't seduce the drinker immediately with large doses of ripe fruit or sweet oak. It opens with a savoury nose where mealy notes and a hint of European-style earthiness surround fine citrus and melon fruit aromas. In the mouth it's soft and creamy, restrained and long-tasting with well-integrated toasty oak, all framed in crisp acidity. Serve it with buttery gnocchi.

| | |
|---|---|
| Quality | ♟♟♟♟ |
| Value | ★★★★ |
| Grapes | chardonnay |
| Region | Yarra Valley, Vic. |
| Cellar | ▮ 3 |
| Alc./Vol. | 13.2% |
| RRP | $21.50 |

## Albert River Chardonnay

Chardonnay is an adaptable critter, and does well in warmer spots. This vineyard is in Queensland's Gold Coast hinterland. We looked very hard for *tropical* fruit character in this chardonnay.
CURRENT RELEASE 2000    The nose has sweet ripe aromas reminiscent of honey, candied fruits and confectionery with a seasoning of sweet oak and some buttery richness. In the mouth it has smooth flavours with slightly over-the-top fruit-sweet character married to measured oak. The finish is soft. Put on your white shoes and try it with a Gold Coast selection of spanner crabs, prawns and tropical fruit.

| | |
|---|---|
| Quality | ♟♟♟♟ |
| Value | ★★★ |
| Grapes | chardonnay |
| Region | South Burnett, Qld |
| Cellar | ▮ 1 |
| Alc./Vol. | 13.0% |
| RRP | $19.00 |

## Allandale Chardonnay

| | |
|---|---|
| Quality | 🍷🍷🍷🍷 |
| Value | ★★★★ |
| Grapes | chardonnay |
| Region | Hunter Valley, NSW |
| Cellar | 🍾 2 |
| Alc./Vol. | 14.0% |
| RRP | $20.00 |

Allandale chardonnay is about as far from dainty cool-climate chardonnay as possible. Made in an unashamedly full-throttle style, it's ideal if you like big flavour in your white wines.

CURRENT RELEASE 2000    This has a big, soft nose with rich lashings of melted butter aromas, a hint of cracked yeast, and fruit that's exuberantly ripe with peachy smells and even a hint of pineapple. In the mouth there's a round, fruit-sweet palate. It shows more toasty oak than the nose, but it's kept in check well. A substantial mouthful of chardonnay with a clean, soft finish. Serve it chilled with or without cold chicken drumsticks.

## Allandale Verdelho

| | |
|---|---|
| Quality | 🍷🍷🍷🍷 |
| Value | ★★★⌐ |
| Grapes | verdelho |
| Region | Hunter Valley, NSW |
| Cellar | 🍾 2 |
| Alc./Vol. | 14.0% |
| RRP | $18.00 |

Verdelho has been in the Hunter for ever, but it's enjoying renewed interest lately as an easy-drinking crowd-pleaser.

CURRENT RELEASE 2000    This is a succulent drop, in keeping with the accepted modern style of Hunter verdelhos, which are wines to enjoy in the fruity flush of youth. This has good ripeness with juicy tropical fruit and lime sherbet notes. It tastes full of grapey flavour which is nicely intense, leading through to a dry finish. Try it with a vegetable terrine.

## Amberley Chenin Blanc

| | |
|---|---|
| Quality | 🍷🍷⌐ |
| Value | ★★ |
| Grapes | chenin blanc |
| Region | Margaret River, WA |
| Cellar | 🍾 1 |
| Alc./Vol. | 12.5% |
| RRP | $15.95 |

Another of the many 'cooking' whites made from chenin blanc in Western Australia. This style is starting to look a bit passé.

CURRENT RELEASE 2000    The nose is rather neutral and light-on with a fresh, simple grapiness, some tropical touches and aromas of apples. In the mouth residual sugar dominates giving a flat sweetness to the middle palate, which is formless, short and a bit too soft in acidity. Serve very cold at a party.

## Amberley Sauvignon Blanc

While most makers produce a single blend to use up both their semillon and sauvignon blanc, Amberley makes two different wines, a blend with a hint of oak and this straight unwooded sauvignon.

CURRENT RELEASE 2000    This has a lively aroma that provides appetising scents of passionfruit, citrus, herbs and green fruit. The nose indicates excatly what's to follow: a fresh, tangy, clean palate with tropical fruit-sweetness and herbaceous flavours of good length and intensity. Serve it with Vietnamese rice paper rolls.

| | |
|---|---|
| Quality | ♟ ♟ ♟ ♟ |
| Value | ★ ★ ★ ♪ |
| Grapes | sauvignon blanc |
| Region | Margaret River, WA |
| Cellar | ▮ 2 |
| Alc./Vol. | 13.0% |
| RRP | $19.00 |

## Amberley Semillon Sauvignon Blanc

Amberley is at the northern end of the greater Margaret River district, a sub-region with wines that perhaps lack the same clear-cut identity of Willyabrup or Margaret River proper.

CURRENT RELEASE 2000    The nose has an overt, almost New Zealand-accented, fruit aroma that suggests lemon pastilles, crushed spiky leaves and gooseberry. A hint of subtle nutty oak adds a bit of substance. It tastes crisp and tangy with lime and tropical fruit flavours, a fruit-sweet soft mid-palate, and a whisper of skilfully underplayed oak. Serve it with a fresh asparagus and chicken stirfry.

| | |
|---|---|
| Quality | ♟ ♟ ♟ ♟ |
| Value | ★ ★ ★ |
| Grapes | semillon; sauvignon blanc |
| Region | Margaret River, WA |
| Cellar | ▮ 3 |
| Alc./Vol. | 12.8% |
| RRP | $22.00 |

## Andrew Harris Chardonnay

Mudgee has a much longer chardonnay history than most Australian vignobles, and vies for credit as the pioneering modern chardonnay region with the Hunter. Andrew Harris set up in the area only a decade ago.

CURRENT RELEASE 2000    Melon and tropical-fruit varietal aromas meet the nose along with an alkaline, slightly soapy aroma and a hint of resinous oak. The palate is full and fruity with a straightforward commercial personality of persistent juicy tropical flavour, a touch of barrel influence and tangy acidity. A crowd-pleasing style to drink with stirfried prawns.

| | |
|---|---|
| Quality | ♟ ♟ ♟ |
| Value | ★ ★ ★ |
| Grapes | chardonnay |
| Region | Mudgee, NSW |
| Cellar | ▮ 2 |
| Alc./Vol. | 13.5% |
| RRP | $15.80 |

## Andrew Peace Chardonnay

| | |
|---|---|
| Quality | 🍷🍷🍷 |
| Value | ★★★★ |
| Grapes | chardonnay |
| Region | Murray Valley, Vic. |
| Cellar | 🍷 1 |
| Alc./Vol. | 14.0% |
| RRP | $15.50 |

The label on this wine from Swan Hill boasts a number of glittery medals, and unlike some of its competitors' 'medals', these ones are fair dinkum. The judges were right, it's really pretty good at the price.

CURRENT RELEASE 2000    A good example of the 'bottled sunshine' style that's charmed export markets, this has a sweet, juicy nose full of tropical fruit-salady aromas. Oak provides a bit of backbone and seasoning, but the fruit character carries the day. It's driven by ripe, melony chardonnay fruit in the mouth which has reasonable persistence and a dry finish. Try it with chicken club sandwiches.

## Angoves Bear Crossing Chardonnay

| | |
|---|---|
| Quality | 🍷🍷 |
| Value | ★★★ |
| Grapes | chardonnay |
| Region | Murray Valley, SA |
| Cellar | 🍷 1 |
| Alc./Vol. | 13.0% |
| RRP | $10.00 |

The 'bear' on the road sign-inspired label is a koala, and a proportion of the price of each bottle goes to the Australian Koala Foundation. Admirable work.

CURRENT RELEASE 2000    The colour here is slightly dull but the wine inside is a reasonable drop. Melon perfumes the fruit-driven nose, and there's a light seasoning of oak. In the mouth it's pleasant enough, easy and fruity with just a hint of wood. The palate pulls up a bit short but it finishes clean and dry. Try it with quick-fried calamari and chilli jam.

## Annie's Lane Chardonnay

| | |
|---|---|
| Quality | 🍷🍷🍷🍷 |
| Value | ★★★★ |
| Grapes | chardonnay |
| Region | Clare Valley, SA |
| Cellar | 🍷 2 |
| Alc./Vol. | 13.0% |
| RRP | $16.00 |

The Clare Valley isn't renowned as a chardonnay region, in fact most of the growers there opt for riesling as a premium white variety.

CURRENT RELEASE 2000    A soft, attractive chardonnay that seems to have gained a little in depth and complexity over past releases. The nose has fig syrup, butterscotch and spicy oak aromas of good character, and it tastes easy and smooth. The fruit flavour is ripe and satisfying, and a dab of toasty oak dresses up the chalky-dry finish. Serve it with sugar-cured tuna.

## Annie's Lane Semillon

The old Quelltaler semillons employed lots of oak which made them an oddity in pre-chardonnay days, when white wines rarely had the benefit of wood. Now oaky whites are everywhere; Annie's Lane, from the old Quelltaler plantings, is an exception. Maker: Caroline Dunn.

CURRENT RELEASE 2000   An appetising nose of good intensity introduces this bright semillon. It has aromas of lemon, herbs and a hint of hand cream, ahead of a smooth palate, which has a more-ish balance between ripe yet stylish fruit, and clean acidity. Great value and excellent with pan-fried fish, or as a drink on its own.

| | |
|---|---|
| Quality | 🍷🍷🍷🍷 |
| Value | ★★★★★ |
| Grapes | semillon |
| Region | Clare Valley, SA |
| Cellar | 3 |
| Alc./Vol. | 12.0% |
| RRP | $15.50 Ⓢ |

## Arlewood Semillon

One of the smaller Margaret River producers, Arlewood has plans to double its production in the next few years, so we might see their wines a bit more often.

CURRENT RELEASE 2000   A lively nose here: zippy lemon, mint and herbal aromas, gently dusted with oak to add dimension. The palate is smooth with good depth, and a touch of fruit-sweetness mid-palate gives that tropical Margaret River accent. Crisp acidity and a hint of oak keep it interesting and augur well for short-term bottle development. Serve it with mild chilli prawns.

| | |
|---|---|
| Quality | 🍷🍷🍷 |
| Value | ★★★ |
| Grapes | semillon |
| Region | Margaret River, WA |
| Cellar | 1–4 |
| Alc./Vol. | 13.7% |
| RRP | $19.00 |

## Artamus Chardonnay

Ian Parmenter is the affable presenter of that friendly little cooking spot called 'Consuming Passions' on ABC TV. He and his partner, Ann Dewar, planted this vineyard on a hobby basis in 1994. Maker: Michael Gadd.

CURRENT RELEASE 1999   A likeable first effort, this bright yellow–green wine has a nose of light melony aromas, mellow barrel influence, a subtle leafy touch and hints of chalky minerals. The palate is well put together with fine texture, smooth juicy flavour, and some pleasant nuttiness from nicely integrated oak. An easy-drinking companion for steamed scampi, perhaps with hints of ginger and coriander.

| | |
|---|---|
| Quality | 🍷🍷🍷🍷 |
| Value | ★★★★★ |
| Grapes | chardonnay |
| Region | Margaret River, WA |
| Cellar | 2 |
| Alc./Vol. | 13.0% |
| RRP | $17.10 (delivered from cellar door) |

## Ashwood Grove Chardonnay

| | |
|---|---|
| Quality | 🍷🍷🍷 |
| Value | ★★★★ |
| Grapes | chardonnay |
| Region | Murray Valley, Vic. |
| Cellar | 🍷 1 |
| Alc./Vol. | 13.5% |
| RRP | $12.50 |

Oceans of chardonnay like this sit at the heart of the Murray Valley wineries' recent success. Ashwood Grove is a typical example.

CURRENT RELEASE 2000    This has ripe stone-fruit, cashew and sweaty characters, with sweet toasty oak adding seasoning. It survives well with a big chill, so it's a good hot-weather wine at an everyday price. Richer foods may work here, but it's probably just as much a 'no food' wine to sip at social gatherings. Drink it young before it loses freshness.

## Baldivis Estate Chardonnay

| | |
|---|---|
| Quality | 🍷🍷🍷🍷 |
| Value | ★★★⁴ |
| Grapes | chardonnay |
| Region | Margaret River, WA |
| Cellar | 🍷 4 |
| Alc./Vol. | 14.0% |
| RRP | $28.00 |

The already well-established Baldivis Estate was purchased by the controversial new Margaret River operator Palandri Wines in 2000. They are developing it as a quality label under the winemaking direction of Tony Carapetis.

CURRENT RELEASE 2000    The bright straw colour belies the weight and concentration of the wine. The rich nose shows nutty yeast lees, earth and oak characters surrounding quite syrupy, ripe, peachy chardonnay fruit. It's a very concentrated wine of length and power, with a big seasoning of toasty oak. The oak stops short of being too dominant but only by a whisker. A good first effort. Try it with stirfried lobster with ginger.

## Baldivis Estate Semillon Sauvignon Blanc

| | |
|---|---|
| Quality | 🍷🍷🍷🍷 |
| Value | ★★★ |
| Grapes | semillon; sauvignon blanc |
| Region | Margaret River & Great Southern, WA |
| Cellar | 🍷 3 |
| Alc./Vol. | 12.5% |
| RRP | $23.00 |

Semillon–sauvignon blends are a big part of the Western Australian wine scene. Cheaper versions, sometimes with input from other grapes, provide the basis for many a 'Classic Dry White', but the better examples usually bear varietal labelling.

CURRENT RELEASE 2000    Zap! This is a wake-up call for the palate. It opens with a zesty thrill of up-front fruit, herbaceous aromas and hints of the passionfruit/fruit-salady notes that sauvignon blanc brings. The palate is brisk and tangy with medium fruit intensity and a clean, high-acid finish. Good with a crab salad.

## Balgownie Estate Chardonnay

Many recent changes at this renowned vineyard. First, Mildara sold it to private investors in Queensland; then long-time winemaker Lindsay Ross departed. Balgownie was never allowed to market an estate chardonnay when Mildara owned it. Silly billies! This wine proves how good it can be.

CURRENT RELEASE 2000   This delicious, finessy chardonnay won the trophy for best chardonnay in a class of 138 at the 2001 Boutique Wine Awards. It's a very fine, fresh and youthful – yet complex – chardonnay smelling of toast, creamed nuts and stone fruits. The palate is intense and deep. All components are in superb harmony. Try it with grilled scampi.

| | |
|---|---|
| Quality | 🍷🍷🍷🍷🍷 |
| Value | ★★★★ |
| Grapes | chardonnay |
| Region | Bendigo, Vic. |
| Cellar | 🍾 5+ |
| Alc./Vol. | 13.0% |
| RRP | $30.00 |

## Bannockburn Chardonnay

With the estate vines back on-stream after the '98 hailstorm vintage, which resulted in a multi-region blend, it's business as usual for one of Australia's most consistent chardonnays. Maker: Gary Farr.
*Previous outstanding vintages: '88, '90, '91, '92, '94, '95, '96, '97, '98*

CURRENT RELEASE 1999   This is a powerful, complex style that needs air and really comes up in the glass. It has a full brassy-yellow colour and smells of ground meal, toasty oak, melon and tropical fruits. There are cooked-fruit, pepper and pencil-wood aromas too. The palate has a chewy richness and is about texture as much as flavour. A wine for drinking – not tasting. It will improve with age but goes well now with turkey risotto.

| | |
|---|---|
| Quality | 🍷🍷🍷🍷🍷 |
| Value | ★★★★ |
| Grapes | chardonnay |
| Region | Geelong, Vic. |
| Cellar | 🍾 5 |
| Alc./Vol. | 14.0% |
| RRP | $47.00 |

## Belgenny Vineyard Chardonnay

| | |
|---|---|
| Quality | 🍷🍷🍷🍷 |
| Value | ★★★★⟩ |
| Grapes | chardonnay |
| Region | Hunter Valley, NSW |
| Cellar | 🍾 3 |
| Alc./Vol. | 13.5% |
| RRP | $22.00 Ⓢ |

Belgenny is a new name with a historic past. Norman Seckold planted the vineyard in 1989, naming it after the original home of the pioneering Macarthur family at Camden, Sydney. In 1837 Seckold's great-great-grandfather Frederick was one of the Macarthurs' German 'vine dressers'.

CURRENT RELEASE 2000    This is a delicious, vibrant and relatively restrained young wine, Hunter chardonnay tending to age fast and being best when young and fresh. At one year of age, it still has youthful melon and raw-cashew aromas, nicely understated oak and green tints in the colour. Medium-bodied and finessy, it promises a fine future. Serve with fish pie.

## Belgenny Vineyard Partners Reserve Chardonnay

| | |
|---|---|
| Quality | 🍷🍷🍷🍷🍷 |
| Value | ★★★★★ |
| Grapes | chardonnay |
| Region | Hunter Valley, NSW |
| Cellar | 🍾 4 |
| Alc./Vol. | 14.0% |
| RRP | $23.00 Ⓢ |

This is the big brother from Belgenny, but surprisingly you'll only have to pay an extra dollar for it. The Belgenny wines are all made by Greg Silkman at the contract winemaking outfit, Monarch.

CURRENT RELEASE 2000    This is similarly reserved, fresh, and pristinely fruity as the regular chardonnay, but is more concentrated and powerful in the mouth, and has a fraction more oak character. Nevertheless, it is still finely balanced and well made. It has quite high viscosity, a hallmark of chardonnay, and this gives a slight impression of sweetness. Smooth, seamless finish. Try it with Cantonese fish balls.

## Belgenny Vineyard Semillon

| | |
|---|---|
| Quality | 🍷🍷🍷 |
| Value | ★★★⟩ |
| Grapes | semillon |
| Region | Hunter Valley, NSW |
| Cellar | ➤ 2–5+ |
| Alc./Vol. | 10.0% |
| RRP | $18.00 |

If low alcohol and high acid are indications the makers are angling for a traditional Hunter style, this is on track. It won a bronze medal at the Rutherglen Show.

CURRENT RELEASE 2000    This shows some of the herbaceous characters that typify 2000 Hunter semillons. It's pale yellow in hue with a passionfruity, slightly sweaty aroma and hints of cured grass/hay. The taste is light-bodied, lean and zesty, with a distinct tartness which indicates cellaring. No oak has been used. It needs time to fill out and until then is best drunk with fresh oysters.

## Best's Great Western Riesling

Best's was started in 1866 by Henry Best, younger brother of Joseph Best, who started the winery across the road which became Seppelt Great Western. The Thomson family has owned it since 1920.

CURRENT RELEASE 2000    This is a delicate, ethereal riesling which needs subtle food. The restrained aromas remind of flowers, slate and passionfruit with a slightly tea-leafy edge. It is soft and dry to taste and just lacks a little in intensity. Try it with crab cakes.

| | |
|---|---|
| Quality | ▮▮▮▮ |
| Value | ★★★★ |
| Grapes | riesling |
| Region | Great Western, Vic. |
| Cellar | ▮ 7 |
| Alc./Vol. | 12.5% |
| RRP | $15.80 |

## Bethany Riesling

The drought conditions that led up to the 2000 vintage were so devastating the Schrapels were forced to buy grapes in, from two growers in the Adelaide Hills and Eden Valley.

CURRENT RELEASE 2000 The colour is medium–deep yellow, which reflects the advanced maturity of this wine. It is not your usual restrained style. The aromas remind of peach, melon jam and honeysuckle, and the wine is fairly broad and could do with more focus and finesse. There could be some botrytised fruit in it. It's a wine to drink now, not keep, and suits fish cakes.

| | |
|---|---|
| Quality | ▮▮▮▮ |
| Value | ★★★⁴ |
| Grapes | riesling |
| Region | Eden Valley 80%, Adelaide Hills 20%, SA |
| Cellar | ▮ 1 |
| Alc./Vol. | 12.0% |
| RRP | $15.00 |

## Bethany The Manse

This eclectic blend is an easygoing, inexpensive dry white and offers exactly what we'd hope for in what the marketeers call an 'entry level' wine. Makers: Geoff and Rob Schrapel.

CURRENT RELEASE 2000    It's starting to show some early development but that's not a problem. It smells of lemon, herbs and grass/hay – very pleasant and well made – with semillon flavours predominating. It's light-bodied and smooth, and easy to enjoy right now, perhaps with spaghetti carbonara.

| | |
|---|---|
| Quality | ▮▮▮ |
| Value | ★★★⁴ |
| Grapes | semillon; riesling; chardonnay |
| Region | Barossa Valley, SA |
| Cellar | ▮ 1 |
| Alc./Vol. | 13.0% |
| RRP | $13.00 Ⓢ |

## Bloodwood Estate Chardonnay

| | |
|---|---|
| Quality | 🍷🍷🍷🍷 |
| Value | ★★★★ |
| Grapes | chardonnay |
| Region | Orange, NSW |
| Cellar | 🍷 3+ |
| Alc./Vol. | 12.8% |
| RRP | $20.00 |

Bloodwood lays claim to being the pioneer vineyard of Orange. The wines are made elsewhere by Jon Reynolds, who moved a bit closer last year into the new Cabonne winery. Sydney's Five Way Cellars seems to act as an unofficial agent.

CURRENT RELEASE 1999 This is the best chardonnay we can recall from this vineyard. In true cool-grown form, it's tight, fine and reserved. Nutty, mealy, mineral and sur-lie aromas are there, but admirably subtle. The structure is crisp, dry and angular, with fine peach and cashew flavours that linger well. It's lovely now with lighter fish dishes, and should repay short-term cellaring.

## Blues Point Chardonnay Semillon

| | |
|---|---|
| Quality | 🍷🍷🍷 |
| Value | ★★★⁺ |
| Grapes | chardonnay; semillon |
| Region | not stated |
| Cellar | 🍷 1 |
| Alc./Vol. | 12.5% |
| RRP | $10.95 ⑤ |

If Southcorp is still selling the '99 vintage in mid-2001, it's probably a sign that this trendy 'concept' brand is already on the downhill run of its product life cycle. Blue bottles and blue plastic corks can only entertain for so long.

CURRENT RELEASE 1999 This is still drinking remarkably well for its age. The aroma is shy, plain and rather broad, with dusty, herbal, vegetable/basil scents. The flavour is simple and rather boring, with some cabbagy hints: light-weight, soft, dry and perfectly acceptable at the price. It goes with fish fingers.

## Bridgewater Mill Sauvignon Blanc

| | |
|---|---|
| Quality | 🍷🍷🍷🍷 |
| Value | ★★★ |
| Grapes | sauvignon blanc |
| Region | Coonawarra, Adelaide Hills & Clare Valley, SA |
| Cellar | 🍷 2 |
| Alc./Vol. | 13.0% |
| RRP | $19.50 |

Petaluma's Bridgewater Mill is a picturesque old mill in the Adelaide Hills that serves not only as a headquarters for the wine company but also as a sparkling wine production centre, a restaurant and a tourist destination.

CURRENT RELEASE 2000 Thrilling varietal character makes this a young wine to take notice of. It smells zesty and appealing with passionfruit, snappy snow-pea and herbaceous aromas. The palate is more giving than many sauvignons with soft mid-palate fruit of good intensity, and it balances out with a mouth-watering tang and a chalky dry finish.

## Brindabella Hills Chardonnay

*Childhood at Brindabella* was one of Miles Franklin's memorable novels about bush life in early Australia. It was written well before the national capital was built nearby. Maker: Dr Roger Harris.

CURRENT RELEASE 1999    For those who like subtle chardonnay, this is a pearler. It has a restrained bouquet and is tightly focused on palate. The flavours recall white peach and nectarine. It is gently oaked, and its appeal builds with each sip. Don't over-chill it, and try it with Pacific oysters with chopped onion, herbs and balsamic.

| | |
|---|---|
| Quality | ▼▼▼▼ |
| Value | ★★★┤ |
| Grapes | chardonnay |
| Region | Orange, NSW; Canberra Region, ACT; Yarra Valley, Vic. |
| Cellar | ▮ 3 |
| Alc./Vol. | 13.0% |
| RRP | $24.00 |

## Broke Estate Lacrima Angelorum

The names mean 'angels' tears', as opposed to Lacryma Christi which is that famous Italian dry white fashioned from the tears of Christ himself. This is from the Broke Fordwich sub-region of the Hunter.

CURRENT RELEASE 1999    This was picked at 20 degrees Baumé from cut-cane vines. It has a spicy/herbal aroma with hints of apricot jam and very attractive simple flavours. The taste has medium sweetness and finishes fairly abruptly with a dry after-palate. A pleasant but not spectacular sweetie. Try it with fruit salad.

| | |
|---|---|
| Quality | ▼▼▼ |
| Value | ★★┤ |
| Grapes | not stated |
| Region | Hunter Valley, NSW |
| Cellar | ▮ 2 |
| Alc./Vol. | 12.6% |
| RRP | $38.00 (cellar door) |

## Brokenwood Graveyard Vineyard Chardonnay

One of the authors had his fingers in the '98 version of this wine. No correspondence will be entered into. The 2000 could be the best yet under this label. Official makers are Iain Riggs and P.J. Charteris.

CURRENT RELEASE 2000    This took a while to spread its wings in the glass. The nose reveals quite a lot of timber, airing to reveal rich, fruit compote aromas. It's a big, gutsy, oaky chardonnay which makes a good mate for the shiraz from the same vineyard. The taste is rich and there's a chewy quality to the dense palate. It will improve with cellaring and goes well with turkey.

| | |
|---|---|
| Quality | ▼▼▼▼ |
| Value | ★★★ |
| Grapes | chardonnay |
| Region | Hunter Valley, NSW |
| Cellar | ▮ 4 |
| Alc./Vol. | 14.0% |
| RRP | $35.00 |

## Brokenwood ILR Aged Reserve Semillon

| | |
|---|---|
| Quality | 🍷🍷🍷🍷🍷 |
| Value | ★★★★★ |
| Grapes | semillon |
| Region | Hunter Valley, NSW |
| Cellar | 🍶 3+ |
| Alc./Vol. | 11.0% |
| RRP | $35.00 |

Penguin Best
Semillon

Iain Riggs, boss cocky at Brokenwood, is dedicated to producing great semillon. To that end, he began a program of holding back some of his semillon for maturation, to be re-issued as ILR Reserve, in much the same way as Tyrrells and Mount Pleasant. This wine is proof he's succeeding handsomely.
**CURRENT RELEASE 1996 This is a great semillon! The colour is full yellow and it has a rich, complex bouquet which includes toasty, buttery and slightly rubbery regional nuances. The palate is where it excels. It has great length and style, a powerfully intense, mature lemon/lanolin, toast flavour that retains its finesse while impressing with intensity and persistence. Spectacular with pan-fried John Dory.**

## Brookland Valley Verse One Chardonnay

| | |
|---|---|
| Quality | 🍷🍷🍷🍷 |
| Value | ★★★★ |
| Grapes | chardonnay |
| Region | Margaret River, WA |
| Cellar | 🍶 3 |
| Alc./Vol. | 13.8% |
| RRP | $21.00 |

Brookland Valley, whose symbol is that noted flautist Pan, commissioned the pixie-ish flautist Jane Rutter to record a CD of music to go with the Verse One wines. CURRENT RELEASE 2000 We actually preferred the Verse One to the more expensive Brookland chardonnay. It's lighter and easier to drink. The nose displays tropical fruit aromas including mango and passionfruit, and the clean, fresh, tangy appeal continues on the palate. Oak adds richness and length to the palate and it has oodles of appeal. It goes well with grilled scallops.

## Brookland Valley Verse One Semillon Sauvignon Blanc

| | |
|---|---|
| Quality | 🍷🍷🍷🍷🍷 |
| Value | ★★★★★ |
| Grapes | semillon; sauvignon blanc |
| Region | Margaret River, WA |
| Cellar | 🍶 2+ |
| Alc./Vol. | 12.5% |
| RRP | $16.00 ⑤ |

Verse One is Brookland Valley's lower-priced range of wines, but it is still in the premium class. The business is now 50 per cent-owned by BRL Hardy.
CURRENT RELEASE 2000 This is a very smart wine that in no way resembles a second-class citizen. It's pale lemon hued, and smells of delicate citrus, grassy and cashew fruit with a hint of free sulfur which will soon bind up. The palate is bracingly tangy, with good weight, presence and persistence. It's crunchy and has plenty of substance. It would go well with fish pie.

### Brown Brothers King Valley Gewurztraminer

Browns' is one of the most staunchly family-owned wine companies. It's hard to imagine them doing what the Oatleys have done with Rosemount, but hey! You never know. Maker: Terry Barnett and team.
CURRENT RELEASE 2000    This has a very scented, varietal aroma which reminds of bath powder: pungently flowery and spicy. In the mouth there's plenty of authentic gewurz flavour again, although it's not very complex. It's an instantly appealing wine, and would drink well with a dressed salad of cold duck, rocket and lychees.

| | |
|---|---|
| Quality | ♟♟♟♟ |
| Value | ★★★★ |
| Grapes | gewurztraminer |
| Region | King Valley, Vic. |
| Cellar | 3 |
| Alc./Vol. | 13.5% |
| RRP | $19.00 Ⓢ |

### Brown Brothers Spatlese Lexia

This is the Brown Bros equivalent of the restaurateur's garlic bread: it's a money-spinner that sells itself. Lexia is a synonym for muscat gordo blanco.
CURRENT RELEASE 2000    The colour is green-tinged light yellow, and it has an intense jasmine or bath powder-like scent of fragrant muscat fruit. It's quite sweet but also very fruity, with clean balancing acidity. It lacks a little finesse, but will please a lot of people. Put it alongside fresh fruit salad.

| | |
|---|---|
| Quality | ♟♟♟ |
| Value | ★★★⁴ |
| Grapes | muscat gordo blanco |
| Region | North East Vic. |
| Cellar | 1 |
| Alc./Vol. | 10.5% |
| RRP | $12.45 Ⓢ |

### Brown Brothers Victoria Chardonnay

We always thought the Brown Brothers bow label was one factor in the company's success: it's distinctive, it's attractive, and it's subtly different in colour and shape on various wines. So what do they do? They go and change it to this bland, boring *and* standardised new label. Yuk!
CURRENT RELEASE 2000    This is a decent wine at a fair price. It smells of passionfruit, confectionery and vanilla – pretty, but just lacks intensity all round. It's light and a bit short on the palate, with a slight oak/phenolic coarseness at the finish. It does have flavour and the price, as always, is affordable. It goes with cold turkey.

| | |
|---|---|
| Quality | ♟♟♟⁹ |
| Value | ★★★ |
| Grapes | chardonnay |
| Region | North East Vic. |
| Cellar | 2 |
| Alc./Vol. | 14.0% |
| RRP | $19.00 Ⓢ |

## Brown Brothers Victoria Semillon

| | |
|---|---|
| **Quality** | 🍷🍷🍷🍷 |
| **Value** | ★★★★ |
| **Grapes** | semillon |
| **Region** | North East Vic. |
| **Cellar** | 4 |
| **Alc./Vol.** | 13.5% |
| **RRP** | $16.50 (S) |

Intelligently, the Browns keep their semillon back for a while to allow bottle-aged character to develop, adding interest to a grape that can be austere.

CURRENT RELEASE 1998 This has been wood-aged, and some toasty, cedary aromas combine with lemon, stalky herbal semillon fruit. There's a hint of toasty developed character too. The taste is dry, lean and lemony with, again, attractive wood-fermented characters. Pair it with baked whole snapper.

## Burton McLaren Vale Chardonnay

| | |
|---|---|
| **Quality** | 🍷🍷🍷🍷 |
| **Value** | ★★★★ |
| **Grapes** | chardonnay |
| **Region** | McLaren Vale, SA |
| **Cellar** | 2 |
| **Alc./Vol.** | 14.0% |
| **RRP** | $18.35 |

This is a new label – no doubt it's one of the 121 new producers that came on-stream during the year 2000. That's one every 72 hours! Optimists all.

CURRENT RELEASE 2000 Here is a very decent debut and should ensure this new chum is noticed. It's fruit-accented, with melon-like and nougat/confection aromas. Clean and light- to medium-bodied, it has a fresh-acid finish which lingers nicely. What it lacks in finesse, it more than makes up with flavour. Serve with stuffed chicken wings.

## Bushrangers Bounty Chardonnay

| | |
|---|---|
| **Quality** | 🍷🍷🍷½ |
| **Value** | ★★★★ |
| **Grapes** | chardonnay |
| **Region** | Cowra, NSW |
| **Cellar** | 2 |
| **Alc./Vol.** | 13.0% |
| **RRP** | $14.00 |

Along with Mulyan, this is one of the brands of the Fagan family, who purchased their property from the winemaking medico Dr William Redfern (after whom the suburb was named) in 1886. Jenni and Peter Fagan planted their first vines in 1994.

CURRENT RELEASE 2000 Good value here! This is a very fresh, sprightly and somewhat steely young chardonnay, which emphasises fruit rather than wood. The aromas remind of nectarine and green apples, with tangy acids and a hint of sweetness to soften the ride. It would drink well with pork and apple sauce.

## Cape Mentelle Chardonnay

Margaret River chardonnay is one of Australia's great white wines and Cape Mentelle makes one of the best.

*Previous outstanding vintages: '94, '95, '97, '98*

CURRENT RELEASE 1999 Decanting chardonnays can work wonders and here's a case in point. Our sample opened up rather dumb but improved with air. It revealed a classy nose led by juicy tropical-fruit regional aromas of real strength. There are rich eggy, creamy notes too, all enhanced by smoky French oak. The palate is silky-soft in texture and full in body with an object lesson in integration of classy oak. Try it with grilled Western Australian marron.

**Quality** 🍷🍷🍷🍷🍷
**Value** ★★★★½
**Grapes** chardonnay
**Region** Margaret River, WA
**Cellar** 5
**Alc./Vol.** 14.0%
**RRP** $32.50

## Cape Mentelle Semillon Sauvignon

This wine shows how a style can evolve over the years. What started off dominated by tangy, cut-grass-type fruit is now a more complex benchmark that beautifully combines bright fruit character with very subtle barrel-ferment and lees elements.

CURRENT RELEASE 2000 An appetising nose of fresh gooseberry and citrus aromas along with some stone-fruit richness, although a bit less complex than last year's effort. It's better in the mouth with succulent fruit flavour which is smooth and fresh, allied to a whisper of nuttiness from some barrel treatment. The finish is chalky, dry and crisp. Try it with seafood mousse.

**Quality** 🍷🍷🍷🍷½
**Value** ★★★★
**Grapes** semillon; sauvignon blanc
**Region** Margaret River, WA
**Cellar** 3
**Alc./Vol.** 13.5%
**RRP** $22.00

## Cascabel Eden Valley Riesling

Winemaking partners Susana Fernandez and Duncan Ferguson have taken an adventurous tack with their McLaren Vale vineyard, planting some Spanish varieties – perhaps reflecting Susana's Iberian background.

CURRENT RELEASE 2000 An absolutely classic Eden Valley riesling nose introduces this wine in a fresh and appetising manner, with lifted floral scents, strong lime juice and hints of spice. The palate has real intensity and depth of citrus and spice flavours, finishing dry and crisp. A great companion to fettucine with prawns, coriander and lime.

**Quality** 🍷🍷🍷🍷½
**Value** ★★★★½
**Grapes** riesling
**Region** Eden Valley, SA
**Cellar** 5
**Alc./Vol.** 12.0%
**RRP** $16.50

## Cassegrain Fromenteau Chardonnay Reserve

| | |
|---|---|
| Quality | ♟ ♟ ♟ ♟ |
| Value | ★ ★ ★ |
| Grapes | chardonnay |
| Region | Hastings Valley, NSW |
| Cellar | 🍾 2 |
| Alc./Vol. | 13.5% |
| RRP | $24.95 |

Growing vines on the sub-tropical nothern end of the New South Wales coast may seem more a lifestyle decision than an attempt to make quality wine. But John Cassegrain has weathered the vicissitudes to make some good wines. Chardonnay may be the pick.

CURRENT RELEASE 1998    This is a well-made flavoury chardonnay that treads a commendable middle course between ripe fruit and secondary complexities. The nose has peachy fruit with a herbal touch and subtle nutty, creamy aromas. The palate is medium-bodied, smooth and dry to taste with a lick of toasty oak underneath. A seafood platter here.

## Castle Rock Chardonnay

| | |
|---|---|
| Quality | ♟ ♟ ♟ ♟ |
| Value | ★ ★ ★ ★ ♪ |
| Grapes | chardonnay |
| Region | Great Southern, WA |
| Cellar | 🍾 4 |
| Alc./Vol. | 13.0% |
| RRP | $21.00 |

Castle Rock is in the Porongorup Ranges near Albany. Chardonnay from this region shows much more cool-climate personality than that of other Western Australian vineyards.

CURRENT RELEASE 1999    This could, we suppose, be termed a chablis style, although it lacks any real similarity to the French wine of that name. It has very subtle grapefruit and white peach aromas with well-modulated light oak fitting in well. It's very appealing in the mouth with light, tangy fruit flavour, subtle secondary influences and tangy acidity. Good with delicate seafoods like crab.

## Castle Rock Riesling

| | |
|---|---|
| Quality | ♟ ♟ ♟ ♟ ♪ |
| Value | ★ ★ ★ ★ ★ |
| Grapes | riesling |
| Region | Great Southern, WA |
| Cellar | ➡ 2–8+ |
| Alc./Vol. | 12.0% |
| RRP | $18.00 |

If you're uncertain about the value of ageing white wines, this is a good place to start. Castle Rock is one of the Great Southern's finest and most ageworthy rieslings, only really coming into its own after a few years in bottle.

CURRENT RELEASE 2000    At the moment it has rather shy fruit character which is light and delicate, with a hint of blossom in the aroma, and some lime and lemon scents. The palate is similarly delicate, but it has a minerally backbone and enough high acid to help it flourish in the future. Buy a dozen and drink them over time, observing how they unfold. Serve it with fresh oysters now, lightly smoked salmon when mature.

## Chain of Ponds Riesling

The Amadio family has 135 hectares of vines in the Gumeracha and Kersbrook regions of the Adelaide Hills. They recently employed the zany marketer Zar Brooks, the man who put *War and Peace* on the d'Arenberg back labels, so we're waiting to see what effect he'll have.

CURRENT RELEASE 2000　If riesling were more fashionable you can bet the Hills would be full of it. This wine attests to the area's suitability. It's a fine wine, intensely lemony and slightly tropical, and very alive on the palate. There is a trace of astringency but it's probably just the exuberance of youth. Try it with grilled flounder.

| | |
|---|---|
| Quality | ♀♀♀♀ |
| Value | ★★★★ |
| Grapes | riesling |
| Region | Adelaide Hills, SA |
| Cellar | 6+ |
| Alc./Vol. | 12.5% |
| RRP | $21.00 |

## Chapel Hill Reserve Chardonnay

Chapel Hill Reserve epitomises an oaky style that's starting to look a bit passé, especially when confronted by a new generation of chardonnays with wood incorporated with subtlety and restraint.

CURRENT RELEASE 2000　Made with big wood input, this wine also has some fruit richness and creaminess in there and attractive mealy notes. But it's the oak you notice and it starts to pall on the palate after a while. This makes it difficult to drink more than a small amount, with the finish adding a bone-dry oaky aftertaste. Try it with prawn satays.

| | |
|---|---|
| Quality | ♀♀♀♀ |
| Value | ★★★ |
| Grapes | chardonnay |
| Region | McLaren Vale & Padthaway, SA |
| Cellar | 3 |
| Alc./Vol. | 13.5% |
| RRP | $22.00 |

## Chapel Hill Unwooded Chardonnay

Pam Dunsford was one of the first to push the unwooded chardonnay bandwagon and she's often made better wines than most.

CURRENT RELEASE 2001　This is a very fresh youngster with a slight whiff of sulfur and light pear and melon-like aromas. There's a minerally touch as well that differentiates it from some of the fruit-sweet unoaked chardonnays about the place. The palate is clean-tasting with light fruit and a chalky feel that gives it some savoury interest. Try it with yabbies.

| | |
|---|---|
| Quality | ♀♀♀♀ |
| Value | ★★★ |
| Grapes | chardonnay |
| Region | various, SA |
| Cellar | 3 |
| Alc./Vol. | 12.5% |
| RRP | $14.95 |

## Chapel Hill Verdelho

| | |
|---|---|
| Quality | ▼ ▼ ▼ |
| Value | ★ ★ ★ |
| Grapes | verdelho |
| Region | McLaren Vale, SA |
| Cellar | ▮ 3 |
| Alc./Vol. | 13.5% |
| RRP | $17.50 |

Verdelho gives the sort of fruity young whites that should be real crowd-pleasers, particularly in the summer months. Maker: Pamela Dunsford.

CURRENT RELEASE 2001    Still very young, this has a fresh unevolved nose with some tropical fruit aromas and smells that normally belong at the cosmetic counter. The palate has some succulent fruit-salady flavours and zesty acidity. It's a simple white for summer entertaining that should improve in bottle over the next year or so. A great wine for chicken sandwiches.

## Charles Sturt University Chardonnay

| | |
|---|---|
| Quality | ▼ ▼ ▼ ▵ |
| Value | ★ ★ ★ ★ ┤ |
| Grapes | chardonnay |
| Region | Wagga Wagga & Tumbarumba, NSW |
| Cellar | ▮ 2 |
| Alc./Vol. | 12.6% |
| RRP | $12.00 |

At Charles Sturt they not only teach students winemaking, they cleverly make wine and sell it to help finance the institution. Prices are always reasonable and quality is generally high.

CURRENT RELEASE 2000    This has a degree of refinement that belies its modest price tag. Very subtle barrel-ferment nuttiness adds interest to a core of dry stone-fruit aroma, and the palate is fresh, smooth and easy to quaff. It has enough tang to keep things lively and is good value. Exciting stuff with prawn cutlets.

## Chestnut Grove Verdelho

| | |
|---|---|
| Quality | ▼ ▼ ▼ |
| Value | ★ ★ ★ |
| Grapes | verdelho |
| Region | Pemberton, WA |
| Cellar | ▮ 3 |
| Alc./Vol. | 13.5% |
| RRP | $18.00 |

Verdelho was quite at home in Western Australia's Swan Valley, then it proved its adaptability by making the migration to Pemberton with minimal fuss.

CURRENT RELEASE 2000    Pale in colour, this has a very verdelho nose of medium intensity that's reminiscent of fruit jubes and fresh tropical juices. The simple, fruity, slightly sweet palate makes for an easy, crowd-pleasing white of no great personality. Try it with a chicken pie.

## Cheviot Bridge Chardonnay

The hills near Yea, just beyond the Yarra Valley, have long been a source of excellent chardonnay under the Murrindindi label. New vineyard plantings in the region, such as Cheviot Bridge, are reinforcing its reputation.

CURRENT RELEASE 2000   This is still an undeveloped youngster with citrus, nectarine and white peach characters, with a hint of butterscotch and sympathetically handled spicy, toasty oak. The flavour is long, subtle and intense, and will benefit by building complexity in the bottle. Judging by the Murrindindi chardonnay, it should cellar well in the short to medium term. Try it with seafood risotto.

| | |
|---|---|
| Quality | 🍷🍷🍷🍷 |
| Value | ★★★⭒ |
| Grapes | chardonnay |
| Region | Yea, Vic. |
| Cellar | 🍾 4 |
| Alc./Vol. | 13.0% |
| RRP | $27.00 |

## Clairault Sauvignon Blanc

Margaret River is one of those Australian regions with good form when it comes to sauvignon blanc. Blended with semillon, it's the stuff of many good-quality dry whites, and it also works well straight up.

CURRENT RELEASE 2000   Pristine varietal characters here in the form of an attractive clean nose combining tangy tropical fruit, citrus and herbal notes. In the mouth it has intense ripe sauvignon fruit of nice persistence and good body, ending in a well-balanced acid finish. A fresh, clean wine to accompany dolmades and dips.

| | |
|---|---|
| Quality | 🍷🍷🍷🍷 |
| Value | ★★★ |
| Grapes | sauvignon blanc |
| Region | Margaret River, WA |
| Cellar | 🍾 2 |
| Alc./Vol. | 13.0% |
| RRP | $22.00 |

## Clonakilla Riesling

The Canberra district looks to suit riesling. Clonakilla is among the region's best winemakers, and as expected their riesling is one of the top drops.

CURRENT RELEASE 2001   The classical riesling pale straw colour with a distinct green tinge to it is evident here. The nose has an intense, slightly musky aroma with hints of wild flowers and lime. It has the sort of subdued intensity that holds promise for future development, and the palate confirms it with a tight structure around a soft, fruit-sweet mid-palate, with a hint of residual sugar and a dry lemony finish. Serve it with Vietnamese spring rolls.

| | |
|---|---|
| Quality | 🍷🍷🍷🍷 |
| Value | ★★★★ |
| Grapes | riesling |
| Region | Murrumbateman, NSW (Canberra district) |
| Cellar | 🍾 5 |
| Alc./Vol. | 12.0% |
| RRP | $18.00 |

## Clonakilla Semillon Sauvignon Blanc

| | |
|---|---|
| Quality | 🍷🍷🍷 |
| Value | ★★★ |
| Grapes | semillon; sauvignon blanc |
| Region | Murrumbateman, NSW (Canberra district) |
| Cellar | 🍷 1 |
| Alc./Vol. | 12.0% |
| RRP | $16.00 |

Although his ground-breaking shiraz viognier gets the plaudits, Clonakilla's Tim Kirk quietly goes about the business of making a number of other good wines from this small Canberra region vineyard.
CURRENT RELEASE 2000    Pale and green-tinged in colour, this is a fresh youngster with tangy, light aromas of herbs, fruit salad, grass and lemon. There is a slightly soapy note to the nose as well. The palate is light yet reasonably intense, with pleasant dry flavours which finish off a little short. Good with steamed asparagus.

## Clonakilla Viognier

| | |
|---|---|
| Quality | 🍷🍷🍷🍷 |
| Value | ★★★↓ |
| Grapes | viognier |
| Region | Murrumbateman, NSW (Canberra district) |
| Cellar | 🍷 2 |
| Alc./Vol. | 12.5% |
| RRP | $28.00 |

The Kirks of Clonakilla have been playing around with viognier for a few years now, primarily as a small component added to their shiraz to give a beguiling Rhone-like fragrance, but also as a white varietal. This straight viognier is always in very limited supply.
CURRENT RELEASE 2000    Want to try something different? Well here it is. The nose has voluptuously aromatic scents that suggest apricots, pot-pourri, linen presses, lychee and talcum powder. Really. In the mouth it's round, exotic, viscous in texture and very long on the finish. Acidity is soft yet the palate isn't flabby.
Try it with rosemary-studded roast pork.

## Cloudy Bay Chardonnay

| | |
|---|---|
| Quality | 🍷🍷🍷🍷🍷 |
| Value | ★★★★ |
| Grapes | chardonnay |
| Region | Marlborough, NZ |
| Cellar | 🍷 3 |
| Alc./Vol. | 14.0% |
| RRP | $32.40 |

Sauvignon blanc gets the international plaudits for New Zealand, but chardonnay is their real white 'grand vin'. Cloudy Bay is always an excellent example.
CURRENT RELEASE 1999    Secondary lees, barrel and malolactic characters are always a part of the Cloudy Bay Chardonnay style, but they are never allowed to dominate the fruit input. The result is wines that combine succulent regional chardonnay aromas with enough complexity to keep you hooked. This is exactly that – citrus and melon fruit intermixed with spice and cashew characters in real harmony. It has good body and depth of flavour with some austerity on the finish. A good sup with noodles and lobster pieces.

## Cloudy Bay Sauvignon Blanc

Cloudy Bay defined New Zealand sauvignon blanc and took it to the world. Such is its esteem these days that it sells out in a flash, so you might have to hunt to find a bottle.

CURRENT RELEASE 2000    Not many wines are as consistent as this one. The 2000 edition follows the pattern exactly – a thrilling, succulent combination of bracing aromas and flavours like passionfruit, gooseberry, tomato leaves and lime. There's juicy fruit-sweet flavour, good depth and length with that hallmark zing of acidity that keeps it so appetising. Try it with tomato, basil and mozzarella bruschette.

| | |
|---|---|
| Quality | ♥♥♥♥♥ |
| Value | ★★★★ |
| Grapes | sauvignon blanc |
| Region | Marlborough, NZ |
| Cellar | 🍷 2 |
| Alc./Vol. | 13.5% |
| RRP | $21.50 |

## Cockatoo Ridge Reserve Chardonnay

The Cockatoo Ridge Reserve's coat of arms on this trendy battleship-grey label has what looks like a two-headed cocky on it, and we're not seeing double either. The Reserve is a step up from the standard label.

CURRENT RELEASE 1999    This ripe commercial style of chardonnay should be a crowd-pleaser. The nose has sweet stone-fruit and citrus aromas with subtle buttery and nutty nuances. In the mouth there is smooth fruit in a medium-bodied package with a clean finish, and some toasty oak perfumes the palate lightly. Serve it with chicken pie.

| | |
|---|---|
| Quality | ♥♥♥♥ |
| Value | ★★★ |
| Grapes | chardonnay |
| Region | Coonawarra, SA |
| Cellar | 🍷 2 |
| Alc./Vol. | 13.5% |
| RRP | $19.90 |

## Cockfighter's Ghost Chardonnay

Cockfighter was a horse who drowned long ago in the Wollombi Brook next to this Hunter Valley vineyard. The wonderfully atmospheric label captures the feel of that fateful dark, stormy night all those years ago.

CURRENT RELEASE 1999    This has a tropical, sweet-fruited nose typical of ripe Hunter chardonnay. It's reminiscent of figs, nuts and has smooth, understated oak influence. The palate has fine tropical-fruit flavour in good balance with creamy smooth barrel influence. A well-mannered Hunter chardonnay that doesn't overdo things. Serve it with little roasted spatchcocks.

| | |
|---|---|
| Quality | ♥♥♥♥ |
| Value | ★★★★┤ |
| Grapes | chardonnay |
| Region | Hunter Valley, NSW |
| Cellar | 🍷 2 |
| Alc./Vol. | 13.0% |
| RRP | $18.95 |

## Coldstream Hills Chardonnay

| | |
|---|---|
| Quality | 🍷🍷🍷🍷 |
| Value | ★★★ |
| Grapes | chardonnay |
| Region | Yarra Valley, Vic. |
| Cellar | 🍾 3 |
| Alc./Vol. | 13.5% |
| RRP | $26.00 ⑤ |

Coldstream Hills occupies a lovely spot. Its north-facing slopes look over the Yarra Valley from the southern hills; a pastoral landscape of great beauty. The wines aren't bad either.

CURRENT RELEASE 1999    An appealing chardonnay with mellow fruit and secondary characters well put together. There are syrupy fig and stone-fruit aromas of good concentration with very subtle oak input to aid texture rather than flavour. The palate is smooth, long and rather gentle, although there's no problem with fruit intensity. A good middle-of-the-road chardonnay to go with Chinese stirfried prawns.

## Coldstream Hills Reserve Chardonnay

| | |
|---|---|
| Quality | 🍷🍷🍷🍷🍷 |
| Value | ★★★★ |
| Grapes | chardonnay |
| Region | Yarra Valley, Vic. |
| Cellar | 🍾 2 |
| Alc./Vol. | 14.0% |
| RRP | $42.00 |

Chardonnay works so well in the Yarra Valley that it's difficult to believe that it hasn't been there always, but in the boom times of the 1800s it was of little importance.

CURRENT RELEASE 1998    This chardonnay brings great harmony with it, although the fact that it's 100 per cent barrel-fermented, half in new French oak, means that it shows notable wood character. The bouquet is mellow with fig, cashew, cream and nutty oak aromas that lead to a fine, long palate with smooth flavour dovetailed into French oak. The finish is dry and long. Suitable for chicken in a creamy sauce.

## Coolangatta Estate Alexander Berry Chardonnay

| | |
|---|---|
| Quality | 🍷🍷🍷🍷🍷 |
| Value | ★★★★ |
| Grapes | chardonnay |
| Region | Shoalhaven, NSW |
| Cellar | 🍾 5 |
| Alc./Vol. | 13.8% |
| RRP | $22.00 (cellar door) |

The Coolangatta Estate property is a hidden gem, located near the mouth of the Shoalhaven River in southern New South Wales. It is an unlikely place to make fine wine, but the track record of this wine would fill most Australian chardonnay makers with envy.

CURRENT RELEASE 2000    A delicious, refined wine that drinks well right now although history suggests it will age very nicely. It has a clean, buttery, creamy bouquet which suggests maturation on lees. The all-round impression is of harmony and subtle charm. It is tightly structured and long, with real finesse. And it has a future. Great with grilled scampi.

## Crabtree Watervale Riesling

The grapes from Robert Crabtree's 70-year-old riesling vines are made into a more modern style of Clare–Watervale riesling than most, and the wine probably isn't quite as ageworthy.

CURRENT RELEASE 2000   A lovely fresh sweet-sour character pervades this young riesling and makes it delectable drinking as a youngster. There's a succulent nose with slightly estery passionfruit, lime and herbal aromas, and it tastes similarly limey and juicy, yet clean and dry finishing. Try it with grilled whiting.

| | |
|---|---|
| Quality | ▼▼▼▼◗ |
| Value | ★★★★◗ |
| Grapes | riesling |
| Region | Clare Valley, SA |
| Cellar | ◖ 5 |
| Alc./Vol. | 12.0% |
| RRP | $16.00 |

## Craig Avon Chardonnay

Ken Lang of Craig Avon is a persistent man, growing, vinifying and promoting his Mornington Peninsula wines with real dedication and determination. Chardonnay is usually the pick of the crop.

CURRENT RELEASE 1999   An appealing wine on the nose, this has honeydew melon and stone-fruit aromas with a bit of cashew-like richness. Unlike some of its Mornington brethren it's not overworked, oak is subtle and there's an attractive nuttiness to it. The medium-bodied palate is smooth and soft with a light, dry finish. Serve it with snapper cutlets.

| | |
|---|---|
| Quality | ▼▼▼▼ |
| Value | ★★★ |
| Grapes | chardonnay |
| Region | Mornington Peninsula, Vic. |
| Cellar | ◖ 2 |
| Alc./Vol. | 13.4% |
| RRP | $37.00 |

## Craiglee Chardonnay

When it was one of the vineyard jewels of nineteenth-century Victoria, Craiglee had no chardonnay planted. Despite this, it now looks an ideal spot to grow it, and Craiglee can sometimes produce the best chardonnay for miles around. Maker: Patrick Carmody.

CURRENT RELEASE 2000   This bright youngster has great balance, avoiding the excesses of so many overworked big Aussie chardonnays. Melon and citrus aromas are well integrated with hints of vanilla and spice from classy oak. In the mouth it has lovely texture and a fine, subtle and long flavour. It's very stylish, with good depth, measured richness and soft acidity. Works well with crab cakes.

| | |
|---|---|
| Quality | ▼▼▼▼◗ |
| Value | ★★★★ |
| Grapes | chardonnay |
| Region | Sunbury, Vic. |
| Cellar | ◖ 4+ |
| Alc./Vol. | 14.0% |
| RRP | $30.00 |

# Cranswick Estate Vignette Botrytis Semillon

| | |
|---|---|
| Quality | 🍷🍷🍷︎ |
| Value | ★★★★ |
| Grapes | semillon |
| Region | Riverina, NSW |
| Cellar | 🍾 2 |
| Alc./Vol. | 11.0% |
| RRP | $12.75 (375 ml) |

It's unusual to see a Riverina botrytised semillon at such a keen price. This is an unoaked version that was released last year and is still in the shops.
CURRENT RELEASE 1999    If you want to see botrytis character straight up, without the influence of French oak, try this. It has a sweet juicy nose full of grapey scents, apricot and cumquat-like botrytis aromas and a malty touch. The flavour is consistent with the nose, and the palate is sweet and tangy. It finishes pretty light and lacks the complexity of wines with a higher pedigree, but it's good value. Try it with crème brûlée.

# Cullen Chardonnay

| | |
|---|---|
| Quality | 🍷🍷🍷🍷︎ |
| Value | ★★★ |
| Grapes | chardonnay |
| Region | Margaret River, WA |
| Cellar | ➠ 2–7+ |
| Alc./Vol. | 14.0% |
| RRP | $55.00 |

A true star in the Margaret River firmament, winemaker Vanya Cullen is one of this country's great wine talents.
*Previous outstanding vintages: '90, '92, '93, '94, '95, '96, '97*
CURRENT RELEASE 1999  The '99 has an understated nose of mineral, citrus, melon and nutty elements robed in classy oak. In the mouth it's fine and long, tight in structure and very restrained. Rather unevolved at the moment but time should see it build into something special. A good match for Chinese-style steamed scampi.

# Cullen Semillon Sauvignon Blanc

| | |
|---|---|
| Quality | 🍷🍷🍷🍷🍷 |
| Value | ★★★★★ |
| Grapes | semillon 60%; sauvignon blanc 40% |
| Region | Margaret River, WA |
| Cellar | 🍾 6 |
| Alc./Vol. | 14.0% |
| RRP | $28.00 |

In 2000 Vanya Cullen decided that the quality of her Margaret River semillon was such that she would reverse the usual order of things, where sauvignon blanc makes up the majority of the blend, and give semillon the major role. It's worked superbly.
*Previous outstanding vintages: '93, '95, '96, '97, '98, '99*
CURRENT RELEASE 2000    Like dry Bordeaux made from these varieties, this very impressive wine doesn't rely on simple varietal fruit for its personality. Those varietal clues make way for a seamless combination of rich peach and gentle herbal hints, subtle nutty oak, and smooth acidity. It's a complete, satisfying wine of great depth, and it finishes long and subtle. A wine for contemplation. A good food match would be buttery baked snapper cutlets.

## Currency Creek Sauvignon Blanc

Currency Creek lies at the southern end of South
Australia's Mount Lofty Ranges, where they meet the
sea. The mild maritime environment suits sauvignon
blanc well.

CURRENT RELEASE 2000  Most people these days
probably have no idea what gooseberries smell and
taste like, despite the authors describing sauvignon
blanc that way. Unfortunately that's exactly what this
wine smells like: a green fruit aroma with a hint of
grapey sweetness that's fresh and appealing (just like
gooseberries really). The palate is clean with a fruity,
soft mid-palate and balanced acidity on a chalky-dry
finish. A good wine for a salad niçoise.

| | |
|---|---|
| Quality | ♊♊♊♊ |
| Value | ★★★ |
| Grapes | sauvignon blanc |
| Region | Currency Creek, SA |
| Cellar | ▮ 2 |
| Alc./Vol. | 12.0% |
| RRP | $20.50 |

## D'Arenberg The Olive Grove Chardonnay

D'Arenberg may be an ultra-traditional McLaren Vale
producer in some ways but that hasn't stopped them
from getting on the bandwagon with the new-fangled
chardonnay grape.

CURRENT RELEASE 2000  At D'Arenberg they make
two chardonnays, a full-on fat mouthful called The
Other Side, and this Olive Grove wine which is a bit
less daunting. It has a succulent ripe nose of melon
and citrus fruit aromas with a measured seasoning of
dusty oak. The fruity palate is medium in body with
good depth, subtle oak flavour, and sherbety
balancing acid. Serve it with cold chicken and salad.

| | |
|---|---|
| Quality | ♊♊♊♊ |
| Value | ★★★★ |
| Grapes | chardonnay |
| Region | McLaren Vale, SA |
| Cellar | ▮ 2 |
| Alc./Vol. | 13.5% |
| RRP | $16.00 |

## D'Arenberg The Stump Jump Riesling Marsanne

Riesling marsanne blends aren't common, possibly
because they both have such distinctive personalities
on their own, but mixed marriages can work well, so
why not?

CURRENT RELEASE 2000  The nose has floral accents,
but it's more winey and less 'pretty' than young
riesling on its own. The palate has reasonable depth
and straightforward flavour with moderate acidity.
An everyday white with none of the fireworks (and
none of the passion) of some mixed marriages. Try it
with chicken schnitzel.

| | |
|---|---|
| Quality | ♊♊♊ |
| Value | ★★★ |
| Grapes | riesling; marsanne |
| Region | McLaren Vale, SA |
| Cellar | ▮ 2 |
| Alc./Vol. | 12.0% |
| RRP | $11.00 ⑤ |

## Dalrymple Chardonnay

| | |
|---|---|
| Quality | ♟♟♟♟ |
| Value | ★★★⯪ |
| Grapes | chardonnay |
| Region | Pipers River, Tas. |
| Cellar | 🍾 3 |
| Alc./Vol. | 13.5% |
| RRP | $22.60 |

The Dalrymple vineyard is a joint exercise between former Melbourne publicist Jill Mitchell and her sister Anne and brother-in-law, medical specialist Dr Bert Sundstrup, who makes the wines. Special attention is paid to viticulture in this damp, high-vigour site.

CURRENT RELEASE 1999   Some of the pungency found in Dalrymple's sauvignon blanc is also found in the chardonnay. There's an exaggerated passionfruit, tropical and grapefruit aroma, driven by the grape rather than the oak, which plays a supportive role. It has good concentration and length, and fine structure. Try it with fish in a red capsicum aioli.

## Dalrymple Sauvignon Blanc

| | |
|---|---|
| Quality | ♟♟♟♟♟ |
| Value | ★★★★★ |
| Grapes | sauvignon blanc |
| Region | Pipers River, Tas. |
| Cellar | 🍾 1 |
| Alc./Vol. | 12.6% |
| RRP | $24.00 |

You might expect Tasmania to produce more good sauvignon blancs than it does. The climate should be well suited. In fact, sauvignon is a difficult variety to grow and this is borne out by the poor average standard of the wines – at least in Australia. Dalrymple's regularly shines.

CURRENT RELEASE 2000   This is sauvignon blanc writ large! The passionfruity, tropical-fruit pungency of the grape comes through strongly and its intensity on the palate doesn't disappoint. Some may see a certain sweaty note in the wine but others will love it. It has plenty of strength and persistence in the mouth. Try it with mussel soup.

## Dalwhinnie Chardonnay

| | |
|---|---|
| Quality | ♟♟♟⯪ |
| Value | ★★⯪ |
| Grapes | chardonnay |
| Region | Pyrenees, Vic. |
| Cellar | ⬤— 1–4+ |
| Alc./Vol. | 13.5% |
| RRP | $39.70 |

The Pyrenees region needs make no excuses about its red wines, but whites have been less easily mastered. Dalwhinnie is making real effort with this wine, but it's not there yet. Maker: Don Lewis.

CURRENT RELEASE 1999   The bouquet is clean and nutty with hints of cashew, peach, and toasty barrel-ferment characters. It turns rather lean and drying in the mouth, with a touch of harshness. Short-term cellaring should bring some rewards. One to serve with yabbies in a seafood reduction sauce.

# David Traeger Verdelho

Traeger used to be a winemaker at Mitchelton. In 1986 he set up his own business in the same district and this unabashedly commercial verdelho has been his biggest success story.

CURRENT RELEASE 2000    This is very easy to like. It smells floral and lightly spicy, with a hint of vanilla, and is starting to show some forward development. The flavour is soft and full in the mouth, with much less sweetness than some past vintages. It has loads of flavour and finishes cleanly, with a slight grip. Goes well with Thai fish cakes.

| | |
|---|---|
| Quality | ▼ ▼ ▼ ▼ |
| Value | ★ ★ ★ |
| Grapes | verdelho |
| Region | various, Vic. |
| Cellar | 🍾 2 |
| Alc./Vol. | 14.0% |
| RRP | $18.50 |

# Deakin Estate Chardonnay

Some Riverland wineries try to make their chardonnay into something more by adding chips and God knows what else in the name of oak character. Why bother, when they often muck up the wine's main asset: its nice, clean, simple fruit. Here's one that succeeds.

CURRENT RELEASE 2000    Quite delicious but essentially plain fruit is the hallmark of this good-value chardonnay. Simple melon and cashew aromas; possibly unwooded. It's light and one-dimensional but clean and fruity and well made. It's short and has a smidgin of sweetness, but is balanced. It goes well with corn fitters.

| | |
|---|---|
| Quality | ▼ ▼ ▼ ▼ |
| Value | ★ ★ ★ ★ |
| Grapes | chardonnay |
| Region | Murray Valley, Vic. |
| Cellar | 🍾 1 |
| Alc./Vol. | 13.5% |
| RRP | $10.50 Ⓢ |

# Deakin Estate Sauvignon Blanc

This brand, part of the sizeable Wingara group which also owns Katnook, was named after Australia's second prime minister, Alfred Deakin, whose work helped start the Murray Valley irrigation scheme in the 1890s. If it weren't for irrigation, the Riverland wine industry might never have been.

CURRENT RELEASE 2000    The colour is appropriately pale yellow and the wine has retained its freshness and delicacy thus far. The aromas are subdued but clean and correct; it's light and fresh to taste and while it lacks intensity of varietal fruit, it has good quality and respectable depth of lightly herbal, stone-fruit flavour. Good with fish and chips.

| | |
|---|---|
| Quality | ▼ ▼ ▼ |
| Value | ★ ★ ★ ★ |
| Grapes | sauvignon blanc |
| Region | Murray Valley, Vic. |
| Cellar | 🍾 1 |
| Alc./Vol. | 13.5% |
| RRP | $10.50 Ⓢ |

## De Bortoli Sacred Hill Traminer Riesling

| | |
|---|---|
| Quality | ♀ ♀ ♀ ♀ |
| Value | ★ ★ ★ ★ ★ |
| Grapes | gewurztraminer; riesling |
| Region | not stated |
| Cellar | ▮ 2 |
| Alc./Vol. | 10.5% |
| RRP | $7.00 ⑤ |

It's hard work uncovering good cheap white wines these days. De Bortoli often comes up with the goods. The wine has a terrific cork: a full-length bleached one-piece – not a cheap and nasty agglomerate nor a lump of plastic.

CURRENT RELEASE 2000   One sniff of this and you'll be a goner. Won over, we mean. The colour is light yellow and the aroma is immediately arresting: pungent, grapey, lolly-ish, confectionery muscat fruit – thanks to the gewurz. It's fresh and vibrantly fruity. The sweetness is close to spatlese level, but it's clean and well-made and will win lots of friends. Try it with fresh grapes and crème fraiche.

## De Bortoli Windy Peak Rhine Riesling

| | |
|---|---|
| Quality | ♀ ♀ ♀ ♀ |
| Value | ★ ★ ★ ★ ★ |
| Grapes | riesling |
| Region | various, Vic. |
| Cellar | ▮ 3 |
| Alc./Vol. | 13.5% |
| RRP | $14.00 |

We would have thought De Bortoli would have dropped the 'Rhine' from 'Riesling' by now. Whatever name it's called by, this is great value.

CURRENT RELEASE 2000   Pronounced varietal character lends the nose aromas of lime zest, floral talc and pine. In the mouth it's surprisingly rich and full with clever use of residual sugar giving it strong flavour impact ahead of a long, dry finish. Great value with coriander and ginger chicken.

## De Bortoli Yarra Valley Chardonnay

| | |
|---|---|
| Quality | ♀ ♀ ♀ ♀ ♀ |
| Value | ★ ★ ★ ★ |
| Grapes | chardonnay |
| Region | Yarra Valley, Vic. |
| Cellar | ▮ 4 |
| Alc./Vol. | 13.5% |
| RRP | $25.00 |

The De Bortoli Dixon's Creek base is a focal point of the northern Yarra Valley with a restaurant, good tasting facilities and excellent wines. Worth a visit if ever you're in that neck of the woods.

CURRENT RELEASE 1999   This still has a bright youthful colour for an oaked chardonnay. The bouquet is subtle and complex with restrained fruit and eggy chardonnay smells mixed in with oatmeal, spice and oak aromas. The medium-weight palate isn't as plump as the '98 at the same stage but it has good intensity of fine flavour. It finishes clean and long. Serve fettucine with scallops here.

### Deen De Bortoli Vat 6 Verdelho

Deen De Bortoli was the second generation De Bortoli to make wine at the family pile at Bilbul, near Griffith. Vittorio begat Deen, who begat Darren and Leanne, who've since begat a few of their own to carry on. CURRENT RELEASE 2000    This soft, fruity Riverina white won't break the bank. It overflows with aromas of confectionery and spices. Delicate stone-fruit flavours flood the mouth, and a suggestion of sweetness adds to its immediate appeal. The label says oak has been used, but it doesn't really show. Pair it with a salad of tomato, bocconcini, basil and olive oil.

| | |
|---|---|
| Quality | ♟ ♟ ♟ |
| Value | ★ ★ ★ ♪ |
| Grapes | verdelho |
| Region | Riverina, NSW |
| Cellar | 🍾 1 |
| Alc./Vol. | 13.0% |
| RRP | $11.60 Ⓢ |

### Deen De Bortoli Vat 7 Chardonnay

The De Bortoli clan have jazzed up the packaging of this range. But why no smiling head-shot of the happy squire himself? He's a very photogenic guy! CURRENT RELEASE 2000    As usual, this offers terrific flavour for the price. It comes over all smoky at first, with burnt-toast oak which asserts itself on the bouquet but less so in the mouth. It tastes softly fruity and while it's not hugely complex, it has loads of appeal. Especially at the price. Try it with whitebait fritters.

| | |
|---|---|
| Quality | ♟ ♟ ♟ ♪ |
| Value | ★ ★ ★ ★ |
| Grapes | chardonnay |
| Region | Riverina, NSW |
| Cellar | 🍾 2 |
| Alc./Vol. | 13.5% |
| RRP | $11.75 Ⓢ |

### Delatite Dead Man's Hill Gewurztraminer

The Ritchie family has farmed the same land for four generations. Robert and Vivienne started the vineyard in 1968, and followed it with a winery. Their daughter Rosie is winemaker and son David is viticulturist. **CURRENT RELEASE 2000    Anyone sceptical about traminer should try this: it's a gorgeous wine. The fragrant spicy aromas recall lychees and frangipani, and the varietal character is not only clear, but complex. In the mouth it's rich and concentrated, with terrific depth and length. It's perfect with tuna sashimi and truffle oil dressing.**

| | |
|---|---|
| Quality | ♟ ♟ ♟ ♟ ♟ |
| Value | ★ ★ ★ ★ ★ |
| Grapes | gewurztraminer |
| Region | Mansfield, Strathbogie and Whitfield, Vic. |
| Cellar | 🍾 5 |
| Alc./Vol. | 13.0% |
| RRP | $22.00 |

Penguin Best White Blend/Other Variety

## Delatite Riesling

| | |
|---|---|
| Quality | ♟♟♟♟ |
| Value | ★★★★⁴ |
| Grapes | riesling |
| Region | Mansfield & Strathbogie Ranges, Vic. |
| Cellar | ▪ 7+ |
| Alc./Vol. | 11.5% |
| RRP | $18.00 |

Delatite has over the past 20 years established itself as one of the finest Australian riesling makers. Lately they've been including fruit from other vineyards: this is 85 per cent Delatite, and 15 per cent growers in Mansfield and the Strathbogie Ranges. Maker: Rosie Ritchie.

CURRENT RELEASE 2000 This is a delicate cool-climate riesling: you can almost sniff the alpine air rolling off the ski fields. There are lemon-juice and lightly herbal, passionfruit aromas while the palate is dry, crisp and tart. It has moderate length and fine balance and could reward ageing. Serve with crab timbales.

## Delatite Sauvignon Blanc

| | |
|---|---|
| Quality | ♟♟♟⌡ |
| Value | ★★★ |
| Grapes | sauvignon blanc |
| Region | Mansfield, Vic. |
| Cellar | ▪ 1 |
| Alc./Vol. | 13.5% |
| RRP | $18.00 |

The film *The Man from Snowy River* was shot at the little village of Merrijig, near the Delatite vineyard. This wine is 100 per cent estate grown. Maker: Rosie Ritchie.

CURRENT RELEASE 2000 This is our sort of sauvignon: we could drink several glasses at a sitting. Its crisp grassy aroma is not excessively pungent, but has subtler snapped-twig and crushed-herb notes. It is clean and delicate in the mouth, fresh and full of vitality. It's best drunk as young as possible, perhaps with fresh Pacific oysters and lemon juice.

## Delatite Unoaked Chardonnay

| | |
|---|---|
| Quality | ♟♟♟♟ |
| Value | ★★★★ |
| Grapes | chardonnay |
| Region | Mansfield, Vic. |
| Cellar | ▪ 2 |
| Alc./Vol. | 12.5% |
| RRP | $18.00 |

This is one of the better unwooded chardonnays doing the rounds. Too often, this genre is an excuse to sell sweetened-up, second-rate grapes under an excessive price tag. The grapes are all Mansfield region, 60 per cent from the Delatite vineyard. Maker: Rosie Ritchie.

CURRENT RELEASE 2000 The colour is pale lemon and it smells enticingly of fragrant passionfruit and grapefruit, absolutely pristine and spring-water fresh. Light-bodied yet with good intensity, it's lively and refreshing, with plenty of mouth-watering acidity. Try it with deep-fried whiting and salad.

## Derwent Estate Chardonnay

This is a tiny, 4.5-hectare vineyard at Granton on the Derwent River. The wines are contract-made by neighbour Stefano Lubiana. This wine scored a high gold and trophy for best chardonnay at the 2001 Tasmanian Regional Wine Show.

CURRENT RELEASE 2000   An impressive fruit-driven style, it smells deliciously grapefruity, with hints of peach and tropical fruits, and very subtly handled oak. The flavours run deep, rich and long on the palate. It is very refined and has amazing persistence, without obvious oak or alcohol. Great with grilled Tasmanian crayfish.

| | |
|---|---|
| Quality | ▼▼▼▼▼ |
| Value | ★★★★★ |
| Grapes | chardonnay |
| Region | Derwent Valley, Tas. |
| Cellar | 🍷 5 |
| Alc./Vol. | 13.5% |
| RRP | $25.00 (cellar door) |

## Devil's Lair Chardonnay

Devil's Lair was founded by Perth brewing tycoon Phil Sexton in 1985 and acquired by Southcorp in 1996. Sexton has gone on to establish more breweries and, it's rumoured, another vineyard.

CURRENT RELEASE 1999   A very complex chardonnay, with layers of flavour and concentrated fruit in typical Margaret River style. It's also restrained and that augurs well for its future. Flavours of butter, toasted nuts, peach and caramel abound. It's still reserved and maybe a tad austere, but age should bring forth some rewards. Drink with pan-fried scallops.

| | |
|---|---|
| Quality | ▼▼▼▼▼ |
| Value | ★★★ |
| Grapes | chardonnay |
| Region | Margaret River, WA |
| Cellar | ➥ 1–5+ |
| Alc./Vol. | 14.0% |
| RRP | $41.00 ⑤ |

## Devil's Lair Fifth Leg

We tasted three bottles before we found one that wasn't corked, which may or may not be an issue. It's a variation on a blend theme that's common in Margaret River. The 2000 was made by Janice McDonald.

CURRENT RELEASE 2000   A delicious, unwooded dry white that's dominated by the sauvignon blanc component at this stage. It has a glowing light yellow hue and a distinctive aroma of passionfruit, lemon and gooseberry. It's smooth and seamless on the palate with delicious subtlety and balance. The varietal character is not too pungent. Try it with trout with almonds.

| | |
|---|---|
| Quality | ▼▼▼▼▼ |
| Value | ★★★✦ |
| Grapes | sauvignon blanc; semillon; chardonnay |
| Region | Margaret River, WA |
| Cellar | 🍷 4 |
| Alc./Vol. | 13.5% |
| RRP | $21.60 |

## Diamond Valley Yarra Valley Chardonnay

| | |
|---|---|
| Quality | 🍷🍷🍷🍷🍷 |
| Value | ★★★★★ |
| Grapes | chardonnay |
| Region | Yarra Valley, Vic. |
| Cellar | 🍾 4 |
| Alc./Vol. | 13.0% |
| RRP | $20.60 |

This high-flying boutique is still owned by the family that founded it, and shows no sign of selling out. That means continuity of style direction and real commitment to quality. Here's to that!

CURRENT RELEASE 1999   This is an exciting, exotic and slightly 'out there' style of chardonnay. The slight bottle-pong to begin quickly unfolds into complex nutty, toasty, mealy and funky complexities, with lots of barrel-ferment character. The intensity and focus of the savoury flavours is totally arresting. The oak is restrained. Try it with tuna sashimi with truffle oil.

## Dominion Wines Alexander Park Chardonnay

| | |
|---|---|
| Quality | 🍷🍷🍷🍷 |
| Value | ★★★✦ |
| Grapes | chardonnay |
| Region | Strathbogie Ranges, Vic. |
| Cellar | 🍾 2 |
| Alc./Vol. | 13.0% |
| RRP | $18.00 Ⓢ |

This is a new outfit with a 90-hectare vineyard in the Strathbogie Ranges, offering contract winemaking for other small growers. Winemaker is Rob Dolan, formerly of Yarra Ridge and a long-time Mildara Blass employee.

CURRENT RELEASE 2000   A pretty decent first outing. It's clean, fruit-driven, peachy stuff that doesn't tax the concentration too much. Simple but good, it has nuances of pineapple and little discernible oak impact. Try it with a prawn, lychee and rocket salad.

## Dowie Doole Chenin Blanc

| | |
|---|---|
| Quality | 🍷🍷🍷🍷 |
| Value | ★★★★✦ |
| Grapes | chenin blanc |
| Region | McLaren Vale, SA |
| Cellar | 🍾 2 |
| Alc./Vol. | 13.5% |
| RRP | $14.00 |

Few wineries have a go with chenin blanc. Of those that do, most pitch it too low, with a lot of residual sugar. Maker: Mike Farmilo.

CURRENT RELEASE 2000   A very attractive chenin, not green or sweet, but blessed with a seamlessly smooth palate and a delicious balance of straw, lemon and creamy aromas. It is generous but lively, and ever-so-drinkable. Try it chilled with salad niçoise.

| | |
|---|---|
| Quality | 🍷🍷🍷✦ |
| Value | ★★★ |
| Grapes | chenin blanc |
| Region | McLaren Vale, SA |
| Cellar | 🍾 2 |
| Alc./Vol. | 12.5% |
| RRP | $16.25 |

CURRENT RELEASE 2001   We're not sure this is as good as the 2000, but it's still a fine drink and will be better after a few months in bottle. Peppermint/lolly confectionery aromas are very youthful, and the taste is light, simple and sherbety, and finishes slightly short. It's likely to fill out with a little time and drink at its best around Christmas 2001. It goes with fish and chips.

## Eldridge Estate Chardonnay

David Lloyd takes his winemaking and viticulture very seriously. His inquiring mind has led to some surprising innovations and his wine quality is on a path of steady improvement.

CURRENT RELEASE 1999   This chardonnay combines winemaking input with good cool-climate grapes to produce a wine of attractive complexity and finesse. There are melon and citrus aromas and flavours with lots of creamy, nutty and mealy touches to add dimension. It's smooth in texture with good length and lively acid balance. A good companion to baked snapper.

| | |
|---|---|
| Quality | 🍷🍷🍷🍷🍷 |
| Value | ★★★⁺ |
| Grapes | chardonnay |
| Region | Mornington Peninsula, Vic. |
| Cellar | 🍾 2 |
| Alc./Vol. | 13.5% |
| RRP | $32.00 |

## Elgee Park Family Reserve Riesling

Victoria's picturesque Mornington Peninsula is a holiday retreat for thousands of Melburnians. Historically the beaches and verdant hinterland attracted the visitors, but these days the wineries are another drawcard. Elgee Park is the vineyard where it all started.

CURRENT RELEASE 2000   Perhaps a shade less ripe than the '99 edition, this still has real charm. Lime juice, floral aromas, a trace of leafy regional character and a slightly sweaty touch meet the nose. The palate is pleasantly intense with rich varietal flavour counterpointed by dry, tangy acidity. Works well with spring rolls wrapped in leafy Vietnamese mint.

| | |
|---|---|
| Quality | 🍷🍷🍷🍷 |
| Value | ★★★⁺ |
| Grapes | riesling |
| Region | Mornington Peninsula, Vic. |
| Cellar | 🍾 3 |
| Alc./Vol. | 13.0% |
| RRP | $17.00 |

## Elmswood Estate Chardonnay

Elmswood Estate is a new name from the southern end of the Yarra Valley. The wines are competently made and regionally typical. Elmswood produces two chardonnays which are basically the same wine, one made with the benefit of oak and one without. This is the oaked version.

CURRENT RELEASE 2000    There's good light varietal character on the nose of the stone-fruit kind, along with some subtle oak and winery treatment that adds nutty, yeasty and milky touches. In the mouth it's light, soft and round with a fruit-sweet middle palate, well-integrated lightly toasty oak and a soft, clean finish. Serve it with prosciutto and melon.

| | |
|---|---|
| Quality | 🍷🍷🍷🍷 |
| Value | ★★★ |
| Grapes | chardonnay |
| Region | Yarra Valley, Vic. |
| Cellar | 🍾 2 |
| Alc./Vol. | 13.3% |
| RRP | $25.00 |

## etc. Chardonnay

| | |
|---|---|
| Quality | ♥ ♥ ♥ |
| Value | ★ ★ ★ |
| Grapes | chardonnay |
| Region | various |
| Cellar | ⬦ 1 |
| Alc./Vol. | 13.0% |
| RRP | $12.00 ⑤ |

Groovy packaging. No capital letters. Silly name. This type of labelling is clearly designed to appeal to some demographic the wine industry thinks it's missing out on, but we can't quite work out who they are.
CURRENT RELEASE 1999   There is a light, unfussed peachy nose that's immediately appealing. Fruit controls things; oak has taken a holiday. In the mouth that fresh personality is confirmed with clean melony flavour and a soft dry finish. A gulpable chardonnay to serve at a casual picnic lunch.

## Evans and Tate Margaret River Classic

| | |
|---|---|
| Quality | ♥ ♥ ♥ ♥ |
| Value | ★ ★ ★ |
| Grapes | not stated |
| Region | Margaret River, WA |
| Cellar | ⬦ 1 |
| Alc./Vol. | 12.5% |
| RRP | $18.00 ⑤ |

This pretty well sums up the Classic Dry White syndrome that's prevalent in Western Australia. They are usually fresh and lively wines made for early consumption. They also have a friendlier price tag than some other Western whites. Maker: Virginia Willcock.
CURRENT RELEASE 2000   A pale wine with a simple, clean nose of grapey and lemony aromas with herbal and herbaceous touches. In the mouth there's some tropical fruit and grassy flavours with a slightly skinsy firm finish. A white to drink young with fresh shellfish.

## Evans and Tate Margaret River Semillon

| | |
|---|---|
| Quality | ♥ ♥ ♥ ♥ |
| Value | ★ ★ ★ ⟩ |
| Grapes | semillon |
| Region | Margaret River, WA |
| Cellar | ⬤— 1–4 |
| Alc./Vol. | 13.0% |
| RRP | $19.50 |

Evans and Tate are big players in the Western Australian wine scene. Now headquartered in the Margaret River region, they were pioneers of the new Jindong sub-region under the energetic direction of boss Frank Tate.
CURRENT RELEASE 2000   Here is a young semillon with fresh lemon, apple and herbal aromas coupled to a measure of nutty oak. The palate has more than expected fruit-sweetness mid-palate. The taste of oak doesn't intrude too much and it finishes dry, yet remains quite straightforward without complex integration of fruit and oak flavours. Good drinking now, but needs time in bottle to sort itself out, then drink with stirfried seafood.

## Evans and Tate Two Vineyards Chardonnay

The inexorable southward march of viticulture in the West has changed the wine scene dramatically in the last couple of decades. Evans and Tate began in the Swan Valley, but now they've moved lock, stock and barrel(s) to Margaret River.
CURRENT RELEASE 2000    This is a pale chardonnay with pear and melon-like fruit aromas and a straightforward, succulent, fruit-driven palate that's smooth and easy to glug. Clever use of fruit-sweetness and a touch of oak ensure this will be popular for casual entertaining. The finish is clean and dry with a hint of oak on the aftertaste. Serve it with Asian-inspired goodies.

| | |
|---|---|
| Quality | 🍷🍷🍷 |
| Value | ★★★ |
| Grapes | chardonnay |
| Region | Margaret River, WA |
| Cellar | 🍾 2 |
| Alc./Vol. | 13.5% |
| RRP | $19.50 Ⓢ |

## Eyton Chardonnay

Under the ownership of the late Newell Cowan and his daughter Diedre, the old Yarra Vale vineyard has been transformed since 1993 into this Yarra Valley showplace called Eyton-on-Yarra.
CURRENT RELEASE 1999    This style has meandered a bit in the past, sometimes showing shaded fruit character and lack of ripeness. Here we don't have that problem, but it does have a very substantial oak and malolactic input. Stone fruit and melon is there in the middle, but nutty, buttery and spicy oak influences border on playing too big a part. More time in bottle should tone things down a bit. Meanwhile drink it with chargrilled salmon.

| | |
|---|---|
| Quality | 🍷🍷🍷🍷 |
| Value | ★★★↓ |
| Grapes | chardonnay |
| Region | Yarra Valley, Vic. |
| Cellar | 🍾 3 |
| Alc./Vol. | 13.0% |
| RRP | $22.00 |

## Eyton Dalry Road Chardonnay

The Dalry Road wines are Eyton's second label, lightly oaked styles for casual enjoyment. Maker: Matt Aldridge.
CURRENT RELEASE 2000    Dalry Road may be an uncomplicated chardonnay, but it's not so simple as to be totally uninteresting. The nose has melony fruit with an attractive slightly syrupy aroma. There's also a subtle touch of caramelly oak, reflecting the fact that a small portion is fermented in used French oak. It's still a style where fruit dominates, but those secondary elements are a bonus. Try it with grilled fish.

| | |
|---|---|
| Quality | 🍷🍷🍷 |
| Value | ★★★ |
| Grapes | chardonnay |
| Region | Yarra Valley, Vic. |
| Cellar | 🍾 2 |
| Alc./Vol. | 12.0% |
| RRP | $18.50 |

## Fettlers Rest Gewurztraminer

| | |
|---|---|
| **Quality** | 🍷🍷🍷½ |
| **Value** | ★★★ |
| **Grapes** | gewurztraminer |
| **Region** | Geelong, Vic. |
| **Cellar** | 4 |
| **Alc./Vol.** | 12.5% |
| **RRP** | $20.00 |

When this vineyard was named Idyll, its traminer was legendary. We can't resist making the observation that the label has improved.

CURRENT RELEASE 2000 An unusual wine, it has an exotic bouquet which combines vanilla, malt and caramel developed characters with tropical/lychee gewurz varietal characters. The taste is full and soft in the mouth, somewhat broad but smooth and balanced. A good partner for onion quiche.

## Fonty's Pool Manjimup Chardonnay

| | |
|---|---|
| **Quality** | 🍷🍷🍷🍷 |
| **Value** | ★★★½ |
| **Grapes** | chardonnay |
| **Region** | Manjimup, WA |
| **Cellar** | 4 |
| **Alc./Vol.** | 14.0% |
| **RRP** | $21.00 |

Manjimup, Pemberton, the Warren Valley, Blackwood Valley . . . the region has many aliases, and the protagonists can't agree. David Hohnen chose Manjimup because it's Aboriginal and therefore has a true Aussie ring to it. Maker: Eloise Jarvis at Cape Mentelle.

CURRENT RELEASE 1999 Hohnen sees this as a chablis style compared to the richer Cape Mentelle. Fair comment: it's high in acid and understated in style. There's a whiff of green melon and lightly toasted cashew nut. It's a subtle, medium-weight chardonnay in the mouth, with lightness yet intensity, and that cool-climate acid really lingers. Try it with oysters.

## Fossil Creek Verdelho

| | |
|---|---|
| **Quality** | 🍷🍷🍷½ |
| **Value** | ★★★½ |
| **Grapes** | verdelho |
| **Region** | Cowra, NSW |
| **Cellar** | 1 |
| **Alc./Vol.** | 13.5% |
| **RRP** | $15.00 |

Cowra has proved a happy hunting ground for verdelho. Fossil Creek vineyard has its wine contract-made by Hunter winemaker Andrew Margan. The area's fossils are of fish that are estimated at 360 million years old.

CURRENT RELEASE 2000 This is a very likeable verdelho. It's medium- to full-bodied, soft and rich, and smells of melon and confectionery. It's fruity but dry to taste and you don't need a licence in advanced wine tasting to be able to appreciate it. Pasta with pippies would work well.

## Frankland Estate Isolation Ridge Chardonnay

This company sponsors an annual riesling scholarship, sending a deserving member of the wine trade to Europe, and a biennial international riesling tasting at which German and Austrian winemakers show their wares alongside Aussies and Kiwis.

CURRENT RELEASE 1999    Here's a chardonnay straight out of left field to knock you off balance. It smells oxidised to the point of sherry, but it's also an enjoyable drink and quite complex. The powerful bouquet is loaded with stirred-lees and oak-barrel characters, and it's nutty, dry and savoury to taste. There is intensity as well as tight structure and length; puzzling! It goes well with chicken kebabs.

| | |
|---|---|
| Quality | ♀ ♀ ♀ |
| Value | ★ ★ ┥ |
| Grapes | chardonnay |
| Region | Great Southern, WA |
| Cellar | ♦ 3 |
| Alc./Vol. | 14.0% |
| RRP | $23.00 |

## Frankland Estate Isolation Ridge Riesling

The Smith/Cullam family has 30 hectares of vines on its aptly named Isolation Ridge vineyard at Frankland, south-west Western Australia. The site seems especially suited to riesling. A tiny portion of this wine was matured in aged barrels.

CURRENT RELEASE 2000    This is one of the best ever Frankland Estate rieslings, albeit very much in their typical full-flavoured, warm, dry style. It smells of various herbs and flowers. There's plenty of alcohol adding to its rich, almost chewy texture and the finish lingers on and on. It goes well with crab timbale.

| | |
|---|---|
| Quality | ♀ ♀ ♀ ♀ ♀ |
| Value | ★ ★ ★ ★ |
| Grapes | riesling |
| Region | Great Southern, WA |
| Cellar | ♦ 8 |
| Alc./Vol. | 14.0% |
| RRP | $23.00 |

## Freycinet Chardonnay

The Bull family's 9-hectare vineyard, near Bicheno, is the source of much magic in the form of pinot noir and chardonnay. The wines are all estate-grown and remarkably consistent. Maker: Claudio Radenti.

CURRENT RELEASE 1999    Fine, subtle and needing time to develop to its full potential – that's Tassie wine. The Freycinet style shows a fair degree of creamy malolactic butteriness, and the '99 is very much in that vein. As the corporate winemakers say: lots of artefact. There are minerally characters too and the palate is tight and dry, finishing firm and promising more if cellared. It goes with barbecued prawns.

| | |
|---|---|
| Quality | ♀ ♀ ♀ ♀ |
| Value | ★ ★ ★ |
| Grapes | chardonnay |
| Region | East Coast, Tas. |
| Cellar | ♦ 3 |
| Alc./Vol. | 13.5% |
| RRP | $33.00 |

## Freycinet Riesling

| | |
|---|---|
| Quality | ▼▼▼▼▼ |
| Value | ★★★★⅃ |
| Grapes | riesling |
| Region | East Coast, Tas. |
| Cellar | 🍾 8 |
| Alc./Vol. | 12.5% |
| RRP | $19.35 |

This topped a very strong class of young Tassie rieslings in the 2001 Tasmanian Regional Wine Show. Maker: Claudio Radenti.

CURRENT RELEASE 2000   Surprisingly for a young Tasmanian riesling, this is very approachable. It's soft and accessible, smelling of Pink Lady apples, with a slight cosmetic lift, while the palate is clean, crisp and seamless. A very fine and harmonious wine. Try it with scallop and rocket salad.

## Fromm La Strada Dry Riesling

| | |
|---|---|
| Quality | ▼▼▼▼▼ |
| Value | ★★★★★ |
| Grapes | riesling |
| Region | Marlborough, NZ |
| Cellar | 🍾 10+ |
| Alc./Vol. | 12.5% |
| RRP | $29.00 |

Swiss-born Hatsch Kalberer is – perhaps predictably – a dab hand at riesling, sweet and dry, although his fame probably rests more on pinot noir at this stage. The Fromms have 21 hectares of vines in Marlborough. CURRENT RELEASE 2000   Fabulous stuff! And spooky . . . it's like a fine German riesling from the Rheingau. It's pale coloured and in every way restrained, promising a long life. The haunting perfume recalls grapefruit, minerals and green apple. The palate is just scintillating, with briskly acidic, taut, vibrant citrus flavours and that fantastic tension between sweetness and acid that you see in the great German and Austrian rieslings. Deliciously steely flavours ripple through a long, long palate. Very exciting indeed.

## Gapsted Ballerina Canopy Chardonnay

| | |
|---|---|
| Quality | ▼▼▼▼ |
| Value | ★★★★ |
| Grapes | chardonnay |
| Region | Alpine & King Valleys, Vic. |
| Cellar | 🍾 2 |
| Alc./Vol. | 13.5% |
| RRP | $20.00 |

The cool highlands of north-eastern Victoria are the focus of an expanding wine industry of increasing importance. Just how important is shown by the size of the 7000-tonne Gapsted winery on the road to the snowfields of Falls Creek, Mount Hotham and Mount Buffalo. CURRENT RELEASE 1999   The nose is complete and satisfying, with many of the best elements of modern chardonnay. Aromas and flavours are of ripe stone fruit, butter-cream, nutty nougat and caramelly oak. The palate is creamy textured and medium-bodied with good balance and soft integrated acidity. Serve it with seafood risotto.

## Gartelmann Chardonnay

Gartelmann vineyard was originally planted in 1970. It is one of those smaller Hunter Valley estates that are sometimes hard to find outside New South Wales, but worth looking for.

CURRENT RELEASE 1999 A big, obvious Hunter chardonnay – slurp it down, with or without food. The nose is ripe and honeyed, reminiscent of pineapple and other tropical fruit, and dressed up in nutty barrel-ferment and sweet oak aromas. In the mouth it's ripe and peachy with good depth, zippy acidity, and an aftertaste perfumed with toasty oak. A good wine for sweet and sour prawns.

**Quality** 🍷🍷🍷🍷
**Value** ★★★
**Grapes** chardonnay
**Region** Hunter Valley, NSW
**Cellar** 🍾 1
**Alc./Vol.** 12.5%
**RRP** $19.00 (cellar door)

## Gartelmann Semillon

Jorg and Jan Gartelmann bought the established George Hunter Estate in 1996 as a lifestyle move after Jorg had heart problems.

CURRENT RELEASE 1999 A classically built regional wine, this has typically reserved lemon and mineral aromas, and a dry, medium-intensity palate that's just starting to show some of the richness that bottle age brings. A good match for delicate grilled fish.

**Quality** 🍷🍷🍷🍷
**Value** ★★★
**Grapes** semillon
**Region** Hunter Valley, NSW
**Cellar** 🍾 5
**Alc./Vol.** 11.0%
**RRP** $17.00

CURRENT RELEASE 2000 In common with many 2000 Hunter semillons, this has an extra dimension of ripe richness, compared to the '99 edition. The lemony fruit is less subdued than usual with zesty ripe semillon fruit to the fore, yet it still seems a little dumb in youth. That said, it looks to have the backbone and intensity to build real aged complexity with time.

**Quality** 🍷🍷🍷🍷
**Value** ★★★
**Grapes** semillon
**Region** Hunter Valley, NSW
**Cellar** 🍾 6
**Alc./Vol.** 11.0%
**RRP** $17.00

## Geoff Weaver Lenswood Sauvignon Blanc

| | |
|---|---|
| Quality | ♥♥♥♥♥ |
| Value | ★★★★ |
| Grapes | sauvignon blanc |
| Region | Adelaide Hills, SA |
| Cellar | 🍾 3 |
| Alc./Vol. | 13.7% |
| RRP | $21.00 |

The Adelaide Hills lay claim to being Australia's premier place for sauvignon blanc. Climate plays a big part but the region also boasts a band of very experienced and expert winemakers like Geoff Weaver.

CURRENT RELEASE 2000   This has more vinosity and less simple varietal character than many of its peers. It smells herbaceous but there's a tight minerally, chalky thread through it making it savoury and appetising. In the mouth, a tang of primary fruit flavour gives way to texture, firmness, structure and length. A very good example to try with tomato bruschetta and some rocket salad.

## Giaconda Aeolia

| | |
|---|---|
| Quality | ♥♥♥♥♥ |
| Value | ★★★ |
| Grapes | roussanne |
| Region | Beechworth, Vic. |
| Cellar | 🍾 4 |
| Alc./Vol. | 13.5% |
| RRP | $85.00 |

Rick Kinzbrunner's Giaconda mainstays are chardonnay, pinot noir and the Bordeaux varieties. In recent years he's also had a bit to do with some Beechworth plantings of the Rhone grapes viognier, roussanne and shiraz. The wines are just coming on-stream.

CURRENT RELEASE 2000   Straight roussannes are rare birds and Giaconda's first release makes a success of this enchanting variety. This subtle wine creeps up on you. The nose has floral, pear and herbal/heathland aromas allied to a restrained oak input. It's a gentle wine of great harmony. The palate is a smooth progression of complex, subtle flavours that are winey, fine and texturally interesting. It has a long aftertaste. Serve it with sautéed yabby tails.

## Giaconda Chardonnay

Unlike some cult wines, Giaconda chardonnay has achieved its status with a softly-softly approach that relies on quality rather than hype. Maker Rick Kinzbrunner is a quiet chap who lets his wonderful wine do the talking.

*Previous outstanding vintages: '88, '90, '92, '93, '94, '95, '96, '97, '98*

CURRENT RELEASE 1999  Is Giaconda Australia's best chardonnay? Some compare it to great Californian chards, but to us the obvious comparisons here are with Burgundy. It's subtle and delicate, yet there's inner strength and complexity so more is revealed with each sip. This latest is right on song, a great wine yet still immature. It has the usual lees, cream, toasted nut and matchstick aromas interwoven with subtle fruit. The profound palate is rich and long, and it's hard to separate flavour interest from textural interest, such is its balance and harmony. A great companion to a chargrilled salmon fillet.

| | |
|---|---|
| Quality | ♟♟♟♟♟ |
| Value | ★★★★ |
| Grapes | chardonnay |
| Region | Beechworth, Vic. |
| Cellar | ➛ 1–6+ |
| Alc./Vol. | 13.0% |
| RRP | $85.00 |

## Giesen Marlborough Sauvignon Blanc

The Giesens originally hail from Germany. Their winery started as a modest, family-run operation but it has grown like Topsy and now they export their wine all over the world.

CURRENT RELEASE 2000  The nose has tangy, herbaceous, snow-pea aromas with some richer tropical fruit too. In the mouth succulent fruit-sweetness and grassy flavours are counterpointed by higher than usual acidity. A typically thrilling Marlborough sauvignon which would suit New Zealand green-lipped mussels perfectly.

| | |
|---|---|
| Quality | ♟♟♟♟♟ |
| Value | ★★★★ |
| Grapes | sauvignon blanc |
| Region | Marlborough, NZ |
| Cellar | ▮ 2 |
| Alc./Vol. | 13.0% |
| RRP | $17.50 |

## Gramp's Semillon

| | |
|---|---|
| Quality | ♟ ♟ ♟ ♟ |
| Value | ★ ★ ★ ⁺ |
| Grapes | semillon |
| Region | Barossa Valley, SA |
| Cellar | 🍷 2 |
| Alc./Vol. | 12.0% |
| RRP | $16.50 ⑤ |

Johann Gramp planted the vineyard that grew into the Orlando empire over 150 years ago. His family name lives into the 2000s as a sub-brand of Orlando's Barossa enterprise.

CURRENT RELEASE 1999    A straightforward dry white of good character that shows what value there is in Barossa semillon. The nose has pleasant light lemon and richer lanolin aromas, and the palate is clean and quite richly flavoured with soft acidity making it an agreeable drink-now proposition. Serve it with whiting.

## Grant Burge Barossa Vines Chardonnay

| | |
|---|---|
| Quality | ♟ ♟ ♟ |
| Value | ★ ★ ★ ⁺ |
| Grapes | chardonnay |
| Region | Barossa Valley, SA |
| Cellar | 🍷 2 |
| Alc./Vol. | 14.0% |
| RRP | $12.00 ⑤ |

Grant Burge is very much the Barossa man, so it's not surprising that he can source good regional material, even in wines of relatively modest standing like this one. CURRENT RELEASE 2001    Ripe chardonnay makes a statement here. The nose has light sunshine-in-a-bottle aromas reminiscent of pineapple and melon. Barrel influence is just enough to season that ripe fruit character without dominating. The palate is still a bit closed up in youth, but it's satisfying and easy to understand yet with a finish that's a wee bit too firm. Try it with cold chicken salad.

## Grant Burge Thorn Riesling

| | |
|---|---|
| Quality | ♟ ♟ ♟ ♟ |
| Value | ★ ★ ★ ⁺ |
| Grapes | riesling |
| Region | Eden Valley, SA |
| Cellar | 🍷 3 |
| Alc./Vol. | 11.5% |
| RRP | $15.00 |

Between the vineyards he owns and his contacts right through the Barossa and Eden Valleys, Grant Burge has vast resources when it comes to putting together his range.

CURRENT RELEASE 2000    A pale green-tinged riesling with light lime juice and delicate floral aromas. It smells fragrant and clean and the palate is intense and clean-tasting. Freshness and aromatic qualities are its chief virtues, it doesn't have the firm structure and minerally strength of the top wines. It's pleasant drinking though, even more so with a Vietnamese salad.

## Grant Burge Virtuoso

Virtuoso has the sort of snappy packaging that's part of the push to encourage a younger demographic to drink table wine. There must be a better way.
CURRENT RELEASE 2000    The nose has some light juicy aromas in a fruit-salady vein with a hint of herbaceousness. The palate has similar flavours which are rather one-dimensional with simple grapey character. It lacks a bit of generosity and finishes with slightly hard acidity.

| | |
|---|---|
| Quality | ♀ ♀ ♀ |
| Value | ★ ★ ★ |
| Grapes | sauvignon blanc; semillon |
| Region | Barossa Valley, SA |
| Cellar | ◑ 2 |
| Alc./Vol. | 12.5% |
| RRP | $16.50 |

## Grant Burge Zerk Semillon

Semillon has a long history in the Barossa Valley, where it was once known confusingly as madeira. The fruit for this wine comes from a 70-year-old vineyard owned by Robert and Janine Zerk.
CURRENT RELEASE 2000    This is a typical example of substantial Barossa semillon. The varietal character is richer and deeper, reminiscent of lemon butter, and a hint of oak adds some complexity without dominating. In the mouth it's medium-bodied and rather more oaky than the nose suggests, but good depth of citrus-accented fruit carries it well. The finish is crisp and dry. Try it with sautéed scallops.

| | |
|---|---|
| Quality | ♀ ♀ ♀ ♀ |
| Value | ★ ★ ★ |
| Grapes | semillon |
| Region | Barossa Valley, SA |
| Cellar | ◑ 3 |
| Alc./Vol. | 12.0% |
| RRP | $14.90 |

## Greg Norman Estates Chardonnay

Psst! Want to know a secret? The Great White Shark didn't really make this wine – the winemakers of the Mildara cum Beringer Blass organisation did.
CURRENT RELEASE 1999    Greg Norman should be right proud to have his name on this chardonnay; it's pretty good. The nose has plenty going on with melon and syrupy stone-fruit aromas, robed in caramelly, nutty oak. The palate has creamy texture and good length of flavour with a balanced lick of toasty oak to add savour. A likeable drop to enjoy with fried fish (shark?) and chips.

| | |
|---|---|
| Quality | ♀ ♀ ♀ ♀ |
| Value | ★ ★ ★ ⭑ |
| Grapes | chardonnay |
| Region | Yarra Valley, Vic. |
| Cellar | ◑ 2 |
| Alc./Vol. | 13.0% |
| RRP | $21.00 |

## Grosset Piccadilly

| | |
|---|---|
| Quality | ♟ ♟ ♟ ♟ ⸜ |
| Value | ★ ★ ★ |
| Grapes | chardonnay |
| Region | Adelaide Hills, SA |
| Cellar | ⬤ 1–4 |
| Alc./Vol. | 13.5% |
| RRP | $40.00 |

Piccadilly is a place in the Adelaide Hills. It's also the source of Jeffrey Grosset's chardonnay, an ideal site for wines of great finesse.

CURRENT RELEASE 2000    This chardonnay has an intense nose that's powerful yet at the same time very restrained. Stone-fruit, creamy touches and a herbal hint meet a fair measure of smoky oak in this one, and it's long and promising. It's really too young at the moment, and slightly disjointed and edgy, but given time to mellow and build complexity it should be a beauty. Serve it with bug tails.

## Grosset Polish Hill

| | |
|---|---|
| Quality | ♟ ♟ ♟ ♟ ♟ |
| Value | ★ ★ ★ ★ ⸜ |
| Grapes | riesling |
| Region | Clare Valley, SA |
| Cellar | ⬤ 2–10 |
| Alc./Vol. | 13.0% |
| RRP | $35.00 |

Jeffrey Grosset is one of a high-profile group of Clare Valley vignerons who have adopted screw tops as seals for their rieslings. Other wine producers are looking on with interest and more will surely follow.
*Previous outstanding vintages: '90, '92, '93, '94, '96, '97, '98, '99*
CURRENT RELEASE 2000    Bright, pale and greenish in colour, this riesling has everything in the right place. The nose has understated power; it's very aromatic, spicy and lime-scented with an essency quality that separates it from the ruck. The concentrated palate has that spice and lime, as well as great length and a tight minerally backbone. A big riesling that needs cellaring, then serve with cold seafood.

## Grosset Semillon Sauvignon Blanc

| | |
|---|---|
| Quality | ♟ ♟ ♟ ♟ ⸜ |
| Value | ★ ★ ★ ⸜ |
| Grapes | semillon; |
| | sauvignon blanc |
| Region | Clare Valley & |
| | Adelaide Hills, SA |
| Cellar | ⬤ 3 |
| Alc./Vol. | 13.0% |
| RRP | $28.00 |

This is Jeff Grosset's quiet achiever; it doesn't have the benchmark status of his Clare rieslings but it is still a very good wine indeed.

CURRENT RELEASE 2000    There's a 'winey' feel that's more than just the smell and taste of grapes. It combines soft citrus, green fruits and fruit-salad aromas into a subtle and integrated whole that's full of interest. The palate is fresh and tangy yet refined and it has real length and subtle intensity. Serve with baked ramekins of fresh asparagus, eggs and savoury breadcrumbs.

## Grosset Watervale Riesling

The Watervale is the second of Grosset's rieslings, and while it doesn't enjoy quite the reputation of its Polish Hill stablemate, it has similar superb purity of regional and varietal character.

*Previous outstanding vintages: '90, '92, '93, '94, '95, '96, '97, '98, '99*

CURRENT RELEASE 2000 Archetypal Watervale riesling, a slightly broader, less well-defined wine than its sibling. The nose is perfumed, floral and intense with some exotic limey fruit. The palate has a lively spicy flavour with the usual Grosset undercurrent of dissolved minerals. It has a powdery dry, firm finish, and really needs time to come together. Plain grilled fish fillets suit it well.

| | |
|---|---|
| **Quality** | 5 glasses |
| **Value** | ★★★★½ |
| **Grapes** | riesling |
| **Region** | Clare Valley, SA |
| **Cellar** | 1–8 |
| **Alc./Vol.** | 13.0% |
| **RRP** | $30.00 |

## Hanging Rock The Jim Jim Sauvignon Blanc

Hanging Rock takes in grapes from a multitude of vineyards all over Victoria, but this comes from the Ellises' own vineyard, The Jim Jim, beside the winery.

CURRENT RELEASE 2000 It's a refreshing dry white, ideal for summer sipping. The aromas of crushed leaves, blackcurrant, herbs and citrus invite you in and the palate is crisp, dry and tangy, with bracing cool-climate Macedon acidity. It would be perfect with raw oysters.

| | |
|---|---|
| **Quality** | 3½ glasses |
| **Value** | ★★★ |
| **Grapes** | sauvignon blanc |
| **Region** | Macedon Ranges, Vic. |
| **Cellar** | 1 |
| **Alc./Vol.** | 12.0% |
| **RRP** | $22.00 |

## Heathcote Winery Curagee Viognier

Heathcote isn't a region closely associated with this trendy new grape, but it could become so in future, if this maker's results are any guide. The fruit was sourced from the Newton's Lane vineyard and was barrel-fermented in older oak. Maker: Mark Kelly.

CURRENT RELEASE 2000 A quite delicious viognier! Nutty, spicy, hints of musk, lashings of fresh tropical fruit. It's light and lively on the tongue, smooth and beautifully balanced, without excessive alcohol. There's an agreeable measure of richness to the palate, too. Pair it with pan-fried scallops and rocket.

| | |
|---|---|
| **Quality** | 4½ glasses |
| **Value** | ★★★½ |
| **Grapes** | viognier |
| **Region** | Heathcote, Vic. |
| **Cellar** | 3 |
| **Alc./Vol.** | 13.5% |
| **RRP** | $40.00 |

## Heggies Riesling

| | |
|---|---|
| Quality | 🍷🍷🍷🍷🍷 |
| Value | ★★★★★ |
| Grapes | riesling |
| Region | Eden Valley, SA |
| Cellar | 🍾 10+ |
| Alc./Vol. | 11.0% |
| RRP | $16.50 ⑤ |

Penguin Best
Riesling

This marque has improved out of sight in recent years. In the past, some of the wines were just *too* delicate, and took forever to come round. Ironically, the first-ever vintage, 1979, is still fabulous today, and is probably yet to be surpassed. Maker: Louisa Rose.

**CURRENT RELEASE 2000    This is one of the best young Heggies we've seen. It's steely, delicate and refined but has enough appreciable fruit to enjoy now, including some up-front flowery, jasmine-like aromas. Classically stylish, bracingly tangy and very long on the palate, it's a most impressive youngster. Goes well with green salad with prawns and lychees.**

## Henschke Tilly's Vineyard

| | |
|---|---|
| Quality | 🍷🍷🍷🍷 |
| Value | ★★★ |
| Grapes | various |
| Region | Barossa Valley, SA |
| Cellar | 🍾 2 |
| Alc./Vol. | 13.4% |
| RRP | $17.25 |

Any new parent stuck for a distinctive name for a babe should consult Henschke labels. They're a mine of great old-fashioned ones. This wine's named after Clotilde 'Tilly' Henschke.

CURRENT RELEASE 1999    This is Henschke's workhorse dry white, and the '99 is passable if unexciting. It has a full yellow shade and smells simple, herbal, peachy, with some toasty characters from oak and early bottle-age. The palate is tight, with a lemony leanness giving an echo of riesling (they're coy about the blend) leading to a dry and slightly grippy finish. Try it with grilled chicken salad.

## Hewitson Eden Valley Riesling

| | |
|---|---|
| Quality | 🍷🍷🍷🍷🍷 |
| Value | ★★★★★ |
| Grapes | riesling |
| Region | Eden Valley, SA |
| Cellar | 🍾 12+ |
| Alc./Vol. | 11.5% |
| RRP | $18.55 |

Dean Hewitson worked at Petaluma for 10 years, and obviously learnt a thing or two about riesling while he was there.

CURRENT RELEASE 2000    This is classical Eden Valley riesling, superbly made and promising to live on and on. It has an instant-attraction nose: fine flowery and citrusy aromas that are very fresh but at the same time complex. The taste is intense yet subtle, and the fruit is full of vitality. Crisp acid, fine balance and cellarability. Try it with pan-fried whiting.

## Highfield Marlborough Sauvignon Blanc

The rather grand winery building at Highfield reflects the international ownership of this company. A proportion of the wine was barrel-fermented to add complexity and depth. Maker: Alistair Soper.
CURRENT RELEASE 2000    A simply brilliant wine that epitomises the strengths of Marlborough. Pale yellow–green colour. The nose is very intense, with fragrant, tangy lantana, nettle and tropical fruit aromas. It's light-bodied and perhaps a fraction short, but with sauvignon blanc it's immediate palate that matters. In this regard it's absolutely delicious. Slurp with caesar salad.

| | |
|---|---|
| Quality | ♥ ♥ ♥ ♥ ♥ |
| Value | ★ ★ ★ ┤ |
| Grapes | sauvignon blanc |
| Region | Marlborough, NZ |
| Cellar | ▮ 2 |
| Alc./Vol. | 13.0% |
| RRP | $27.00 |

## Hollick Reserve Chardonnay

Odd use of the word 'reserve'. It usually means the superior bottling when there are more than one, but Hollick has only one chardonnay so far as we know. The wine was all barrel-fermented and part of it underwent malolactic.
CURRENT RELEASE 2000    This was just a babe in arms at the time of tasting (May '01) and promised to fill out with a few months' ageing. It's light yellow; the nose is subtle and straightforward, showing herb and lime-leaf aromas. The flavour is fruit-led and the acidity quite elevated, giving a slight hardness to the finish, countered by an impression of sweetness. Try it with fish patties.

| | |
|---|---|
| Quality | ♥ ♥ ♥ ♥ |
| Value | ★ ★ ★ |
| Grapes | chardonnay |
| Region | Coonawarra, SA |
| Cellar | ▮ 4 |
| Alc./Vol. | 13.5% |
| RRP | $20.00 |

## Hollick Sauvignon Blanc Semillon

Ian Hollick is a viticulturist first and foremost, but he has succeeded in holding together a high-quality winemaking division as well. His erstwhile long-time partner, Pat Tocaciu, has been replaced by the experienced David Norman.
CURRENT RELEASE 2000    It's light lemon in colour and the aromas are subtle, clean, herbal and citrus whiffs rising sedately from the glass. It comes into its own in the mouth, where it's clean and tangy with quite elevated acidity which makes for a fresh, lively taste and a refreshing finish. It needs food, and would team well with grilled whiting and lemon juice.

| | |
|---|---|
| Quality | ♥ ♥ ♥ ♥ |
| Value | ★ ★ ★ ★ ┤ |
| Grapes | sauvignon blanc 85%; semillon 15% |
| Region | Coonawarra, SA |
| Cellar | ▮ 2 |
| Alc./Vol. | 12.0% |
| RRP | $16.15 |

## Hope Estate Chardonnay

| | |
|---|---|
| **Quality** | 🍷🍷🍷🍷½ |
| **Value** | ★★★★½ |
| **Grapes** | chardonnay |
| **Region** | Hunter Valley, NSW |
| **Cellar** | 🍾 2 |
| **Alc./Vol.** | 13.0% |
| **RRP** | $18.00 |

The Hope Estate winery is the reborn Saxonvale. The blurb tells us this was made from hand-picked grapes and fermented in French barriques. The winemaker is Peter Howland.

CURRENT RELEASE 1999 This is a full-on, opulent, generously flavoured Hunter style, with a touch of class. It's medium yellow in hue and the developed bouquet shows butter, toast and vanilla aromas which suggest a liberal approach to oak. The palate is very rich, full-bodied and generous, with layered flavours that linger long on the farewell. It's not over-oaked. The finish is all honey and smoke. Delicious, and would go with roast chicken.

## Hope Estate Semillon

| | |
|---|---|
| **Quality** | 🍷🍷🍷🍷 |
| **Value** | ★★★★ |
| **Grapes** | semillon |
| **Region** | Hunter Valley, NSW |
| **Cellar** | ➡ 2–10+ |
| **Alc./Vol.** | 12.5% |
| **RRP** | $16.00 |

Sometimes Hunter semillon can be forbiddingly acid as a youngster. If the guys at Hope Estate were planning on a wine to cellar, they've succeeded!

CURRENT RELEASE 2000 The 2000 vintage is a great one for Hunter semillon, and the wines have a distinctive pea-pod, snow-pea aroma. This also has straw and lemongrass nuances, and the palate is unashamedly lean, dry, tart and austere. If you drink it now, try fresh oysters with it.

## Hotham Bridgeland Chardonnay

| | |
|---|---|
| **Quality** | 🍷🍷🍷🍷🍷 |
| **Value** | ★★★★ |
| **Grapes** | chardonnay |
| **Region** | Margaret River, WA |
| **Cellar** | 🍾 4 |
| **Alc./Vol.** | 14.0% |
| **RRP** | $35.00 |

The Bridgeland label is dedicated to Hotham's new suite of up-market wines made from Margaret River grapes. Maker: James Pennington.

CURRENT RELEASE 2000 This is a character-filled wine which surprised the hell out of us. Coming out of left field in an unlabelled bottle, it topped one of our regular tastings. Not that surprising for the region. It's a youthful, lively chardonnay which presents a lot of smoky barrel-ferment character at first, then airs to reveal deep tropical fruit with a well-integrated smoky, toasted oak background. It's soft and open-knit, with excellent depth and persistence. It goes with smoked chicken.

## Hotham Valley Reserve Semillon

This winery is located at Wandering, Western Australia; not really part of any recognised region, but it takes grapes from various places as well as the home vineyard. Maker: Jim Pennington.

CURRENT RELEASE 2000   The colour is very pale and it smells of herbs, fresh-cut grass, capsicum, bracken and a twinge of volatility. There is some lemony fruit on the palate and again that kick of volatility. The finish is dry and it lingers quite well. Serve it with yabbie salad.

| | |
|---|---|
| Quality | ♟ ♟ ♟ |
| Value | ★ ★ ⁴ |
| Grapes | semillon |
| Region | Wandering, WA |
| Cellar | 🍾 4 |
| Alc./Vol. | 13.0% |
| RRP | $22.60 Ⓢ |

## Hungerford Hill Cowra Chardonnay

To look at the labels and read the blurb, you might think the people behind Hungerford Hill have been sniffing something other than wine. They are fairly bizarre – but entertaining. The winemaker in '99 was Ian Walsh.

CURRENT RELEASE 1999   This is an attractive wine, and far more conventional than its label. It has a slight harshness from the wood, but is an otherwise fine drink. It smells peachy and toasty, with caramel developed overtones. In the mouth, it has plenty of character and depth and finishes dry and long. It would partner smoked chicken.

| | |
|---|---|
| Quality | ♟ ♟ ♟ ♟ |
| Value | ★ ★ ★ ★ ⁴ |
| Grapes | chardonnay |
| Region | Cowra, NSW |
| Cellar | 🍾 1 |
| Alc./Vol. | 13.5% |
| RRP | $14.85 Ⓢ |

## Hunter's Chardonnay

Jane Hunter has an admirable policy of releasing her chardonnay after a period of bottle-age. That's to the wine's advantage, but would scarcely contribute to the winery profits.

CURRENT RELEASE 1997   Wow, Montrachet move over! This is a serious chardonnay, and quite Burgundian to boot. Bottle-age has added extra layers of complexity resulting in butterscotch, tropical-fruit, toasty, smoky aromas which translate perfectly to the palate. It's full-bodied, very rich and complex, mouth-filling and enlivened by fine acidity. It has great power and persistence, and would go well with chargrilled lobster.

| | |
|---|---|
| Quality | ♟ ♟ ♟ ♟ ♟ |
| Value | ★ ★ ★ ★ ★ |
| Grapes | chardonnay |
| Region | Marlborough, NZ |
| Cellar | 🍾 3 |
| Alc./Vol. | 13.0% |
| RRP | $24.00 |

## Huntington Estate Semillon

| | |
|---|---|
| Quality | 🍷🍷🍷🍷🍷 |
| Value | ★★★★★ |
| Grapes | semillon |
| Region | Mudgee, NSW |
| Cellar | 🍾 10+ |
| Alc./Vol. | 11.0% |
| RRP | $12.50 (cellar door) |

Mudgee is strictly red wine country, *non*? Well, no: it produces some delectable semillon and some passable chardonnay. This is reliably one of the region's finest whites. Maker: Susie Roberts.

CURRENT RELEASE 2000  Huntington sells its semillon at a bargain-basement price, but don't be deceived: it's a terrific drop! The fresh, tangy, lemon and straw/hay aromas have a snow-pea herbaceous edge which is typical of New South Wales semillons from the 2000 vintage. The taste is vivacious and deep in fruit. The finish is long and impeccably balanced. Perfect with cold seafood and salads.

## Incognito Chardonnay

| | |
|---|---|
| Quality | 🍷🍷🍷🍷🍷 |
| Value | ★★★★★ |
| Grapes | chardonnay |
| Region | Adelaide Hills, SA |
| Cellar | 🍾 4 |
| Alc./Vol. | 13.0% |
| RRP | $21.00 |

Incognito is a second label of Shaw and Smith, designed to accommodate grapes from the younger vines on their own Adelaide Hills vineyard, and also for parcels of high-quality fruit brought in from elsewhere. This is made from chardonnay grown on Shaw and Smith's Woodside vineyard.

CURRENT RELEASE 2000  A very impressive young wine with a bright appearance and a fine, subtle nose of citrus and nectarine fruit, balanced leesy touches and restrained oak. There's good mouth-feel, fine-textured and long, and the flavour has a gentle, more-ish intensity that keeps you refilling your glass. It finishes long and clean with nice austerity. Try it with delicate grilled fish.

## Ingoldby Chardonnay

| | |
|---|---|
| Quality | 🍷🍷🍷🍷 |
| Value | ★★★★ |
| Grapes | chardonnay |
| Region | McLaren Vale, SA |
| Cellar | 🍾 2 |
| Alc./Vol. | 13.5% |
| RRP | $17.00 Ⓢ |

Ingoldby Chardonnay is typical of the sound flavourful chardonnays that underpin Australian wine's success in foreign markets. It's little wonder really; wines like this are like bottled Aussie sunshine, great in cool northern climes.

CURRENT RELEASE 2000  Right on song in 2000, this has all the usual pear, peach and melon fruit allied to a smartly tuned dusting of spicy oak on the nose. It tastes smooth and flavoursome with easy-to-drink ripe chardonnay fruit, good length of flavour, a sympathetic seasoning of wood and a dry finish. Works well with seafood pasta.

## Isabel Estate Sauvignon Blanc

One of the best New Zealand sauvignon blancs, a benchmark for the new wave of wines that employ winery fiddling and a little oak to make a more serious drop than the zippy fruit version.

CURRENT RELEASE 2000    Pale with a green tinge, this young sauvignon has a nose of sweet tropical fruit, grass and gooseberry aromas, touches of nuts and minerals, and a little of the distinctive arm-pit aroma that Marlborough vineyards can give to this variety. It tastes of green fruits, but it has ample richness and round fleshy texture. The finish is dry and long. Good with stirfried calamari with black pepper and ginger.

| | |
|---|---|
| Quality | 🍷🍷🍷🍷🍷 |
| Value | ★★★★⁺ |
| Grapes | sauvignon blanc |
| Region | Marlborough, NZ |
| Cellar | 🍷 3 |
| Alc./Vol. | 13.0% |
| RRP | $23.00 |

## Jeanneret Riesling

Ben Jeanneret's venture, commenced in 1992, is one of the smaller producers at Clare. His four hectares of vines at Sevenhill are organically farmed.

CURRENT RELEASE 2000    The Jeanneret 2000 is not a steely, forbidding, lock-me-in-the-cellar style, but a charming, full, generously flavoured, soft, round wine. It has aromas of garden herbs and small flowers. It's quite precocious, drinking well already, and would go well with leek and potato soup.

| | |
|---|---|
| Quality | 🍷🍷🍷🍷 |
| Value | ★★★★ |
| Grapes | riesling |
| Region | Clare Valley, SA |
| Cellar | 🍷 5 |
| Alc./Vol. | 12.5% |
| RRP | $16.00 |

## Jim Barry Watervale Riesling

In the late 1980s the Barry family bought the Florita vineyard, source of many great Leo Buring rieslings of the past, thus guaranteeing themselves a supply of great riesling grapes. Like many current Clare rieslings, this is sealed with a screw-cap.

CURRENT RELEASE 2001    In the first flush of youth, this has pristine varietal aromas of flowers, spices, lemon and lime. The palate is steely and firm, with plenty of body and dimension, although it's not as nuanced as some of its compatriots. It has excellent length and concentration, and should richly reward even limited cellaring. Enjoy it with trout risotto.

| | |
|---|---|
| Quality | 🍷🍷🍷🍷🍷 |
| Value | ★★★★★ |
| Grapes | riesling |
| Region | Clare Valley, SA |
| Cellar | 🍷 6+ |
| Alc./Vol. | 12.0% |
| RRP | $14.50 Ⓢ |

## Jindalee Chardonnay

| | |
|---|---|
| Quality | 🍷 🍷 🍷 |
| Value | ★ ★ ★ ★ |
| Grapes | chardonnay |
| Region | Murray Valley, Vic. |
| Cellar | 🍾 1 |
| Alc./Vol. | 13.5% |
| RRP | $10.00 Ⓢ |

The bottle was sealed with a plastic stopper instead of a cork, which is designed to guard the wine against cork taint. A noble idea, but we wouldn't cellar a wine with a plastic cork until more research has been done on the subject.

CURRENT RELEASE 2000   This is a vital, fresh young white with a suspicion of sauvignon blanc in its tropical passionfruit and gooseberry aromas. These can come from chardonnay when harvested slightly green – or the winemaker could have blended another variety in for effect. There's also a little apparent sweetness, which will ensure its popularity. It goes with mushroom vol-au-vents.

## Kaesler Old Vine Semillon

| | |
|---|---|
| Quality | 🍷 🍷 🍷 🍷 |
| Value | ★ ★ ★ ★ |
| Grapes | semillon |
| Region | Barossa Valley, SA |
| Cellar | 🍾 3 |
| Alc./Vol. | 10.5% |
| RRP | $19.00 |

Semillon was once for some unknown reason also known as madeira in the Barossa. These days it's always called semillon and it's a staple white grape for many of the more traditional producers like Kaeslers.

CURRENT RELEASE 2000   This has a fresh nose with the pleasant lemon and straw varietal aromas of semillon fruit. The palate has attractive intensity, depth and richness, and a crisp mouth-watering finish. What is surprising is that a young wine of such good mouth-weight should be so low in alcohol at only 10.5 per cent. A most un-Barossa thing, but it works. Pan-fry some whiting or garfish to go with this.

## Katnook Estate Riesling

| | |
|---|---|
| Quality | 🍷 🍷 🍷 🍷 |
| Value | ★ ★ ★ ⅃ |
| Grapes | riesling |
| Region | Coonawarra, SA |
| Cellar | ➥ 2–8+ |
| Alc./Vol. | 12.5% |
| RRP | $19.00 |

Katnook winemaker Wayne Stehbens is a dab hand with many grape varieties, including riesling. The wines taste great young and they age as well as any.

CURRENT RELEASE 2000   A very pale youngster this, but don't be put off by its anaemic appearance. As usual the nose has lovely purity of varietal aroma. There are floral scents, some pear and touches of lime, and the palate has medium intensity, but it will build more as the very firm, tangy acidity softens and flavour develops. A good cellaring proposition. Try it with poh pia – fresh Malaysian spring rolls.

## Katnook Estate Sauvignon Blanc

Coonawarra isn't generally recognised for sauvignon blanc, but Katnook's example is often among Australia's best.
CURRENT RELEASE 2000    Loads of varietal character here, and of the best sort, combining a tangy cut reminiscent of grass and green fruits with the succulent aromas of tropical fruits and lime. The palate has concentrated fruit with a minerally touch, and the finish is dry and atypically soft for young sauvignon. Vietnamese spring rolls suit this admirably.

| | |
|---|---|
| Quality | 🍷🍷🍷🍷🍷 |
| Value | ★★★ |
| Grapes | sauvignon blanc |
| Region | Coonawarra, SA |
| Cellar | 🍷 2 |
| Alc./Vol. | 13.5% |
| RRP | $27.00 |

## Kelly Riesling

Mornington Peninsula rieslings are rare, most probably because at the time most of the MP vineyards were being planted, *nothing* was an unfashionable as riesling. Nevertheless it seems to suit the place well.
CURRENT RELEASE 2000    This has a steely nose with some zesty lime scent. It's fresh and rather austere in aroma, and it tastes similarly dry and firm with limey fruit and tingling acidity. Not the most giving of young rieslings but it should improve with time. Try it now with flathead fillets.

| | |
|---|---|
| Quality | 🍷🍷🍷🍷 |
| Value | ★★★ |
| Grapes | riesling |
| Region | Mornington Peninsula, Vic. |
| Cellar | 🍷 4 |
| Alc./Vol. | 12.0% |
| RRP | $17.00 |

## Kim Crawford Sauvignon Blanc

Kim Crawford started off making sauvignon blanc in the pristine Marlborough fashion, but is now using a small proportion of barrel-ferment and malolactic ferment material to add complexity.
CURRENT RELEASE 2000    No mistaking the variety here. The smells of prickly green bushes and herbs meet the nose first, then a hint of smokiness adds an extra dimension. The palate is clean and crisp, herbaceous to taste yet a little softer in texture than usual. An evolving style of New Zealand sauvignon. This suits seared scallops with minty cucumber salad.

| | |
|---|---|
| Quality | 🍷🍷🍷🍷🍷 |
| Value | ★★★★ |
| Grapes | sauvignon blanc |
| Region | Marlborough, NZ |
| Cellar | 🍷 2 |
| Alc./Vol. | 12.5% |
| RRP | $20.00 |

## Kingston Estate Verdelho

**Quality** 🍷🍷🍷
**Value** ★★★
**Grapes** verdelho
**Region** Murray Valley, SA
**Cellar** 1
**Alc./Vol.** 13.0%
**RRP** $12.95

Most winemakers fashion verdelho into a simple, fruity, unoaked white wine, but at Kingston Estate they employ a little oak to add dimension to it.

CURRENT RELEASE 2000 The nose has a hint of caramel and nutty touches from oak, which subdues any varietal personality. The palate has a sort of oaky neutrality – you can't say it's over-wooded, it's not – but you can't discern much verdelho fruit either. It finishes dry and might be good with mee goreng.

## Knappstein Dry Style Gewurztraminer

**Quality** 🍷🍷🍷½
**Value** ★★★½
**Grapes** gewurztraminer
**Region** Clare Valley, SA
**Cellar** 2
**Alc./Vol.** 13.5%
**RRP** $18.50

Gewurztraminer was once a variety that excited the imagination of many Australian winemakers. Now it's just a curiosity, with a handful of makers persisting with it. Maker: Andrew Hardy.

CURRENT RELEASE 2000 The nose has a mix of varietal clues and also a hint of limey, almost riesling-like fruit. There are aromatic ginger, talcum powder and smoky aromas of good intensity. In the mouth it has floral and spicy flavours, good body and some firmness underneath. True to its label, it's quite dry and leaves the mouth with a musky, exotic aftertaste. Grab a bottle if you're after a change and serve with Thai ginger chicken.

## Knappstein Hand-Picked Riesling

**Quality** 🍷🍷🍷🍷
**Value** ★★★★
**Grapes** riesling
**Region** Clare Valley, SA
**Cellar** 6+
**Alc./Vol.** 12.0%
**RRP** $19.50

The Knappstein name has long been associated with riesling in Clare, although Tim Knappstein is now successfully ensconced in the Adelaide Hills. Today the winery belongs to Petaluma and Andrew Hardy calls the winemaking shots.

CURRENT RELEASE 2000 Pale and greenish in colour, this is right in the varietal mainstream with penetrating aromas of lime, stone fruit, and apple. The palate is lively with limey flavour and bracing acidity. It has good intensity, but perhaps not quite the firm backbone of some of its neighbours. Enjoyable drinking nevertheless and likely to really develop into something with bottle-age. Serve it with nasi goreng.

## Knappstein Semillon Sauvignon Blanc

Knappstein's semillon sauvignon follows a developing trend to give these blends more depth and complexity via oak and yeast lees influence. Maker: Andrew Hardy CURRENT RELEASE 2000 A bit over 50 per cent of this wine was barrel-fermented, but wood doesn't dominate as a result. The nose has citrus, herbal and white peach aromas that are made richer by a hint of oak. In the mouth it has full flavour – smooth, clean and persistent. Oak influence is subtle, making the wine deeper and more serious-tasting rather than adding a strong flavour dimension. Serve it with baked snapper.

| | |
|---|---|
| Quality | ♥ ♥ ♥ ♥ ♥ |
| Value | ★ ★ ★ ★ |
| Grapes | semillon; sauvignon blanc |
| Region | Clare Valley, Adelaide Hills & Coonawarra, SA |
| Cellar | ♦ 3 |
| Alc./Vol. | 13.5% |
| RRP | $20.75 |

## Knight Granite Hills Riesling

The mature riesling vines of Granite Hills perform well in the cool highlands of Victoria's Macedon region where other varieties can struggle. Maker: Llew Knight. CURRENT RELEASE 2000 Zippy lime, floral, passionfruit and citrus peel varietal characters show some evidence of botrytis here, and the wine has a fruity citrus-accented flavour with a whisper of residual sugar mid-palate. It feels a little oily in the mouth, but some rather shrill acidity provides a lively wake-up call at the end. An unusual riesling that might work well with cured salmon.

| | |
|---|---|
| Quality | ♥ ♥ ♥ ♥ |
| Value | ★ ★ ★ |
| Grapes | riesling |
| Region | Macedon Ranges, Vic. |
| Cellar | ♦ 4 |
| Alc./Vol. | 13.0% |
| RRP | $19.00 |

## Kopparossa Unwooded Chardonnay

A new name based at Naracoorte, near Coonawarra, with wines made by very experienced winemakers Mike Press and Gavin Hogg. Incidentally some of the fruit for this wine was grown in Penola High School's own vineyard.
CURRENT RELEASE 2000 This probably has exactly what people are looking for in unoaked chardonnay. It starts with a fragrant, uncomplicated nose of juicy tropical melon and fruit-salad aromas, and follows with a pleasantly fruity, soft palate of reasonable depth. A good-quality quaffer for summery dishes.

| | |
|---|---|
| Quality | ♥ ♥ ♥ ♥ |
| Value | ★ ★ ★ |
| Grapes | chardonnay |
| Region | Coonawarra, SA |
| Cellar | ♦ 2 |
| Alc./Vol. | 13.5% |
| RRP | $15.00 |

## Kulkunbulla The Glandore Semillon

| | |
|---|---|
| Quality | ▼▼▼▼▼ |
| Value | ★★★⬧ |
| Grapes | semillon |
| Region | Hunter Valley, NSW |
| Cellar | 🍷 10 |
| Alc./Vol. | 10.8% |
| RRP | $28.00 |

The Kulkunbulla syndicate makes several semillons but this is the best, and the only one made entirely from grapes grown on Brokenback. Glandore was a derelict winery on the property, dating back to the early 1900s. CURRENT RELEASE 2000   Kulkunbulla's flagship is made in classic ageing Hunter style and should cellar at least a decade. But it's a beaut drop now, with seafood or salads. The youthful aromas remind of straw, lemon and a hint of acetone, while the palate holds delicate but intense flavour that is gentle, dry and seamless. The price is quite a statement for a little-known, young semillon.

## Lake Breeze Chardonnay

| | |
|---|---|
| Quality | ▼▼▼▼ |
| Value | ★★★★ |
| Grapes | chardonnay |
| Region | Langhorne Creek, SA |
| Cellar | 🍷 2 |
| Alc./Vol. | 13.5% |
| RRP | $14.00 (cellar door) |

The Langhorne Creek region, including this maker, is better known for its reds. But occasionally it throws up a surprise in white. Maker: Greg Follett. CURRENT RELEASE 2000   An interesting chardonnay: it's soft and medium-bodied, and the bouquet shows off peachy fruit, and some coconutty-oak and meaty characters. It tastes as though it's been aged on its lees and there are some aldehyde overtones. There's a hint of sweetness and while not particularly complex, it's a good drink. Try it with cold chicken sandwiches.

## Lamonts Chardonnay

| | |
|---|---|
| Quality | ▼▼▼▼▼ |
| Value | ★★★★ |
| Grapes | chardonnay |
| Region | Swan Valley, WA |
| Cellar | 🍷 3 |
| Alc./Vol. | 14.0% |
| RRP | $20.00 |

This maker's wines, especially the whites, invariably impress and surprise those who are sceptical about the potential of the Swan Valley. Maker Mark Warren is obviously a real talent. CURRENT RELEASE 2000   This is a stylish and complex chardonnay which shows heaps of toasty, slightly feral, barrel-fermented characters and perhaps just a whisper of greenness. There's lovely grapefruit flavour in the mouth: deep, rich and pleasingly textured. It would go well with sautéed veal.

## Lamonts Verdelho

Lamonts is not just any old winery: it's also home to one of the best eating spots in the Swan Valley region. Chef Corin Lamont is one of the foodie gurus of Western Australia. Maker: Mark Warren.
CURRENT RELEASE 2000    Lovers of tropical fruit styles will love this. It also offers peach, straw and gooseberry aromas, while the palate has good intensity and a lingering finish – and it's not propped up by sugar, as are many verdelhos. A powerful, very cleanly made dry white which can stand a big chill. Drink now, with salady things.

| | |
|---|---|
| Quality | ▯▯▯▯ |
| Value | ★★★┤ |
| Grapes | verdelho |
| Region | Swan Valley, WA |
| Cellar | ▮ 2 |
| Alc./Vol. | 13.1% |
| RRP | $17.60 |

## Lark Hill Riesling

In the cool altitudes of Bungendore, Lark Hill makes fine rieslings in a style that comes closer to Germanic than most in Australia. Maker: Sue Carpenter.
CURRENT RELEASE 2000    The aromas recall tropical fruits, especially pawpaw, and a trace of sweetness balances frisky cool-climate acidity. Intense and rich – yet subtle and refined – in the mouth, it has a powerful finish and should age beautifully. Try it with cold duck and lychee salad.

| | |
|---|---|
| Quality | ▯▯▯▯ |
| Value | ★★★★ |
| Grapes | riesling |
| Region | Canberra Region, NSW |
| Cellar | ▮ 7 |
| Alc./Vol. | 12.0% |
| RRP | $18.00 (cellar door) |

## Leeuwin Estate Art Series Chardonnay

Many rate this Australia's best chardonnay. In a frenzy of money-grubbing price-hikes by 'icon' wine producers, the Horgans have been admirably restrained. The label of this vintage features a painting by Margaret River's outstanding artist, Robert Juniper.
*Previous outstanding vintages: '82, '83, '85, '87, '89, '90, '92, '93, '95, '96, '97*
CURRENT RELEASE 1998    Our sample was faintly corked, but the quality shone through so clearly we still rated it five glasses! Taint or no taint, it 'comes up' with breathing, and shows fabulous multi-dimensional flavour and aroma that will leave you gasping. It's powerful but restrained and shows tropical fruit, grilled nut, cedar and vanilla flavours, and more. It's very intense and persistent in the mouth, finishing clean and dry. Perfect with chargrilled crayfish tails.

| | |
|---|---|
| Quality | ▯▯▯▯▯ |
| Value | ★★★★ |
| Grapes | chardonnay |
| Region | Margaret River, WA |
| Cellar | ▮ 5+ |
| Alc./Vol. | 14.0% |
| RRP | $75.50 |

## Leeuwin Estate Prelude Vineyard Chardonnay

| | |
|---|---|
| Quality | 🍷🍷🍷🍷 |
| Value | ★★★⁴ |
| Grapes | chardonnay |
| Region | Margaret River, WA |
| Cellar | 🍷 3+ |
| Alc./Vol. | 14.0% |
| RRP | $30.00 |

This is the second-string chardonnay from this maker. Leeuwin Estate is named after Cape Leeuwin, which marks one end of the promontory which forms the Margaret River winegrowing region. Makers: Bob Cartwright and John Brocksopp.

CURRENT RELEASE 1999    The oak is subtler and the fruit more floral and less concentrated than the Art Series. It's a lighter wine all round, but very good, with pleasing depth and richness of palate. Its passionfruit/tropical flavour fills the mouth nicely and is lingering and dry on the finish. Serve it with prawn wontons.

## Lenswood Vineyards Sauvignon Blanc

| | |
|---|---|
| Quality | 🍷🍷🍷🍷⁵ |
| Value | ★★★⁴ |
| Grapes | sauvignon blanc |
| Region | Adelaide Hills, SA |
| Cellar | 🍷 2+ |
| Alc./Vol. | 13.0% |
| RRP | $22.15 |

Penguin Best
Sauvignon
Blanc

Tim and Annie Knappstein have precisely 26.7 hectares of vines in the Lenswood sub-region of the Adelaide Hills. They don't own a winery but make their wines at other people's. Tim is a perfectionist and a veritable seeker of the holy grail when it comes to quality.

**CURRENT RELEASE 2000    Not a pungent drop, but a subtly varietal wine with gently herbal, cashew nut and tropical fruit aromas, this is a triumph of substance over style. It has a full, rich, ripe-tasting flavour of considerable strength. The finish is very long and dry, with just a trace of hardness. A very fine wine. Goes well with Chinese dumplings.**

## Lenswood Vineyards Semillon

| | |
|---|---|
| Quality | 🍷🍷🍷🍷⁵ |
| Value | ★★★★ |
| Grapes | semillon |
| Region | Adelaide Hills, SA |
| Cellar | 🍷 6 |
| Alc./Vol. | 13.8% |
| RRP | $25.00 |

Tim Knappstein has been making wine since 1966 and, for all his achievements, is still a hands-on winemaker – and proud of it! No paper-shuffler, this.

CURRENT RELEASE 1999    Half the wine was barrel-fermented but the oak is very discreet. It's tight and subtle although possessed of hidden power (and no shortage of alcohol!). It has aromas of herb, nettle, lemon and melon with a light smokiness. The palate is smooth and seamless. It teams well with snapper with a light, truffly vinaigrette.

## Lenton Brae Chardonnay

Here's yet another fast-improving Margaret River chardonnay, making a spirited bid to fight its way to the top of the heap among the myriad contenders. CURRENT RELEASE 2000 This shows typical concentrated fruit of the region and a tidy, dry palate. There are some nutty, aldehydic aromas which may derive from maturation on lees, together with peach and tropical fruit nuances. It has a degree of subtlety and doesn't overreach in the oak department. It would suit scallops à la nage, simmered in a fish stock.

| | |
|---|---|
| Quality | ♟ ♟ ♟ ♟ |
| Value | ★ ★ ★ ⸍ |
| Grapes | chardonnay |
| Region | Margaret River, WA |
| Cellar | ▮ 4 |
| Alc./Vol. | 13.5% |
| RRP | $24.80 |

## Lenton Brae Semillon Sauvignon Blanc

The attractive winery, built of stabilised rammed earth, was designed by architect and founder Bruce Tomlinson. The winemaker is his son Ed Tomlinson. CURRENT RELEASE 2000 Typical Margaret River aromas of dry twigs and crisp green herbs are apparent in this fresh white blend, along with some hints of tropical fruits. It finishes clean and dry, but without great length, and is a satisfying accompaniment to vegetable terrines.

| | |
|---|---|
| Quality | ♟ ♟ ♟ ♟ |
| Value | ★ ★ ★ |
| Grapes | semillon; sauvignon blanc |
| Region | Margaret River, WA |
| Cellar | ▮ 2 |
| Alc./Vol. | 13.5% |
| RRP | $18.25 |

## Leo Buring Leonay Riesling

This label and its predecessor, the Special Bin label with a number such as DWC17 of 1973, mark the pinnacle of Leo Buring riesling. Often very austere when young, they're built to last and are released after a period of cellaring. Depending on the year, a wine from Eden Valley and/or Clare Valley may be made. *Previous outstanding vintages: '90, '91, '92, '94, '95, '97* CURRENT RELEASE 1998 At three years this is still in its shell, a restrained, delicate, shy riesling with aromas of dried flowers, minerals, slate and lemon. It may appear lean and ungenerous at first sip, but let it breathe and come up to room temperature and you'll discover its entertaining subtleties. It is a delicious riesling and promises to reveal yet more charms with further maturity. It goes well now with crab meat.

| | |
|---|---|
| Quality | ♟ ♟ ♟ ♟ ♟ |
| Value | ★ ★ ★ ★ |
| Grapes | riesling |
| Region | Eden Valley, SA |
| Cellar | ▮ 8+ |
| Alc./Vol. | 12.5% |
| RRP | $34.00 |

## Levi's Wine Semillon

| | |
|---|---|
| Quality | ▮▮▮▮ |
| Value | ★★★★ |
| Grapes | semillon |
| Region | Hilltops, NSW |
| Cellar | ▮ 6 |
| Alc./Vol. | 11.9% |
| RRP | $16.50 |

An unusual wine in several respects. It was made at Vicary's winery, Luddenham, in outer western Sydney, from Hilltops (Young) grapes. And it is a kosher wine, suitable for Passover. It's not easy to track down, but you'll find it at The Wine Emporium, in Sydney's Surry Hills. This shop specialises in kosher and organic wines, and wines suitable for vegans.

CURRENT RELEASE 2000    No doubt about it: this is one of the best kosher wines we've ever tasted. Crisp and clean, it has fresh snow-pea aromas typical of the 2000 vintage throughout New South Wales and is tight, dry, delicate and flinty to taste. It's good with food now (try salads and vegetables) and should also cellar for several years.

## Lillydale Chardonnay

| | |
|---|---|
| Quality | ▮▮▮ |
| Value | ★★★ |
| Grapes | chardonnay |
| Region | Yarra Valley, Vic. |
| Cellar | ▮ 1 |
| Alc./Vol. | 13.5% |
| RRP | $17.50 ⑤ |

McWilliams owns the Lillydale winery in the Yarra, and Max McWilliam is their winemaker. This chardonnay often sports a gold-medal sticker but doesn't always live up to it.

CURRENT RELEASE 1999    This won a trophy at Melbourne in '99, but in all honesty we'd have to say it hasn't retained its initial charms. The bouquet is big, obvious and up-front with charred oak and development giving a rubbery character. The palate is also quite developed, with slightly overblown, cooked-fruit flavours. It has flavour and body, and is lowly priced for the Yarra.

| | |
|---|---|
| Quality | ▮▮▮▮ |
| Value | ★★★★ |
| Grapes | chardonnay |
| Region | Yarra Valley, Vic. |
| Cellar | ▮ 4+ |
| Alc./Vol. | 13.5% |
| RRP | $18.00 ⑤ |

CURRENT RELEASE 2000    The first thing you notice is the nice bright colour, light yellow, and the wine is bright and fresh in every way. The bouquet offers butterscotch, cream, toasted nuts and confectionery while the taste is restrained, delicate and very drinkable. It has frisky acidity and a tangy, almost steely, undeveloped palate without much evidence of oak. Lovely now with crab mousse, and has a future.

## Lillydale Sauvignon Blanc

The former Lillydale Vineyards is now just Lillydale. It's not actually at Lilydale (the town has one 'l'), but Seville.
CURRENT RELEASE 2000    Curious sauvignon blanc, this! It smells strongly of peppermint; almost makes you want to bring out the toothbrush. Could it be coming from oak? The palate holds dusty, grassy as well as minty flavours and it's pleasant enough to drink. It's short and simple, but balanced, with a clean, dry finish. It would suit whitebait fritters.

| | |
|---|---|
| Quality | 🍷 🍷 🍷 |
| Value | ★ ★ ★ |
| Grapes | sauvignon blanc |
| Region | Yarra Valley, Vic. |
| Cellar | 🍾 1 |
| Alc./Vol. | 12.0% |
| RRP | $18.00 ⑤ |

## Lindemans Bin 65 Chardonnay

An earlier vintage ('98) was our Penguin Wine of the Year, but the 2000 isn't in the same class, probably due to a lesser-quality season. Still, it's a hell of an achievement to make millions of litres of such a drinkable white wine. Maker: Philip John and team.
CURRENT RELEASE 2000    The colour is light–medium yellow and it's ageing gracefully. The fruit-led aromas recall peach and nectarine and it's still a fresh, clean wine. There are some greener herbal flavours, too, and while it has plenty of fruit it's not particularly fine. It's good value and goes with barbecued chicken kebabs.

| | |
|---|---|
| Quality | 🍷 🍷 🍷 🍷 |
| Value | ★ ★ ★ ★ |
| Grapes | chardonnay |
| Region | South East Australia |
| Cellar | 🍾 1 |
| Alc./Vol. | 13.0% |
| RRP | $9.30 ⑤ |

## Lindemans Bin 95 Sauvignon Blanc

The Lindemans bin wines are about as adventurous label-wise as a packet of cancer-sticks, but they sure do deliver where it counts.
CURRENT RELEASE 2001    This baby is full of estery, squashy, passionfruit, newly fermented aromas. There's a hint of sweatiness, too. It's very light and just a tad flimsy in the mouth. It starts with a trace of sweetness and finishes short, with greenish herby flavours. But it's good value at under a tenner. It goes well with salads.

| | |
|---|---|
| Quality | 🍷 🍷 🍷 |
| Value | ★ ★ ★ |
| Grapes | sauvignon blanc |
| Region | not stated |
| Cellar | 🍾 1 |
| Alc./Vol. | 12.0% |
| RRP | $9.30 ⑤ |

## Lindemans Classic Hunter Semillon Bin 7871

| | |
|---|---|
| Quality | 🍷🍷🍷🍷🍷 |
| Value | ★★★★★ |
| Grapes | semillon |
| Region | Hunter Valley, NSW |
| Cellar | 🍶 4+ |
| Alc./Vol. | 11.0% |
| RRP | $44.00 |

Every couple of years Lindemans brings out a bevy of aged wines – whites, reds and fortifieds – which have been matured in ideal conditions and regularly checked by the winemakers to determine the right time to release them. They're doing us all a favour.

CURRENT RELEASE 1991    This is a fabulous semillon, drinking at its peak but showing no sign of fading. The full yellow colour still has some green glints. The waxy, lemony, herbal bouquet is still youthful but also complex, and the palate is fine and seamless. It has great delicacy and marvellous length. Try it with roast turkey breast.

## Lindemans Limestone Coast Chardonnay

| | |
|---|---|
| Quality | 🍷🍷🍷 |
| Value | ★★★★ |
| Grapes | chardonnay |
| Region | Limestone Coast, SA |
| Cellar | 🍶 1 |
| Alc./Vol. | 12.5% |
| RRP | $12.00 Ⓢ |

The Limestone Coast zone covers a vast tract of the south-east of South Australia, including Coonawarra, Padthaway, Wrattonbully (formerly Koppamurra), Mt Benson, Robe and Kingston. It's not to be confused with Limestone Ridge, which is a Lindemans Coonawarra brand.

CURRENT RELEASE 2000    This is a fairly simple, basic but acceptable budget-priced chardonnay that relies on charred oak chips for its character. The palate is broad and plain, the flavour and slight astringency of wood tending to take centre-stage. It works okay with barbecued chicken burgers.

## Lindemans Padthaway Winemakers Reserve Chardonnay

| | |
|---|---|
| Quality | 🍷🍷🍷🍷🍷 |
| Value | ★★★★ |
| Grapes | chardonnay |
| Region | Padthaway, SA |
| Cellar | 🍶 2 |
| Alc./Vol. | 13.5% |
| RRP | $28.50 Ⓢ |

For the last few years Lindemans has kept a parcel of its best Padthaway chardonnay separate and held it back for further maturation. Makers: Greg Clayfield and Philip John. *Previous outstanding vintage: '97*

CURRENT RELEASE 1998    This is a rich and multi-layered chardonnay that should be a crowd-pleaser. Like a Rod Stewart song or a favourite old jumper, it's a comfy, familiar style. Medium–full yellow in hue, it smells of buttered toast, creamed honey, with obvious age but still quite fresh and retaining some primary fruit. In the mouth it shows balance, softness and style. Perfect with roast Barossa chook.

## Little's Reserve Traminer

The Littles have a substantial 51 hectares of vineyards and a winery in Palmer's Lane, Pokolbin. Winemaker is Ian Little.

CURRENT RELEASE 2000    Little's is one of very few traminers in the Hunter, and even fewer have much varietal character. The spicy aromas are rich and slightly pungent, with a hint of hair-oil. It tastes full-bodied and broad in the mouth and while it is rich, it turns slightly hard on the finish. A good match for mild chilli crab.

| | |
|---|---|
| Quality | ♀♀♀♀ |
| Value | ★★★ |
| Grapes | gewurztraminer |
| Region | Hunter Valley, NSW |
| Cellar | 🍷 3 |
| Alc./Vol. | 12.0% |
| RRP | $16.00 |

## Lowe Chardonnay

David Lowe and Jane Wilson have realised long-held plans and built a new winery and home on the Lowe family property at Mudgee. They still have cellar-door sales in the Hunter – at Peppers Creek winery – and also consult to other people. He makes the whites; she the reds.

CURRENT RELEASE 1999    There's a lot happening in this deceptively subtle wine. You'll pick up herbal, melon fruit and delicate hints of creamy, buttery and oaky complexing factors. It's a lean, refined style, consciously different from traditional fat Hunter chardonnay. Very drinkable now and should hold well in the cellar. Food: yabbie salad.

| | |
|---|---|
| Quality | ♀♀♀♀ |
| Value | ★★★★ |
| Grapes | chardonnay |
| Region | Hunter Valley, Mudgee & Orange, NSW |
| Cellar | 🍷 4 |
| Alc./Vol. | 13.5% |
| RRP | $23.00 |

## Lowe Hunter Semillon

David Lowe made this from 70-year-old vines on Judge Tony Bainton's property at Broke. It was once owned by Peter Fox – now there's a hallowed name from the past. Peter was chief financial backer to Len Evans in the early '80s when he was buying wineries in France.

CURRENT RELEASE 2000    This is a lovely, seamless semillon, with a smidgin of the herbal character of the vintage, in this case a green-stick or snapped-twig aroma. It will develop great character and complexity with a little age. On the palate it's dry, but soft, gentle and rounded, making it very enjoyable as a youngster. Try it with fish and chips.

| | |
|---|---|
| Quality | ♀♀♀♀♀ |
| Value | ★★★★ |
| Grapes | semillon |
| Region | Hunter Valley, NSW |
| Cellar | 🍷 7+ |
| Alc./Vol. | 11.5% |
| RRP | $21.00 |

## Madfish WA Premium White

| | |
|---|---|
| Quality | 🍷🍷🍷🍷 |
| Value | ★★★★ |
| Grapes | chardonnay; sauvignon blanc |
| Region | South West WA |
| Cellar | 🍾 2 |
| Alc./Vol. | 13.5% |
| RRP | $17.00 |

Madfish wines are an offshoot of the growing Howard Park enterprise. The mad fish in question are found in Madfish Bay near Denmark in southern Western Australia. CURRENT RELEASE 2000   A light, clean-smelling wine, with the 2000 reversing the style of the '99 in looking more chardonnay-influenced than sauvignon blanc. It has a gentle fruitiness that's grapey and soft with only a hint of grassiness. Very easy drinking with Cantonese-style steamed fish with spring onion.

## Main Ridge Chardonnay

| | |
|---|---|
| Quality | 🍷🍷🍷🍷🍷 |
| Value | ★★★⭒ |
| Grapes | chardonnay |
| Region | Mornington Peninsula, Vic. |
| Cellar | 🍾 4 |
| Alc./Vol. | 13.5% |
| RRP | $39.00 |

Main Ridge's Nat White is always working to improve the quality of the wine from his small, deliberately low-yielding vineyard, facing the difficulties of a marginal climate with unceasing good humour. CURRENT RELEASE 1999   A stylish bouquet introduces a fine complex chardonnay that shows gentle, subdued fruit character, with butter, oatmeal and nutty complexities. The lightish to medium-weight palate is creamy with complex flavour, good length and clean acidity. An understated chardonnay to enjoy with grilled whiting.

## Margan Semillon

| | |
|---|---|
| Quality | 🍷🍷🍷🍷🍷 |
| Value | ★★★★ |
| Grapes | semillon |
| Region | Hunter Valley, NSW |
| Cellar | 🍾 5+ |
| Alc./Vol. | 13.0% |
| RRP | $17.50 |

Hunter semillons enjoyed a great year in 2000, with the only criticism we've heard being that they were so ripe, juicy, herbaceous and full that they weren't like Hunter semillons! Work that one out if you can. CURRENT RELEASE 2000   This has the typically precocious character of the 2000 vintage Hunter sems, which has some people wondering about their ageworthiness. Whatever happens, this has lots going for it right now. The nose has lemon sherbet, green herb and grapey aromas of real intensity. In the mouth it is smooth, deep and rich with much higher than usual alcohol. This full-on personality is balanced by tangy acidity. A wine to drink with pan-fried fish fillets.

## Massoni Chardonnay

The technical note for the latest Massoni wines contains the handy information that the wine is completely suitable for vegans. It's good to know that now vegans can at least have a drink to cheer them up from the depths of gastronomic misery.
*Previous outstanding vintages: '94, '97*
CURRENT RELEASE 1999    This is an excellent Mornington chardonnay with a youthful, bright appearance and great complexity. The nose has citrus, melon and pineappley aromas along with malt caramel touches and a whiff of bacony French oak. It smells tangy yet rich and it tastes that way too. It's smooth and harmonious with zippy acidity carrying a very long finish. Try it with a meaty fish like tuna.

| | |
|---|---|
| Quality | 🍷🍷🍷🍷 |
| Value | ★★★→ |
| Grapes | chardonnay |
| Region | Mornington Peninsula, Vic. |
| Cellar | 🍷 3 |
| Alc./Vol. | 14.1% |
| RRP | $35.00 |

## McGuigan Bin 7000 Chardonnay

McGuigan wines are at the very commercial end of the spectrum, offering good drinkability at reasonable price.
CURRENT RELEASE 2000    A straightforward chardonnay that's been cleverly put together to fit fashion and price point well. It has a sweet fruit nose with hints of caramel and smoky oak. The palate is medium-bodied and smoothly fruity with a touch of toasty oak on the finish. Serve it with mee goreng.

| | |
|---|---|
| Quality | 🍷🍷🍷 |
| Value | ★★★ |
| Grapes | chardonnay |
| Region | Hunter Valley, NSW |
| Cellar | 🍷 2 |
| Alc./Vol. | 13.0% |
| RRP | $12.00 ⑤ |

## McGuigan Bin 8000 Sauvignon Blanc

Be wary of wines with gold medals and the like adorning the label. Some of them warrant close examination. The 'medal' on this wine reads 'Vintage 2001 from vineyard to bottle in 4 weeks', with no mention of an award at all.
CURRENT RELEASE 2001    This certainly arrived on the market in no time flat. As a result it was very zesty, a quality it has retained in the short term. The nose has tropical fruit, talcum powder and herbaceous aromas, and it tastes pleasant and fresh with a trace of sweetness mid-palate ahead of tangy acidity. Serve it as an aperitif with some salty little nibbles.

| | |
|---|---|
| Quality | 🍷🍷🍷 |
| Value | ★★★ |
| Grapes | sauvignon blanc |
| Region | Hunter Valley, NSW |
| Cellar | 🍷 1 |
| Alc./Vol. | 11.5% |
| RRP | $12.00 ⑤ |

## McWilliams Eden Valley Riesling

| | |
|---|---|
| Quality | ♡ ♡ ♡ ♡ ♡ |
| Value | ★ ★ ★ ★ ★ |
| Grapes | riesling |
| Region | Eden Valley, SA |
| Cellar | 🍷 2 |
| Alc./Vol. | 12.5% |
| RRP | $15.00 |

These McWilliams regionally labelled wines look lacklustre, but quality is good and they are very sharply priced, with this aged riesling heading the pack for value. CURRENT RELEASE 1997 Quite mature right now, this is a golden wine with a developed, richly attractive bouquet reminiscent of dried flowers, lime marmalade and buttered toast. It has a viscous feel in the mouth, rich and deeply flavoured with lime juice cordial and toasty flavours ahead of a clean, tangy, bone dry finish. Try it with Thai fish cakes.

## McWilliams Hanwood Chardonnay

| | |
|---|---|
| Quality | ♡ ♡ ♡ ♡ |
| Value | ★ ★ ★ ★ ★ |
| Grapes | chardonnay |
| Region | Riverina, NSW |
| Cellar | 🍷 2 |
| Alc./Vol. | 13.5% |
| RRP | $11.00 Ⓢ |

Last year we were amazed by the quality of this modestly priced wine; nothing's changed with the release of the latest vintage. Either the bean-counters at McWilliams have taken leave of their senses, or the company's registered itself as a charitable institution. Maker: Jim Brayne and team.
CURRENT RELEASE 2000 Serve this masked to any smarty-pants wine buffs you know and ask them how much you paid for it. Chances are they'll over-estimate it by two or three times – it's that good. It has a complex nose of melon, nuts, yeast lees and toffee, and the rich medium-bodied palate has smooth, creamy flavour and texture, good persistence and a tangy finish. Try it with goujons of salmon.

## McWilliams Hunter Valley Semillon

With their Mount Pleasant and Riverina vineyards, McWilliams have as much experience with semillon as anyone. This Hunter example has the sort of label that almost guarantees that it will be ignored on the shelf; despite that, it's an agreeable drop.

CURRENT RELEASE 2000    A more forward style of Hunter semillon than its Mount Pleasant stablemates with a tropical fruit touch to the usual lemon and straw varietal aromas. The palate is dry and clean-tasting with more depth than the classical style, perhaps another case of the 2000 vintage endowing grapes with more than usual ripeness. Try it with grilled fish.

| | |
|---|---|
| Quality | 🍷🍷🍷🍷 |
| Value | ★★★★ |
| Grapes | semillon |
| Region | Hunter Valley, NSW |
| Cellar | 🍷 3 |
| Alc./Vol. | 12.5% |
| RRP | $16.00 |

## McWilliams Limited Release Botrytis Semillon

McWilliams Riverina sweeties don't get quite the raves of De Bortolis et al, but for our money they're as good as any, and often have a degree of elegance that's lacking elsewhere. Maker: Jim Brayne and team.

CURRENT RELEASE 1997    Like liquid gold, this glitters and sparkles on the table. The nose has archetypal Riverina botrytis aromas and flavours of liqueur apricots, peaches, mandarin and rock candy. It tastes voluptuously smooth and sweet, yet it has freshness and tang. Rich and powerfully sweet with volatility in check, this is a beaut sweet white. Serve it with blue cheese for a grown-up sweet experience.

| | |
|---|---|
| Quality | 🍷🍷🍷🍷🍷 |
| Value | ★★★★★ |
| Grapes | semillon |
| Region | Riverina, NSW |
| Cellar | 🍷 4 |
| Alc./Vol. | 12.0% |
| RRP | $20.00 (375 ml) |

## McWilliams Mount Pleasant Elizabeth

A venerable label that's offered exceptional value for money for many years. As an example of a classic Aussie wine with bottle-age it has few peers at the price.
*Previous outstanding vintages: '83, '86, '87, '89, '91, '93, '94, '95*

CURRENT RELEASE 1997    Few wines are as consistent as this Hunter semillon. At four years of age the '97 is starting to show a bit of development, but it's still worth some cellar time. The bouquet has a toasty touch to lemon and herbal varietal/regional cues. It tastes subtle, dry and vinous with fine texture and good length. Works well with grilled prawns.

| | |
|---|---|
| Quality | 🍷🍷🍷🍷 |
| Value | ★★★★★ |
| Grapes | semillon |
| Region | Hunter Valley, NSW |
| Cellar | 🍷 5+ |
| Alc./Vol. | 11.0% |
| RRP | $17.00 Ⓢ |

## McWilliams Mount Pleasant Hunter Valley Chardonnay

| | |
|---|---|
| Quality | ▼▼▼▼ |
| Value | ★★★★★ |
| Grapes | chardonnay |
| Region | Hunter Valley, NSW |
| Cellar | ▮ 2 |
| Alc./Vol. | 13.5% |
| RRP | $15.00 ⑤ |

Real Hunter aficionados have never stopped saying that the region's white wine strength rests with semillon rather than chardonnay, but chardonnay can still be pretty good.

CURRENT RELEASE 1998  More subtle than many Hunter chardonnays, this has attractive melon-like aromas, with some complexity coming from melted butter and nutty touches derived from barrel and malolactic influence. The palate is smooth and persistent with good harmony between chardonnay fruit and oak. Try it with fish cakes.

| | |
|---|---|
| Quality | ▼▼▼▼ |
| Value | ★★★★¹ |
| Grapes | chardonnay |
| Region | Hunter Valley, NSW |
| Cellar | ▮ 4 |
| Alc./Vol. | 13.5% |
| RRP | $15.00 ⑤ |

CURRENT RELEASE 1999  The newest release of this wine shows a tad more toasty oak influence than its predecessor but we'd expect that to mellow with time. Otherwise it follows the pattern faithfully: melony fruit, some buttery, nutty complexity, smooth flavour, good length, and easy fruit/oak balance. The finish is clean and dry. Try it with grilled prawns and herb butter.

## McWilliams Mount Pleasant Lovedale Semillon

| | |
|---|---|
| Quality | ▼▼▼▼▼ |
| Value | ★★★★ |
| Grapes | semillon |
| Region | Hunter Valley, NSW |
| Cellar | ▮ 10+ |
| Alc./Vol. | 10.5% |
| RRP | $40.00 |

The Lovedale vineyard is a prized patch of Hunter vineyard that produces very special wine in the right conditions. It is only occasionally bottled separately from the normal Elizabeth.

*Previous outstanding vintages: '74, '75, '79, '84, '86, '95*

CURRENT RELEASE 1996  Bright yellow–green, this has a relatively unevolved bouquet. There are refined regional aromas of citrus and soap with a bit of richness developing and only a hint of the honeyed toastiness that often comes with bottle-age. The palate is subtle, clean and long-tasting, with a silky texture and a very fine finish. Still a pup, this will develop into a Hunter star. A fine companion to delicate seafoods.

# McWilliams Mount Pleasant Maurice O'Shea Chardonnay

Maurice O'Shea was winemaker at Mount Pleasant for thirty-odd years, a man ahead of his time in the fields of wine and gastronomy. Today he is remembered in Mount Pleasant's flagship wines.

CURRENT RELEASE 1998   The regional style is good but it usually lacks the finesse of cooler-climate chardonnay. This is a case in point, a good drink but a bit simple for a wine that's meant to be a range leader. Oak is quite pronounced, with honeyed peachy chardonnay fruit behind it in good measure. Good but not great, this will suit veal in a creamy sauce.

| | |
|---|---|
| Quality | 🍷🍷🍷🍷 |
| Value | ★★★ |
| Grapes | chardonnay |
| Region | Hunter Valley, NSW |
| Cellar | 🍾 3 |
| Alc./Vol. | 13.5% |
| RRP | $33.00 |

# Meerea Park Alexander Munro Chardonnay

Chardonnay can be delicate and light, or it can be big and potent. This fits the latter category, and how! CURRENT RELEASE 1999   There's power a-plenty in this Hunter chardonnay, and at the moment most of it comes from a big serve of toasty oak. The nose has lots of it and it makes the palate rather too harsh for easy drinking. A core of ripe peachy fruit of real concentration and alcoholic warmth is buried in the middle, but whether it will emerge remains to be seen. Try it with fried chicken.

| | |
|---|---|
| Quality | 🍷🍷🍷🍷 |
| Value | ★★★ |
| Grapes | chardonnay |
| Region | Hunter Valley, NSW |
| Cellar | 🍾 4 |
| Alc./Vol. | 13.5% |
| RRP | $25.00 |

# Meerea Park Epoch Semillon

Unwooded Hunter semillon is one of only a couple of wines that could truly be labelled uniquely Australian. With bottle-age they attain real stature.

CURRENT RELEASE 2000   The nose is neutral à la Hunter sem tradition, with light citrus, hand cream and herbal scents that don't actually leap out of the glass. But the palate is very 2000 vintage Hunter with an unusual dimension of richness and concentration. The varietal flavour has a suggestion of fruit-sweetness that's usually lacking and the finish is long-lasting and clean as a whistle. Try it with crab terrine.

| | |
|---|---|
| Quality | 🍷🍷🍷🍷🍷 |
| Value | ★★★★ |
| Grapes | semillon |
| Region | Hunter Valley, NSW |
| Cellar | 🍾 5+ |
| Alc./Vol. | 12.0% |
| RRP | $18.00 |

## Meerea Park Forefathers Chardonnay

| | |
|---|---|
| Quality | 🍷🍷🍷🍷 |
| Value | ★★★★ |
| Grapes | chardonnay |
| Region | Hunter Valley, NSW |
| Cellar | 🍾 3 |
| Alc./Vol. | 13.0% |
| RRP | $18.00 |

In common with a number of smallish Hunter wineries, the Meerea Park wines didn't get far past the cellar-door sales market until recently, but now they have limited distribution elsewhere. Maker: Rhys Eather.

CURRENT RELEASE 1999    A well-made, honest Hunter chardonnay. The nose has ripe fruit in the obvious peachy Hunter style, but the cloves and spices of good French oak, and some nutty lees and malolactic influences add attractive complexity. In the mouth it has medium body with smooth, creamy texture, ripe fruit flavour and balanced oak, ahead of a clean, dry finish. Try it with baked snapper.

## Meerea Park Lindsay Hill Viognier

| | |
|---|---|
| Quality | 🍷🍷🍷🍷 |
| Value | ★★★ |
| Grapes | viognier |
| Region | Hunter Valley, NSW |
| Cellar | 🍾 1 |
| Alc./Vol. | 14.0% |
| RRP | $21.00 |

Is viognier the next big thing? We doubt it, but many Australian winemakers are messing around with it, with mixed success. Its distinctive varietal character is an acquired taste.

CURRENT RELEASE 2000    An exuberant example of viognier, this has powerful ripe varietal aromas that suggest musk, flowers, spice and honey. That big nose is matched perfectly to a dense, super-rich palate which finishes with typically soft acidity. The aftertaste is decadently perfumed and long. Works well with smelly washed-rind cheeses.

## Metier Chardonnay

| | |
|---|---|
| Quality | 🍷🍷🍷🍷🍷 |
| Value | ★★★★ |
| Grapes | chardonnay |
| Region | Yarra Valley, Vic. |
| Cellar | 🍾 3 |
| Alc./Vol. | 13.4% |
| RRP | $32.00 |

Grown and made in the Yarra Valley by Martin Williams, Metier is a full-on wine which employs all the tricks of the trade when it comes to building chardonnay of complex personality.

CURRENT RELEASE 1998    This very 'worked' style of chardonnay isn't everybody's cuppa, but fans can't get enough. Martin Williams is interested in building as much textural interest and 'feel' into his wine as aroma and flavour. The result is a powerful, persistent wine of buttery richness, oatmeal and nutty notes, grapefruit and nectarine varietals and refined spicy oak. Crisp acidity retains palate freshness nicely. Try it with blanquette of veal.

## Milburn Park Chardonnay

These days Milburn Park wines emphasise value for money throughout the range, rather than absolute quality. Maker: Krister Jonsson (Australia's only Swedish winemaker!).

CURRENT RELEASE 2000    This is an acceptable sort of chardonnay with a hint of sophistication lacking in many, perhaps due to the inclusion of some cool-climate material. The nose has light stone-fruit, oak and minerally notes, and it tastes of pear and peach, with a light veneer of slightly chippy oak. The mouth-feel is smooth and agreeable with a soft finish. Try it with seafood pasta.

| | |
|---|---|
| Quality | ♥♥♥♥ |
| Value | ★★★→ |
| Grapes | chardonnay |
| Region | Murray & Alpine Valleys, Vic. |
| Cellar | 🍶 2 |
| Alc./Vol. | 14.0% |
| RRP | $14.00 Ⓢ |

## Miranda High Country Sauvignon Blanc

The Miranda concern has spread its wings from its Riverina base into South Australia's Barossa Valley and Victoria's King Valley. The High Country range springs from the latter outpost.

CURRENT RELEASE 2000    A fresh young sauvignon of reasonable quality at a fair price. The nose has some zippy herbaceousness and light citrus/tropical fruit. In the mouth it has medium intensity of grassy flavour but it lacks a little depth. Very brisk acidity provides a lively zip to the finish, emphasising that rather shy ripe fruit character. Try it with mussels topped with a tomato salsa.

| | |
|---|---|
| Quality | ♥♥♥♥ |
| Value | ★★★ |
| Grapes | sauvignon blanc |
| Region | King Valley, Vic. |
| Cellar | 🍶 1 |
| Alc./Vol. | 11.0% |
| RRP | $13.00 Ⓢ |

## Miranda Mirool Creek Semillon Sauvignon Blanc

The New South Wales Riverina has always pumped out lakes of inexpensive table wine. It used to be innocuous at best, but these days the standard is better than ever before. Miranda is one of the names to watch for passable cheapies.

CURRENT RELEASE 2000    This simple dry white doesn't make any great claims, but in the under-$10 category you could do much worse. It combines tropical fruit aromas with herbal touches on the nose, and the fruity palate is soft and easy with pleasant smoothness and a clean finish. An everyday white to serve with fish and chips.

| | |
|---|---|
| Quality | ♥♥♥ |
| Value | ★★★ |
| Grapes | semillon; sauvignon blanc |
| Region | Riverina, NSW |
| Cellar | 🍶 1 |
| Alc./Vol. | 12.0% |
| RRP | $9.00 Ⓢ |

## Mitchelton Airstrip Marsanne Roussanne Viognier

| | |
|---|---|
| Quality | 🍷 🍷 🍷 🍷 ᵜ |
| Value | ★ ★ ★ ⅃ |
| Grapes | marsanne; roussanne; viognier |
| Region | Goulburn Valley, Vic. |
| Cellar | 🍷 2 |
| Alc./Vol. | 13.5% |
| RRP | $24.95 |

The patch of land that was once Mitchelton's airstrip is now a sea of mature marsanne vines. You'll have to leave the Gulfstream at home and drive there now. CURRENT RELEASE 2000    A wine with true white Rhone personality with a fascinating, complex aroma of floral notes, apricot, peach and a hint of graphite from barrel fermentation. It tastes smooth and fragrant with soft, aromatic stone-fruit flavour, good palate structure and length. A well-made unusual white that will go well with mild cheeses.

## Mitchelton Blackwood Park Botrytis Riesling

| | |
|---|---|
| Quality | 🍷 🍷 🍷 🍷 ᵜ |
| Value | ★ ★ ★ ★ ⅃ |
| Grapes | riesling |
| Region | Goulburn Valley, Vic. |
| Cellar | 🍷 3 |
| Alc./Vol. | 13.0% |
| RRP | $14.50 (375 ml) |

Part of the Mitchelton vineyard is in a slight hollow next to the Goulburn River in Central Victoria. This gives rise to the perfect misty, mild autumn weather that is favourable to botrytis cinerea, the noble rot. This consistently good sweet white wine is the result. CURRENT RELEASE 2000    In 2000 the Blackwood Park vineyard enjoyed some 80–90 per cent botrytis infection, a very high figure. The nose has intense cumquat marmalade-like aromas along with some exotic spice and juicy sweet lime. The palate has citrus peel and sweet lime flavours that are well concentrated with a good 'cut' of acidity giving an impression of firm dryness to the finish. An unusual companion to a rich chicken liver pâté.

## Mitchelton Blackwood Park Riesling

| | |
|---|---|
| Quality | 🍷 🍷 🍷 🍷 🍷 |
| Value | ★ ★ ★ ★ ★ |
| Grapes | riesling |
| Region | Goulburn Valley, Vic. |
| Cellar | 🍷 6+ |
| Alc./Vol. | 13.0% |
| RRP | $15.00 Ⓢ |

This could be Victoria's best riesling – it's certainly one of the most consistent and ageworthy. Maker: Don Lewis. *Previous outstanding vintages : '85, '90, '91, '92, '94, '95, '96, '97, '98, '99* CURRENT RELEASE 2000    The 1999 was our Penguin Best White Wine in last year's *Guide*, and we approached the 2000 model with keen anticipation. Unfortunately it was corked, a reminder of how much better screw-tops are on this type of wine. Our second example was great, a thrilling wine not far behind last year's winner. It has a spring-like, pristine fruit character boasting lime, floral, stone-fruit and spicy elements in a crisp, long-tasting package. Great with Thai salads.

## Mitchelton Chardonnay

A couple of management changes at Mitchelton in recent years have given the brand a slight touch of the stutters, but Don Lewis's winemaking remains spot-on. CURRENT RELEASE 1998    While most producers are trotting out their '99s, Mitchelton's '98 is still available. It has quite a bit of good-quality French oak in its make-up, but the requisite melon and citrus fruit character is there in good measure too, along with some nutty, mealy touches. It hasn't quite the fruit richness of the 1997 vintage, but the middleweight palate still has a smooth feel to it, moderate depth and good acidity. Try it with seafood crepes.

| | |
|---|---|
| Quality | ♟♟♟♟ |
| Value | ★★★ |
| Grapes | chardonnay |
| Region | Goulburn Valley, Vic. |
| Cellar | 🍷 2 |
| Alc./Vol. | 13.5% |
| RRP | $20.00 |

## Mitchelton Vineyard Series Chardonnay

The Vineyard Series is a new Mitchelton label, which supersedes a slightly confused arrangement of differing wine ranges. It's based broadly on the Rhone varieties that are winemaker Don Lewis's speciality. CURRENT RELEASE 1999    This bright greeny–yellow wine has a bouquet of medium intensity with fig and melon aromas, seasoned with some nutty oak touches. In the mouth it has smooth flavour with an attractive veneer of creamy oak adding interest and complexity. A well-balanced wine of restrained personality that should age well short-term. Serve it with pasta with a creamy seafood sauce.

| | |
|---|---|
| Quality | ♟♟♟♟ |
| Value | ★★★⯪ |
| Grapes | chardonnay |
| Region | Goulburn Valley & Strathbogie Ranges, Vic. |
| Cellar | 🍷 3 |
| Alc./Vol. | 13.5% |
| RRP | $20.00 |

## Moorilla Estate Riesling

Not only are good wines produced at Moorilla Estate, but they have a fascinating museum of antiquities and art in the original estate house designed by Sir Roy Grounds. CURRENT RELEASE 2000    A pale, greenish-tinged wine with an exotic varietal nose of apple, lime and musk that's a little reminiscent of Alsace. There also looks to be some botrytis influence in its make-up. Those aromatic qualities, and hints of bakery spices, persist on the long palate, which has a little more depth than usual. Lively acidity keeps it clean and fresh. Good with salmon gravlax.

| | |
|---|---|
| Quality | ♟♟♟♟⯪ |
| Value | ★★★★ |
| Grapes | riesling |
| Region | various, Tas. |
| Cellar | 🍷 8 |
| Alc./Vol. | 13.0% |
| RRP | $22.00 |

## Moss Wood Semillon

| | |
|---|---|
| Quality | 🍷🍷🍷🍷🍷 |
| Value | ★★★★⯪ |
| Grapes | semillon |
| Region | Margaret River, WA |
| Cellar | 🍾 1–4 |
| Alc./Vol. | 14.0% |
| RRP | $26.00 |

To many Australian wine enthusiasts (especially Sydneysiders) semillon equals Hunter Valley. But it's a variety that performs well in other parts of Australia like Margaret River.

CURRENT RELEASE 2000    Pale straw in colour, this has a really interesting European-accented nose with minerally elements woven through soft citrus fruit. The impression is 'winey' rather than 'fruity', and the palate follows the theme. It's smooth in texture and medium-bodied with richly satisfying dry flavour and well-integrated firm acidity. A serious Margaret River semillon to sip with a seafood terrine.

## Mount Avoca Chardonnay

| | |
|---|---|
| Quality | 🍷🍷🍷⯪ |
| Value | ★★★ |
| Grapes | chardonnay |
| Region | Pyrenees, Vic. |
| Cellar | 🍾 1–4 |
| Alc./Vol. | 12.5% |
| RRP | $21.00 |

There's something about chardonnays packed in claret bottles; it's silly we know, but somehow they just don't look right. Mount Avoca's is made by Matthew Barry.

CURRENT RELEASE 1999    A bright appearance and a nose with notable spicy oak. Underneath it ripe, syrupy chardonnay fruit aroma strives to get through, but the wood wins out. In the mouth it has some fruit-sweetness but once again oak intrudes a bit much. Try it with barbecued pork fillet with a creamy mustardy sauce.

## Mount Horrocks Cordon Cut Riesling

| | |
|---|---|
| Quality | 🍷🍷🍷🍷⯪ |
| Value | ★★★ |
| Grapes | riesling |
| Region | Clare Valley, SA |
| Cellar | 🍷 2 |
| Alc./Vol. | 11.0% |
| RRP | $29.00 (375 ml) |

Cordon cutting involves cutting the fruit-bearing cane when the grapes are already ripe to allow them to shrivel a bit. It achieves concentration of flavouring elements without botrytis. In the final analysis, the best cordon cut sweet wine won't be quite as complex as the best botrytised sticky, but in a good year Mount Horrocks must come close.

CURRENT RELEASE 2000    This has a rather developed pale golden colour, and the rich nose and palate are reminiscent of luscious sweet stone fruits like apricots and peaches. There's also a citrus note that provides a sweet–sour tang. A lovely sweet wine, more straightforward than some, but a delight to drink with fresh mangoes and cream.

## Mount Horrocks Riesling

| | |
|---|---|
| Quality | 🍷🍷🍷🍷🍷 |
| Value | ★★★★★ |
| Grapes | riesling |
| Region | Clare Valley, SA |
| Cellar | 🍷 5+ |
| Alc./Vol. | 13.0% |
| RRP | $25.00 |

Stephanie Toole's Mount Horrocks rieslings are made using exacting standards resulting in a powerful wine of great intensity. She is also a member of the Clare Valley screw-top brigade.

CURRENT RELEASE 2000    This screw-top riesling, as expected, was fresh and alive on the nose with concentrated spices, flowers and lime juice aromas. There's a minerally touch and the beginnings of the complexity that comes with bottle-age. It tastes intense and mouth-filling, with tight cinnamon/spicy flavours and a long, fragrant, floral aftertaste. First-class riesling to enjoy with fritto misto.

## Mount Horrocks Semillon

| | |
|---|---|
| Quality | 🍷🍷🍷🍷🍷 |
| Value | ★★★⁺ |
| Grapes | semillon |
| Region | Clare Valley, SA |
| Cellar | 🍷 3 |
| Alc./Vol. | 14.0% |
| RRP | $21.00 |

Clare Valley semillon is one of the unsung heroes of Aussie wine. These days its star is on the rise and clever winemaking has made this a more serious contender. CURRENT RELEASE 2000    Fermentation and maturation in French oak for eight months has worked wonders here, giving a touch of creamy, nutty lees and barrel influence. This adds dimension to a core of herbal, lemon-scented fruit. The palate has surprising presence: citrus-like flavours are interwoven with attractive nutty touches, richness and length are exemplary and it finishes with a clean tang. A chardonnay alternative to enjoy with light chicken dishes.

## Mount Langi Ghiran Pinot Gris

| | |
|---|---|
| Quality | 🍷🍷🍷 |
| Value | ★★★ |
| Grapes | pinot gris |
| Region | Grampians, Vic. |
| Cellar | 🍷 2 |
| Alc./Vol. | 13.5% |
| RRP | $22.00 |

Whither pinot gris? There's a bit about in Australia's cooler vineyards, but its coming of age here is taking time. At Mount Langi Ghiran, Trevor Mast's example is getting better.

CURRENT RELEASE 2000    This has more real varietal character than last year's edition, possibly a case of increasing vine age improving fruit quality. The colour is bright and the nose has banana, nutty and stone-fruit aromas, with a hint of honeyed richness. The palate is smooth and soft, but still not as richly endowed as the classic Alsatian style. A good wine for some chicken liver mousse.

## Mount Langi Ghiran Riesling

| | |
|---|---|
| Quality | ▼▼▼▼▼ |
| Value | ★★★★ |
| Grapes | riesling |
| Region | Grampians, Vic. |
| Cellar | ▬ 1–4+ |
| Alc./Vol. | 13.0% |
| RRP | $18.00 |

Trevor Mast's winemaking training included time spent in Germany learning a lot about riesling. Despite that, rieslings from his Mount Langi Ghiran vineyard are typically Australian in style.

CURRENT RELEASE 2000    A more reserved, serious wine than the '99 edition, this has attractive freshness on the bouquet with lime, minerals and an almost minty touch. The clean, subdued aromas track through the palate which is dry and understated, yet with real underlying richness and a firm backbone. Good with salmon sushi.

## Mount Mary Triolet

| | |
|---|---|
| Quality | ▼▼▼▼▼ |
| Value | ★★★✦ |
| Grapes | semillon; sauvignon blanc; muscadelle |
| Region | Yarra Valley, Vic. |
| Cellar | ▮ 5 |
| Alc./Vol. | 12.5% |
| RRP | $50.00 |

Where a lot of wineries regard their semillon sauvignon blanc blends as lightweight everyday sups, at Mount Mary the Bordeaux white blend is serious wine.

CURRENT RELEASE 1999    This is a complex white wine worthy of the best tables. The bouquet has a distinct European touch. Aromas of herbs, minerals, nuts and honey provide savoury interest, and the palate is concentrated and long-flavoured, minerally and dry. There's a dry austerity that is very appealing, and high acidity to underpin its proven ageing ability.

## Mount Riley Sauvignon Blanc

| | |
|---|---|
| Quality | ▼▼▼▼ |
| Value | ★★★★✦ |
| Grapes | sauvignon blanc |
| Region | Marlborough, NZ |
| Cellar | ▮ 2 |
| Alc./Vol. | 12.8% |
| RRP | $15.50 |

As Marlborough sauvignon blanc has been enjoying worldwide popularity prices have crept up a little for the top wines. Thankfully you can still get a taste of what it's all about with a reasonable price tag from Mount Riley. Maker: Bill Hennessy.

CURRENT RELEASE 2000    A bright, green-tinged colour looks the goods here, and the nose has archetypal regional/varietal character. There's a grapey, clean aroma with hints of green fruits, citrus and minerals. In the mouth it has moderate intensity of tangy flavour with good length and a clean, relatively soft finish. A crisp young sauvignon to accompany the freshest shellfish.

# Mountadam Chardonnay

Adam Wynn and his late father David were pioneers of chardonnay in South Australia at Mountadam. The wine is a more refined expression of chardonnay that deserves good food to be at its best, unlike the 'fruit-bomb' style made by many SA vignerons.

CURRENT RELEASE 1998 Mountadam's twentieth-anniversary chardonnay typifies the subtle and complex house style. The bouquet and full palate are relatively understated, yet they have a more-ish character that keeps you refilling your glass. Stone-fruit character is interwoven with nutty/leesy elements, a touch of butterscotch, and a light veneer of spicy oak. Good with stirfried chicken, almonds and Chinese broccoli.

| | |
|---|---|
| Quality | ❦ ❦ ❦ ❦ ❦ |
| Value | ★ ★ ★ ✦ |
| Grapes | chardonnay |
| Region | Eden Valley, SA |
| Cellar | ▮ 4 |
| Alc./Vol. | 13.8% |
| RRP | $34.00 |

# Neagle's Rock Riesling

The 2000 vintage was good in Clare, certainly better than '99, but the early signs are that 2001 will be better still. Here's yet another excellent Clare riesling to add to an already impressive list.

CURRENT RELEASE 2000 Normally wine marketers don't make particularly good vignerons, but Steve Wiblin and Jane Willson are rapidly putting runs on the board. Their 2000 is a typical Clare riesling: smooth and rich, scented with wild flowers and garden herbs, and just starting to build toastiness. It's good to drink now or cellar, and goes well with fish and chips.

| | |
|---|---|
| Quality | ❦ ❦ ❦ ❦ |
| Value | ★ ★ ★ ★ |
| Grapes | riesling |
| Region | Clare Valley, SA |
| Cellar | ▮ 5+ |
| Alc./Vol. | 12.0% |
| RRP | $16.00 |

# Nepenthe Lenswood Chardonnay

In antiquity, nepenthe was supposed to be a natural drug that helped you to forget your troubles. The founder of this winery is Ed Tweddell, who headed up F.H. Faulding pharmaceuticals. Get the idea?

CURRENT RELEASE 1999 Most of Nepenthe's whites have a vegetal/petroleum character, which may just be due to young vines, and this has a trace too. The colour is quite a developed, medium yellow and the bouquet also has cashew and melon aromas. The palate is light and fruity, but lacks a little intensity and focus. The usual Adelaide Hills subtlety is there. For drinking with delicate fodder, like crab salad.

| | |
|---|---|
| Quality | ❦ ❦ ❦ ❦ |
| Value | ★ ★ ★ |
| Grapes | chardonnay |
| Region | Adelaide Hills, SA |
| Cellar | ▮ 2 |
| Alc./Vol. | 13.5% |
| RRP | $26.00 |

## Normans Adelaide Hills Chardonnay

| | |
|---|---|
| Quality | ♈ ♈ ♈ ♈ |
| Value | ★ ★ ★ |
| Grapes | chardonnay |
| Region | Adelaide Hills, SA |
| Cellar | 🍷 2 |
| Alc./Vol. | 14.5% |
| RRP | $25.00 |

The public company Normans is now associated with a new public company floated by Margaret River's Chateau Xanadu. Winemaker in '99 was Peter Fraser. CURRENT RELEASE 1999 There's a slightly rough oak note in the bouquet and, in hindsight, ours may have been a less than perfect bottle. The palate is lean and somewhat short on fruit freshness, the high alcohol strength tending to unbalance the wine. It does have flavour – and some of the trademark finesse of the Adelaide Hills region. Try it with vegetable quiche.

## Normans Encounter Bay Chardonnay

| | |
|---|---|
| Quality | ♈ ♈ ♈ ♈ |
| Value | ★ ★ ★ ★ |
| Grapes | chardonnay |
| Region | not stated |
| Cellar | 🍷 1 |
| Alc./Vol. | 13.5% |
| RRP | $12.00 ⑤ |

This wine backs up what we call the New Brand Syndrome. That's when a wine company puts out a new brand, often with quality well above the market standard. It's a ploy designed to get attention and establish the brand quickly. CURRENT RELEASE 2000 This is showing some early development, with its medium–light yellow hue and soft, apricot, squash-like aromas. The taste is quite rich and intense for a wine of this price. It's medium-bodied with heaps of fruit, and a lingering finish. It would drink well with grilled mullet and leek sauce.

## Orlando Jacob's Creek Reserve Chardonnay

| | |
|---|---|
| Quality | ♈ ♈ ♈ ♈ |
| Value | ★ ★ ★ ⁍ |
| Grapes | chardonnay |
| Region | various, SA |
| Cellar | 🍷 2 |
| Alc./Vol. | 13.0% |
| RRP | $14.95 ⑤ |

The white part of the Jacob's Creek Reserve trio is a very handy chardonnay. Like the two reds, it offers exemplary value for money. CURRENT RELEASE 2000 The colour is a bright yellow–green and the nose has juicy tropical fruit aromas with a touch of citrus and nutty bits to give interest. The medium-bodied palate is soft and smooth with good balance and ripe fruit flavour. Acidity is a little tart, but it keeps the palate clean and fresh. This is great value, especially since it is often discounted from its already reasonable price. A good all-round chardonnay to serve with fettucine all'alfredo.

## Orlando Jacob's Creek Riesling

Of all the famous Jacob's Creek wines, the riesling often surprises us the most. Perhaps it's the old out-of-fashion riesling syndrome at work, but the wine can be quite attractive and of a varietal purity that belies its modest status.

CURRENT RELEASE 2000   The aromas are of lime and minerals that give a reasonable varietal impression, but the wine seems less intense than some previous examples. The palate is light and fresh with citrus flavour and a crisp finish. Serve it with fish and chips.

| | |
|---|---|
| Quality | 🍷 🍷 🍷 |
| Value | ★ ★ ★ |
| Grapes | riesling |
| Region | various, SA |
| Cellar | 🍾 1 |
| Alc./Vol. | 12.0% |
| RRP | $11.00 ⑤ |

## Orlando St Hilary Chardonnay

Padthaway chardonnay provides the sort of wine that Australians love, yet the region remains a curiously placed back-lot in the scheme of things. Perhaps it's just as well as it keeps the prices down. St Hilary shows what value results.

CURRENT RELEASE 1999   Oak is less apparent in this vintage than the last; it's still there, but deft winemaking has integrated it better from the start. A nose of attractive stone fruit and subtle nutty, creamy complexity starts things off, and the medium-weight palate has excellent fruit/oak/acid balance that makes it very easy to drink. This is great buying, and it's often discounted. Try it with sweetbreads.

| | |
|---|---|
| Quality | 🍷 🍷 🍷 🍷 |
| Value | ★ ★ ★ ★ ⁺ |
| Grapes | chardonnay |
| Region | Padthaway, SA |
| Cellar | 🍾 2 |
| Alc./Vol. | 13.0% |
| RRP | $18.00 ⑤ |

## Orlando Trilogy Semillon Sauvignon Blanc Muscadelle

This three-way blend is best known in the white wines of Bordeaux, which are either unctuously sweet or dry and austere. Orlando's version is a dry style but it bears little resemblance to the French prototype.

CURRENT RELEASE 2000   This is a clean, zippy wine with fresh herbaceous and citrus aromas. The palate is fresh with tropical lime flavour and a grassy sauvignon thread running through it. It seems to have gained a bit of interest over the '99 vintage but it's still a bit of a lightweight. Fair value and good with tempura.

| | |
|---|---|
| Quality | 🍷 🍷 🍷 ! |
| Value | ★ ★ ★ ★ |
| Grapes | semillon; sauvignon blanc; muscadelle |
| Region | Adelaide Hills, McLaren Vale, Barossa Valley & Eden Valley, SA |
| Cellar | 🍾 2 |
| Alc./Vol. | 11.5% |
| RRP | $13.00 ⑤ |

## Padthaway Estate Chardonnay

| | |
|---|---|
| Quality | 🍷🍷🍷🍷 |
| Value | ✱✱✱ |
| Grapes | chardonnay |
| Region | Padthaway, SA |
| Cellar | 🍾 1 |
| Alc./Vol. | 13.5% |
| RRP | $19.00 |

Winemaker Ulrich Grey-Smith fermented 55 per cent of this wine in barrels. Why not 100 per cent? Probably, he wanted to retain more primary fruit, by fermenting some of the wine in steel tanks. Some winemakers don't like a lot of barrel-fermented character.

CURRENT RELEASE 2000   The bouquet is shy, airing to display some pineapple aromas together with lightly dusty oak. It's quite full and rich in the mouth, with a little broadness and a clean, dry finish. It doesn't have a lot of persistence. It would drink well with fish patties.

## Palandri Aurora Chardonnay

| | |
|---|---|
| Quality | 🍷🍷🍷🍷 |
| Value | ✱✱✱✱✦ |
| Grapes | chardonnay |
| Region | various, WA |
| Cellar | 🍾 3 |
| Alc./Vol. | 13.0% |
| RRP | $15.00 Ⓢ |

Palandri is one of the more ambitious vineyard developers in Western Australia's recent history. Investors were doubtless attracted by the promise of big tax advantages and dividends.

CURRENT RELEASE 2000   The aromas take you straight to Western Australia: gooseberry-style fruit with sidenotes of passionfruit and hair oil. It's subtly wooded and has good depth of palate flavour, without any special complexity. We like its balance and drinkability. It goes with lightly baked salmon.

## Palandri Aurora Semillon Sauvignon Blanc

| | |
|---|---|
| Quality | 🍷🍷🍷🍷 |
| Value | ✱✱✱✱✦ |
| Grapes | semillon; sauvignon blanc |
| Region | mainly Margaret River, WA |
| Cellar | 🍾 2 |
| Alc./Vol. | 12.5% |
| RRP | $15.00 Ⓢ |

This start-up operation is sourcing fruit from all over the shop till its own vines are in full bearing. This is 66 per cent Margaret River, the remainder Great Southern, Pemberton and Warren Valley. Maker: Tony Carapetis.

CURRENT RELEASE 2000   This is a pretty smart debut from Palandri, the most controversial new winemaking outfit in Western Australia. Skilfully blended, it has a fragrant gooseberry sauvignon aroma and a light, soft, straightforward but fruity palate, with passionfruit the key flavour. It's keen value and goes with vegetable terrines.

## Paracombe Sauvignon Blanc

The Drogemullers have seven grape varieties in their 13.3 hectares of vineyard, and have their wines made under contract elsewhere. They sell by mail order, with limited retail distribution.

CURRENT RELEASE 2000    The colour is pale and the bouquet shows some cool-climate (and possibly shaded-bunch) sweaty/passionfruit aromas, while the palate lacks a little intensity, but it is a pleasant drink nevertheless. It is clean and well made, and will be enjoyed by most drinkers. The potential is there for some crackerjack wines in future.

| | |
|---|---|
| Quality | ♥♥♥♥ |
| Value | ★★★ |
| Grapes | sauvignon blanc |
| Region | Adelaide Hills, SA |
| Cellar | 🍷 1 |
| Alc./Vol. | 12.0% |
| RRP | $19.00 (mail order) |

## Pauletts Riesling

Neil Paulett makes one of the Clare region's finest rieslings. The family has 17 hectares of vines in the Polish Hill River sub-region. Son Matthew is in charge of the vineyards.

CURRENT RELEASE 2000    As usual, this is a restrained, delicate, early-harvest style of riesling, which promises to develop beautifully with age. It has flowery, minerally aromas together with some residual fermentation esters. It tastes a little on the light side in its youth, but could surprise as it fills out. It has fine balance and drinks well young with freshly shucked oysters.

| | |
|---|---|
| Quality | ♥♥♥♥ |
| Value | ★★★★ |
| Grapes | riesling |
| Region | Clare Valley, SA |
| Cellar | 🍷 8+ |
| Alc./Vol. | 11.0% |
| RRP | $19.80 |

## Penfolds Adelaide Hills Chardonnay

This wine arose out of the Penfolds chardonnay experiments that culminated in Yattarna. Although the latter is a blend of several regions, it always involves a fair dollop of Hills fruit.

CURRENT RELEASE 1999    The bouquet is quite marked by oak at this stage, smelling of toasty wood, grilled nuts and cedar. The palate is lighter than expected, with appealing fineness and subtlety, although it finishes a trifle short. Give it a few months to harmonise further. Then serve it with barbecued king prawns.

| | |
|---|---|
| Quality | ♥♥♥♥ |
| Value | ★★★ |
| Grapes | chardonnay |
| Region | Adelaide Hills, SA |
| Cellar | 🍷 4 |
| Alc./Vol. | 13.5% |
| RRP | $28.00 Ⓢ |

## Penfolds Clare Valley Reserve Aged Riesling

| | |
|---|---|
| Quality | 🍷🍷🍷🍷🍷 |
| Value | ★★★★⸳ |
| Grapes | riesling |
| Region | Clare Valley, SA |
| Cellar | 🍾 5+ |
| Alc./Vol. | 12.9% |
| RRP | $29.00 |

The blurb describes this as a 'high-elevation, cool-climate Clare Valley' wine. The vineyard's altitude may well be high, but in years like 1997 the climate was anything but cool! Maker: Neville Falkenberg and team. CURRENT RELEASE 1997 HH found a disturbing number of corked bottles, but the good ones are great. It has a medium–full yellow colour and lovely developed riesling bouquet of lemon butter, lightly browned toast and hints of paraffin. The palate still has youthful tang and delicious sweet citrus/herbal flavours, with lime juice to the fore. It's concentrated and very, very long. Terrific with pan-fried flounder.

## Penfolds Rawsons Retreat Semillon Chardonnay

| | |
|---|---|
| Quality | 🍷🍷🍷🍷 |
| Value | ★★★★⸳ |
| Grapes | semillon; chardonnay |
| Region | not stated |
| Cellar | 🍾 1 |
| Alc./Vol. | 12.5% |
| RRP | $10.20 Ⓢ |

Retreat? Isn't that bad marketing psychology? Or were they remembering F-Troop? The bugler was told to blow Retreat, but they were all so incompetent, the order was reversed into victory! CURRENT RELEASE 2000 This is a competent glass of light dry white. It has a grassy, herbal aroma laced with rather a lot of garden mint, which may come from the fruit or perhaps oak chips. The profile is light, lean and dry, with pleasing crispness and ample drinkability. It's an odd wine, but very good value. Try it with fish balls.

## Penfolds Yattarna Chardonnay

| | |
|---|---|
| Quality | 🍷🍷🍷🍷 |
| Value | ★★ |
| Grapes | chardonnay |
| Region | Adelaide Hills, SA; Tumbarumba, NSW; McLaren Vale, SA & Drumborg, Vic. |
| Cellar | 🍷 1–4+ |
| Alc./Vol. | 13.5% |
| RRP | $110–$150 |

The first Yattarna, 1995, has already blown out into a golden, blowsy, typical Aussie chardonnay, just as we predicted, making a mockery of its release price. The '97 and '98 are far finer wines. Makers: Ian McKenzie, Neville Falkenberg, Philip John and the Southcorp white winemaking team (most of whom have now departed). *Previous outstanding vintage: '97* CURRENT RELEASE 1998 Great things are expected of this vintage, which Penfolds believes even better than the magnificent '97. It's still in its shell, however. A very restrained, future-orientated style which smells of grapefruit, nuts and lemon. It's lean on the palate and seems to lack length compared to the '97. In time it may unfold more goodies. Drinks well with grilled crayfish.

## Penley Estate Chardonnay

The label says it's estate-grown, but doesn't say where. We assume it's all Coonawarra, although some earlier chardonnays have included McLaren Vale. Only 20 per cent of it underwent malolactic.

CURRENT RELEASE 2000    The unusual petro-chemical aromas recall vegetables and medicaments, which remind us of some Hunter chardonnays. It's a big, full-bodied, rather broad wine with fig-jam flavours and some aged characters. There could be a slight botrytis influence. It really fills the mouth. Try it with Thai ma-hor.

| | |
|---|---|
| Quality | 🍷🍷🍷🍷 |
| Value | ★★★⭑ |
| Grapes | chardonnay |
| Region | Coonawarra, SA |
| Cellar | 🍾 2 |
| Alc./Vol. | 13.5% |
| RRP | $20.20 |

## Petaluma Riesling

Not only is this a top-priced riesling, it's also a big production these days. It figures on just about every restaurant wine-list for starters. Maker: Brian Croser and team.

CURRENT RELEASE 2000    This is a great riesling and one of the best Petalumas for some years. The colour is brilliant yellow–green and it has a fabulous fragrance of lime, lemon and garden herbs. It manages to taste rich, powerful and concentrated in the mouth without lacking finesse. Indeed, it dances on the tongue. It's great now and will be for many years. Serve with pan-fried whiting.

| | |
|---|---|
| Quality | 🍷🍷🍷🍷🍷 |
| Value | ★★★★★ |
| Grapes | riesling |
| Region | Clare Valley, SA |
| Cellar | 🍾 10+ |
| Alc./Vol. | 12.8% |
| RRP | $23.50 |

## Petaluma Viognier

The label tells us only 250 cases of this wine were produced, which is a bit of a tease, really. As far as the market's concerned, it won't even touch the sides.

CURRENT RELEASE 2000    The nose is typical viognier: softly spicy and musky, with a scent reminiscent of bath-soap. It's clean and well made as you'd expect from Petaluma, with plenty of interest. There's an oily texture and fruit-sweetness thanks to very ripe grapes and a high glycerol/alcohol content. It goes with lightly spiced Thai food.

| | |
|---|---|
| Quality | 🍷🍷🍷🍷 |
| Value | ★★★ |
| Grapes | viognier |
| Region | Adelaide Hills, SA |
| Cellar | 🍾 3 |
| Alc./Vol. | 14.0% |
| RRP | $35.00 |

## Peter Lehmann Blue Eden Riesling

| | |
|---|---|
| Quality | 🍷🍷🍷🍷🍷 |
| Value | ★★★★⸹ |
| Grapes | riesling |
| Region | Eden Valley, SA |
| Cellar | 🍷 5+ |
| Alc./Vol. | 12.0% |
| RRP | $19.20 |

This newie from Lehmann has an intriguing package. The blue bottle has a coiled asp baked onto the glass and the label is a bracelet around the neck, which carries on about Adam and Eve in the garden of Eden, etc. Maker: Andrew Wigan and team.

CURRENT RELEASE 2000    A smart riesling indeed, even if it does have a touch of gamy/sweatiness among the authentic floral and citrus varietal aromas. It's lovely and juicy in the mouth, dried wild flowers pervading, and has a soft, open structure. It would drink well with delicate oven-baked scampi.

## Peter Lehmann Clancy's Classic Dry White

| | |
|---|---|
| Quality | 🍷🍷🍷 |
| Value | ★★★ |
| Grapes | sauvignon blanc; semillon |
| Region | not stated |
| Cellar | 🍷 1 |
| Alc./Vol. | 12.0% |
| RRP | $11.80 Ⓢ |

The name is a link to that famous Banjo Paterson poem, 'Clancy of the Overflow'. HH remembers the late actor Leonard Teale launching this brand with a stunning recitation in Perry's restaurant, Sydney, around 1990.

CURRENT RELEASE 2000    The nose reminds of slightly underripe sauvignon blanc, with its green herb, bracken and capsicum notes. The taste is dry, straightforward, clean and a touch green, but perfectly acceptable at the price. There's a hint of a tannin grip to finish. Pair it with fried whitebait.

## Peter Lehmann Semillon Chardonnay

| | |
|---|---|
| Quality | 🍷🍷🍷🍷 |
| Value | ★★★★ |
| Grapes | semillon; chardonnay |
| Region | Barossa Valley, SA |
| Cellar | 🍷 2 |
| Alc./Vol. | 12.5% |
| RRP | $11.80 Ⓢ |

These days, Peter Lehmann is a publicly listed wine company. The blending of semillon and chardonnay is a peculiarly Australian habit, but why not? It works. The grapes came from Light Pass and Vine Vale on the Barossa floor.

CURRENT RELEASE 2000    This is an attractive lighter-bodied dry white, cleverly made with a proportion of barrel ferment. Its aromas remind of citrus/lemon rind and mineral, with a lightly nutty undercurrent. It has good flavour and a little more weight and depth than most whites in its price-bracket. It's nicely proportioned and would go with pan-fried flathead.

## Pewsey Vale Riesling

Pewsey is perennially one of the best buys in riesling – it's affordable, it drinks well young and ages superbly. The vineyard was first planted by Eden Valley pioneer Joseph Gilbert in 1847. Maker: Louisa Rose.
CURRENT RELEASE 2000   Here's a delicious riesling that's drinking well now, but whose pedigree shows it will reward several years' cellaring. Pale lemon hue; fresh, delicate citrus aromas; intense and refined in the mouth with the merest hint of sweetness to broaden its appeal. It suits cold seafood and salad.

| | |
|---|---|
| Quality | ▼▼▼▼▼ |
| Value | ★★★★★ |
| Grapes | riesling |
| Region | Eden Valley, SA |
| Cellar | 🍾 8 |
| Alc./Vol. | 12.0% |
| RRP | $15.00 Ⓢ |

## Pewsey Vale The Contours Riesling

Yalumba has decided to keep back some stock of Pewsey riesling and re-issue it when mature as a 'Museum Reserve'. The '95 was the first, and it was at least as fine as this one. Maker: Louisa Rose.
CURRENT RELEASE 1996   Eden Valley riesling at its best! The colour is medium–full yellow and the bouquet has filled out, offering creamy, buttered-toast and vanilla aromas with some traces of primary fruit lingering. The palate is rich and smooth from bottle-age but doesn't lack vibrancy. A superb wine and a real treat at the price. Serve with pan-fried flathead.

| | |
|---|---|
| Quality | ▼▼▼▼▼ |
| Value | ★★★★★ |
| Grapes | riesling |
| Region | Eden Valley, SA |
| Cellar | 🍾 3+ |
| Alc./Vol. | 12.5% |
| RRP | $25.00 |

## Phillip Island Wines Chardonnay

There are two labels from the Phillip Island winery: this is the estate-grown label; the other is for bought-in grapes. The island is officially part of the Gippsland region. Makers: the Lance and Bentley families.
CURRENT RELEASE 2000   The colour is light yellow and it smells of milk powder – a sure sign of malolactic fermentation in a cool-climate wine. In the mouth, it's still very delicate and restrained, needing time to come out of its shell. The finish is a trifle pinched. The oak is gently handled and it finishes properly dry. Cellar, then serve with cheese goujons.

| | |
|---|---|
| Quality | ▼▼▼▼ |
| Value | ★★★ |
| Grapes | chardonnay |
| Region | Gippsland, Vic. |
| Cellar | ⟷ 1–4+ |
| Alc./Vol. | 13.5% |
| RRP | $27.00 |

## Picarus Chardonnay

| | |
|---|---|
| Quality | ▼▼▼▼ |
| Value | ★★★⟩ |
| Grapes | chardonnay |
| Region | Limestone Coast, SA |
| Cellar | ▮ 1 |
| Alc./Vol. | 13.6% |
| RRP | $27.00 |

Some effort has gone into the packaging of this new range, with the label blurb telling us earnestly that the vineyard sites were carefully chosen. The grapes came from Coonawarra, Padthaway and Mount Benson. CURRENT RELEASE 1999   The full yellow colour and developed bouquet suggest this is a wine to drink, not keep. It has a nice integration of toasty, pineapple and quince aromas and a suggestion of barrel fermentation. It's rich and full in the mouth but the combination of acid and alcohol results in a somewhat astringent finish. The flavours are attractive and it is a lively drink. Pair it with chicken kebabs.

## Pierro Chardonnay

| | |
|---|---|
| Quality | ▼▼▼▼▼ |
| Value | ★★★ |
| Grapes | chardonnay |
| Region | Margaret River, WA |
| Cellar | ▮ 4+ |
| Alc./Vol. | 14.0% |
| RRP | $57.00 |

Busselton sawbones Mike Peterkin has firmly established Pierro as one of the nation's leading chardonnays. The grapes are all grown on Pierro's own meticulously managed vineyard at Caves Road, Willyabrup. *Previous outstanding vintages: '86, '89, '90, '93, '94, '96, '97* CURRENT RELEASE 1999   A typical Pierro chardonnay with lots of oak and rich flavour, it also retains some tightness of structure and still has potential to fill out and improve. Light–medium yellow colour; toasted nut aromas with butter and vanilla nuances. The palate is rich and deep with generous sweet fruit flavour but not overblown. Mineral and oaky flavours on the finish still need time to soften. It's just right with crayfish.

## Pikes Riesling

| | |
|---|---|
| Quality | ▼▼▼▼▮ |
| Value | ★★★★⟩ |
| Grapes | riesling |
| Region | Clare Valley, SA |
| Cellar | ▮ 10+ |
| Alc./Vol. | 12.0% |
| RRP | $18.20 |

The Polish Hill River area makes finer, lighter riesling than other parts of Clare. It has a slatey character and spine-tingling acidity. Maker: Neil Pike; viticulturist: Andrew Pike. CURRENT RELEASE 2000   Another delicious riesling from 'Pikey'. It offers beautiful aromas of flowers and citrus blossom, with a hint of doughy esteriness. In the mouth you'll find the characteristic tangy, shivery acid of young Pikes riesling, which can be almost harsh at this stage, but will enable a long life during which great character will build. The structure is taut and tight and it goes well with crab mousseline.

## Pipers Brook Cuvée Clark Reserve

John Clark was the first MD of Pipers Brook. This is a sweet German-style wine with a whopping 230 grams per litre of residual sugar! Maker: Andrew Pirie.

**CURRENT RELEASE 2000   A great sticky, with an even greater future! This fine, restrained wine has a light yellow hue and delicate floral riesling and smoky botrytis aromas. It's clean, with bell-clear varietal character, very sweet but not at all unbalanced. The rich, unctuous palate has great flavour and texture. A very fine wine with great poise and potential.**

| | |
|---|---|
| Quality | ▼▼▼▼▼ |
| Value | ★★★★ |
| Grapes | riesling |
| Region | Pipers Brook, Tas. |
| Cellar | ▮ 8+ |
| Alc./Vol. | 10.1% |
| RRP | $34.00 (375 ml) |
| | (cellar door) |

Penguin Best
Sweet Wine

## Pipers Brook Estate Chardonnay

This company is the biggest wine producer in Tasmania, with vineyards at Pipers Brook, in the West Tamar, and in the Pipers River region.
CURRENT RELEASE 1999   It's restrained and somewhat closed, in typical house style. The colour is light and the nose is slightly sulfury with mineral, vanilla, nutty scents which open out with some airing. It's delicate and properly dry to taste, with finesse and subtle charms. The palate is grapefruity and seamlessly structured. It needs time to reveal its full worth. Cellar, then serve with sautéed yabbies.

| | |
|---|---|
| Quality | ▼▼▼▼▼ |
| Value | ★★★➤ |
| Grapes | chardonnay |
| Region | Pipers Brook, Tas. |
| Cellar | ▮ 6 |
| Alc./Vol. | 13.1% |
| RRP | $33.50 |

## Pipers Brook Summit Chardonnay

This wine is made in tiny quantities, and is sourced from the oldest vines, which were 25 years old for this particular vintage. It can impress initially, but tends to develop oddly with age – such as the '97, which is now full of tinned-pea and petroleum aromas.
CURRENT RELEASE 1998   As ever, an idiosyncratic style that polarises tasters, some enjoying its apricot and quince-like aromas and very tart acidity, others, including the authors, not. There's no denying the intensity of flavour, however. The colour is quite forward in development – a medium–deep yellow – and there is a question of botrytis influence. Because of the acid, it needs to be served with food. Try grilled Tassie crayfish.

| | |
|---|---|
| Quality | ▼▼▼▼ |
| Value | ★★➤ |
| Grapes | chardonnay |
| Region | Pipers Brook, Tas. |
| Cellar | ▮ 3 |
| Alc./Vol. | 13.5% |
| RRP | $55.00 |

## Pipers Brook Vineyard Riesling

| | |
|---|---|
| Quality | 🍷🍷🍷🍷᛫ |
| Value | ★ ★ ★ |
| Grapes | riesling |
| Region | Pipers River, Tas. |
| Cellar | ⬤— 1–8+ |
| Alc./Vol. | 13.2% |
| RRP | $23.00 |

The Pipers Brook back label goes to some lengths to explain how cool the vineyard's climate is. Even to the extent of a map with lines of latitude and '41 degrees south' clearly marked. Maker: Andrew Pirie.

*Previous outstanding vintages: '82, '84, '85, '90, '91, '92, '93, '94, '95, '99*

CURRENT RELEASE 2000    The bouquet is unusual in youth, displaying grass/hay and compost aromas together with lemon, creating an individual and not unattractive fragrance. The palate flavour is delicate, fine, crisp and tangy, and finishes quite dry. It will benefit from a little time to fill out. The indications are that it'll turn into a very good wine.

## Plantagenet Omrah Sauvignon Blanc

| | |
|---|---|
| Quality | 🍷🍷🍷🍷 |
| Value | ★ ★ ★ ★ ᛫ |
| Grapes | sauvignon blanc |
| Region | Great Southern, WA |
| Cellar | ▮ 1 |
| Alc./Vol. | 12.0% |
| RRP | $16.00 ⑤ |

The Omrah brand stands for wines made from bought-in grapes. Funny name, but it has a history. It's the name of a grower's vineyard that used to sell grapes to Plantagenet. Maker: Gavin Berry.

CURRENT RELEASE 2000    You could be excused for going to New Zealand on this one. It has a tangy, crisp, high-acid zestiness that identifies it as unequivocally cool-climate. There are some sweaty and kiwifruit overtones. It's clean and fresh in the mouth with that cleansing quality that typifies the sauvignon grape. Very gulpable with crab cakes.

## Plunkett Chardonnay

| | |
|---|---|
| Quality | 🍷🍷🍷 |
| Value | ★ ★ ★ |
| Grapes | chardonnay |
| Region | Strathbogie Ranges, Vic. |
| Cellar | ▮ 5 |
| Alc./Vol. | 13.0% |
| RRP | $18.00 (cellar door) |

You know you're deep in the country when the name of the road is Lambing Gully. The Plunketts planted their first vines in 1968, long before they ventured into winemaking.

CURRENT RELEASE 1999    For a two-year-old this is a very restrained chardonnay. It has a shy aroma, with a hint of airfix glue, and tastes very light, lean and undeveloped. It's dry and tangy from crisp acidity, and oak plays a minor role. It could benefit from cellaring. Try it with fresh oysters.

## Prentice Victoria Chardonnay

Neil Prentice is a very small-scale winemaker who uses other people's wineries (Rochford and Tuck's Ridge) and sources fruit from various regions, especially Whitfield, near Brown Brothers' pioneering block in the highest part of the King Valley region.
CURRENT RELEASE 1998    The date on the label is no indication of the style: this is a very backward wine, still light yellow in shade and showing undeveloped (and somewhat unripe) cool-climate characters. It smells pea-poddy, minerally and chalky, and in the mouth it is lean and tart with delicate flavour. It will probably never fill out, so drink now, with mussels marinière.

| | |
|---|---|
| Quality | ♟ ♟ ♟ |
| Value | ★ ★ ★ |
| Grapes | chardonnay |
| Region | not stated |
| Cellar | ▮ 3 |
| Alc./Vol. | 13.6% |
| RRP | $15.00 |

## Preston Peak Reserve Chardonnay

The cellar door is located at Preston, Queensland, and draws on vineyards there and at Wyberba. There's a minor boom in viticulture going on in Queensland.
Maker: Philippa Hambleton.
CURRENT RELEASE 1999    There's a distinct lack of freshness, possibly attributable to malolactic fermentation, resulting in a smoky, wet-dog kind of bouquet which could just be construed as complexity. It has good depth of flavour and the only question mark concerns that funkiness. It would go with smoked chicken and salad.

| | |
|---|---|
| Quality | ♟ ♟ ♟ |
| Value | ★ ★ ⸍ |
| Grapes | chardonnay |
| Region | Granite Belt, Qld |
| Cellar | ▮ 2 |
| Alc./Vol. | 12.5% |
| RRP | $28.00 |

## Providence Miguet Chardonnay

Providence is the new(ish) name for La Provence, which was established by a Frenchman, Jean Miguet, in 1956. Owner Stuart Bryce subtitles his best vintages Miguet in homage to the founder. This is the first such chardonnay release. It will go on sale early 2002.
CURRENT RELEASE 2000    This is a very fine chardonnay, with the accent firmly on the fruit; oak and other non-grape characters are very much in the background. It has a bouquet of pawpaw and other tropical fruits, a hint of apricot, and the taste is refined, subtle and yet very rewarding in length and intensity. It's a model cool-climate chardonnay, and would go well with grilled crayfish tails.

| | |
|---|---|
| Quality | ♟ ♟ ♟ ♟ ♟ |
| Value | ★ ★ ★ ★ ⸍ |
| Grapes | chardonnay |
| Region | Pipers River, Tas. |
| Cellar | ▮ 5+ |
| Alc./Vol. | 13.0% |
| RRP | $25.50 (cellar door) |

## Queen Adelaide Riesling

| | |
|---|---|
| Quality | ▼▼▼ |
| Value | ★ ★ ★ |
| Grapes | riesling |
| Region | various |
| Cellar | ▮ 1 |
| Alc./Vol. | 12.0% |
| RRP | $7.50 $ |

The Woodley name was once an important one in South Australian wine, with pioneering vineyards and celebrated labels known all over the country. Today it's all but gone, with the Queen Adelaide brand, now reserved for Southcorp cheapies, one of the last reminders.

CURRENT RELEASE 2000    There's nothing flash about this young wine, but you can certainly get worse for more money. It's a simple, estery, fruit-juicy white with a light limey palate that just hints at sweetness. Served icy cold at a party it should pass muster, but our recommendation is to consult this *Guide* and spend a few extra dollars for a better alternative.

## R.L. Buller & Son Victoria Chardonnay

| | |
|---|---|
| Quality | ▼▼▼▼ |
| Value | ★ ★ ★ ★ ┥ |
| Grapes | chardonnay |
| Region | Murray Valley, Vic. |
| Cellar | ▮ 1 |
| Alc./Vol. | 13.0% |
| RRP | $11.00 $ |

It's a puzzle how a boutique winery like Buller's can sell wine as cheaply as this little beaut, which discounts to $8. Other boutiques claim they're not profitable at $25. Maker: Richard Buller.

CURRENT RELEASE 1999    A real crowd-pleaser, and what a bargain. At two years this is still fresh and lively, and the generous depth of apricot, nougat, fruit-compote flavours makes it great value. It has a sweetish entry while good acidity gives it a clean, tangy finish. Bravo! Serve it with chicken and apricots.

## Ravenswood Lane Gathering Sauvignon Blanc

| | |
|---|---|
| Quality | ▼▼▼ |
| Value | ★ ★ ┥ |
| Grapes | sauvignon blanc |
| Region | Adelaide Hills, SA |
| Cellar | ▮ 2 |
| Alc./Vol. | 12.5% |
| RRP | $27.00 |

This Adelaide Hills vineyard uses some chummy brand names . . . Beginning, Gathering, Reunion, etc. Grapegrower John Edwards selects his own wines from the tanks at Hardys, who put their share into the Starvedog Lane brand.

CURRENT RELEASE 2000    The wine seems a tad dilute, but the flavours are certainly attractive. The colour is palish, the aromas are of herbs and gooseberries. It tastes like the grapes were ripe, and the finish is clean and dry – if a trifle salty. It could work well with asparagus salad.

## Redbank Pinot Gris

Pinot gris is a new line for the Robb family of Redbank, in the Pyrenees region. They've wisely opted for a different district for the grapes. In this case, it's the King Valley.

CURRENT RELEASE 2000 The colour has a faint coppery tinge – not unusual in pinot gris. The clean, fresh aromas remind of grass-hay, with subtle spice and flowery inflexions. The taste is soft and fruity, with a semblance of sweetness which comes from the very ripe grapes and high alcohol. While it's not very subtle, it certainly has generous flavour. Goes well with salmon risotto.

| | |
|---|---|
| **Quality** | 🍷🍷🍷½ |
| **Value** | ★★★ |
| **Grapes** | pinot gris |
| **Region** | King Valley, Vic. |
| **Cellar** | 2 |
| **Alc./Vol.** | 14.5% |
| **RRP** | $21.00 ($) |

## Redgate Reserve Sauvignon Blanc

Some of the Redgate labels depict exactly that – a red gate. A wee bit too literal? The winemaker since 1995, Andrew Forsell, did 10 years at California's Iron Horse and before that, Fergussons in the Yarra Valley.

CURRENT RELEASE 2000 Oak plays a prominent role here, but the intense sauvignon fruit comes through strongly too. The aromas recall sweet confectionery, peppermint and gooseberry, and the oak lends a complexing nutty, toasty aspect. The palate flavour is very good, although some may think it pushes oak to the extreme. It drinks well with warm goat's cheese tartlets.

| | |
|---|---|
| **Quality** | 🍷🍷🍷🍷 |
| **Value** | ★★★½ |
| **Grapes** | sauvignon blanc |
| **Region** | Margaret River, WA |
| **Cellar** | 3 |
| **Alc./Vol.** | 13.5% |
| **RRP** | $21.00 |

## Redgate Sauvignon Blanc Semillon

Blends of these two varieties, in varying proportions, are all the rage in Margaret River. And why not? They're frequently better drinks than either variety on its own. And that's what blending is about: the sum is greater than the components on their own.

CURRENT RELEASE 2000 This is a fine, reserved, tightly wound dry white which avoids excess pungency and smacks instead of fully ripe grapes. It has a pale colour and a fragrant aroma of musk, green apple and gooseberry. It tastes of pure, crisp varietal fruit with a clean, slightly short finish. It would team well with scallop and rocket salad.

| | |
|---|---|
| **Quality** | 🍷🍷🍷🍷 |
| **Value** | ★★★★ |
| **Grapes** | sauvignon blanc; semillon |
| **Region** | Margaret River, WA |
| **Cellar** | 2 |
| **Alc./Vol.** | 13.0% |
| **RRP** | $18.40 |

## Reynolds Orange Chardonnay

| | |
|---|---|
| Quality | 🍷 🍷 🍷 |
| Value | ★ ★ ✦ |
| Grapes | chardonnay |
| Region | Orange, NSW |
| Cellar | 🍷 1 |
| Alc./Vol. | 13.0% |
| RRP | $20.50 |

This won a gold medal at the national wine show in Canberra, but maybe there's some bottle variation . . . The Reynolds name is now the main brand of the ambitious new Orange district venture, Cabonne Limited. CURRENT RELEASE 1999  The wine is fairly developed now, with a full yellow colour and an obvious, toasty bouquet reflecting bottle-age and oak. On the palate it's fairly broad and overblown and although it has plenty of flavour, it lacks finesse. Team it up with grilled chicken.

## Richmond Grove Barossa Valley Riesling

| | |
|---|---|
| Quality | 🍷 🍷 🍷 🍷 🍷 |
| Value | ★ ★ ★ ★ ★ |
| Grapes | riesling |
| Region | Barossa Valley, SA |
| Cellar | 🍷 8+ |
| Alc./Vol. | 12.0% |
| RRP | $15.80 ⑤ |

It would be logical for John 'Mr Riesling' Vickery to make an Eden Valley riesling as well as Watervale and Barossa ones. But parent company Orlando doesn't like this idea: it already has a couple of Eden Valley beauties under the Orlando brand.
CURRENT RELEASE 2000  Though seldom quite as distinguished as its sister from Watervale, this can often be delicious nevertheless – usually when younger rather than older. It has a strongly herbal aroma with green lime inflexions, and excellent fruit intensity. There's a suggestion of sweetness mid-palate and it just needs time to build more character. It should be superb in a year or so. Serve with pasta alla vongole.

## Richmond Grove Watervale Riesling

| | |
|---|---|
| Quality | 🍷 🍷 🍷 🍷 🍷 |
| Value | ★ ★ ★ ★ ★ |
| Grapes | riesling |
| Region | Clare Valley, SA |
| Cellar | 🍷 10+ |
| Alc./Vol. | 12.0% |
| RRP | $15.80 ⑤ |

This company has bitten the bullet and bottled much of its riesling under Stelvin screw-caps. The reason is that cork-taint affects an unacceptable percentage of wines and is especially damaging to delicate whites such as riesling. CURRENT RELEASE 2000  John Vickery has done it again. This is a superb young riesling. It is bracingly fresh, scented with green apple, lime, lemon and grapefruit. It's very intense on nose and palate; very long and concentrated with fine acidity in perfect harmony. It's delicious now with oysters.

# Riddoch Chardonnay

The marketers have taken to plastering the label with such endorsements as 'from Katnook Estate' and a mug shot of John Riddoch. Thank heavens they stopped short of saying 'Home of the Jimmy Watson Trophy' . . . !

CURRENT RELEASE 1999    This chardonnay has a lot of – what they call in the trade – artefact. In other words, it's more about winemaking complexities than primary fruit. Smoky butterscotch, honey and pineapple are the main aromas, and it's soft and very gentle on the tongue, with apparently quite low acid. It's a straightforward, but pleasing, typical chardonnay with a juicy tropical taste. Try it with boudin blanc.

| | |
|---|---|
| Quality | ▼▼▼▼ |
| Value | ★★★⁺ |
| Grapes | chardonnay |
| Region | Coonawarra, SA |
| Cellar | ▮ 2 |
| Alc./Vol. | 13.5% |
| RRP | $17.75 Ⓢ |

# Riddoch Sauvignon Blanc

Katnook Estate is one of this country's finest sauvignon blanc producers, and its second-rank Riddoch wine is often just as good as the Katnook, although a shade lighter. Maker: Wayne Stehbens.

CURRENT RELEASE 2000    Another delicious wine under this label. Fresh lemon aromas come rocketing from the glass, and it's more like semillon than sauvignon – in other words, not pungent like a Kiwi rendition. It's light- to medium-bodied, smooth and lemony/smoky/nutty; beautifully balanced and ready to go. It suits a plate of fresh Sydney rock oysters.

| | |
|---|---|
| Quality | ▼▼▼▼▼ |
| Value | ★★★★★ |
| Grapes | sauvignon blanc |
| Region | Coonawarra, SA |
| Cellar | ▮ 3 |
| Alc./Vol. | 12.5% |
| RRP | $17.00 Ⓢ |

# Riverby Estate Riverstone Run Riesling

This is a single-vineyard wine from Marlborough. The name refers to a bit of history: the Wairau River changed course in the 1930s, exposing the flat shingle country that is now carpeted in very famous vineyards.

CURRENT RELEASE 2000    This is different – and delicious! Mineral, slate, wet-pebble and passionfruit aromas pour from the glass. It's delicate in the mouth, steely and fine, with subtle but concentrated flavour; a dry style with structure and length. Great now, but should mature well. Try it with green-lip mussels.

| | |
|---|---|
| Quality | ▼▼▼▼▼ |
| Value | ★★★★ |
| Grapes | riesling |
| Region | Marlborough, NZ |
| Cellar | ▮ 7+ |
| Alc./Vol. | 13.0% |
| RRP | $19.00 |

## Rochford Chardonnay

| | |
|---|---|
| Quality | ▟ ▟ ▟ ▟ ▛ |
| Value | ★ ★ ★ ★ |
| Grapes | chardonnay |
| Region | Macedon Ranges, Vic. |
| Cellar | ▮ 3 |
| Alc./Vol. | 13.5% |
| RRP | $21.00 |

Victoria's charming Macedon region is a cool, marginal place to grow grapes, and results with some grape varieties have on balance been disappointing. Chardonnay has been iffy too, but its fabled site adaptability has made it a safer bet.

CURRENT RELEASE 1999    A bright yellow–green wine with some interesting complexity. The nose has good balance with melon, nectarine and cashew aromas mixed in with butter/cream and nutty touches. In the mouth it has full rich flavour with creamy smooth texture, yet it's not overblown. There's good length of flavour and the typically tangy finish of good Macedon chardonnay. Try this with poached salmon.

## Rosemount Hill of Gold Chardonnay

| | |
|---|---|
| Quality | ▟ ▟ ▟ ▟ |
| Value | ★ ★ ★ ★ |
| Grapes | chardonnay |
| Region | Mudgee, NSW |
| Cellar | ▮ 3 |
| Alc./Vol. | 13.5% |
| RRP | $20.00 ⑤ |

Hill of Gold is the name of an existing Mudgee vineyard which Rosemount bought in the late 1990s. It was established by Peter Edwards in 1974. He was a Burgundy nut, and the name is a loose translation of Cote d'Or.

CURRENT RELEASE 2000    This wine has a degree of subtlety unusual in Rosemount chardonnays, presumably because of the terroir. The colour is light- to mid-yellow and it smells of dried flowers and candied fruits. The oak is nicely harmonised and discreet. It has delicacy and length on the palate. It could repay short-term cellaring, and teams well with gratinéed parmesan and asparagus.

## Rosemount Roxburgh Chardonnay

| | |
|---|---|
| Quality | ▟ ▟ ▟ ▛ |
| Value | ★ ★ |
| Grapes | chardonnay |
| Region | Hunter Valley, NSW |
| Cellar | ▮ 2 |
| Alc./Vol. | 14.0% |
| RRP | $52.00 |

This dinosaur of a wine is Rosemount's idea of a great Australian chardonnay. Although they've been slowly lightening and refining it over the years, it is still looking increasingly outdated. Maker: Philip Shaw and team.

CURRENT RELEASE 1998    The nose is classic Hunter chardonnay from a hot (that is: good red, but not-so-good white) year. It's full of developed, burnt-rubber and medicinal characters, with precious little primary fruit. The taste is similarly broad and clumsy, and it's a head-and-shoulders wine, lacking after-palate. Still, we're sure it will have some admirers. Food: chicken Maryland.

## Rosemount Semillon

Rosemount makes two semillons; this one appears under the regular diamond label and offers keen value. It doesn't say so on the package, but it's all Hunter wine. CURRENT RELEASE 2000    A great vintage for semillon in the Hunter, and it shows. This is a very accessible wine in youth. It smells distinctively of semillon from that vintage: intense grassy, herbal aromas which turn tangy and crisp in the mouth. It's fine, dry, lively and refreshing to drink on a summery day with cold seafood and salads.

| | |
|---|---|
| Quality | ▼▼▼▼▼ |
| Value | ★★★★★ |
| Grapes | semillon |
| Region | Hunter Valley, NSW |
| Cellar | ▌ 6+ |
| Alc./Vol. | 12.5% |
| RRP | $16.20 Ⓢ |

## Rosemount Show Reserve Semillon

With their Hunter semillon, Rosemount hand-pick the grapes and do all they can to ensure these thin-skinned grapes don't lose too much juice before they go down the chute. This was made from the 30-year-old vines on the Giants Creek and Roxburgh vineyards. CURRENT RELEASE 2000    The colour is light yellow and the wine evokes an exotic European style, with hints of solids and oxidative handling. It has straw and resin aromas while the taste is delicate, unevolved and somewhat ethereal. It should benefit from some time in the cellar. Try it with pasta and pipis.

| | |
|---|---|
| Quality | ▼▼▼▼ |
| Value | ★★★ |
| Grapes | semillon |
| Region | Hunter Valley, NSW |
| Cellar | ▌ 5 |
| Alc./Vol. | 13.5% |
| RRP | $25.00 |

## Rosemount Yarra Valley Chardonnay

| | |
|---|---|
| Quality | ♥♥♥♥ |
| Value | ★★★★ |
| Grapes | chardonnay |
| Region | Yarra Valley, Vic. |
| Cellar | 🍾 3 |
| Alc./Vol. | 13.0% |
| RRP | $18.00 |

Rosemount is one of the most energetic wine companies: they are constantly trying new ideas and new regions, even if the grapes are a long way from the company's wineries. Now, however, they're associated with the Coldstream Hills winery. So Yarra Valley chardonnay? No worries.

CURRENT RELEASE 1999    Racy is the word to describe this crisp but complex chardonnay. Rosemount's trademark butterscotch, honey, malt complexities are there in force to sniff, but the palate – while rich – retains tight structure and tangy acidity, which faithfully reflects the region. A fine wine to serve with crab cakes.

| | |
|---|---|
| Quality | ♥♥♥♥ |
| Value | ★★★ |
| Grapes | chardonnay |
| Region | Yarra Valley, Vic. |
| Cellar | 🍾 3 |
| Alc./Vol. | 13.5% |
| RRP | $18.20 Ⓢ |

CURRENT RELEASE 2000    Despite nine months in new barrels, this has subtle oak flavours and is soft and easy on the gums. It smells of creamed nuts and mixed spices, reflecting skilfully harmonised fruit and oak. The taste is soft and smooth, with a semblance of sweetness and a pleasing touch of richness on the mid-palate. A good match for slow-braised calamari.

## Rosily Vineyard Chardonnay

| | |
|---|---|
| Quality | ♥♥♥♥♥ |
| Value | ★★★★⁺ |
| Grapes | chardonnay |
| Region | Margaret River, WA |
| Cellar | 🍾 4+ |
| Alc./Vol. | 13.9% |
| RRP | $20.00 |

Rosily is a new venture in Margaret River which has fielded an impressive range of dry whites from the 2000 vintage. The 13.5-hectare vineyard, planted in 1994, is at Willyabrup.

CURRENT RELEASE 2000    The colour is rather pale and the aromas of melon and toast, together with some dairy-like malolactic characters, are fresh and inviting. The palate displays the kind of power and intensity for which the region is famous. The palate is long-lingering, with a flinty, mineral finish. It would team well with a yabbie salad.

## Rosily Vineyard Semillon

This is a first release from Rosily, which takes its name from a member of the early French expeditions to the west coast of Australia. Comte François de Rosily was a member of two expeditions to Western Australia and served as France's chief hydrographer.

CURRENT RELEASE 2000    This is a pretty good first effort, although the oak is somewhat obvious, showing assertive peppermint and pine-sap aromas. The palate is lean and very dry, the oak tannins helping firm up the finish. A pleasant wine, but certainly not a definitive expression of the grape! Try it with smoked cod.

| | |
|---|---|
| Quality | ♀♀♀♀ |
| Value | ★★★ |
| Grapes | semillon |
| Region | Margaret River, WA |
| Cellar | 🍶 3+ |
| Alc./Vol. | 13.5% |
| RRP | $18.00 |

## Ross Hill Orange Chardonnay

This vineyard is in Griffin Road, Orange, not far from Bloodwood Estate, and the altitude is a lofty 760 metres. The vines were just four years old in '99. Owners are Peter and Terri Robson.

CURRENT RELEASE 1999    For a two-year-old, this is a fairly subtle wine, lightly oaked and delicate, reflecting its cool-climate origins. It is clean and has a touch of austerity. There are hidden charms that reveal themselves after a few sips. It's dry and well balanced and could reward cellaring. It goes well now with fresh oysters.

| | |
|---|---|
| Quality | ♀♀♀♀ |
| Value | ★★★ |
| Grapes | chardonnay |
| Region | Orange, NSW |
| Cellar | 🍶 5 |
| Alc./Vol. | 13.0% |
| RRP | $18.00 (cellar door) |

## Rothbury Estate Brokenback Chardonnay

Brokenback is one of the Hunter's finest white wine vineyards. Rothbury has a portion of it, as do Tyrrells and Kulkunbulla. Rothbury uses the Brokenback name to signify its top semillon and chardonnay these days.

CURRENT RELEASE 2000    This is a fresh, youthful chardonnay that's yet to show its Hunter identity as it surely will. It smells of passionfruity, herbal, tropical fruit and tastes delicate in the mouth, with nutty oak in good balance. It finishes with a suggestion of sweetness and will probably show more character if cellared till 2002. Then try it with roast chicken.

| | |
|---|---|
| Quality | ♀♀♀♀ |
| Value | ★★★ |
| Grapes | chardonnay |
| Region | Hunter Valley, NSW |
| Cellar | 🍶 5+ |
| Alc./Vol. | 12.5% |
| RRP | $21.10 |

## Rothbury Estate Brokenback Semillon

| | |
|---|---|
| Quality | 🍷🍷🍷🍷🍷 |
| Value | ★★★★ |
| Grapes | semillon |
| Region | Hunter Valley, NSW |
| Cellar | 🍷 7 |
| Alc./Vol. | 11.0% |
| RRP | $21.00 Ⓢ |

We hope the maturity of this wine doesn't mean Beringer Blass is having trouble selling it. Especially at a time when big companies seem to be less and less interested in fringe varieties. It's won a gold medal at the 2000 Hobart Show.

CURRENT RELEASE 1998    This is a very fine semillon from what was a 'big' Hunter year, not conducive to long-ageing whites. The colour is still light to mid-yellow and it's starting to build the classic toasty, lanolin, resin and candle-wax regional bouquet. In the mouth it's bone-dry and quite restrained, with lemon-butter flavours and surprising austerity. It will benefit from cellaring. Try it with pan-fried flounder.

## Rothbury Estate Verdelho

| | |
|---|---|
| Quality | 🍷🍷🍷🍷 |
| Value | ★★★★⁴ |
| Grapes | verdelho |
| Region | Hunter Valley, NSW |
| Cellar | 🍷 1 |
| Alc./Vol. | 13.5% |
| RRP | $13.75 Ⓢ |

The Hunter Valley is one of the verdelho strongholds. Between the Hunter and Western Australia you'd probably have 90 per cent of the verdelho in the country. Maker: Alan Harris.

CURRENT RELEASE 2000    Gold medallist and top verdelho at the 2000 Hunter Show, this has tremendous depth of flowery fruit. While some verdelhos are slightly sweet, it finishes clean and relatively dry. From a top Hunter vintage, it has some richness and is a real crowd-pleaser. Serve it with mussels braised with fennel.

## Rothvale Reserve A Chardonnay

| | |
|---|---|
| Quality | 🍷🍷🍷🍷 |
| Value | ★★★⁴ |
| Grapes | chardonnay |
| Region | Hunter Valley, NSW |
| Cellar | 🍷 3+ |
| Alc./Vol. | 13.5% |
| RRP | $25.00 |

The A stands for American Oak, as there is an F (French oak) version, too. Rothvale is one of the most exciting new names to emerge in the Hunter in recent years. Owner Max Patton is obviously a human dynamo.

CURRENT RELEASE 2000    Coconutty American oak shows quite strongly at this stage, but will undoubtedly mellow into the wine if given a few more months' rest in a quiet place. There are peachy chardonnay flavours aplenty as well, and the wine is flawlessly clean and well made. You could serve it with chicken mornay.

## Ryecroft Reserve Adelaide Hills Chardonnay

The label is signed by Ros Oatley, daughter of
Rosemount founder Bob and wife of managing
director, Keith Lambert. She's a sort of de facto brand
manager for Ryecroft, a Rosemount sub-brand.
CURRENT RELEASE 2000    This is a delicate young
babe, with a palish colour and a subtle, fresh nose
of nougat and estery, slightly sweaty fermentation
aromas. The bouquet has yet to really develop.
In the mouth it's delicate and almost a touch bland.
It's pleasant without being exciting and could
improve in bottle. Try it with crab timbales.

| | |
|---|---|
| Quality | ♟ ♟ ♟ ↓ |
| Value | ★ ★ ★ |
| Grapes | chardonnay |
| Region | Adelaide Hills, SA |
| Cellar | ▮ 4 |
| Alc./Vol. | 13.5% |
| RRP | $19.90 Ⓢ |

## Rymill Sauvignon Blanc

The Rymill operation is one of Coonawarra's most
important. The family owns extensive vineyards, sells
grapes and makes wine for others under contract – as
well as making and marketing its own fine range of
wines. Maker: John Innes.
CURRENT RELEASE 2000    The colour is pale yellow
and it has a herbaceous scent that recalls fresh-cut
capsicum. It's light and rather delicate to taste, and
finishes pleasingly dry and clean. The balance is good,
although it could use more impact. It would be a good
match for sushi.

| | |
|---|---|
| Quality | ♟ ♟ ♟ |
| Value | ★ ★ ★ |
| Grapes | sauvignon blanc |
| Region | Coonawarra, SA |
| Cellar | ▮ 1 |
| Alc./Vol. | 11.0% |
| RRP | $15.50 Ⓢ |

## Saddlers Creek Semillon

John Johnstone has 15 hectares of vines and has made
his mark at least as strongly with innovative packaging
as with wine quality. This is a fine follow-up to his
excellent 2000.
CURRENT RELEASE 2001    This wine is just jumping
out of its bottle to get down your throat. It is
marvellously fresh and clean, delivering crisp, bouncy,
citrusy semillon flavour remarkably well considering its
youth. Still, it's a delicate, restrained style despite its
intensity of flavour. It drinks well now – with salad
niçoise – but should also age well.

| | |
|---|---|
| Quality | ♟ ♟ ♟ ♟ ↓ |
| Value | ★ ★ ★ ★ |
| Grapes | semillon |
| Region | Hunter Valley, NSW |
| Cellar | ▮ 10 |
| Alc./Vol. | 12.0% |
| RRP | $20.00 |

## Salisbury Estate Sauvignon Blanc

| | |
|---|---|
| Quality | 🍷🍷🍷 |
| Value | ★★★ |
| Grapes | sauvignon blanc |
| Region | Murray Valley, Vic. |
| Cellar | 🍾 1 |
| Alc./Vol. | 13.5% |
| RRP | $9.00 ⑤ |

An unprepossessing pale blue label does little for the appeal of this young Murray Valley sauvignon, but the wine is okay at the price.

CURRENT RELEASE 2000   There's a grassy varietal aroma here of medium intensity, and the palate follows a similar theme, although the flavour is rather neutral and quite short. But it has some weight and 'heat' in the mouth probably due to relatively high alcohol. The finish is clean and dry. An acceptable drop to serve with fish and chips.

## Sandalford Chardonnay

| | |
|---|---|
| Quality | 🍷🍷🍷🍷 |
| Value | ★★★↓ |
| Grapes | chardonnay |
| Region | Margaret River, Mount Barker & Swan Valley, WA |
| Cellar | 🍾 2 |
| Alc./Vol. | 14.0% |
| RRP | $17.00 |

A multi-regional blend that comprises grapes from across a wide spectrum of Western Australian climatic regions. The sum of the parts is probably better than some of the components on their own.

CURRENT RELEASE 1999   Quite a worked style this, with a somewhat developed yellow colour. It has stone-fruit and melon aromas combined with rich butter/caramel touches and dusty, nutty oak. The wine has a slightly 'hot' feel and it's full-bodied with powerful flavours of tangy ripe chardonnay fruit, nicely integrated with toasty oak. It's already showing some development and looks about ready to drink right now, with chicken scallopine.

## Schinus Chardonnay

| | |
|---|---|
| Quality | 🍷🍷🍷🍷 |
| Value | ★★★↓ |
| Grapes | chardonnay |
| Region | Goulburn Valley, Vic. |
| Cellar | 🍾 2 |
| Alc./Vol. | 13.5% |
| RRP | $15.00 ⑤ |

Although Garry Crittenden's Schinus operation is based at Dromana on the Mornington Peninsula, grapes are sourced from further afield. Among other things this helps to keep the price down.

CURRENT RELEASE 2000   Fruit is what this wine is all about. The nose has a lively melon and peach aroma that's juicy and appealing. More barrel influence than usual spices things somewhat, and it tastes pleasantly straightforward if a little hollow mid-palate. It finishes dry and rather firm. Sits well alongside seafood tempura.

## Schinus Sauvignon Blanc

The back label of this wine says, 'Each vintage our viticulture moves inexorably ahead.' They probably have an inexhaustible supply of such phrases, although their use when inexpedient is inexcusable, and sometimes inexplicable. Unfortunately they're inexpungible. Luckily the wine is inexpensive.
CURRENT RELEASE 2000    This is a fresh, fruity sauvignon with attractive gooseberry fruit on the nose and a smooth, undemanding tropical fruit palate with balanced acidity. It all combines nicely for easy drinking and would work well at a seafood buffet.

| | |
|---|---|
| Quality | ♛ ♛ ♛ ♛ |
| Value | ★ ★ ★ ★ |
| Grapes | sauvignon blanc |
| Region | not stated |
| Cellar | ▮ 1 |
| Alc./Vol. | 13.0% |
| RRP | $15.00 ⑤ |

## Seaview Chardonnay

A heritage of quality and a long-cherished identity comes to naught when the Southcorp brand managers try to make their mark in the organisation. As a result Seaview is now a cheap supermarket brand, and its better wines are unrecognisable under the E&C label.
CURRENT RELEASE 1999    Despite Seaview's decline as a brand, this inexpensive chardonnay remains good value. It has attractive melon aromas with a touch of caramel and a thread of oak running through it. In the mouth it repeats the nose exactly with soft flavour and a smooth, dry finish. Serve it with garlic prawns.

| | |
|---|---|
| Quality | ♛ ♛ ♛ |
| Value | ★ ★ ★ ★ |
| Grapes | chardonnay |
| Region | various, South East Australia |
| Cellar | ▮ 2 |
| Alc./Vol. | 13.0% |
| RRP | $11.00 ⑤ |

## Seppelt Corella Ridge Chardonnay

Corella Ridge is one of the wines in the ill-starred Seppelt Victoria range. Whether it's the fault of the odd labelling, or the work of Seppelt brand managers, it's never quite made it as it should have. Wine quality is very good and sometimes outstanding.
CURRENT RELEASE 1998    A year or two older than most of the competition, this has benefited from the experience, where some would be getting flabby. The colour is still a bright greenish straw, and the nose has some citrus and honeydew aromas edged in spicy oak. The palate is medium-bodied with similar flavours to the nose, a dash of toasty oak and a clean finish. Serve it with seafood pastries.

| | |
|---|---|
| Quality | ♛ ♛ ♛ ♛ |
| Value | ★ ★ ★ ★ ★ |
| Grapes | chardonnay |
| Region | various, Vic. |
| Cellar | ▮ 1 |
| Alc./Vol. | 13.5% |
| RRP | $14.50 ⑤ |

## Seppelt Drumborg Sauvignon Blanc

**Quality** 🍷🍷🍷🍷
**Value** ★★★
**Grapes** sauvignon blanc
**Region** Drumborg, Vic.
**Cellar** 2
**Alc./Vol.** 12.0%
**RRP** $23.00

At one stage Seppelt's Drumborg vineyard was almost given up as a bad joke due to wind, sometimes too much rain and sometimes not enough, and difficulties in adapting viticultural technique to such a marginal climate. But persistence paid off, and today it's the source of some very interesting wines.

CURRENT RELEASE 2000 Drumborg suits sauvignon blanc well. Seppelt's latest is a nifty young example with attractive tropical, passionfruity aromas and a flinty touch that adds dimension. It tastes clean and zippy with similar fruit flavours ahead of a penetrating dry finish. Suits a mussel salad.

## Seppelt Mornington Peninsula Pinot Gris

**Quality** 🍷🍷🍷🍷
**Value** ★★★★½
**Grapes** pinot gris
**Region** Mornington Peninsula, Vic.
**Cellar** 3
**Alc./Vol.** 14.0%
**RRP** $15.00 (S)

An adventure for Seppelt, whose portfolio can contain wines that fall outside the safe commercial constraints of most Southcorp brands. It also gives an imprimatur of sorts to Mornington Peninsula pinot gris, and is much better value than some.

CURRENT RELEASE 2000 There's a whiff of sulfur on the nose here that initially masks honeyed, nutty, smoky aromas. The whole effect is rather Alsatian, and it's reinforced in the honeyed richness of the palate. The flavour is exotically different, with some alcoholic warmth to boot, and it finishes soft and long. Give it a good chill and serve it with classic quiche lorraine.

## Seppelt Partalunga Chardonnay

This vineyard in the Adelaide Hills should be better-known than it is. The occasional releases of chardonnay are refined, ageworthy wines of real distinction, but they seem to get lost somewhere in the maze of products that is the Southcorp portfolio. CURRENT RELEASE 1996   No that's not a misprint, the currently available Partalunga Chardonnay *is* the '96. It's proof-positive that *some* Australian chardonnays do age well. It has an attractive yellow–green colour and a nose and palate where fruit and oak have melted together into a complex whole. There's a rich bouquet of honeyed peach, nuts, minerals and subtle oak. The palate has a smooth texture but it's surprisingly tight, austere and restrained in flavour. The finish is dry and firm. Try it with a vegetable paella.

| | |
|---|---|
| Quality | 🍷🍷🍷🍷🍷 |
| Value | ★★★★ |
| Grapes | chardonnay |
| Region | Adelaide Hills, SA |
| Cellar | 🍾 1 |
| Alc./Vol. | 13.0% |
| RRP | $25.00 |

## Seppelt Terrain Series Chardonnay

The economies of scale available to our big wine names mean that their cheaper labels offer incomparable value in world terms. The flavours may not be super-subtle but who cares? CURRENT RELEASE 2000   A well-proportioned chardonnay that offers a lot for the price. It has melon-like fruit on the nose and a gentle dusting of oak. The palate is similarly flavoured, medium-bodied, a trifle short in keeping with its pedigree, and soft yet dry finishing. Easy sipping with grilled marinated chicken.

| | |
|---|---|
| Quality | 🍷🍷🍷🍷 |
| Value | ★★★⤙ |
| Grapes | chardonnay |
| Region | various, South East Australia |
| Cellar | 🍾 2 |
| Alc./Vol. | 13.0% |
| RRP | $11.50 Ⓢ |

## Sevenhill Riesling

The Sevenhill vineyard was one of the earliest in the Clare Valley. It was originally set up by the Jesuits to provide sacramental wine, and it continues to be run by them to this day. Maker: Brother John May S.J. CURRENT RELEASE 2000   This is a broader style of Clare riesling without the cut and structure of some of its neighbours' wines. That said, it has plenty of aroma and flavour in the lemon/lime spectrum, with attractive floral hints. The palate is quite full-bodied with a clean but relatively soft finish. Try it with pan-fried flounder.

| | |
|---|---|
| Quality | 🍷🍷🍷🍷 |
| Value | ★★★⤙ |
| Grapes | riesling |
| Region | Clare Valley, SA |
| Cellar | 🍾 4 |
| Alc./Vol. | 12.0% |
| RRP | $16.50 |

## Seville Estate Chardonnay

| | |
|---|---|
| Quality | ♥♥♥♥♥ |
| Value | ★★★★↓ |
| Grapes | chardonnay |
| Region | Yarra Valley, Vic. |
| Cellar | ▮ 3 |
| Alc./Vol. | 13.5% |
| RRP | $26.00 |

Under Brokenwood ownership, Seville Estate, in the southern part of the lovely Yarra Valley, is becoming a more diverse enterprise. The hitherto very private vineyard is now open to the public with a cellar door sales facility which is well worth visiting.

CURRENT RELEASE 1999    Made from the best barrels of Seville chardonnay, this is a richly complex wine. The nose is lush with stone-fruit and citrus aromas which are intense, almost syrupy. Smoky oak and mealy secondary characters add dimension. In the mouth it's ripe yet tangy with good depth and body finishing clean, dry and long.

## Shadowfax Burong Vineyard Chardonnay

| | |
|---|---|
| Quality | ♥♥♥♥ |
| Value | ★★★ |
| Grapes | chardonnay |
| Region | Geelong, Vic. |
| Cellar | ▮ 2 |
| Alc./Vol. | 13.8% |
| RRP | $24.00 |

Burong vineyard is at Winchelsea, between Geelong and Colac. Geelong and environs have proven ability to produce great wine, and compared to the Mornington Peninsula, across Port Phillip Bay, access is easier, land is cheaper and climate marginally better; yet still budding vignerons flock down the Mornington side.

CURRENT RELEASE 1999    A lively, fruit-dominant young chardonnay with juicy melon and stone-fruit aromas and restrained nutty oak. In the mouth it has soft varietal flavour of good intensity and persistence. It makes clean-tasting, easy drinking as a youngster, and will suit a light seafood terrine well.

## Shadowfax Pinot Gris

| | |
|---|---|
| Quality | ♥♥♥↓ |
| Value | ★★★ |
| Grapes | pinot gris |
| Region | Geelong, Vic. |
| Cellar | ▮ 2 |
| Alc./Vol. | 14.1% |
| RRP | $20.00 |

Shadowfax was a winged horse in Tolkien's *Lord of the Rings*. A name in keeping with the slightly arty-farty atmosphere of this establishment.

CURRENT RELEASE 2000    In common with some other pinot gris wines, this has a hint of pink that gives it a disconcertingly dull look alongside the more usual 'whiter than white' type of wine. But overcome that and you'll be pleased by its lightly perfumed, honeyed aromas and rich nutty/grapey/musky palate. It has a mellow, smooth texture and soft acidity. Try it with a herbed veal sautée.

# Shadowfax Riesling

The Shadowfax winery is a weird bit of architecture, mostly rusty metal with splashes of colour here and there. This Mad Max-ish building provides quite a contrast to the classically proportioned Werribee Park Mansion nearby.

CURRENT RELEASE 2000    A promising newie made from grapes grown outside traditional riesling regions. This has a delicate but not wimpish nose reminiscent of citrus, fragrant floral scents and cinnamon/spice, and it tastes of spice and lime in good intensity. The palate has a classical riesling build, delicate yet with underlying firmness and strength. Good to serve with smoked trout.

| | |
|---|---|
| Quality | ▼▼▼▼ |
| Value | ★★★⌐ |
| Grapes | riesling |
| Region | Geelong & Macedon Ranges, Vic. |
| Cellar | ▮ 4 |
| Alc./Vol. | 13.9% |
| RRP | $18.00 |

# Shaw and Smith Reserve Chardonnay

This fine chardonnay is now made in Shaw and Smith's new winery in the Adelaide Hills. It's always one of South Australia's best.

*Previous outstanding vintages: '94, '97, '98*

CURRENT RELEASE 1999    With each new vintage, the Reserve seems to gain in finesse. This has a subtle, inviting fruit aroma of nectarine and grapefruit seamlessly interwoven with nutty, mealy and creamy undertones. The palate is smooth, long and crisp, and while nicely mouth-filling, it retains the superfine texture and flavour that is the house style. Oak is restrained throughout. Serve with buttery grilled salmon.

| | |
|---|---|
| Quality | ▼▼▼▼▼ |
| Value | ★★★★⌐ |
| Grapes | chardonnay |
| Region | Adelaide Hills, SA |
| Cellar | ▮ 4 |
| Alc./Vol. | 13.0% |
| RRP | $31.00 |

# Shaw and Smith Sauvignon Blanc

The cousins Martin Shaw and Michael Hill Smith helped pioneer the idea of the Adelaide Hills as a source of zesty sauvignon blanc.

CURRENT RELEASE 2000    This wine opens with a juicy riot of the passionfruit and zesty herbaceous aromas that typify this thrilling style. The palate follows with piercing, pristine varietal flavour that's tangy and fresh, yet it's not all just frippery, there's real presence and length of flavour as well. Try it with a salad niçoise.

| | |
|---|---|
| Quality | ▼▼▼▼▼ |
| Value | ★★★★ |
| Grapes | sauvignon blanc |
| Region | Adelaide Hills, SA |
| Cellar | ▮ 2 |
| Alc./Vol. | 13.0% |
| RRP | $21.00 |

## Shottesbrooke Chardonnay

| | |
|---|---|
| Quality | ♥♥♥♥ |
| Value | ★★★ |
| Grapes | chardonnay |
| Region | McLaren Vale, SA |
| Cellar | 🍾 3 |
| Alc./Vol. | 14.0% |
| RRP | $18.20 |

McLaren Vale gives fans of big, ripe chardonnay plenty of what they like . . . flavour. This makes up for what they often lack in subtlety. This is an example.

CURRENT RELEASE 2000    A rich, ripe, fruit-sweet chardonnay that dances a two-step with quite strong toasty oak and barrel-ferment characters on the nose. In the mouth there's more of the same, with that charry vanillin oak leading the way over the ripe fruit, and following right through to the end. Less wood would be good. Try it with charry chicken kebabs.

## Shottesbrooke Fleurieu Sauvignon Blanc

| | |
|---|---|
| Quality | ♥♥♥♥ |
| Value | ★★★ |
| Grapes | sauvignon blanc |
| Region | McLaren Vale, SA |
| Cellar | 🍾 1 |
| Alc./Vol. | 13.0% |
| RRP | $18.20 |

Nick Holmes was once the winemaker at the long-established Ryecroft. His own wines are sourced from higher hillside McLaren Vale/Fleurieu Peninsula vines.

CURRENT RELEASE 2000    This has a clean aroma and flavour of herbal, grapey sauvignon blanc with light stone-fruit touches. It's also quite rich on nose and palate, with more 'oomph' than the light zesty sauvignons that fashion dictates. The finish is clean and relatively soft. Serve it with a vegetable terrine.

## Smithbrook Sauvignon Blanc

| | |
|---|---|
| Quality | ♥♥♥♥♥ |
| Value | ★★★★ |
| Grapes | sauvignon blanc |
| Region | Great Southern, WA |
| Cellar | 🍾 2 |
| Alc./Vol. | 12.5% |
| RRP | $17.00 |

Smithbrook is another Petaluma outpost, this time in the south of Western Australia. It currently enjoys a lower profile than the others.

CURRENT RELEASE 2000    The nose has snappy herbaceous aromas that are pungent and lively, as well as succulent passionfruit and citrus touches. The palate has a sharpish, appetising nature that would make a Kiwi winemaker take notice, with blackcurranty flavour in the middle, good persistence and a tangy dry finish. Try it with Chinese stirfried snow peas and green vegetables with oyster sauce.

## St Hallett Poacher's Blend

Poacher's Blend is an ideal easy-drinking white, even if the only thing you can poach is an egg.
CURRENT RELEASE 2000    A bright and breezy young white with an appealing grape-juicy aroma that's succulent and appetising. In the mouth it's soft and medium intense, with a clever little dab of residual sugar to round it out. It has delicious drinkability and a tangy, dry finish. Try it with a poached trout, whichever way you poach it.

| | |
|---|---|
| Quality | ♀ ♀ ♀ ♀ |
| Value | ★ ★ ★ ★ ⁺ |
| Grapes | not stated |
| Region | Barossa Valley, SA |
| Cellar | ▮ 2 |
| Alc./Vol. | 12.0% |
| RRP | $12.50 |

## St Huberts Roussanne

The interest currently shown in the Australian wine world for the grape varieties of the Rhone Valley in France is very sensible. If shiraz works here, and mourvedre and marsanne, why won't the others?
CURRENT RELEASE 2000    A simple rendition of roussanne, this is a pale wine with a distinctive aroma of herbs and wild flowers. The clean, rather neutral palate is light, slightly aromatic and dry, but it falls away a bit at the end. Try it with trout.

| | |
|---|---|
| Quality | ♀ ♀ ♀ ♀ |
| Value | ★ ★ ⁺ |
| Grapes | roussanne |
| Region | Yarra Valley, Vic. |
| Cellar | ▮ 2 |
| Alc./Vol. | 11.8% |
| RRP | $25.50 |

## St Huberts Sauvignon Blanc

Sauvignon blanc isn't one of the Yarra Valley's headline grapes. It performs well enough but gets lost amongst all the Yarra chardonnay.
CURRENT RELEASE 2000    This has a lively nose with some sweet passionfuit aromas, a touch of tart apple and a zippy grassiness that gives a savoury touch. The palate is lively with some tropical fruit flavours to start but crisp grassy notes take over mid-palate. A likeable straightforward sauvignon of good quality. Try it with little ramekins of asparagus and baked eggs.

| | |
|---|---|
| Quality | ♀ ♀ ♀ ♀ |
| Value | ★ ★ ★ ⁺ |
| Grapes | sauvignon blanc |
| Region | Yarra Valley, Vic. |
| Cellar | ▮ 2 |
| Alc./Vol. | 12.5% |
| RRP | $21.50 |

## St Leonards Orange Muscat

| | |
|---|---|
| Quality | ▼▼◗ |
| Value | ★★◗ |
| Grapes | orange muscat |
| Region | Rutherglen, Vic. |
| Cellar | ▮ 1 |
| Alc./Vol. | 14.0% |
| RRP | $14.50 |

Orange muscat is another permutation of the muscat/frontignac/lexia/gordo family. Like its siblings, it's dominated by inimitable grapey aromatics. CURRENT RELEASE 2000    A scent like a handful of crushed fresh muscat grapes leaps out of the glass here. It's a juicy aroma that suggests sweetness, but the palate is really quite dry, with a hardness that's a part of many dry white table wines made from muscat. Despite all that grapey promise, this is not a very generous wine. Try it very well chilled on a summer's afternoon, but beware that 14 per cent alcohol.

## Stefano Lubiana Riesling

| | |
|---|---|
| Quality | ▼▼▼▼◗ |
| Value | ★★★◗ |
| Grapes | riesling |
| Region | Derwent Valley, Tas. |
| Cellar | ▮ 4 |
| Alc./Vol. | 13.0% |
| RRP | $24.50 |

Tasmania and riesling seem meant for each other. The style is often more European than the mainland mainstream with a pristine delicacy that's captivating. CURRENT RELEASE 2000    This is an aromatic young riesling with an exotic nose that's sweetly fragrant with oriental fruit, lime and floral aromas. The palate has delicate lime and spice flavours that are light yet intense. The finish is crisp and clean. Good with sushi.

## Stefano Lubiana Sauvignon Blanc

| | |
|---|---|
| Quality | ▼▼▼▼ |
| Value | ★★★ |
| Grapes | sauvignon blanc |
| Region | Derwent Valley, Tas. |
| Cellar | ▮ 2 |
| Alc./Vol. | 13.2% |
| RRP | $25.00 |

We don't see many sauvignon blancs from the Apple Isle, but such is Stefano Lubiana's skill as a winemaker that his version was bound to be an attention-getter. CURRENT RELEASE 2000    A nose of herbs, lime sherbet, pawpaw and briary undergrowth makes a bracing introduction to this young Taswegian. The palate has good depth with fruity yet dry flavours, and a long, tasty finish. There's a hint of the Loire about this, and it would suit smoked Tassie trout perfectly.

## Stonier Chardonnay

The merger of Stonier into the Petaluma camp has meant that now there are a couple of different Brians calling the shots at Stonier. To avoid confusion in future, please refer to Brian Croser as B1 and Brian Stonier as B2.

CURRENT RELEASE 1999    Stonier make two chardonnays; this one is made to sip a bit younger than the more complex Reserve wine. It's a bright young wine with juicy melon and citrus aromas, touched by a little nutty complexity and a whisper of good oak. The palate is soft and medium in body, with good depth of melony chardonnay flavour which is kept fresh by a tangy crisp finish. Serve with baby snapper.

| | |
|---|---|
| Quality | ♟ ♟ ♟ ♟ |
| Value | ★ ★ ★ ★ |
| Grapes | chardonnay |
| Region | Mornington Peninsula, Vic. |
| Cellar | 🍶 2 |
| Alc./Vol. | 13.0% |
| RRP | $21.00 |

## Stonier Reserve Chardonnay

This is one of the Mornington Peninsula's best wines. Maker Tod Dexter understands perfectly how to create chardonnay of both impact and elegance.
*Previous outstanding vintages: '94, '95, '96, '97*
CURRENT RELEASE 1999    This is a fine internationally styled chardonnay with a nose of classical restraint. There are aromas of melon, nuts, honey, burnt match and minerals which give it real classical poise. The palate is creamy-smooth, clean and persistent with subtle fruit character integrated seamlessly with smooth oak, secondary winemaker-induced flavours and fine acidity. A wine for salmon.

| | |
|---|---|
| Quality | ♟ ♟ ♟ ♟ ♟ |
| Value | ★ ★ ★ ✦ |
| Grapes | chardonnay |
| Region | Mornington Peninsula, Vic. |
| Cellar | 🍶 3+ |
| Alc./Vol. | 13.5% |
| RRP | $39.00 |

## T'Gallant Chardonnay

Kevin McCarthy and Kathleen Quealy were among the first boutique winemakers to espouse the unwooded style of cool-grown chardonnay and market it as a premium wine style.

CURRENT RELEASE 2000    It's an appealing and obviously unwooded style, perfumed with passionfruit and honeydew melon. It tastes light bodied and fairly simple as chardonnays go, but it's clean, fresh and avoids the saccharine, flabby palates of so many unoaked chards. It goes with seafood and salads.

| | |
|---|---|
| Quality | ♟ ♟ ♟ ♟ |
| Value | ★ ★ ★ ✦ |
| Grapes | chardonnay |
| Region | Mornington Peninsula, Vic. |
| Cellar | 🍶 4 |
| Alc./Vol. | 14.0% |
| RRP | $21.30 |

## Tahbilk Chardonnay

| | |
|---|---|
| Quality | ♥♥♥♥ |
| Value | ★★★★⁺ |
| Grapes | chardonnay |
| Region | Goulburn Valley, Vic. |
| Cellar | ▮ 2 |
| Alc./Vol. | 13.0% |
| RRP | $16.50 Ⓢ |

By comparison with some of our big wine companies, who throw away heritage built up over many scores of years as though it didn't mean a thing, at a place like Tahbilk things move slowly. After agonising long and hard over the change, they've now dropped 'Chateau' from their name; it's simply Tahbilk, but the wonderful old label remains almost unchanged. Good on 'em for showing some respect.

CURRENT RELEASE 1999    Tahbilk chardonnay is a flavoury style with a ripe nose of pear, toffee, light nuttiness and some leesy touches. The palate is rich and ripe with good length and a fine powdery-textured clean finish. Smooth oak is well integrated throughout. Try it with chicken and white wine sauce.

## Tahbilk Marsanne

| | |
|---|---|
| Quality | ♥♥♥◗ |
| Value | ★★★ |
| Grapes | marsanne |
| Region | Goulburn Valley, Vic. |
| Cellar | ▮ 5+ |
| Alc./Vol. | 12.5% |
| RRP | $12.90 Ⓢ |

This is still labelled 'Chateau' Tahbilk, but that French word will be dropped from future Tahbilk wines, making a truly Australian statement. Apart from that the label will retain the same timeless old design we've come to know and love.

CURRENT RELEASE 1999    The last couple of decades have seen the gradual evolution of Tahbilk Marsanne into a more modern, fresher white wine than it was. The '99 is a good example with true hints of marsanne's distinctive honeysuckle varietal aroma and flavour, along with some citrus and waxy notes. It tastes soft, simple, dry and easy to like. Oh, and judging by past performance it should age well too. Serve it with lemon risotto.

# Tahbilk Viognier

| | |
|---|---|
| Quality | 🍷🍷🍷🍷🍷 |
| Value | ★★★★⁺ |
| Grapes | viognier |
| Region | Goulburn Valley, Vic. |
| Cellar | 🍾 1 |
| Alc./Vol. | 12.5% |
| RRP | $16.00 |

The Goulburn Valley is a home away from home for the white Rhone grapes. Both Tahbilk and next-door neighbour Mitchelton fool around with them with good results.

CURRENT RELEASE 2000    Looking for a change? Try this. It has a gorgeous perfume like a garden full of spring flowers. There's also a touch of dried apricots. The viognier aroma is fresher and brighter than the dried pot-pourri scent of some viogniers and equally charming. The palate is smooth and round, with the typical unctuous texture of this grape variety. This is a silky, exotic low-acid white wine that really *is* different. Try it with Thai chicken dishes.

# Talijancich Verdelho

| | |
|---|---|
| Quality | 🍷🍷🍷 |
| Value | ★★★ |
| Grapes | verdelho |
| Region | Swan Valley, WA |
| Cellar | 🍾 1 |
| Alc./Vol. | 13.5% |
| RRP | $34.00 |

These people have a puzzling policy for their verdelho dry whites. The standard wine is kept back for 18 months before release, and they suggest it will cellar for 10 years. They also market an aged Special Reserve, the current vintage being 1994.

CURRENT RELEASE 1994 *Special Reserve*    At seven years the colour is deep yellow and it smells of buttered toast, malt and vanilla. There's a little sweetness on entry and the palate is full, soft and broad but fairly undistinguished. If people who like this are prepared to pay $34, well and good, but we do wonder what's the point of cellaring it. Serve with roast chicken.

| | |
|---|---|
| Quality | 🍷🍷🍷 |
| Value | ★★★ |
| Grapes | verdelho |
| Region | Swan Valley, WA |
| Cellar | 🍾 1 |
| Alc./Vol. | 13.5% |
| RRP | $16.90 |

CURRENT RELEASE 1998    It's certainly young for its age, with a light lemon–green colour. The bouquet has a slightly meaty character and the taste is remarkably light and youthful, with some residual sweetness. A pleasant drink, but we're not convinced it's worth cellaring. It suits yabbie salad.

## Talijancich Voices

| | |
|---|---|
| Quality | 🍷🍷🍷❜ |
| Value | ★★★★❜ |
| Grapes | chenin blanc; chardonnay; semillon |
| Region | Swan Valley, WA |
| Cellar | 🍾 2 |
| Alc./Vol. | 13.0% |
| RRP | $13.70 |

The triangular label with its somewhat naïve picture has a lot of charm. Is this a Swan Valley idea of a 'concept wine'?

CURRENT RELEASE 1998    So, it's already three years old and your expectations aren't high. But the colour is still youthful and it smells very appealing. Aromas of gooseberry, lemon and the subtlest toasty bottle-age characters creep through too. It's light-bodied and has a smoothly balanced finish. It goes well with pan-fried John Dory.

## Tallarook Chardonnay

| | |
|---|---|
| Quality | 🍷🍷🍷🍷❜ |
| Value | ★★★★ |
| Grapes | chardonnay |
| Region | Tallarook, Vic. |
| Cellar | 🍾 5+ |
| Alc./Vol. | 13.9% |
| RRP | $27.50 |

Cool climate, low cropping, north-facing slope, hand harvested, whole-bunch pressed, 50 per cent wild yeast fermentation, partial malolactic, lees contact, minimal filtration – and the winemaker was a Master of Wine. Could you be any more trendy than that?! Perhaps they also make a donation from every bottle to Land Rights for Gay Whales.

CURRENT RELEASE 1999    This is a sophisticated chardonnay – every bit the show pony. The bouquet is dominated by smoky, toasty barrel characters, while the taste is intense yet refined, with rich and very long flavours which recall toasted nuts and cedar. It could benefit from some age, but drinks well already with a smoked chicken sandwich.

## Tamar Ridge Josef Chromy Selection Riesling

| | |
|---|---|
| Quality | 🍷🍷🍷🍷🍷 |
| Value | ★★★★★ |
| Grapes | riesling |
| Region | West Tamar, Tas. |
| Cellar | 🍾 12+ |
| Alc./Vol. | 12.0% |
| RRP | $24.20 (cellar door) |

Joe Chromy and Julian Alcorso have demonstrated their commitment to making great wine in several ways, not least by holding this proprietor's selection wine back for extended bottle-age before release. It was released on 1 July 2001.

CURRENT RELEASE 1999    The perfume is ethereal, seductive and thoroughly marvellous. The palate follows on just as impressively: very intense, fine as silk and incredibly long. It is a beautiful wine, thoroughly deserving its two trophies (including best white of show) at the 2001 Tasmanian Regional Wine Show. It should age superbly. Serve with cold crayfish and salad.

## Tamar Ridge Riesling

Joe Chromy sold Heemskerk and Rochecombe and started again, with his vineyard at Kayena (now 55 hectares), where he's built an impressive state-of-the-art winery. Julian Alcorso makes the wine.
CURRENT RELEASE 2000    Zingy Tasmanian riesling at its best, with that spine-tingling acidity and zappy palate freshness you just don't see in warmer areas. The nose is intensely limey, with some herbal nuances, while the palate is steely and firm to finish, with a clean, dry aftertaste. Pair it with Tassie oysters.

| | |
|---|---|
| Quality | 🍷🍷🍷🍷🍷 |
| Value | ★★★★⁺ |
| Grapes | riesling |
| Region | West Tamar, Tas. |
| Cellar | 🍷 8 |
| Alc./Vol. | 12.0% |
| RRP | $18.00 |

## Tamar Ridge Sauvignon Blanc

Winemaker Julian Alcorso has brought to Tamar Ridge the same magic touch with white wines he showed in his many years before the mast at Moorilla Estate. His boss at Tamar Ridge is beef baron Joe Chromy, who for a while owned Heemskerk and Rochecombe.
CURRENT RELEASE 2000    This is a racy style, with a little Tasmanian sweatiness that doesn't mar it. There are also pineapple overtones and in the mouth some mineral qualities. It's light and soft and ready to enjoy with food. Try it with Tassie Pacific oysters.

| | |
|---|---|
| Quality | 🍷🍷🍷🍷 |
| Value | ★★★⁺ |
| Grapes | sauvignon blanc |
| Region | Tamar Valley, Tas. |
| Cellar | 🍷 1 |
| Alc./Vol. | 13.0% |
| RRP | $18.50 |

## Tarline Chardonnay

Tarline is a new brand for the established wine company Normans. It's a vehicle for the wines from the Strathbogie Ranges vineyard Normans bought from Mildara a few years ago, originally Tisdall's Mount Helen.
CURRENT RELEASE 2000    There are definite green flavours in this wine; indeed it tastes as though there's some semillon blended in. The nose offers nutty, vanilla and caramel oak-derived scents over herbal fruit, and it's soft, round and light-bodied in the mouth. A straightforward, clean wine with a pleasant dry finish. Try it with vegetable gado gado – Indonesian salad.

| | |
|---|---|
| Quality | 🍷🍷🍷 |
| Value | ★★★★ |
| Grapes | chardonnay |
| Region | Strathbogie Ranges, Vic. |
| Cellar | 🍷 2 |
| Alc./Vol. | 13.0% |
| RRP | $15.00 Ⓢ |

## Tatachilla Adelaide Hills Chardonnay

| | |
|---|---|
| Quality | ♟ ♟ ♟ ♟ |
| Value | ★ ★ ★ ⟩ |
| Grapes | chardonnay |
| Region | Adelaide Hills, SA |
| Cellar | 🍾 2 |
| Alc./Vol. | 13.0% |
| RRP | $20.00 Ⓢ |

The grapes came from vineyards at Lenswood and Hahndorf. Tatachilla has made its name with reds, but the whites are increasingly impressive.

CURRENT RELEASE 1999   A lighter-bodied chardonnay – and it's easy to drink more than one glass. It smells of freshly shelled nuts and ripe honeydew melon. Oak character is tucked neatly into the background and it has some creamy lees-derived flavours. A delicate, refined wine which could go well with crudités and aioli.

## Tatachilla Growers

| | |
|---|---|
| Quality | ♟ ♟ ♟ |
| Value | ★ ★ ★ ⟩ |
| Grapes | chenin blanc; semillon; sauvignon blanc |
| Region | McLaren Vale, SA |
| Cellar | 🍾 2 |
| Alc./Vol. | 12.5% |
| RRP | $12.00 Ⓢ |

This is named in tribute to the grapegrowers from whom Tatachilla buys most of its grapes. This wine is a blend of three varieties. Makers: Michael Fragos and Justin McNamee.

CURRENT RELEASE 2000   There are some greenish aromas and some attendant hardness on the finish, which points to underripe fruit. But it also has some appeal, with creamy, nutty, vanilla aromas and a herbaceous, sauvignon-like edge. The palate has tangy acid and a fresh, tart, slightly green finish. Try it with asparagus and hollandaise.

## Tatachilla Padthaway Chardonnay

| | |
|---|---|
| Quality | ♟ ♟ ♟ |
| Value | ★ ★ ★ |
| Grapes | chardonnay |
| Region | Padthaway, SA |
| Cellar | 🍾 2 |
| Alc./Vol. | 13.0% |
| RRP | $15.60 Ⓢ |

Tatachilla is part of a new private company, Banksia Wines Limited, along with St Hallett and Hillstowe. Between them, they cover Barossa, McLaren Vale, Adelaide Hills and Padthaway.

CURRENT RELEASE 2000   This is the fighting varietal in Tatachilla's chardonnay arsenal. It's a fairly basic wine, smelling nettly, dusty and lightly herbaceous. It's lightly weighted in the mouth and has some acid hardness. Food will help, so serve it with fish balls.

## Taylors St Andrews Chardonnay

Taylors is a big wine company these days, and still 100 per cent family owned. It has 550 hectares of vineyards at Auburn in the Clare Valley. Makers: Adam Eggins and Neil Jericho.

CURRENT RELEASE 1998    The '98 vintage was great for reds in South Australia, but perhaps the whites lack a little finesse. This is already quite mature and a tad clumsy, despite a fresh-looking light yellow–green hue. Slightly fat, overblown bouquet of toasty oak, rubber tyres and straw. Palate is very full-bodied and rather heavy. It needs to be well chilled. Try it with roast spatchcock.

| | |
|---|---|
| Quality | 🍷🍷🍷🍷 |
| Value | ★★⁺ |
| Grapes | chardonnay |
| Region | Clare Valley, SA |
| Cellar | 🍾 2 |
| Alc./Vol. | 14.0% |
| RRP | $32.25 |

## Te Mata Hawkes Bay Chardonnay

This is a new release from Te Mata Estate, designed to fill the vacuum created below the high price and relative scarcity of its top chardonnay, Elston. Maker: Peter Cowley.

CURRENT RELEASE 2000    It's certainly a lighter, plainer, less impressive wine than Elston, produced no doubt from some of the newer vineyards Te Mata has planted of late. Straw/hay and light gooseberry aromas are fairly straightforward and the palate has reasonable depth and character. It finishes clean and dry but doesn't really sing. Try it with a vegetarian meal.

| | |
|---|---|
| Quality | 🍷🍷🍷🍷 |
| Value | ★★★ |
| Grapes | chardonnay |
| Region | Hawkes Bay, NZ |
| Cellar | 🍾 3 |
| Alc./Vol. | 13.0% |
| RRP | $25.00 |

## Temple Bruer Botrytis Riesling

This is one of Australia's most serious vineyards on the subject of sustainable viticulture. The Bruers run all their vineyards by organic principles and some are biodynamic – which is their aim for all their vineyards. Maker: Nick Bruer.

CURRENT RELEASE 1999    The colour is deep golden and the wine is quite forward in development – but no more than most Aussie botrytis wines. It's a delicious drink, boasting smoky, toffee aromas, and the taste is lusciously sweet, rich and concentrated. It would cope with a very sweet dessert, even crème brûlée.

| | |
|---|---|
| Quality | 🍷🍷🍷🍷🍷 |
| Value | ★★★★⁺ |
| Grapes | riesling |
| Region | Langhorne Creek, SA |
| Cellar | 🍾 2 |
| Alc./Vol. | 12.5% |
| RRP | $17.00 (375 ml) |

## Tempus Two Botrytis Semillon

| | |
|---|---|
| Quality | ▼▼▼▼ |
| Value | ★★★ |
| Grapes | semillon |
| Region | Riverina, NSW |
| Cellar | 🍾 5 |
| Alc./Vol. | 12.5% |
| RRP | $18.00 (250 ml) |

Tempus Two is a small wine company begun by Lisa McGuigan and Veronica Lourey, which is part of Dad's public company Brian McGuigan Wines, but independently run by the girls. They're doing 25 000 cases a year.

CURRENT RELEASE 1997   The bottle looks more like perfume than wine: small, elegantly shaped and bearing a pewter label. It's a delicious sticky: smoky, tropical fruit aromas with lots of botrytis, and the palate is lighter-bodied, fine and sweet with superb balance. It's reserved for its age and really delish. It would go with pavlova.

## The Gorge Verdelho

| | |
|---|---|
| Quality | ▼▼▼ |
| Value | ★★★★ |
| Grapes | verdelho |
| Region | Hunter Valley, NSW |
| Cellar | 🍾 2 |
| Alc./Vol. | 12.5% |
| RRP | $14.00 |

This did well in the 2001 Boutique Wine Awards, winning a high bronze medal. The Gorge wines have been made since 1996 by David Hook (no relation to the author), whose Pothana vineyard supplies most of the grapes. Hook has a winery on-site which handles 250 tonnes of grapes.

CURRENT RELEASE 2001   Verdelho varietal character is alive and well at The Gorge. It sings out of this wine with full voice, ringing attractive musky, confectionery notes. Being just a babe, it shows some freshly fermented estery aromas. The palate is soft and carries a little sweetness. It should prove a crowd-pleaser. Serve it with scallop brochettes.

## The Mill Cowra Chardonnay

| | |
|---|---|
| Quality | ▼▼▼▼ |
| Value | ★★★★⟩ |
| Grapes | chardonnay |
| Region | Cowra, NSW |
| Cellar | 🍾 2 |
| Alc./Vol. | 12.8% |
| RRP | $13.45 |

The O'Dea family of Windowrie Estate build their cellar-door sales in an old granite flour mill, built in 1861, which had lain derelict for 91 years. Maker: Tobias Ansted.

CURRENT RELEASE 2000   Delicious, lightly oaked, attractively priced chardonnay from the Windowrie Estate vineyards. The colour is light yellow, the aromas recall melon and cashew, with nutty barrel-ferment complexity. It's soft but not sweet. Clean, straightforward, fresh and very appealing to drink now, perhaps with prosciutto and melon.

## Tim Adams Riesling

Adams makes his riesling in an unashamedly long-term cellaring style. He buys the grapes from three growers, at Watervale, Sevenhill and Waninga in the Skillogalee Valley.

CURRENT RELEASE 2000  The colour is light yellow and the aromas are minerally, earthy and dusty with a glimpse of lime peeping through. It's more a teaser of things to come than anything. The taste is very lean and taut, with searing acidity that demands it be drunk with fish – such as sole meunière – or cellared. An uncompromising style!

| | |
|---|---|
| Quality | ♀♀♀♀ |
| Value | ★★★★ |
| Grapes | riesling |
| Region | Clare Valley, SA |
| Cellar | ➡ 2–9+ |
| Alc./Vol. | 11.5% |
| RRP | $18.00 |

## Tim Adams Semillon

Tim Adams gave this wine some pretty hearty wood treatment: fermentation and maturation in new American and French oak hogsheads for five months. It's a wonder it doesn't taste woodier.

CURRENT RELEASE 1999  Age is starting to soften this wine and allowing the palate to fill out. It's still a light mid-yellow with a fresh young aroma of lemon juice and lemon butter. The palate is fuller and broader than many, with lots of stuffing. Toasty, straw-developed flavours come through in the mouth. The finish is dry and lingering. It would go well with fish and chips.

| | |
|---|---|
| Quality | ♀♀♀♀ |
| Value | ★★★★ |
| Grapes | semillon |
| Region | Clare Valley, SA |
| Cellar | ♦ 7 |
| Alc./Vol. | 12.5% |
| RRP | $17.25 |

## Tintilla Semillon

Tintilla began in 1994 when the Lusby family began planting what is now a 10-hectare vineyard on Hermitage Road, Pokolbin. The semillon is on classic Hunter, sandy riverbed soil. The wines up till 2001 were made by Jon Reynolds.

CURRENT RELEASE 2000  This was the top semillon in the Winewise Small Vigneron Awards 2001, and has plenty of the snow-pea aroma that typifies Hunter 2000 semillons. It also has intense flavour that's long and lively in the mouth, balanced and dry on the finish. It's a classic, a great drink now and should also cellar well.

| | |
|---|---|
| Quality | ♀♀♀♀♀ |
| Value | ★★★★★ |
| Grapes | semillon |
| Region | Hunter Valley, NSW |
| Cellar | ♦ 10+ |
| Alc./Vol. | 11.5% |
| RRP | $16.50 (cellar door) |

## Tollana Adelaide Hills Sauvignon Blanc

| | |
|---|---|
| Quality | ♟ ♟ ♟ ♟ |
| Value | ★★★★ |
| Grapes | sauvignon blanc |
| Region | Adelaide Hills, SA |
| Cellar | 🍷 2 |
| Alc./Vol. | 13.0% |
| RRP | $18.30 ⑤ |

At time of writing Tollana's future was under a seriously dark and threatening cloud, amid the Rosemount–Southcorp rationalisations. It would be a pity to see it go. It's been a byword for value for many years. But that's economic rationalism.

CURRENT RELEASE 2000   The Adelaide Hills produces some of Australia's best sauvignon blanc. The wine is pale yellow and smells subtly of the fragrant sauvignon grape: herbal, lemony and lightly passionfruity. It's a good wine, light but pleasant, with decent intensity and some persistence on the finish. It goes with lemon sole.

## Tollana Bay F2 Reserve Riesling

| | |
|---|---|
| Quality | ♟ ♟ ♟ ♟ ♟ |
| Value | ★★★★★ |
| Grapes | riesling |
| Region | Eden Valley, SA |
| Cellar | 🍷 4+ |
| Alc./Vol. | 11.5% |
| RRP | $29.00 |

The story goes that the grapes were harvested from a single section of the Tollana Eden Valley vineyard, Woodbury, because they showed special promise. Will we continue to see such one-off gems under the new streamlined Southcorp regime? Let's hope so.

CURRENT RELEASE 1994   This mature new-release shows some richness from bottle-age but also great freshness and life considering it's seven years old. The bouquet has candle-wax, bready, creamy aromas and the palate is soft and smooth. It's just starting to fill out with age, but is still understated, finishing clean and dry. It would suit pan-fried whiting.

## Tollana Botrytis Riesling

| | |
|---|---|
| Quality | ♟ ♟ ♟ ♟ |
| Value | ★★★★ |
| Grapes | riesling |
| Region | Eden Valley, SA |
| Cellar | 🍷 2 |
| Alc./Vol. | 12.0% |
| RRP | $18.00 ⑤ |
| | (375 ml) |

Tollana bottles are now collector's items: they have Neville Falkenberg's signature on the back-label. He was one of the first people to get the golden wristwatch when Southcorp merged with Rosemount.

CURRENT RELEASE 1998   This golden-coloured sweetie is fairly mature and ready to go, smelling of honey, vanilla, malt and quince paste. It's rich and broad on the palate, and finishes quite dry, the acid leaving a trace of hardness that doesn't detract from the pleasure it gives. Try it with crème caramel.

## Tollana Chardonnay

For years, astute bargain hunters have lined their cellars with Tollana wines. They are still exceptional value, and still the prices are way low, which suggests that you and we are the only ones that know the secret!

**CURRENT RELEASE 1999    Adelaide Hills has been added to the blend this year, and it's probably the best yet. This is a fine and delicious chardonnay, restrained but intense and laden with stone-fruit, quince and nougat aromas. Oak has been used sparingly. It's bright and lively in the mouth, with subtle richness and a long, finely balanced finish. Yum with chargrilled chicken breast.**

| | |
|---|---|
| Quality | ♟♟♟♟♟ |
| Value | ★★★★★ |
| Grapes | chardonnay |
| Region | Eden Valley & Adelaide Hills, SA |
| Cellar | ▮ 3 |
| Alc./Vol. | 13.5% |
| RRP | $14.50 ⑤ |

 Penguin Best Bargain White

## Tollana Eden Valley Riesling

Tollana wines are always great value, but somehow they've never sold the numbers that impress big wine company bean-counters. Is it lack of promotion, the label, the name, or what?

CURRENT RELEASE 2000    A lovely big mouthful of riesling, this is soft, dry and quite full in the mouth for Eden Valley. The aromas are doughy, bready and floral with some toast developing. It has very fine balance in the mouth: a delicious riesling to serve with goat's cheese and salad. It drinks well now but should cellar too.

| | |
|---|---|
| Quality | ♟♟♟♟ |
| Value | ★★★★★ |
| Grapes | riesling |
| Region | Eden Valley, SA |
| Cellar | ▮ 6+ |
| Alc./Vol. | 12.5% |
| RRP | $11.60 ⑤ |

## Tower Estate Verdelho

Tower Estate is the latest winemaking project of Len Evans, with a syndicate of 12 other partners. These include Rick Stein, the fish man, and fellow Hunter wineman Brian McGuigan. Maker: Dan Dineen.

CURRENT RELEASE 2000    This is definitive verdelho. It has pristine musk and herb aromas, and is richly fruity and smooth, without the usual verdelho prop of residual sugar. It's beautifully balanced and would work well with a fish pie.

| | |
|---|---|
| Quality | ♟♟♟♟ |
| Value | ★★★ |
| Grapes | verdelho |
| Region | Hunter Valley, NSW |
| Cellar | ▮ 2 |
| Alc./Vol. | 13.5% |
| RRP | $20.00 |

## Tranquil Vale Semillon

| | |
|---|---|
| Quality | 🍷🍷🍷🍷 |
| Value | ★★★★ |
| Grapes | semillon |
| Region | Hunter Valley, NSW |
| Cellar | 🍾 5+ |
| Alc./Vol. | 11.0% |
| RRP | $20.00 |

'A jug of wine under the bough, a loaf of bread and thou' sort of thing. This is a Hunter newie (established 1996) with eight hectares of vines at Luskintyre.

CURRENT RELEASE 2000   Grassy, snow-pea aromas burst from a glass of this typical 2000 vintage unwooded Hunter semillon. It tastes tangy and juicy, crisp and clean, with maybe just a smidgin of sweetness helping tame that jumpy green herby fruit and jazzy acidity. It should cellar well, and goes nicely with a Waldorf salad.

## Trentham Estate Chardonnay

| | |
|---|---|
| Quality | 🍷🍷🍷🍷 |
| Value | ★★★★ |
| Grapes | chardonnay |
| Region | Murray Valley, NSW |
| Cellar | 🍾 2 |
| Alc./Vol. | 13.5% |
| RRP | $14.00 ⑤ |

These Murphys . . . they are setting a mean pace when it comes to the issue of pricing. They may not be in a trendy region and the wines might not have long lives, but the quality/price ratio is hard to beat.

CURRENT RELEASE 2000   Showing fairly forward development (typical of hot-climate whites), this is full gold and already smells toasty, with complex grilled nut and poached peach aromas, as well as hint of herb. It is smooth and full-bodied, with a slightly chewy texture which is quite agreeable. It goes down well with roast stuffed chicken.

## Trentham Estate Murphy's Lore Semillon Chardonnay

| | |
|---|---|
| Quality | 🍷🍷🍷🍷 |
| Value | ★★★★★ |
| Grapes | semillon; chardonnay |
| Region | Murray Valley, NSW |
| Cellar | 🍾 1 |
| Alc./Vol. | 12.5% |
| RRP | $10.65 ⑤ |

Murphy's Lore is a new budget-priced range from the Murphy family's Trentham Estate. As usual, the quality and value are high.

CURRENT RELEASE 2000   It's developing quite quickly but that's probably a positive in a drink-now white. The colour is medium yellow and it smells fresh, with a hint of oak and some appealing candied-fruit aromas. It is remarkably complex and rich for the price, the palate assisted by a hint of sweetness. It's soft and lingers well, and goes with spaghetti marinara.

## Trentham Estate Sauvignon Blanc

Trentham is a family affair: Tony Murphy is the winemaker and his brother Pat is viticulturist. The grapes are drawn mainly from their own 46-hectare spread of vines.

CURRENT RELEASE 2000   Yet another amazing value-for-money wine from Trentham! This is a delicious wine. While it is fairly reserved in its varietal expression, for a lot of drinkers that's no bad thing. It has a creamy, melony, cashew nutty, fresh aroma. The palate is juicy, bright and lively, with remarkable intensity of attractive fruit flavour. Drink it young, with a vegetable terrine.

| | |
|---|---|
| Quality | ♟ ♟ ♟ ♟ ♟ |
| Value | ★ ★ ★ ★ ★ |
| Grapes | sauvignon blanc |
| Region | Murray Valley, NSW |
| Cellar | ▮ 1 |
| Alc./Vol. | 12.5% |
| RRP | $12.00 ⑤ |

## Turkey Flat Semillon

Turkey Flat vineyard was established in 1847 and has been in the Schulz family all along. This is an unwooded style, but it's so big and soft it's not easy to tell whether it's seen wood or not.

CURRENT RELEASE 1999   Two years of age are starting to tell. The colour is medium–full yellow and it smells of straw, hay bales, lemon and tobacco. It's big, soft, broad and lacks a little in the structure department. What they call cuddly in the Barossa. It is perfect for roast stuffed chicken.

| | |
|---|---|
| Quality | ♟ ♟ ♟ ♟ |
| Value | ★ ★ ★ |
| Grapes | semillon |
| Region | Barossa Valley, SA |
| Cellar | ▮ 2 |
| Alc./Vol. | 12.1% |
| RRP | $18.00 |

## Tyrrells Long Flat White

The Long Flat wines are sporting new livery, including chief executive Bruce Tyrrell's signature on the back where his late father Murray's used to be. In faint lettering you can read 'semillon sauvignon blanc' beside the bolder 'Long Flat White'.

CURRENT RELEASE 2001   So many cheap whites taste like off-cuts, but this is an impressive wine for the price. Pale lemon colour; delicate fragrant aroma of green melon rind, citrus and herbs; a sweetish entry with zesty acids balancing nicely. It's crisp and tart, without oak, and – in all – a very pleasing drink. It goes with cold seafood and salads.

| | |
|---|---|
| Quality | ♟ ♟ ♟ ♟ |
| Value | ★ ★ ★ ★ ✦ |
| Grapes | semillon; sauvignon blanc |
| Region | not stated |
| Cellar | ▮ 2 |
| Alc./Vol. | 11.5% |
| RRP | $9.70 ⑤ |

## Tyrrells Moon Mountain Chardonnay

| | |
|---|---|
| Quality | ♛ ♛ ♛ ♛ |
| Value | ★ ★ ★ |
| Grapes | chardonnay |
| Region | Hunter Valley, NSW |
| Cellar | ▮ 4 |
| Alc./Vol. | 13.7% |
| RRP | $22.00 ⑤ |

Moon Mountain is an individual vineyard which seems to produce a decidedly un-Hunter-like chardonnay: a restrained, finessy style. Maker: Andrew Spinaze.

CURRENT RELEASE 2000    Still quite undeveloped, this has a green-tinged colour and a shy, nectarine-scented aroma. Oak has been lightly handled, and there are subtle peach and dried-apricot flavours, coupled with sherbety acids and fine balance. It would drink well with a creamy chicken dish.

## Tyrrells Old Winery Sauvignon Blanc Semillon

| | |
|---|---|
| Quality | ♛ ♛ ♛ ♛ ♛ |
| Value | ★ ★ ★ ★ ★ |
| Grapes | sauvignon blanc; semillon |
| Region | McLaren Vale, SA & Hunter Valley, NSW |
| Cellar | ▮ 2 |
| Alc./Vol. | 11.0% |
| RRP | $15.65 ⑤ |

Sauvignon blanc is not one of the Hunter's strengths. So it's no wonder Tyrrells' winemaker Andrew Spinaze has ventured down to McLaren Vale to buy some grapes.

CURRENT RELEASE 2000    The blend has worked well: this has plenty of sauvignon friskiness as well as strength on palate, thanks to Hunter semillon. The aromas remind of cut grass, capsicum and gooseberry, and the taste is tartly acidic and lets you know you're alive. The finish is likewise jumpy, crisp and dry. It's a lighter style but well balanced and quite delicious with calamari and salad.

## Tyrrells Old Winery Verdelho

| | |
|---|---|
| Quality | ♛ ♛ ♛ ♛ |
| Value | ★ ★ ★ ★ |
| Grapes | verdelho |
| Region | Hunter Valley, NSW |
| Cellar | ▮ 2 |
| Alc./Vol. | 12.5% |
| RRP | $15.60 ⑤ |

Liquorland's statistics show verdelho is one of the fastest-growing wines in its retail shops. It grew by 32.7 per cent in the year 2000, and more brands came onto the market.

CURRENT RELEASE 2000    This is a refreshingly racy style of verdelho. At time of tasting it had slightly subdued, undeveloped minerally aromas and a tangy palate with sherbety acid. The sweet fruit is balanced by crisp acid and the overall effect is most seductive. It's a good aperitif style and would go well with oysters. Drink young.

## Tyrrells Stevens Reserve Semillon

This is part of Tyrrells' individual vineyard range, which is sporting some spiffy new labelling. The grapes came from George and Neil Stevens' highly regarded vineyard at Pokolbin. Maker: Andrew Spinaze.

CURRENT RELEASE 1997   This is still a baby, but what a treat to be able to buy it at four years, rather than one (or less!). Thanks to Tyrrells, we can enjoy a classic semi-mature Hunter semillon, full of vibrant lemony freshness, or cellar it some more. The crunchy delicacy and thrilling acidity really make it a delicious drink now, but it'll be even better in a few years. It's great with raw oysters, lemon juice and sourdough bread.

| | |
|---|---|
| Quality | 🍷🍷🍷🍷🍷 |
| Value | ★★★★⁴ |
| Grapes | semillon |
| Region | Hunter Valley, NSW |
| Cellar | 🍾 6+ |
| Alc./Vol. | 10.8% |
| RRP | $21.30 |

## Tyrrells Vat 1 Semillon

Murray Tyrrell AM, doyen of the Tyrrell family and one of the great people of the wine industry, died in October 2000, aged 79. He pioneered both pinot noir and chardonnay, but his heart was with semillon.

CURRENT RELEASE 1995   A great example of aged Hunter semillon, in all its subtly layered glory. Low in alcohol and unwooded, it retains its finesse even as it builds mellow mature complexities. Toasty, straw, honey and nutty aromas; lean and dry, seamless and fine on the palate. It's great with any pan-fried fish finished with verjuice.

| | |
|---|---|
| Quality | 🍷🍷🍷🍷🍷 |
| Value | ★★★★ |
| Grapes | semillon |
| Region | Hunter Valley, NSW |
| Cellar | 🍾 6+ |
| Alc./Vol. | 11.3% |
| RRP | $50.00 |

## Tyrrells Vat 47 Pinot Chardonnay

| | |
|---|---|
| Quality | 🍷🍷🍷🍷 |
| Value | ★★★ |
| Grapes | chardonnay |
| Region | Hunter Valley, NSW |
| Cellar | 🍷 5+ |
| Alc./Vol. | 13.5% |
| RRP | $50.00 |

This famous wine has always been labelled 'pinot' chardonnay, as patriarch Murray Tyrrell always believed that was the true name of the grape. The '99 came from three separate blocks, all on sandy soil and planted with own-rooted vines. Maker: Andrew Spinaze.

CURRENT RELEASE 1999   Vat 47 is consistently one of the Hunter's finest, most ageworthy chardonnays. The '99 is fresh and restrained, with bacony aromas, good intensity and length. The oaky characters will benefit from another year to better integrate. It's already very appealing but you ain't seen nothin' yet! Serve with creamy, ripe brie.

## Vasse Felix Noble Riesling

| | |
|---|---|
| Quality | 🍷🍷🍷 |
| Value | ★★★★ |
| Grapes | riesling |
| Region | Great Southern, WA |
| Cellar | 🍷 5 |
| Alc./Vol. | 12.5% |
| RRP | $19.00 (375 ml) |

The grapes were sourced from the Forest Hill vineyard at Mount Barker, which was the first vineyard to be planted in the south-west. It's since been sold and the new owners have struck a smart new Forest Hill label. No sticky yet, so enjoy this *pro tem*.

CURRENT RELEASE 1999   This little trimmer is a tightly structured, fairly reserved sticky with a mid-yellow hue and a bouquet of dried apricot, fruit compote and straw. It's not a high-sugar style, but has lovely balance of sweetness, flavour and botrytis. The finish carries well. It suits Meredith Blue cheese.

## Vavasour Marlborough Sauvignon Blanc

| | |
|---|---|
| Quality | 🍷🍷🍷🍷 |
| Value | ★★★★ |
| Grapes | sauvignon blanc |
| Region | Marlborough, NZ |
| Cellar | 🍷 3 |
| Alc./Vol. | 13.5% |
| RRP | $20.00 |

Vavasour is located in the Awatere Valley, which is adjacent to the main part of Marlborough, the Wairau Valley. It is a little drier and warmer. This is 85 per cent Awatere, 12 per cent Wairau. Maker: Glenn Thomas.

CURRENT RELEASE 2000   Marlborough sauvignon writ large! It has all the subtlety of an All Black winger on the charge. The nose is pungent capsicum, asparagus and lawn-clippings. There are also complexing chalky/mineral aromas in the background. It has great intensity and persistence. Pair it with a mussel salad and you won't be disappointed.

## Voyager Estate Chardonnay

Stuart Pym has left Voyager and gone to Devil's Lair. On a voyage from a Cape Dutch extravaganza to a demon's den? His loyal deputy Cliff Royle has taken his place. Voyager wines have established a premium reputation in a short time.

CURRENT RELEASE 1999   This fronts as quite oaky at first, and it needs time for that wood to integrate further. There are sweet confectionery aromas from malolactic, and sappy, sawn-timber scents as well, but the fruit is hidden. It has a great deal of presence in the mouth, and will benefit from further bottle-age. Try it with barbecued chicken.

| | |
|---|---|
| Quality | ♟♟♟♟ |
| Value | ★★★ |
| Grapes | chardonnay |
| Region | Margaret River, WA |
| Cellar | ➡ 1–5+ |
| Alc./Vol. | 13.5% |
| RRP | $33.00 |

## Voyager Estate Sauvignon Blanc Semillon

This two-way blend has become one of the signature wines of Margaret River. This one has a higher alcohol reading than most. Maker: Stuart Pym, who's since resigned.

CURRENT RELEASE 2000   The colour is very pale, and the fresh tangy gooseberry, herbaceous, highly aromatic nose reminds of New Zealand versions. The alcohol leaves a slight impression of sweetness, and the flavour is a little disjointed, somewhat lacking finesse. A gutsy, full-throttle style to serve with pasta marinara.

| | |
|---|---|
| Quality | ♟♟♟♟ |
| Value | ★★★ |
| Grapes | sauvignon blanc; semillon |
| Region | Margaret River, WA |
| Cellar | ♟ 3 |
| Alc./Vol. | 13.7% |
| RRP | $19.35 |

## Water Wheel Bendigo Chardonnay

Always great value, Water Wheel's unfussed style of chardonnay makes friends everywhere due to its generous flavour.

CURRENT RELEASE 2000   This is the lush, juicy Water Wheel style and then some. It has a syrupy rich nose reminiscent of pineapple, peach and cashew, with oak playing a cameo role. In the mouth it's fruit-sweet and relatively viscous in texture. Unlike most chardonnays this is best consumed quite cold. Try it with a chicken salad.

| | |
|---|---|
| Quality | ♟♟♟♟ |
| Value | ★★★★ |
| Grapes | chardonnay |
| Region | Bendigo, Vic. |
| Cellar | ♟ 1 |
| Alc./Vol. | 13.5% |
| RRP | $14.00 |

## Water Wheel Bendigo Sauvignon Blanc

| | |
|---|---|
| Quality | ▼▼▼▽ |
| Value | ★★★★ |
| Grapes | sauvignon blanc |
| Region | Bendigo, Vic. |
| Cellar | 🍾 1 |
| Alc./Vol. | 14.0% |
| RRP | $15.50 Ⓢ |

The name of this winery harks back to the days when the original building was a flour mill. The grinding wheels were water-driven, as they mostly were – in this case by the flow of the Loddon River. Maker: Peter Cumming.
CURRENT RELEASE 2000    Not all boutiques charge an arm and a leg for their wine. Thanks be to the Cumming family. This is a decent dry white although its varietal character is subdued. The colour is pale and the aromas are delicate, recalling straw, hay and bracken. The palate is jumpy with acid and the finish carries some alcohol warmth. It goes with a salad niçoise.

## Westend 3 Bridges Chardonnay

| | |
|---|---|
| Quality | ▼▼▼▽ |
| Value | ★★★ |
| Grapes | chardonnay |
| Region | Riverina, NSW |
| Cellar | 🍾 1 |
| Alc./Vol. | 13.5% |
| RRP | $17.75 |

Bill Calabria's Westend winery is another Riverina enterprise that's made the transition from production of bulk wines and cheaper lines, to the sort of good-quality, reasonably priced products that the modern Riverina wine scene is judged by.
CURRENT RELEASE 2000    This is a tasty oaked chardonnay of direct appeal. The nose has peaches-and-cream aromas and some tropical fruit clothed in a fair amount of oak, which takes things over a bit. The palate has the same balance of strong oak, fruit-sweet tropical flavour, and buttery richness, and it has good depth. Could do with a shade less wood for our liking. Serve it with honey prawns.

## Westend 3 Bridges Golden Mist

| | |
|---|---|
| Quality | ▼▼▼▼ |
| Value | ★★★ |
| Grapes | semillon |
| Region | Riverina, NSW |
| Cellar | 🍾 4 |
| Alc./Vol. | 10.5% |
| RRP | $20.00 (375 ml) |

Another of the burgeoning number of sweet botrytised semillons coming out of the Riverina. Makers: Bill Calabria and James Ceccato.
CURRENT RELEASE 1999    A classic 'Riverina Gold' nose of intense apricot liqueur, marmalade, honey and vanilla. In the mouth it's sweet and luscious, yet not as persistent as some of its peers. It has high acidity and a hint of volatility to cut the sweetness back a little. A good sweetie to serve with panna cotta.

## Westend Richland Sauvignon Blanc

Bill Calabria's Westend wines have taken on a higher profile in recent times, with better wine quality and a concerted effort to market more effectively in Australian capital city and export markets.
CURRENT RELEASE 2000  Belying its warm-climate origins, this young white has a piercingly bright herbaceous nose in the take-no-prisoners sauvignon blanc school. It has sharp varietal identity but a little more depth and fruit sweetness might improve it somewhat. The palate follows as expected with lively grassy/ herby flavour and a zippy finish. Try it with crudités and dips.

| | |
|---|---|
| Quality | 🍷🍷🍷 |
| Value | ★★★★ |
| Grapes | sauvignon blanc |
| Region | Riverina, NSW |
| Cellar | 🍷 1 |
| Alc./Vol. | 11.5% |
| RRP | $11.00 Ⓢ |

## Wicked Wines Envy Chardonnay

A metallic green normally sprayed on hot panel vans and old Valiants graces this bottle. It's designed to appeal to that nebulous, and patently tasteless, group known as Gen X.
CURRENT RELEASE 2000  As with the other Wicked Wines, don't let looks fool you here. It's a creditable early drinking style with pleasant melon and herbal aromas; oak is well hidden. The palate is clean-tasting and medium-bodied, with smooth tropical fruit in the middle and maybe a tiny little seasoning of oak to finish it off. The palate falls a fraction short but what the hell. Slurp it down at suitably wicked parties.

| | |
|---|---|
| Quality | 🍷🍷🍷 |
| Value | ★★★ |
| Grapes | chardonnay |
| Region | not stated |
| Cellar | 🍷 1 |
| Alc./Vol. | 12.5% |
| RRP | $12.00 Ⓢ |

## Will Taylor Clare Valley Riesling

Behind Will Taylor's carefully thought-out merchant label is a desire to bottle absolutely classic Australian wine styles of peerless quality. So far he's succeeding very well.
CURRENT RELEASE 2000  An excellent Clare riesling, this has real aromatic intensity along with the backbone for longevity. The nose has lime, floral and juicy grapey notes, and the palate has good depth of concentrated mineral and citrus flavours. It finishes long and clean. Try it with Thai duck salad.

| | |
|---|---|
| Quality | 🍷🍷🍷🍷 |
| Value | ★★★★ |
| Grapes | riesling |
| Region | Clare Valley, SA |
| Cellar | 🍷 6+ |
| Alc./Vol. | 11.8% |
| RRP | $20.00 |

## Will Taylor Hunter Valley Semillon

**Quality** 🍷🍷🍷🍷
**Value** ★★★½
**Grapes** semillon
**Region** Hunter Valley, NSW
**Cellar** 2–10
**Alc./Vol.** 12.3%
**RRP** $20.00

Hunter semillons are just about the most shy white wines you can get when they're young, and true aficionados take it as an article of faith that they'll improve with age, as this one should.

CURRENT RELEASE 2000 If you're a chardonnay fan you'll think the nose on this semillon so neutral that it's hardly there; look deeper and you'll find sprightly citrus and lanolin aromas. Delicate, yes, but with a sort of inner intensity full of promise. The dry lemony palate is tight in structure. Surprisingly it's quite high in alcohol for a Hunter sem. Despite this it's a bit more austere than most of the 2000s. Should be an interesting cellaring proposition. A wine for delicate fish.

## Will Taylor Sauvignon Blanc

**Quality** 🍷🍷🍷🍷
**Value** ★★★½
**Grapes** sauvignon blanc
**Region** Adelaide Hills, SA
**Cellar** 2
**Alc./Vol.** 13.0%
**RRP** $20.00

In keeping with his intention of bottling only the regional and varietal classics of Australia, Will Taylor seeks his sauvignon blanc in the Adelaide Hills.

CURRENT RELEASE 2000 This is an altogether fuller, riper sauvignon than most in them thar Hills, with less of the piercing herbaceousness and more fruit-juicy sweet aromas. There's a hint of grassiness behind tropical-scented fruit in the mouth, but that fruit richness stands out. It finishes dry and clean. Try it with mussels marinière.

## Willow Bridge Estate Chenin Blanc

**Quality** 🍷🍷🍷
**Value** ★★
**Grapes** chenin blanc
**Region** Ferguson Valley, WA
**Cellar** 1
**Alc./Vol.** 12.5%
**RRP** $16.00

Chenin Blanc has a long history in Western Australia but these days it's certainly not the most trendy white variety around. Willow Bridge Estate is a new name to us, from the Ferguson Valley. Maker: Rob Bowen.

CURRENT RELEASE 2000 A fruity nose suggesting grapes and apples has a certain juicy appeal but there's a slightly sweaty touch as well. The palate is soft and simple, with clean grapey flavour, a hint of residual sugar and a soft finish. Not a bad everyday white wine but a bit pricey in the scheme of things. Serve it with a prawn salad.

## Willow Creek Sauvignon Blanc

Willow Creek is another attractive destination for the visitor to the lovely Mornington Peninsula. There's a good restaurant among the vines and the wines are well worth trying.

CURRENT RELEASE 2000    Pristine sauvignon varietal character is spot-on here. The nose is musky, almost exotic, and it has attractive herbaceous, pawpaw and grapey notes. It tastes clean and tangy but the mid-palate has unusual softness with blackcurranty flavours of good intensity. Works well with mussels.

| | |
|---|---|
| Quality | ♟ ♟ ♟ ♟ |
| Value | ★★★ |
| Grapes | sauvignon blanc |
| Region | Mornington Peninsula, Vic. |
| Cellar | 🍶 2 |
| Alc./Vol. | 13.0% |
| RRP | $20.00 |

## Wirra Wirra Hand-Picked Riesling

McLaren Vale isn't exactly the best place to grow riesling in Australia, but riesling vines have been there a long time, and Wirra Wirra has been one of the best. These days it includes fruit from other districts to add complexity. Maker: Ben Riggs.

CURRENT RELEASE 2000    There's a little more depth of greenish–yellow colour in this than in young rieslings from the Clare and Eden Valleys. It's not as fine in aroma and flavour as those wines either, but the nose is really characterful with rich, vinous, citrus aromas. The palate is rich too with good depth and length ahead of a long tasty finish. Serve it with fried prawns.

| | |
|---|---|
| Quality | ♟ ♟ ♟ ♟ |
| Value | ★★★★ |
| Grapes | riesling |
| Region | McLaren Vale & Coonawarra, SA; Grampians, Vic. |
| Cellar | 🍶 3 |
| Alc./Vol. | 13.0% |
| RRP | $15.50 |

## Wolf Blass Yellow Label Riesling

Much of Wolf Blass's fame was built on this riesling with the yellow label. Distributed just about everywhere, it maintains an enviable record for value.

CURRENT RELEASE 2000    In this vintage, Blass Yellow Label has a little more intensity than usual. Lime, floral tones and a hint of talcum powder mark the fragrant nose. The aromatics continue in the mouth with surprisingly concentrated varietal flavour framed in good acidity and firm structure. Try Thai seafood salad with this.

| | |
|---|---|
| Quality | ♟ ♟ ♟ ♟ |
| Value | ★★★★┦ |
| Grapes | riesling |
| Region | various, SA |
| Cellar | 🍶 3 |
| Alc./Vol. | 11.0% |
| RRP | $12.95 ⑤ |

## Wyndham Estate Show Reserve Chardonnay

| | |
|---|---|
| Quality | ♥ ♥ ♥ ⟨ |
| Value | ★ ★ ★ |
| Grapes | chardonnay |
| Region | Hunter Valley, NSW |
| Cellar | ▮ 2 |
| Alc./Vol. | 12.5% |
| RRP | $18.20 |

Wyndham's premier range arrived last year with a couple of reds and this white. Although this is a Show Reserve there are no awards listed anywhere on the label; perhaps it was one of the also-rans.
CURRENT RELEASE 1999    Made in the too-much-bloody-oak style beloved of chardonnay drinkers a decade or two ago, this wine really is a bit passé in a world getting used to the subtleties of modern Oz chard. The nose has vanilla and caramel-like wood aromas with very subdued melon fruit. On the palate oaky flavours to the fore, everything else bringing up the rear. The palate texture is good, but all that wood! Serve it with gruyère-style cheese.

## Wynns Chardonnay

| | |
|---|---|
| Quality | ♥ ♥ ♥ ⟨ |
| Value | ★ ★ ★ ★ |
| Grapes | chardonnay |
| Region | Coonawarra, SA |
| Cellar | ▮ 3 |
| Alc./Vol. | 13.0% |
| RRP | $14.00 ⑤ |

Like other wines in the keenly priced Wynns Coonawarra basic range, this chardonnay can often leave much more expensive wines behind for quality and value.
CURRENT RELEASE 2000    There's more toasty oak apparent in this vintage than the last couple, and it tends to dominate attractive melony fruit aromas and nutty subtleties. The palate has good depth and ripeness with smooth melon and citrus flavour in the middle, but again there's a tad more oak than there is fruit character to back it up. Will probably be more harmonious in a year or so. Try it now with barbecued prawn brochettes.

## Wynns Riesling

| | |
|---|---|
| Quality | ♥ ♥ ♥ ♥ ⟨ |
| Value | ★ ★ ★ ★ ★ |
| Grapes | riesling |
| Region | Coonawarra, SA |
| Cellar | ▮ 5 |
| Alc./Vol. | 12.0% |
| RRP | $12.00 ⑤ |

Despite predictions of climbing prices for riesling, the bargains still abound. Wynns' Coonawarra is one of the greatest.
CURRENT RELEASE 2000    Bargain-basement territory here. Everything about it would lead you to expect a higher price tag – vivacious lime, talc and floral aromas of pristine varietal purity, and a palate of intense citrus flavours. It's delicate but that doesn't mean it's weak. Balance is excellent right now, and bottle-age will reward the patient with richness and complexity. Good with stirfried Malaysian-style calamari.

# Xanadu Chardonnay

A good wine to drink in any stately pleasure dome, whether it be in Xanadu or elsewhere. Maker: Jurg Muggli.

CURRENT RELEASE 1999    This is always a subtle style with smooth integration of subdued fruit character and nutty winemaking influences. There is a bit of the typical tropical fruit of Margaret River, but it's less voluminous than in some of its peers. The palate is balanced, fine in texture and smooth, leading through to some tangy acidity and a long finish perfumed with gentle fruit and oak. Very good with scallop pastries.

| | |
|---|---|
| Quality | ♟♟♟♟ |
| Value | ★★★↓ |
| Grapes | chardonnay |
| Region | Margaret River, WA |
| Cellar | ▮ 4 |
| Alc./Vol. | 13.0% |
| RRP | $25.00 |

# Xanadu Semillon

Xanadu's semillon is a serious white wine, made in a style more in keeping with chardonnay than this underrated variety. The result is pretty interesting.

CURRENT RELEASE 2000    A bright straw colour looks good, and the nose is complex with nutty and yeasty touches, a creamy, lactic layer, and soft, herbal fruit aromas. A touch of oaky spice reinforces a chardonnay-like dimension, despite a different varietal profile. It's rich in the mouth and very complex, with fine balance and a long finish flavoured with a hint of toasty oak. Serve it with soy-sauce chicken.

| | |
|---|---|
| Quality | ♟♟♟♟♟ |
| Value | ★★★★ |
| Grapes | semillon |
| Region | Margaret River, WA |
| Cellar | ▮ 5 |
| Alc./Vol. | 13.5% |
| RRP | $23.00 |

# Yalumba Barossa Riesling

Few Australian wineries have as much experience with riesling as Yalumba. They also keep a wine museum built up over many years, and sometimes open very old examples of Barossa and Eden Valley riesling to stun tasters with their ageing ability.

CURRENT RELEASE 2000    A straightforward Barossa riesling with pleasant aromas of citrus fruits and flowers. The palate is light and you could call it delicate, or does it just lack a bit of stuffing in the middle? It has a dry finish but it pulls up a little short for our liking. Take it along to a party.

| | |
|---|---|
| Quality | ♟♟♟ |
| Value | ★★★↓ |
| Grapes | riesling |
| Region | Barossa Valley, SA |
| Cellar | ▮ 2 |
| Alc./Vol. | 10.5% |
| RRP | $12.00 |

## Yalumba Christobel's Classic Dry White

| | |
|---|---|
| Quality | ♟ ♟ ♙ |
| Value | ★ ★ ⸴ |
| Grapes | sauvignon blanc; semillon |
| Region | various, SA |
| Cellar | ▮ 1 |
| Alc./Vol. | 12.0% |
| RRP | $12.00 Ⓢ |

Classic Dry White is a nebulous title that can mean anything and generally does. Yalumba's version is fairly typical of the genre.

CURRENT RELEASE 2000    The nose is herbal with light grapey and green-pea aromas that give a gentle, almost neutral impression. The washed-out nose translates accurately to the palate which is simple, lightly grassy and clean enough to be inoffensive. A 'nothing' sort of wine to serve at a party when nobody's paying much attention to what they're drinking.

## Yalumba Hand–Picked Riesling

| | |
|---|---|
| Quality | ♟ ♟ ♟ ♟ ♟ |
| Value | ★ ★ ★ |
| Grapes | riesling |
| Region | Eden Valley, SA |
| Cellar | ▮ 10+ |
| Alc./Vol. | 12.5% |
| RRP | $29.00 |

Yalumba pioneered the Stelvin screw-top on some of their rieslings back in 1969. Perceived consumer negativity towards this sort of closure led to it being dropped, but now, in answer to the cork-taint problem, it's back on this smartly turned-out bottle.

CURRENT RELEASE 2000    The colour is pale and green-tinged in the best Eden Valley riesling tradition. There's a pungent, spicy, floral and light citrus aroma that gets top marks for intensity. The palate is round, rich and long with flavours of spices and lime, leading to a firm signature of acidity. An excellent style that needs time. Try it with Thai-style roast duck salad.

## Yarra Ridge Chardonnay

| | |
|---|---|
| Quality | ♟ ♟ ♟ ♟ |
| Value | ★ ★ ★ |
| Grapes | chardonnay |
| Region | Yarra Valley, Vic. |
| Cellar | ▮ 2 |
| Alc./Vol. | 12.5% |
| RRP | $20.00 |

This Yarra Valley outpost of the Beringer–Blass consortium is a substantial clearing house for the region's grapes. Wine quality under the estate label is good.

CURRENT RELEASE 2000    This is a crowd-pleaser of a chardonnay which delivers the goods without any rough edges or quirky qualities. The nose has smoothly integrated melon-fruit and oak influence, and the palate follows suit exactly. It's medium-bodied and soft, with adequate richness and a pleasantly light and crisp finish. The perfect wine to satisfy a room full of chardonnay-socialists. Serve it with chicken club sandwiches.

## Yarra Ridge Sauvignon Blanc

Yarra Ridge is one of the major players in the Yarra Valley, producing three different levels of wine under Reserve, standard and Mount Tanglefoot labels. Maker: Nick Walker.

CURRENT RELEASE 2000 Although this lacks the personality and depth of the 1999 vintage, it's still a reasonable effort. On the nose it's all straightforward sauvignon blanc with tropical fruit and tomato-leaf aromas, and the palate is soft but rather attenuated in flavour. Zippy acidity keeps it lively. Good with Vietnamese rice paper rolls.

| | |
|---|---|
| Quality | ♥♥♥♥ |
| Value | ★★★ |
| Grapes | sauvignon blanc |
| Region | Yarra Valley, Vic. |
| Cellar | ▮ 1 |
| Alc./Vol. | 12.5% |
| RRP | $19.95 ⑤ |

## Yering Station Chardonnay

Yering Station's winemaker Tom Carson is a gifted performer with Yarra Valley grapes, making wines of good style and regional integrity.

CURRENT RELEASE 2000 Chardonnay responds well to winery manipulation that paints some interesting colours on a sometimes blank canvas. This wine is an example with subtle hints of nuts, yeast lees and restrained oak from winemaker's additions dressing up melon and pear fruit aromas. They add a little richness all right, but there's also a beery quality that detracts a bit. The palate has good texture, moderate fruit character and body with a soft, dry finish. Try it with chicken stirfry.

| | |
|---|---|
| Quality | ♥♥♥♥ |
| Value | ★★★ |
| Grapes | chardonnay |
| Region | Yarra Valley, Vic. |
| Cellar | ▮ 3 |
| Alc./Vol. | 13.5% |
| RRP | $20.70 |

## Yering Station Marsanne

Marsanne was known as one of 'the best and most useful' grape varieties in the Yarra Valley in the 1870s, and lately the fascination with the Rhone grape varieties has prompted Yering Station to have another go.

CURRENT RELEASE 2000 Victoria is one of the world's greatest marsanne outposts and the wines deserve to be more popular. This example has an interesting nose with aromas of honey, white stone fruit, flowers and herbs. It's 'winey' rather than fruity, and has a honeyed but dry palate with a hint of nuttiness. The aftertaste is long and smooth. Try it with prawn satays.

| | |
|---|---|
| Quality | ♥♥♥♥ |
| Value | ★★★ |
| Grapes | marsanne |
| Region | Yarra Valley, Vic. |
| Cellar | ▮ 4 |
| Alc./Vol. | 12.5% |
| RRP | $19.50 |

## Yering Station Reserve Chardonnay

| | |
|---|---|
| Quality | ▼▼▼▼▼ |
| Value | ★★★★★ |
| Grapes | chardonnay |
| Region | Yarra Valley, Vic. |
| Cellar | 🍾 4 |
| Alc./Vol. | 13.5% |
| RRP | $50.00 |

 Penguin Best White Wine & Best Chardonnay

The Reserve wines from Yering Station were a big hit as soon as they arrived. The chardonnay results from careful fruit selection allied to Rolls-Royce treatment in the winery. **CURRENT RELEASE 1999    A beautifully put-together Yarra chardonnay with a bouquet that combines subtlety and power in rather Burgundian fashion. There are sweet fruit, cashew, butter-cream and matchsticky aromas as well as some spicy French oak seasoning. The palate is fine and oh-so-smooth with a nutty thread of classy oak woven through the clean chardonnay flavour. The aftertaste is long and savoury. Dust off the credit card to buy a bottle, and get a lobster to go with it.**

## Yering Station Sauvignon Blanc

| | |
|---|---|
| Quality | ▼▼▼▼ |
| Value | ★★★↓ |
| Grapes | sauvignon blanc |
| Region | Yarra Valley, Vic. |
| Cellar | 🍾 2 |
| Alc./Vol. | 12.0% |
| RRP | $16.00 |

Yering Station is the Yarra Valley's first vineyard resurrected and some of the original buildings are still in use in the new incarnation. Anyone visiting the Yarra Valley should make a pilgrimage to this place.
CURRENT RELEASE 2000    This smells uncompromisingly varietal and if sauvignon blanc makes you wince you should avoid it. But if you're a sauvignon fan you'll love it: it has intense tomato-stalk, herb and grapey aromas, with a hint of floral perfume. In the mouth it's snappy with lively herbaceousness and high acidity. Try it with a grilled prosciutto, tomato and asparagus salad.

## Yering Station Viognier

| | |
|---|---|
| Quality | ▼▼▼▼ |
| Value | ★★★↓ |
| Grapes | viognier |
| Region | Yarra Valley, Vic. |
| Cellar | 🍾 2 |
| Alc./Vol. | 12.5% |
| RRP | $20.50 |

Viognier is the flavour of the month for some of our winemakers. Whether it attains fashionability is a moot point.
CURRENT RELEASE 2000    Viognier has one of the most distinctive aromas of all white grapes and this shows it well. There are interesting 'foreign' smells here with suggestions of exotic spice, flowers, kernelly/nutty touches and a hint of spicy oak. It's very fragrant and the palate is smooth with gentle floral and nutty flavours finishing light and long with soft acidity. Try it with soft cheeses.

## Zarephath Chardonnay

Zarephath is a name from the Bible, and the grapes were grown by a Benedictine community in Porongurup, Western Australia. From right out of left field, it's a real surprise package. Maker: Brenden Smith, at West Cape Howe winery.

CURRENT RELEASE 2000    Streets ahead of any altar wine we can recall! It has plenty of toasty barrel-ferment character, and is rich and nutty in the mouth with typical chardonnay, velvet-smooth texture. The flavours are nicely layered and there's a suggestion of sweetness on the finish. It drinks well with vegetable terrines.

| | |
|---|---|
| Quality | ♟♟♟♟ |
| Value | ★★★★ |
| Grapes | chardonnay |
| Region | Great Southern, WA |
| Cellar | 🍾 4 |
| Alc./Vol. | 13.0% |
| RRP | $19.50 |

## Zarephath Riesling

Great name! Who cares what it means, it's gonna stop 'em in their tracks when they spot it on the retailer's shelf. The packaging is good too.

CURRENT RELEASE 2000    The Porongurup Ranges are a great locale for riesling, so it's no surprise that experienced local Brenden Smith has turned out a ripper here. The aromas are typical riesling: clean, soft and fragrantly flowery. The palate is intense but also quite acidic. This gives a slight hardness to the finish, so we suggest serving it with food, such as John Dory poached in wine and lemon juice.

| | |
|---|---|
| Quality | ♟♟♟♟ |
| Value | ★★★★ |
| Grapes | riesling |
| Region | Great Southern, WA |
| Cellar | 🍾 7+ |
| Alc./Vol. | 13.0% |
| RRP | $16.50 |

# Sparkling Wines

### Andrew Harris Double Vision Sparkling Shiraz

| | |
|---|---|
| **Quality** | 🍷🍷🍷 |
| **Value** | ★★⁺ |
| **Grapes** | shiraz |
| **Region** | Mudgee, NSW |
| **Cellar** | 🍶 4 |
| **Alc./Vol.** | 14.0% |
| **RRP** | $40.30 |

Great name! Harris's flagship red was named The Vision (roll images of Driza-Boned, Akubra'd man silhouetted against a blazing sunset) so it seemed logical to follow it with a double vision. Maker: Frank Newman.

CURRENT RELEASE 1997    This is a spirited, youthful red fizz that leaves you with a lick of Mudgee astringency. The colour retains purple tints and it smells sweetly ripe and plummy, with meaty and earthy notes. The mousse is good and it's fluffy in the mouth. There's both acid and tannin on the finish. Pair it with pork spare ribs and plum sauce.

### Banrock Station Sparkling Shiraz

| | |
|---|---|
| **Quality** | 🍷🍷🍷 |
| **Value** | ★★★★⁺ |
| **Grapes** | shiraz |
| **Region** | Murray Valley, SA |
| **Cellar** | 🍶 2 |
| **Alc./Vol.** | 14.0% |
| **RRP** | $12.80 ⑤ |

Banrock is the trendy Riverland wine of BRL Hardy. It's been a giant killer in some judgings. Maker: master fizzicist Ed Carr.

CURRENT RELEASE non-vintage    Being inexpensive, it's quite a young wine: a fruity, straightforward style, smelling of jam and licorice. It enters the mouth fairly sweet, but acid cleans up the finish nicely. It is very keen value for money. Try it with pork ribs and plum sauce.

## Barossa Valley Estate E & E Sparkling Shiraz

According to the Melbourne-based Australian Sparkling
Red Association, there are more than 80 different brands
of red bubbly out there at present. Most are made in
tiny quantities.

*Previous outstanding vintages: '94, '95*

CURRENT RELEASE 1996    Very typical of the E & E
style, the latest vintage shows a major contribution from
oak. It's big and full-flavoured with quite pronounced
sweetness which tends to do battle with oak and tannin.
It has vanilla, fruitcake, dark-chocolate flavours and a
big, dry finish. The style is arresting, but it's a bit too
aggressive to really enjoy. It will probably reward
cellaring. Then crack a bottle with Peking duck.

| | |
|---|---|
| Quality | ▼▼▼▼ |
| Value | ★★★ |
| Grapes | shiraz |
| Region | Barossa Valley, SA |
| Cellar | ➤ 2–6 |
| Alc./Vol. | 14.5% |
| RRP | $42.00 |

## Blues Point Brut Reserve

Is this named after the awful Blues Point Tower on
Sydney Harbour, we wonder? It comes in a blue bottle,
and was one of the first 'concept wines' to hit the
startled market.

CURRENT RELEASE *non-vintage*    It's quite good value,
really. There are no pretences to finesse, but it has
flavour and drinkability. The bubbles are on the large
side, while the bouquet is all about quince, nectarine
and faintly herbal fruit overlaid by a little toasty
development. The palate is slightly sweet on entry and
somewhat broad, but it's a very acceptable party fizz.

| | |
|---|---|
| Quality | ▼▼▼ |
| Value | ★★★★ |
| Grapes | not stated |
| Region | not stated |
| Cellar | ▌1 |
| Alc./Vol. | 11.5% |
| RRP | $11.25 ⑤ |

## Briar Ridge Pinot Chardonnay

| | |
|---|---|
| Quality | ♟ ♟ ♟ |
| Value | ★ ★ ★ |
| Grapes | pinot noir, chardonnay |
| Region | Hunter Valley, NSW |
| Cellar | ▮ 3 |
| Alc./Vol. | 10.3% |
| RRP | $21.00 |

Briar Ridge recently joined the Mildara Blass (or should we say Beringer Blass) stable, linking up with fellow Hunter winery, Rothbury Estate. Maker: Neil McGuigan.
CURRENT RELEASE 1999    The colour is very light yellow and it seems a little stripped. Either that or the delicate base wine really needed more time on lees to build character. There are aromas of honey, minerals and dusty earth. The palate reveals slightly green, young herbal fruit. It has flavour but is a bit on the bland side. No faults, but maybe another year on lees would have helped. It can handle oysters.

## Brown Brothers King Valley Pinot Chardonnay

| | |
|---|---|
| Quality | ♟ ♟ ♟ |
| Value | ★ ★ ★ |
| Grapes | pinot noir, chardonnay |
| Region | King Valley, Vic. |
| Cellar | ▮ 1 |
| Alc./Vol. | 12.0% |
| RRP | $17.35 ⑤ |

Browns' standard bubbly comes from lower-altitude vineyards in the King Valley than the Whitlands vintage. It's also cheaper and produced in quantities that make it easier to track down.
CURRENT RELEASE *non-vintage*    The colour is medium yellow and there are whiffs of crème anglaise and pear-like fruit. The palate is fairly light and uncomplicated with a trace of sweetness on entry. It's balanced to be a crowd-pleaser. It would go well with salted pistachios.

## Brown Brothers Whitlands Pinot Chardonnay Brut

| | |
|---|---|
| Quality | ♟ ♟ ♟ ♟ |
| Value | ★ ★ ★ |
| Grapes | pinot noir, chardonnay |
| Region | King Valley, Vic. |
| Cellar | ▮ 3+ |
| Alc./Vol. | 12.5% |
| RRP | $36.20 |

This bottle seemed younger than when we last sampled this vintage! Perhaps they are disgorging it in batches, which is fairly common practice. The longer a wine stays on its lees, the more slowly it ages.
CURRENT RELEASE 1996    Light yellow in the glass, this smells fresh, delicate and youthful. There are overtones of fresh nuts and a subtle yeast-lees undertone. In the mouth, it's delicate and steely, with plenty of acid and a dryness from low dosage. It finishes with good length and some style. Serve it with cheese goujons.

## Canobolas–Smith Shine

This sparkling chardonnay was made at Charles Sturt University, Wagga, from Murray and Toni Smith's Canobolas–Smith grapes. It's had three years on its yeast lees, and is available at cellar door only.
CURRENT RELEASE 1997   This impressive bubbly is very youthful and crisp, with pristine apple/pear chardonnay flavours and a fine veneer of smoky, bready yeast autolysis. The palate is tremendously fine, intense and vivacious, finishing crisp and clean with balanced acidity and quite good length for a blanc de blancs style. Try it with goat's cheese tartlets.

| | |
|---|---|
| Quality | 🍷🍷🍷🍷🍷 |
| Value | ★★★⁺ |
| Grapes | chardonnay |
| Region | Orange, NSW |
| Cellar | 🍾 5+ |
| Alc./Vol. | 12.5% |
| RRP | $30.00 (cellar door) |

## Celebration

This is the fizz that flowed during Nicole Kidman's party at Fox Studios to launch her new flick, *Moulin Rouge*. The base wines are made by John Wade from Smithbrook grapes and fizzed up at Bridgewater Mill.
*Previous outstanding vintage: '96*
CURRENT RELEASE 1997   There's an echo of the ultra-refined Croser style here; it's light yellow in hue and smells fresh and fruit-dominant, without obvious yeast character. Straw, nougat, melon and malt characters can be detected. It's delicate, subtle and shy in the mouth, with a very dry but not austere finish. The mousse is fluffy and a hint of regional passionfruit is revealed as it warms. Try it with oysters.

| | |
|---|---|
| Quality | 🍷🍷🍷🍷 |
| Value | ★★★⁺ |
| Grapes | pinot noir 65%; chardonnay 35% |
| Region | Pemberton, WA |
| Cellar | 🍾 3+ |
| Alc./Vol. | 12.9% |
| RRP | $27.00 |

## Chandon Blanc de Blancs

| | |
|---|---|
| Quality | 🍷🍷🍷🍷🍷 |
| Value | ★★★★⁺ |
| Grapes | chardonnay |
| Region | various, southern Australia |
| Cellar | 🍶 2 |
| Alc./Vol. | 13.0% |
| RRP | $34.00 Ⓢ |

Penguin Best Sparkling Wine

This 100 per cent chardonnay sparkler is often our favourite of the whole range. We like its finesse, freshness and subtle complexity.

**CURRENT RELEASE 1997    A bright straw colour and a fine creaming bubble whet the appetite visually here, and the bouquet is complex yet understated. There are biscuit and bread touches to citrus and light melony aromas, all harmoniously folded together. The palate follows suit with smooth texture and good length of flavour. The secondary yeasty flavours don't dominate too much, allowing it to remain fresh and light on the palate. A lovely aperitif.**

## Chandon Prestige Cuvée

| | |
|---|---|
| Quality | 🍷🍷🍷🍷🍷 |
| Value | ★★★⁺ |
| Grapes | pinot noir; chardonnay |
| Region | various Vic., SA & Tas. |
| Cellar | 🍶 2 |
| Alc./Vol. | 13.0% |
| RRP | $42.00 |

The first true Prestige Cuvée from Chandon was labelled 1993 Millennium Cuvée for the 2000 celebrations. We've now had another look at Chandon's 1994 flagship wine, first reviewed in last year's *Guide* but still found on the shelves here and there, to see how it is a year older.
CURRENT RELEASE 1994    The colour has deepened slightly. On the nose it's a rich, developed wine with biscuit, vanilla custard, bread and meringue aromas of real complexity. In the mouth there is deep, cracked yeasty flavour, good body and a long finish. It's lost some freshness since last year, the trade-off being an increase in richness. On balance we think it was better when first released. Try it with chicken liver brioche.

## Chandon Sparkling Red

| | |
|---|---|
| Quality | 🍷🍷🍷🍷 |
| Value | ★★★★⁺ |
| Grapes | pinot noir; shiraz |
| Region | various, southern Australia |
| Cellar | 🍶 3 |
| Alc./Vol. | 13.0% |
| RRP | $22.00 |

This is the first sparkling red from Chandon, a wine that differs somewhat from the traditional Australian idea of 'sparkling burg'.
CURRENT RELEASE *non-vintage*    The nose has juicy red berry, pinot noir-ish aromas that are a lot less less jammy than most red fizz. There are also soft hints of vanilla bean and undergrowthy notes which carry through the medium-weight palate. Gentle sweetness touches the mid-palate which finishes in dry, fine-grained tannins. Try it with the Christmas turkey.

## Chandon Vintage Brut

We saw an early disgorgement of this wine and reviewed it in the last *Guide*. It's still current and since these wines improve markedly with time on lees and in bottle, we thought we should have a look at it again.
CURRENT RELEASE 1997    The passage of time has added depth and complexity to what was already a very good drop. If anything that creamy, subtle Chandon thing has become more harmonious and seamless on the palate. It's long and fine with subtle biscuity notes and a crisp, clean finish. Sip it with sushi.

| | |
|---|---|
| Quality | 🍷🍷🍷🍷🍷 |
| Value | ★★★★ |
| Grapes | pinot noir; chardonnay; pinot meunier |
| Region | various Vic.; Coonawarra, SA & Pemberton, WA |
| Cellar | 🍾 2 |
| Alc./Vol. | 12.5% |
| RRP | $33.50 |

## Chandon Vintage Brut Rosé

High-quality rosé sparkling wines are usually made in a more solid, fuller-flavoured style than the white, a character that seems at odds with the pretty pink colour.
CURRENT RELEASE 1997    A bit bigger and richer than it was a year ago, this has a lot of red berry-scented pinot noir in the bouquet. It also has the vanilla custard/cream aromas of the house style, full body and a smooth, deeply flavoured palate. There's also a firm thread that runs through it, reinforcing its 'serious' nature. Try it with gravlax.

| | |
|---|---|
| Quality | 🍷🍷🍷🍷🍷 |
| Value | ★★★★ |
| Grapes | pinot noir; chardonnay |
| Region | various |
| Cellar | 🍾 2 |
| Alc./Vol. | 12.5% |
| RRP | $33.50 |

## Deakin Estate Brut

This wine once landed the Penguin award for best value sparkling wine. We're pleased to report it's as good as ever and still great value. These days Deakin's an all-girl affair with winemakers Linda Jakubans and Kim Hart.
CURRENT RELEASE *non-vintage*    There's no pretence at finesse here, the wine is WYSIWYG (what you see is what you get). The colour is light–mid yellow and it smells of candy, vanilla and meringue, with some developed character. The bead is rather coarse and while it may lack finesse and length, it has plenty of flavour and richness. Serve it with devils on horseback.

| | |
|---|---|
| Quality | 🍷🍷🍷 |
| Value | ★★★★ |
| Grapes | mainly chardonnay |
| Region | Murray Valley, Vic. |
| Cellar | 🍾 1 |
| Alc./Vol. | 13.0% |
| RRP | $10.50 |

## Eyton Pinot Chardonnay

| | |
|---|---|
| Quality | 🍷🍷🍷🍷 |
| Value | ★★★ |
| Grapes | pinot noir; chardonnay |
| Region | Yarra Valley, Vic. |
| Cellar | 🍷 2 |
| Alc./Vol. | 12.5% |
| RRP | $30.00 |

No winery is a more appropriate place than this to sip a civilised flute of fizz. Eyton has a smart restaurant, a pristine winery, and art on the walls. And their own very good sparkling wine.

CURRENT RELEASE 1997    This is always a stylish drop. The latest has a bright appearance with a complex, developed bouquet showing rich bready, yeasty notes, apple fruit and some sweet citrus. The palate is smooth and seems to have quite a high level of liqueuring which gives it an off-dry mid-palate. Bracing acidity on the finish balances that hint of sweetness. An attractive all-rounder, good for a pre-theatre tipple or a party.

## Fleur de Lys Chardonnay Pinot Noir Pinot Meunier

| | |
|---|---|
| Quality | 🍷🍷🍷🍷 |
| Value | ★★★★ |
| Grapes | chardonnay; pinot noir; pinot meunier |
| Region | not stated |
| Cellar | 🍷 2 |
| Alc./Vol. | 12.0% |
| RRP | $12.60 ⑤ |

This comes from the Southcorp fizz factory at Great Western and was originally marketed under the Seppelt banner. The non-vintage is in a conventional bubbly bottle, the vintage in a fancier one.

CURRENT RELEASE *non-vintage*    The name is French but the style's dinky-di Aussie. The bouquet offers broader fig, quince and nectarine-like aromas and some evidence of age on lees. It's fruity, light and somewhat short on the palate, with peach and nectarine fruit flavours and a little sweetness. It would go well with devils on horseback.

## Fleur de Lys Vintage Pinot Noir Chardonnay

| | |
|---|---|
| Quality | 🍷🍷🍷🍷 |
| Value | ★★★★★ |
| Grapes | pinot noir; chardonnay |
| Region | not stated |
| Cellar | 🍷 3 |
| Alc./Vol. | 12.5% |
| RRP | $18.50 ⑤ |

There's a time-honoured tradition of trying to give sparkling wine the romance of Champagne. As far as we know, fleur de lys doesn't grow in Australia . . . Chief winemaker Ian McKenzie retired in 2001 after 43 vintages.

CURRENT RELEASE 1994    How the makers justify so much time on lees is not for us to ponder: this is superior bubbly and great value for money. It has a bready, figgy bouquet showing fruitcake, dried-fruit and straw aromas. It's smooth, fine and dry in the mouth, with generous flavour that lingers well. In all, a wine that's full of body and character. Try it with grilled figs and prosciutto.

# Fox Creek Vixen

Sparkling reds have become something of a cult item among younger wine drinkers. Even the very youthful, purple, callow styles have their devotees. They're certainly a lot of fun, until you spill them on your best party frock.

CURRENT RELEASE *non-vintage*   Opaque purple in hue, this smells of raw, undeveloped, plummy, floral fruit. There's good-quality fruit there but it surely would have benefited from further ageing. It has a stack of flavour and tannin, and finishes with a little astringency. It needs food: try it with Chinese glazed pork.

| | |
|---|---|
| Quality | ♥♥♥♥ |
| Value | ★★★ |
| Grapes | shiraz; cabernet franc |
| Region | McLaren Vale, SA |
| Cellar | ➥ 1–5+ |
| Alc./Vol. | 14.0% |
| RRP | $22.50 |

# Hardy's Omni Red

The classic style Australian sparkling reds are aged wines. But, if they're well made, they don't have to be old to bring a lot of pleasure.

CURRENT RELEASE *non-vintage*   The colour is medium–full red/purple and it smells tantalisingly fresh – simple cherry plum ripe shiraz. It has loads of vitality and makes up in youthful exuberance for what it lacks in maturity. There's a whisper of tannin on the finish that's not quite countered by the sweetness of the dosage. Nice with meatballs in tomato sauce.

| | |
|---|---|
| Quality | ♥♥♥♥ |
| Value | ★★★★★ |
| Grapes | shiraz |
| Region | not stated |
| Cellar | 🍷 3 |
| Alc./Vol. | 14.0% |
| RRP | $10.00 Ⓢ |

# Jansz Australia Premium Cuvée

The label tells us this was based on several vintages of Jansz (presumably the Tasmanian wine) plus base wines from other cool-climate regions in Tasmania, South Australia and Victoria. It's a pretty good drink for such a schizo!

CURRENT RELEASE *non-vintage*   The colour is light yellow and it has a simple, but fresh, clean and fruity bouquet of green apple, straw and fresh nuts. It's light–medium weight and the flavours in the mouth are very satisfying. It just needs a little more oomph at the finish, but then it is good value at $20. Try it with sushi.

| | |
|---|---|
| Quality | ♥♥♥♥ |
| Value | ★★★★ |
| Grapes | not stated |
| Region | various, Tas., SA & Vic. |
| Cellar | 🍷 3 |
| Alc./Vol. | 12.0% |
| RRP | $20.00 |

## Jansz Tasmania Vintage

| | |
|---|---|
| Quality | ♙♙♙♙ |
| Value | ★★★ |
| Grapes | chardonnay; pinot noir |
| Region | Pipers Brook, Tas. |
| Cellar | 🍾 2 |
| Alc./Vol. | 13.5% |
| RRP | $35.00 |

The Jansz name is owned by Yalumba these days, and they've extended the brand with a non-vintage version which is blended from here, there and everywhere. The vintage is the original, and gets three years on lees. CURRENT RELEASE 1996    This is quite a mature wine now, and it has a complex aged bouquet of caramel and vanilla with a whiff of oak and a background of regional character peculiar to Pipers Brook, which might be described as silage or compost. The palate is high in acid but has a creamy texture and seriously complex flavour, finishing dry. It needs crab cakes.

## Joseph Sparkling Red

| | |
|---|---|
| Quality | ♙♙♙♙♙ |
| Value | ★★★⟩ |
| Grapes | mainly shiraz |
| Region | mainly Adelaide Plains, SA |
| Cellar | 🍾 7+ |
| Alc./Vol. | 13.5% |
| RRP | $55.00 |

Joe Grilli goes to a lot of trouble to make this. He uncorks old Australian dry reds to contribute extra aged character to the blend, and some vintage port in the *liqueur* for the *dosage*. It works! CURRENT RELEASE *non-vintage*    The age is unknown (and probably incalculable!), but a useful degree of maturity is reflected in the brick-red hue. There's a welter of fruitcake, plum, prune, raisin, licorice and dark chocolate aromas, and the vintage port in the liqueur peeps through. Complex, high-extract and silky smooth, it's a character-filled drink. Try it with baked honey-glazed ham.

## Killawarra Sparkling Shiraz Cabernet

| | |
|---|---|
| Quality | ♙♙♙♙ |
| Value | ★★★★ |
| Grapes | shiraz; cabernet sauvignon |
| Region | various, SA |
| Cellar | 🍾 2 |
| Alc./Vol. | 13.0% |
| RRP | $16.50 Ⓢ |

Don't bother looking for Killawarra's vineyards anywhere, it's a Southcorp brand with a commercial identity and little else. That said, the Killawarra sparkling red is always a very tidy drop and great value. CURRENT RELEASE *non-vintage*    A deep-coloured bubbly with a lively foaming appearance that delivers the goods. The nose has good intensity with sweet juicy dark berry aromas, earthy, foresty undertones and a touch of licorice to it. It tastes full and rewarding with rich fruit and good persistence of flavour.

# Knight Granite Hills Pinot Chardonnay

Like Tasmania (and Champagne for that matter), much of the Macedon region is pretty chilly for growing wine grapes. As a result getting adequate ripeness is a problem, but such cold conditions can provide ideal fruit for sparkling wines like this.
CURRENT RELEASE 1996    This was an unusually cool year that seems to have suited Llew Knight's sparkling plans. Here we have a nose and palate that suggest stone fruit, strawberry, rock candy and a hint of toasty yeast autolysis. It has richness, depth and good weight in the mouth with a dry, long finish. Serve it with smoked trout and toast.

| | |
|---|---|
| Quality | ♥♥♥♥ |
| Value | ★★★ |
| Grapes | chardonnay; pinot noir |
| Region | Macedon Ranges, Vic. |
| Cellar | 🍾 2 |
| Alc./Vol. | 12.5% |
| RRP | $39.00 |

# Lacache

Interesting wine, this! It's made in Margaret River, presumably at Cape Mentelle, by Harold Osborne, David Hohnen's Californian mate who is charged with the creation (and continuation) of Cloudy Bay's Pelorus. There's a similarity of style here . . .
CURRENT RELEASE 1995    The colour is deep yellow with a distinct brassy hue, no doubt from the red pinot noir grapes. It smells very oaky and developed. In the mouth it is rich, full-bodied, smooth and dry, but you need to like the taste of wood. Totally opposite to mainstream Oz fizz, which emphasises freshness. A very eccentric style.

| | |
|---|---|
| Quality | ♥♥♥ |
| Value | ★★★┪ |
| Grapes | pinot noir 85%; pinot blanc 15% |
| Region | Margaret River, WA |
| Cellar | 🍾 1 |
| Alc./Vol. | 13.0% |
| RRP | $30.65 |

# Miranda High Country Sparkling Chardonnay

Miranda's operation in Victoria's King Valley has inspired a lot of new wines in recent years. This new sparkler shows how versatile high country, cool-climate chardonnay can be.
CURRENT RELEASE1999    A pale, green-tinged wine with a lively sparkle, this has fresh cool-grown varietal aromas of stone fruit and citrus. The palate matches the nose well with light succulent fruit flavour and a crisp zippy finish. Good with crudités before a casual meal with friends.

| | |
|---|---|
| Quality | ♥♥♥♥ |
| Value | ★★★★ |
| Grapes | chardonnay |
| Region | King Valley, Vic. |
| Cellar | 🍾 1 |
| Alc./Vol. | 12.5% |
| RRP | $13.00 |

## Mount Eyre Neptune

| | |
|---|---|
| Quality | 🍷🍷🍷ᵞ |
| Value | ★⁺ |
| Grapes | semillon |
| Region | Hunter Valley, Vic. |
| Cellar | 🍾 2 |
| Alc./Vol. | 11.0% |
| RRP | $35.00 |

It's nice to see sparkling wines that fall outside the safe chardonnay–pinot noir make-up that's de rigueur for Aussie fizz these days. Not that we're arguing against chard and pinot; we remember how ordinary sparklers could be before they arrived – but variety is the spice of life, isn't it?

CURRENT RELEASE 2000    A pale wine with a light sparkle that isn't very lively, nor is it persistent. The nose has pleasantly fresh aromas of lemon, tart apples and a light lanolin touch that says Hunter semillon. The palate is light and reserved in fruit, with some depth of flavour but a forgettable finish. All rather underwhelming. Interesting with seafood canapés.

## Padthaway Estate Eliza Pinot Chardonnay

| | |
|---|---|
| Quality | 🍷🍷🍷🍷 |
| Value | ★★★⁺ |
| Grapes | pinot noir; |
| | chardonnay; |
| | pinot meunier |
| Region | Padthaway, SA |
| Cellar | 🍾 3 |
| Alc./Vol. | 12.5% |
| RRP | $25.00 |

Eliza and Robert Lawson were the original settlers of Padthaway Estate. Robert's memory is celebrated on Orlando's Lawson's Shiraz. Makers: Ulrich Grey-Smith and Nigel Catt.

CURRENT RELEASE 1998    The colour is very faint pink and the bouquet contains straw/hay aromas and an element of herbaceousness. It's not very complex but it has plenty of flavour with finesse and balance. It's fine and dry to taste, but not austere, and makes a lovely aperitif with gravlax trout.

## Penley Estate Pinot Noir Chardonnay

| | |
|---|---|
| Quality | 🍷🍷🍷🍷ᵞ |
| Value | ★★★★ |
| Grapes | pinot noir; |
| | chardonnay |
| Region | Coonawarra, SA |
| Cellar | 🍾 3 |
| Alc./Vol. | 11.5% |
| RRP | $34.40 |

Penley's guiding light Kym Tolley is noted for reds rather than bubbly, but this is quite a turn-up. It's his best sparkling yet, as far as we've seen. Kym should know a thing or two about the style: he made fizz for Southcorp in his younger days.

CURRENT RELEASE 1994    This is a superior sort of bubbly. Remarkably fresh and young for its age, it features melon, apple and lightly herbal aromas with an appealing overlay of yeast autolysis. It is fine and savoury with lots of secondary flavours and a smooth, dry, finely balanced finish. Serve it with freshly shelled nuts such as pistachios.

## Plunkett Chardonnay Pinot Noir

This won a gold medal at the Victorian Wines Show in 2000, and topped the bubbly class with a silver in the 2001 Boutique Wine Awards. It's had two years on lees and is 80 per cent chardonnay.

CURRENT RELEASE 1997   The colour is pale with a slightly pink tinge. The aromas are nutty and smoky and it tastes youthful for its age. There is some evidence of malolactic fermentation in its creaminess. It's pleasingly delicate, chardonnay-dominant and dry on the palate. A fine aperitif style that would go well with freshly shucked oysters.

| | |
|---|---|
| Quality | 🍷🍷🍷🍷 |
| Value | ★★★★ |
| Grapes | chardonnay; pinot noir |
| Region | Strathbogie Ranges, Vic. |
| Cellar | 🍾 2+ |
| Alc./Vol. | 12.0% |
| RRP | $25.00 (cellar door) |

## Preece Chardonnay Pinot Noir

Colin Preece would be proud to be associated with the wines that appear under his name at Mitchelton. The legendary Great Western winemaker helped set up the Mitchelton winery and vineyards in the late 1960s.

CURRENT RELEASE 1997   This had 18 months on its yeast lees and is a remarkably fine wine for the money. It shows creamy, melon and meringue aromas, while the taste is clean, light and fresh from every angle, and the finish lingers well. It's a fine aperitif, served with pistachio nuts.

| | |
|---|---|
| Quality | 🍷🍷🍷🍷 |
| Value | ★★★★ |
| Grapes | chardonnay; pinot noir |
| Region | various, Vic. |
| Cellar | 🍾 2 |
| Alc./Vol. | 12.0% |
| RRP | $19.00 ⑤ |

## Radenti Chardonnay Pinot Noir

This is Freycinet's bubbly, but the brand name is Radenti because the giant Spanish sparkling winemaker Freixenet (pronounced fresh-annette) sooled the lawyers onto Freycinet (fray-sennay) re its name. The fact that they're pronounced quite differently and one is Spanish, the other French, didn't cut any ice. This won a high silver medal at the 2001 Tasmanian Regional Wine Show.

CURRENT RELEASE 1996   It is an unusual style: a little oak has been used which is fairly evident in the coconutty aromas. The palate is very fine and long, with creamy texture and plenty of fine acidity. It finishes clean and dry. Tuna sashimi would work well.

| | |
|---|---|
| Quality | 🍷🍷🍷🍷🍷 |
| Value | ★★★⭤ |
| Grapes | chardonnay; pinot noir |
| Region | East Coast, Tas. |
| Cellar | 🍾 4+ |
| Alc./Vol. | 12.0% |
| RRP | $34.00 (cellar door) |

## Red Hill Estate Sparkling Pinot Noir Meunier Chardonnay

| | |
|---|---|
| Quality | 🍷🍷🍷🍷 |
| Value | ★★★ |
| Grapes | pinot noir; pinot meunier; chardonnay |
| Region | Mornington Peninsula, Vic. |
| Cellar | 🍾 3 |
| Alc./Vol. | 13.0% |
| RRP | $40.00 |

Whew! That's a name and a half. Fortunately it's easier to drink than say. The Red Hill Estate vineyard is better suited to sparkling than table wine, as it's located in one of the coolest parts of the Mornington Peninsula high country.

CURRENT RELEASE 1997    True to house style, this is a refined sparkler with a delicate pink colour. The bouquet features restrained strawberry-like fruit together with pastry scents, and is quite complex. The palate is soft, rich and long, ending with a cleansing flick of acidity. It would go well with sushi.

## Richmond Grove NV Brut

| | |
|---|---|
| Quality | 🍷🍷🍷 |
| Value | ★★★⯪ |
| Grapes | chardonnay; pinot noir |
| Region | not stated |
| Cellar | 🍾 1 |
| Alc./Vol. | 12.0% |
| RRP | $13.00 Ⓢ |

The natty silvery label shows the new-look Chateau Leonay with its newly built towers. Poor old Leo Buring could never afford to finish his dream Flemish castle himself.

CURRENT RELEASE *non-vintage*    This has some interesting 'champagne character' which is not really expected at the lowly price. There are candied, vanillin, cakey and raisiny aromas that get you in. The palate carries a little sweetness and is quite broad, without a lot of finesse. Goes with almond bread as an aperitif.

## Riddoch Sparkling Shiraz

| | |
|---|---|
| Quality | 🍷🍷🍷⯪ |
| Value | ★★★ |
| Grapes | shiraz |
| Region | Coonawarra, SA |
| Cellar | 🍾 3 |
| Alc./Vol. | 12.5% |
| RRP | $22.00 |

The latest issue of Riddoch wines have a subscript 'from Katnook Estate'. No doubt it's intended to enhance their appeal in the marketplace. Maker: Wayne Stehbens.

CURRENT RELEASE *non-vintage*    The base wine has been aged in oak, and it shows. The aromas are of coconut and vanilla along with herbal/celery notes and a suggestion of aldehyde. The palate flavour is fairly basic and pulls up a trifle short, with sweetness as well as a firm grip. It needs food: try it with stirfried beef in black-bean sauce.

### Rosemount Kirri Billi Pinot Chardonnay

The wine spent 23 months on its yeast lees, following secondary fermentation in the bottle. The makers are coy about the source of the grapes, fudging it with a vague 'cool areas' statement.

CURRENT RELEASE 1998    The colour is brassy to pale pink, reflecting the use of red grapes. The nose also speaks of pinot noir: smoky, earthy aromas dominate. In the mouth it's rather delicate and lacks both fruit intensity and acid zip. A lot of people will probably enjoy it for its softness, though. Try it as a solo aperitif.

| | |
|---|---|
| Quality | ♟♟♟♟ |
| Value | ★★★ |
| Grapes | pinot noir; chardonnay |
| Region | not stated |
| Cellar | ▮ 3 |
| Alc./Vol. | 12.5% |
| RRP | $25.00 |

### Rosemount Sparkling Chardonnay

The diamond label has been a big hitter for Rosemount. Is this what appeals to the baseball-mad Americans, we wonder? This relatively new addition to the range makes prominent use of the yellow diamond label.

CURRENT RELEASE *non-vintage*    This is a straightforward, simple wine with an aroma that recalls muscat or perhaps riesling, more than chardonnay. It is a fruit-driven style and cracked yeast character plays little part. There's a touch of sweetness on entry and an overtone of quince. Serve it with cream cheese and celery.

| | |
|---|---|
| Quality | ♟♟♟ |
| Value | ★★★ |
| Grapes | chardonnay |
| Region | not stated |
| Cellar | ▮ 1 |
| Alc./Vol. | 12.5% |
| RRP | $16.00 ⓢ |

### Rumball Sparkling Shiraz SB13

Peter Rumball has become a real specialist in sparkling reds. Indeed, his is almost a one-wine company. He buys fruit from various regions and blends the base wine, then gives it a couple of years on lees.

CURRENT RELEASE *non-vintage*    This edition has a deep red–purple colour showing its youth, and the aromas recall licorice, plum and confectionery, with an odd pencil-wood overtone, which may reflect some oak-age. It's quite full-bodied, with plenty of flavour, sweetness, and even a lick of tannin to finish, making it just a bit firm to slurp with gay abandon. Serve with pork spare ribs.

| | |
|---|---|
| Quality | ♟♟♟♟ |
| Value | ★★★⭒ |
| Grapes | shiraz |
| Region | various, South East Australia |
| Cellar | ▮ 8+ |
| Alc./Vol. | 12.5% |
| RRP | $21.50 |

## Seaview Blanc de Blancs Chardonnay

| | |
|---|---|
| Quality | ⚇⚇⚇⚇⚇ |
| Value | ★★★★★ |
| Grapes | chardonnay |
| Region | various, SA |
| Cellar | 🍷 1 |
| Alc./Vol. | 12.0% |
| RRP | $18.50 |

The better Seaview sparkling wines are sold in heavy, slightly skittle-like bottles to differentiate them from Seaview's supermarket cheapies. Their quality can vary from year to year, but at their best they are excellent value.

CURRENT RELEASE 1996   Persistent fine bubbles and a bright, pale colour give this wine a quality look from the outset. The bouquet is richly endowed with nutty, yeasty touches, stewed apple and cream aromas, backed up with a dab of citrus. In the mouth it's smooth and rich with good flavour development, full body and a long aftertaste. A sparkling wine for food, it works well with mushroom risotto.

## Seaview Grande Cuvée

| | |
|---|---|
| Quality | ⚇⚇⚇ |
| Value | ★★★ |
| Grapes | not stated |
| Region | various |
| Cellar | 🍷 |
| Alc./Vol. | 12.0% |
| RRP | $8.00 ⑤ |

This sparkler belongs on floor stacks in supermarkets. It won't make the earth move, or even tremble a little, but essentially there's nothing wrong with it – and it's cheap!

CURRENT RELEASE *non-vintage*   There's a neutrality about these cheap bubblies that's a virtue. When wines at this price point have 'character' it's usually offensive. There is a little personality here though, with soft grapiness, a touch of sweetness, and a clean taste that won't offend. Drink it at the yo-ho-ho sort of staff Christmas party that's usually held by a harbour, bay or river.

## Seaview Pinot Noir Chardonnay Vintage Brut

| | |
|---|---|
| Quality | ⚇⚇⚇⚇ |
| Value | ★★★ |
| Grapes | pinot noir; chardonnay |
| Region | various, SA |
| Cellar | 🍷 2 |
| Alc./Vol. | 12.5% |
| RRP | $20.80 ⑤ |

Something had to give with this wine. Either the price went up a bit or the quality came down a tad. The latter course prevailed and the last couple of vintages have been less impressive than some of the bargains of the early '90s.

CURRENT RELEASE 1998   A bright colour and fine, persistent bubble look the goods here, but the nose is disappointing with a slight stemminess intruding on red-fruit, custard and cracked yeast aromas. The palate is smooth and easy to start, but a skinsy sort of astringency comes in halfway down, making the finish a bit hard. Try it with cheese gougères.

## Seppelt Original Sparkling Shiraz

Sparkling reds almost disappeared in the1970s, a result of a complete lack of public interest in the style, rather than the arrival of cheap Cold Duck as some maintain. Seppelt kept the faith through those bad years with wines just like this one.

CURRENT RELEASE 1996    Complex aged qualities are part and parcel of the distinctive Seppelt style. Here we have earthy, tarry touches to dark, spiced plum fruit aromas. It tastes mellow and ripe in sweet berry flavours which cream across the palate, dovetailing easily into soft melted tannins at the end. A classic Australian wine to serve with Peking duck.

| | |
|---|---|
| Quality | 🍷🍷🍷🍷🍷 |
| Value | ★★★★★ |
| Grapes | shiraz |
| Region | Barossa Valley, SA & Great Western, Vic. |
| Cellar | 🍷 4 |
| Alc./Vol. | 14.0% |
| RRP | $19.00 Ⓢ |

## Seppelt Salinger

Salinger is released at five or six years of age but you wouldn't know it. It's super-fresh and full of youthful vitality.

CURRENT RELEASE 1994    The colour is a bright pale straw and the bouquet is lively. Appley fruit and understated patisserie cream aromas meet the nose. In the mouth it continues in the surprisingly youthful vein, the flavours are light and fresh and a hint of bottle ferment character hides in the background. The finish is dry and powdery. A wine to enjoy with pre-dinner nibbles.

| | |
|---|---|
| Quality | 🍷🍷🍷🍷 |
| Value | ★★★⭢ |
| Grapes | chardonnay; pinot noir |
| Region | various, South East Australia |
| Cellar | 🍷 2 |
| Alc./Vol. | 12.5% |
| RRP | $26.00 Ⓢ |

## Seppelt Show Sparkling Shiraz

Thirty years ago, these old wines used to sit around in the back of Seppelt warehouses as a curiosity for the initiated and a nuisance for the stocktakers. These days their true value is appreciated by a larger audience, and the small amounts available sell out quickly.

CURRENT RELEASE 1990    This encapsulates the aged Great Western style perfectly. The nose is complex; there are scrumptious aromas of sweet berries, plums and spicy old oak, along with savoury mushroom, leather and earthy notes. The palate is smooth and long with understated richness, controlled sweetness in the middle and a soft kiss of tannin on the finish. Try it chilled with a fancy glazed ham.

| | |
|---|---|
| Quality | 🍷🍷🍷🍷🍷 |
| Value | ★★★★ |
| Grapes | shiraz |
| Region | Great Western, Vic. |
| Cellar | 🍷 4 |
| Alc./Vol. | 13.5% |
| RRP | $65.00 |

## Stone Bridge St Allourn Cuvée

| | |
|---|---|
| Quality | 🍷🍷🍷🍷⁕ |
| Value | ★★★★★ |
| Grapes | pinot noir; chardonnay |
| Region | Great Southern, WA |
| Cellar | 🍷 2 |
| Alc./Vol. | 10.7% |
| RRP | $30.00 (cellar door) |

Stone Bridge Cuvée is an oddity – a methode champenoise sparkling wine from southern Western Australia. Winemaker Kate Hooker is a graduate of the Champagne school at Avize in France, so it's not surprising that she has put her expertise to work at her family's Manjimup vineyard. Results are very encouraging.

CURRENT RELEASE Cuvée 1997    This opens up with a fine foaming bead and a glittering light yellow–green colour. The bouquet is stylish and rich, with citrus, vanilla cream, strawberry and slightly herbal notes providing a promising introduction. Despite relatively low alcohol, the palate has enough intensity. It's clean-tasting with attractive flavour and creamy texture leading through to a dry, slightly firm finish.

## Taltarni Brut

| | |
|---|---|
| Quality | 🍷🍷🍷 |
| Value | ★★★★ |
| Grapes | chardonnay; pinot noir; pinot meunier |
| Region | Pyrenees, Vic. & Pipers Brook, Tas. |
| Cellar | 🍷 2 |
| Alc./Vol. | 13.0% |
| RRP | $19.50 |

In its early days this was known as Cuvée Dalys and was a non-vintage. Now it's a blend of Pyrenees and Tasmanian fruit, which makes a lot of sense as the Pyrenees is best suited to red table wines. It's had 18 months on lees.

CURRENT RELEASE 1998    This is a very delicate, even slightly bland, sparkler which has a light brassy–yellow colour and a bready, nutty, caramel, confectionery bouquet. The balance is good and it's dry and smooth. Just don't overchill it: you'll kill the flavour. Good with sautéed yabbies.

## Taltarni Brut Taché

| | |
|---|---|
| Quality | 🍷🍷🍷 |
| Value | ★★★★ |
| Grapes | chardonnay; pinot noir; pinot meunier |
| Region | Pyrenees, Vic. & Pipers Brook, Tas. |
| Cellar | 🍷 2 |
| Alc./Vol. | 13.0% |
| RRP | $19.50 |

Apologies to those who've read it before, but taché means 'stained' in French. (Doesn't sound all that appealing, but perhaps it's a poor translation.) This refers to the colour: it's basically a white bubbly tinted with a little red wine.

CURRENT RELEASE 1998    The colour is a dirty stain – oops – we mean an attractive light salmon pink with a youthful purple tinge! Lightly smoky overtones mingle with simple cherry, melon and apple aromas. A pleasing flavour but it's mainly on the front palate: it falls away at the finish. Good drinking with whitebait.

## Tamar Ridge Josef Chromy Selection

At five years, this is still a baby, and was no doubt selected as the flagship wine because of its long ageing potential. It was released in mid-2001. Beef baron Joe Chromy is the owner.

CURRENT RELEASE 1996 There's a certain 'young Champagne' style about this wine, which explains why sparkling winemakers are so excited about Tassie grapes. It's still a delicate, tart, jumpy youngster, showing a little sulfur when we tried it, but the palate has great length and texture, and it promises to develop into a superb bubbly. It cries out for tuna sashimi with truffle oil.

| | |
|---|---|
| **Quality** | 🍷🍷🍷🍷½ |
| **Value** | ★★★½ |
| **Grapes** | pinot noir 100% |
| **Region** | Pipers River, Tas. |
| **Cellar** | 1–5+ |
| **Alc./Vol.** | 12.0% |
| **RRP** | $36.00 |

## Tamar Ridge RV Sparkling

RV stands for Rochecombe Vineyard. This was all sold in Tassie, but it won the trophy for best sparkling wine at the 2001 Tasmanian Regional Wine Show, so we include it for the record. It's a graphic example of how well a fine Tassie base wine can age and improve with extended time on lees.

CURRENT RELEASE 1995 The aromas are creamy, smoky and vanilla, reminding strongly of pinot noir, with some pastry-like overtones. The palate is superb: very fine, creamy, subtle and long, a sparkling of excellent balance and refinement. It goes well with sushi.

| | |
|---|---|
| **Quality** | 🍷🍷🍷🍷🍷 |
| **Value** | ★★★★ |
| **Grapes** | pinot noir; chardonnay |
| **Region** | Pipers River, Tas. |
| **Cellar** | 3+ |
| **Alc./Vol.** | 12.0% |
| **RRP** | $25.00 |

## Tempus Two Sparkling Chardonnay

This brand, owned by McGuigan Brothers but with Lisa McGuigan and Veronica Lourey heading it up, is based in the Hunter Valley. They are planning to build a winery/restaurant/cellar door outlet very soon.

CURRENT RELEASE 1997 The pewter label and slick packaging more than do the wine justice. It's a full yellow, developed, rather broad style with herbal and apricot jam aromas. The palate is broad and fairly straightforward, with a distinct lack of subtlety. Chill well and serve with smoked oysters.

| | |
|---|---|
| **Quality** | 🍷🍷½ |
| **Value** | ★★½ |
| **Grapes** | chardonnay |
| **Region** | not stated |
| **Cellar** | 1 |
| **Alc./Vol.** | 12.5% |
| **RRP** | $25.00 (S) |

## Wayne Thomas Card Table Cabernet Franc

| | |
|---|---|
| Quality | 🍷🍷🍷🍷 |
| Value | ★★★ |
| Grapes | cabernet franc |
| Region | McLaren Vale, SA |
| Cellar | 🍷 3 |
| Alc./Vol. | 14.0% |
| RRP | $41.50 |

McLaren Vale identity Wayne Thomas established Thomas Fern Hill wines in the 1970s and set up the Wayne Thomas operation after selling Fern Hill in the '90s. Fruit for the wines comes entirely from contract growers.

CURRENT RELEASE 1997   Effervescence is a bit less explosive than in most red bubbly, and the nose has traditional ripe plum and berry aromas, spices, licorice and dusty oak. The palate has good balance with earthy, almost shiraz-like fruit intermingling with subtle old oak flavours. Sweetness is well controlled, texture is smooth, and soft tannins support a long, tasty finish. Try it with pork and black beans.

## Wyndham Estate Vintage Chardonnay Brut

| | |
|---|---|
| Quality | 🍷🍷🍷 |
| Value | ★★★★ |
| Grapes | chardonnay |
| Region | not stated |
| Cellar | 🍷 1 |
| Alc./Vol. | 12.0% |
| RRP | $13.50 ⓢ |

As chardonnay plantings have expanded in Australia, they have provided makers of sparkling wines with much better base material than the hotch-potch they used before.

**CURRENT RELEASE 1999   This is good fizz at a good price. The nose has clean apple and citrus chardonnay aromas, along with a hint of biscuity bottle-ferment character. It tastes pleasantly smooth and easy with reasonable length and relatively soft acidity. Well suited to the party crowd.**

Penguin Best
Bargain
Bubbly

## Yarra Burn Pinot Noir Chardonnay Pinot Meunier

| | |
|---|---|
| Quality | 🍷🍷🍷🍷 |
| Value | ★★★⭒ |
| Grapes | pinot noir; |
| | chardonnay; |
| | pinot meunier |
| Region | Yarra Valley, Vic. |
| Cellar | 🍷 3 |
| Alc./Vol. | 12.5% |
| RRP | $21.65 ⓢ |

The name is quite a mouthful, but they are giving the consumer plenty of info regarding the exact grape varieties.

CURRENT RELEASE 1999   Pale in colour with a fine bead, this has attractive fresh pear, citrus and herb aromas with hints of fresh bready yeast, leading to a smoothly textured palate that's long and fine flavoured. It seems a little riper than previous examples, yet it still finishes with a brisk tang. Serve it as a pre-dinner drink with some crudités.

## Yellowglen Red

This product was launched with a black and white (and red) press ad featuring a young woman in a red bra and red knickers trying things on in a clothes store . . . the point of it escapes us completely.
CURRENT RELEASE *non-vintage*    A straightforward sparkling red with a fruit-of-the-forest nose and a slight aroma of licorice. The palate is soft and reasonably intense with a smooth texture enhanced by sweetness. Moderate, balanced tannins complete the picture nicely. If you like you can wear red undies when you try it, and if that makes you feel adventurous, serve it as a dessert wine with profiteroles and chocolate sauce. Really.

| | |
|---|---|
| Quality | ♟ ♟ ♟ |
| Value | ★ ★ ★ |
| Grapes | not stated |
| Region | not stated |
| Cellar | ▮ 1 |
| Alc./Vol. | 13.0% |
| RRP | $12.00 Ⓢ |

## Yellowglen Y Sparkling Burgundy

Yellowglen must be about the only mob who still call their sparkling red Sparkling Burgundy. It's not really P.C. to do so and soon use of the French wine name 'burgundy' will be outlawed in line with trade regulations and so forth.
CURRENT RELEASE *non-vintage*    Rather like a semi-dry red table wine with bubbles, this wine is a satisfying amalgam of ripe blackberry fruit, mint, meaty aromas, savoury spices and sweet vanilla/coconut oak in a medium-bodied package. Nose and palate don't have much subtlety but that's not what sparkling burg is all about. It tastes smooth, ripe and sweetish, finishing dry with slightly grippy tannins. Try it with pork rillettes and brioche.

| | |
|---|---|
| Quality | ♟ ♟ ♟ ♟ |
| Value | ★ ★ ★ ⁴ |
| Grapes | not stated |
| Region | not stated |
| Cellar | ▮ 3 |
| Alc./Vol. | 13.5% |
| RRP | $22.50 |

# Fortified Wines

## All Saints Classic Rutherglen Muscat

| | |
|---|---|
| Quality | ♟♟♟♟ |
| Value | ★★★♪ |
| Grapes | red frontignac |
| Region | Rutherglen, Vic. |
| Cellar | ⬧ |
| Alc./Vol. | 18.0% |
| RRP | $24.00 (500 ml) |

A new muscat blend from All Saints. Although there was a 'Classic' in the old range, it has become the 'Grand', and now this is the new Classic. Confused? See All Saints Grand Rutherglen Tokay.

CURRENT RELEASE *non-vintage* This has a more open, grapey personality than the older All Saints fortified blends. It has a mahogany colour suggesting some age and an attractive nose of raisined muscatels, Turkish delight and vanilla with some earthy notes. The palate follows suit, sweet and grapey with some earthy spirit input and a clean finish. Try this with a cheese platter.

## All Saints Grand Rutherglen Muscat

| | |
|---|---|
| Quality | ♟♟♟♟♟ |
| Value | ★★★★ |
| Grapes | red frontignac |
| Region | Rutherglen, Vic. |
| Cellar | ⬧ |
| Alc./Vol. | 18.0% |
| RRP | $32.00 (375 ml) |

All Saints fortified wines have undergone a revamp in line with the new Rutherglen labelling protocols. Nothing wrong with that, but why did they drop stylish packaging in favour of cheap-looking bright red and orange labels? Thankfully the wines transcend the tacky presentation.

CURRENT RELEASE *non-vintage* Mahogany colour and great viscosity suggest some very old, special material in this blend. The nose confirms it with syrupy toffee, honey, concentrated muscatel and Saunders Malt Extract aromas (we're showing our age here!). The gorgeously intense palate has deeply reduced essency raisin and grilled nut flavours that are long and luscious. A grown-up experience with soft blue cheese and fruit bread.

## All Saints Grand Rutherglen Tokay

This used to be labelled 'Classic', but when new terminology was put in place to describe the age and quality of Rutherglen fortifieds, this solera was substantially above the Classic requirements.
CURRENT RELEASE *non-vintage* A mouth-filling, luscious tokay with moderate oak and rancio characters dominated by syrupy, malty, sweet tea and honey aromas, ahead of a big raisiny, lush and sweet palate. It lingers rich and long on the palate, all concentration and strength. Try it with vanilla-bean ice cream for a decadent grown-up sundae-type experience.

| | |
|---|---|
| Quality | 🍷🍷🍷🍷🍷 |
| Value | ★★★★ |
| Grapes | muscadelle |
| Region | Rutherglen, Vic. |
| Cellar | 🍾 |
| Alc./Vol. | 18.0% |
| RRP | $32.00 (375 ml) |

## All Saints Rare Rutherglen Muscat

Under Brown Brothers ownership initially, and then just Peter Brown on his own, the old All Saints vineyards and winery have been given a new lease of life. The fortified wines are consistently among Rutherglen's best.
CURRENT RELEASE *non-vintage* Some wines in this blend are over 50 years old and you can see it in the walnut-brown colour and smell it on the intensely concentrated nose. Nose and palate share wonderful ultra-complex raisined sweetness with hints of orange peel, toffee, floral perfume and roasted nuts. It finishes long and fine. All Saints describe this as a 'Rutherglen masterpiece' and we won't contradict them on that. Serve it with some muscatels and nuts.

| | |
|---|---|
| Quality | 🍷🍷🍷🍷🍷 |
| Value | ★★★★ |
| Grapes | red frontignac |
| Region | Rutherglen, Vic. |
| Cellar | 🍾 |
| Alc./Vol. | 18.0% |
| RRP | $65.00 (375 ml) |

## All Saints Rare Rutherglen Tokay

Awful new packaging may have sabotaged the appearance of the All Saints fortified wines, but the quality remains superb.
CURRENT RELEASE *non-vintage* A syrupy brownish–khaki colour indicates great age, and so does the super-concentrated bouquet. It is exquisitely complex: a delicious cocktail of syrupy malt-toffee, raisins and roasted nuts. The palate reproduces those wonderful scents, profound and lusciously sweet but remaining clean and uncloying. The aftertaste lasts for yonks. Sip it on its own with espresso coffee.

| | |
|---|---|
| Quality | 🍷🍷🍷🍷🍷 |
| Value | ★★★★ |
| Grapes | muscadelle |
| Region | Rutherglen, Vic. |
| Cellar | 🍾 |
| Alc./Vol. | 18.0% |
| RRP | $65.00 (375 ml) |

## Angoves Fino Dry Flor

| | |
|---|---|
| Quality | 🍷🍷🍷 |
| Value | ★★★★ |
| Grapes | pedro ximenez; palomino |
| Region | Murray Valley, SA |
| Cellar | 🍶 |
| Alc./Vol. | 16.0% |
| RRP | $14.90 |

Angoves Fino has long languished on bottle-shop shelves, known only to a few eccentric sherry fans.
CURRENT RELEASE *non-vintage*  This is a less penetrating, more 'winey' sherry style than the best Spanish examples or Aussie wines like Seppelt. The full nose still has good nutty characters derived from flor yeast and oak age, but it's not as savoury as the best. The softer, fuller feel continues on the palate where nutty, yeasty flavours end in an appetising dry tang. Try it with assorted tapas.

## Baileys Founder Tawny Port

| | |
|---|---|
| Quality | 🍷🍷🍷 |
| Value | ★★⊣ |
| Grapes | not stated |
| Region | North East Vic. |
| Cellar | 🍶 |
| Alc./Vol. | 18.0% |
| RRP | $20.50 Ⓢ |

Baileys is located in the Warby Ranges near Glenrowan, scene of Ned Kelly's last stand. For the benefit of foreigners, Kelly was Australia's most famous bushranger, which is to say, highwayman and outlaw. It says something about Australians that they made him a folk hero.
CURRENT RELEASE *non-vintage*  The wine is a straightforward young-ish style, smelling of dusty, dry leather and caramel. It is quite sweet and syrupy to taste, a little lumpy and the finish fails to really satisfy. The muscats and tokays from this maker are better.

## Brown Brothers Reserve Muscat

| | |
|---|---|
| Quality | 🍷🍷🍷🍷 |
| Value | ★★★★★ |
| Grapes | red frontignac |
| Region | North East Vic. |
| Cellar | 🍶 |
| Alc./Vol. | 18.0% |
| RRP | $16.70 |

Penguin Best Bargain Fortified

The Brown brethren recently had a reshuffle in the team, and Ross Brown is now chief executive while John Brown junior becomes chairman. Browns is still a model family wine company.
**CURRENT RELEASE *non-vintage*  Never mind the price, this is amazing value for money. It seems to have received a substantial boost of older material recently, to give it extra richness and depth. The bouquet features intense muscat fruit together with a lovely rancio touch, and the mouth has layered, smooth malt/toffee richness that lingers on and on. Amazing value! Serve with creamy blue cheese, such as blue castello.**

## Brown Brothers Reserve Port

Odd that the word reserve appears on a $13 bottle of port. Could it be a throwback to the rather dated notion of Royal Reserve port?

CURRENT RELEASE *non-vintage*   Not too much ancient reserve stock involved in this. It's a youthful, fruity, slightly muscat-scented port which is good value for money. The colour is medium amber–tawny, and it is simple, sweet and grapey. You do find the cheaper ports are nearly always the sweetest. Sip with a Cuban cigar and strong espresso.

| | |
|---|---|
| Quality | ♉♉♉♉ |
| Value | ★★★★ |
| Grapes | not stated |
| Region | North East Vic. |
| Cellar | ♦ |
| Alc./Vol. | 18.0% |
| RRP | $13.50 |

## Brown Brothers Very Old Muscat

There is no law governing the use of names such as 'very old' on wine labels. Suffice to say, the more reputable wineries always give good value, and in Browns' case, these words signify their oldest and best fortifieds.

CURRENT RELEASE *non-vintage*   The colour is like burnished walnut; the bouquet is very complex, with deep raisiny muscat-fruit aromas plus toffee and rancio aged characters. It has excellent depth of flavour in the mouth and waves of complexities that keep you fascinated to the last drop. Delicious with brandied figs and mascarpone.

| | |
|---|---|
| Quality | ♉♉♉♉♉ |
| Value | ★★★★ |
| Grapes | red frontignac |
| Region | North East Vic. |
| Cellar | ♦ |
| Alc./Vol. | 18.0% |
| RRP | $34.60 |

## Brown Brothers Very Old Port

A lot of people assume the name of this company referred to the brothers John, Roger, Peter and Ross. Not so. It was the previous generation, but in fact the business was only big enough in those days to support one brother: John Charles Brown, the recently retired chairman.

CURRENT RELEASE *non-vintage*   The back label declares it's an average seven years of age, and the taste is in keeping with that. It has a darkish tawny colour and a youthful, but slightly muffled, red-grape, fruity aroma. It's again rich and sweet on the palate, with youthful red-fruit flavours, and would benefit from some older material in the blend. Try it with King Island cheddar.

| | |
|---|---|
| Quality | ♉♉♉♉ |
| Value | ★★★ |
| Grapes | not stated |
| Region | North East Vic. |
| Cellar | ♦ |
| Alc./Vol. | 18.0% |
| RRP | $25.45 |

## Brown Brothers Very Old Tokay

| | |
|---|---|
| Quality | ♟♟♟♟ |
| Value | ★★★♪ |
| Grapes | muscadelle |
| Region | North East Vic. |
| Cellar | ♦ |
| Alc./Vol. | 18.0% |
| RRP | $34.60 |

The Browns consider there are rare benefits in being a family-owned wine company. They've clubbed together with other distinguished family wineries from other countries to form a mutually supportive, information-sharing group.

CURRENT RELEASE *non-vintage*   This is a youthful but thoroughly delicious tokay that faithfully displays the true essence of the style. It has a medium amber–orange hue, and an aromatic bouquet featuring tea leaves, malt extract and Turkish delight. The taste is lollyish with a finish that remains very sweet. Try it with strong coffee on the side.

## Campbells Liquid Gold Tokay

| | |
|---|---|
| Quality | ♟♟♟♟♪ |
| Value | ★★★ |
| Grapes | muscadelle |
| Region | Rutherglen, Vic. |
| Cellar | ♦ |
| Alc./Vol. | 17.5% |
| RRP | $40.00 (500 ml) |

Attractive packaging and labelling has improved the 'feel' of Campbells products in the marketplace in recent years. The Liquid Gold fortifieds are a good example.

CURRENT RELEASE *non-vintage*   This is such an easy-drinking fortified wine that you should take great care with it. It doesn't have much wood-aged character, but that's offest by its intense varietal character and smooth, luxurious texture. Fresh tea, honey and butterscotch tokay characters are there, and clean, integrated spirit matches it perfectly. Sip this with a good friend you'd like to know better.

## Campbells Rutherglen Muscat

| | |
|---|---|
| Quality | ♟♟♟♟ |
| Value | ★★★♪ |
| Grapes | red frontignac |
| Region | Rutherglen, Vic. |
| Cellar | ♦ |
| Alc./Vol. | 17.5% |
| RRP | $18.95 (375 ml) |

Campbells' basic Rutherglen Muscat and Tokay are smartly packaged in classy-looking clear half-bottles that look good on any table. This is aimed at broadening the wines' appeal and it works.

CURRENT RELEASE *non-vintage*   The colour says 'young' – a light red with a tawny–pink edge, and the nose is straightforward with an attractive raisined/grapey perfume with a hint of Turkish delight. The palate is sweet and simple with light, grapey flavours of good intensity. It doesn't have the oomph of the classics, but you can't drink them all the time and this freshness is a real plus. Sip it casually with a plate of cheese.

## Campbells Rutherglen Tokay

The Campbells fortified wines simply labelled 'Rutherglen' are made from fresh young material without the complexity that long cask-age can bring. CURRENT RELEASE *non-vintage* This is a delicious example of young tokay, uncomplicated by the gorgeous complexities of age maybe, but with a distinctive appeal of its own. It's light golden–amber in colour with a bouquet of sweet cold tea and homemade toffee. The flavour is harmonious with a lush, but not heavy, texture and a long sweet finish. Try it chilled with ice cream.

| | |
|---|---|
| Quality | 🍷🍷🍷🍷 |
| Value | ★★★★ |
| Grapes | muscadelle |
| Region | Rutherglen, Vic. |
| Cellar | 🍾 |
| Alc./Vol. | 17.5% |
| RRP | $18.95 (375 ml) |

## Chambers Special Muscat

Bill Chambers is a Rutherglen legend who makes some of the region's richest and most profound wines. He had a lot to do with the prestige image (and prices) some of the wines now enjoy.
CURRENT RELEASE *non-vintage* A classic Rutherglen with a middling amber–red colour and a penetrating varietal bouquet of concentrated crushed raisins, malt-toffee and vanilla. The complex palate has super-intense raisiny flavour and nuttiness, tangy acidity and a finish that lasts for ages. A delicious thing to have with nougat and good coffee.

| | |
|---|---|
| Quality | 🍷🍷🍷🍷🍷 |
| Value | ★★★★ |
| Grapes | red frontignac |
| Region | Rutherglen, Vic. |
| Cellar | 🍾 |
| Alc./Vol. | 18.0% |
| RRP | $30.00 (375 ml) (cellar door) |

## Chambers Special Tokay

Bill Chambers is a master with tokay too. By the way, the original tokay wine was an unfortified, botrytised sweet white from Hungary, served to the czars in crystal flasks. Aussie tokay is a fortified made from the French muscadelle variety.
CURRENT RELEASE *non-vintage* This is an extraordinary, hard-to-find wine with a walnut-brownish amber colour of great depth with an olive-coloured edge to it. The bouquet is concentrated with malt, burnt toffee, syrupy tea and mocha characters. There's even a whisper of anchovy about it (no, we're not going crazy), and the palate has an exotic sweetness, great length and a savoury meaty note. Amazingly good. Try it with soft blue cheese and accompaniments.

| | |
|---|---|
| Quality | 🍷🍷🍷🍷🍷 |
| Value | ★★★★┤ |
| Grapes | muscadelle |
| Region | Rutherglen, Vic. |
| Cellar | 🍾 |
| Alc./Vol. | 18.0% |
| RRP | $50.00 (375 ml) |

## D'Arenberg Nostalgia Rare Tawny

Quality 🍷🍷🍷🍷½
Value ★★★½
Grapes grenache; shiraz; mourvèdre; pedro ximenez; muscat of Alexandria
Region McLaren Vale, SA
Cellar 🍾
Alc./Vol. 19.5%
RRP $35.00 (375 ml)

Funny how ports have names like Club, Show, Director's Special, Old Boys and Nostalgia. It all reeks of fusty, smoky men's clubs and ancient leather armchairs. It does nothing to open up the port market to young people and women.

CURRENT RELEASE *non-vintage* This is a very fine 12-year-old, and we can just picture portly old men with cigars shlocking it away beneath a portrait of the Queen. It has a lovely sweet vanilla/honey bouquet and mellow, elegant and lingering flavour with a clean dry finish. Beaut with Tim Tams.

## D'Arenberg Vintage Fortified Shiraz

Quality 🍷🍷🍷🍷
Value ★★★½
Grapes shiraz
Region McLaren Vale, SA
Cellar 3–20+
Alc./Vol. 18.5%
RRP $21.30 (375 ml)

We reviewed this last year but it's still available, and because it's so good we're sending it around again. Maker: Chester 'Wild Thing' Osborn.

CURRENT RELEASE 1998 This is a serious vintage port style. The colour is very dark purple–red and it smells of bell-clear blackberry fruit mingling with fine spirit, which lends a beguiling licorice/anise note. It's a vibrant, and very big, concentrated, tannic youngster that needs a lot of cellar-time. Lock it away and, when mature, drink with stilton.

## Galway Pipe 20 Year Old Tawny Port

Quality 🍷🍷🍷🍷🍷
Value ★★★★★
Grapes various
Region Barossa Valley, SA
Cellar 🍾
Alc./Vol. 17.5%
RRP $45.00

This is a special edition bottled to commemorate the arrival of the twenty-first century. Given the slow speed with which port leaves the shelves, there's still a bit around and it's still fresh.

CURRENT RELEASE *non-vintage* Twenty years in barrel has given this wine a true tawny colour. The nose is complex with rich aromas of peel, toffee, spice, roasted nut rancio and lovely brandified spirit. The palate is sweet and intense with luscious clean flavours of dried fruits, nuts and soft spirit. It's a lovely after-dinner drink.

## Grant Burge 20 Year Old Tawny Port

The decline in port consumption has left old relics like this fortified wine gently ageing away in the forgotten corners of wineries.

CURRENT RELEASE *non-vintage*    This smart package is one of a handful of newly released fortifieds from Grant Burge. It's bright tawny in colour with a lot of rancio character on the nose giving a nutty tone to raisiny aged fruit and old oak aromas. The palate has richness and depth with sweet dried fruit and chocolatey scorched-almond flavours. It finishes fine, long and clean.

| | |
|---|---|
| Quality | 🍷🍷🍷🍷🍷 |
| Value | ★★★★ |
| Grapes | grenache; mourvèdre; shiraz |
| Region | Barossa Valley, SA |
| Cellar | 🍾 |
| Alc./Vol. | 20.0% |
| RRP | $30.00 |

## Hardys Show Port

This wine harks back to the days when wineries mixed up special blends to enter in the wine shows. Often, the show blend was not actually available for sale. This was, and some of the earlier releases had vintage dates. The oldest the authors can remember drinking was the 1954.

CURRENT RELEASE *non-vintage*    Another beautiful port from BRL Hardy, albeit in a more oaky style. The bouquet is somewhat vanilla-dominant, but the great depth and complexity of really old base wine shines through. It's quite rich and full-bodied in the mouth, showing fruit as well as heaps of age. Wonderful flavour and enormous length. Perfect when sipped around a roaring log fire in the snowfields.

| | |
|---|---|
| Quality | 🍷🍷🍷🍷🍷 |
| Value | ★★★★ |
| Grapes | not stated |
| Region | McLaren Vale, SA |
| Cellar | 🍾 |
| Alc./Vol. | 19.0% |
| RRP | $43.00 |

## Haselgrove 'H' VP Shiraz

| | |
|---|---|
| Quality | ▼▼▼▼⁵ |
| Value | ★★★⁴ |
| Grapes | shiraz |
| Region | McLaren Vale, SA |
| Cellar | ➡ 3–15+ |
| Alc./Vol. | 19.5% |
| RRP | $41.00 (375 ml) 🍾 |

Haselgrove was, until mid-2001, a subsidiary of the public wine company Cranswick Estate, along with Alambie Wines (including the Salisbury Estate label). It's quite coincidental that the winemaker is a Haselgrove – Nick. It'll soon be illegal to name a wine 'port', hence the initials VP here.

CURRENT RELEASE 1999    This is an excellent young vintage port style, clean and vital with loads of sweet berry flavour and balanced sweetness. There is tannin on the finish but it's not overdone: you can drink the wine young if you like. The aromas are of clean floral spirit and ripe plum/blackberry fruit. Serve with stilton cheese.

| | |
|---|---|
| Quality | ▼▼▼▼ |
| Value | ★★★ |
| Grapes | shiraz |
| Region | McLaren Vale, SA |
| Cellar | ➡ 2–12+ |
| Alc./Vol. | 19.0% |
| RRP | $39.00 (375 ml) 🍾 |

CURRENT RELEASE 1997    The current release VP is a more serious style than the '99, with firmer tannins and a fair grip to the finish. There's a slightly fatty spirit aroma and it's starting to show mellow, developed characters, with shy aniseed and berry touches. Best cellared further, but can be enjoyed with a creamy blue cheese such as Meredith.

## Joseph The Fronti IV

| | |
|---|---|
| Quality | ▼▼▼▼ |
| Value | ★★★ |
| Grapes | frontignac |
| Region | Adelaide Plains, SA |
| Cellar | 🍾 |
| Alc./Vol. | 18.5% |
| RRP | $49.00 |

This is kinda like a dry tawny port, but made from frontignac, the same grape as Rutherglen dessert-style muscat. It tastes quite different, though. 'IV' doesn't mean you take it intravenously: it's the fourth blend of the wine.

CURRENT RELEASE non-vintage    A good fortified, although lacking the intense muscat-fruit aromatics of the Rutherglen model. The colour is medium–full amber, with orange tints. The bouquet is subdued vanilla, fruitcake and caramel without great depth of rancio character. It breathes to display some tea-leafy aromas. Soft and smooth in the mouth, well balanced, and less sweet, therefore less overpowering, than a liqueur muscat. It goes with dried fruits and nuts.

## Lauriston Show Port

This is a brand of the BRL Hardy empire. It was acquired via the Berri Renmano Ltd stable, swallowed by Hardys years ago. It's now but a memory, represented by the B, R and L.

**CURRENT RELEASE** *non-vintage* It's always been a great port, and continues thus. The nose is jam-packed with complex rancio scents, slightly lifted and very forceful, with great mellowness and balance. In the mouth, it is superbly harmonious, rich and nicely dry finishing, with a tremendously long aftertaste. Sip sparingly with the finest chocolates you can buy.

| | |
|---|---|
| Quality | 🍷🍷🍷🍷🍷 |
| Value | ★★★★ |
| Grapes | not stated |
| Region | Murray Valley, SA |
| Cellar | 🍷 |
| Alc./Vol. | 19.0% |
| RRP | $29.00 (500 ml) Ⓢ |

## Lindemans Celebration Spirit Tawny Port

This is a special blend, bottled for the Sydney XXVII Olympiad, for which Lindemans shelled out zillions of dollars to be the exclusive sponsor.

**CURRENT RELEASE** *non-vintage* **A lovely port indeed, and – as you might hope – a great ambassador for Australia. It has a medium–light amber hue with a yellow rim, and smells wonderfully complex and aged, with hints of old amontillado sherry and heaps of rancio. The flavour is concentrated and intense, revealing a generous dollop of very old material, and it has layer upon layer of complex flavours that resonate in the mouth long after it's gone. Drink with pride.**

| | |
|---|---|
| Quality | 🍷🍷🍷🍷🍷 |
| Value | ★★★★★ |
| Grapes | shiraz; grenache |
| Region | not stated |
| Cellar | 🍷 |
| Alc./Vol. | 19.5% |
| RRP | $26.00 |

 Penguin Best Fortified Wine

## Lindemans Macquarie Tawny Port

Lindemans was a New South Wales-based company for most of its existence; no doubt that's why they decided to name a port after an early Governor of the colony. But, shame and scandal, this is a Barossa Valley wine. Glory be.

**CURRENT RELEASE** *non-vintage* It's hard to imagine being disappointed by Macquarie, it's been consistently good for so long. Generous raisiny fruit and a background of aged rancio character result in considerable complexity. It would go down well with coffee and after-dinner mints.

| | |
|---|---|
| Quality | 🍷🍷🍷🍷 |
| Value | ★★★★⁺ |
| Grapes | grenache; shiraz |
| Region | Barossa Valley, SA |
| Cellar | 🍷 |
| Alc./Vol. | 19.0% |
| RRP | $12.50 Ⓢ |

## Morris 'Canister' Liqueur Muscat

| | |
|---|---|
| Quality | ♥ ♥ ♥ ♥ ♥ |
| Value | ★ ★ ★ ★ ★ |
| Grapes | red frontignac |
| Region | Rutherglen, Vic. |
| Cellar | ╽ |
| Alc./Vol. | 17.5% |
| RRP | $16.50 (500 ml) |

There are very few poor fortifieds made in Rutherglen, even in the lower-graded younger wines. These Morris wines, known unofficially as the 'Canister' range because of the cylindrical tubes they are packed in, are excellent examples of what we mean.

CURRENT RELEASE *non-vintage*    Fresh grapey sweetness is the thing with this type of Rutherglen muscat, and this one delivers as well as any. This has a bright ruddy colour, and a lively nose of intense raisin aromas with floral hints. It tastes sweet and luscious with the bouquet repeated perfectly in intense raisiny grapiness. The finish is long and fragrant. Serve it with blue cheese, nuts and fruit bread.

## Morris 'Canister' Liqueur Tokay

| | |
|---|---|
| Quality | ♥ ♥ ♥ ♥ ♥ |
| Value | ★ ★ ★ ★ ★ |
| Grapes | muscadelle |
| Region | Rutherglen, Vic. |
| Cellar | ╽ |
| Alc./Vol. | 17.5% |
| RRP | $16.50 (500 ml) |

Which do you prefer, tokay or muscat? It's useless asking us, we're besotted by both of them.

CURRENT RELEASE *non-vintage*    Bright amber in colour, this wine continues the great Morris tradition. It has the essential tokay personality in a fresh, intense package. Those wood-aged characteristics of great old wines are largely lacking here, instead it has the immediate charm of tea-leaf, honey and caramel varietal aromas and flavours, lush sweetness and a tangy signature. Try with petits fours and coffee.

## Morris Old Premium Amontillado Sherry

| | |
|---|---|
| Quality | ♥ ♥ ♥ ♥ ♥ |
| Value | ★ ★ ★ ★ ⅋ |
| Grapes | palomino; |
| | pedro ximimez |
| Region | Rutherglen, Vic. |
| Cellar | ╽ |
| Alc./Vol. | 22.0% |
| RRP | $46.00 (500 ml) |

Only a handful of Australian wineries persevere with sherry these days. Morris's occasional releases maintain the faith well.

CURRENT RELEASE *non-vintage*    This superb Australian sherry style has balance and finesse. The brilliant amber liquid glistens invitingly in the glass. Vanilla, nutty and toffee-like aromas indicate long wood-age, while a fresh whiff of flor yeastiness gives it an appetising tang. The palate has a suggestion of sweetness yet the overall impression is savoury, clean and dry with good depth, bracing acidity and a persistent, mouth-watering finish. A brilliant aperitif, but also at home with classic soups like consommé.

## Morris Old Premium Liqueur Muscat

Some would say that the Morris Old Premiums are the archetypal essence of Rutherglen Liqueur wines; they have a point.

CURRENT RELEASE *non-vintage* This has the deep olive-tinged mahogany colour and great viscosity that indicates a blend containing the oldest and best material. The bouquet and palate have concentrated aged raisin, nutty rancio, mocha and toffee characters, with a deep satin and velvet texture. The palate is exquisite, with extraordinary complexity and length, yet it's fresh and tangy at the same time. We can see why this is a wine by which others are judged. A wine for coffee and contemplation.

| | |
|---|---|
| **Quality** | 🍷🍷🍷🍷🍷 |
| **Value** | ***** |
| **Grapes** | red frontignac |
| **Region** | Rutherglen, Vic. |
| **Cellar** | 🍾 |
| **Alc./Vol.** | 17.5% |
| **RRP** | $46.00 (500 ml) |

## Morris Old Premium Liqueur Tokay

One of the secrets of producing great Rutherglen fortifieds is the art of blending old with new. The Morris clan have had it mastered for generations.

CURRENT RELEASE *non-vintage* Dark walnut in colour with an olive-green edge, this looks the goods. It reminds us a wee bit of the Saunders Malt Extract that propelled toddlers a generation or two ago, or maybe we're waxing nostalgic. There's also the complex cold tea, vanilla and roasted almond aromas of a great tokay blend. The palate is a tour de force with concentration, depth and complexity of flavour. The finish lasts and lasts and lasts . . . Serve it on its own in homage to the winemakers of Rutherglen.

| | |
|---|---|
| **Quality** | 🍷🍷🍷🍷🍷 |
| **Value** | ***** |
| **Grapes** | muscadelle |
| **Region** | Rutherglen, Vic. |
| **Cellar** | 🍾 |
| **Alc./Vol.** | 18.0% |
| **RRP** | $46.00 (500 ml) |

## Normans King William 12 Year Old Tawny

Normans is a South Australian company whose origins lie in the capital city Adelaide itself. The main drag in Adelaide is King William Street.

CURRENT RELEASE *non-vintage* We tried two bottles and both showed an aroma we pedants refer to as 'vinegar fly'. It won't bother most drinkers: the wine is otherwise full of character and genuine aged flavour, and will bring pleasure to almost everyone. It is mellow, soft, sweet and gentle: a decent drink and appropriately priced. Try it with a slice of fudge.

| | |
|---|---|
| **Quality** | 🍷🍷🍷½ |
| **Value** | *** |
| **Grapes** | not stated |
| **Region** | various, SA |
| **Cellar** | 🍾 |
| **Alc./Vol.** | 18.0% |
| **RRP** | $19.35 (S) |

## Penfolds Club Tawny Port

**Quality** 🍷🍷🍷
**Value** ★★★½
**Grapes** shiraz; grenache; mataro
**Region** Barossa Valley, SA
**Cellar** 🍾
**Alc./Vol.** 18.0%
**RRP** $9.60 (S)

This basic, entry-level Penfolds port still offers respectable value for money. And it sells heaps. You can be content that you're being given fair exchange here.

CURRENT RELEASE *non-vintage* The colour is light amber and it smells sweet, simple and grapey, with some spirity warmth and no real depth of aged material. It is clean, well made and fruity, with a marked sweet finish. A bottle to pass around to keep you warm while fishing on a cold night.

## Penfolds Magill Bluestone Tawny

**Quality** 🍷🍷🍷🍷
**Value** ★★★★
**Grapes** shiraz; mataro; muscadelle
**Region** Barossa Valley, SA
**Cellar** 🍾
**Alc./Vol.** 19.0%
**RRP** $22.50 (S)

The Magill cellars were built more than a century ago from bluestone quarried locally in the Adelaide foothills. It's puzzling that Penfolds has two ports (this and the Hyland Thomas) at much the same price-point.

CURRENT RELEASE *non-vintage* The bouquet invites you to take a sip: vanilla, plum, prune and subtle oak-aged characters mingle with a hint of floral, brandy spirit resulting in a complex port nose. The palate is very elegant, showing genuine wood-aged character and with only moderate sweetness throughout. This results in a clean finish that invites another sip. And another . . .

## Penfolds Thomas Hyland Tawny Port

**Quality** 🍷🍷🍷🍷
**Value** ★★★
**Grapes** shiraz; grenache; mataro
**Region** Barossa Valley, SA
**Cellar** 🍾
**Alc./Vol.** 19.0%
**RRP** $22.75 (S)

This is a relatively new addition to the Pennies port range. The namesake married Georgina Penfold, daughter of the founders Chris and Mary Penfold. Their offspring were named Penfold-Hyland.

CURRENT RELEASE *non-vintage* This is a step up the quality ladder from the likes of Club and Club Reserve: it has an element of fine wood-aged character, alongside raisined grape and prune fruit aromas. The palate is full and complex, with a fairly dry finish – an altogether more serious wine. Try it with date slice.

## R.L. Buller & Son Premium Fine Old Muscat

Buller's is very much a family affair. Established in 1921 by Reginald Langdon Buller, it's run by his grandsons Andrew and Rick Buller and their mother, Val. Their father, the late Richard senior, was made a 'Legend of Rutherglen' by his peers – the top honour for Rutherglenites.

CURRENT RELEASE *non-vintage*   This is Buller's mid-range muscat, and shows some lovely aged characters. The colour is medium tawny with a brown–yellow rim. The aroma is not especially muscaty but has secondary smells: leathery, oaky and rancio. It's sweet, rich and luscious in the mouth, with a little alcohol heat on the finish. It would go well with chocolate florentines.

| | |
|---|---|
| Quality | ▼▼▼▼ |
| Value | ★★★ |
| Grapes | red frontignac |
| Region | Rutherglen, Vic. |
| Cellar | ▮ |
| Alc./Vol. | 18.5% |
| RRP | $20.00 |

## R.L. Buller & Son Premium Fine Old Tawny

The Bullers have two wineries and vineyards: 32 hectares at Rutherglen and 27 hectares at Swan Hill. CURRENT RELEASE *non-vintage*   A decent middle-aged tawny port, this. The colour is medium brick-red with a tawny edge, and it shows some cask-aged plus some younger, red-fruit aromas. It's of elegant weight and – pleasingly – the finish is relatively dry. Shell some walnuts and serve with dried muscatels.

| | |
|---|---|
| Quality | ▼▼▼▼ |
| Value | ★★★ |
| Grapes | not stated |
| Region | Rutherglen, Vic. |
| Cellar | ▮ |
| Alc./Vol. | 18.5% |
| RRP | $20.00 |

## R.L. Buller & Son Victoria Muscat

The Victoria brand is Buller's basic line, and judging from the label, probably doesn't come from Rutherglen. They are certainly inexpensive.

CURRENT RELEASE *non-vintage*   The colour is light and quite red in tone, which indicates youth. The aromas are meaty, leathery and not as fresh as we'd like to see in such a youngster. It tastes pretty sweet but there is a certain harshness to the palate. Best served over ice cream as a topping.

| | |
|---|---|
| Quality | ▼▼▼ |
| Value | ★★★ |
| Grapes | red frontignac |
| Region | not stated |
| Cellar | ▮ |
| Alc./Vol. | 17.8% |
| RRP | $11.00 |

## R.L. Buller & Son Victoria Tawny

| | |
|---|---|
| Quality | ♟ ♟ ♟ |
| Value | ★ ★ ★ ⸱ |
| Grapes | not stated |
| Region | not stated |
| Cellar | ▯ |
| Alc./Vol. | 17.8% |
| RRP | $11.00 |

Rutherglen is fortified wine country, and Buller's is one of the fortified makers that most staunchly defend the area's name. We reckon they'd still make port even if the market dried up completely.

CURRENT RELEASE *non-vintage*    This is a nice style and a refreshing change from the sugary wines you find in most bottles of cheaper port. It smells young and plummy, with spirit and prune/juicy grape aromas without a lot of age. The finish is a highlight: it's clean and dry, with attractive anise-like bitterness drying the aftertaste. It would go with Pyengana cheddar.

## Saltram Mr Pickwick Particular Port

| | |
|---|---|
| Quality | ♟ ♟ ♟ ♟ ⸱ |
| Value | ★ ★ ★ ⸱ |
| Grapes | not stated |
| Region | Barossa Valley, SA |
| Cellar | ▯ |
| Alc./Vol. | 19.0% |
| RRP | $67.00 |

The label on this wine has a terrific retro feel that takes us way back, maybe not to Dickens's London, but certainly to the '70s.

CURRENT RELEASE *non-vintage*    A sweet, intense old tawny that shows aged nutty/raisiny characters of old-fashioned style. It's not as dry as some of the more esteemed old wines around and the texture is heavier than most. In fact the palate has real sweet depth of the sort that once marked a 'liqueur port'. It finishes reasonably long and sweet. Serve a steamed golden syrup pudding to go with this.

## Sandalford Sandalera

| | |
|---|---|
| Quality | ♟ ♟ ♟ ♟ ⸱ |
| Value | ★ ★ ★ ★ |
| Grapes | verdelho; chenin blanc & others |
| Region | Swan Valley, WA |
| Cellar | ▯ |
| Alc./Vol. | 18.0% |
| RRP | $33.00 (500 ml) |

This unusual old fortified wine takes advantage of ridiculously ripe, sweet Swan Valley grapes, and long wood-age in a hot climate, to forge a unique style for Australia.

CURRENT RELEASE *non-vintage*    If you're looking for a comparative wine style, start thinking of sweet Madeira; nothing in Australia is quite like it. Loads of toasted nut rancio aromas and a lot of volatile acidity in combination give it a savoury, appetising presence, but it remains a sweet wine with a core of syrupy, spicy fruitcake-like flavour. It finishes long and tasty with an almond touch. Good after dinner with some little almond biscotti.

## Seppelt Mount Rufus Tawny Port DP 4

Mount Rufus is a hill near Seppeltsfield in the Barossa Valley, not far from cellars full of sleeping fortified wine. CURRENT RELEASE *non-vintage*   The base model port styles like this have been having a rough trot in the marketplace since .05, healthy lifestyles and fashion shrank their following to almost nothing. This is a fruity younger wine with simple grape and dried-fruit aromas. The palate has reasonable depth with a hint of nuttiness. It's smooth and has a dry finish. All in all good value. Try it with a cheese platter.

| | |
|---|---|
| Quality | ♟ ♟ ♟ |
| Value | ★ ★ ★ ⁴ |
| Grapes | not stated |
| Region | Barossa Valley, SA |
| Cellar | ▮ |
| Alc./Vol. | 18.0% |
| RRP | $8.00 |

## Seppelt Para Liqueur 21 Year Old Vintage Tawny

Each year a quantity of Para Liqueur is put aside to be released years later as a single-vintage tawny. Some arrives on the market as an ideal twenty-first birthday present, and some remains in the cellars to become a century-old curio in the future.
CURRENT RELEASE 1980   This is a classic Australian style with an aged nose that doesn't suggest great sweetness. Instead there's a wonderful dusty bouquet of nutty aromas, spice and leather Chesterfields, surrounding a core of sweet toffee. The palate is unctuous and complex, perfectly balanced by nutty, drying rancio characters. The finish is long and fragrant. Serve it with a cheese board.

| | |
|---|---|
| Quality | ♟ ♟ ♟ ♟ ♟ |
| Value | ★ ★ ★ ★ ★ |
| Grapes | grenache; shiraz; mataro |
| Region | Barossa Valley, SA |
| Cellar | ▮ |
| Alc./Vol. | 20.5% |
| RRP | $42.00 |

## Seppelt Rutherglen Show Muscat DP 63

Seppelt once had vineyards and a winery at Rutherglen but not any more. These days Rutherglen material is matured and blended by James Godfrey at Seppeltsfield in the Barossa.
CURRENT RELEASE *non-vintage*   This is made in a different style to the voluptuous Rutherglen wines like Chambers, All Saints and the like. It has good intensity of raisiny muscat fruit with roasted almond/rancio complexity, but it's more tightly focused and somehow less lush. The flavour is still rich and deeply intense, with a long, sweet raisiny finish. Very tasty with espresso coffee and palmiers.

| | |
|---|---|
| Quality | ♟ ♟ ♟ ♟ ⁴ |
| Value | ★ ★ ★ ★ ⁴ |
| Grapes | red frontignac |
| Region | Rutherglen, Vic. |
| Cellar | ▮ |
| Alc./Vol. | 17.5% |
| RRP | $25.00 (375 ml) |

## Seppelt Show Amontillado DP 116

| | |
|---|---|
| Quality | 🍷🍷🍷🍷🍷 |
| Value | ★★★★★ |
| Grapes | palomino |
| Region | Barossa Valley, SA |
| Cellar | 🍾 |
| Alc./Vol. | 22.0% |
| RRP | $20.00 (375 ml) |

Amontillado is a wood-aged fino, with added depth and flavour coming from time spent in cask. The Spanish prototypes are usually a bit drier than local examples like this.

CURRENT RELEASE *non-vintage* A brilliant deep, old gold colour introduces this wine with an appropriate glitter. The nose has vanillin and nutty aromas, with a hint of toffee and candied peel. Sweetness on the middle palate eases into some toasty notes on a long, super-tangy, austere finish. A superbly balanced sherry style that's equally at home as an aperitif or as an accompaniment to a soup course based on good veal or beef stock.

## Seppelt Show Fino DP 117

| | |
|---|---|
| Quality | 🍷🍷🍷🍷🍷 |
| Value | ★★★★★ |
| Grapes | palomino |
| Region | Barossa Valley, SA |
| Cellar | 🍾 |
| Alc./Vol. | 15.5% |
| RRP | $20.00 (375 ml) |

The last few years have seen a bit of a resurgence in sherry drinking in the capitals, as the cool café set look for new thrills. Finos like this are becoming almost chic. A good thing too. As a refined and elegant aperitif, fino sherry is hard to beat. It stimulates the appetite and encourages conversation. This may well be Australia's best example of the style, especially now that the level of alcohol has been brought back to the common Spanish standard of 15.5 per cent.

CURRENT RELEASE *non-vintage* Pale and brilliant in colour, it has a distinctive, sea-breezy fresh aroma that's hard to describe, but maybe kernelly, nutty and lightly yeasty will almost do. That savoury lightness and freshness continues in the mouth with classic dry flor-yeasty flavour. Great served cool with a selection of tapas like green olives, spiced almonds and anchovies.

## Seppelt Show Oloroso DP 38

Good olorosos are glorious wines, complex, profound and lingering. If you've never tried one, do yourself a favour and buy a bottle of this.

CURRENT RELEASE *non-vintage*   A wonderful wine. The colour is an inviting deep amber–copper and it smells of vanilla, nuts, dried fruits and spices. It tastes gorgeous with sweet nutty/vanillin flavours that are long and subtly complex. The finish is clean, savoury and appetising, with a lingering toasted-almond aftertaste. Great after dinner with cake and coffee.

| | |
|---|---|
| Quality | 🍷🍷🍷🍷🍷 |
| Value | ★★★★★ |
| Grapes | palomino |
| Region | Barossa Valley, SA |
| Cellar | 🍾 |
| Alc./Vol. | 20.5% |
| RRP | $20.00 (375 ml) |

## Seppelt Show Tawny DP 90

No Australian wine has ever enjoyed the astonishing wine-show success of this one. Long wood-ageing (some components are a century old) combined with careful selection and blending has created a masterpiece. Blended by James Godfrey.

CURRENT RELEASE *non-vintage*   You need to readjust your sights here if you're used to very sweet, lush-textured ports. Fashioned like a superb old Portuguese tawny port, Seppelt DP 90 is all about refinement, something it has achieved by supremely skilled blending and access to superb wines of varying cask-age. Pale tawny in colour, it has a fine, elegant bouquet that suggests grilled nuts, butter toffee, leather and old brandy. The palate has lovely finesse and super intensity of long fragrant nutty flavour. There's sweetness but it's subdued, the finish is quite dry, and the aromatic aftertaste lasts for ages. Simply a great wine. Sip it with dried fruits, almonds and walnuts.

| | |
|---|---|
| Quality | 🍷🍷🍷🍷🍷 |
| Value | ★★★★ |
| Grapes | mostly shiraz & grenache |
| Region | Barossa Valley, SA |
| Cellar | 🍾 |
| Alc./Vol. | 21.5% |
| RRP | $92.00 (500 ml) |

## Seppelt Trafford Tawny DP 30

| | |
|---|---|
| Quality | 🍷🍷🍷🍷 |
| Value | ★★★★┤ |
| Grapes | shiraz; grenache |
| Region | Barossa Valley, SA |
| Cellar | 🍾 |
| Alc./Vol. | 18.0% |
| RRP | $12.00 |

The quality of the fortified wines blended at Seppeltsfield remains high despite a chronic lack of demand for them. The result is some terrific value.

CURRENT RELEASE *non-vintage* A fortified wine with a light, clean nose of some style. It has grape, dried-fruit and clean spirit aromas. In the mouth it has good balance of intense sweet flavour. Some aged nuttiness is found on the finish, suggesting clever blending work to give a hint of aged character to a reasonably priced wine. Good with chocolates, coffee and conversation.

## Stanton and Killeen Grand Rutherglen Muscat

| | |
|---|---|
| Quality | 🍷🍷🍷🍷🍷 |
| Value | ★★★┤ |
| Grapes | red frontignac |
| Region | Rutherglen, Vic. |
| Cellar | 🍾 |
| Alc./Vol. | 18.5% |
| RRP | $63.50 (500 ml) |

While Chris Killeen makes good Rutherglen red table wine in a more modern style than most, his fortifieds follow the traditional pattern superbly. This muscat has an average age of 25 years.

CURRENT RELEASE *non-vintage* This mahogany-coloured drop has a richly concentrated nose of muscaty essence along with some plum pudding and nutty touches. A whiff of Madeira-like volatility adds to the complexity. The palate is rich and sweet with a powerful raisin and vanilla caramel flavour. High acid balances and keeps it dryish on the finish. Try with coffee and chocolates.

## Stanton and Killeen Rutherglen Muscat

| | |
|---|---|
| Quality | 🍷🍷🍷🍷 |
| Value | ★★★ |
| Grapes | red frontignac |
| Region | Rutherglen, Vic. |
| Cellar | 🍾 |
| Alc./Vol. | 17.5% |
| RRP | $19.00 |

In the new Rutherglen classification anything labelled simply 'Rutherglen' with the grape variety attached is the base-level wine, but that isn't damning it with faint praise – it's usually pretty good.

CURRENT RELEASE *non-vintage* An immediately appealing sweet fortified with a fresh grapey/muscatel nose of pretty floral notes. In the mouth it's deliciously sweet, with little of the raisiny character of very old muscats but loads of the fresh grapiness of young wines. It's easy to like and is an interesting answer to the problem of wine to serve with lighter chocolate desserts. Chill it if you like.

## Talijancich Julian James White Liqueur

This is a family business established in 1932 and the winemaker today is Jim Talijancich. The wine's name reflects the generations elapsed between the founder, Jim's grandfather James, and his son, Julian. The wine has an average age of 10 years, the oldest material being from 1969.

CURRENT RELEASE *non-vintage*   This has a complex toffee/malt nose similar to a Rutherglen tokay. There are rosewater and caramel notes, and a hint of slightly fatty spirit. It's an attractive young tokay style with good freshness and balance. Serve it with dried muscatels and blue cheeses.

| | |
|---|---|
| Quality | ♟♟♟♟ |
| Value | ✸✸✸ |
| Grapes | mainly muscadelle & pedro ximenez |
| Region | Swan Valley, WA |
| Cellar | ▮ |
| Alc./Vol. | 18.0% |
| RRP | $29.00 (500 ml) |

## Wirra Wirra Fortified Muscat

Based on some muscat that's been left cooking under the verandah at Wirra Wirra winery for 14 years, this shows that Victoria's North East doesn't have a monopoly on this style.

CURRENT RELEASE *non-vintage*   A tawny–amber colour indicates age here, and the nose has sweet muscatel, toffee and floral aromas, but without quite the same essency raisined character of the best Vics. In the mouth it's sweet and grapey with syrupy texture and good depth and length. It's not too heavy and some attractively clean spirit marks an aromatic finish. Try it with steamed puddings.

| | |
|---|---|
| Quality | ♟♟♟♟♟ |
| Value | ✸✸✸ |
| Grapes | red frontignac |
| Region | McLaren Vale, SA |
| Cellar | ▮ |
| Alc./Vol. | 18.5% |
| RRP | $24.50 (375 ml) |

## Wirra Wirra Fortified Sweet White

Wines like this did a roaring trade in the days when most of the world map bore the pink of the British Empire. They were probably called variously white port, madeira, or anything else the winemaker chose.

CURRENT RELEASE *non-vintage*   This has an amber colour and a nose that's sweet, honeyed, spirity and intriguing. The fruit character is a bit stewed and old-fashioned, and there's a level of volatility. The palate is deeply flavoured and unctuously sweet: reminiscent of raisins, caramel, syrup and roasted nuts on the finish. A lovely treat with an aromatic espresso coffee.

| | |
|---|---|
| Quality | ♟♟♟♟ |
| Value | ✸✸✸ |
| Grapes | not stated |
| Region | McLaren Vale, SA |
| Cellar | ▮ |
| Alc./Vol. | 18.5% |
| RRP | $28.50 (375 ml) |

# Wine Terms

The following are commonly used winemaking terms.

**Acid**   There are many acids that occur naturally in grapes and it's in the winemaker's interest to retain the favourable ones because these promote freshness and longevity.

**Agrafe**   A metal clip used to secure champagne corks during secondary bottle fermentation.

**Alcohol**   Ethyl alcohol ($C_2H_5OH$) is a by-product of fermentation of sugars. It's the stuff that makes people happy and it adds warmth and texture to wine.

**Alcohol by Volume (A/V)**   The measurement of the amount of alcohol in a wine. It's expressed as a percentage, e.g. 13.0% A/V means there is 13.0% pure alcohol as a percentage of the total volume.

**Aldehyde**   An unwanted and unpleasant organic compound formed between acid and alcohol by oxidation. It's removed by sulfur dioxide.

**Allier**   A type of oak harvested in the French forest of the same name.

**Aperitif**   A wine that stimulates the appetite.

**Aromatic**   A family of grape varieties that have a high terpene content. Riesling and gewürztraminer are examples, and terpenes produce their floral qualities.

**Autolysis**   A Vegemite or freshly baked bread taste and smell imparted by spent yeast cells in sparkling wines.

**Back Blend**   To add unfermented grape juice to wine or to add young wine to old wine in fortifieds.

**Barrel Fermentation**   The process of fermenting a red or white wine in a small barrel, thereby adding a creamy texture and toasty or nutty characters, and better integrating the wood and fruit flavours.

**Barrique**   A 225-litre barrel.

**Baumé**   The measure of sugar in grape juice used to estimate potential alcohol content. It's usually expressed as a degree, e.g. 12 degrees Baumé juice will produce approximately 12.0% A/V if it's fermented to dryness. The alternative brix scale is approximately double Baumé and must be divided by 1.8 to estimate potential alcohol.

**Bentonite**   A fine clay (drillers mud) used as a clarifying (fining) agent.

**Blend**   A combination of two or more grape varieties and/or vintages. *See also* Cuvée.

**Botrytis Cinerea**   A mould that thrives on grapevines in humid conditions and sucks out the water of the grapes thereby concentrating the flavour. Good in white wine but not so good in red. (There is also a loss in quantity.)

**Breathing**   Uncorking a wine and allowing it to stand for a couple of hours before serving. This introduces oxygen and dissipates bottle odours. Decanting aids breathing.

**Brix**   *see* Baumé.

**Brut**   The second lowest level of sweetness in sparkling wine; it does not mean there is no added sugar.

**Bush Vine**   Although pruned the vine is self-supporting in a low-to-the-ground bush. (Still common in the Barossa Valley.)

**Carbonic Maceration**   Fermentation in whole (uncrushed) bunches. This is a popular technique in Beaujolais. It produces bright colour and soften tannins.

**Charmat Process**   A process for making sparkling wine where the wine is fermented in a tank rather than in a bottle.

**Clone (Clonal)**   A recognisable subspecies of vine within a varietal family, e.g. there are numerous clones of pinot noir and these all have subtle character differences.

**Cold Fermentation**   (Also Controlled Temperature Fermentation) Usually applied to white wines where the ferment is kept at a low temperature (10–12 degrees Centigrade).

**Cordon**   The arms of the trained grapevine that bear the fruit.

**Cordon Cut**   A technique of cutting the fruit-bearing arms and allowing the berries to dehydrate to concentrate the flavour.

**Crush**   Crushing the berries to liberate the free-run juice (*q.v.*). Also used as an expression of a wine company's output: 'This winery has a 1000-tonne crush'.

**Cuvée**   A Champagne term meaning a selected blend or batch.

**Disgorge**   The process of removing the yeast lees from a sparkling wine. It involves freezing the neck of the bottle and firing out a plug of ice and yeast. The bottle is then topped up and recorked.

**Dosage**   Sweetened wine added to a sparkling wine after disgorgement.

**Downy Mildew**   A disease that attacks vine leaves and fruit. It's associated with humidity and lack of air circulation.

**Drip Irrigation**   An accurate way of watering a vineyard. Each vine has its own dripper and a controlled amount of water is applied.

**Dryland Vineyard**   A vineyard that has no irrigation.

**Esters**   Volatile compounds that can occur during fermentation or maturation. They impart a distinctive chemical taste.

**Fermentation**   The process by which yeast converts sugar to alcohol with a by-product of carbon dioxide.

**Fining**   The process of removing solids from wine to make it clear. There are several methods used.

**Fortify**   The addition of spirit to increase the amount of alcohol in a wine.

**Free-run Juice**   The first juice to come out of the press or drainer (as opposed to pressings).

**Generic**   Wines labelled after their district of origin rather than their grape variety, e.g. Burgundy, Chablis, Champagne etc. These terms can no longer legally be used on Australian labels. *Cf.* Varietal.

**Graft**   Changing the nature/variety of a vine by grafting a different variety onto a root stock.

**Imperial**   A 6-litre bottle (contains eight 750-ml bottles).

**Jeroboam**   A 4.5-litre champagne bottle.

**Laccase**   A milky condition on the surface of red wine caused by noble rot. The wine is usually pasteurised.

**Lactic Acid**   One of the acids found in grape juice; as the name suggests, it's milky and soft.

**Lactobacillus**   A micro-organism that ferments carbohydrates (glucose) or malic acid to produce lactic acid.

**Lees**   The sediment left after fermentation. It consists mainly of dead yeast cells.

**Malic Acid**   One of the acids found in grape juice. It has a hard/sharp taste like a Granny Smith apple.

**Malolactic Fermentation**   A secondary process that converts malic acid into lactic acid. It's encouraged in red wines when they are in barrel. If it occurs after bottling, the wine will be fizzy and cloudy.

**Mercaptan**   Ethyl mercaptan is a sulfur compound with a smell like garlic, burnt rubber or asparagus water.

**Méthode Champenoise**   The French method for producing effervescence in the bottle; a secondary fermentation process where the carbon dioxide produced is dissolved into the wine.

**Methoxypyrazines**   Substances that give sauvignon blanc and cabernet sauvignon that added herbaceousness when the grapes aren't fully ripe.

**Mousse**   The froth or head on sparkling wines.

**Must**   *see* Free-run juice.

**Noble Rot**   *see* Botrytis cinerea.

**Non-vintage**   A wine that is a blend of two or more years.

**Oak**   The least porous wood, genus *Quercus*, and used for wine storage containers.

**Oenology**   The science of winemaking.

**Organic Viticulture**   Growing grapes without the use of pesticides, fungicides or chemical fertilisers. Certain chemicals, e.g. copper sulfate, are permitted.

**Organic Wines**   Wines made from organically grown fruit without the addition of chemicals.

**Oxidation**   Browning and dullness of aroma and flavour caused by excessive exposure to air.

**pH**   The measure of the strength of acidity. The higher the pH the higher the alkalinity and the lower the acidity. Wines with high pH values should not be cellared.

**Phenolics**   A group of chemical compounds which includes the tannins and colour pigments of grapes. A white wine described as 'phenolic' has an excess of tannin, making it taste coarse.

**Phylloxera**   A louse that attacks the roots of a vine, eventually killing the plant.

**Pigeage**   To foot-press the grapes.

**Pressings**   The juice extracted by applying pressure to the skins after the free-run juice has been drained.

**Pricked**   A wine that is spoilt and smells of vinegar, due to excessive volatile acidity. *Cf.* Volatile.

**Puncheon**   A 500-litre barrel.

**Racking**   Draining off wine from the lees or other sediment to clarify it.

**Saignée**   French for bleeding: the winemaker has run off part of the juice of a red fermentation to concentrate what's left.

**Skin Contact**   Allowing the free-run juice to remain in contact with the skins; in the case of white wines, usually for a very short time.

**Solero System**   Usually a stack of barrels used for blending maturing wines. The oldest material is at the bottom and is topped up with younger material from the top barrels.

**Solids**   Minute particles suspended in a wine.

**Sulfur Dioxide (SO₂)**   (Code 220) A chemical added since Roman times to wine as a preservative and a bactericide.

**Sur Lie**   Wine that has been kept on lees and not racked or filtered before bottling.

**Taché**   A French term that means 'stained', usually by the addition of a small amount of red wine to sparkling wine to turn it pink.

**Tannin**   A complex substance derived from skins, pips and stalks of grapes as well as the oak casks. It has a preservative function and imparts dryness and grip to the finish.

**Terroir**   Arcane French expression that describes the complete growing environment of the vine, including climate, aspect, soil, etc., and the direct effect this has on the character of its wine.

**Varietal**   An industry-coined term used to refer to a wine by its grape variety, e.g. 'a shiraz'. *Cf.* Generic.

**Véraison**   The moment when the grapes change colour and gain sugar.

**Vertical Tasting**   A tasting of consecutive vintages of one wine.

**Vigneron**   A grapegrower or vineyard worker.

**Vinegar**   Acetic acid produced from fruit.

**Vinify**   The process of turning grapes into wine.

**Vintage**   The year of harvest, and the produce of a particular yeast.

**Volatile**   Excessive volatile acids in a wine.

**Yeast**   The micro-organism that converts sugar into alcohol.

# Tasting Terms

The following terms refer to the sensory evaluation of wine.

**Aftertaste**   The taste (sensation) after the wine has been swallowed. It's usually called the finish.

**Astringent (Astringency)**   Applies to the finish of a wine. Astringency is caused by tannins that produce a mouth-puckering sensation and coat the teeth with dryness.

**Balance**   'The state of . . .'; the harmony between components of a wine.

**Bilgy**   An unfortunate aroma like the bilge of a ship. Usually caused by mouldy old oak.

**Bitterness**   A sensation detected at the back of the tongue. It's not correct in wine but is desirable in beer.

**Bouquet**   The aroma of a finished or mature wine.

**Broad**   A wine that lacks fruit definition; usually qualified as soft or coarse.

**Cassis**   A blackcurrant flavour common in cabernet sauvignon. It refers to a liqueur produced in France.

**Chalky**   An extremely dry sensation on the finish.

**Cheesy**   A dairy character sometimes found in wine, particularly sherries.

**Cigar Box**   A smell of tobacco and wood found in cabernet sauvignon.

**Cloudiness**   A fault in wine that is caued by suspended solids that make it look dull.

**Cloying**   Excessive sweetness that clogs the palate.

**Corked**   Spoiled wine that has reacted with a tainted cork, and smells like wet cardboard. (The taint is caused by trichloroanisole.)

**Creamy**   The feeling of cream in the mouth, a texture.

**Crisp**   Clean acid on the finish of a white wine.

**Depth**   The amount of fruit on the palate.

**Dry**   A wine that does not register sugar in the mouth.

**Dull**   Pertaining to colour; the wine is not bright or shining.

**Dumb**   Lacking nose or flavour on the palate.

**Dusty**   Applies to a very dry tannic finish; a sensation.

**Earthy**   Not as bad as it sounds, this is a loamy/mineral character that can add interest to the palate.

**Finesse**   The state of a wine. It refers to balance and style.

**Finish**   *see* Aftertaste.

**Firm**   Wine with strong, unyielding tannins.

**Flabby**   Wine with insufficient acid to balance ripe fruit flavours.

**Fleshy**   Wines of substance with plenty of fruit.

**Flinty**   A character on the finish that is akin to sucking dry creek pebbles.

**Garlic**   *see* Mercaptan (in Wine Terms).

**Grassy**   A cut-grass odour, usually found in semillon and sauvignon blancs.

**Grip**   The effect on the mouth of tannin on the finish; a puckering sensation.

**Hard**   More tannin or acid than fruit flavour.

**Herbaceous**   Herbal smells or flavour in wine.

**Hollow**   A wine with a lack of flavour in the middle palate.

**Hot**   Wines high in alcohol that give a feeling of warmth and a slippery texture.

**Implicit Sweetness**   A just detectable sweetness from the presence of glycerin (rather than residual sugar).

**Inky**   Tannate of iron present in a wine which imparts a metallic taste.

**Integrated (Well)**   The component parts of a wine fit together without gaps or disorders.

**Jammy**   Ripe fruit that takes on the character of stewed jam.

**Leathery**   A smell like old leather, not necessarily bad if it's in balance.

**Length (Long)**   The measure of the registration of flavour in the mouth. (The longer the better.)

**Lifted**   The wine is given a lift by the presence of either volatile acid or wood tannins, e.g. vanillin oak lift.

**Limpid**   A colour term usually applied to star-bright white wine.

**Madeirised**   Wine that has aged to the point where it tastes like a madeira.

**Mouldy**   Smells like bathroom mould; dank.

**Mouth-feel**   The sensation the wine causes in the mouth; a textural term.

**Musty**   Stale, flat, out-of-condition wine.

**Pepper**   A component in either the nose or the palate that smells or tastes like cracked pepper.

**Pungent**   Wine with a strong nose.

**Rancio**   A nutty character found in aged fortifieds that is imparted by time on wood.

**Residual Sugar**   The presence of unfermented grape sugar on the palate; common in sweet wines.

**Rough**   Unpleasant, aggressive wines.

**Round**   A full-bodied wine with plenty of mouth-feel (*q.v.*).

**Sappy**   A herbaceous character that resembles sap.

**Short**   A wine lacking in taste and structure. *See also* Length.

**Spicy**   A wine with a high aromatic content; spicy character can also be imparted by wood.

**Stalky**   Exposure to stalks, e.g. during fermentation. Leaves a bitter character in the wine.

**Tart**   A lively wine with a lot of fresh acid.

**Toasty**   A smell of cooked bread.

**Vanillin**   The smell and taste of vanilla beans; usually imparted by oak ageing.

**Varietal**   Refers to the distinguishing qualities of the grape variety used in the wine.

# Directory of Wineries

**Abbey Vale**
Wildwood Rd
Yallingup WA 6282
(08) 9755 2277
fax (08) 9755 2286
www.abbeyvale.com.au

**Abercorn**
Cassilis Rd
Mudgee NSW 2850
(02) 6373 3106
www.abercornwine.com.au

**Affleck Vineyard**
RMB 244
Millynn Rd
(off Gundaroo Rd)
Bungendore NSW 2651
(02) 6236 9276

**Alambie Wines**
(see Cranswick Estate)

**Albert River Wines**
1–117 Mundoolun
Connection Road
Tamborine Qld 4270
(07) 5543 6622
fax (07) 5543 6627
www.albertriverwines.com.au

**Alkoomi**
Wingeballup Rd
Frankland WA 6396
(08) 9855 2229
fax (08) 9855 2284
www.alkoomiwines.com.au

**All Saints Estate**
All Saints Rd
Wahgunyah Vic. 3687
(02) 6033 1922
fax (02) 6033 3515
www.allsaintswine.com.au

**Allandale**
Lovedale Rd
Pokolbin NSW 2320
(02) 4990 4526
fax (02) 4990 1714
www.allandalewinery.com.au

**Allanmere**
Lovedale Rd
Pokolbin NSW 2320
(02) 4930 7387
www.allanmere.com.au

**Allinda**
119 Lorimer's Lane
Dixon's Creek Vic. 3775
(03) 5965 2450
fax (03) 5965 2467

**Amberley Estate**
Wildwood & Thornton Rds
Yallingup WA 6282
(08) 9755 2288
fax (08) 9755 2171

**Anderson Winery**
Lot 13 Chiltern Rd
Rutherglen Vic. 3685
(03) 6032 8111

**Andraos Bros. Wines**
150 Vineyard Road
Sunbury Vic. 3429
(03) 9740 9703
fax (03) 9740 9795
www.andraosbros.com.au

**Andrew Garrett
Vineyard Estates**
134A The Parade
Norwood SA 5067
(08) 8364 0555
fax (08) 8364 5799
www.andrewgarrett.com.au

**Andrew Harris**
Sydney Rd
Mudgee NSW 2850
(02) 6373 1213
fax (02) 6373 1296

**Angove's**
Bookmark Ave
Renmark SA 5341
(08) 8595 1311
fax (08) 8595 1583
www.angoves.com.au

**Annie's Lane**
(see Beringer Blass)

**Antcliffe's Chase**
RMB 4510
Caveat
via Seymour Vic. 3660
(03) 5790 4333

**Apsley Gorge**
'The Gulch'
Bicheno Tas. 7215
(03) 6375 1221
fax (03) 6375 1589

**Armstrong Vineyards**
(not open to public)
(08) 8277 6073
fax (08) 8277 6035

**Arrowfield**
Denman Rd
Jerry's Plains NSW 2330
(02) 6576 4041
fax (02) 6576 4144
www.arrowfieldwines.com.au

**Arthurs Creek Estate**
(not open to public)
(03) 9714 8202

**Ashton Hills**
Tregarthen Rd
Ashton SA 5137
(08) 8390 1243
fax (08) 8390 1243

**Ashwood Grove**
(not open to public)
(03) 5030 5291

**Austins Barrabool**
50 Lemins Rd
Waurn Ponds Vic. 3216
(03) 5241 8114
fax (03) 5241 8122

**Avalon**
RMB 9556
Whitfield Rd
Wangaratta Vic. 3677
(03) 5729 3629

**Babich Wines**
Babich Rd
Henderson NZ
(09) 833 8909

**Baileys**
Taminick Gap Rd
Glenrowan Vic. 3675
(03) 5766 2392
fax (03) 5766 2596
www.beringerblass.com.au

**Baldivis Estate**
Lot 165 River Rd
Baldivis WA 6171
(08) 9525 2066
fax (08) 9525 2411

**Balgownie**
Hermitage Rd
Maiden Gully Vic. 3551
(03) 5449 6222
fax (03) 5449 6506
www.balgownie.com

**Ballingal Estate**
700 Kidman Way
Griffith NSW 2680
(02) 6962 4122

**Balnaves**
Penola-Naracoorte Rd
Coonawarra SA 5263
(08) 8737 2946
fax (08) 8737 2945
www.balnaves.com.au

**Bannockburn**
(not open to public)
Midland Hwy
Bannockburn Vic. 3331
(03) 5281 1363
fax (03) 5281 1349

**Banrock Station**
(see Hardys)

**Barak's Bridge**
(see Yering Station)

**Barambah Ridge**
79 Goschnicks Rd
Redgate via Murgon
Qld 4605
(07) 4168 4766
fax (07) 4168 4770

**Barossa Settlers**
Trial Hill Rd
Lyndoch SA 5351
(08) 8524 4017

**Barossa Valley Estate**
Seppeltsfield Rd
Marananga SA 5355
(08) 8562 3599
fax (08) 8562 4255
www.brlhardy.com.au

**Barratt**
(not open to public)
PO Box 204
Summertown SA 5141
(08) 8390 1788
fax (08) 8390 1788

**Barrington Estate**
700 Yarraman Rd
Wybong NSW 2333
(02) 6547 8118
fax (02) 6547 8039
www.barringtonestate.com.au

**Barwang**
(see McWilliam's)

**Basedow**
161–165 Murray St
Tanunda SA 5352
(08) 8563 3666
fax (08) 8563 3597
www.basedow.com.au

**Bass Phillip**
Tosch's Rd
Leongatha South
Vic. 3953
(03) 5664 3341

**Batista**
PO Box 88
Manjimup WA 6258
Tel/fax (08) 9772 3530

**Belgenny**
Level 8
261 George St
Sydney NSW 2000
(02) 9247 5577
fax (02) 9247 7273
www.belgenny.com.au

**Beresford**
49 Fraser Ave
Happy Valley SA 5159
(08) 8322 3611
fax (08) 8322 3610
www.beresfordwines.com.au

**Beringer Blass**
77 Southbank Blvd
Southbank Vic. 3000
(03) 9633 2000
fax (03) 8626 3451
www.beringerblass.com.au

**Berrys Bridge**
Forsters Road
Carapooee
St Arnaud Vic. 3478
(03) 5496 3220
fax (03) 5496 3322

**Best's Great Western**
Western Hwy
Great Western Vic. 3377
(03) 5356 2250
fax (03) 5356 2430

**Bethany**
Bethany Rd
Bethany
via Tanunda SA 5352
(08) 8563 2086
fax (08) 8563 2086
www.bethany.com.au

**Bianchet**
187 Victoria Rd
Lilydale Vic. 3140
(03) 9739 1779
fax (03) 9739 1277
www.bianchet.com

**Bindi**
(not open to public)
145 Melton Rd
Gisborne Vic. 3437
(03) 5428 2564
fax (03) 5428 2564

**Birdwood Estate**
PO Box 194
Birdwood SA 5234
(08) 8263 0986

**Blackjack Vineyard**
Calder Hwy
Harcourt Vic. 3452
(03) 5474 2528
fax (03) 5475 2102

**Blass**

(see Wolf Blass)

**Bleasdale**

Wellington Rd
Langhorne Creek SA 5255
(08) 8537 3001
www.bleasdale.com.au

**Blewitt Springs**

Recreational Rd
McLaren Vale SA 5171
(08) 8323 8689
www.hillsview.com.au

**Bloodwood Estate**

4 Griffin Rd
via Orange NSW 2800
(02) 6362 5631
www.bloodwood.com.au

**Blue Pyrenees Estate**

Vinoca Rd
Avoca Vic. 3467
(03) 5465 3202
fax (03) 5465 3529
www.bluepyrenees.com.au

**Blues Point**

(see Southcorp)

**Bookpurnong Hill**

Bookpurnong Road
Bookpurnong Hill
Loxton SA 5333
(08) 8584 1333
fax (08) 8584 1388
www.salenaestate.com.au

**Boston Bay**

Lincoln Hwy
Port Lincoln SA 5605
(08) 8684 3600
www.bostonbaywines.com.au

**Botobolar**

Botobolar Lane
PO Box 212
Mudgee NSW 2850
(02) 6373 3840
fax (02) 6373 3789
www.botobolar.com

**Bowen Estate**

Penola-Naracoorte Rd
Coonawarra SA 5263
(08) 8737 2229
fax (08) 8737 2173

**Boyntons of Bright**

Ovens Valley Hwy
Porepunkah Vic. 3740
(03) 5756 2356

**Brands Laira**

Naracoorte Hwy
Coonawarra SA 5263
(08) 8736 3260
fax (08) 8736 3208
www.mcwilliams.com.au

**Brangayne**

49 Pinnacle Rd
Orange NSW 2800
(02) 6365 3229

**Bremerton**

Strathalbyn Rd
Langhorne Creek SA 5255
(08) 8537 3093
fax (08) 8537 3109
www.bremerton.com.au

**Briagolong Estate**

118 Boisdale St
Maffra Vic. 3860
(03) 5147 2322
fax (03) 5147 2400

**Brian Barry**

(not open to public)
(08) 8363 6211

**Briar Ridge**

Mount View
Mt View NSW 2321
(02) 4990 3670
fax (02) 4998 7802
www.briarridge.com.au

**Bridgewater Mill**

Mount Barker Rd
Bridgewater SA 5155
(08) 8339 3422
fax (08) 8339 5253

**Brindabella Hills**

Woodgrove Cl.
via Hall ACT 2618
(02) 6230 2583

**Broke Estate**

Wollombi Rd
Broke NSW 2330
Tel/fax (02) 6579 1065

## Brokenwood
McDonalds Rd
Pokolbin NSW 2321
(02) 4998 7559
fax (02) 4998 7893
www.brokenwood.com.au

## Brook Eden
Adams Rd
Lebrina Tas. 7254
(03) 6395 6244

## Brookland Valley
Caves Rd
Willyabrup WA 6284
(08) 9755 6250
fax (08) 9755 6214
www.brlhardy.com.au

## Brown Brothers
Meadow Crk Rd
(off the Snow Rd)
Milawa Vic. 3678
(03) 5720 5500
fax (03) 5720 5511
www.brown-brothers.com.au

## Browns of Padthaway
PMB 196
Naracoorte SA 5271
(08) 8765 6063
fax (08) 8765 6083
www.browns-of-padthaway.com

## Buchanan Wines
Glendale Rd
Loira
West Tamar Tas. 7275
(03) 6394 7488
fax (03) 6394 7581

## Buller & Sons, R.L.
Calliope
Three Chain Rd
Rutherglen Vic. 3685
(02) 6032 9660
www.rlbullerandson.com.au

## Buller (R.L.) & Son
Murray Valley Hwy
Beverford Vic. 3590
(03) 5037 6305
fax (03) 5037 6803
fax (03) 6032 8005
www.rlbullerandson.com.au

## Burge Family Winemakers
Barossa Hwy
Lyndoch SA 5351
(08) 8524 4644
fax (08) 8524 4444
www.burgefamily.com.au

## Burnbrae
Hargraves Rd
Erudgere
Mudgee NSW 2850
(02) 6373 3504
fax (02) 6373 3601

## Calais Estate
Palmers Lane
Pokolbin NSW 2321
(02) 4998 7654
fax (02) 4998 7813

## Callatoota Estate
Wybong Rd
Wybong NSW 2333
(02) 6547 8149

## Cambewarra Estate
520 Illaroo Rd
Cambewarra NSW 2541
(02) 4446 0170
fax (02) 4446 0170

## Campbells
Murray Valley Hwy
Rutherglen Vic. 3685
(02) 6032 9458
fax (02) 6032 9870
www.campbellswines.com.au

## Canobolas-Smith
Cargo Rd
Orange NSW 2800
(02) 6365 6113
fax (02) 6365 6113

## Canonbah Bridge
Merryanbone Station
Warren NSW 2824
(02) 6833 9966
www.canonbah.com.au

## Cape Clairault
via Caves Rd
or Bussell Hwy
CMB Carbunup River
WA 6280
(08) 9755 6225
fax (08) 9755 6229

## Cape Mentelle
Wallcliffe Rd
Margaret River WA 6285
(08) 9757 3266
fax (08) 9757 3233

## Capelvale
Lot 5
Capel North West Rd
Capel WA 6271
(08) 9727 2439
fax (08) 9727 2164
www.capelvale.com

## Capercaillie
Londons Rd
Lovedale NSW 2325
(02) 4990 2904
fax (02) 4991 1886
www.capercailliewine.com.au

## Casella Carramar Estate
Wakley Rd
Yenda NSW 2681
(02) 6968 1346

## Cassegrain
Fern Bank Crk Rd
Port Macquarie NSW 2444
(02) 6583 7777
fax (02) 6584 0353

## Castle Rock Estate
Porongurup Rd
Porongurup WA 6324
(08) 9853 1035
fax (08) 9853 1010
www.castlerockestate.com.au

## Chain of Ponds
Gumeracha Cellars
PO Box 365
Main Rd
Gumeracha SA 5233
(08) 8389 1415
fax (08) 8336 2462
www.chainofpondswines.com.au

## Chambers Rosewood
Corowa-Rutherglen Rd
Rutherglen Vic. 3685
(02) 6032 8641
fax (02) 6032 8101

## Chandon
Maroondah Hwy
Coldstream Vic. 3770
(03) 9739 1110
fax (03) 9739 1095
www.chandon.com.au

## Chapel Hill
Chapel Hill Rd
McLaren Vale SA 5171
(08) 8323 8429
fax (08) 8323 9245
www.chapelhillwine.com.au

## Charles Cimicky
Gomersal Rd
Lyndoch SA 5351
(08) 8524 4025
fax (08) 8524 4772

## Charles Melton
Krondorf Rd
Tanunda SA 5352
(08) 8563 3606
fax (08) 8563 3422
www.charlesmeltonwines.com.au

## Charles Sturt University
Boorooma St
North Wagga Wagga
NSW 2678
(02) 6933 2435
fax (02) 6933 2107
www.csu.edu.au/winery

## Chateau Leamon
Calder Hwy
Bendigo Vic. 3550
(03) 5447 7995
www.chateauleamon.com.au

## Chatsfield
O'Neill Rd
Mount Barker WA 6324
(08) 9851 1704
fax (08) 9841 6811
www.chatsfield.com.au

## Chestnut Grove
PO Box 335
Manjimup WA 6258
(08) 9772 4345
fax (08) 9772 4543
www.chestnutgrove.com.au

## Chrismont
Upper King Valley Road
Cheshunt Vic. 3678
(03) 5729 8220
fax (03) 5729 8253

## Clarendon Hills
(not open to public)
(08) 8364 1484

**Classic McLaren**
PO Box 245
McLaren Vale SA 5171
Tel/fax (08) 8323 9551

**Cleveland**
Shannons Rd
Lancefield Vic. 3435
(03) 5429 1449
fax (03) 5429 2017
www.cleveland.winerydirect.
com.au

**Clonakilla**
Crisps Lane
Murrumbateman
NSW 2582
(02) 6227 5877
www.clonakilla.com.au

**Cloudy Bay**
(see Cape Mentelle)

**Clover Hill**
(see Taltarni)

**Cobaw Ridge**
Perc Boyer's Lane
East Pastoria
via Kyneton Vic. 3444
(03) 5423 5227

**Cockfighter's Ghost**
(see Poole's Rock)

**Cofield**
Distillery Rd
Wahgunyah Vic. 3687
(03) 6033 3798

**Coldstream Hills**
31 Maddens Lane
Coldstream Vic. 3770
(03) 5964 9388
fax (03) 5964 9389
www.southcorp.com.au

**Connor Park**
59 Connor Road
Leichardt Vic. 3516
(03) 5437 5234
fax (03) 5437 5204
www.bendigowine.com.au

**Constable Hershon**
1 Gillards Rd
Pokolbin NSW 2320
(02) 4998 7887
fax (02) 4998 7887

**Coolangatta Estate**
Coolangatta Resort
via Berry NSW 2535
(02) 4448 7131
fax (02) 4448 7997
www.coolangattaestate.com.au

**Coombend**
Swansea Tas. 7190
(03) 6257 8256
fax (03) 6257 8484

**Coopers Creek
Winery**
Highway 16
Haupai
Auckland NZ
(09) 412 8560

**Cope Williams
Winery**
Glenfern Rd
Romsey Vic. 3434
(03) 5429 5428
fax (03) 5429 2655
www.cope-williams.com.au

**Coriole**
Chaffeys Rd
McLaren Vale SA 5171
(08) 8323 8305
fax (08) 8323 9136

**Cowra Estate**
Boorowa Rd
Cowra NSW 2794
(02) 6342 3650

**Crabtree Watervale
Cellars**
North Tce
Watervale SA 5452
(08) 8843 0069
fax (08) 8843 0144

**Craig Avon**
Craig Avon Lane
Merricks North Vic. 3926
(03) 5989 7465

**Craigie Knowe**
Cranbrook Tas. 7190
(03) 6223 5620

**Craiglee**
Sunbury Rd
Sunbury Vic. 3429
(03) 9744 4489
fax (03) 9744 4489

**Craigmoor**
Craigmoor Rd
Mudgee NSW 2850
(02) 6372 2208

**Craigow**
Richmond Rd
Cambridge Tas. 7170
(03) 6248 5482

**Craneford**
Main St
Springton SA 5235
(08) 8568 2220
fax (08) 8568 2538
www.cranefordwines.com

**Cranswick Estate**
Walla Ave
Griffith NSW 2680
(02) 6962 4133
fax (02) 6962 2888
www.cranswick.com.au

**Crawford River**
Condah Vic. 3303
(03) 5578 2267

**Crofters**
(see Houghton)

**Cullens**
Caves Rd
Willyabrup
via Cowaramup WA 6284
(08) 9755 5277

**Currency Creek**
Winery Rd
Currency Creek SA 5214
(08) 8555 4069

**Dalfarras**
(see Tahbilk)

**Dalry Road**
(see Eyton on Yarra)

**Dalrymple**
Pipers Brook Rd
Pipers Brook Tas. 7254
(03) 6382 7222

**Dalwhinnie**
Taltarni Rd
Moonambel Vic. 3478
(03) 5467 2388

**Dal Zotto**
Edi Road
Cheshunt Vic. 3678
(03) 5729 8321
fax (03) 5729 8490

**D'Arenberg**
Osborn Rd
McLaren Vale SA 5171
(08) 8323 8206
www.darenberg.com.au

**Darling Estate**
(by appointment only)
Whitfield Rd
Cheshunt Vic. 3678
(03) 5729 8396
fax (03) 5729 8396

**Darling Park**
Lot 1 Browne Lane
Red Hill 3937
(03) 5989 2732
fax (03) 5989 2254

**David Traeger**
399 High St
Nagambie Vic. 3608
(03) 5794 2514

**David Wynn**
(see Mountadam)

**Deakin Estate**
(see Katnook)

**De Bortoli**
De Bortoli Rd
Bibul NSW 2680
(02) 6964 9444
fax (02) 6964 9400
www.debortoli.com.au

**De Bortoli**
Pinnacle Lane
Dixons Creek Vic. 3775
(03) 5965 2423
Fax (03) 5965 2464
www.debortoli.com.au

**Delamere**
4238 Bridport Rd
Pipers Brook Tas. 7254
(03) 6382 7190

**Delatite**
Stoney's Rd
Mansfield Vic. 3722
(03) 5775 2922
fax (03) 5775 2911

### Demondrille
RMB 97 Prunevale Rd
Prunevale
via Harden NSW 2587
(02) 6384 4272
fax (02) 6384 4292

### Dennis's of McLaren Vale
Kangarilla Rd
McLaren Vale SA 5171
(08) 8323 8665
fax (08) 8323 9121
www.daringacellars.com.au

### Derwent Estate
Lyell Hwy
Granton Tas 7030
Tel/fax (03) 6263 5802

### Devil's Lair
(not open to public)
PO Box 212
Margaret River WA 6285
(08) 9757 7573
fax (08) 9757 7533
www.southcorp.com.au

### Diamond Valley Vineyards
Kinglake Rd
St Andrews Vic. 3761
(03) 9710 1484
fax (03) 9710 1369
www.diamondvalley.com.au

### Dominion Wines
Upton Rd, via Avenel
Strathbogie Ranges
Vic. 3664
(03) 5796 2718
fax (03) 5796 2719

### Doonkuna Estate
Barton Hwy
Murrumbateman
NSW 2582
(02) 6227 5811
fax (02) 6227 5085

### Dowie Doole
182 Main Rd
McLaren Vale SA 5171
(08) 8323 7314
fax (08) 8323 7305

### Drayton's Bellevue
Oakey Creek Rd
Pokolbin NSW 2320
(02) 4998 7513
fax (02) 4998 7743
www.draytonswines.com.au

### Dromana Estate
Bittern-Dromana Rd
Dromana Vic. 3936
(03) 5987 3800
office (03) 5987 3177
fax (03) 5981 0714
www.dromanaestate.com.au

### Duncan Estate
Spring Gully Rd
Clare SA 5453
(08) 8843 4335

### Eden Ridge
(see Mountadam)

### Elan Vineyard
17 Turners Rd
Bittern Vic. 3918
(03) 5983 1858

### Elderton
3 Tanunda Rd
Nuriootpa SA 5355
(08) 8862 1058 or
1800 88 8500
fax (08) 8862 2844
www.eldertonwines.com.au

### Eldridge Estate
120 Arthurs Seat Road
Red Hill Vic. 3937
(03) 5989 2644
fax (03) 5989 2089
www.eldridge-estate.com.au

### Elgee Park
(no cellar door)
Junction Rd
Merricks Nth
PO Box 211
Red Hill South Vic. 3926
(03) 5989 7338
fax (03) 5989 7553
www.elgeeparkwines.com.au

### Eppalock Ridge
Metcalfe Pool Rd
Redesdale Vic. 3444
(03) 5425 3135

**Evans & Tate**
Lionel's Vineyard
Payne Rd
Jindong WA 6280
(08) 9755 8855
fax (08) 9755 4362
www.evansandtate.com.au

**Evans Family**
Palmers Lane
Pokolbin NSW 2320
(02) 4998 7333

**Eyton on Yarra**
Cnr Maroondah Hwy &
Hill Rd
Coldstream Vic. 3770
(03) 5962 2119
fax (03) 5962 5319
www.eyton.com.au

**Felton Road**
Bannockburn RD2
Central Otago NZ
(03) 445 0885
fax (03) 445 0881

**Fergusson's**
Wills Rd
Yarra Glen Vic. 3775
(03) 5965 2237
www.fergussonwinery.com.au

**Fermoy Estate**
Metricup Rd
Willyabrup WA 6284
(08) 9755 6285
fax (08) 9755 6251
www.fermoy.com.au

**Fern Hill Estate**
Ingoldby Rd
McLaren Flat SA 5171
(08) 8383 0167
fax (08) 8383 0107
www.fernhillestate.com.au

**Fettler's Rest**
(see Jindalee)

**Fiddler's Creek**
(see Blue Pyrenees Estate)

**Fire Gully**
(see Pierro)

**Flanagans Ridge**
(see Mildara)

**Fleur De Lys**
(see Seppelt)

**Flinders Bay**
(see Old Station)

**Fontys Pool**
(see Cape Mentelle)

**Forrest Estate**
Blicks Rd
Renwick
Blenheim NZ
(03) 572 9084
fax (03) 572 9084

**Fox Creek**
Malpas Rd
Willunga SA 5172
(08) 8556 2403
fax (08) 8556 2104
www.foxcreekwines.com.au

**Fox River**
(see Goundrey)

**Frankland Estate**
Frankland Rd
Frankland WA 6396
(08) 9855 1555
fax (08) 9855 1549

**Freycinet Vineyard**
Tasman Hwy
Bicheno Tas. 7215
(03) 6257 8574
fax (03) 6257 8454

**Fromm La Strada**
RD2, Godfrey Rd
Blenheim NZ
(03) 572 9355
fax (03) 572 9366

**Gabriel's Paddocks**
Deasy's Rd
Pokolbin NSW 2321
(02) 4998 7650
fax (02) 4998 7603
www.gabrielspaddocks.com.au

**Galafrey**
Quangellup Rd
Mount Barker WA 6324
(08) 9851 2022
fax (08) 9851 2324

**Galah Wines**
Box 231
Ashton SA 5137
(08) 8390 1243

**The Gap**
(see Mount Langi Ghiran)

## Gapsted Wines
Great Alpine Road
Gapsted Vic. 3737
(03) 5751 1992
fax (03) 5751 1368
www.gapstedwines.com

## Garden Gully
Western Hwy
Great Western Vic. 3377
(03) 5356 2400

## Garry Crittenden
(see Dromana Estate)

## Gembrook Hill
(by appointment only)
Launching Place Road
Gemrook Vic. 3783
(03) 5968 1622
fax (03) 5968 1699

## Geoff Merrill
291 Pimpala Rd
Woodcroft SA 5162
(08) 8381 6877
fax (08) 8322 2244

## Geoff Weaver
(not open to public)
2 Gilpin Lane
Mitcham SA 5062
(08) 8272 2105
fax (08) 8271 0177
www.geoffweaver.com.au

## Giaconda
(not open to public)
(03) 5727 0246
www.giaconda.com.au

## Gilbert's
Albany Hwy
Kendenup WA 6323
(08) 9851 4028
(08) 9851 4021

## Glenara
126 Range Rd Nth
Upper Hermitage SA 5131
(08) 8380 5277
fax (08) 8380 5056
www.glenara.com.au

## Glenguin
Lot 8 Milbrodale Rd
Broke NSW 2330
(02) 6579 1011
fax (02) 6579 1009

## Golden Grove Estate
Sundown Rd
Ballandean Qld 4382
(07) 4684 1291
www.goldengrove.com.au

## Goona Warra
Sunbury Rd
Sunbury Vic. 3429
(03) 9744 7211
fax (03) 9744 7648

## The Gorge
(see Pothana Vineyard)

## Goundrey
Muir Hwy
Mount Barker WA 6324
(08) 9851 1777
fax (08) 9848 1018
www.goundreywines.com.au

## Gramp's
(see Orlando)

## Grand Cru Estate
Ross Dewell's Rd
Springton SA 5235
(08) 8568 2378

## Grant Burge
Jacobs Creek
Barossa Valley Hwy
Tanunda SA 5352
(08) 8563 3700
Fax (08) 8563 2807
www.grantburgewines.com.au

## Green Point
(see Chandon)

## The Green Vineyards
1 Albers Rd
Upper Beaconsfield
Vic. 3808
(03) 5944 4599

## Greenock Creek
Radford Rd
Seppeltsfield SA 5360
(08) 8562 8103
fax (08) 8562 8259

## Grosset
King St
Auburn SA 5451
(08) 8849 2175
fax (08) 8849 2292
www.grosset.com.au

**Grove Estate**
Murringo Rd
Young NSW 2594
(02) 6382 6999
fax (02) 6382 4527

**Grove Mill**
Waihopai Valley Rd
Marlborough NZ
(03) 572 8200
fax (03) 572 8211

**Gulf Station**
(see De Bortoli)

**Hainault**
255 Walnut Road
Bickley WA 6076
(08) 9293 8339
fax (08) 9293 8339

**Half Mile Creek**
(see Beringer Blass)

**Hamilton**
Willunga Vineyards
Main South Rd
Willunga SA 5172
(08) 8556 2288
fax (08) 8556 2868
www.hamiltonwinegroup.com.au

**Hamilton's Ewell**
Barossa Valley Way
Nuriootpa SA 5355
(08) 8562 4600
fax (08) 8562 4611
www.hamiltonewell.com.au

**Hanging Rock**
Jim Rd
Newham Vic. 3442
(03) 5427 0542
fax (03) 5427 0310
www.hangingrock.com.au

**Hanson Wines**
'Oolorong'
49 Cleveland Ave
Lower Plenty Vic. 3093
(03) 9439 7425

**Happ's**
Commonage Rd
Dunsborough WA 6281
(08) 9755 3300
fax (08) 9755 3846
www.happs.com.au

**Harcourt Valley**
Calder Hwy
Harcourt Vic. 3453
(03) 5474 2223

**Hardys**
Reynella Rd
Reynella SA 5161
(08) 8392 2222
fax (08) 8392 2202
www.brlhardy.com.au

**Harewood Estate**
Scotsdale Rd
Denmark WA 6333
(08) 9840 9078
fax (08) 9840 9053

**Haselgrove Wines**
Sand Rd
McLaren Vale SA 5171
(08) 8323 8706
fax (08) 8323 8049
www.haselgrove.com.au

**Hay Shed Hill**
Harmans Mill Rd
Willyabrup WA 6285
(08) 9755 6234
fax (08) 9755 6305

**Heathcote Winery**
183 High St
Heathcote Vic. 3523
(03) 5433 2595
fax (03) 5433 3081
www.heathcotewinery.com.au

**Heathfield Ridge**
Cnr Caves Rd and
Riddoch Hwy
Naracoorte SA 5271
(08) 8762 4133
fax (08) 8762 0141
www.hthfieldwine.com.au

**Heemskerk**
Pipers Brook Tas. 7254
(03) 6382 7133
fax (03) 6382 7242

**Heggies**
(see Yalumba)

**Helm's**
Yass River Rd
Murrumbateman
NSW 2582
(02) 6227 5536 (A.H.)
(02) 6227 5953

**Henschke**
Moculta Rd
Keyneton SA 5353
(08) 8564 8223
fax (08) 8564 8294
www.henschke.com.au

**Heritage Wines**
Seppeltsfield Rd
Marananga
via Tununda SA 5352
(08) 8562 2880

**Hewitson**
16 McGowan Ave
Unley SA 5061
(08) 8271 5755
fax (08) 8271 5570
www.hewitson.com.au

**Hickinbotham**
Nepean Hwy
Dromana Vic. 3936
(03) 5981 0355
fax (03) 5981 0355
www.hickinbothamwinemakers.
com.au

**Highbank**
Penola-Naracoorte Rd
Coonawarra SA 5263
(08) 8737 2020
www.highbank.com.au

**Highfield**
Brookby Rd
RD 2 Blenheim NZ
(03) 572 8592
fax (03) 572 9257

**Highwood**
(see Beresford)

**Hill Smith Estate**
(see Yalumba)

**Hillstowe Wines**
104 Main Rd
Hahndorf SA 5245
(08) 8388 1400
fax (08) 8388 1411
www.hillstowe.com.au

**Hollick**
Racecourse Rd
Coonawarra SA 5263
(08) 8737 2318
fax (08) 8737 2952
www.hollick.com

**Holm Oak**
11 West Bay Rd
Rowella, Tas 7270
(03) 6394 7577
fax (03) 6394 7350

**Homes**
(see Massoni)

**Honeytree**
16 Gillards Rd
Pokolbin NSW 2321
Tel/fax (02) 4998 7693

**Hope Estate**
Cobcroft Rd
Broke NSW 2330
(02) 6579 1161
fax (02) 6579 1373

**Horseshoe Vineyard**
Horseshoe Road
Horses Valley
Denman NSW 2328
(02) 6547 3528

**Hotham Valley**
(by appointment only)
South Wandering Rd
Wandering WA 6308
(08) 9884 1525
fax (08) 9884 1079

**Houghton**
Dale Rd
Middle Swan WA 6056
(08) 9274 5100
fax (08) 9250 3872
www.brlhardy.com.au

**Howard Park**
Scotsdale Rd
Denmark WA 6333
(08) 9848 2345
fax (08) 9848 2064

**Hugh Hamilton
Wines**
PO Box 615
McLaren Vale SA 5171
(08) 8323 8689
fax (08) 8323 9488
www.hamiltonwines.com.au

**Hugo**
Elliott Rd
McLaren Flat SA 5171
(08) 8383 0098
fax (08) 8383 0446

**Huia**
Boyces Rd
RD3
Blenheim NZ
(03) 572 8326
fax (03) 572 8331

**Hungerford Hill**
(see Tulloch or Lindemans)

**Hunter's Wines**
Rapaura Rd
Blenheim NZ
(03) 572 8489
fax (03) 572 8457

**Huntington Estate**
Cassilis Rd
Mudgee NSW 2850
(02) 6373 3825
fax (02) 6373 3730

**Inglewood**
18 Craig Street
Artarmon NSW 2064
(02) 9436 3022
fax (02) 9439 7930

**Ingoldby**
Kangarilla Rd
McLaren Vale SA 5171
(08) 8383 0005
www.beringerblass.com.au

**Innisfail**
(not open to public)
(03) 5276 1258

**Ivanhoe**
Marrowbone Rd
Pokolbin NSW 2320
(02) 4998 7325
www.ivanhoewines.com.au

**James Irvine**
Roeslers Rd
Eden Valley SA 5235
PO Box 308
Angaston SA 5353
(08) 8564 1046
fax (08) 8564 1046

**Jamiesons Run**
(see Beringer Blass)

**Jane Brook**
Toodyay Rd
Middle Swan WA 6056
(08) 9274 1432
fax (08) 9274 1211
www.janebrook.com.au

**Jansz**
(see Yalumba)

**Jasper Hill**
Drummonds Lane
Heathcote Vic. 3523
(03) 5433 2528
fax (03) 5433 3143

**Jeanneret**
Jeanneret Rd
Sevenhill SA 5453
(08) 8843 4308
fax (08) 8843 4251
www.ascl.com/j-wines

**Jeir Creek Wines**
Gooda Creek Rd
Murrumbateman
NSW 2582
(02) 6227 5999

**Jenke Vineyards**
Jenke Rd
Rowland Flat SA 5352
(08) 8524 4154
fax (08) 8524 4154
www.jenkevineyards.com

**Jim Barry**
Main North Rd
Clare SA 5453
(08) 8842 2261
fax (08) 8842 3752

**Jindalee**
(not open to public)
13 Shepherd Court
North Geelong Vic. 3251
(03) 5277 2836
fax 5277 2840
www.jindaleewines.com.au

**Jingalla**
Bolganup Dam Rd
Porongurup WA 6324
(08) 9853 1023
fax (08) 9853 1023

**John Gehrig**
Oxley Vic. 3678
(03) 5727 3395

**Joseph**
(see Primo Estate)

**Juniper Estate**
Harmans Road South
Cowaramup WA 6284
(08) 9451 7277
fax (08) 9458 6015
www.juniperestate.com.au

**Kangarilla Road Winery**
Kangarilla Rd
McLaren Flat SA 5171
(08) 8383 0533
fax (08) 8383 0044

**Kara Kara**
Sunraysia Hwy
St Arnaud Vic. 3478
(03) 5496 3294
fax (03) 5496 3294
www.pyrenees.org.au/
karakara.htm

**Karina Vineyards**
RMB 4055
Harrisons Rd
Dromana Vic. 3936
(03) 5981 0137

**Karl Seppelt**
(see Grand Cru Estate)

**Karrivale**
Woodlands Rd
Porongurup WA 6324
(08) 9853 1009
fax (08) 9853 1129

**Karriview**
RMB 913
Roberts Rd
Denmark WA 6333
(08) 9840 9381

**Katnook Estate**
Riddoch Hwy
Coonawarra SA 5263
(08) 8737 2394
fax (08) 8737 2397
www.katnookestate.com.au

**Kays Amery**
Kays Rd
McLaren Vale SA 5171
(08) 8323 8211
fax (08) 8323 9199

**Kies Estate**
Barossa Valley Way
Lyndoch SA 5351
(08) 8524 4110

**Killawarra**
(see Southcorp Wines)

**Killerby**
Minnimup Rd
Gelorup WA 6230
(08) 9795 7222
fax (08) 9795 7835
www.killerby.com.au

**Kings Creek**
237 Myers Rd
Bittern Vic. 3918
(03) 5983 2102
fax (03) 5983 5153

**Kingston Estate**
Sturt Hwy
Kingston-on-Murray
SA 5331
(08) 8583 0244
fax (08) 8583 0304

**Knappstein Wines**
2 Pioneer Ave
Clare SA 5453
(08) 8842 2600
fax (08) 8842 3831
www.knappsteinwines.com.au

**Knights**
Burke and Wills Track
Baynton
via Kyneton Vic. 3444
(03) 5423 7264
mobile 015 843 676
fax (03) 5423 7288

**Koppamurra**
(no cellar door)
PO Box 110
Blackwood SA 5051
(08) 8271 4127
fax (08) 8271 0726
www.koppamurrawines.com.au

**Krondorf**
(see Beringer Blass)

## Kulkunbulla
PO Box 6265
Silverwater DC NSW 1811
(02) 9848 2103
fax (02) 9898 0200

## Kyeema
(not open to public)
PO Box 282
Belconnen ACT 2616
(02) 6254 7557

## Laanecoorie
(cellar door by
arrangement)
RMB 1330
Dunolly Vic. 3472
(03) 5468 7260

## Lacache
(see Cape Mentelle)

## Lake Breeze
Step Rd
Langhorne Creek SA 5255
(08) 8537 3017
fax (08) 8537 3267

## Lake's Folly
Broke Rd
Pokolbin NSW 2320
(02) 4998 7507
fax (02) 4998 7322
www.lakesfolly.com.au

## Lamont's
Bisdee Rd
Millendon WA 6056
(08) 9296 4485
fax (08) 9296 1663
www.lamonts.com.au

## Lancefield Winery
Woodend Rd
Lancefield Vic. 3435
(03) 5433 5292

## Langmeil
Cnr Langmeil & Para Rds
Tanunda SA 5352
(08) 8563 2595
fax (08) 8563 3622
www.langmeilwinery.com.au

## Lark Hill
RMB 281
Gundaroo Rd
Bungendore NSW 2621
(02) 6238 1393

## Laurel Bank
(by appointment only)
130 Black Snake Lane
Granton Tas. 7030
(03) 6263 5977
fax (03) 6263 3117

## Lawsons Dry Hills Wines
Alabama Rd
Blenheim NZ
(03) 578 7674
fax (03) 578 7603

## Leasingham
7 Dominic St
Clare SA 5453
(08) 8842 2555
fax (08) 8842 3293
www.brlhardy.com.au

## Leconfield
Riddoch Hwy
Coonawarra SA 5263
(08) 8737 2326
fax (08) 8737 2285
www.leconfield.com.au

## Leeuwin Estate
Stevens Rd
Margaret River WA 6285
(08) 9757 6253
fax (08) 9757 6364
www.leeuwinestate.com.au

## Leland Estate
PO Lenswood SA 5240
(08) 8389 6928

## Lengs & Cooter
24 Lindsay Tce
Belair SA 5052
(08) 8278 3998
(08) 8278 3998
fax (08) 8278 3998

## Lenswood Vineyards
3 Cyril John Crt
Athelstone SA 5076
(08) 8365 3766
fax (08) 8365 3766
www.knappsteinlenswood.
com.au

## Lenton Brae
Caves Rd
Willyabrup WA 6280
(08) 9755 6255
fax (08) 9755 6268

## Leo Buring
(see Southcorp Wines)

**Leydens Vale**
(see Blue Pyrenees Estate)

**Lillydale Vineyards**
Davross Crt
Seville Vic. 3139
(03) 5964 2016
www.mcwilliams.com.au

**Lillypilly Estate**
Farm 16
Lilly Pilly Rd
Leeton NSW 2705
(02) 6953 4069
fax (02) 6953 4980
www.lillypilly.com

**Lindemans**
McDonalds Rd
Pokolbin NSW 2320
(02) 4998 7501
fax (02) 4998 7682
www.southcorp.com.au

**Littles Winery**
Lot 3 Palmers Lane
Pokolbin NSW 2320
(02) 4998 7626
fax (02) 4998 7867
www.littleswinery.com

**Logan**
(not open to public)
(02) 9958 6844
www.loganwines.com.au

**Long Gully**
Long Gully Rd
Healesville Vic. 3777
(03) 5962 3663
fax (03) 59807 2213

**Longleat**
Old Weir Rd
Murchison Vic. 3610
(03) 5826 2294
fax (03) 5826 2510
www.longleatwines.com

**Lovegrove**
Heidelberg Kinglake Road
Cottlesbridge Vic. 3099
(03) 9718 1569
fax (03) 9718 1028

**Lowe Family**
Ashbourne Vineyard
Tinja Lane
Mudgee NSW 2850
(02) 4998 7121
fax (02) 4998 7393
www.lowewine.com.au

**Madew**
(by appointment only)
Westering Vineyard
Federal Hwy
Lake George NSW 2581
(02) 4848 0026
fax (02) 4848 0026

**Madfish**
(see Howard Park)

**Maglieri**
Douglas Gully Rd
McLaren Flat SA 5171
(08) 8323 8648
www.beringerblass.com.au

**Main Ridge**
Lot 48 Williams Rd
Red Hill Vic. 3937
(03) 5989 2686

**Majella**
Lynn Rd
Coonawarra SA 5263
(08) 8736 3055
fax (08) 8736 3057
www.majellawines.com.au

**Malcolm Creek**
(not open to public)
(08) 8264 2255

**Marienberg**
2 Chalk Hill Rd
McClaren Vale SA 5171
(08) 8323 9666
fax (08) 8323 9600
www.marienberg.com.au

**Maritime Estate**
Tuck's Rd
Red Hill Vic. 3937
(03) 5989 2735

**Martindale Hall**
(see Andrew Garrett
Vineyard Estates)

**Massoni Home**
(by appointment only)
Mornington-Flinders Rd
Red Hill Vic. 3937
(03) 5981 8008
fax (03) 5981 2014
www.massoniwines.com

**Maxwell**
Cnr Olivers & Chalkhill Rds
McLaren Vale SA 5171
(08) 8323 8200

**McAlister**
(not open to public)
RMB 6810
Longford Vic. 3851
(03) 5149 7229

**McGuigan**
Cnr Broke & McDonalds Rds
Pokolbin NSW 2320
(02) 4998 7700
fax (02) 4998 7401

**McLarens on the
Lake**
(see Andrew Garrett
Vineyard Estates)

**McWilliam's**
Hanwood NSW 2680
(02) 6963 0001
fax (02) 6963 0002
www.mcwilliams.com.au

**Meadowbank**
Glenora Tas. 7140
(03) 6286 1234
fax (03) 6286 1133

**Merricks Estate**
Cnr Thompsons La. &
Frankston-Flinders Rd
Merricks Vic. 3916
(03) 5989 8416
fax (03) 9629 4035

**Miceli**
60 Main Creek Rd
Arthur's Seat Vic. 3936
(03) 5989 2755

**Middleton Estate**
Flagstaff Hill Rd
Middleton SA 5213
(08) 8555 4136
fax (08) 8555 4108

**Milburn Park**
(see Cranswick Estate)

**The Mill**
(see Windowrie Estate)

**Mintaro Cellars**
Leasingham Rd
Mintaro SA 5415
(08) 8843 9046

**Miramar**
Henry Lawson Dr.
Mudgee NSW 2850
(02) 6373 3874

**Miranda Wines**
57 Jordaryan Ave
Griffith NSW 2680
(02) 6962 4033
fax (02) 6962 6944
www.mirandawines.com.au

**Mirrool Creek**
(see Miranda)

**Mitchell**
Hughes Park Rd
Sevenhill via Clare SA 5453
(08) 8843 4258

**Mitchelton Wines**
Mitcheltstown
Nagambie 3608
(03) 5794 2710
fax (03) 5794 2615
www.mitchelton.com.au

**Molly Morgan**
Talga Rd
Allandale NSW 2321
(02) 4930 7695
fax (02) 9235 1876
www.mollymorgan.bizland.com

**Monichino**
1820 Berry's Rd
Katunga Vic. 3640
(03) 5864 6452
fax (03) 5864 6538

**Montana**
PO Box 18-293
Glen Innis
Auckland NZ
(09) 570 5549

**Montara**
Chalambar Rd
Ararat Vic. 3377
(03) 5352 3868
fax (03) 5352 4968

**Montrose**
Henry Lawson Dr.
Mudgee NSW 2850
(02) 6373 3853

**Moondah Brook**
(see Houghton)

**Moondarah**
(see Prentice)

**Moorilla Estate**
655 Main Rd
Berridale Tas. 7011
(03) 6249 2949

**Moorooduc Estate**
Derril Rd
Moorooduc Vic. 3933
(03) 5978 8585

**Morning Cloud**
(cellar door by
appointment)
15 Ocean View Ave
Red Hill South Vic. 3937
(03) 5989 2762
fax (03) 5989 2700

**Mornington
Vineyards Estate**
(by appointment only)
Moorooduc Rd
Mornington Vic. 3931
(03) 5974 2097
www.dromanaestate.com.au

**Morris**
off Murray Valley Hwy
Mia Mia Vineyards
Rutherglen Vic. 3685
(02) 6026 7303
fax (02) 6026 7445

**Moss Brothers**
Caves Rd
Willyabrup WA 6280
(08) 9755 6270
fax (08) 9755 6298
www.mossbrothers.com.au

**Moss Wood**
Metricup Rd
Willyabrup WA 6280
(08) 9755 6266
fax (08) 9755 6303
www.mosswood.com.au

**Mount Avoca**
Moates Lane
Avoca Vic. 3467
(03) 5465 3282
www.mountavoca.com

**Mount Helen**
(see Mildara)

**Mount Horrocks**
Curling St
Auburn SA 5451
(08) 8849 2243
fax (08) 8849 2265
www.mounthorrocks.com

**Mount Hurtle**
(see Geoff Merrill)

**Mount Ida**
(see Mildara)

**Mount Langi Ghiran**
Warrak Rd
Buangor Vic. 3375
(03) 5354 3207
fax (03) 5354 3277

**Mount Mary**
(not open to public)
(03) 9739 1761
fax (03) 9739 0137

**Mount Pleasant**
Marrowbone Rd
Pokolbin NSW 2321
(02) 4998 7505
fax (02) 4998 7761
www.mcwilliams.com.au

**Mount Prior
Vineyard**
Cnr River Rd & Popes La.
Rutherglen Vic. 3685
(02) 6026 5591
fax (02) 6026 5590

**Mount William
Winery**
Mount William Rd
Tantaraboo Vic. 3764
(03) 5429 1595
fax (03) 5429 1998

**Mountadam**
High Eden Ridge
Eden Valley SA 5235
(08) 8564 1101
www.mountadam.com

**Mulyan**
North Logan Rd
Cowra NSW 2794
(02) 6342 1336
fax (02) 6341 1015
www.mulyan.com.au

**Murrindindi**
(not open to public)
(03) 5797 8217

**Nautilus**
(see Yalumba)

**Neagle's Rock**
Main North Rd
Clare SA 5453
(08) 8842 1169

**Nepenthe Vineyards**
(not open to public)
(08) 8389 8218
www.nepenthe.com.au

**Neudorf**
Neudorf Rd RD2
Upper Moutere
Nelson NZ
(03) 543 2643
fax (03) 543 2955

**Ngatarawa**
305 Ngatarawa Rd
Bridge Pa
Hastings NZ
(06) 879 7603

**Nicholson River**
Liddells Rd
Nicholson Vic. 3882
(03) 5156 8241

**Ninth Island**
(see Pipers Brook)

**Nobilo**
Station Rd
Huapai, Auckland 1250 NZ
(09) 412 9148
fax (09) 412 7124

**Normans**
Grants Gully Rd
Clarendon SA 5157
(08) 8383 6138
fax (08) 8383 6089
www.normanswines.com.au

**Notley Gorge**
(vineyard only)
Loop Road
Glengarry Tas. 7275
(03) 6396 1166
fax (03) 6396 1200

**Oakridge Estate**
864 Maroondah Hwy
Coldstream Vic. 3770
(03) 5964 3379
fax (03) 5964 2061
www.oakridgeestate.com.au

**Oakvale Winery**
Broke Rd
Pokolbin NSW 2320
(02) 4998 7520
www.oakvalewines.com.au

**Old Kent River**
Turpin Rd
Rocky Gully WA 6397
(08) 9855 1589
fax (08) 9855 1589

**Old Station**
PO Box 40
Watervale SA 5452
(02) 9144 1925

**Orlando**
Barossa Valley Way
Rowland Flat SA 5352
(08) 8521 3111
fax (08) 8521 3102
www.jacobscreek.com.au

**Osborn's**
Ellerina Rd
Merricks North Vic. 3926
(03) 5989 7417
fax (03) 5989 7510

**Padthaway Estate**
Riddoch Hwy
Padthaway SA 5271
(08) 8765 5039
fax (08) 8765 5097

**Palandri**
Bussell Hwy
Margaret River WA 6285
(08) 9755 5711
fax (08) 9755 5722
www.palandri.com.au

**Palliser Estate**
Kitchener St
Martinborough NZ
(06) 306 9019
fax (06) 306 9946

**Palmer Wines**
Caves Rd
Willyabrup WA 6280
(08) 9797 1881
fax (08) 9797 0534

**Pankhurst Wines**
Woodgrove Rd
Hall ACT 2618
(02) 6230 2592

**Panorama**
1848 Cygnet Coast Rd
Cradoc Tas. 7109
Tel/fax (03) 6266 3409

**Paracombe**
Paracombe Rd
Paracombe SA 5132
(08) 8380 5058
fax (08) 8380 5488

**Paradise Enough**
(weekends & holidays only)
Stewarts Rd
Kongwak Vic. 3951
(03) 5657 4241
www.paradiseenough.com.au

**Paringa Estate**
44 Paringa Rd
Red Hill South Vic. 3937
(03) 5989 2669

**Parker Coonawarra Estate**
(cellar door sales at
Bushmans Inn, Penola)
110B Elizabeth Bay Rd
Elizabeth Bay NSW 2011
(02) 9357 3376
fax (02) 9358 1517

**Passing Clouds**
Powlett Rd
via Inglewood
Kingower Vic. 3517
(03) 5438 8257

**Pattersons**
St Werburghs Rd
Mount Barker WA 6324
(08) 9851 2063
fax (08) 9851 2063

**Paul Conti**
529 Wanneroo Rd
Woodvale WA 6026
(08) 9409 9160
fax (08) 9309 1634

**Paulett's**
Polish Hill River Rd
Sevenhill SA 5453
(08) 8843 4328
fax (08) 8843 4202

**Paul Osicka**
Graytown Vic. 3608
(03) 5794 9235
fax (03) 5794 9288

**Peel Estate**
Fletcher Rd
Baldivis WA 6210
(08) 9524 1221

**Pegasus Bay**
Stockgrove Rd
Waipara
Amberley RD 2
North Canterbury NZ
(03) 314 6869
fax (03) 355 5937

**Pendarves Estate**
Lot 12 Old North Rd
Belford NSW 2335
(02) 6574 7222
www.winedoctor.md/wine.htm

**Penfolds**
(see Southcorp Wines)

**Penley Estate**
McLean's Rd
Coonawarra 5263
(08) 8736 3211
fax (08) 8736 3124
www.penley.com.au

**Pepperjack**
(see Beringer Blass)

**Peppers Creek**
Cnr Ekerts & Broke Rds
Pokolbin NSW 2321
(02) 4998 7532

**Pepper Tree Wines**
Halls Rd
Pokolbin NSW 2320
(02) 4998 7539
fax (02) 4998 7746
www.peppertreewines.com.au

**Petaluma**
(not open to public)
(08) 8339 4122
fax (08) 8339 5253

**Peter Lehmann**
Para Rd
Tanunda SA 5352
(08) 8563 2500
fax (08) 8563 3402
www.peterlehmannwines.
com.au

**Petersons**
PO Box 182
Mount View Rd
Mount View NSW 2325
(02) 4990 1704

**Pewsey Vale**
(see Yalumba)

**Pfeiffer**
Distillery Rd
Wahgunyah Vic. 3687
(02) 6033 3889

**Phillip Island Wines**
Lot 1 Berrys Beach Rd
Phillip Island Vic. 3922
(03) 5956 8465
www.phillipislandwines.com.au

**Pibbin Farm**
Greenhill Rd
Balhannah SA 5242
(08) 8388 4794

**Picardy**
(not open to public)
(08) 9776 0036
fax (08) 9776 0036
www.picardy.com.au

**Picarus**
C/- Winetrust Estates
(no cellar door sales)
(02) 9816 4088

**Piccadilly Fields**
(not open to public)
(08) 8390 1997

**Pierro**
Caves Rd
Willyabrup WA 6280
(08) 9755 6220
fax (08) 9755 6308

**Pikes Polish Hill Estate**
Polish Hill River Rd
Seven Hill SA 5453
(08) 8843 4370
fax (08) 8843 4353
www.pikeswines.com.au

**Pipers Brook**
3959 Bridport Hwy
Pipers Brook Tas. 7254
(03) 6382 7197
fax (03) 6382 7226
www.pbv.com.au

**Pirie**
(see Pipers Brook)

**Pirramimma**
Johnston Rd
McLaren Vale SA 5171
(08) 8323 8205
fax (08) 8323 9224

**Pizzini**
King Valley Road
Wangaratta Vic. 3768
(03) 5729 8278
fax (03) 5729 8495

**Plantagenet**
Albany Hwy
Mount Barker WA 6324
(08) 9851 2150
fax (08) 9851 1839

**Plunkett's**
Cnr Lambing Gully Rd &
Hume Fwy
Avenel Vic. 3664
(03) 5796 2150
fax (03) 5796 2147
www.plunkett.com.au

**Poole's Rock**
(not open to public)
Lot 41 Wollombi Road
Broke NSW 2330
(02) 6579 1251
fax (02) 6579 1277

### Port Phillip Estate
261 Red Hill Rd
Red Hill Vic. 3937
(03) 5989 2708
fax (03) 5989 2891
www.portphillip.net

### Portree Vineyard
RMB 700
Lancefield Vic. 3435
(03) 5429 1422
fax (03) 5429 2205
www.portreevineyard.com.au

### Pothana Vineyard
Pothana Lane
Belford NSW 2335
(02) 6574 7164
fax (02) 6574 7209

### Preece
(see Mitchelton)

### Prentice
(no cellar door sales)
PO Box 4
Red Hill South, Vic. 3937
(03) 5989 9063
fax (03) 5989 9068

### Preston Peak
Wallangarra Rd
Wyberba
Wallangarra Qld 4383
Tel/fax (07) 4630 9499

### Primo Estate
Cnr Old Port Wakefield &
Angle Vale Rds
Virginia SA 5120
(08) 8380 9442
fax (08) 8380 9696
www.primoestate.com.au

### Prince Albert
Lemins Rd
Waurn Ponds Vic. 3221
(03) 5243 5091
fax (03) 5241 8091

### Providence
236 Lalla Rd
Lalla Tas. 7267
(03) 6395 1290
fax (03) 6395 2088
www.providence-
vineyards.com.au

### Punters Corner
Cnr Riddoch Hwy &
Racecourse Rd
Coonawarra SA 5263
(08) 8737 2007

### Queen Adelaide
(see Seppelt)

### Quelltaler Estate / Annie's Lane
Main North Rd
Watervale SA 5452
(08) 8843 0003
fax (08) 8843 0096
www.beringerblass.com.au

### Radenti
(see Freycinet)

### Ravenswood Lane
Ravenswood Lane
Hahndorf SA 5245
(08) 8388 1250
fax (08) 8388 7233
www.ravenswoodlane.com.au

### Redbank
Sunraysia Hwy
Redbank Vic. 3478
(03) 5467 7255

### Red Edge
(not open to public)
(03) 9337 5695

### Redgate
Boodjidup Rd
Margaret River WA 6285
(08) 9757 6488
fax (08) 9757 6308
www.redgatewines.com.au

### Red Hill Estate
53 Red Hill-Shoreham Rd
Red Hill South Vic. 3937
(03) 5989 2838
www.redhillestate.com.au

### Redman
Riddoch Hwy
Coonawarra SA 5263
(08) 8736 3331
fax (08) 8736 3013

### Renmano
Renmark Ave
Renmark SA 5341
(08) 8586 6771
fax (08) 8586 5939
www.brlhardy.com.au

**Reynell**
(see Hardys)

**Reynolds Yarraman**
Quandong Winery
Cargo Rd
Cudal NSW 2864
(02) 6364 2330
fax (02) 6364 2388
www.reynoldswine.com.au

**Ribbon Vale Estate**
Lot 5 Caves Rd
via Cowaramup
Willyabrup WA 6284
(08) 9755 6272

**Richmond Grove**
(see Orlando)

**Riddoch**
(see Katnook)

**Rimfire**
C/- PO Maclagan Qld 4352
(07) 4692 1129
www.rimfirewinery.com.au

**Riverby Estate**
RD 3 Jacksons Rd
Blenheim NZ
(03) 572 9509

**Robertson's Well**
(see Beringer Blass)

**Robinvale Wines**
Sealake Rd
Robinvale Vic. 3549
(03) 5026 3955
fax (03) 5026 1123
www.organicwines.com

**Rochecombe**
(see Heemskerk)

**Rochford**
Romsey Park
via Woodend Rd
Rochford Vic. 3442
(03) 5429 1428
www.rochfordwines.com.au

**Rockford**
Krondorf Rd
Tanunda SA 5352
(08) 8563 2720
info@rockfordwines.com.au

**Romsey Park**
(see Rochford)

**Romsey Vineyards**
(see Cope Williams)

**Rosabrook Estate**
Rosa Brook Rd
Margaret River WA 6285
(08) 9757 2286
fax (08) 9757 3634

**Rosemount**
Rosemount Rd
Denman NSW 2328
(02) 6547 2467
fax (02) 6547 2742
www.southcorp.com.au

**Rosevears Estate**
1A Waldhorn Drive
Rosevears Tas. 7277
(03) 6330 1800
fax (03) 6330 1810

**Rosily Vineyard**
Yelverton Rd
Willyabrup WA
Tel/fax (08) 9755 6336

**Rossetto**
Farm 576
Beelbangera NSW 2680
(02) 6963 5214
fax (02) 6963 5542

**Rothbury Estate**
Broke Rd
Pokolbin NSW 2321
(02) 4998 7555
fax (02) 4998 7553
www.beringerblass.com.au

**Rothvale**
Deasy's Rd
Pokolbin NSW 2321
(02) 4998 7290

**Rouge Homme**
(see Lindemans)

**Rufus Stone**
(see Tyrrell's)

**Rumball**
(no cellar door)
(08) 8332 2761
fax (08) 8364 0188

### Ryan Family Wines
Broke Estate
Wollombi Rd
Broke NSW 2330
(02) 6579 1065
fax (02) 6579 1065
www.ryanwines.com.au

### Ryecroft
Ingoldby Rd
McLaren Flat SA 5171
(08) 8383 0001
www.southcorp.com.au

### Rymill
The Riddoch Run
Vineyards (off Main Rd)
Coonawarra SA 5263
(08) 8736 5001
fax (08) 8736 5040
www.rymill.com.au

### Saddlers Creek Winery
Marrowbone Rd
Pokolbin NSW 2321
(02) 4991 1770
fax (02) 4991 1778
www.saddlerscreekwines.com.au

### Salisbury
(see Cranswick Estate)

### Salitage
Vasse Hwy
Pemberton WA 6260
(08) 9776 1599
fax (08) 9776 1504
www.salitage.com.au

### Saltram
Angaston Rd
Angaston SA 5353
(08) 8564 3355
www.beringerblass.com.au

### Sandalford
West Swan Rd
Caversham WA 6055
(08) 9274 5922
fax (08) 9274 2154
www.sandalford.com

### Sandhurst Ridge
156 Forest Drive
Marong Vic. 3515
(03) 5435 2534
fax (03) 5435 2548
www.bendigowine.org.au

### Sandstone Vineyard
(cellar door by
appointment)
Caves & Johnson Rds
Willyabrup WA 6280
(08) 9755 6271
fax (08) 9755 6292

### Saxonvale
Fordwich Estate
Broke Rd
Pokolbin NSW 2330
(02) 6579 1009

### Scarborough Wines
Gillards Rd
Pokolbin NSW 2321
(02) 4998 7563

### Scarpantoni
Kangarilla Rd
McLaren Flat SA 5171
(08) 8383 0186
fax (08) 8383 0490
www.scarpantoni-wines.com.au

### Schinus
(see Dromana Estate)

### Scotchman's Hill
Scotchmans Rd
Drysdale Vic. 3222
(03) 5251 3176
fax (03) 5253 1743
www.scotchmanshill.com.au

### Seaview
Chaffeys Rd
McLaren Vale SA 5171
(08) 8323 8250
www.southcorp.com.au
(see Nobilo)

### Seppelt
Seppeltsfield
via Tanunda SA 5352
(08) 8562 8028
fax (08) 8562 8333
www.southcorp.com.au

### Sevenhill
College Rd
Sevenhill
via Clare SA 5453
(08) 8843 4222
fax (08) 8843 4382
www.sevenhillcellars.com.au

**Seville Estate**
Linwood Rd
Seville Vic. 3139
(03) 5964 2622
fax (03) 5964 2633

**Shantell**
Melba Hwy
Dixons Creek Vic. 3775
(03) 5965 2264
fax (03) 9819 5311
www.shantellvineyard.com.au

**Sharefarmers**
(see Petaluma)

**Shaw & Smith**
(tastings by appointment)
Lot 4 Jones Rd
Balhannah SA 5242
(08) 8398 0500
fax (08) 8398 0600

**Shottesbrooke**
1 Bagshaws Rd
McLaren Flat SA 5171
(08) 8383 0002
fax (08) 8383 0222
www.shottesbrooke.com.au

**Simon Hackett**
(not open to public)
(08) 8331 7348

**Skillogalee**
Skillogalee Rd
via Sevenhill SA 5453
(08) 8843 4311
fax (08) 8843 4343
skilly@capri.net.au

**Smithbrook**
(not open to public)
(08) 9772 3557
fax (08) 9772 3579
www.smithbrook.com.au

**Sorrenberg**
Alma Rd
Beechworth Vic. 3747
(03) 5728 2278

**Southcorp Wines**
Tanunda Rd
Nuriootpa SA 5355
(08) 8568 9389
fax (08) 8568 9489
www.southcorp.com.au

**Springwood Park**
(see Andrew Garrett
Vineyard Estates)

**St Hallett**
St Halletts Rd
Tanunda SA 5352
(08) 8563 7000
fax (08) 8563 7001
www.sthallett.com.au

**St Huberts**
Maroondah Hwy
Coldstream Vic. 3770
(03) 9739 1118
fax (03) 9739 1015
www.beringerblass.com.au

**St Leonards**
St Leonard Rd
Wahgunyah Vic. 3687
(02) 6033 1004
fax (02) 6033 3636
www.allsaintswine.com.au

**St Mary's Vineyard**
V and A Lane
via Coonawarra SA 5263
(08) 8736 6070
fax (08) 8736 6045

**St Matthias**
(see Moorilla Estate)

**Stafford Ridge**
Geoff Weaver
(not open to public)
(08) 8272 2105
www.geoffweaver.com.au

**Stanley Brothers**
Barossa Valley Way
Tanunda SA 5352
(08) 8563 3375
fax (08) 8563 3758
www.stanleybros.mtx.net

**Stanton & Killeen**
Murray Valley Hwy
Rutherglen Vic. 3685
(02) 6032 9457

**Stein's Wines**
Pipeclay Rd
Mudgee NSW 2850
(02) 6373 3991
fax (02) 6373 3709

**Stephen John Wines**
Government Rd
Watervale SA 5452
(08) 8843 0105
fax (08) 8843 0105

**Stoneleigh**
Corbans Wines
Great Northern Rd
Henderson NZ
(09) 836 6189

**Stoney Vineyard/ Domaine A**
Teatree Rd
Campania Tas. 7026
(03) 6260 4174
fax (03) 6260 4390

**Stonier's Winery**
362 Frankston-Flinders Rd
Merricks Vic. 3916
(03) 5989 8300
fax (03) 5989 8709
www.stoniers.com.au

**Stumpy Gully**
1247 Stumpy Gully Rd
Moorooduc Vic. 3933
(03) 5978 8429
fax (03) 5978 8419

**Summerfield**
Main Rd
Moonambel Vic. 3478
(03) 5467 2264
fax (03) 5467 2380

**Tahbilk**
Tabilk Vic. 3607
via Nagambie
(03) 5794 2555
fax (03) 5794 2360
www.tahbilk.com.au

**Talijancich**
26 Hyem Rd
Herne Hill WA 6056
(08) 9296 4289
fax (08) 9296 1762

**Tallarook**
(not open to public)
(03) 9818 3455
www.tallarook.com

**Taltarni Vineyards**
off Moonambel-Stawell Rd
Moonambel Vic. 3478
(03) 5467 2218
fax (03) 5467 2306
www.taltarni.com.au

**Talunga**
Lot 101 Adelaide-
Mannum Rd
Gumeracha SA 5233
(08) 8389 1222
fax (08) 8389 1233

**Tamar Ridge**
Auburn Road
Kayena Tas. 7270
(03) 6394 7002
fax (03) 6394 7003

**Tamburlaine Wines**
McDonalds Rd
Pokolbin NSW 2321
(02) 4998 7570
fax (02) 4998 7763
www.mywinery.com

**Tanglewood Downs**
Bulldog Creek Rd
Merricks North
(03) 5974 3325

**Tapestry**
Merrivale Wines
Olivers Rd
McLaren Vale SA 5171
(08) 8323 9196
fax (08) 8323 9746
www.merrivale.com.au

**Tarrawarra**
Healesville Rd
Yarra Glen Vic. 3775
(03) 5962 3311
fax (03) 5962 3311
www.tarrawarra.com.au

**Tatachilla Winery**
151 Main Rd
McLaren Vale SA 5171
(08) 8323 8656
fax (08) 8323 9096
www.tatachillawinery.com.au

**Taylors**
Mintaro Rd
Auburn SA 5451
(08) 8849 2008
www.taylorswines.com.au

**Te Mata Estate**
Te Mata Road
Havelock North
Hawkes Bay NZ
(06) 877 4399
fax (06) 877 4397

**Temple Bruer**
Angas River Delta
via Strathalbyn SA 5255
(08) 8537 0203
fax (08) 8537 0131
www.templebruer.net.au

**Tempus Two**
(see McGuigan)

**T'Gallant**
Lot 2 Mornington-
Flinders Rd
Main Ridge Vic. 3937
(03) 5989 6565
fax (03) 5989 6577

**Thalgara Estate**
De Beyers Rd
Pokolbin NSW 2321
(02) 4998 7717

**Thomas Fernhill
Estate**
Ingoldby Rd
McLaren Flat SA 5171
(08) 8383 0167
fax (08) 8383 0107
www.fernhillestate.com.au

**Thomas Wines**
PO Box 606
Cessnock NSW 2325
Tel/fax (02) 4991 6801

**Tim Adams**
Wendouree Rd
Clare SA 5453
(08) 8842 2429
fax (08) 8842 2429
www.timadamswines.com.au

**Tim Gramp**
PO Box 810
Unley SA 5061
(08) 8379 3658
fax (08) 8338 2160

**Tintilla**
Hermitage Rd
Pokolbin NSW 2335
(02) 6574 7093
fax (02) 6574 7094

**Tisdall**
Cornelia Creek Rd
Echuca Vic. 3564
(03) 5482 1911
fax (03) 5482 2516

**Tollana**
(see Southcorp Wines)

**Tom**
(see Andrew Garrett
Vineyard Estates)

**Torbreck**
Roennfeldt Rd
Marananga SA 5360
(08) 8562 4155
fax (08) 8562 4195

**Torresan Estate**
Manning Rd
Flagstaff Hill SA 5159
(08) 8270 2500

**Tower Wines**
Broke & Halls Rds
Pokolbin NSW 2321
(02) 4998 7989
www.towerestatewines.com.au

**Trentham Estate**
Sturt Hwy
Trentham Cliffs
via Gol Gol NSW 2738
(03) 5024 8888
fax (03) 5024 8800
www.trenthamestate.com.au

**Tuck's Ridge**
37 Red Hill-Shoreham Rd
Red Hill South Vic. 3937
(03) 5989 8660
fax (03) 5989 8579

**Tulloch**
De Beyers Rd
Pokolbin NSW 2321
(02) 4998 7503
fax (02) 4998 7682
www.southcorp.com.au

**Tunnel Hill**
(see Tarrawarra)

**Turkey Flat**
James Rd
Tanunda SA 5352
(08) 8563 2851
fax (08) 8563 3610
www.turkeyflatvineyards.com.au

**Turramurra Estate**
295 Wallaces Rd
Dromana Vic. 3936
(03) 5987 1146
fax (03) 5987 1286
www.turramurra.citysearch.
com.au

**Tyrrell's**
Broke Rd
Pokolbin NSW 2321
(02) 4993 7000
fax (02) 4998 7723
www.winefutures.com.au

**Vasse Felix**
Cnr Caves & Harmans Rds
Cowaramup WA 6284
(08) 9755 5242
fax (08) 9755 5425
www.vassefelix.com.au

**Vavasour**
Redwood Pass Rd
Lower Dashwood
Marlborough NZ
(03) 575 7481
fax (03) 575 7240

**Veritas**
94 Langmeil Rd
Tanunda SA 5352
(08) 8563 2330

**Virgin Hills**
(not open to public)
(03) 5423 9169
www.virginhills.com.au

**Voyager Estate**
Stevens Rd
Margaret River WA 6285
(08) 9757 6358
fax (08) 9757 6405

**Wandin Valley Estate**
Wilderness Rd
Rothbury NSW 2321
(02) 4930 7317
fax (02) 4930 7814
www.wandinvalley.com.au

**Waninga**
Hughes Park Rd
Sevenhill
via Clare SA 5453
(08) 8843 4395
fax (08) 8843 4395

**Wantirna Estate**
(not open to public)
(03) 9801 2367

**Warburn Estate**
(see Ballingal Estate)

**Wards Gateway Cellars**
Barossa Valley Hwy
Lyndoch SA 5351
(08) 8524 4138

**Warramate**
27 Maddens Lane
Gruyere Vic. 3770
(03) 5964 9219

**Warrenmang**
Mountain Ck Rd
Moonambel Vic. 3478
(03) 5467 2233
fax (03) 5467 2309
www.bazzani.com.au/
warrenmang

**Waterwheel Vineyards**
Lyndhurst St
Bridgewater-on-Loddon
Bridgewater Vic. 3516
(03) 5437 3060
fax (03) 5437 3082

**Wedgetail**
(not open to public)
(03) 9714 8661

**Wellington**
(Hood Wines)
489 Richmond Rd
Cambridge Tas. 7170
(03) 6248 5844
fax (03) 6248 5855

**Wendouree**
Wendouree Rd
Clare SA 5453
(08) 8842 2896

**Westend**
1283 Brayne Rd
Griffith NSW 2680
(02) 6964 1506
fax (02) 6962 1673

**Westfield**
Memorial Ave
Baskerville WA 6056
(08) 9296 4356

**Wignalls**
Chester Pass Rd
Albany WA 6330
(08) 9841 2848
www.wignallswines.com.au

**Wild Duck Creek**
Springflat Rd
Heathcote Vic. 3523
(03) 5433 3133

**Wildwood**
St Johns Lane
via Wildwood Vic. 3428
(03) 9307 1118
www.wildwoodvineyards.com.au

**Will Taylor**
1 Simpson Pde
Goodwood SA 5034
(08) 8271 6122

**Willespie**
Harmans Mill Rd
Willyabrup WA 6280
(08) 9755 6248
fax (08) 9755 6210

**Willow Creek**
166 Balnarring Rd
Merricks North Vic. 3926
(03) 5989 7448
fax (03) 5989 7584
www.willow-creek.com

**The Willows Vineyard**
Light Pass Rd
Barossa Valley SA 5355
(08) 8562 1080

**The Wilson Vineyard**
Polish Hill River
via Clare SA 5453
(08) 8843 4310
www.wilsonvineyard.com.au

**Wilton Estate**
Whitton Stock Route
Yenda NSW 2681
(02) 6968 1303
fax (02) 6968 1328

**Winchelsea Estate**
C/- Nicks Wine Merchants
(03) 9639 0696

**Windowrie Estate**
Windowrie Rd
Canowindra NSW 2804
(02) 6344 3264
fax (02) 6344 3227
www.windowrie.com

**Wingfields**
(see Water Wheel)

**Winstead**
Winstead Rd
Bagdad Tas. 7030
(03) 6268 6417

**Wirilda Creek**
Lot 32 McMurtrie Rd
McLaren Vale SA 5171
(08) 8323 9688

**Wirra Wirra**
McMurtrie Rd
McLaren Vale SA 5171
(08) 8323 8414
fax (08) 8323 8596
www.wirra.com.au

**Wolf Blass**
Sturt Hwy
Nuriootpa SA 5355
(08) 8562 1955
fax (08) 8562 2156
www.beringerblass.com.au

**Wood Park**
Kneebone Gap Rd
Bobinawarrah Vic. 3678
(03) 5727 3367
fax (03) 5727 3682

**Woodstock**
Douglas Gully Rd
McLaren Flat SA 5171
(08) 8383 0156
fax (08) 8383 0437
www.woodstockwine.com.au

**Woody Nook**
Metricup Rd
Metricup WA 6280
(08) 9755 7547
fax (08) 9755 7547

**Wyanga Park**
Baades Rd
Lakes Entrance Vic. 3909
(03) 5155 1508
fax (03) 5155 1443

**Wyndham Estate**
Dalwood Rd
Dalwood NSW 2321
(02) 4938 3444
fax (02) 4938 3422
www.wyndhamestate.com.au

**Wynns**
Memorial Dr.
Coonawarra SA 5263
(08) 8736 3266
fax (08) 8736 3202
www.southcorp.com.au

**Xanadu**
Terry Rd (off Railway Tce)
Margaret River WA 6285
(08) 9757 2581
fax (08) 9757 3389

**Yaldara**
Gomersal Rd
Lyndoch SA 5351
(08) 8524 4200
fax (08) 8524 467
www.simeon.com.au

**Yalumba**
Eden Valley Rd
Angaston SA 5353
(08) 8561 3200
fax (08) 8561 3392
www.yalumba.com

**Yarra Burn**
Settlement Rd
Yarra Junction Vic. 3797
(03) 5967 1428
fax (03) 5967 1146
www.brlhardy.com.au

**Yarra Glen**
(see Andrew Garrett
Vineyard Estates)

**Yarra Ridge**
Glenview Rd
Yarra Glen Vic. 3775
(03) 9730 1022
fax (03) 9730 1131
www.beringerblass.com.au

**Yarra Valley Hills**
(see Dromana Estate)

**Yarraman Road**
(see Barrington Estate)

**Yarra Yering**
Briarty Rd
Gruyere Vic. 3770
(03) 5964 9267

**Yellowglen**
White's Rd
Smythesdale Vic. 3351
(03) 5342 8617
www.beringerblass.com.au

**Yeringberg**
(not open to public)
(03) 9739 1453
fax (03) 9739 0048

**Yering Station**
Melba Hwy
Yering Vic. 3775
(03) 9730 1107
fax (03) 9739 0135
www.yering.com

**Zarephath**
Moorialup Rd
East Porongurup WA 6324
Tel/fax (08) 9853 1152
www.zarephathwines.com

**Zema Estate**
Penola-Naracoorte Rd
Coonawarra SA 5263
(08) 8736 3219
fax (08) 8736 3280
www.zema.com.au

# Index of Varieties

## Fortified wines

# Red wines

# White wines